2007

$35.00

Published by
America's Test Kitchen
17 Station Street
Brookline, MA 02445

ISBN-13: 978-1-933615-21-9
ISBN-10: 1-933615-21-4
ISSN: 1068-2821

To get home delivery of *Cook's Illustrated*, call 800-526-8442 inside the U.S., or 515-247-7571 if calling from outside the U.S., or subscribe online at www.cooksillustrated.com.

In addition to *Cook's Illustrated* Annual Hardbound Editions available from each year of publication (1993–2007), America's Test Kitchen offers the following cookbooks and DVD sets:

The America's Test Kitchen Family Cookbook

The Best Recipe Series
The Best International Recipe
The Best Make-Ahead Recipe
The Best 30-Minute Recipe
The Best Light Recipe
The Cook's Illustrated Guide to Grilling and Barbecue
Best American Side Dishes
Cover & Bake
The New Best Recipe
Steaks, Chops, Roasts, and Ribs
Baking Illustrated
Restaurant Favorites at Home
Perfect Vegetables
Italian Classics
The Best American Classics
The Best Soups & Stews

Additional books from America's Test Kitchen
America's Best Lost Recipes
The Best of America's Test Kitchen 2008
The Best of America's Test Kitchen 2007
834 Kitchen Quick Tips
The Kitchen Detective
1993–2007 Cook's Illustrated Master Index

Cook's Country Hardbound Annual Editions
2007 Cook's Country Annual Edition
2006 Cook's Country Annual Edition
2005 Cook's Country Annual Edition

The America's Test Kitchen Series Companion Cookbooks
Behind the Scenes with America's Test Kitchen (2008)
Test Kitchen Favorites (2007)
Cooking at Home with America's Test Kitchen (2006)
America's Test Kitchen Live! (2005)
Inside America's Test Kitchen (2004)
Here in America's Test Kitchen (2003)
The America's Test Kitchen Cookbook (2002)

The America's Test Kitchen Series DVD Sets (from our hit public television series)
The *America's Test Kitchen* 2007 Season (4 DVD set)
The *America's Test Kitchen* 2006 Season (4 DVD set)
The *America's Test Kitchen* 2005 Season (4 DVD set)
The *America's Test Kitchen* 2004 Season (4 DVD set)
The *America's Test Kitchen* 2003 Season (4 DVD set)
The *America's Test Kitchen* 2002 Season (4 DVD set)
The *America's Test Kitchen* 2001 Season (2 DVD set)

To order any of our cookbooks and DVDs listed above, give us a call at 800-611-0759 inside the U.S., or at 515-246-6911 if calling from outside the U.S. You can order subscriptions, gift subscriptions, and any of our books by visiting our online store at www.cooksillustrated.com

BC = Back Cover

COOK'S ILLUSTRATED INDEX 2007

A

B

H

I

J

K

O

P

U

V

W

Y

Z

NUMBER EIGHTY-FOUR

JANUARY & FEBRUARY 2007

Herb-Crusted Pork Loin
Big Flavor, Big Crunch

Perfect Pound Cake

Rating Dutch Ovens
$40 Pot Nearly Beats $250 Favorite

Steak Frites
Juicy Steak, Super-Crisp Fries

No-Stuff Manicotti

Fudge without Fear
Forget Your Candy Thermometer!

Thai Chicken Soup
Secret Ingredient Yields Big Flavor

French Onion and Bacon Tart

Sichuan Green Beans

Potato Primer

White Chicken Chili

Soy Sauce Taste Test

How to Roast Cauliflower

www.cooksillustrated.com

$5.95 U.S./$6.95 CANADA

CONTENTS

January & February 2007

COOKING GREENS Not just a plate garnish, curly kale has an assertive, earthy flavor when cooked. Darker Tuscan kale (or black kale) has wrinkled leaves, which are more tender and delicately flavored. Collard greens are usually boiled or braised along with pork; their pungent flavor pairs well with rich meat and bean dishes. Peppery mustard greens come from the plant that yields the seeds used to make mustard. Beet greens, most often found with their bulbous roots still attached, are earthy and flavorful and do not have to be cooked much beyond a quick sauté. They are closely related to chard, which has broad, crinkly leaves, prominent stems, and a slightly bitter, mineraly flavor. Radicchio is not green at all but rather a tight head of burgundy leaves; it can be eaten raw but is also good grilled or sautéed. Mild, fresh-tasting escarole is good raw in salads and cooked in soups. Dandelion greens have a mildly bitter, tangy flavor; young, tender leaves are fine for salads, but mature leaves are better braised. Spinach, which can have flat or curly leaves, requires little or no cooking.

COVER (*Lemons*): Elizabeth Brandon, BACK COVER (*Cooking Greens*): John Burgoyne

For list rental information, contact: Specialists Marketing Services, Inc., 1200 Harbor Blvd., 9th Floor, Weehawken, NJ 07087; 201-865-5800.
Editorial Office: 17 Station St., Brookline, MA 02445; 617-232-1000; fax 617-232-1572. Subscription inquiries, call 800-526-8442.
Postmaster: Send all new orders, subscription inquiries, and change-of-address notices to Cook's Illustrated, P.O. Box 7446, Red Oak, IA 51591-0446.

RABBITS RUN IN CIRCLES

Just last week my wife, Adrienne, asked me to have the "birds and bees" talk with our eleven-year-old, Charlie. I, of course, kept putting it off, while Charlie pestered me every night to sit down and answer all his questions about relations with the opposite sex. So, after a full week of delays, he and I did, in fact, retire to the library for the great discussion. I posed like a wise and thoughtful Harvard don; Charlie sat eagerly on the edge of a footstool. What followed was blessedly unexpected. He asked only two questions, both of which had little to do with the core issues at hand. I quickly satisfied his need for information and then pretended I had done a marvelous job. When informed of the content of our discussion, my wife was not pleased—I had (thankfully) shirked my paternal duty.

Tom, our former neighbor and President Emeritus of the Old Rabbit Hunters' Association, has had similar conversations with me over the last 20 years, albeit on the topics of dogs and rabbits. My first lesson was that rabbits tend to run in circles, so a good hunter, instead of hotfooting it through the woods after an energetic bunny, will simply stay put and allow the dog to do his job. The rabbit, unless it holes up somewhere, always comes back around. (The amusing part, from Tom's perspective, was that he did not inform me of this well-known rabbit-hunting strategy for a couple of years, during which time I tried to run down a couple dozen "browns" on foot, which resulted in a display of ineptitude that Tom, I am told, enjoyed immensely.)

Then I learned the difference between a rabbit and a hare, how to train a rabbit dog to not chase deer, where rabbits are likely to sit, the fact that rabbits do not dig holes—they use natural cover or lairs abandoned by other animals (most of my rabbit expertise had come from old Bugs Bunny cartoons in which Bugs had done a lot of digging)—the difference between 12-, 16- and 20-gauge shotguns, how a semiautomatic gun works, what a choke is and how to adjust it, how to skin an animal, and then, through my own trials and tests, how to cook one. He also taught me to not rush a shot (his infamous comment after I discharged three wide shots in a row still stings: "Need more ammo?"), the difference between a 13-inch and a 15-inch rabbit dog, and why you should leave your hunting jacket by the side of the road in the event your dog gets lost. (He will find the coat and sit on it until you return.)

Christopher Kimball

In cooking, there are folks who are fundamentally curious as to process—why bad things happen to good recipes—and sympathetic toward the notion of culinary education. Readers of this publication fall into that category. Others are content to believe that cooking is about no more than positive attitude—anyone with sufficient enthusiasm can cook a great meal. This golden age of the American amateur has been a long time coming. In the 1959 movie *Some Like It Hot,* Jack Lemmon joined an all-girl band and ended up in a sleeper car with pajama-clad Marilyn Monroe all through sheer bluster, boundless comic energy, and a borrowed dress. Now there is a guy who could have had a successful cooking show!

I am proud to say that my Vermont neighbors are of a different persuasion—they actually know a lot more then they let on. I remember a visit last summer with our demure neighbor Jack. Jack can be found every Sunday afternoon taking in the sun on a homemade wooden bench outside Jean's roadside sauna. But, as it turns out, Jack spent World War II flying P-40s, chasing Rommel out of Africa.

One day last summer, he told me a war story about developing a mechanical problem that sprayed oil all over the windshield of his plane. He had to roll back the canopy and make an emergency landing while flying the plane pretty much blind, looking out sideways. He bellied in, the plane digging a long trench, and then jumped out onto the wing brandishing his .45, not knowing if he was behind enemy lines. A dozen friendly locals showed up, made him a good hot lunch, and sent a messenger to the nearby British airfield. He was back at work the next day. Other neighbors, often spurred on by large quantities of dandelion wine, have related that they had wartime careers reminiscent of *The Big Red One*, including fighting at Anzio and Sicily.

Much like our son, Charlie, many folks have enthusiasms that don't reach beneath the surface. But with no more than an extra spoonful of curiosity, we soon discover that rabbits run in circles, why stew meat often cooks up tough and dry (and what to do about it), and that your unassuming neighbor—the guy who is particularly fond of a big slice of pie—landed on Utah Beach on June 6, 1944. As Calvin Coolidge said, "No man has ever listened himself out of a job." Pretty good advice, even in the kitchen.

FOR INQUIRIES, ORDERS, OR MORE INFORMATION:

www.cooksillustrated.com

At www.cooksillustrated.com, you can order books and subscriptions, sign up for our free e-newsletter, or renew your magazine subscription. Join the website and you'll have access to 14 years of *Cook's* recipes, cookware tests, ingredient tastings, and more.

COOKBOOKS

We sell more than 40 cookbooks by the editors of *Cook's Illustrated.* To order, visit our bookstore at www.cooksillustrated.com or call 800-611-0759 (or 515-246-6911 from outside the U.S.).

COOK'S ILLUSTRATED Magazine

Cook's Illustrated magazine (ISSN 1068-2821), number 84, is published bimonthly by Boston Common Press Limited Partnership, 17 Station St., Brookline, MA 02445. Copyright 2007 Boston Common Press Limited Partnership. Periodicals postage paid at Boston, Mass., and additional mailing offices, USPS #012487. POSTMASTER: Send address changes to Cook's Illustrated, P.O. Box 7446, Red Oak, IA 51591-0446. For subscription and gift subscription orders, subscription inquiries, or change-of-address notices, call 800-526-8442 in the U.S. or 515-247-7571 from outside the U.S., or write us at Cook's Illustrated, P.O. Box 7446, Red Oak, IA 51591-0446.

ILLUSTRATION: RANDY GLASS

NOTES FROM READERS

COMPILED BY SANDRA WU

Pepper Picking

What is the difference between jarred pimentos and jarred roasted red peppers?

MELISA CAREY
ENFIELD, CONN.

Fresh pimentos are thin-skinned, heart-shaped sweet peppers with a slightly bitter, aromatic flavor reminiscent of paprika (a spice made from pimento pods). Jarred pimentos have been boiled to remove their skins and then packed in a brine of citric acid or vinegar.

PIMENTO PEPPER: PUNGENT AND SOFT

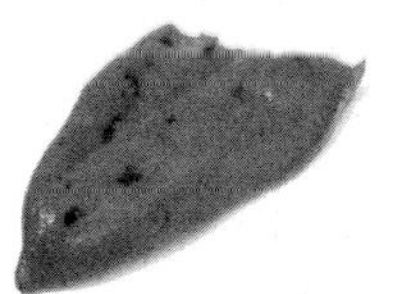

ROASTED RED PEPPER: SMOKY AND TENDER

Depending on whether the peppers are boiled (top photo) or roasted (bottom photo), pimentos can be labeled as either pimentos or roasted red peppers.

Jarred roasted red peppers can be made from a variety of peppers, including pimentos and bell peppers. As their name suggests, jarred roasted red peppers are roasted to remove their skins and then packed in an acidic brine.

We compared nationally available Goya pimentos with our favorite brand of roasted red peppers, Divina (made from Florina peppers, a type of pimento grown in northern Greece). Straight from the jar, the Goya pimentos had a "pungent," "complex" flavor with some bitterness and astringency. Their texture was soft and slimy. The Divina roasted red peppers, on the other hand, had a smoky, sweet flavor and tender, toothsome texture. When we sampled red pepper dip and arroz con pollo made with both peppers, opinions were split; some tasters preferred the briny pimentos while others favored the smoky red peppers.

If you're only going to buy one product, we recommend the sweeter, smokier flavor and firmer texture of roasted red peppers, but pimentos can be used in place of roasted red peppers in many recipes, as long as you don't mind their slightly bitter, briny flavor.

Wild versus Farmed Salmon

I often see wild Alaskan salmon for sale at the market. How is it different from farmed salmon?

MEAGHAN SHEA
QUEENS, N.Y.

Setting environmental and sustainability issues aside, we compared wild salmon fillets with farmed salmon fillets, noting variations in fattiness, flavor, aroma, and color. We tasted fresh wild Alaskan king salmon ($15.99 a pound), which is available year-round either fresh, frozen, or thawed (wild-caught salmon from Washington, Oregon, or California is available only seasonally), alongside fresh farmed salmon ($11.99 a pound) from Norway in a basic pan-fried application as well as in a salmon cake recipe. Sometimes labeled "Atlantic salmon," farmed salmon is also widely bred in Canada, Chile, and the United Kingdom.

Both raw and cooked, the wild salmon had a rich, rosy-pink hue, while the farmed salmon was lighter pink. Wild salmon attain their color by absorbing a carotenoid called *astaxanthin* from their krill-based diet, while farmed salmon eat fish feed supplemented with various sources of astaxanthin to enhance their grayish color. The feed is available in a variety of compositions, enabling fish farmers to select the precise pink to reddish hue of the flesh they'd like to sell (much like using a color swatch).

The wild salmon exuded more oil in the pan than the farmed salmon but tasted leaner overall, with a "buttery, pleasant texture" and a sweet, fresh flavor. The farmed salmon, which get less exercise and consume more fat than wild salmon, tasted "fishy," with "slimy, soft" flesh and a "musty, fatty" aftertaste. When mashed, seasoned, formed into cakes, and pan-fried, the differences remained. Tasters overwhelmingly preferred the wild salmon, which had a rich, full but delicate flavor. In comparison, the farmed salmon had a "canned" flavor.

The flavor and texture of wild and farmed salmon will vary depending on a host of factors, including the species of salmon, the season, and the place of origin. In this particular instance, however, we found that the wild Alaskan salmon was preferable to the Norwegian farmed salmon.

Salting Sweets

Every cake and cookie recipe I've come across calls for salt. What purpose does it serve?

JEAN HAZELTON
EAU CLAIRE, WIS.

Salt is a flavor enhancer that is just as important in sweet foods as it is in savory ones, so we assumed that a cake or cookie made without salt wouldn't taste as good as one that included it. Still, we wanted to understand exactly how the flavor would change. To do so, we tasted two batches of yellow layer cake and sugar cookies: one batch with salt, the other without.

The flavor differences in the cake, which called for ¾ teaspoon salt, were astounding. The salt-free cake tasted sweet—"like cotton candy"—yet bland. Tasters called it "mild," "flat," "dull," and "boring" and could barely detect vanilla flavor. The cake that included salt was also sweet, but the flavors of butter and vanilla were much more balanced and pronounced. The differences were more difficult to nail down in the sugar cookies, which were coated generously with sugar and contained only ¼ teaspoon salt. Still, some tasters could detect the flavors of butter and vanilla more readily in the "salted" cookies.

How does salt work its magic? While many cooks think of salt as simply a flavor enhancer, it can also mask less agreeable tastes like bitterness. We proved this theory true in the test kitchen by adding a pinch of salt to inherently bitter foods like coffee and eggplant, and the perceived bitterness was cut in half. By suppressing bitterness, salt allows more desirable flavors—including sweetness and spices—to come through. Ingredients that can contribute bitter flavors in baking include yeast, leavening agents, proteins in flour, bittersweet chocolate, and vanilla.

To summarize, if a recipe calls for a pinch of salt, don't be tempted to omit it. Otherwise, you might be left with a singularly sweet and sugary dessert with little complexity. Also, be sure when baking to use unsalted butter so that all the salt comes from a single source and the finished product doesn't actually come out salty.

Seeding Canned Tomatoes

When using canned whole tomatoes in recipes, should I leave the seeds in or take them out? Will the presence of seeds affect the flavor?

CLARK DUNSON
SAN MATEO, CALIF.

To determine whether removing the seeds from canned whole tomatoes is worth the effort, we used seed-in and seedless samples in a quick salsa and in a marinara sauce. The salsa made with seed-in tomatoes had a bit more brightness, while the salsa made with seedless tomatoes was slightly sweeter. But the differences were minor.

In the marinara sauce, the differences were still subtle, but more noticeable than in the salsa. This has more to do with the moisture added by the gelatinous material surrounding the seeds than the flavor of the seeds. Because the seed-in tomatoes are so juicy, we had to cook the sauce made with them longer. As a result, the sauce made with seed-in tomatoes was duller than the sauce made with seedless tomatoes, which had a fresher, fruitier tomato flavor.

So where do we stand? In uncooked applications like salsa, don't bother seeding canned tomatoes. In cooked recipes (such as marinara sauce or tomato soup), where excess moisture from the seeds would prolong the cooking time, we recommend removing the seeds. To do so, break the tomatoes open over a strainer set in a large bowl and use your fingers to scoop out the seeds and surrounding gelatinous material. Make sure to reserve the seedless juice—you might need some of it to adjust the consistency of a sauce or soup.

Spray-On Seed Sticker

When I made your Multigrain Bread recipe (March/April 2006) and used nonstick cooking spray to help the oats adhere to the crust, some of the oats fell off after baking. I noticed that The Baker's Catalogue sells a product called Quick Shine that supposedly helps seeds stick to dough. Is it worth buying?

JEREMY HURWITZ
ATLANTA, GA.

➢We went back into the test kitchen and baked Multigrain Bread, finding, like you did, that nonstick cooking spray wasn't completely effective at adhering oats to the dough. The water (the other recommendation we made in the recipe) did a better job of keeping the oats in place. But could we do even better?

AEROSOL SPRAY FOR BREAD

Quick Shine, an aerosol spray containing water, milk protein, canola oil, and stabilizers, purports to help toppings such as seeds stay stuck to bread dough once the loaf is baked. To find out how well it works, we made three loaves of Multigrain Bread, using water on one, Quick Shine on another, and a homemade "glue" of beaten egg and milk on the last loaf. We coated half of each loaf with oats and the other half with sesame seeds.

None of the oats and seeds had trouble sticking to the raw bread dough, and after the bread was finished baking, the loss of oats and seeds from the exteriors of all three loaves was equally minimal. So does Quick Shine work? Sure. But at $11.95 plus shipping for a 16-ounce can, we'll stick with water.

Pink Turkey Meat

Why is turkey meat still sometimes pink even after it is fully cooked? Is it safe to eat?

JOSEPH VOLPICELLI
BOSTON, MASS.

➢Having prepared thousands of turkeys in the test kitchen, we too have experienced the occasional slice of pink turkey meat. First off, always rely on an instant-read thermometer to ascertain doneness when roasting poultry. In the case of turkey, look for 165 degrees in the thickest portion of the breast and 170 to 175 degrees in the thickest part of the thigh.

So what about the unsettling color? Just because a slice of turkey has a pinkish tint doesn't necessarily mean it is underdone. In general, the red or pink color in meat is due to the red protein pigment called myoglobin in the muscle cells that store oxygen. Because the areas that tend to get the most exercise—the legs and thighs—require more oxygen, they contain more myoglobin (and are therefore darker in color) than the breasts. When oxygen is attached to myoglobin in the cells, it is bright red. As turkey (or chicken) roasts in the oven, the oxygen attached to the myoglobin is released, and the meat becomes lighter and browner in color. However, if there are trace amounts of other gases formed in a hot oven or grill, they may react to the myoglobin to produce a pink color, even if the turkey is fully cooked.

When cooking turkey or other poultry, don't be afraid if you see a little bit of pink. As long as you've let your thermometer be your guide, the meat is perfectly safe to eat.

WHAT IS IT?

This contraption looks like a bottle cap opener, but I can't figure out what the hooks on top are for. Any ideas?

AMY SHENG
BEDFORD, MASS.

In its closed position, this 4½-inch tool does function as a bottle cap opener, but when the folding cover is pulled open, the sharp-toothed shaft of a cork puller is revealed (see illustration at right). This antique (circa 1925) gadget is called the E-Z Cork Puller.

Cork pullers are said to be helpful for dislodging a cork that is very tightly sealed in a wine bottle. Unlike a corkscrew, the barbed blade of a cork puller is inserted between the cork and the inside of the bottle neck (not directly into the center of the cork). Next, the handle is turned counterclockwise until the barbs grip the cork. Lastly, one's index and middle fingers grasp the "hooks," or finger grips, to pull straight up to remove the cork. Despite its ingenious design, we found that yanking the cork out of a wine bottle using the E-Z Cork Puller required a strong grip and brute force. We're content to stick with modern corkscrews for all of our wine bottle–opening needs.

Not So Easy: Using the antique E-Z Cork Puller requires serious upper-arm strength.

Using Prechopped Nuts

I often buy prechopped nuts because they are much cheaper than whole nuts. Can I use them in recipes that call for whole nuts that are to be toasted before being chopped?

HOLLY BROWN
LANSING, MICH.

➢We were doubtful there would be significant differences between chopped-then-toasted and toasted-then-chopped nuts, but we headed into the kitchen anyway to try both kinds of nuts plain as well as in a mixed green salad and a pecan pie.

Because the prechopped nuts had more surface area, they were able to get more toasted all around and subsequently had a slightly fuller, "nuttier" flavor when tasted plain. Tossed in a salad dressed with vinaigrette and garnished with dried cranberries, however, the differences were less obvious. The same results held true in the pecan pie.

The short answer? The order in which you chop and toast nuts doesn't really matter, so by all means buy the cheaper chopped variety.

Storing Minced Garlic

I use a lot of minced garlic. Rather than buying the jarred variety, can I mince my own fresh garlic, cover it with oil, and refrigerate it?

DONNA SMITH
MIDDLESBORO, KY.

➢As tempting as this shortcut might seem, it isn't safe. There is a risk of botulism developing in garlic that is stored in oil for more than a few days, even when it is refrigerated. Botulism grows in anaerobic (oxygen-free) conditions. Placing garlic into an anaerobic climate such as a container of oil creates a hospitable environment for producing the toxin. (Commercially made jarred minced garlic and garlic-flavored oil both contain acidic additives that kill harmful bacteria.) To make the task of mincing garlic less tedious, we recommend using a garlic press. It works just as well as mincing by hand, is much faster, and tastes infinitely better than the jarred stuff.

SEND US YOUR QUESTIONS We will provide a complimentary one-year subscription for each letter we print. Send your inquiry, name, address, and daytime telephone number to Notes from Readers, Cook's Illustrated, P.O. Box 470589, Brookline, MA 02447, or to notesfromreaders@bcpress.com.

ILLUSTRATION: JOHN BURGOYNE

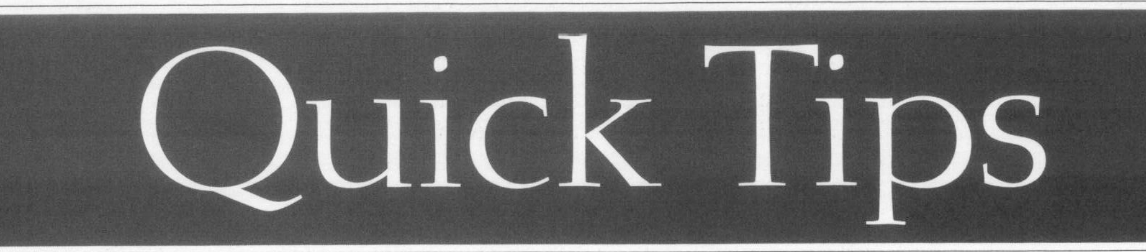

Quick Tips

⋟ COMPILED BY DAVID PAZMIÑO ⋞

Transferring Fish Fillets

A large fish fillet or whole fish can make an impressive presentation, but it can be a challenge to remove the delicate fish from a baking sheet without it falling apart. For an easier transfer, Renee Saxman of Rochester, Minn., reaches for a flexible cutting board.

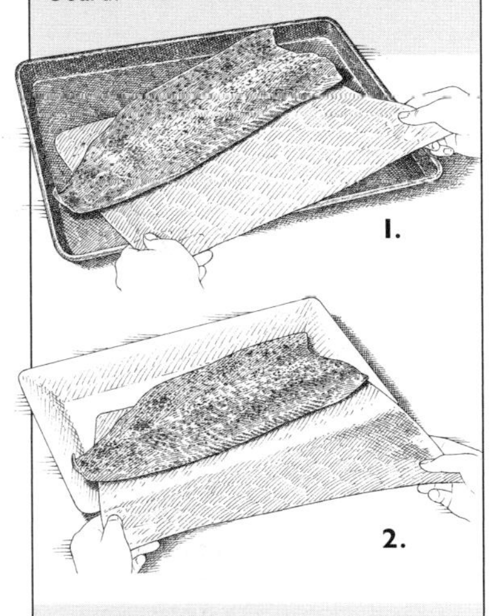

1. Slide a thin, flexible plastic cutting board under the fish.
2. Gently slide the fish onto a serving platter, using a spatula if necessary.

Cast-Iron Care

Cast-iron pans often build up crud that can be difficult to dislodge with a sponge, and cleaning cast iron with a soapy scrubber pad will affect the seasoning. Mary Flynn of Naples, Fla., found that aluminum foil makes an effective (and safe) scrubbing device. After using paper towels to wipe excess grease from a cooled pan, she follows the steps below.

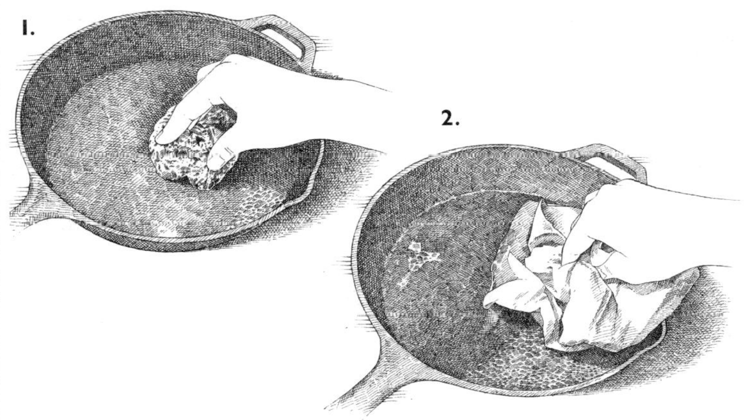

1. Scrub the pan with a wad of heavy-duty aluminum foil, removing stuck-on food.
2. Rinse and dry the pan, then reseason it by using paper towels to wipe it with about 1 tablespoon oil.

Safer Potato Piercing

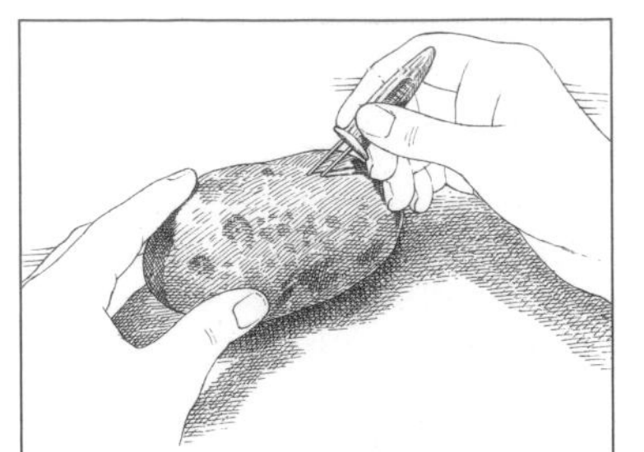

Forks and knives sometimes get stuck when piercing raw potatoes to allow steam to escape during microwaving. Alison Baez of Palmetto Bay, Fla., discovered a better tool for the job. She pricks the skin of the potato with the sharp tip of a corncob holder.

Extra Refrigerator Storage Space

Finding room for a large casserole dish in a cramped refrigerator is a familiar challenge for many cooks. Amy Riley of Reynoldsburg, Ohio, came up with this space-saving solution. Create an extra "shelf" by stacking a baking sheet on top of the casserole dish, then place smaller items on the baking sheet.

Warp-Free Muffin Tins

Mary Ann Gibson of Lompoc, Calif., often bakes half-batches of muffins and finds that the empty cups heat up rapidly during baking, causing the tin to warp. Her solution is to place two ice cubes in each empty cup. Once in the oven, the ice melts and the water prevents the metal from getting too hot.

Foolproof Lattice Top Transfer

Fragile strips of dough for lattice pies or tarts often break when they are transferred from the countertop to the pie. Trudy Mavin of Berkeley Heights, N.J., found a way to make this delicate task foolproof. After rolling out pie dough on parchment paper, she proceeds as follows.

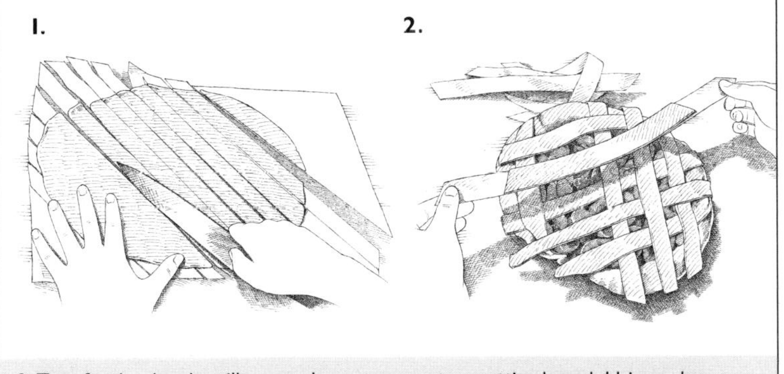

1. Transfer the dough, still on parchment paper, to a cutting board. Using a sharp knife, cut through the dough and parchment paper to form strips. (If the dough is too soft to cut, place it in the freezer until firm, about 5 minutes.)
2. Using the parchment paper to lift the dough, transfer the strips to the top of the pie, gently pulling the paper away to create a decorative lattice pattern.

No-Slip Peppermill

When hands get wet during cooking, using a plastic or glass peppermill becomes a slippery, frustrating task. John Dahl of San Anselmo, Calif., came up with a simple remedy. Secure a thick rubber band (often found on bunches of broccoli) at the top of the peppermill. Grip the rubber band while grinding.

Send Us Your Tip We will provide a complimentary one-year subscription for each tip we print. Send your tip, name, and address to Quick Tips, Cook's Illustrated, P.O. Box 470589, Brookline, MA 02447, or to quicktips@americastestkitchen.com.

ILLUSTRATION: JOHN BURGOYNE

Opening Tight Lids

Many jars are difficult to open because of a tight vacuum seal created during manufacturing. Tired of struggling, Joanne Lewis of Brookfield, Wis., discovered that a church key could be used to facilitate the process.

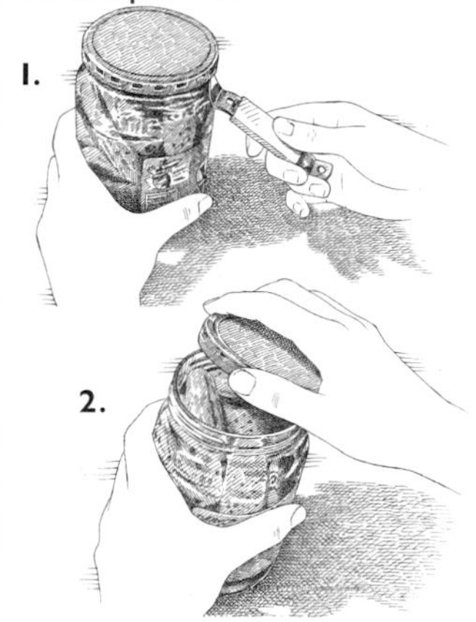

1. Fit the tip of the church key under the edge of the lid and gently lift the key to break the seal.
2. The lid should now be easy to unscrew.

Draining Sauerkraut

To avoid dirtying a colander for a small job, Mary Clugstone of Binghamton, N.Y., drains sauerkraut in the plastic bag in which it is packaged.

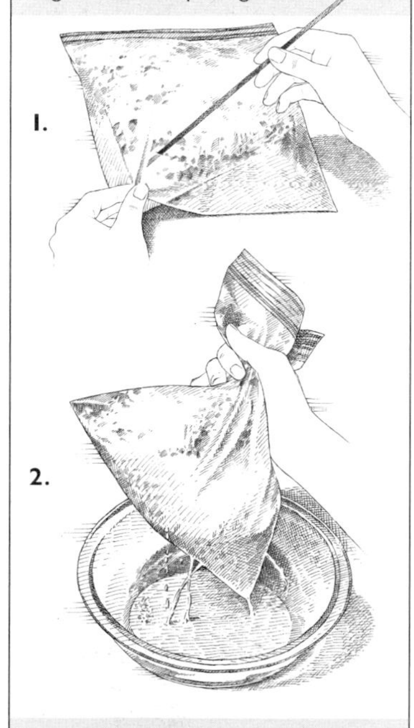

1. Poke several holes in the bottom of the sauerkraut bag with a skewer or sharp knife. (Jarred sauerkraut can be transferred to a zipper-lock bag.)
2. Gently squeeze the bag over a large bowl or sink to drain the liquid through the holes.

No-Stick Proposition

Weary of battling with stuck-on price tags and labels on dishware, glasses, and wine bottles, Lynda Bernel of Lakeville, Mass., came up with a novel way to release them. Point a hair dryer set on high at the price tag or label until the glue softens, allowing it to be peeled off with ease.

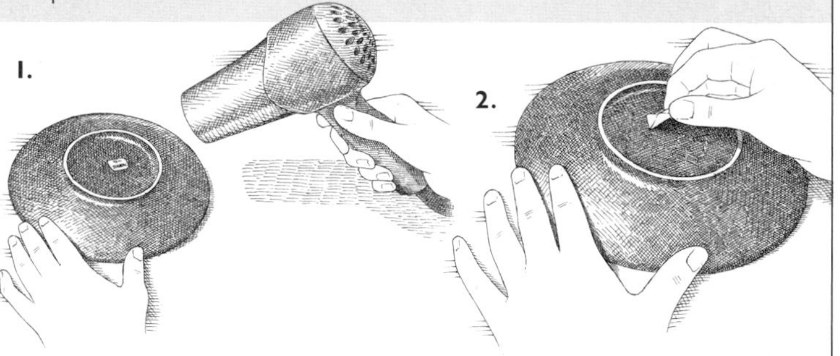

Overnight Bread Cooling

Peggy Wegman of Auburndale, Mass., often bakes bread in the evening and finds that her loaves never cool sufficiently before bedtime. Instead of wrapping a slightly warm loaf in plastic wrap (a method that yields a soggy crust) or leaving it out on a rack (an approach that can attract kitchen critters), she takes the following approach. Place the loaf on a cooling rack and turn a large colander upside down over the loaf, allowing it to cool safely while preserving the crisp crust.

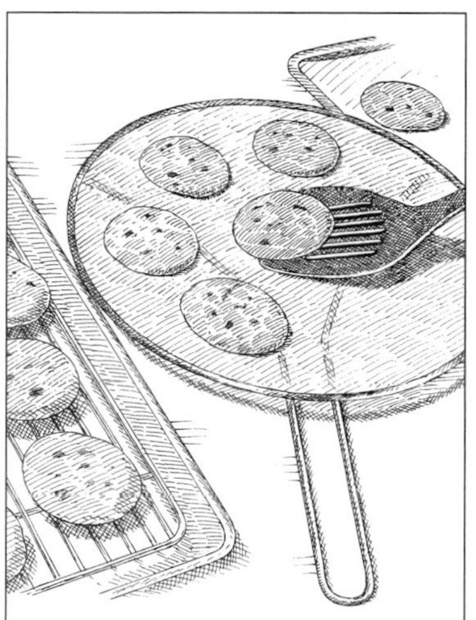

Impromptu Cookie Cooling Rack

Finding himself with a baking sheet full of hot cookies and a shortage of cooling racks, Jerry Ammons of San Francisco, Calif., transferred the cookies to a splatter screen to cool.

Keeping Flapjacks Hot

A warm oven can be used to keep pancakes hot, but this method sometimes results in a dried-out breakfast. Rebecca Cohen of New York, N.Y., uses the following trick for keeping pancakes hot and moist as they come out of the skillet.

1. Bring 2 cups water to a simmer in a large saucepan. Place a large heatproof plate on top of the saucepan.
2. As the pancakes are cooked, place them on the warm plate until serving time.

Double-Duty Onion Bag

In need of a scrub pad for cleaning dirty pots and pans, Suni McLeod of Little Rock, Ark., cleverly improvised with an onion bag.

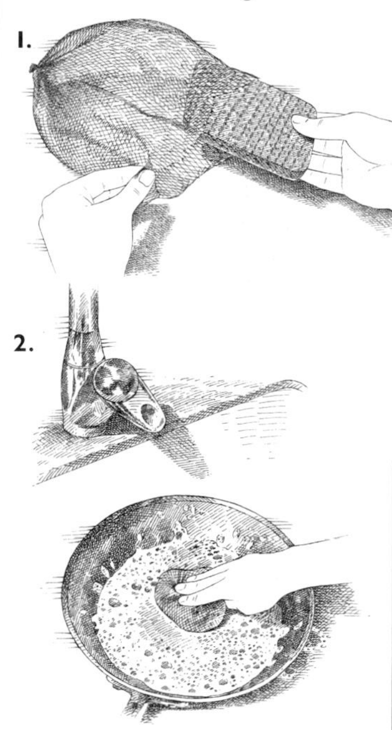

1. Wrap an empty perforated plastic onion bag around a sponge.
2. Use the wrapped sponge and hot soapy water to scrub cookware.

Hassle-Free Garlic Paste

Making garlic paste with the blade of a chef's knife takes practice. Suzanne Phillips of Akron, Ohio, sidesteps knife work with this easy method.

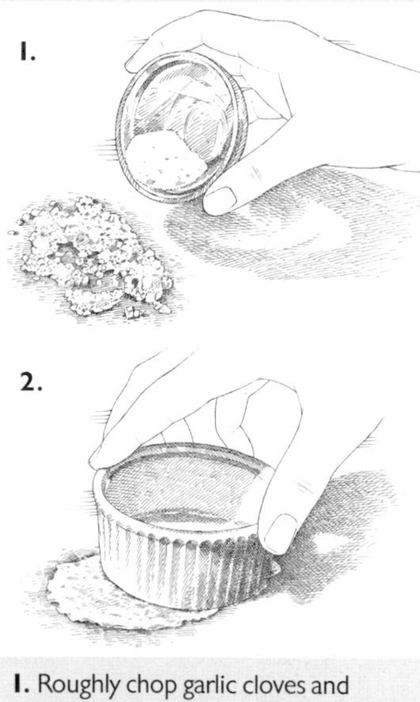

1. Roughly chop garlic cloves and sprinkle with a pinch of salt.
2. Using the flat, unglazed underside of a small ramekin, press the garlic against the cutting board, smearing it to make a smooth paste.

The Best White Chili

This Southwestern-style chili often cooks up bland and watery, with chewy bits of rubbery chicken that make home cooks ask, "Where's the beef?"

⋟ BY SANDRA WU ⋞

White chicken chili is a fresher, lighter cousin of the thick red chili most Americans know and love. While its origins date back to the health and Southwestern crazes of the 1980s, white chicken chili has since shown up in a number of Midwestern family cookbooks and has become a regular on the chili cook-off circuit. Its appeal is not surprising. First, because the recipe uses chicken rather than beef, many folks appreciate it for being healthier. Next, because there are no tomatoes to mask the other flavors, the chiles, herbs, and spices take center stage. Unlike red chili, which uses any combination of dried chiles, chili powders, and cayenne pepper, white chicken chili gets its backbone from fresh green chiles. So much so, in fact, that the recipe is sometimes called *chili verde*, or green chili.

The ingredients in white chicken chili are fairly consistent: diced or ground chicken, green chiles (usually fresh but sometimes canned or pickled), onions, white beans, garlic, spices, and chicken broth. But most of the recipes I tried were too watery and bland, bearing a closer resemblance to chicken and bean soup than actual chili. While the floating bits of mushy beans and overcooked chicken were hard to overlook, the chiles themselves were often barely noticeable. But amid all these bad recipes, I saw the possibility of creating something great—a rich, stew-like chili with moist, tender chicken, perfectly cooked beans, and a complex flavor profile.

Garnishes are key components in white chili. Cilantro and scallions add freshness, while lime juice provides a welcome burst of acidity.

Chicken and Chiles

The basic procedure for making white chicken chili is fairly simple. Most recipes start by browning the chicken. Next, the browned chicken is set aside and the chiles, onion, garlic, and spices are sautéed in the same pot. Finally, the chicken is added back in along with chicken broth and white beans and simmered until the chicken has cooked through.

Ground chicken was moist but had a chewy, spongy texture and an unattractive crumbly appearance. The choice between white and dark meat was a close call. Chicken thighs tasted richer and meatier, but they took twice as long to cook as the milder-flavored breasts and tended to compete with the fresh flavors of the chiles and seasonings. Boneless, skinless chicken breasts were attractive but lent little flavor to the broth. I had better luck with bone-in, skin-on breasts. I browned the pieces first to help develop fond (the flavorful bits on the bottom of the pot) and render out fat, which I saved to cook with the aromatics.

I was ready to move on to the main order of business: the chiles. Some recipes rely solely on canned or jarred green chiles. While offering convenience, they were also too vinegary and pickled. That left me with six widely available fresh chiles to choose from: poblanos, Anaheims, banana peppers, Italian peppers, jalapeños, and serranos. Banana peppers and Italian peppers were uninspiring. Extremely hot serranos were also out. I hoped to find a one-size-fits-all chile but discovered that more than one variety was necessary to provide the complexity and modest heat I was looking for. A trio of poblanos, Anaheims, and jalapeños did just that, with each chile bringing its own inimitable characteristics (see "The Chosen Chiles" on page 7) to the table.

Following the lead of other recipe writers, I briefly sautéed the chopped chiles along with diced onions, garlic, and spices over relatively high heat before adding the broth, beans, and chicken. This technique often yielded chiles that retained too much texture and had a flat, vegetal flavor. Roasting softened the chiles but provided an unwanted smokiness that muddied the dish. I found my solution back on the stovetop by lowering the heat and covering the pot to help soften the chiles and other vegetables. In 10 minutes, the chiles and onions were softened, and the flavors of the garlic and spices were nicely bloomed. As for the spices, tasters liked the standard cumin but preferred aromatic coriander to the more commonly used dried oregano.

RECIPE DIAGNOSIS: White Chicken Chili

We tried a variety of white chicken chili recipes from cookbooks and Internet sites. Here are three common problems we encountered and our solutions.

PROBLEM: BLAND, WATERY SAUCE
SOLUTION: PUREE VEGETABLES Process part of chile-onion mixture and beans with broth to thicken the base.

PROBLEM: FLOATING BITS OF RUBBERY CHICKEN
SOLUTION: SHREDDED CHICKEN BREAST Brown, poach, and shred bone-in, skin-on chicken breasts for hearty texture and full chicken flavor.

PROBLEM: NOT ENOUGH CHILE FLAVOR
SOLUTION: TRIO OF FRESH CHILES Use a combination of fresh jalapeño, poblano, and Anaheim chiles.

PHOTOGRAPHY: CARL TREMBLAY

Thicker and Thin

At this point, I was ready to deal with the chicken. After removing the skin, I poached the breasts until they were just done (about 20 minutes) and set them aside while the base continued to cook. Canned beans were my go-to choice, as dried beans were unnecessarily time-consuming. I favored larger cannellini beans over navy beans, which were too reminiscent of minestrone.

To fix the wateriness problem that had plagued so many of my test recipes, I tried adding a small amount of masa harina (a corn flour product), which we've used to thicken a red chili recipe in the past. While it technically worked, the masa also imparted a gelatinous texture and strong "corny" flavor. I was back to the drawing board. Most white chili recipes don't call for pureeing any of the ingredients, but I decided to try anyway. If it worked in vegetable soups, then why not in chili? Pureeing a cup each of the sautéed chile-onion mixture, beans, and broth not only gave my chili a nicely thickened consistency but also ensured that chile flavor was present in every drop.

With a host of complex Southwestern flavors, interesting textures, and filling but not heavy ingredients, this white chicken chili had come full circle. While I could never imagine myself eating a big bowl of thick, meaty red chili outside of the cold winter months, I would definitely make this light and flavorful white chili all year round. Starting now.

KEY STEPS TO BUILDING FLAVOR

1. BROWN CHICKEN
Brown the bone-in, skin-on chicken breasts before poaching them to achieve deep chicken flavor.

2. SAUTÉ VEGETABLES
To create a flavorful chile-centered base, sauté the trio of chiles and onion along with the spices and garlic.

3. PUREE VEGETABLES
To thicken the chili, process 1 cup each of the sautéed chile mixture, beans, and broth in the food processor.

4. STIR IN FRESH CHILE
Add one minced raw jalapeño to the finished dish for a last-minute burst of chile flavor.

WHITE CHICKEN CHILI

SERVES 6 TO 8

Adjust the heat in this dish by adding the minced ribs and seeds from the jalapeño as directed in step 6. If Anaheim chiles cannot be found, add an additional poblano and jalapeño to the chili. This dish can also be successfully made by substituting chicken thighs for the chicken breasts. If using thighs, increase the cooking time in step 4 to about 40 minutes. Serve chili with sour cream, tortilla chips, and lime wedges.

- 3 pounds bone-in, skin-on chicken breast halves, trimmed of excess fat and skin
- Table salt and ground black pepper
- 1 tablespoon vegetable oil
- 3 medium jalapeño chiles
- 3 medium poblano chiles, stemmed, seeded, and cut into large pieces
- 3 medium Anaheim chiles, stemmed, seeded, and cut into large pieces
- 2 medium onions, cut into large pieces (2 cups)
- 6 medium garlic cloves, minced or pressed through garlic press (about 2 tablespoons)
- 1 tablespoon ground cumin
- 1½ teaspoons ground coriander
- 2 (15-ounce) cans cannellini beans, drained and rinsed
- 3 cups low-sodium chicken broth
- 3 tablespoons juice from 2 to 3 limes
- ¼ cup minced fresh cilantro leaves
- 4 scallions, white and light green parts sliced thin

1. Season chicken liberally with salt and pepper. Heat oil in large Dutch oven over medium-high heat until just smoking. Add chicken, skin side down, and cook without moving until skin is golden brown, about 4 minutes. Using tongs, turn chicken and lightly brown on other side, about 2 minutes. Transfer chicken to plate; remove and discard skin.

2. While chicken is browning, remove and discard ribs and seeds from 2 jalapeños; mince flesh. In food processor, process half of poblano chiles, Anaheim chiles, and onions until consistency of chunky salsa, ten to twelve 1-second pulses, scraping down sides of workbowl halfway through. Transfer mixture to medium bowl. Repeat with remaining poblano chiles, Anaheim chiles, and onions; combine with first batch (do not wash food processor blade or workbowl).

3. Pour off all but 1 tablespoon fat from Dutch oven (adding additional vegetable oil if necessary) and reduce heat to medium. Add minced jalapeños, chile-onion mixture, garlic, cumin, coriander, and ¼ teaspoon salt. Cover and cook, stirring occasionally, until vegetables soften, about 10 minutes. Remove pot from heat.

4. Transfer 1 cup cooked vegetable mixture to now-empty food processor workbowl. Add 1 cup beans and 1 cup broth and process until smooth, about 20 seconds. Add vegetable-bean mixture, remaining 2 cups broth, and chicken breasts to Dutch oven and bring to boil over medium-high heat. Reduce heat to medium-low and simmer, covered, stirring occasionally, until chicken registers 160 degrees (175 degrees if using thighs) on instant-read thermometer, 15 to 20 minutes (40 minutes if using thighs).

5. Using tongs, transfer chicken to large plate. Stir in remaining beans and continue to simmer, uncovered, until beans are heated through and chili has thickened slightly, about 10 minutes.

6. Mince remaining jalapeño, reserving and mincing ribs and seeds (see note above), and set aside. When cool enough to handle, shred chicken into bite-sized pieces, discarding bones. Stir shredded chicken, lime juice, cilantro, scallions, and remaining minced jalapeño (with seeds if desired) into chili and return to simmer. Adjust seasonings with salt and pepper and serve.

The Chosen Chiles

We found that using a combination of poblanos, Anaheims, and jalapeños was the key to achieving vibrant chile flavor. Here's what each chile brings to the table.

JALAPEÑO
This small, smooth-skinned, forest-green chile provides heat and a bitter, green bell pepper–like flavor.

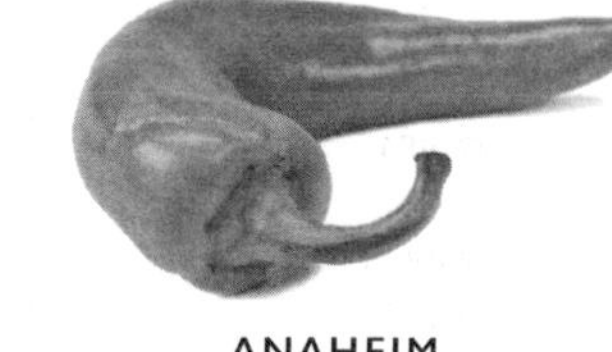

ANAHEIM
This long, medium-green, mildly spicy chile has an acidic, lemony bitterness.

POBLANO
This large, heart-shaped, blackish-green chile is mild to medium-hot and packs a rich, vegetal, slightly sweet flavor.

Authentic Steak Frites

A good rendition of this bistro standard is hard to find in American restaurants. Short of flying to Paris, how could we reliably enjoy this French classic?

⋟ BY KEITH DRESSER ⋞

When most people travel to Paris, the first thing they do is visit Notre Dame, the Eiffel Tower, or the Louvre. Not me. When I get off the plane, I head to a bistro and order steak frites. I know steak frites might seem like a pedestrian choice—it's just steak with a side of fries—but in Paris, the steak is always perfectly cooked and the fries are fluffy on the inside and crisp on the outside, even when bathed in juices from the meat.

I've ordered my fair share of steak frites in American restaurants, but they often miss the mark. The fries are usually too soggy and the steak just isn't as flavorful. Since I don't regularly dine in Parisian bistros, I set out to re-create steak frites in my own kitchen.

My Two Left Frites

From past test kitchen work, I knew that high-starch russet potatoes make the best fries. Most recipes call for blanching the sliced potatoes in moderately hot oil to cook them through and then finishing them in hotter oil to render them golden and crispy. Following these steps was easy; achieving the desired result of a super-crisp fry that stood up to the steak and its juices was monumentally difficult. No matter what I tried, the fries were too tough, too soggy, or too greasy.

When I cooked the potatoes in a single batch, the fries were very greasy. By cooking the potatoes in two batches, I was able to increase the ratio of oil to potatoes. This also reduced the drop in oil temperature that naturally occurs when the potatoes are added. When I added all of the potatoes to the oil, the oil temperature dropped 125 degrees and the oil was no longer boiling. When I added half the potatoes, the oil temperature dropped just 75 degrees.

Squaring the Spud

The best way to uniformly cut fries is to start by trimming a thin slice from each side of the potato. Once the potato is "squared," you can slice it into 1/4-inch planks and then cut each plank into 1/4-inch fries.

For super-crisp fries, we coat the potatoes with an unlikely ingredient.

Why does this matter? When the oil is very hot (well above 212 degrees), moisture on the surface of the potato turns to steam, with hot oil taking the place of the escaping moisture. As the surface of the potato becomes hotter and hotter, the outer coating of starch begins to seal, making it more difficult for the oil and water to exchange. If the oil isn't hot enough, the sealing process doesn't occur and the oil will seep into the potatoes. Minimizing the temperature drop when the potatoes are added to the hot oil is an insurance policy against greasiness.

To find out whether the type of fat played a role in crispness, I tried cooking the potatoes in vegetable oil, peanut oil, and shortening. The fries cooked in vegetable oil were bland and almost watery. The fries cooked in vegetable shortening and peanut oil were both crisp, but the shortening left a heavy aftertaste, while the fries cooked in peanut oil were light and earthy-tasting.

Crispy Tricks

Following these steps resulted in better fries. However, the fries were still not crisp enough to stand up to the steak juices. Some recipes suggest soaking the potatoes in cold water before they are cooked. Compared with potatoes that were fried without presoaking, the soaked potatoes made slightly crispier fries with more even coloration. Other recipes call for "resting" the fries between the first and second frying. After 10 minutes of resting, I noticed that the starches on the exterior of the blanched fries had formed a thin film that indeed helped the fries become crisp once they were fried again. I was making progress, but I still wasn't completely satisfied.

It was time to try some more unusual ideas, so I turned to the Internet. I landed on the website of a company that makes frozen fries and learned that they spray their potatoes with a thin potato starch–based coating. After more research, I realized starch was also a key ingredient in many fast-food fries. Could an extra layer of starch be the key to crispier fries?

I alternately tossed uncooked potatoes with cornstarch, potato starch, and arrowroot and fried up each batch. I saw an immediate improvement. Our science advisor explained that the starch was absorbing some of the surface moisture on the potatoes to form a gel-like coating. This coating made a super-protective sheath around each fry, helping create the shatteringly crisp crust I had been working toward. After more tests, I determined that two tablespoons of cornstarch provided a flavorless coating that guaranteed crisp fries.

Steak My Claim

In France, steak frites is usually prepared with a cut called *entrecôte* (literally, "between the ribs"). Although you won't find this steak in American supermarkets, it's similar to our rib-eye steak—both are cut from the same area as prime rib. The one big difference is that entrecôte steaks are quite thin, usually just ½ to ¾ inch thick.

Even if your butcher will cut entrecôte steaks, I discovered that they're not the best choice for my recipe. These thin steaks work well in restaurants, where blazing hot burners reign and steaks are cooked one at a time. With a weaker home stove and four steaks in the pan, I found that thicker rib-eyes gave me more time to get a nice sear on

Go to www.cooksillustrated.com

- Click on the Cook's Extra button for our **French Bistro Menu** and recipe for **Oven Fries**. Menu and recipe available until June 1, 2007.

PHOTOGRAPHY: CARL TREMBLAY

One Steak Becomes Two

In order to have four steaks that fit in a skillet at the same time, it is necessary to buy two 1-pound steaks and cut them in half according to their thickness. If your steaks are 1¼ to 1¾ inches thick, cut them in half vertically into small, thick steaks. If your steaks are thicker than 1¾ inches, cut them in half horizontally into two thinner steaks.

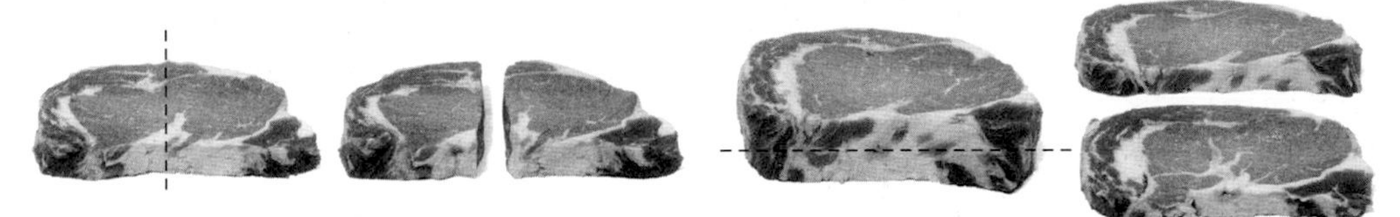

THIN STEAK: Cut in half vertically. **THICK STEAK:** Cut in half horizontally.

the meat without overcooking the middle.

I had finally created a recipe that could almost rival the Parisian bistro meals I remember. The only hitch: The steak was a little bland. Maybe French beef is better? Then I recalled that most bistros spoon a flavored butter over the steak. Spread over the steaks while they rested, the herb butter added the exclamation point to this bistro classic. I no longer have to fly across the Atlantic to enjoy great steak frites.

STEAK FRITES

SERVES 4

Make sure to dry the potatoes well before tossing them with the cornstarch. For safety, use a Dutch oven with a capacity of at least 7 quarts. Use refined peanut oil (such as Planters) to fry the potatoes, not toasted peanut oil. A 12-inch skillet is essential for cooking four steaks at once. The recipe can be prepared through step 4 up to 2 hours in advance; turn off the heat under the oil, turning the heat back to medium when you start step 6. The ingredients can be halved to serve two—keep the oil amount the same and forgo blanching and frying the potatoes in batches. If you prefer not to fry, follow our recipe for Oven Fries (see Cook's Extra on page 8).

- 2½ pounds russet potatoes (about 4 large), scrubbed, sides squared off, and cut lengthwise into ¼-inch by ¼-inch fries (see photo on page 8)
- 2 tablespoons cornstarch
- 3 quarts peanut oil
- 1 tablespoon vegetable oil
- 2 boneless rib-eye steaks (1 pound each), cut in half (see photos, above)
- Kosher salt and ground black pepper
- 1 recipe Herb Butter (recipe follows)

1. Rinse cut potatoes in large bowl under cold running water until water turns clear. Cover with cold water and refrigerate for 30 minutes or up to 12 hours.

2. Pour off water, spread potatoes onto kitchen towels, and thoroughly dry. Transfer potatoes to large bowl and toss with cornstarch until evenly coated. Transfer potatoes to wire rack set in rimmed baking sheet and let rest until fine white coating forms, about 20 minutes.

3. Meanwhile, in large, heavy-bottomed Dutch oven fitted with clip-on-the-pot candy thermometer, heat peanut oil over medium heat to 325 degrees.

4. Add half of potatoes, a handful at a time, to hot oil and increase heat to high. Fry, stirring with mesh spider or large-hole slotted spoon, until potatoes start to turn from white to blond, 4 to 5 minutes. (Oil temperature will drop about 75 degrees during this frying.) Transfer fries to thick paper bag or paper towels. Return oil to 325 degrees and repeat with remaining potatoes. Reduce heat to medium and let fries cool while cooking steaks, at least 10 minutes.

5. Heat vegetable oil in 12-inch skillet over medium-high heat until smoking. Meanwhile, season steaks with salt and pepper. Lay steaks in pan, leaving ¼ inch between them. Cook, not moving steaks, until well browned, about 4 minutes. Using tongs, flip steaks and continue to cook until instant-read thermometer inserted in center registers 120 degrees for rare to medium-rare, 3 to 7 minutes. Transfer steaks to large plate, top with butter, and tent loosely with foil; let rest while finishing fries.

6. Increase heat under Dutch oven to high and heat oil to 375 degrees. Add half of fries, a handful at a time, and fry until golden brown and puffed, 2 to 3 minutes. Transfer to thick paper bag or paper towels. Return oil to 375 degrees and repeat with remaining fries. Season fries with salt and serve immediately with steaks.

EQUIPMENT TESTING:

Spider Skimmers

If you peek into a restaurant kitchen, you'll see chefs working over steaming stockpots or vats of bubbling oil using shallow, woven wire baskets on long handles to retrieve blanched vegetables, french fries, and thin-skinned wontons. Suffice it to say that most chefs wouldn't part with their "spiders," as they are called, which effortlessly scoop out multiple handfuls of food with one swoop and leave all the hot cooking oil, water, or broth behind.

But is one species of spider superior to the others? While cooking skinny french fries and plump cheese ravioli, we noted that several models trapped too much liquid and sharp wire edges snagged delicate ravioli wrappers. Wood handles soaked up oil and water, discoloring the wood and absorbing odors. One model, the Typhoon Extra-Large Wire Skimmer ($15), avoided all these flaws and is our clear favorite. –Elizabeth Bomze

STURDY SPIDER
The Typhoon Extra-Large Wire Skimmer sports a solid metal handle that won't soak up oil or odors and a uniform mesh face that lets liquid pass through with ease.

HERB BUTTER

MAKES ENOUGH FOR 4 STEAKS

- 4 tablespoons unsalted butter, softened
- ½ medium shallot, minced (about 2 tablespoons)
- 1 garlic clove, minced or pressed through garlic press (about 1 teaspoon)
- 1 tablespoon minced fresh parsley leaves
- 1 tablespoon minced fresh chives
- ¼ teaspoon table salt
- ¼ teaspoon ground black pepper

Combine all ingredients in medium bowl.

RECIPE SHORTHAND | STEAK FRITES

Successful steak frites requires some careful timing. The first four steps can be completed up to 2 hours before dinner. Once you start cooking the steaks, you need to work quickly to get the steak and fries on the table.

1. Rinse cut potatoes. **2.** Toss potatoes with cornstarch. **3.** Air-dry potatoes. **4.** Blanch potatoes, in two batches, in 325-degree oil; let cool. **5.** Cook steaks. **6.** Finish fries, in two batches, in 375-degree oil.

ILLUSTRATION: JAY LAYMAN

Perfecting Herb-Crusted Pork Roast

A fresh herb crust seems like a good way to enliven a boneless pork roast—but not if the crust has little flavor and falls off.

BY CHARLES KELSEY

Boneless center-cut pork roast is a poster child for the "other white meat" campaign. Its uniform shape and compact eye of meat make it an attractive, easy-to-slice roast. This cut is also widely available and won't break the bank. Now for the bad news. The center-cut roast comes from the leanest part of the pig, and it's very bland. It needs adornment. Enter the herb crust.

Typically a mix of fresh herbs and bread crumbs applied before roasting, an herb crust can be attached any number of ways. Some recipes brush the roast with mustard—or some other sticky, complementary ingredient—and then coat it with herbs and crumbs. Others make an herb paste (think pesto) to attach the bread crumbs. Other recipes simply rely on the roast's exterior moisture to keep the herb crust affixed.

My initial testing of existing recipes produced dismal results. Roasts emerged with pale crusts and minimal herb flavor. Recipes with a measly tablespoon or two of fresh herbs and a handful of bread crumbs were the worst. But more herbs and crumbs didn't solve the problem; they just tended to fall right off, although the pesto-like pastes worked best. My tasters had one last complaint: The solid expanse of lean meat seemed to overshadow the crust, and the best bites from each slice were those closest to the crust. Tasters hypothesized that somehow infusing the meat with herb flavor would unify the crust and meat so that even if you didn't get a bite with crust, you'd still get pork with great herb flavor. I had my work cut out for me.

For flavor in every bite, we spread an herb paste in the middle and on top of the roast. A cheesy crumb crust is the crowning touch.

RECIPE DIAGNOSIS:

When Good Meat Goes Bad

Our initial testing revealed a host of problems with most recipes for herb-crusted pork loin.

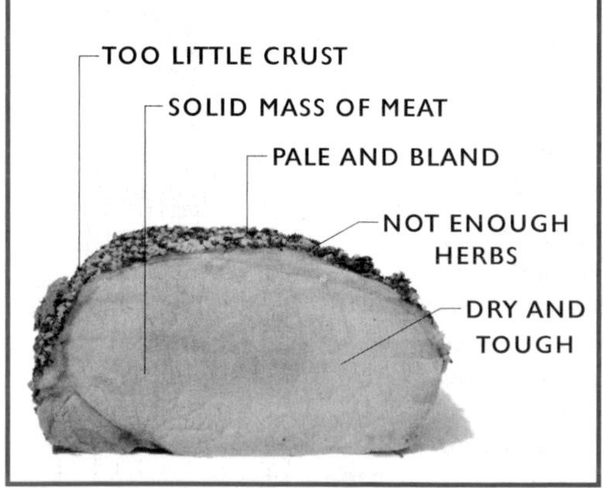

Laying the Groundwork

I took a big step back and reviewed some pork roasting basics. Based on previous test kitchen research, I knew that brining the roast in a salt-sugar solution for an hour before cooking would boost moisture and season the meat. I also knew that browning the roast would be crucial for maximum flavor. Previous test results showed that searing the roast in a skillet on the stovetop before finishing the meat in a 325-degree oven works best. (The relatively low oven temperature allows the roast to cook evenly, so the exterior doesn't overcook while you wait for the center to come up to temperature.)

But even when I brined this roast before browning, it was still pretty lackluster. I decided to deal with the blandness issue first; I would work on the crust later. I tried adding chopped herbs and smashed garlic cloves to the brine, assuming that the brine would carry the herb and garlic flavors deep into the meat. My hunch was only half correct. Tasters detected garlic flavor, but the herbs were missing in action. Even when I threw fistfuls of herbs into the brine bucket, no one could taste them.

Confused, I wondered why the garlic flavor would come through but not the herbs. I spoke with our food scientist, who explained that garlic's flavor compounds are water soluble, so they can pass into the meat during brining. The flavor compounds in herbs are oil soluble and don't mix with the water in the brine, so herb flavor can't penetrate the meat.

If herbs need oil to carry their flavor, I assumed that marinating the roast in a mixture of oil, herbs, and garlic would do the trick. But even after 24 hours, the herb flavor had barely penetrated the exterior of the roast. Inspired by a recipe from my research, I tried cutting random slits deep into the roast before smearing on a thick herb paste. This technique showed promise, as tasters finally praised a roast for good herb flavor in every bite. With multiple slits, however, this roast was far from attractive. Could I do better?

After some experimentation, I found that cutting a single horizontal pocket across the middle of the roast was the solution I'd been searching for. The pocket was easy to make and could hold a handsome ¼ cup of herb paste. Finally, each bite of pork contained herb flavor.

I discovered it was best to cut the pocket before brining. Also, tying the stuffed roast with twine kept the paste in place as the meat went from the counter to the skillet for browning.

Crust Building

Now that the roast itself was more flavorful, it was time to work on the exterior crust. I slathered the browned roast with more herb paste, covered it with crumbs, and popped it into the oven. About an hour later, the roast emerged with an attractive golden brown crust. Following protocol, I let the meat rest for 10 minutes (which gave the

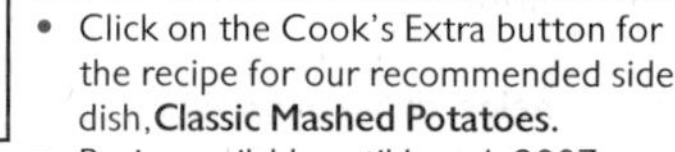

ILLUSTRATION: JOHN BURGOYNE

STEP-BY-STEP | PREPARING HERB-CRUSTED PORK ROAST

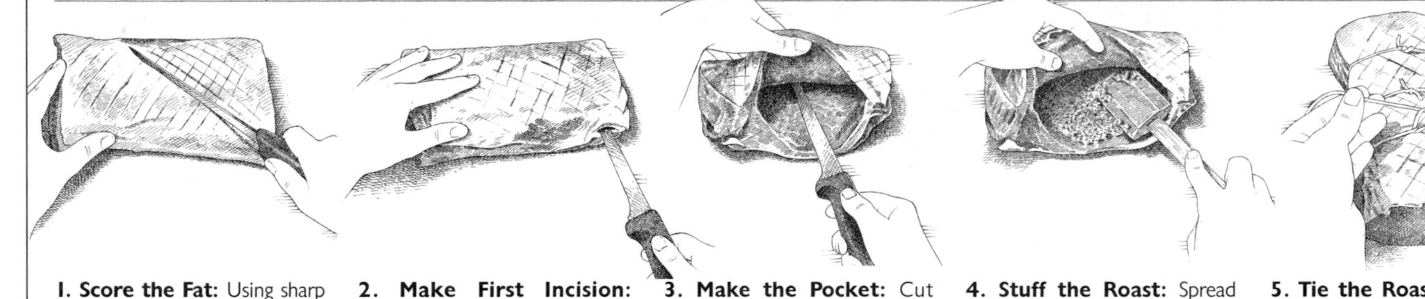

1. Score the Fat: Using sharp boning knife, lightly score fat cap on roast to make ¼-inch crosshatch pattern.

2. Make First Incision: Starting ½ inch from end of roast, insert knife into middle of roast, with blade parallel to work surface.

3. Make the Pocket: Cut along side of pork, stopping ½ inch short of other end. Pull open roast and use gentle strokes to cut deeper pocket.

4. Stuff the Roast: Spread ¼ cup herb paste evenly into pocket, using spatula and fingers to make sure paste reaches corners of pocket.

5. Tie the Roast: Fold roast over to original shape and tie at even intervals along its length with 3 pieces of kitchen twine.

juices time to redistribute and allowed the roast to slowly finish cooking from its carryover heat) and then sliced away. My knife blade revealed perfectly cooked, juicy pork, but the crust didn't stay firmly attached. Upon closer inspection, I noticed the herb paste was sliding off the rendered fat cap. Scoring a crosshatch pattern into the fat cap before searing the roast gave the paste something to grip and helped unify the crust and meat even more.

My last tasks were to tweak the herb paste and ramp up the flavor of the bread crumbs. Tasters wanted a simple mix of herbs in the paste and felt strongly that the bulk should be made up by a neutral, soft herb, such as parsley (basil worked too). Tasters liked quite a bit of woodsy thyme and a touch of intense rosemary to bolster parsley's mild flavor. Garlic was a welcome addition to the herb paste, as was grated Parmesan cheese, which made the paste tackier and easier to affix to the meat. A bit of Parmesan and minced shallot seasoned the bread crumbs, and some olive oil helped the crumbs crisp perfectly in the oven.

I had finally transformed this plain-Jane cut into a tasty roast that offered herb flavor in every bite.

HERB-CRUSTED PORK ROAST

SERVES 4 TO 6

If only "enhanced" pork is available (the label will state that the pork was injected with a water-salt solution; see photo, page 30), do not brine the roast. Instead, simply season the stuffed and tied roast with salt before browning. Note that you should not trim the pork of its layer of fat. While it is possible to substitute dried rosemary for fresh, do not substitute dried thyme for fresh or the herb crust will be dry and dusty tasting. The roasting time will vary widely depending on the thickness of the meat. The roast can be brined, stuffed, and tied a day ahead, but don't prepare the bread crumb topping until you are ready to cook.

- 1 boneless center-cut pork loin roast, 2½ to 3 pounds (see note above)
- Table salt
- ¼ cup sugar
- 1 large slice white sandwich bread, torn into pieces
- 1 ounce Parmesan or pecorino cheese, grated (about ½ cup)
- 1 medium shallot, minced (about 3 tablespoons)
- 4 tablespoons plus 2 teaspoons olive oil
- Ground black pepper
- ⅓ cup packed fresh parsley or basil leaves
- 2 tablespoons minced fresh thyme leaves
- 1 teaspoon minced fresh rosemary leaves or ½ teaspoon dried
- 1 large garlic clove, minced or pressed through garlic press (about 1½ teaspoons)

1. Following illustration 1 above, lightly score fat cap on pork, making ¼-inch crosshatch pattern. Following illustrations 2 and 3, cut pocket in roast. Dissolve ½ cup salt and sugar in 2 quarts water in large container; submerge roast, cover with plastic wrap, and refrigerate for 1 hour. Rinse roast under cold water and dry thoroughly with paper towels.

2. Meanwhile, adjust oven rack to lower-middle position and heat oven to 325 degrees. Pulse bread in food processor until coarsely ground, about sixteen 1-second pulses (you should have 1 cup crumbs). Transfer crumbs to medium bowl (do not wash food processor workbowl) and add 2 tablespoons Parmesan, shallot, 1 tablespoon oil, ⅛ teaspoon salt, and ⅛ teaspoon pepper. Using fork, toss mixture until crumbs are evenly coated with oil.

3. Add parsley or basil, thyme, rosemary, garlic, remaining 6 tablespoons Parmesan, 3 tablespoons oil, ⅛ teaspoon salt, and ⅛ teaspoon pepper to now-empty food processor workbowl and process until smooth, about twelve 1-second pulses. Transfer herb paste to small bowl.

4. Following illustrations 4 and 5, spread ¼ cup herb paste inside roast and tie. Season roast with pepper (and salt, if using enhanced pork).

5. Heat remaining 2 teaspoons oil in 12-inch skillet over medium-high heat until just smoking. Add roast, fat side down, and brown on all sides, 8 to 10 minutes, lowering heat if fat begins to smoke. Transfer roast to wire rack set in rimmed baking sheet lined with aluminum foil.

6. Using scissors, snip and remove twine from roast; discard twine. Following photos below, spread remaining herb paste over roast and top with bread crumb mixture. Transfer baking sheet with roast to oven and cook until thickest part of roast registers 145 degrees on instant-read thermometer, 50 to 75 minutes. Remove roast from oven and let rest 10 minutes. Internal temperature should rise to 150 degrees. Using spatula and meat fork, transfer roast to carving board, taking care not to squeeze juices out of pocket in roast. Cut roast into ½-inch slices and serve immediately.

HERB-CRUSTED PORK ROAST WITH MUSTARD AND CARAWAY

Follow recipe for Herb-Crusted Pork Roast, substituting 1 tablespoon minced garlic for shallot in bread crumb mixture, replacing rosemary with 4 teaspoons whole-grain mustard and 1 tablespoon toasted caraway seeds, and reducing oil in step 3 to 2 tablespoons.

Building a Better Crust

Apply the Paste: After browning roast in skillet and removing kitchen twine, use rubber spatula to spread remaining herb paste evenly over top of roast.

Affix the Crumbs: Sprinkle Parmesan-laced bread crumbs on top of roast and then gently press them in with hands. Finish cooking roast in oven.

ILLUSTRATION: JOHN BURGOYNE

Streamlining Manicotti

Manicotti may look homey, but blanching and stuffing pasta tubes is a tedious chore, and the ricotta filling can be uninspired and watery. We wanted a simpler, better recipe.

⋟ BY REBECCA HAYS ⋞

I have a love/hate relationship with manicotti. Well-made versions of this Italian-American classic—pasta tubes stuffed with rich ricotta filling and blanketed with tomato sauce—can be eminently satisfying. So what's not to love? Putting it all together. For such a straightforward collection of ingredients (after all, manicotti is just a compilation of pasta, cheese, and tomato sauce), the preparation is surprisingly fussy. Blanching, shocking, draining, and stuffing slippery pasta tubes require more patience (and time) than I usually have. In addition, a survey of manicotti recipes proved that most recipe writers don't get the filling right; too often, the ricotta-based mixture turns out bland and runny.

Test Tubes

Testing started with the pasta component. Cheese-stuffed pastas have been consumed in Italy since medieval times, and traditional recipes used either homemade *crespelle* (thin, eggy, crêpe-like pancakes) or rectangular sheets of homemade pasta as wrappers for the filling. (Both are terrific, though neither fit into my streamlined schematic.) Over time, most Italian-American recipes evolved to use ready-made dried pasta shells instead of homemade wrappers. For manicotti, pasta tubes are parboiled, shocked in ice water to stop the cooking, drained, and stuffed with ricotta filling. It was on this approach that I focused my attention.

Some recipes require a pastry bag for filling the long, hollow cylinders with ricotta; others explain how to snip the corner from a zipper-lock bag to create a mock pastry bag. Many recipes take a different approach altogether, suggesting a small soupspoon for stuffing the tubes. With a bowl of basic ricotta filling at my side, I took a deep breath and gave each method a try. The pastry bag was messy but workable. However, many cooks don't own a pastry bag, and I didn't want to write a recipe requiring a specialty tool. Using a zipper-lock bag to force the ricotta into a slick parboiled pasta tube was maddening; most of the cheese oozed out of the bag, with an embarrassingly small amount actually making it into the tube. The soupspoon was equally frustrating; I eventually gave up on it and used my fingers instead. Noticing my impatience, a colleague suggested slitting a blanched noodle lengthwise, packing it with filling, and putting the stuffed tube into a casserole seam side down. Not bad, but this method still called for blanching, shocking, and draining the noodles.

I found a "quick" recipe that seemed worth trying on the back of one of the manicotti boxes. It called for stuffing uncooked pasta tubes with ricotta, covering them with a watery sauce, then baking. Filling raw pasta tubes with cheese was marginally easier than stuffing limp parboiled noodles, but it wasn't without missteps: A few shattered along the way. Still, I followed the recipe through, watering down a jar of tomato sauce with a cup of boiling water and pouring it over the manicotti. After 45 minutes in the oven, this manicotti was inedible, with some of the pasta shells remaining uncooked and the pink, watered-down sauce tasting, well, like water.

Nearly at my wit's end, I remembered the crespelle and fresh pasta sheets, which didn't have any of the assembly problems associated with manicotti tubes. Spreading the filling onto a flat wrapper had to be easier than cramming it into a floppy tube. I scanned the fine print on a package of store-bought crêpes, hoping to use them instead of crespelle, but alas, they were far too sugary. Fresh pasta sheets aren't sold at many supermarkets. It was then that I thought of no-boil lasagna noodles. What if I softened the noodles in water, turning them into pliable sheets of pasta? This method worked like a charm. After a quick soak in boiling water, no-boil lasagna noodles could be spread with filling and rolled up in a few easy minutes.

Forget tricky stuffing methods. Our recipe relies on no-boil lasagna noodles and a simple filling technique.

NO SHORTCUT AT ALL

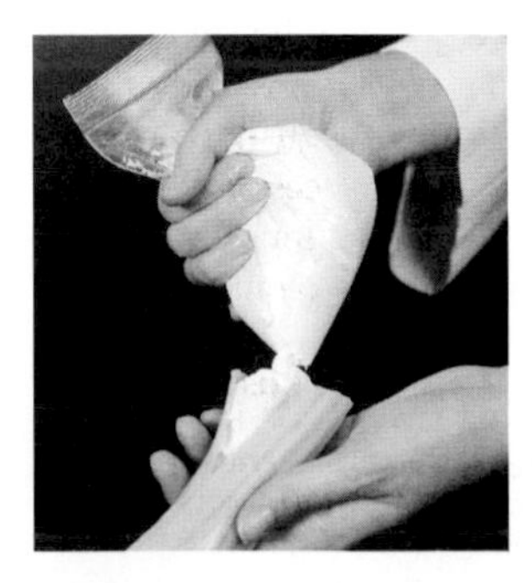

Many recipes replace the traditional pastry bag with a zipper-lock plastic bag. But using a plastic bag to stuff parboiled manicotti shells is a messy, frustrating job that is eliminated by our simple recipe.

The Big Cheese

It was a given that ricotta would serve as the base for the filling, but was whole milk, part-skim, or even fat-free ricotta preferable? All were fine, but part-skim ricotta provided an ideal level of richness, allowing the other flavors to shine.

In addition to ricotta, shredded low-moisture mozzarella and Parmesan are generally added to the filling. I wondered if other cheeses might fare better. After testing cream cheese, fresh mozzarella, fontina, Asiago, pecorino, and aged provolone, I decided to stick with tradition, opting for mozzarella and Parmesan.

Without eggs, the filling separates, becoming loose and watery. After experimenting with various amounts of whole eggs and yolks, I settled on two whole eggs. But eggs alone didn't completely ward off a runny filling. The proper amounts of mozzarella and Parmesan also proved key; specifically, a generous amount of mozzarella was necessary.

As for seasonings, a few specks of parsley plus salt and pepper are the norms. Looking for improvement, I explored other options, eventually settling on a combination of fresh parsley and basil (dried herbs were too harsh).

PHOTOGRAPHY: CARL TREMBLAY

STEP-BY-STEP | MANICOTTI 1, 2, 3

In our streamlined recipe, the ricotta filling is spread onto softened no-boil lasagna noodles, eliminating the slippery task of stuffing parboiled manicotti shells.

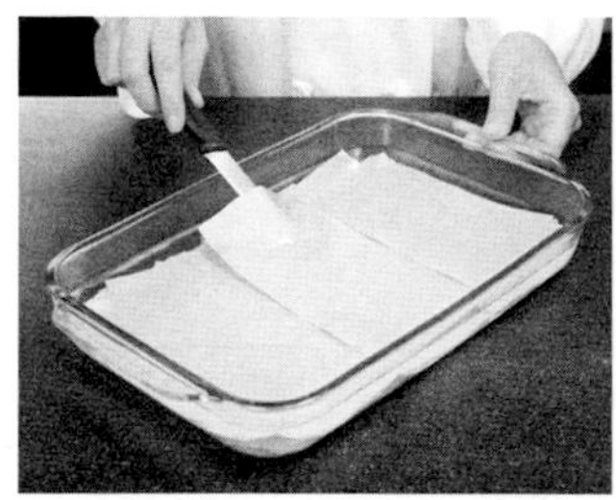

1. Soak no-boil lasagna noodles in boiling water for 5 minutes until pliable, using tip of paring knife to separate noodles and prevent sticking.

2. Using soupspoon, spread about ¼ cup filling onto three-quarters of each noodle, leaving top quarter of noodle exposed.

3. Roll each noodle by hand and place in baking dish, seam side down.

Finishing Touches

A slow-cooked tomato sauce didn't fit into my streamlining goal, so I was relieved when tasters preferred the bright, fresh flavor of a 15-minute sauce made with olive oil, garlic, and diced canned tomatoes pureed in a food processor to give the sauce body quickly. I punched up my quick recipe with fresh basil leaves and a dash of red pepper flakes.

Finally, most baked pasta dishes benefit from a browned, cheesy topping. The best approach was to add a light sprinkling of Parmesan, passing the casserole under the broiler before serving. This, at last, was manicotti that won my complete affection: great tasting and easy to prepare.

BAKED MANICOTTI

SERVES 6 TO 8

We prefer Barilla no-boil lasagna noodles for their delicate texture resembling fresh pasta. Note that Pasta Defino and Ronzoni brands contain only 12 no-boil noodles per package; the recipe requires 16 noodles. The manicotti can be prepared through step 5, covered with a sheet of parchment paper, wrapped in aluminum foil, and refrigerated for up to 3 days or frozen for up to 1 month. (If frozen, thaw the manicotti in the refrigerator for 1 to 2 days.) To bake, remove the parchment, replace the aluminum foil, and increase baking time to 1 to 1¼ hours.

Tomato Sauce

- 2 (28-ounce) cans diced tomatoes in juice
- 2 tablespoons extra-virgin olive oil
- 3 medium garlic cloves, minced or pressed through garlic press (about 1 tablespoon)
- ½ teaspoon red pepper flakes, optional
- Table salt
- 2 tablespoons chopped fresh basil leaves

Cheese Filling and Pasta

- 3 cups part-skim ricotta cheese
- 4 ounces grated Parmesan cheese (about 2 cups)
- 8 ounces mozzarella, shredded (about 2 cups)
- 2 large eggs, lightly beaten
- ¾ teaspoon table salt
- ½ teaspoon ground black pepper
- 2 tablespoons chopped fresh parsley leaves
- 2 tablespoons chopped fresh basil leaves
- 16 no-boil lasagna noodles (see note above)

1. **FOR THE SAUCE:** Adjust oven rack to middle position and heat oven to 375 degrees. Pulse 1 can tomatoes with their juice in food processor until coarsely chopped, 3 or 4 pulses. Transfer to bowl. Repeat with remaining can tomatoes.

2. Heat oil, garlic, and pepper flakes (if using) in large saucepan over medium heat until fragrant but not brown, 1 to 2 minutes. Stir in tomatoes and ½ teaspoon salt and simmer until thickened slightly, about 15 minutes. Stir in basil; adjust seasoning with salt.

3. **FOR THE CHEESE FILLING:** Combine ricotta, 1 cup Parmesan, mozzarella, eggs, salt, pepper, and herbs in medium bowl; set aside.

4. **TO ASSEMBLE:** Pour 1 inch boiling water into 13 by 9-inch broilersafe baking dish, then add noodles one at a time. Let noodles soak until pliable, about 5 minutes, separating noodles with tip of sharp knife to prevent sticking. Remove noodles from water and place in single layer on clean kitchen towels; discard water in baking dish and dry baking dish.

5. Spread bottom of baking dish evenly with 1½ cups sauce. Using soupspoon, spread ¼ cup cheese mixture evenly onto bottom three-quarters of each noodle (with short side facing you), leaving top quarter of noodle exposed. Roll into tube shape and arrange in baking dish seam side down. Top evenly with remaining sauce, making certain that pasta is completely covered.

6. Cover manicotti with aluminum foil. Bake until bubbling, about 40 minutes, then remove foil. Remove baking dish, adjust oven rack to uppermost position (about 6 inches from heating element), and heat broiler. Sprinkle manicotti evenly with remaining 1 cup Parmesan. Broil until cheese is spotty brown, 4 to 6 minutes. Cool 15 minutes, then serve.

TASTING: Ricotta Cheese

Originally crafted from the whey by-product of Romano cheesemaking, ricotta cheese has garnered fame on its own as a white, cushiony filling for baked pasta dishes. As ricotta has gained global popularity, however, preservation methods used by many large-scale manufacturers have turned these once fluffy, buttery, sweet curds into chalky, sour spreads. Seeking at least one noble specimen, we sampled four nationally available brands of part-skim ricotta.

The three commercially processed brands—Dragone, Sargento, and Sorrento—consistently garnered unfavorable adjectives such as "rancid," "grainy," "soggy," and just plain "yucky." At the other end of the spectrum entirely sat Calabro's "fresh," "creamy," and, as one taster put it, "perfect" curds—the hands-down favorite. Baked into rolls of pasta and smothered with homemade tomato sauce and fresh herbs, the differences were slightly less apparent, though not altogether unnoticed.

All three commercial brands are packed with gums and other stabilizers to guarantee shelf-stability for weeks. Calabro's curds, on the other hand, are fresh—drawn from nothing other than Vermont farm whole milk, skim milk, a starter, and a sprinkle of salt. Granted, the latter's shelf life spans only a matter of days, but one spoonful should be enough to guarantee its quick disappearance from your fridge. If you can't find Calabro, read labels and look for another fresh ricotta without gums or stabilizers.

—Elizabeth Bomze

NOT FOR US | FRESH IS BEST

When it comes to ricotta, choose a freshly made cheese without gums or stabilizers. We particularly like Calabro ricotta, which is available nationwide at Whole Foods Markets.

BAKED MANICOTTI WITH SAUSAGE

Follow recipe for Baked Manicotti through step 1. Cook 1 pound hot or sweet Italian sausage, casings removed, in 2 tablespoons olive oil in large saucepan over medium-high heat, stirring to break sausage into ½-inch pieces, until no longer pink, about 6 minutes. Continue as directed, adding garlic and pepper flakes to sausage.

Go to www.cooksillustrated.com
- Click on the Cook's Extra button for **Baked Manicotti with Prosciutto** and **Baked Manicotti Puttanesca**.
- Recipes available until June 1, 2007

Thai-Style Chicken Soup at Home

Authentic Thai chicken soup gains complex flavor in minutes via a handful of exotic ingredients. Could supermarket substitutes deliver comparable results?

BY MATTHEW CARD

Whenever I go out for Thai food, I start my meal with a bowl of *tom khaa gai*, or the easier-to-pronounce translation: Thai chicken soup. It doesn't look like much—a creamy, pale broth laced with chicken slices, mushrooms, and cilantro—but what it lacks in looks it makes up for in flavor. Sweet and sour components balance the richness of lemon grass–and-lime-infused coconut milk, which, in turn, tempers a slow-building chile burn. It makes my own chicken noodle soup seem as enticing as hospital food.

So if Thai chicken soup is so good, why don't I make it at home? Simple: ingredients. Its complex flavor is largely derived from such exotica as galangal, kaffir lime leaves, lemon grass, and bird's eye chiles. I'd be hard pressed to find most of these ingredients at my market. That being said, I wondered if a plausibly authentic version of Thai chicken soup could be prepared with more readily available (i.e., supermarket) substitutions.

Broth Matters

I found a handful of "simplified" or "Americanized" Thai chicken soup recipes that, while largely informative regarding substitutions, mostly missed the mark. Each lacked the taut balancing of hot, sour, salty, and sweet components that makes Thai cooking so compelling. (Appropriately enough, that balance, in Thai, is called *yum*.) So, for the time being at least, I stuck with the authentic recipes. I'd address substitutions once I knew how best to prepare the soup. I spent a long day shopping to find all the required ingredients and set to work.

Variation in Thai chicken soup recipes tends to center on two basic components: broth and garnishes. Traditional recipes typically prepare the broth in one of two methods. The first involves poaching a whole chicken in water with aromatics (just like my own chicken noodle soup), after which the broth is blended with coconut milk and further seasoned; the chicken—now shredded—is stirred in with the mushrooms. In the second approach, chicken broth and coconut milk are simmered with the aromatics, after which thin-sliced raw chicken and the remaining ingredients and seasonings are added. Both methods have their merits, but I much preferred the latter, which took half the effort and time without any apparent injury to flavor. The richness of the coconut milk and assertive seasonings evidently added big flavor fast.

How long did the broth and aromatics need to simmer for the best results? I cobbled together a working recipe from the best I had tried—a blend of chicken broth, coconut milk, lemon grass, shallots, galangal, and cilantro. A scant 10 minutes after the broth had come to a simmer proved perfect. Much longer and the broth tasted bitter, vegetal, and overextracted.

While the simple simmer certainly sufficed, I wondered if sautéing the aromatics before adding the liquid, as is common for Western-style soups, might improve matters. I cooked the shallots, galangal, lemon grass, and cilantro with a little vegetable oil until softened, then added the chicken broth and coconut milk and proceeded with the recipe. Tasted side by side against the original method, the broth prepared with sautéed aromatics tasted much clearer and fuller. A little extra effort, perhaps, but the "fusion" method paid off.

After preparing a few more batches with varying ratios of chicken broth and coconut milk, I settled on equal parts of each. Rich tasting without being cloying, and definitely chicken flavored, the blend was perfectly balanced. I also tried a technique I had come across in a couple of recipes. The coconut milk was added in two parts: half at the beginning and the remainder just before serving. What seemed fussy made a big difference, as the coconut flavor came through most clearly.

No Substitutions, Please

Now came the hard part: making substitutions. Most of the "simplified" recipes I tried or reviewed replaced the lemon grass with lemon zest, but I found the swap objectionable. Lemon zest—in conjunction with the sweet coconut milk—made for a broth with an odd, candy-like flavor. Dried lemon grass also failed to impress, lacking any of the depth of the fresh stuff. Luckily, I discovered lemon grass to be more readily available than I had assumed.

Galangal is a knotty, peppery-flavored rhizome distantly related to ginger, which most food writers suggest is the perfect substitute. While it wasn't perfect to me—ginger lacked the depth of flavor and piney finish of galangal—it would make do.

Kaffir lime leaves, the fresh or dried leaves from a potent variety of tropical lime, lend the broth a particularly floral, deep flavor and alluring aroma. Lime zest is the usual substitute, but one I felt lacked the intensity of the leaves. Once again, the substitute felt like a distant second.

Plenty of chicken, mushrooms, and garnishes make this quick soup a meal.

A Little Dab'll Do Ya!

Why run all over town looking for authentic Thai ingredients like galangal, bird's eye chiles, and kaffir lime leaves when a jar of supermarket Thai red curry paste delivers all those flavors in super-concentrated form?

PHOTOGRAPHY: CARL TREMBLAY

This was a bad trend. Replacing the authentic ingredients was not working as well as I hoped, and the soup was not tasting nearly as good as I expected. Perhaps authentic flavor really wasn't possible without the proper ingredients.

Then I found my magic bullet. At one tasting postmortem, a colleague suggested red curry paste, an ingredient I hadn't considered to that point. While it is never added to traditional Thai chicken soup, the curry paste did include all the exotic ingredients for which I was trying so hard to find acceptable substitutions. I whisked a small spoonful of the paste into the soup in front of me and was struck by the surprising transformation from boring to—dare I say?—authentic.

Curry paste is usually added early on in cooking to mellow its potent flavor, but I found this flattened the flavors too much. Adding a dollop at the very end of cooking—whisked together with pungent fish sauce and tart lime juice—allowed the sharpness of the galangal, the fragrance of the kaffir lime leaves, and the bright heat of the chiles to come through loud and clear. Out went the mediocre ginger and lime zest and in went two teaspoons of easy-to-find red curry paste.

Chicken and Mushrooms

With the broth under my belt, I could finally tackle the chicken and mushrooms. I initially thought that rich-tasting thigh meat would be the best choice to stand up to the full-flavored broth, but it was too fatty; boneless, skinless breast meat was better.

As for the mushrooms, oyster mushrooms are traditional but hard to find. Supermarket options like cremini, shiitake, and white mushrooms each had their merits, but the latter proved to be the closest match to the mild flavor and chewy texture of oyster mushrooms. Sliced thin and submerged in the broth, they quickly softened and absorbed the soup's flavors like a sponge.

A sprinkle of cilantro usually suffices as a finishing touch, but tasters wanted more. The clean, bright heat of thin-sliced serrano chiles and sharp bite of scallions did the trick.

With twenty-odd minutes of cooking and a minimum of hands-on effort, I had Thai chicken soup that tasted every bit as good as that served at my local Thai restaurant. Will I ever make plain old chicken noodle soup again?

TECHNIQUE | SLICING CHICKEN BREASTS

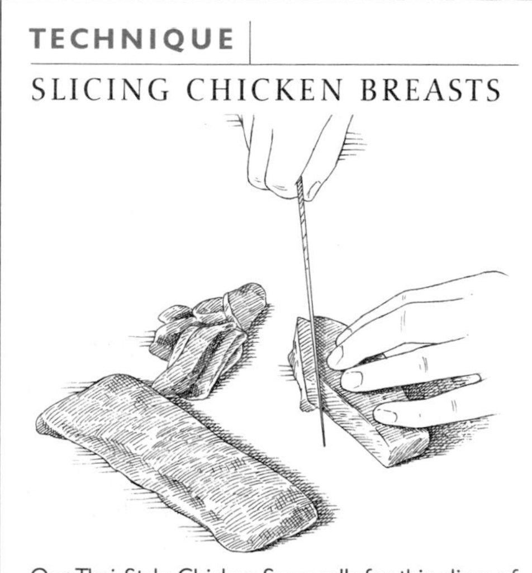

Our Thai-Style Chicken Soup calls for thin slices of boneless, skinless chicken breast that will cook in just a minute or two. To make slicing easier, place the chicken in the freezer for 30 minutes, then cut the breasts in half lengthwise. Firmer, narrower pieces of chicken will be easier to slice on the bias into 1/8-inch-thick slices.

ILLUSTRATION: JOHN BURGOYNE

TASTING: Coconut Milk

Coconut milk is not the thin liquid found inside the coconut itself; that is called coconut water. Coconut milk is a product made by steeping equal parts shredded coconut meat and either warm milk or water. The meat is pressed or mashed to release as much liquid as possible, the mixture is strained, and the result is coconut milk.

We tasted seven nationally available brands (five regular and two light) in coconut pudding, coconut rice, Thai-Style Chicken Soup, and green chicken curry. Among the five regular brands, tasters gravitated to those with more solid cream at the top of the can (most cans recommend shaking before opening to redistribute the solids). These brands also had a much stronger coconut flavor.

In the soup and curry, tasters preferred Chaokoh because of its exceptionally low sugar content (less than 1 gram per 1/3 cup). By comparison, brands with more than twice as much sugar (Ka-Me, Goya, Thai Kitchen) tasted "saccharine." In the sweet recipes, tasters gave velvety Ka-Me top votes for its "fruity" and "complex" flavor. In these recipes, the extra sugar was an advantage.

The light coconut milks we tasted were not nearly as creamy—a serious flaw in desserts but less so in soup. Of the two light brands tasted, we preferred the richer flavor of A Taste of Thai.

—Garth Clingingsmith and Elizabeth Bomze

SWEET AS SUGAR — CREAM OF THE CROP — THE LEAN CHOICE

Among the full-fat coconut milks, Ka-Me (left) is best suited for sweet recipes, while Chaokoh (center) is our favorite for soup. A Taste of Thai light coconut milk (right) was surprisingly good.

THAI-STYLE CHICKEN SOUP

SERVES 6 TO 8 AS AN APPETIZER OR 4 AS A MAIN COURSE

If you want a soup with less fat, it is possible to substitute light coconut milk for one or both cans of regular coconut milk. Fresh lemon grass can be omitted, but the soup will lack some complexity. Don't be tempted to use jarred or dried lemon grass—their flavor is characterless. If you want a spicier soup, add more red curry paste to taste. For a more substantial meal, serve the soup over 2 to 3 cups of cooked jasmine rice. The soup can be prepared through step 1 up to one day ahead of time and refrigerated, but it should be completed immediately before serving, as the chicken and mushrooms can easily overcook.

- 1 teaspoon vegetable oil
- 3 lemon grass stalks, tough outer leaves removed, bottom 5 inches halved lengthwise and sliced thin crosswise
- 3 large shallots, chopped
- 8 sprigs fresh cilantro, chopped coarse
- 3 tablespoons fish sauce
- 4 cups low-sodium chicken broth
- 2 (14-ounce) cans coconut milk, well shaken
- 1 tablespoon sugar
- 1/2 pound white mushrooms, cleaned, stems trimmed, cut into 1/4-inch slices
- 1 pound boneless, skinless chicken breasts, halved lengthwise and sliced on bias into 1/8-inch-thick pieces (see illustration at left)
- 3 tablespoons juice from 2 to 3 limes
- 2 teaspoons Thai red curry paste

Garnish

- 1/2 cup fresh cilantro leaves
- 2 serrano chiles, sliced thin
- 2 scallions, sliced thin on bias
- 1 lime, cut into wedges

1. Heat oil in large saucepan over medium heat until just shimmering. Add lemon grass, shallots, cilantro, and 1 tablespoon fish sauce; cook, stirring frequently, until just softened, 2 to 5 minutes (vegetables should not brown). Stir in chicken broth and 1 can coconut milk; bring to simmer over high heat. Cover, reduce heat to low, and simmer until flavors have blended, 10 minutes. Pour broth through fine-mesh strainer and discard solids in strainer. Rinse saucepan and return broth mixture to pan.

2. Return pan to medium-high heat. Stir remaining can coconut milk and sugar into broth mixture and bring to simmer. Reduce heat to medium, add mushrooms, and cook until just tender, 2 to 3 minutes. Add chicken and cook, stirring constantly, until no longer pink, 1 to 3 minutes. Remove soup from heat.

3. Combine lime juice, curry paste, and remaining 2 tablespoons fish sauce in small bowl; stir into soup. Ladle soup into bowls and garnish with cilantro, chiles, and scallions. Serve immediately with lime wedges.

Potato Primer

Think all potatoes are the same? Think again. Here are the basic information and cooking techniques you need to know for perfect mashed, roasted, boiled, and baked potatoes every time. BY KEITH DRESSER

NEW VERSUS OLD POTATOES

Potatoes can be categorized as "new" or "early" potatoes and "old" or "main crop" potatoes. Both new and old potatoes can come from any variety of potato. New potatoes are thin-skinned, less mature potatoes harvested in the late spring and summer. They are less starchy than "old" potatoes, because they haven't had time to convert their sugar into starch. These potatoes should be used as firm, waxy potatoes, regardless of variety. Old potatoes are fully mature and are harvested in the fall. They are usually starchier and have thick skins. These potatoes are often held in cold storage, or cured, in order for their skins to toughen, which helps protect their flesh for better storage. Most potatoes sold in supermarkets have been cured and can be considered "old" potatoes.

POTATO VARIETIES

Until recently, most markets sold potatoes under generic names, such as "baking potato" or "boiling potato," which helped shoppers choose the right potato for each recipe. But now many markets sell potatoes by varietal name, such as Yukon Gold and Red Creamer. So how do you use these potatoes? We find that potato varieties can be divided into three major categories based on texture. What causes different potatoes to have different textures? In a word, starch.

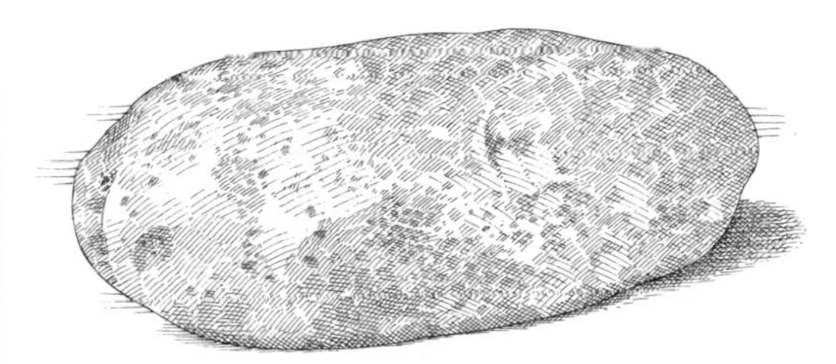

DRY, FLOURY POTATOES

What You Need to Know: Also known as "baking" potatoes, this group contains more total starch (20 percent to 22 percent) and amylose than other categories, giving these varieties a dry, mealy texture.

How to Use Them: The best choice when baking and frying. In our opinion, they are also the best potatoes for mashing, because they can drink up butter and cream. Good when you want to thicken a stew or soup but not if you want distinct chunks of potatoes.

Common Varieties: RUSSET, RUSSET BURBANK, IDAHO

"IN-BETWEEN" POTATOES

What You Need to Know: These potatoes contain less total starch (18 percent to 20 percent) and amylose than dry, floury potatoes but more total starch and amylose than firm, waxy potatoes. Although they are "in-between" potatoes, their texture is more mealy than firm, putting them closer to dry, floury potatoes.

How to Use Them: They can be mashed or baked but won't be as fluffy as dry, floury potatoes; they can be used in salads and soups but won't be quite as firm as waxy potatoes.

Common Varieties: YUKON GOLD, YELLOW FINN, PURPLE PERUVIAN, KENNEBEC, KATAHDIN

FIRM, WAXY POTATOES

What You Need to Know: Also known as "boiling" potatoes, these contain a relatively low amount of total starch (16 percent to 18 percent) and very little amylose, which means they have a firm, smooth, waxy texture. Freshly dug potatoes, which are often called "new" potatoes, fall into this group.

How to Use Them: Perfect when you want the potatoes to hold their shape, as with potato salad; also a good choice when roasting or boiling.

Common Varieties: RED BLISS, FRENCH FINGERLING, RED CREAMER, WHITE ROSE

WHY ARE MY POTATOES GREEN?

The green patches found on some potatoes are caused by prolonged exposure to light or improper storage. This discoloration is produced by chlorophyll and is usually an indication of increased levels of a naturally occurring toxic alkaloid called *solanine*. Ingesting solanine can lead to illness, so if you discover green patches when peeling your potatoes, simply cut off the affected areas.

BUYING AND STORING

BUYING

Look for firm specimens that are free of green spots, sprouts, cracks, and other blemishes. We generally prefer to buy loose potatoes, so we can see what we are getting. Stay away from potatoes in plastic bags, which can act like greenhouses and cause potatoes to sprout, soften, and rot.

STORING

If stored under unsuitable heat and light circumstances, potatoes will germinate and grow. To avoid this, keep potatoes in a cool, dark, dry place. Although some experts warn that refrigerating potatoes can dramatically increase the sugar level, we've never encountered this problem in the test kitchen. Store potatoes in a paper (not plastic) bag and away from onions, which give off gases that will hasten sprouting. Most varieties should keep for several months. The exception is new potatoes—because of their thinner skins, they will keep no more than one month.

THE STARCH MATTERS

Total starch content in potatoes can range from 16 percent to 22 percent. But just as important as the total amount of starch is the type of starch. There are two kinds of starch molecules—amylose and amylopectin—and they behave quite differently. Amylose molecules, which are shaped like long chains, easily separate when cooked in the presence of water. This explains why russet potatoes, which have a high amount of amylose, are the best choice for mashing. In contrast, amylopectin molecules have a compact, branched shape that holds together when cooked and helps the potato remain intact. Varieties with more amylopectin, such as Red Bliss, are the best choice for boiling.

RED BLISS POTATO
Remains Firm When Cooked

RUSSET POTATO
Turns Crumbly When Cooked

COOKING POTATOES

MASHED

Start with dry, floury potatoes and simmer them with their peels on. Yes, this is more work than the usual peel-and-dice method, but keeping water out ensures fluffy mashed potatoes with an earthy flavor. It is also important when mixing the potatoes to add the melted butter before the half-and-half. When butter is added before the half-and-half, the fat coats the starch molecules, inhibiting their interaction with the water in the half-and-half. The result is a silkier, creamier mashed potato.

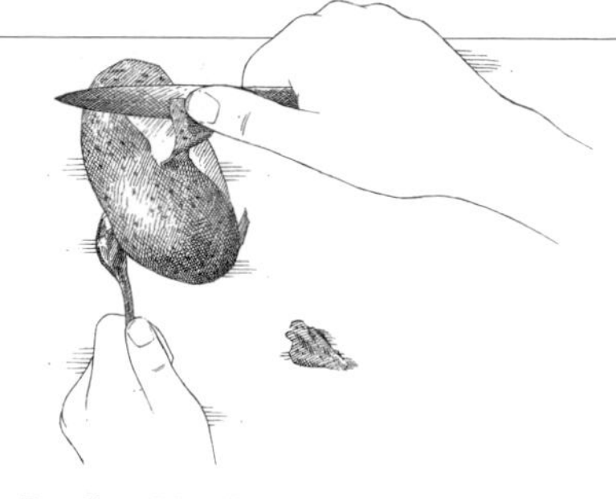

Peeling Hot Potatoes

The most efficient way to peel a just-boiled potato is to spear it with a fork and then use a paring knife to remove the peel.

IF YOU MUST PEEL

Over the years, we've tried many different peelers, and we recommend the OXO I-Series Swivel Peeler ($10). This sturdy, maneuverable, and incredibly sharp peeler simply outdoes the competition.

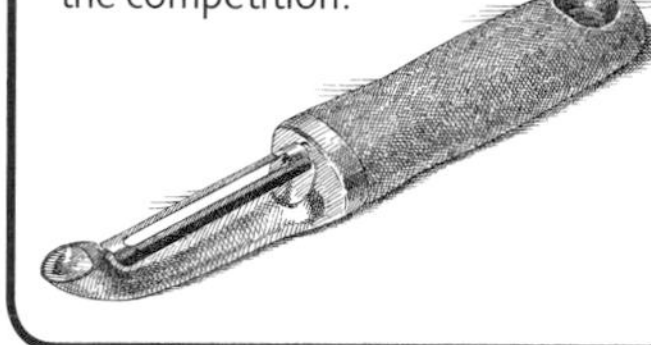

BAKED

Start with a dry, floury potato and bake it at a relatively low temperature, which allows some of the starch in the flesh just inside the skin to break down into sugar and gives the potato a rich flavor. To ensure that the flesh does not steam and become dense, open a baked potato as soon as it comes out of the oven.

Opening a Baked Potato

Use the tines of a fork to make a dotted X on top of each potato. Press in at the ends of the potato to push the flesh up and out. Besides releasing the steam quickly, this method helps trap and hold on to bits of butter.

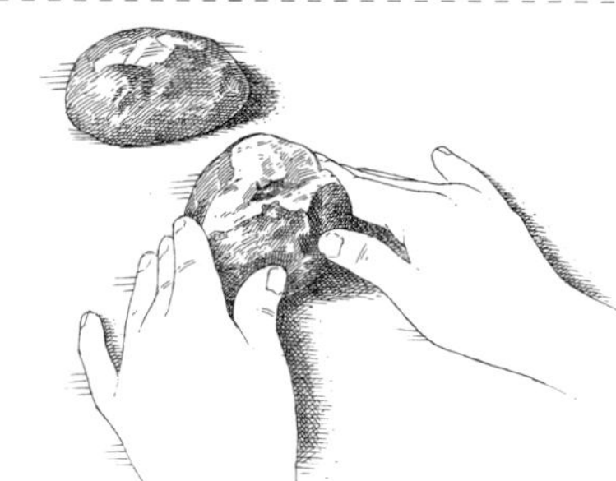

ROASTED

Start with waxy potatoes (they have more moisture than other varieties) and cover the pan with foil for the first half of the roasting time so the potatoes steam in their own moisture and become creamy. Remove the foil and continue roasting until the exteriors are crisp.

Flipping Roast Potatoes

Press a metal spatula against the pan as you slide it under the potatoes to protect the crisp crust. Flip the potatoes so that the other cut sides come in contact with the hot pan.

BOILED

Start with firm, waxy potatoes and boil them with their skin intact. Toss with butter and serve, or, for salad, cut and toss potatoes with vinegar, salt, and pepper. This technique allows the potatoes to easily absorb the vinegar, creating a fuller-flavored salad.

Is It Done Yet?

Poke the potato with a sharp paring knife and then try to lift it out of the water. If the potato clings to the knife even for a second, back into the pot it goes.

THREE TOOLS FOR MASHING

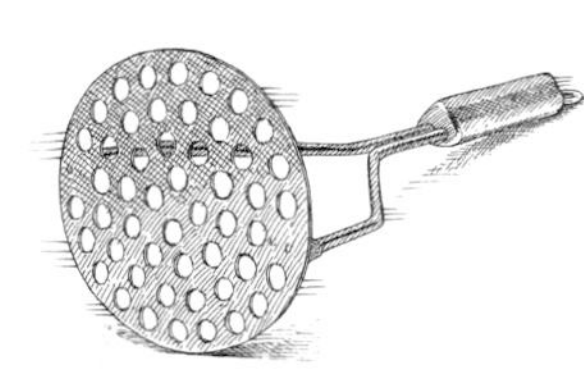

HAND MASHER: For chunky, home-style mashed potatoes, the tool of choice is a hand masher. These mashers come in all shapes and styles, but our choice is the Profi Plus Masher ($15.99). With its perforated disk and comfortable grip, the Profi mashes potatoes with minimum effort.

FOOD MILL: Part food processor and part sieve, a food mill quickly produces silky mashed potatoes while separating out any stray peels. Of the food mills tested in the kitchen, our favorite is the R.S.V.P. Rotary Food Mill ($19.95).

RICER: Like a food mill, the ricer purees the potato while removing any unwanted skins. The drawback to a ricer is that its hopper is quite small and it requires a fair amount of elbow grease, which makes processing a large batch of potatoes laborious. Our favorite is the Cuisipro Potato Ricer ($29.95).

BASIC POTATO RECIPES

MASHED POTATOES SERVES 4

Place 2 pounds scrubbed (and unpeeled) dry, floury potatoes in large saucepan with cold water to cover by about 1 inch. Bring to boil, then simmer over medium-low heat until tender and fully cooked (see illustration below), 20 to 30 minutes. Drain and peel potatoes. Mill, rice, or mash potatoes (see "Three Tools for Mashing"). Stir in 8 tablespoons melted unsalted butter, followed by 1 cup warm half-and-half. Season with 1½ teaspoons table salt and ground black pepper to taste.

BAKED POTATOES SERVES 4

Place 4 medium dry, floury potatoes directly on middle rack in 350-degree oven. Bake potatoes until skewer glides easily through flesh, about 1 hour and 15 minutes. Open immediately (see illustration at left), and serve with butter and salt.

ROASTED POTATOES SERVES 4

Toss 2 pounds firm, waxy potatoes, cut into ¾-inch wedges, with 3 tablespoons olive oil, salt, and pepper. Place potatoes flesh side down on rimmed baking sheet and cover tightly with foil. Cook potatoes on middle rack in 425-degree oven for 20 minutes. Remove foil and continue to roast until sides of potatoes touching pan are golden brown, about 15 minutes. Carefully turn potatoes over and continue to roast until golden brown on the second side, 5 to 10 minutes.

BOILED POTATOES SERVES 4

Place 2 pounds scrubbed firm, waxy potatoes in large saucepan with cold water to cover by about 1 inch. Bring to boil, then simmer over medium-low heat until tender, at least 10 minutes for 1-inch potatoes and up to 18 minutes for 2½-inch potatoes. Drain and toss with butter.

FOR SALAD: Cool potatoes slightly, cut with serrated knife into ¾-inch chunks, and place on rimmed baking sheet. Drizzle with ¼ cup red wine vinegar, ½ teaspoon salt, and ¼ teaspoon pepper. Let stand for 20 minutes, then transfer to bowl and dress as desired.

Introducing French Onion Tart

French Onion Tart is similar to quiche but delivers a more refined slice of pie, with more onions than custard. The problem? Rolling and fitting the dough into a tart pan.

⋟ BY ERIKA BRUCE ⋞

The French have a knack for making incredibly delicious dishes out of very simple ingredients. Case in point: onion tart. French cooks elevate a common vegetable to the status of foie gras by gently simmering it in butter, enriching it with custard (eggs and heavy cream), and baking it in a buttery crust. As the more refined, chic cousin of quiche, this preparation utilizes a slim tart shell and more onions than custard.

At least that's how I remember this tart from trips to France. Re-creating this memory at home was a different story. My crust came out impossibly tough and crackery—a disappointing end to the lengthy chilling, rolling, and resting process of making pastry dough. And after delicately cooking the onions for over an hour, like most French recipes specify, and then finally making the custard and baking the whole thing together, I was more frustrated with this tart than enchanted by it.

But my tantalizing recollections steered me back into the kitchen to find a way to simplify the crust and truncate the overall preparation time. After all, if I could make a successful quiche, with all its varied fillings, then I could certainly tackle this basic onion tart.

Think quiche with more onions and bacon and less eggy custard.

Keeping a Lid on It

Standing by the stovetop for an hour babysitting slowly simmering onions seemed unnecessary. Or so I thought. Starting the onions on high heat and then finishing them on low (the test kitchen's standard method for caramelizing onions) produced more tender onions, but these were far too sweet and one-dimensional for this application. It became apparent that the right cooking technique—one that tenderized the onions without making them candy-sweet—was crucial for a tart with so few ingredients. And a quick cooking method would be nice.

To speed things along, I added liquid to the onions at the onset of cooking (in a nonstick skillet, so as not to encourage browning) in the form of chicken broth, white wine, and water. But all three made the onions waterlogged, and the broth and wine added flavors that overshadowed the onions. I tried finishing the onions in the heavy cream, but this made the onions slimy and over-reduced the cream, resulting in a gluey filling.

Next, I put a lid on the skillet for the first 10 minutes to jump-start the onions over moderate heat without browning them, and then I finished them over low heat with the lid off. This most closely approximated the original low and slow method, but it only shaved about 10 minutes off the cooking time. Becoming exasperated, I just left the lid on the whole time, still turning down the heat after 10 minutes once the onions threatened to brown. Voilà—onions that cooked in half the time! Leaving the lid on allowed them to cook entirely in their own juices, so they became tender more quickly and retained their pure onion flavor. And they cooked more evenly, requiring minimal supervision—just a stir here and there.

It came as no surprise that sweet onions, such as Vidalias, didn't work in this recipe. Red onions stained the filling an odd, brownish-purple color. Both white and yellow onions were solid choices.

Sweet Tart

The proper onion and the right cooking method toned down the overall sweetness of my tart, but I had more work to do. Many versions of this recipe add bacon, and I could see why: Both salty and smoky, it added a welcome savory edge to the filling. If I rendered the bacon before sprinkling it on top, it acted as a nice crisp foil to the creamy filling. And cooking the onions in the rendered bacon fat instead of butter tempered their sweetness even more. I also replaced the usual perfumey nutmeg with woodsy fresh thyme.

Taking a bite of this tart was now a pleasant experience—sweet, soft onions and creamy custard offset by salty bacon and a buttery crust—but I had a hard time getting through an entire piece. It was simply too rich. I wasn't using all that much bacon (just four slices), so I looked to the custard (a mixture of eggs and heavy cream). Reducing the eggs from three to two and switching out cream for half-and-half solved the richness issues. While this tart was still certainly a luxuriant meal, at least now I could eat a whole serving.

Crust Evolution

I now was ready to tackle the other big challenge in this recipe: the crust. Getting an all-butter dough into a tart shell in one piece is time-consuming and stressful—and often requires patching torn dough back together and moving it in and out of the refrigerator to keep it from getting too soft. I wanted to cut out the steps of rolling out and repeatedly chilling the dough. A pat-in-the-pan crust seemed like my best bet.

I tried several recipes, which included everything from shortening to eggs and even cream cheese. But they produced crusts that were all too cookie-like and crumbly and, more important, lacked the intense butteriness of a traditional tart dough. Just patting a standard tart dough into the shell didn't cut it, either: The little pieces of butter, which are normally smeared into the

COOK'S extra

Go to www.cooksillustrated.com

- To make a complete meal, click on the Cook's Extra button for our recipe for **Spinach Salad with Mushrooms, Croutons,** and **Warm Lemon Dressing.**
- Recipe available until June 1, 2007.

PHOTOGRAPHY: CARL TREMBLAY

STEP-BY-STEP | NO ROLLING REQUIRED

While there are many methods of coercing dough into a tart pan, we found this was the simplest and quickest method to ensure an even crust—and no rolling pin is required.

1. Sprinkle walnut-sized clumps of dough evenly into tart pan.

2. Working outward from the center, press dough into even layer, sealing any cracks.

3. Working around edge, press dough firmly into corners of pan with index finger.

4. Go around edge once more, pressing dough up sides and into fluted ridges.

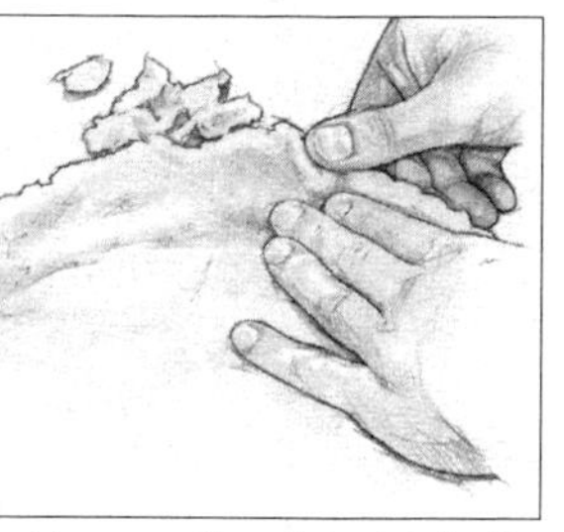

5. Use your thumb to level off top edge. Use this dough to patch any holes.

dough during rolling, melted in the oven, leaving unsightly holes and cracks in their place.

Since cutting back on butter was not an option—this produced a tough, shrunken crust—I turned to the mixing method. In an effort to rid the dough of visible pieces of butter, I beat room-temperature butter until soft and then added flour, salt, sugar (an ingredient that boosted both flavor and browning), and ice water. But this dough was too soft to press into the shell, even though it baked into a promisingly uniform crust. Switching back to cold butter, I cut it completely into the flour mixture using a food processor. Because the butter was fully mixed into the flour, I could now add less ice water than traditional recipes in which the butter is still in small chunks and doesn't hold the dough together as well. Finally, my dough was firm enough to press into the pan, and once baked, it was sturdy enough to hold up to a heavy filling like my onion custard.

With just a few minor changes to a classic recipe, I had produced a crust that was the ideal enclosure for my onion filling. With none of the usual fuss, I could now bring a perfect slice of France to my table at home.

FRENCH ONION AND BACON TART

SERVES 6 TO 8

Either yellow or white onions work well in this recipe, but stay away from sweet onions, such as Vidalias, which will make the tart watery. Use a 9-inch tinned-steel tart pan (see page 30 for details). This tart can be served hot or at room temperature and pairs well with a green salad as a main course. Leftovers should be wrapped in plastic wrap and refrigerated. Reheat on a baking sheet in a 325-degree oven for 10 to 15 minutes.

Crust

- 1¼ cups (6¼ ounces) unbleached all-purpose flour
- 1 tablespoon sugar
- ½ teaspoon table salt
- 8 tablespoons (1 stick) unsalted butter, cut into ½-inch cubes and well chilled
- 2–3 tablespoons ice water

Filling

- 4 ounces bacon (about 4 slices), halved lengthwise, then cut crosswise into ¼-inch pieces
- Vegetable oil, if needed
- 1½ pounds (about 3 medium) yellow or white onions, halved through root end, peeled, and cut crosswise into ¼-inch slices (about 6 cups) (see photo below)
- ¾ teaspoon table salt
- 1 sprig fresh thyme
- 2 large eggs
- ½ cup half-and-half
- ¼ teaspoon ground black pepper

1. **FOR THE CRUST:** Spray 9-inch tart pan with nonstick cooking spray. Combine flour, sugar, and salt in food processor with four 1-second pulses. Scatter butter pieces over flour mixture; pulse to cut butter into flour until mixture resembles coarse sand, about fifteen 1-second pulses. Add 2 tablespoons ice water and process until large clumps form and no powdery bits remain, about 5 seconds, adding up to 1 tablespoon more water if dough will not form clumps. Transfer dough to greased tart pan. Following illustrations above, pat dough into prepared pan. Lay plastic wrap over dough and smooth out any bumps or shallow areas. Place tart shell on plate and transfer to freezer for 30 minutes.

2. Adjust oven rack to middle position and heat oven to 375 degrees. Place frozen tart shell on baking sheet; lightly spray one side of 18-inch square extra-wide heavy-duty aluminum foil with nonstick cooking spray. Press foil greased side down inside tart shell, folding excess foil over edge of pan. Fill with pie weights and bake until top edge just starts to color and surface of dough under foil no longer looks wet, about 30 minutes. Remove from oven and carefully remove foil and weights by gathering edges of foil and pulling up and out. Return baking sheet with tart shell to oven and bake until golden brown, 5 to 10 minutes. Set baking sheet with tart shell on wire rack. Do not turn off oven.

3. **FOR THE FILLING:** While crust is baking, cook bacon in 12-inch nonstick skillet over medium heat until browned and crisp, 8 to 10 minutes. Drain bacon through mesh strainer set over small bowl; transfer bacon to paper towel–lined plate. Return 2 tablespoons bacon fat to skillet, adding vegetable oil to make up difference if necessary.

4. Add onions, salt, and thyme to skillet. Cover and cook until onions release liquid and start to wilt, about 10 minutes. Reduce heat to low and continue to cook, covered, until onions are very soft, about 20 minutes, stirring once or twice (if after 15 minutes onions look wet, remove lid and continue to cook another 5 minutes). Remove pan from heat and let onions cool 5 minutes.

5. Whisk eggs, half-and-half, and pepper together in large bowl. Remove thyme sprig from onions; discard. Stir onions into egg mixture until just incorporated. Spread onion mixture over baked crust (still on baking sheet) and sprinkle bacon evenly on top.

6. Return baking sheet with tart to oven and bake until center of tart feels firm to touch, 20 to 25 minutes. Cool on wire rack at least 10 minutes. When ready to serve, remove tart pan ring; gently slide thin-bladed spatula between tart pan bottom and crust to loosen, then slide tart to serving plate. Cut into wedges and serve.

TECHNIQUE | A CUT ABOVE THE REST

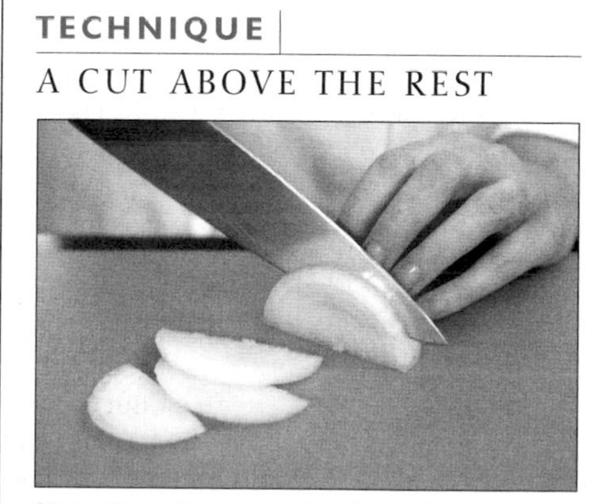

Slicing the onions crosswise allows them to soften and break down more readily than slicing them pole to pole.

How to Roast Cauliflower

High-heat roasting intensifies the flavor of this understated vegetable. We wanted to maximize the golden exterior while ensuring a creamy interior.

BY CHARLES KELSEY

I don't understand why most cooks boil cauliflower. When things go wrong (and they often do), the cauliflower is smelly (from overcooking) and mushy. Even when you avoid overcooking, boiled cauliflower is bland. No wonder delicately flavored cauliflower often gets drowned under a heavy blanket of cheese sauce.

When I want to add flavor to vegetables, I often turn to my oven. Roasting is a great technique for coaxing big flavor from vegetables; the dry heat caramelizes the natural sugars in everything from potatoes to onions. I had never roasted cauliflower, but it seemed worth a try.

I found three basic techniques in my research: roasting the cauliflower straight up, blanching it in water then roasting it, and steaming then roasting it. Each method separated a cauliflower head into florets before roasting on a baking sheet in a very hot oven (around 475 degrees). Each simple preparation coated the cauliflower florets with oil, salt, and pepper at some point in the procedure.

When all three versions were sampled side by side, the blanch-roasting technique was the loser of the bunch. The florets were soggy and had little color (read: flavor). The straight-up roasted cauliflower was well liked for its caramelized exterior, however it cooked unevenly and had some dried-out, gritty florets. Finally, the steam-roasted cauliflower emerged with creamy, evenly cooked florets but so-so browning and flavor.

My goal was to combine the last two methods and produce nicely caramelized cauliflower with a creamy texture. While testing the straight-up roasting technique, I noticed that the cauliflower was shedding its moisture in the first minutes of roasting. I was pretty sure that covering the baking sheet would trap this moisture and add just enough steam to cook the cauliflower properly.

After some tinkering, I discovered that 10 minutes was the perfect amount of time to leave the foil on. The steam kept the florets moist enough to withstand the next 20 minutes of roasting and prevented them from turning dry and gritty.

Served with a drizzle of extra-virgin olive oil or a quickly prepared sauce, roasted cauliflower is a revelation—sweet, creamy, and packed with flavor.

Bigger Than a Pencil

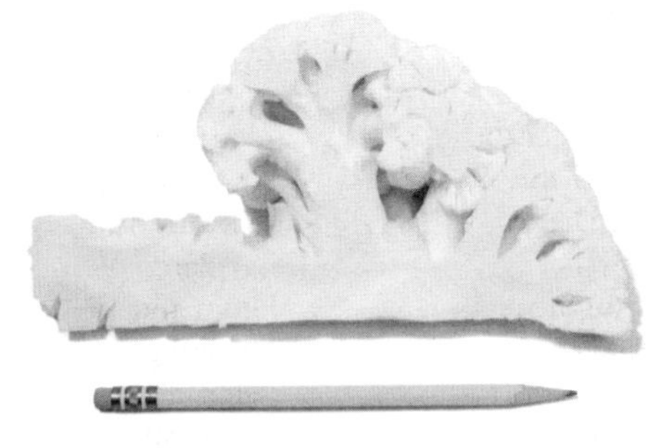

Cutting the cauliflower head from pole to pole into large wedges (about the length of a pencil) exposes more surface area to the hot sheet pan. And leaving the core intact makes it easy to flip the pieces halfway through the caramelization stage so that both sides gain a golden exterior.

ROASTED CAULIFLOWER

SERVES 4 TO 6

This dish stands well on its own, drizzled with extra-virgin olive oil, or with any of the following sauces. Also, some tasters liked spiced versions made with either curry powder or chili powder. Simply stir 2 teaspoons of either spice into the oil before seasoning the cauliflower in step 1.

- 1 medium head cauliflower (about 2 pounds)
- 1/4 cup extra-virgin olive oil, plus extra for drizzling
- Kosher salt and ground black pepper

1. Adjust oven rack to lowest position and heat oven to 475 degrees. Trim outer leaves of cauliflower and cut stem flush with bottom. Cut head into 8 equal wedges so that core and florets remain intact (see photo). Place wedges cut side down on foil- or parchment-lined rimmed baking sheet. Drizzle with 2 tablespoons oil and sprinkle with salt and pepper; gently rub to evenly distribute oil and seasonings. Gently flip cauliflower and season other cut side with remaining 2 tablespoons oil, salt, and pepper.

2. Cover baking sheet tightly with foil and cook for 10 minutes. Remove foil and continue to roast until bottoms of cauliflower pieces are golden, 8 to 12 minutes. Remove sheet from oven, and, using spatula, carefully flip wedges. Return sheet to oven and continue to roast until cauliflower is golden all over, 8 to 12 minutes longer. Season with salt and pepper to taste, drizzle with oil (or sauce), and serve immediately.

SOY-GINGER SAUCE WITH SCALLION

MAKES ENOUGH FOR 1 RECIPE ROASTED CAULIFLOWER

If using this sauce, use vegetable oil to roast the cauliflower instead of olive oil.

- 2 teaspoons vegetable oil
- 2 medium garlic cloves, minced or pressed through garlic press (about 2 teaspoons)
- 1 tablespoon minced fresh ginger
- 2 tablespoons soy sauce
- 2 tablespoons mirin
- 1 tablespoon rice vinegar
- 1/4 cup water
- 1 teaspoon toasted sesame oil
- 1 medium scallion, white and light green parts sliced thin

Heat vegetable oil in small skillet over medium-high heat until shimmering. Add garlic and ginger; cook until fragrant, about 1 minute. Reduce heat to medium-low and add soy, mirin, vinegar, and water. Simmer until slightly syrupy, 4 to 6 minutes. Drizzle sauce and sesame oil over roasted cauliflower and garnish with scallions.

CURRY-YOGURT SAUCE WITH CILANTRO

MAKES ENOUGH FOR 1 RECIPE ROASTED CAULIFLOWER

- 1 tablespoon vegetable oil
- 1 large shallot, minced (about 4 tablespoons)
- 2 teaspoons curry powder
- 1/4 teaspoon red pepper flakes
- 1/3 cup water
- 1/4 cup plain yogurt
- 1 teaspoon juice from 1 lime
- 2 tablespoons minced fresh cilantro leaves
- Table salt and ground black pepper

Heat oil in small skillet over medium-high heat until shimmering. Add shallot and cook until softened, about 2 minutes. Stir in curry powder and pepper flakes; cook until fragrant, about 1 minute. Remove from heat and whisk in water, yogurt, lime juice, cilantro, and salt and pepper to taste. Drizzle sauce over roasted cauliflower.

Bringing Sichuan Green Beans Home

This tangy, spicy dish offers an exotic change of pace from everyday green beans. We set out to overhaul its foreign ingredient list and simplify a troublesome technique.

⋟ BY ERIKA BRUCE ⋞

Whenever I order Chinese food, the one dish I get without fail is Sichuan green beans. The flavors of this addictive concoction—with its wrinkly, sweet beans, sprinkled with morsels of flavorful pork and coated in a pungent sauce—are hot, aromatic, and tangy all at the same time.

Because this preparation lends such flair to the frequently bland green beans, I wanted to create my own recipe. Traditionally, the beans are deep-fried in a wok filled with oil, yielding a wrinkled appearance, slightly chewy texture, and more intense flavor. In an effort to replicate these effects minus the grease and mess, I roasted the beans in a small amount of oil in a 450-degree oven until their skins shriveled and turned golden brown. But instead of the quick five-minute fry, these beans took more than 20 minutes; plus, I had to dirty an additional pan to cook the pork and make the sauce.

Seeking something more streamlined, I tried our traditional stir-frying method, in a large skillet over high heat. This method was indeed quicker and more efficient, but the beans were more crisp than chewy and they weren't flavorful enough. For my next test, I cooked the beans a few minutes longer, until the skins began to shrivel. The beans were now slightly chewy (just like I wanted) and intensely flavorful. By letting the beans stir-fry longer than usual, they had become charred in places, giving them a deeper, caramelized flavor that more than compensated for the fact that they were not being deep-fried.

Once the beans were perfectly cooked, I transferred them to a plate while I made the sauce. Authentic recipes rely on elusive ingredients such as Sichuan preserved mustard stems to produce the characteristic tang and modest heat. I tried substituting pickled ginger, pickled jalapeños, and even dill pickle in my stir-fried beans, but their individual assertive flavors showed through. Fresh mustard was also too strong, but dry mustard added a nice, subtle tang. I tried different vinegars—both rice and white wine vinegar were too sharp, overpowering the other sauce flavors of soy, fresh ginger, and garlic. Dry sherry plus a little sugar produced the right level of both acidity and sweetness.

Lightly charred in spots and coated with a pungent sauce and stir-fried pork, these green beans are something special.

PHOTOGRAPHY: CARL TREMBLAY

My sauce now had the proper tang but still needed more heat. Adding more mustard didn't work, so I tried fresh chiles and red pepper flakes. The pepper flakes had a straightforward punch, but I wanted a deeper heat as well. My tasters said black pepper was too mild and cayenne too hot, but ground white pepper was perfect, adding aromatic warmth and a complex muskiness. A touch of cornstarch made the sauce cling to each bean, delivering more pungent flavor with each bite. Some chopped scallions and a drizzle of sesame oil were the perfect finishing touches.

In restaurants, it is common to find chopped or shredded bits of Chinese barbecued pork mingling with the beans, but I found that simple ground pork worked fine at home. And no advance preparation (such as mincing or marinating in soy sauce) was necessary, as the pork absorbed the strong flavors of the sauce while adding a meaty richness to the dish.

With their crinkled, chewy texture and intriguing spicy tang, Sichuan green beans were no longer lost in translation. They were easily made at home—and without the mess of deep-frying.

STIR-FRIED SICHUAN GREEN BEANS

SERVES 4 AS A SIDE DISH OR 2 AS A MAIN COURSE

To make this dish vegetarian, substitute 4 ounces of shiitake mushrooms, stemmed and minced, for the pork. If using mushrooms, you will need to add a teaspoon of oil to the pan in step 3 before adding the mushrooms. The cooking of this dish goes very quickly, so be sure to have all of the ingredients prepped before you start. For information on Chinese long beans (the traditional choice in this recipe), see page 30. Serve this dish with steamed white rice.

- 2 tablespoons soy sauce
- 1 tablespoon dry sherry
- 1 teaspoon sugar
- 1/2 teaspoon cornstarch
- 1/4 teaspoon ground white pepper
- 1/4 teaspoon red pepper flakes
- 1/4 teaspoon dry mustard
- 2 tablespoons water
- 2 tablespoons vegetable oil
- 1 pound green beans, ends trimmed, cut into 2-inch pieces
- 1/4 pound ground pork
- 3 medium garlic cloves, minced or pressed through garlic press (about 1 tablespoon)
- 1 tablespoon minced fresh ginger
- 3 scallions, white and light green parts sliced thin
- 1 teaspoon toasted sesame oil

1. In small bowl, stir together soy sauce, sherry, sugar, cornstarch, white pepper, pepper flakes, mustard, and water until sugar dissolves; set aside.

2. Heat oil in 12-inch nonstick skillet over high heat until just smoking. Add beans and cook, stirring frequently, until crisp-tender and skins are shriveled and blackened in spots, 5 to 8 minutes (reduce heat to medium-high if beans darken too quickly). Transfer beans to large plate.

3. Reduce heat to medium-high and add pork to now-empty skillet. Cook, breaking pork into small pieces, until no pink remains, about 2 minutes. Add garlic and ginger; cook, stirring constantly, until fragrant, 15 to 20 seconds. Stir sauce to recombine and return beans to pan with sauce. Toss and cook until sauce is thickened, 5 to 10 seconds. Remove pan from heat and stir in scallions and sesame oil. Serve immediately.

Simplifying Fudge

Classic fudge is frustrating and completely unpredictable. After months of tests, we've reimagined this recipe to make it utterly reliable—and surprisingly simple.

BY DAVID PAZMIÑO

With its short ingredient list and seemingly humble pedigree, you wouldn't think fudge is all that hard to master at home. After all, this classic American confection calls for just three main ingredients (sugar, milk, and chocolate) and was popularized 100 years ago by college women who prepared it in their dorms. How difficult could it be to make great fudge in a fully outfitted test kitchen? After four months of testing (and developing tendonitis from stirring 1,000 pounds of fudge), I can tell you that traditional fudge—with its slightly grainy but melt-in-your-mouth creaminess—is anything but easy. The fudge pioneers at colleges like Vassar, Smith, and Wellesley were certainly not cooking on hot plates, and I suspect there were more than a few chemists in the bunch.

Good fudge takes just 15 minutes of work.

Real fudge—the kind you can buy today at boardwalk shops in any touristy beach town—is started by cooking sugar, milk, and chocolate until the resulting mixture (called a syrup) reaches a temperature somewhere between 234 and 242 degrees (depending on the recipe). To test doneness, most sources suggest dropping a small bit of the scalding-hot syrup into cold water and rolling it between your fingers until it feels like a soft ball. To prevent further cooking (which would make the finished fudge gritty and crumbly), the syrup is poured onto a large marble slab, cooled, and pulled to produce the creamy yet slightly dry texture that is the hallmark of good fudge.

To replicate this texture in the test kitchen, I dirtied more pots with cemented and gooey hunks of chocolate than I cared to clean. Without a slab of marble to cool the fudge, I eventually figured out (after more than 150 batches) how to make really good old-fashioned fudge (see "Diary of a Frustrated Test Cook," page 23), but was it foolproof? Crossing my fingers, I sent my recipe to our professional recipe tester, a former pastry chef who lives in Texas. She had problems making the fudge in her hot and humid kitchen. Another colleague tried the recipe at home and failed because he relied on a cheap candy thermometer. It turns out that a cool, dry kitchen and precise digital thermometer are must-haves for my old-fashioned recipe. After four months of work, I conceded that it was time to try another path, one that wouldn't demand ideal conditions and would yield a more forgiving recipe.

Following the Easy Fudge Road

Cookbooks are filled with "easy" fudge recipes that replace the sugar syrup with convenience products—either marshmallow cream (aka Marshmallow Fluff) or sweetened condensed milk—that contain sugar rendered more stable by cooking. After initial testing, it became clear that these recipes have fewer pitfalls than their traditional brethren, but they aren't without flaws.

Marshmallow Fluff, a mixture of cooked sugar and egg whites, was introduced in the 1920s. By the 1950s, "never-fail" and "foolproof" fudge recipes with Fluff were widely published in cookbooks and women's magazines. But as I tested various versions of the basic recipe (which calls for cooking Fluff with sugar, evaporated milk, and butter and then pouring this mixture over chopped chocolate), I realized that precise timing was vital to its success. Sometimes this recipe would yield creamy fudge, but other times it was greasy. Even when this recipe worked, it was more like a chewy candy bar than fudge.

I had better luck with recipes based on sweetened condensed milk—milk and sugar cooked in a vacuum until most of the water in the milk evaporates. No real cooking is necessary to make fudge with sweetened condensed milk. Just heat the sweetened condensed milk and chocolate until the chocolate melts, pour the mixture into a pan, and chill until firm. Unfortunately, the texture of this fudge was more like frosting, and the flavor was reminiscent of a too-sweet milk chocolate bar. But given the simplicity of this method, it seemed worth testing further.

Most fudge recipes with sweetened condensed milk call for semisweet chocolate or a combination of semisweet and milk chocolate. Bittersweet chocolate took the sugary edge off the fudge, but my tasters deemed the overall flavor too sour and "adult." I had better luck supplementing some of the semisweet chocolate with unsweetened chocolate. Two ounces of unsweetened chocolate lessened the sugary intensity while leaving the approachable flavor of semisweet chocolate intact.

Now that the chocolate flavor was boosted and the sweetness was tempered, I needed to find a way to change the texture of my fudge; it was too soft and dense and needed to be firmer and lighter, more like traditional fudge. The only moisture in the recipe was in the sweetened condensed milk, and I figured that cooking off some of this liquid would make the fudge drier and firmer. Unfortunately, simmering sweetened condensed milk proved highly problematic; it easily stuck to the bottom of the pan and burned—not exactly what I had in mind for a foolproof recipe. I was at a loss for how to make my fudge firmer and lighter.

That's when inspiration struck. If I couldn't remove moisture, maybe I could change the texture of my fudge by adding another ingredient.

Go to www.cooksillustrated.com

- Click on the Cook's Extra button for our recipe for **Old-Fashioned Chocolate Fudge.**
- Recipe available until June 1, 2007.

PHOTOGRAPHY: CARL TREMBLAY

Three Key Ingredients to Quick, Reliable Fudge

SWEETENED CONDENSED MILK
Takes the place of traditional sugar syrup.

BAKING SODA
Increases the pH of the fudge and makes the texture firmer.

UNSWEETENED CHOCOLATE
Adds intensity and tames excessive sweetness.

Chemical leaveners have the potential to change the texture of cakes and cookies, so maybe they would work their magic on fudge. I chose baking soda, which reacts with acidic ingredients (everything from buttermilk and lemon juice to chocolate) to produce carbon dioxide and thus lighten and lift baked goods.

Starting with ¼ teaspoon, I mixed baking soda with the chocolates before melting this mixture with the milk. Something was clearly happening: The fudge was becoming drier and less waxy, and it had a more traditional texture. After some research, I discovered that the baking soda was not only reacting with the acids in the chocolate but also altering the pH of the fudge. The proteins in the milk and chocolate are sensitive to changes in pH, losing their ability to retain moisture as the pH increases. One-half teaspoon of baking soda made my fudge drier and firmer without imparting any off flavors.

I had almost finished my marathon fudge odyssey. The baking soda made my fudge firmer, but it was still too dense. Luckily, I had one more trick to try—nuts. Sure enough, a cup of chopped walnuts made my fudge seem lighter and offered a nice counterbalance to the chocolate. My final recipe is utterly reliable and takes just 15 minutes to prepare. It was worth the long, long wait in the test kitchen.

15-MINUTE CHOCOLATE WALNUT FUDGE

MAKES ABOUT 2½ POUNDS

The quality of the chocolate used will affect the flavor and texture of the fudge. We prefer Ghirardelli semisweet and unsweetened chocolate in this recipe. Don't be tempted to make this fudge without the walnuts; they are crucial to the texture. If you prefer, you can use toasted nuts in this recipe. Make sure to remove the fudge from the double boiler before the chocolate is fully melted. If the chocolate stays in the double boiler too long, there is the possibility of the chocolate separating and producing a greasy fudge. This fudge will change texture and become drier the longer it is stored. Store the fudge, tightly wrapped in plastic, in a cool place for up to 2 weeks or in the freezer for 3 months. If frozen, allow ample time to let it reach room temperature before cutting.

- 16 ounces semisweet chocolate, chopped fine
- 2 ounces unsweetened chocolate, chopped fine
- ½ teaspoon baking soda
- ⅛ teaspoon table salt
- 1 (14-ounce) can sweetened condensed milk
- 1 tablespoon vanilla extract
- 1 cup coarsely chopped walnuts

1. Cut 12-inch length extra-wide heavy-duty aluminum foil; fold edges back to form 7½-inch width. With folded sides facing down, fit foil securely into bottom and up sides of 8-inch-square baking pan, allowing excess to overhang pan sides. Spray foil with nonstick cooking spray.
2. Toss chocolates, baking soda, and salt in medium heatproof bowl until baking soda is evenly distributed. Stir in sweetened condensed milk and vanilla. Set bowl over 4-quart saucepan containing 2 cups simmering water. Stir with rubber spatula until chocolate is almost fully melted and few small pieces remain, 2 to 4 minutes.
3. Remove bowl from heat and continue to stir until chocolate is fully melted and mixture is smooth, about 2 minutes. Stir in walnuts. Transfer fudge to prepared pan and spread in even layer with spatula. Refrigerate until set, about 2 hours. Remove fudge from pan using foil and cut into squares.

TO MAKE DOUBLE BATCH: Line 13 by 9-inch pan with two sheets of foil placed perpendicular to each other and double amounts of all ingredients. In step 2, use large heatproof bowl and Dutch oven containing 4 cups simmering water.

15-MINUTE PEANUT BUTTER FUDGE

Follow recipe for 15-Minute Chocolate Walnut Fudge, substituting 18 ounces peanut butter chips for chocolates in step 2 and omitting walnuts.

15-MINUTE ROCKY ROAD FUDGE

Follow recipe for 15-Minute Chocolate Walnut Fudge, substituting 1 cup miniature marshmallows, 1 cup coarsely chopped peanuts, and ½ cup semisweet chocolate chips for walnuts in step 3.

Diary of a Frustrated Test Cook

The most basic old-fashioned fudge recipe cooks granulated sugar, milk, chocolate, corn syrup, butter, and salt until the syrup reaches 234 to 242 degrees on a candy thermometer. The mixture is cooled, then stirred. Sounds simple but, as I found out over many months, this process requires skill and patience. My Old-Fashioned Chocolate Fudge recipe (see Cook's Extra on page 22) is more reliable than most, but it has plenty of quirks. Here's what I learned along the way.

Add More Chocolate: Most older recipes don't have enough chocolate flavor. Using 2 ounces of chocolate per cup of sugar (rather than the standard 1 ounce) and replacing the corn syrup with chocolate syrup (basically corn syrup with cocoa powder) fixed the chocolate issue.

FUDGE-ATHON
David Pazmiño made 1,000 pounds of fudge during his four months of recipe testing.

Precision Counts: When I cooked the syrup to 234 degrees, the fudge was soft and gooey; at 242 degrees, it was dry and crumbly. I discovered that the ideal temperature is 238 degrees, but even then the texture varied depending on the method I used to cool and stir the mixture.

The Quick Chill: Fudge shops pour the hot syrup mixture onto cool marble tables. Without a marble slab, I had to cool the syrup right in the pot, which took 90 minutes. Could I speed it up? Dividing the chocolate, cooking half, and freezing the other half to be added with frozen butter at the end of the cooking process cut the cooling time by 45 minutes. Shocking the hot pot in cool water shaved another 10 minutes from the cooling time.

Big Muscles: Stirring the fudge took more strength than I imagined—and I'm no 98-pound weakling. Eventually, I developed a lazy-man stir: a couple of passes around the perimeter of the pan, lifting the syrup and letting it fall off the spoon so that it would cool more quickly, and then stopping for a minute so the sugar could form the small crystals that make traditional fudge slightly grainy. After about 8 minutes, the fudge began to lose its shine and stiffen. This was better than stirring constantly for 20 minutes, but it still wasn't easy. –D.P.

Seeking Pound Cake Perfection

Don't be fooled by its short ingredient list—pound cake is far from simple. More often than not, it bakes up heavy, squat, and dense.

BY DAWN YANAGIHARA

I am a baker by nature. I like to weigh ingredients and measure dimensions carefully. I am comfortable working with meringues, sugar syrups, and delicate pastries. But a simple pound cake? Over the years, I've been vexed and humbled trying to make a good one. I've never found a recipe for a pound cake that both looked and tasted good. Those that looked good tended to resemble yellow layer cakes: fluffy, bouncy, and open-textured. Those that tasted good were superlatively buttery and fine-pored, with a suede-like texture, but often baked up as flat and firm as bricks.

Pound cake recipes date back to the eighteenth century and originally called for a pound each of flour, sugar, butter, and eggs. But the historical recipes I've tried were too heavy and dense to please modern palates. At some point during pound cake's evolution, baking powder began to appear in recipes, presumably to guarantee that the cake rises in the oven. The downside to adding baking powder is that the cake loses its ultra-plush character and begins to take on coarser yellow cake attributes. I wasn't interested in such a pound cake.

Pound cake has a simple ingredient list, but the mixing method requires precise attention to detail.

Back in 1994, the test kitchen adjusted the proportions in the original pound-of-each recipe to create a delicious version of classic (no leavener) pound cake. But over the years, this five-ingredient recipe has been my nemesis. Sometimes the cake rises nicely, but not always. As one of the most experienced bakers in the test kitchen, I've been nonplussed by my unsuccessful encounters with this temperamental recipe. I decided to put an end to all the nonsense and retool a classic recipe to make it more reliable.

It's No Cakewalk

Most cake recipes, including those for pound cake, start by beating butter and sugar together in a process called creaming. During creaming, the sugar crystals are pushed through the butter and cause the formation of tiny pockets of air. After more than a dozen failed cakes, I learned that the commonly called-for room temperature butter (in the past, we've found that 70 degrees is the ideal butter temperature for most cakes) produces flat, dense pound cakes. Looking into my mixing bowl, I could see that the butter was getting too warm (its temperature rose to 75 degrees by the time I was finished creaming it) and too slack to aerate.

A chemical leavener adds lift to most cake batters. But without any leavener, pound cake demands maximum aeration from the butter—which means keeping the temperature of the batter below 70 degrees. Since creaming heats up the butter, starting with chilly 60-degree butter greatly increases the odds of success. This was my first big discovery.

Just because the butter and sugar are properly creamed doesn't mean success is guaranteed. After a dozen more failures, I learned that too-warm eggs can deflate the batter. And if the eggs were too cold or added too quickly, they were difficult to incorporate and the air was knocked out of the butter by the time I had smooth batter. After more trial and error, I concluded that 60 degrees was perfect for the eggs, too.

Most cake recipes say to add the eggs one at a time, mixing well and scraping the bowl after each addition. Frankly, the pound cake never worked well using this method. The delicate batter just couldn't absorb a whole egg at once yet retain its aeration. Some pound cake recipes require a more extreme method—the eggs are beaten together in a measuring cup then slowly dribbled into the creamed butter and sugar, a process that took up to 5 minutes and tested my patience. Although I was skeptical about this fussy method, I was surprised to find that the resulting batter was in fact more stable and produced substantially better pound cake that rose higher and had a lighter texture. I repeated this experiment over and over again and discovered that a full 5 minutes was unnecessary. The beaten eggs could be added very gradually in 60 to 90 seconds, as long as the mixture was beaten a few additional minutes once the last of the egg was added.

A consultation with our food scientist revealed why slowly adding the eggs produces a more voluminous batter and higher rise in the cake. When added slowly, the egg proteins coat the other ingredients with a thin film; if the eggs are added rapidly, the egg proteins form a thick film. Just as a thin rubber balloon is easier to

TECHNIQUE | SLOW AS YOU GO

Pound cake batter is so delicate that it will deflate if you add the eggs one at a time or add the flour too quickly, as most recipes suggest.

EGGS: With mixer running, pour in beaten egg mixture in slow, steady stream.

FLOUR: Sift flour over batter in three additions, folding in each addition with spatula.

PHOTOGRAPHY: CARL TREMBLAY, ILLUSTRATION: JOHN BURGOYNE

Successful Creaming

Cool butter and thorough mixing are essential to our pound cake recipe. We tried our recipe in four standing and handheld mixers (all set to medium-high speed) and found that the creaming time varied from 5 to 8 minutes. These guidelines will help you determine when the butter is at the correct temperature and when the butter and sugar are properly creamed.

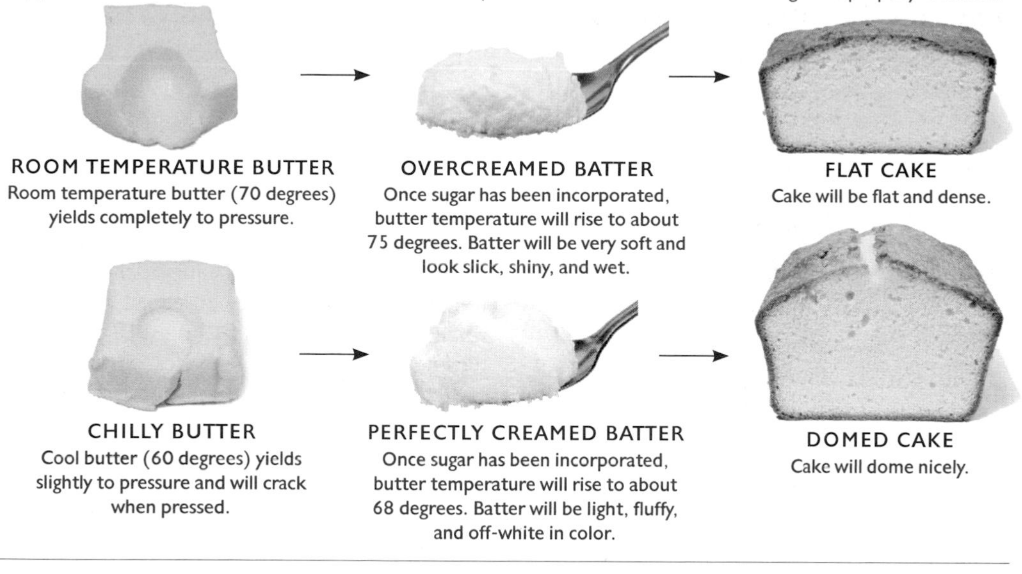

ROOM TEMPERATURE BUTTER
Room temperature butter (70 degrees) yields completely to pressure.

OVERCREAMED BATTER
Once sugar has been incorporated, butter temperature will rise to about 75 degrees. Batter will be very soft and look slick, shiny, and wet.

FLAT CAKE
Cake will be flat and dense.

CHILLY BUTTER
Cool butter (60 degrees) yields slightly to pressure and will crack when pressed.

PERFECTLY CREAMED BATTER
Once sugar has been incorporated, butter temperature will rise to about 68 degrees. Batter will be light, fluffy, and off-white in color.

DOMED CAKE
Cake will dome nicely.

EQUIPMENT TESTING:

Loaf Pans

Seven years after applauding the Baker's Secret Non-Stick Loaf Pan as the best available choice, we wanted to see if anything new could best this bargain pan, which is available for $6 in supermarkets. Seven pound cakes, seven loaves of sandwich bread, and hours of baking later, we had a motley crew of baked goods and some new thoughts about loaf pans.

Bigger pans—Anolon's Suregrip Nonstick Loaf Pan ($16.95) and KitchenAid's Professional Nonstick Loaf Pan ($19.95)—allowed the sandwich bread to bake up a bit fluffier than did smaller pans but yielded dense, square pound cakes. Narrower pans—including the Baker's Secret, Pyrex's Glass Loaf Dish ($4.99), All-Clad Gold Standard Nonstick Loaf Pan ($74.95), Doughmakers Loaf Pan ($14.95), and Williams-Sonoma Goldtouch Nonstick Loaf Pan ($19)—were the only choice for pound cake and fine for sandwich bread.

Our other primary concern was browning. Light-colored aluminum finishes on the All-Clad and Doughmakers pans yielded pale, anemic-looking baked goods. The dark nonstick surface on the Baker's Secret pan actually browned the bread and pound cake a shade too much. Despite its wide availability and low price, it's no longer our top choice. Glass Pyrex browned nicely, but the real star of the show was the Williams-Sonoma Goldtouch. The gold-colored nonstick surface yielded baked goods with a perfectly even, honeyed-copper crust.

—Elizabeth Bomze

GOLD STANDARD
The gold surface on the Williams-Sonoma Goldtouch Nonstick Loaf Pan ($19) took browning to the perfect point.

inflate than a thick one, a thin protein film offers less resistance to a rising cake batter in the oven.

Flour Power

It was time to add the flour—cake flour, to be precise, as all-purpose is too protein-rich and yielded dry, tough cakes in my tests. The mixer did a poor job of incorporating the flour and, as a result, the batter became overworked. As much as I wanted to find a simpler option, I found that sifting the flour over the batter and folding it in by hand was required. Sifting lightens and fluffs the flour, making it easier to incorporate, which also reduces the risk of overworking the batter.

After baking more than 50 cakes, I had finally arrived at a foolproof recipe for classic pound cake, and my confidence as a baker was restored.

CLASSIC POUND CAKE

MAKES ONE 9 BY 5-INCH LOAF

As directed in the recipe, the butter and eggs should be the first ingredients prepared so they have a chance to stand at room temperature and lose their chill while the oven heats, the loaf pan is greased and floured, and the other ingredients are measured. Leftover cake will keep reasonably well for up to 3 days if wrapped tightly in plastic wrap and stored at room temperature.

- 16 tablespoons (2 sticks) unsalted butter, cold, plus extra for greasing pan
- 3 large eggs plus 3 large egg yolks
- 2 teaspoons vanilla extract
- 1 3/4 cups (7 ounces) cake flour, plus extra for dusting loaf pan
- 1/2 teaspoon table salt
- 1 1/4 cups (8 3/4 ounces) sugar

1. Cut butter into 1-tablespoon pieces and place in bowl of standing mixer; let stand at room temperature 20 to 30 minutes to soften slightly (butter should reach no more than 60 degrees). Using dinner fork, beat eggs, egg yolks, and vanilla in liquid measuring cup until combined. Let egg mixture stand at room temperature until ready to use.

2. Adjust oven rack to middle position and heat oven to 325 degrees. Generously butter 9 by 5-inch loaf pan; dust pan liberally with flour and knock out excess.

3. In standing mixer fitted with flat beater, beat butter and salt at medium-high speed until shiny, smooth, and creamy, 2 to 3 minutes, scraping bottom and sides of bowl once with rubber spatula. Reduce speed to medium; with mixer running, gradually pour in sugar (this should take about 60 seconds). Once all sugar is added, increase speed to medium-high and beat until mixture is fluffy and almost white in color, 5 to 8 minutes, scraping bottom and sides of bowl once. With mixer running at medium speed, gradually add egg mixture in slow, steady stream; this should take 60 to 90 seconds. Scrape bottom and sides of bowl; beat mixture at medium-high speed until light and fluffy, 3 to 4 minutes (mixture may look slightly broken). Remove bowl from mixer; scrape bottom and sides.

4. In 3 additions, sift flour over butter/egg mixture; after each addition, fold gently with rubber spatula until combined. Scrape along bottom of bowl to ensure that batter is homogenous.

5. Transfer batter to prepared loaf pan and smooth surface with rubber spatula. Bake until golden brown and wooden skewer inserted into center of cake comes out clean, about 70 to 80 minutes. Cool cake in pan on wire rack for 15 minutes; invert cake onto wire rack, then turn cake right side up. Cool cake on rack to room temperature, about 2 hours. Slice and serve.

ALMOND POUND CAKE

Follow recipe for Classic Pound Cake, reducing vanilla extract to 1 teaspoon and adding 1½ teaspoons almond extract along with vanilla to eggs. Sprinkle 2 tablespoons sliced almonds over surface of batter just before baking.

POUND CAKE WITH ORANGE ESSENCE

Follow recipe for Classic Pound Cake, reducing vanilla extract to 1 teaspoon and adding 1 tablespoon grated then minced orange zest to mixer bowl just after adding eggs.

Searching for Superior Soy Sauce

This Asian condiment should enhance flavor and contribute complexity to your food—not just make it salty.

⋟ BY LISA McMANUS ⋞

Most of us have rarely given soy sauce a second thought, using it as a kind of liquid salt. But this 2,500-year-old ingredient, brewed first in China and since the seventh century in Japan, can offer nearly as much variety, complexity, and flavor as wine or olive oil, and it deserves serious consideration. In most supermarkets today, you will find a shelf of imported soy sauces, as well as American-brewed versions. How do they differ? Which tastes best as a dipping sauce for delicate sushi and savory dumplings? Cooked in stir-fries and glazes for meat and fish? And while we're at it, what is *tamari*?

We decided to sample nationally available brands, choosing a lineup of 12 soy sauces, including both tamari and regular soy sauce, from Japan, China, and the United States. We tasted them three times: first plain, then with warm rice, and finally cooked in a teriyaki sauce with ginger, garlic, and mirin and brushed over broiled chicken thighs. As we tasted them, we noticed a wide range of colors and flavors, from reddish-brown, delicate, and floral to dark brown, pungent, and assertive. Where were these differences coming from? And how well did they play off the other flavors in a dish?

Soy Simple

At its most basic, soy sauce is a fermented liquid made from soybeans and wheat. Soybeans contribute a strong, pungent taste, while wheat lends sweetness. Tamari is a type of soy sauce traditionally made with all soybeans and no wheat—though, confusingly, many tamaris do contain a little wheat. As a result, tamari has a more pungent flavor than soy sauce. Similarly, stronger, earthier Chinese soy sauce tends to be made with a lower proportion of wheat than the sweeter, lighter Japanese soy sauce.

Like many products with a long history, soy sauce is now made both artisanally using traditional methods and industrially using modern technology. All soy sauce begins with whole soybeans or defatted soy meal cooked and mixed with roasted grain, usually wheat (but sometimes barley or rice). This bean/grain mixture is inoculated with a mold called *koji* (technically, *Aspergillus oryzae* or *Aspergillus soyae*) and left for a few days to allow the mold to grow and spread. Then salt water and yeast are added to form a mash called *moromi*. And here comes the biggest difference in quality levels of soy sauce: The mash is fermented for anywhere from two days to four years. The brown liquid that is extruded from the mash is soy sauce, which is usually filtered, pasteurized, and bottled.

Experts claim that each soy sauce gets its particular flavor from the proportion and quality of the ingredients, including the local water where it's brewed, the koji "starter" mold (some companies brag of their proprietary koji, kept alive for centuries), the climate (a certain level of humidity is essential to make the mold grow), and the length of fermentation. Some industrially produced soy sauce starts with hydrolyzed vegetable protein (not necessarily soy) and may be sweetened with corn syrup and colored with caramel to mimic the flavor and color of fermented soy sauce.

A Sauce for All Seasons?

Soy sauce is not all the same—there are five types in Japan alone. In the United States, however, we tend to use one kind of soy sauce for all purposes, and, since we prefer simplicity in the test kitchen, we were hoping one clear winner would emerge from our tasting. No such luck. Our tasters liked one type of soy sauce for plain, uncooked applications and an entirely different one for cooked dishes. How about being able to say the best soy sauce is made in one particular country? Sorry: The tasters chose two different nations' products, depending on how it was used. Method of brewing? Again, they split between an artisanal soy and a mass-produced one (albeit one aged for months, not days). Would saltiness be the favored attribute? No, one had the least amount of salt of the 12 in our lineup, the other had the most. Clearly, these results underscored the fact that there's no "one-size-fits-all" soy sauce.

In the plain tasting, Ohsawa Nama Shoyu (a traditionally brewed import from Japan) came out on top. With 720 milligrams per tablespoon, it has the lowest sodium level of the 12 brands we tasted. When the sauces were drizzled over warm rice and cooked into a teriyaki glaze, our tasters preferred a mass-produced Chinese brand, Lee Kum Kee Tabletop Soy Sauce, which has the highest sodium level of the lineup, at 1,200 milligrams per tablespoon. Ohsawa Nama Shoyu was described as having a "sweet," "delicate," even "floral" taste, while tasters dubbed Lee Kum Kee "salty," "malty," and "delicious." What could explain this flavor divide?

An important clue came when we tested lower-sodium (also called "light") soy sauces. (Lower-sodium soy sauces start as regular soy sauce, then some sodium is removed by filtering or ion exchange.) The lower-sodium soy sauces actually beat the regular soy sauces in a plain taste test but lost out in cooked applications. Why? Cutting down on the salt let some of the other flavors take the stage, leaving a delicate, complex soy taste in the foreground. But once cooked, the delicate flavors dissipated.

These delicate, nuanced flavors develop during the fermentation process, according to Dr. Joseph Frank, professor of food microbiology at the University of Georgia at Athens, who teaches courses in food fermentation and is an expert on soy sauce. "The koji mold produces a variety of enzymes that, when they get put in a salt solution with the soy and toasted wheat, convert proteins to amino acids and starches to sugars. The acids and alcohol that result combine to form esters—flavor compounds that give you fruitiness. This all takes time," he said. "Generally, the longer the soy sauce ages, the more flavor it will develop—like wine."

These flavorful esters are volatile, however, Frank said, and cook off when heated. "If you cook soy sauce for any length of time you'll drive off the aroma—it's sort of like using vanilla. You might want to add more [soy sauce] back at the end of cooking."

In the case of the Lee Kum Kee soy sauce, whose more robust flavor held up during the boiling and reduction of the teriyaki sauce, Frank said, "I think this soy sauce, in its brewing process, is higher in the nonvolatile flavor components, what we call the Maillard components." In the Maillard reaction, sugars and amino acids react to heat, causing browning and bringing about a richer, more savory flavor—like searing meat before making pot roast. "That's what contributes to the depth of flavor in the [teriyaki] glaze," Frank said. And in fact, Lee Kum Kee was the only soy sauce we tasted that had significant sugar content: two grams per tablespoon. Combine that sugar with a high salt content and the overall flavor profile of the dish is improved, Frank noted. "It may not even taste salty [or sweet], per se, but it will change your perception of the flavor."

TASTING SOY SAUCE

Nineteen members of the *Cook's Illustrated* staff tasted 12 soy sauces, including both tamari and regular soy sauce samples. The sauces were rated on their saltiness, complexity, and overall flavor in three applications: plain, drizzled over warm rice, and cooked in a simple teriyaki glaze over chicken thighs. Sodium values are per tablespoon according to product labels. Soy sauces are listed below in order of preference.

RECOMMENDED

LEE KUM KEE Tabletop Soy Sauce
➢ **$1.99 for 5.1 ounces**
➢ **Sodium: 1,200 milligrams**
This Chinese brand won rice and teriyaki tastings. With rice, its flavor was described as "salty, sweet, roasted, pleasant," and "fruity," with a "great aroma." Cooked in teriyaki, it was "salty, malty, and delicious," with "good depth" and "balance." Contains more sodium than other brands tested.

OHSAWA NAMA SHOYU Organic Unpasteurized Soy Sauce
➢ **$6.49 for 10 ounces**
➢ **Sodium: 720 milligrams**
This Japanese brand won the plain tasting, with its flavor described as "clean," "caramel," and "rich and nuanced." A few tasters called it "sweet and dimensional," even "floral," with one adding that it was "lighter in style and flavor than others." Contains less sodium than other brands tested.

RECOMMENDED WITH RESERVATIONS

SAN-J ORGANIC SHOYU Naturally Brewed Soy Sauce
➢ **$3.69 for 20 ounces**
➢ **Sodium: 960 milligrams**
Tasters described this Japanese-style soy sauce made in Virginia as "thin" and "light." With rice, it came across as slightly "earthy," with a "hint of smoke" and "vinegary" notes.

KIKKOMAN All-Purpose Soy Sauce
➢ **$1.79 for 10 ounces**
➢ **Sodium: 920 milligrams**
Many tasters identified this Japanese-style version made in Wisconsin as basic soy sauce: "Tastes very traditional, like what you get in Asian restaurants," one wrote. "Fine, not better [than other soy sauces] in any way," wrote another.

RECOMMENDED WITH RESERVATIONS *(cont.)*

PEARL RIVER BRIDGE Superior Light Soy Sauce
➢ **$1.99 for 16.9 ounces**
➢ **Sodium: 870 milligrams**
Tasters noted a "beefy," "salty," even "smoky" flavor in this Chinese brand, though some described it as "lacking depth," "not rich," and "not very complex" when tasted plain.

EDEN ORGANIC Naturally Brewed Tamari Soy Sauce
➢ **$3.99 for 10 ounces**
➢ **Sodium: 860 milligrams**
The "malty," "caramel" notes of this Japanese-style tamari made in Michigan appealed to some tasters, but many complained of "fishy," "pungent" flavors. Best appreciated in teriyaki—with "sweet," "tangy" character one taster compared to plums.

EDEN ORGANIC Traditionally Brewed Tamari Soy Sauce
➢ **$5.99 for 10 ounces**
➢ **Sodium: 990 milligrams**
When it was tasted plain, tasters raved about the "complex caramel flavors" of this Japanese tamari. Served with warm rice, there were some complaints about saltiness, and in teriyaki it was called "really pungent and strong."

EDEN ORGANIC Shoyu Soy Sauce
➢ **$3.99 for 10 ounces**
➢ **Sodium: 1,040 milligrams**
This Japanese import appealed to some tasters as "nice," with a "light caramel taste" that is "floral and robust." However, salt and alcohol dominated other tasters' perceptions, with one declaring it "smells alcohol-y, tastes like salt."

KIKKOMAN Naturally Brewed Organic Soy Sauce
➢ **$3.99 for 10 ounces**
➢ **Sodium: 1,000 milligrams**
"Pure salt; use sparingly," warned one taster; others agreed but enjoyed this Japanese brand's "nice flavor once the saltiness dissipates—rounded and balanced."

KIKKOMAN Naturally Brewed Tamari Soy Sauce
➢ **$3.29 for 10 ounces**
➢ **Sodium: 980 milligrams**
"Dark, rich, and malty," with "caramel" and "wheat" notes, this Japanese brand came across as "strong and intense," with "full, roasted flavor like coffee" in the teriyaki. It lost points for a "weird fishy aftertaste."

SAN-J Naturally Brewed Tamari Premium Soy Sauce
➢ **$2.99 for 10 ounces**
➢ **Sodium: 960 milligrams**
Some found this Virginia-made tamari "thick, sweet, and tasty," with "good depth." However, many others viewed it less favorably, calling it "nasty," "fishy," "strange," "tinny," "thin and bitter."

NOT RECOMMENDED

LA CHOY Soy Sauce
➢ **$1.79 for 10 ounces**
➢ **Sodium: 1,160 milligrams**
The complaints about this American brand with hydrolyzed soy protein, corn syrup, and caramel color were many: "Ew—tastes so fake!" "grainy, chemical taste," "gross, nasty, bicycle lubricant," "disgusting," "artificial," "burnt," "stinky," and "acidic." In summary, "Could this be any worse?"

Our two winners represent two very different manufacturing styles. Lee Kum Kee is brewed and bottled in a 10 million-square-foot factory in Xinhui, China. It is fermented for three to six months in 20-foot-tall fiberglass holding tanks.

In contrast, Ohsawa Nama Shoyu (*shoyu* is the Japanese word for soy sauce; *nama shoyu* means it's unpasteurized) is made in the Japanese mountain village of Kamiizumi-mura, using the spring water from the mountain. The soy sauce is hand-stirred and fermented in sixty 150-year-old cedar kegs, in a wooden post-and-beam factory surrounded by organic gardens. The flavor of Ohsawa Nama Shoyu develops over an unusually long period of time because it is double-fermented, according to Jean Richardson, president of its importer, San Diego–based Goldmine Natural Foods. After fermenting the sauce in the cedar vats for at least two summers, the makers add more soybeans and wheat and age it another two summers. "This makes a complex bouquet of aroma and flavor," Richardson said. "You don't really get that bite of salt. The aging makes it mellower."

Long-aging and importing costs explain why Ohsawa is the most expensive brand we tasted—$6.49 for 10 ounces. But spending a few extra dollars for a traditional, slow-brewed soy sauce is worth the investment, especially for use as a dipping sauce. However, the more robust Lee Kum Kee is our top choice for cooking.

Inexpensive Dutch Ovens

Our favorite Dutch ovens cost more than $200. Ouch! Is there a cheaper version that performs almost as well? Yes. It costs $40.

BY LISA McMANUS

When we tested Dutch ovens in 1998, the top performers were pots made by All-Clad and Le Creuset. Nearly a decade later, the only flaw we might find in these workhorses is their hefty price—roughly $250. These top-of-the-line pots now have plenty of imitators. Could any of them challenge our pricey favorites? Frankly, we were skeptical. But given that some of the cheaper options cost $200 less than our previous winners, it seemed worth a shot.

Going Dutch

A good Dutch oven (variously called a stockpot, round oven, French oven, or casserole) is a kitchen essential. Heavier and thicker than stockpots, allowing them to retain and conduct heat more effectively, and deeper than a skillet, so they can handle large cuts of meat and cooking liquid, Dutch ovens are the best choice for braises, pot roasts, and stews, as they can go on the stovetop to sear foods and then into the oven to finish cooking. Their tall sides make them useful for deep-frying, and many cooks press Dutch ovens into service for jobs like boiling pasta.

Dutch Oven History

A good Dutch oven has been an essential piece of cookware for hundreds of years. Originally, cooks put these big, deep, covered pots right into the fireplace or campfire. With three short legs for standing in the coals and a flat lid with an upturned lip to hold more hot coals on top, they literally were ovens, baking biscuits and breads, as well as stewing and roasting meats.

Early colonists brought Dutch ovens from Europe, and these portable, versatile pots became a common sight in America, especially among pioneers—even Lewis and Clark carried a Dutch oven on their expedition across the continent. There are several theories about why they are called "Dutch" ovens, the most credible being that they were originally made using a cast-iron process invented by the Dutch.

Dutch ovens have long since come indoors to join the modern kitchen—though some manufacturers (including Lodge) still produce the original legged design for camping.—L.M.

For our first test, we prepared a beef stew that starts on the stovetop and then moves to the oven. In each pan, we browned cubes of beef in batches, and as the meat seared, we observed whether the pan heated evenly and consistently without burning the drippings. After the long, slow cooking in the oven, we tasted the stew to see if the meat had become fork-tender and the broth had reduced to intense flavor. Of all the tests we did, this was the most important, because it focused on the unique abilities of Dutch ovens. As expected, the Le Creuset and All-Clad pots sailed through with flying colors. Surprisingly, so did a few of the others.

We noticed a few trends. Our favorite pots from All-Clad and Le Creuset measure 9¾ inches across, enabling them to brown 3½ pounds of beef in three batches, something narrower pots couldn't do. The Innova, which measures just 7⅝ inches across, required five batches—a big flaw. The Emerilware and Chefmate pans were slightly bigger (8 inches and 8¼ inches, respectively) and handled the beef in four batches—a minor flaw. The stew made in the Chefmate pot was great; the Emerilware pot browned the beef unevenly—an imperfection we also noticed in the too-light pot from Tramontina.

Into Hot Oil

For the next test, we put two quarts of canola oil in each pan, clipped on a deep-fry thermometer, and cooked a pound of frozen french fries to test heat transfer and retention. Here again, our costly favorites met our high expectations but were well matched by a few contenders. The best pans retain heat well enough to prevent the temperature of the oil from dropping too precipitously when food is added. If the temperature drops too far, the fries will be soggy and greasy. The Tramontina pot won this test—the temperature of the oil dropped just 45 degrees when the fries were added and the recovery time for the oil, at 5 minutes and 45 seconds, was also the best. In contrast, oil in the Calphalon pot (the lowest-rated entry in this test) dropped 76 degrees and took more than 10 minutes to recover. As a result, the fries cooked in the Calphalon pot weren't crisp enough. The Innova pot suffered from similar problems.

An unexpected issue emerged during this test. Fries cooked in the Emerilware cast iron pan tasted rusty; evidently, the preseasoned surface had failed. Cast iron is a great choice for a Dutch oven, because it holds onto heat so well. But cast iron will also react with many foods. Some manufacturers (Le Creuset, Chefmate, Mario Batali, and Innova) coat their cast iron with a layer of brightly colored enamel. Other manufacturers preseason their pots—basically spraying them with oil and baking on the seasoning. But, as we discovered, it's possible to wash away the preseasoning. We boiled water in all pots and noticed that the water turned yellow in both of the preseasoned cast iron pots, made by Emerilware and Lodge. As a result, neither pot can be used to boil water for pasta, and we worry that the cast iron may react with acidic cooking liquids, such as wine or tomatoes. Yes, you could reseason the pots yourself, but that seems like a hassle. An enamel coating on the cast iron surface will last a lifetime and makes a Dutch oven much more versatile.

For our last test, we steamed a triple batch of white rice in each Dutch oven to see how they simmered on very low heat. All but one pot made fluffy rice with intact grains. The Innova pot, which had trouble with heat retention in the french-fry test, overcooked the rice.

Ironclad Results

When all the smoke and sizzling fry oil cleared, our favorite pots (the ones we've used almost daily in the test kitchen for nearly 10 years) came out on top. Other than price, it's hard to quibble with the pots made by All-Clad and Le Creuset.

Although we weren't surprised by our winners, we were shocked at their narrow margin of victory. How could a $40 Dutch oven hold its own against pans costing six times as much? The Target Chefmate Casserole looks like a slightly smaller Le Creuset, down to the shape of the handles and the knob on the top. In fact, it kept up with the winners in every test. Because the Chefmate casserole is smaller than our top choices, you will need to brown meat for stew in four batches rather than three, and the biggest pot roasts will be a tight fit. While our test cooks are not ready to trade in their favorite Dutch ovens, the Chefmate is a real find for budget-minded cooks.

If you're willing to spend $100 on a Dutch oven, and you have the biceps to handle it, the Mario Batali pot is comparable in size to the Le Creuset and All-Clad pots and performs nearly as well. Yes, the browning wasn't perfect, but that seems like a minor quibble most cooks would never notice. Two good choices, and both reasonably priced.

RATING DUTCH OVENS

RATINGS
GOOD: ★★★
FAIR: ★★
POOR: ★

We tested seven inexpensive Dutch ovens (priced under $100), along with previous test kitchen winners made by All-Clad and Le Creuset (both priced in excess of $200). Ratings of good, fair, and poor for three kitchen tests (beef stew, french fries, and steamed white rice) were given to each pot; the stew test was given extra weight in determining overall rank. We also boiled water in each pot. Dutch ovens are listed in order of preference. See page 32 for mail-order sources for top-rated pots.

DIAMETER: Of interior cooking surface, as measured in the test kitchen.

WEIGHT: As measured in the test kitchen (includes lid).

STEW: Testers prepared beef stew, browning $3\frac{1}{2}$ pounds of meat in batches, browning onions, and finishing stew in the oven. Testers noted browning and tenderness of meat as well as flavor and consistency of sauce.

FRIES: Testers deep-fried 1 pound frozen french fries in 2 quarts canola oil, noting the time needed to heat oil to 350 degrees, the drop in temperature after fries were added, the time needed for oil to return to 350 degrees, and appearance and taste of the fries.

RICE: Testers prepared 3 cups of plain white rice and assessed the appearance and taste of the cooked rice.

RECOMMENDED	PERFORMANCE	TESTERS' COMMENTS
All-Clad Stainless 8-Quart Stockpot PRICE: $257.95 MATERIALS: Stainless steel with aluminum core	 CAPACITY: 8 qt. DIAMETER: $9\frac{3}{4}$" WEIGHT: 6 lbs. STEW: ★★★ FRIES: ★★★ RICE: ★★★	While this pan runs a little hot, it produced "golden and gorgeous" fond. Starred in the french-fry test, with rapid recovery of cooking temperature after fries were added. The best choice for cooks who prefer a lighter pot.
Le Creuset $7\frac{1}{4}$-Quart Round French Oven PRICE: $229.95 MATERIALS: Enameled cast iron with phenolic lid knob	 CAPACITY: $7\frac{1}{4}$ qt. DIAMETER: $9\frac{3}{4}$" WEIGHT: 13.7 lbs. STEW: ★★★ FRIES: ★★★ RICE: ★★★	The "gold standard" of Dutch ovens put "gorgeous, golden crust" on meat and created great fond. Rice cooked up perfectly, though cleanup required long soaking. A kitchen workhorse that's heavy but not excessively so.
BEST BUY **Chefmate** Round Enameled Cast Iron Casserole for Target PRICE: $39.99 MATERIALS: Enameled cast iron with phenolic lid knob	 CAPACITY: 5 qt. DIAMETER: $8\frac{1}{4}$" WEIGHT: 11.6 lbs. STEW: ★★★ FRIES: ★★★ RICE: ★★★	Similar to Le Creuset, only smaller and a lot cheaper. Less cooking surface meant that stew meat was browned in four batches rather than three—a reasonable trade-off to save $190. Lid has tight fit, and stew barely reduced in oven, although meat was tender and sauce flavorful. Steady, even heating yielded fluffy rice.
Mario Batali Italian Essentials Pot by Copco PRICE: $99.99 MATERIALS: Enameled cast iron with cast stainless lid knob	 CAPACITY: 6 qt. DIAMETER: $9\frac{3}{4}$" WEIGHT: 15.2 lbs. STEW: ★★★ FRIES: ★★★ RICE: ★★★	This roomy pan was slow to heat up but demonstrated quick recovery after fries were added to the oil. The "self-basting" spikes inside the lid work—we never had to shake condensation off this lid after opening it. Browning of beef could have been more even. Testers bemoaned lifting and handling this "super-heavy" pan. Needs bigger handles.

RECOMMENDED WITH RESERVATIONS	PERFORMANCE	TESTERS' COMMENTS
Lodge Pro-Logic Pre-Seasoned Dutch Oven PRICE: $39.99 MATERIAL: Preseasoned cast iron	 CAPACITY: 7 qt. DIAMETER: $9\frac{1}{2}$" WEIGHT: 17.2 lbs. STEW: ★★★ FRIES: ★★★ RICE: ★★★	Although it was hard at first to see the fond developing in this black pot, the meat had "excellent, deep browning." Fries browned well, and the heat recovery was relatively quick. Large looping handles make it easy to manipulate this heavyweight pot. Boiling water picked up a yellow tint and a rusty smell, indicating that our pot had lost its seasoning.
Calphalon One Infused Anodized Dutch Oven PRICE: $99.99 MATERIALS: Heavy-gauge aluminum infused with polymer; stainless steel lid	 CAPACITY: $8\frac{1}{2}$ qt. DIAMETER: $11\frac{7}{8}$" WEIGHT: 6.8 lbs. STEW: ★★★ FRIES: ★★ RICE: ★★★	"So roomy I could almost brown the meat in two batches rather than three." Low sides made it easy to see inside, and it was lightweight and easy to manipulate. In the fries test, the temperature of oil dropped the farthest when potatoes were added, then fluctuated more than the other pans as the temperature very slowly climbed back up.
Tramontina Sterling II 18/10 Stainless Steel Covered Dutch Oven PRICE: $69.95 MATERIALS: Stainless steel with aluminum core bottom	 CAPACITY: 7 qt. DIAMETER $10\frac{5}{8}$" WEIGHT: 6.4 lbs. STEW: ★★ FRIES: ★★★ RICE: ★★★	Pan is big, light, and easy to handle, and it did a nice job browning meat. However, the stew liquid did not reduce at all in the oven and tasted soupy and unfinished; the meat was not fully tender. Oil temperature dropped the least when fries were added and recovered the fastest.
Emerilware from All-Clad Cast Iron Dutch Oven PRICE: $34.95 MATERIAL: Preseasoned cast iron	 CAPACITY: 6 qt. DIAMETER: 8" WEIGHT: 15.9 lbs. STEW: ★★ FRIES: ★★ RICE: ★★★	Deep, narrow pan was slow to heat up but developed a nice fond for stew once it did. Meat had to be browned in four batches rather than three. The stew's broth reduced well in the oven, becoming rich and thick, but the meat wasn't fork-tender. Boiled water appeared yellow, and fries had a distinctly rusty taste, indicating that pot had lost its seasoning.
Innova Color Cast Porcelain Enameled Cast Iron 5-Quart Round Dutch Oven PRICE: $49.99 MATERIAL: Enameled cast iron	 CAPACITY: 5 qt. DIAMETER: $7\frac{5}{8}$" WEIGHT: 11.3 lbs. STEW: ★★ FRIES: ★★ RICE: ★★	We had to brown the meat for the stew in five batches rather than three. The pan runs slightly hot, and rice was overcooked with "blown-out" grains. For fries, this pot was second slowest to heat oil, and the temperature of the oil dropped farther than we'd like when fries were added.

KITCHEN NOTES

BY ERIKA BRUCE

Storing Pound Cake

We had much better luck storing both whole and leftover Pound Cake (page 25) in the freezer, wrapped in a double layer of plastic wrap and foil, than in the refrigerator, where it would quickly stale. The cake usually defrosted nicely on the counter, but sometimes the top became soft and sticky. After some head scratching, we realized the problem only happened when we unwrapped the frozen cake before defrosting it. Keeping the cake wrapped as it thawed (which takes about four hours) ensured a nice, firm crust.

It took us a while to find this solution, because it contradicts the test kitchen's method for defrosting most baked goods. For instance, we've had better luck when we unwrapped cupcakes before defrosting. Why the discrepancy? Pound cakes have much less internal moisture than cupcakes or other baked goods that contain a liquid ingredient such as milk, cream, or yogurt. When unwrapped, liquid-free pound cake has a propensity to draw moisture from the air, causing the crust to become wet; cupcakes, on the other hand, let off moisture, which gets trapped when the wrapping is left on but evaporates when the wrapping is removed.

Who Has the Thyme?

Picking minuscule leaves of fresh thyme can really pluck at your nerves, especially if a recipe calls for a good deal of it. In the test kitchen, we rely on some tricks to make this job go faster. If the thyme has very thin, pliable stems, just chop the stems and leaves together, discarding the tough bottom portions as you go. If the stems are thicker and woodier, hold the sprig of thyme upright, by the top of the stem; then run your thumb and forefinger down the stem to release the leaves and smaller offshoots. The tender tips can be left intact and chopped along with the leaves once the woodier stems have been sheared clean and discarded.

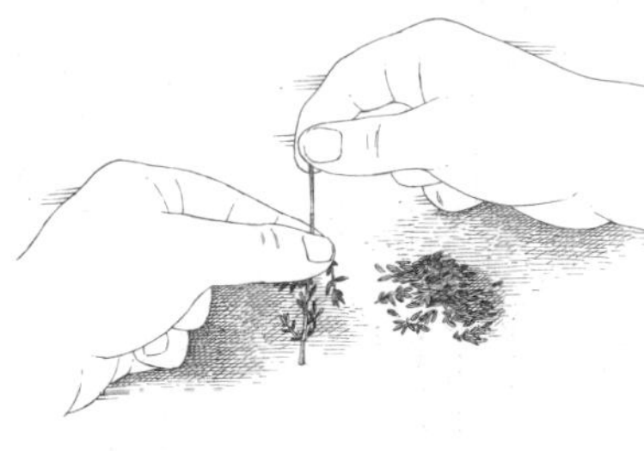

Use a shearing movement to separate thyme leaves from the woody stems.

Enhanced? Not Really

More than half of the fresh pork sold in supermarkets is now "enhanced." Enhanced pork is injected with a salt solution to make lean cuts, such as center-cut roasts and chops, seem moister. But we think natural pork has a better flavor and a quick 1-hour brine adds plenty of moisture. We recommend buying natural pork.

Manufacturers don't use the terms "enhanced" or "natural" on package labels, but if the pork has been enhanced it will have an ingredient list, like the one below. Natural pork contains just pork and won't have an ingredient list.

To determine if pork is "enhanced," look for an ingredient list on the label.

The Best Salt for the Job

For most recipes, the test kitchen has found that inexpensive table salt is just as good as fancy salts. The fine granules are more easily dispersed in batters and doughs, so it's our top choice for baking. We also rely on table salt for soups, stews, sauces, and more. Once salt dissolves, it all tastes pretty much the same, so why waste money on pricey sea salt to season a pot of pasta cooking water? But when it comes to seasoning meat, we don't think table salt is up to the job. The tiny grains slip from our fingers in an uncontrolled manner, creating uneven salt paths and patchy flavoring. This came especially to light during our testing for Steak Frites (page 9). We found that larger-grained salts (such as kosher salt) are easier to control and cling nicely to the meat's surface. When a recipe calls for seasoning meat "to taste," we suggest about ⅛ teaspoon of kosher salt per portion of meat. Kosher salt is inexpensive and readily available, so pick up a box for seasoning meat, chicken, or fish.

Chinese Green Beans

Long beans, also called yard-long or snake beans, are the traditional choice in Chinese stir-fries and other recipes, including Sichuan Green Beans (page 21). These thin, pliable pods can grow up to three feet long. They certainly look exotic, but are these specialty beans worth seeking out at an Asian market?

To find out, we purchased beans from several sources. We found that older, thicker beans can be woody, so look for thin, very flexible beans. After cutting them down to size, we were surprised that even super-thin long beans required the same cooking time as thicker green beans. The long beans were chewier and less sweet than green beans, with a nice nutty flavor. If you find long beans, give them a try—even though our tasters were just as happy with plain old green beans from the supermarket.

LONG BEANS
The Chinese answer to strin[g] beans is surprisingly nutty and chewy.

The Perfect Foil

Regular 12-inch-wide foil is fine for many kitchen tasks, but there are times when it's too narrow and we find ourselves trying to crimp together two sheets to create a single piece. On these occasions, it's much easier to reach for a roll of 18-inch foil. This extra-wide foil is perfect for lining large pans (see 15-Minute

---

EQUIPMENT TESTING: **Tart Pans**

Imagine your disappointment if a French Onion and Bacon Tart (page 19) crumbled as you attempted to liberate it from its pan. During our testing of seven tart pans, we had this unfortunate experience with onion as well as fruit tarts, so it pays to choose your tart pan carefully.

TIN WINS
For buttery tart pastry, stick with tinned steel pans, like this one sold by Kaiser Tinplate.

Tart pans can be divided into three basic categories based on materials: tinned steel (the classic choice), nonstick, and everything else—ranging from heavy ceramic to floppy silicone. What ceramic, as in the Baker's Catalogue Bake-and-Serve Stoneware ($14.96), added in tabletop aesthetics, it quickly lost in practicality—the lack of a removable bottom forced us to chisel the delicate tart from the pan with a sharp knife. The equally flawed, Gumby-like SiliconeZone 10-Inch Tart Pan ($18) required us to bend the pan to pop out our now-cracked pastry.

Because tart pastry is mostly butter, the nonstick surfaces on three of the remaining pans were not only redundant but also unfavorably slick. Without some tackiness, the dough slumped unevenly down the fluted edges of the Calphalon Classic Bakeware Nonstick 10-Inch Round Tart Pan ($19.99), Kaiser Noblesse 9½-Inch Quiche Pan with Removable Base ($14.95), and Nordic Ware 8-Inch Quiche Tart Pan ($13.99).

Tarts baked in the two tinned steel pans—the Kaiser Tinplate 9-Inch Quiche Pan with Removable Bottom ($9) and the Cooking.com Round Tart Pan, 9.5-Inch ($7.95)—browned evenly and released effortlessly. In this case, the classic design is still the best.

—Elizabeth Bomze

ILLUSTRATION: JOHN BURGOYNE

Cauliflower Rainbow

While shopping for Roasted Cauliflower (page 20), we were lured by the riveting green, orange, and purple heads of cauliflower at the market. Were they merely a decorative marketing gimmick, or might these varieties actually taste better than, or cook any differently from, regular cauliflower? In the end, our tasters felt that the broccoflower and purple varieties were well suited to roasting, although neither was any better than plain old white cauliflower.

BROCCOFLOWER
This broccoli-cauliflower hybrid exhibited an assertive broccoli flavor and firm texture.

ROMANESCO CAULIFLOWER
This rare Italian breed boasts a vibrant lime-green color and spiraling turrets, but its delicate flavor and texture suffered when roasted.

PURPLE CAULIFLOWER
A faintly bitter edge and the ability to retain its royal hue after roasting won this variety some accolades.

ORANGE CAULIFLOWER
Loaded with vitamin A but short on moisture, this hybrid was on the dry side.

Chocolate Walnut Fudge, page 23, or Roasted Cauliflower, page 20). It's also the best choice when lining pie or tart shells that need to be prebaked (see French Onion and Bacon Tart, page 19).

Extra-wide foil lets you line baking pans and tart shells with a single piece.

The Proper Process

The rule of thumb in the test kitchen is that chopping vegetables by hand will produce the cleanest-looking and best-tasting result. Although a food processor is certainly quicker, it tends to bruise vegetables. But during the development of our White Chicken Chili (page 7), we ran out of patience while laboriously chopping through cases of onions and chiles, so we threw some into the food processor bowl. Just as we expected, the result was a soupy, irregular mess; the pieces in the bottom of the bowl disintegrated, while the ones on top remained intact. Suspecting overcrowding might be the culprit, we tried splitting the vegetables into two batches and giving them a quick, rough chop by hand beforehand. The result, especially when cooked into a soup or stew, was on par with hand chopping—and a whole lot faster. But for more delicate applications, such as salsa and sauces, hand chopping still reigns supreme.

OVERPROCESSED
If you overload a food processor, you'll have a soupy mess with large chunks.

JUST RIGHT
Perfectly processed chiles and onions (done in two batches) are comparable to vegetables cut with a knife.

RECIPE UPDATE

Well-Done Hamburgers on the Stovetop

We weren't surprised when readers wanted us to adapt our **Well-Done Hamburgers on a Charcoal Grill** (July/August 2006) for the stovetop. Our first intuition was to heat a couple teaspoons of oil in a large traditional skillet over high heat until smoking—we figured high heat would be essential to get a nicely browned crust. But we quickly found this approach was all wrong. The panade—a paste made from bread and milk that keeps our well-done burgers moist—burned over high heat. Turning the heat down to medium allowed a deep-brown crust to develop and helped cook the burgers through. And to ensure that the beautiful sear stays intact, use a nonstick skillet. See Cook's Extra, below, for the recipe.

Arroz con Pollo...with White Meat

After we published our **Latino-Style Chicken and Rice** (September/October 2006), a number of readers wrote in asking the best way to swap the dark meat chicken thighs for white meat breasts. The thighs simmer for close to an hour in the original recipe, a length of time guaranteed to severely dry out tender breast meat. Simmering the breasts in the pot with the liquid ingredients for just 20 minutes turned out to be the answer. The breasts are then transferred to a plate that gets wrapped tightly with foil while the rice is added to the pot and cooks for a half hour. Bone-in, skin-on chicken breasts (as opposed to boneless, skinless cutlets) are necessary to add sufficient chicken flavor. And cutting the breasts in half crosswise exposes more meat surface area to the flavorful marinade and braising liquid—plus it allows for more even cooking. See Cook's Extra, below, for the recipe.

Apple Crumble

A good peach can be difficult to find, even during the stone fruit's peak season. It's no wonder readers asked about making our **Peach Crumble** (July/August 2006) using always-available apples. We found that a three-pound mix of sweet and tart apples makes an excellent crumble; however, because apples are much sturdier than delicate peaches, they must be treated differently. For starters, apples take longer to cook; therefore, we bake them for 20 minutes before adding the topping. (The peaches are not prebaked.) Once the baked topping is added, the crumble goes into the oven for another 25 minutes. Stirring the partially cooked apples before adding the topping is crucial for an evenly cooked filling. Because apples are drier than peaches, we needed only ½ teaspoon cornstarch to nail the right sauce consistency. Finally, we doubled the amount of sugar, because peaches are so much sweeter. See Cook's Extra, below, for the recipe. —Compiled by Charles Kelsey

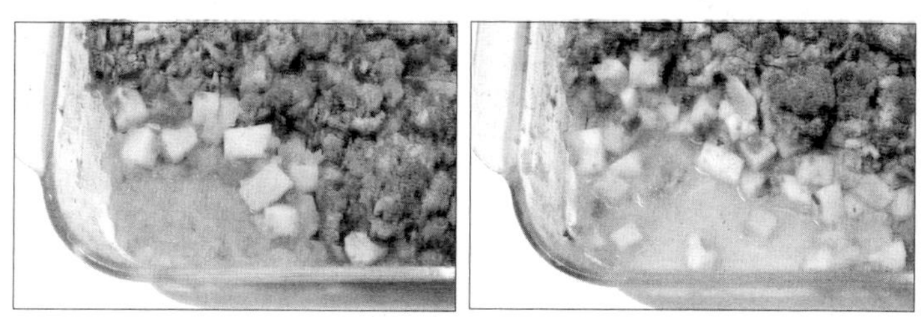

UNSTIRRED **STIRRED**
Partially cooking the apples and giving them a stir before adding the crumble topping ensures perfectly cooked fruit.

IF YOU HAVE A QUESTION about a recipe, let us know. Send your inquiry, name, address, and daytime telephone number to Recipe Update, Cook's Illustrated, P.O. Box 470589, Brookline, MA 02447, or write to recipeupdate@bcpress.com.

Go to www.cooksillustrated.com
- Click on the Cook's Extra button for our recipes for **Stovetop Well-Done Hamburgers, Latin-Style Chicken and Rice with Breast Meat,** and **Apple Crumble.**
- Recipes available until June 1, 2007.

EQUIPMENT CORNER

BY ELIZABETH BOMZE

DO YOU REALLY NEED THIS?

Butter Knife

Before the invention of tablespoon-marked butter wrappers, Americans either messily made do by smearing softened butter into measuring spoons or winged it and hoped for the best. But the recent appearance in stores of unmarked artisanal and European-style block butters (as well as the perennial problem of improperly wrapped marked sticks) can leave many wrapper-dependent chefs helpless in the face of precise cookie and cake recipes. If you don't want to rely on imperfect eyeballing skills, KitchenArt offers the handy Pro Measuring Butter Knife ($7.88)—in Chrome or Satin Finish—a reversible ruler-like paddle knife that accurately measures and neatly cuts both Elgin-style ("stick") or Western-pack-style ("cube") butter, though it's too narrow for pound-block butter's wider plane. For this convenience, we'll happily make a bit of room in our gadget drawer.

A CLEVER KNIFE
KitchenArt's clever Pro Measuring Butter Knife makes short work of gauging teaspoons and tablespoons on unmarked sticks.

EQUIPMENT UPDATE:

Digital Scale

With the combination of an easily deciphered display, generous capacity (to 11 pounds), and roomy platform, the attractively modern Soehnle Futura ($79.99) has been our favorite digital kitchen scale since our 2003 testing. Recently, the Futura has been replaced by Soehnle's new model 65055 ($89.99)—an even sleeker, lighter scale. Though the new model loses just over a pound in maximum capacity, it offers a more durable on-, off-, and zero-setting tare button alongside a gram/pound conversion button—conveniently relocated from the scale's inaccessible underside—and, to a baker's delight, extends the measurement reading one decimal place farther, into the hundredths, starting at 1 gram (or 0.05 ounces). It's our new scale of choice.

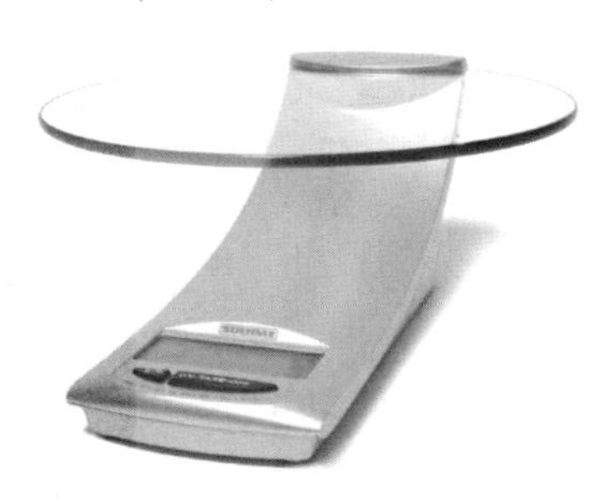

SLEEK AND PRECISE
Upgraded in style and precision, the Soehnle 65055 scale is our new winner.

EQUIPMENT TESTING:

Splatter Screens

Be it bacon, steaks, or fish fillets, pan-frying can be a messy business. Splatter screens—sieve-like mesh or perforated metal disks with handles—aim to overlay a skillet and combat grease splatters. But after frying five pounds of bacon, protected by nine splatter screens, it became clear to us that not all models could earn their keep.

Some screens fell just shy of the skillet's edge. Diameters of 12 inches or less proved insufficient for skillets with an equally large face. And models with overlaying—and painfully heat-absorbing—handles were highly problematic. Gimmicky designs, such as adjustable arms or dual screens designed to fit skillets of varying sizes, did not work.

Traditional lollipop-shaped models were better. Though no single screen perfectly combined splatter-proofing with ergonomic stability, the Amco 13-inch Splatter Screen ($15.95) edged out the well-anchored Norpro model and won for its nearly impermeable mesh face, which corralled the grease and kept our hands clean.

Sources

The following are sources for recommended items. Prices were current at press time and do not include shipping. Contact companies directly to confirm prices and availability; visit www.cooksillustrated.com for updates.

Page 9: SPIDER SKIMMER
- Typhoon Extra-Large Wire Skimmer: $15, product #TY14593, **Golda's Kitchen (866-465-3299, www.goldaskitchen.com).**

Page 25: LOAF PAN
- Williams-Sonoma Goldtouch Nonstick Loaf Pan: $19, item #60-7081524, **Williams-Sonoma (877-812-6235, www.williams-sonoma.com).**

Page 26: SOY SAUCE
- Lee Kum Kee Soy Sauce: $1.99 for 5.1 ounces **(store locator at www.lkk.com).**
- Ohsawa Nama Shoyu: $6.49 for 10 ounces, item #0501-1010, **Gold Mine Natural Food (800-475-3663, www.goldminenaturalfood.com).**

Page 28: DUTCH OVENS
- All-Clad Stainless 8-Quart Stockpot: $257.95, item #100218, **Cooking.com (800-663-8810, www.cooking.com).**
- Le Creuset 7¼-Quart Round French Oven: $229.95, product #102990, **Cooking.com.**
- Chefmate Round Enameled Cast Iron Casserole for Target: $39.99, **Target (www.target.com).**
- Mario Batali 6-Quart Italian Essentials Enamel-on-Cast-Iron Pot: $99.99, product #0-49010, **Amazon.com.**

Page 30: TART PANS
- Round Tart Pan, 9.5-Inch: $7.95, item #103620, **Cooking.com.**
- Kaiser Tinplate 9-Inch Quiche Pan with Removable Bottom: $9, item #610337, **Amazon.com.**

Page 32: BUTTER KNIFE
- KitchenArt Pro Measuring Butter Knife: $7.88, item #90531, **KitchenArt (800-239-8090, www.kitchenart.com).**

Page 32: DIGITAL SCALE
- Soehnle: $89.99, product #65055, **Soehnle (made by Leifheit), The Consumer Link (800-421-1223, www.theconsumerlink.com).**

Page 32: SPLATTER SCREEN
- Amco Splatter Screen 13": $15.95, item #06-0004, **Chef Tools (866-716-2433, www.cheftools.com).**

UNITED STATES POSTAL SERVICE. Statement of Ownership, Management, and Circulation (All Periodicals Publications Except Requester Publications)

1. Publication Title	2. Publication Number	3. Filing Date
Cook's Illustrated	1 0 6 8 - 2 8 2 1	10-01-06
4. Issue Frequency	**5. Number of Issues Published Annually**	**6. Annual Subscription Price**
Bi-Monthly	6 issues	$35.70

7. Complete Mailing Address of Known Office of Publication (Not printer) (Street, city, county, state, and ZIP+4®): 17 Station Street, Brookline, MA 02445
Contact Person:
Telephone (Include area code): 617-232-1000

8. Complete Mailing Address of Headquarters or General Business Office of Publisher (Not printer): same as publisher

9. Full Names and Complete Mailing Addresses of Publisher, Editor, and Managing Editor (Do not leave blank)
Publisher (Name and complete mailing address): Christopher P. Kimball, Boston Common Press, 17 Station Street, Brookline, MA 02445
Editor (Name and complete mailing address): same as publisher
Managing Editor (Name and complete mailing address): Jack Bishop, Boston Common Press, 17 Station Street, Brookline, MA 02445

10. Owner (Do not leave blank. If the publication is owned by a corporation, give the name and address of the corporation immediately followed by the names and addresses of all stockholders owning or holding 1 percent or more of the total amount of stock. If not owned by a corporation, give the names and addresses of the individual owners. If owned by a partnership or other unincorporated firm, give its name and address as well as those of each individual owner. If the publication is published by a nonprofit organization, give its name and address.)

Full Name	Complete Mailing Address
Boston Common Press Limited Partnership	17 Station Street, Brookline, MA 02445
(Christopher P. Kimball)	

11. Known Bondholders, Mortgagees, and Other Security Holders Owning or Holding 1 Percent or More of Total Amount of Bonds, Mortgages, or Other Securities. If none, check box ☐ None

Full Name	Complete Mailing Address
N/A	

12. Tax Status (For completion by nonprofit organizations authorized to mail at nonprofit rates) (Check one)
The purpose, function, and nonprofit status of this organization and the exempt status for federal income tax purposes:
☐ Has Not Changed During Preceding 12 Months
☐ Has Changed During Preceding 12 Months (Publisher must submit explanation of change with this statement)

PS Form 3526, September 2006 (Page 1 of 3 (Instructions Page 3)) PSN 7530-01-000-9931 PRIVACY NOTICE: See our privacy policy on www.usps.com

13. Publication Title: Cook's Illustrated
14. Issue Date for Circulation Data: September/October 2006

15. Extent and Nature of Circulation		Average No. Copies Each Issue During Preceding 12 Months	No. Copies of Single Issue Published Nearest to Filing Date
a. Total Number of Copies (Net press run)		1,163,998	1,206,685
b. Paid Circulation (By Mail and Outside the Mail)	(1) Mailed Outside-County Paid Subscriptions Stated on PS Form 3541 (Include paid distribution above nominal rate, advertiser's proof copies, and exchange copies)	829,967	867,592
	(2) Mailed In-County Paid Subscriptions Stated on PS Form 3541 (Include paid distribution above nominal rate, advertiser's proof copies, and exchange copies)	0	0
	(3) Paid Distribution Outside the Mails Including Sales Through Dealers and Carriers, Street Vendors, Counter Sales, and Other Paid Distribution Outside USPS®	87,664	86,217
	(4) Paid Distribution by Other Classes of Mail Through the USPS (e.g. First-Class Mail®)	0	0
c. Total Paid Distribution (Sum of 15b (1), (2),(3), and (4))		917,631	953,809
d. Free or Nominal Rate Distribution (By Mail and Outside the Mail)	(1) Free or Nominal Rate Outside-County Copies included on PS Form 3541	8,300	3,654
	(2) Free or Nominal Rate In-County Copies Included on PS Form 3541	0	0
	(3) Free or Nominal Rate Copies Mailed at Other Classes Through the USPS (e.g. First-Class Mail)	0	0
	(4) Free or Nominal Rate Distribution Outside the Mail (Carriers or other means)	3,486	3,403
e. Total Free or Nominal Rate Distribution (Sum of 15d (1), (2), (3) and (4)		11,786	7,057
f. Total Distribution (Sum of 15c and 15e)		929,416	960,866
g. Copies not Distributed (See Instructions to Publishers #4 (page #3))		234,582	245,819
h. Total (Sum of 15f and g)		1,163,998	1,206,685
i. Percent Paid (15c divided by 15f times 100)		98.73%	99.27%

16. Publication of Statement of Ownership
☒ If the publication is a general publication, publication of this statement is required. Will be printed in the Jan/Feb 2007 issue of this publication. ☐ Publication not required.

17. Signature and Title of Editor, Publisher, Business Manager, or Owner — Date: 9/12/06

I certify that all information furnished on this form is true and complete. I understand that anyone who furnishes false or misleading information on this form or who omits material or information requested on the form may be subject to criminal sanctions (including fines and imprisonment) and/or civil sanctions (including civil penalties).

PS Form 3526, September 2006 (Page 2 of 3)

RECIPES

January & February 2007

Available on the Web
The following recipes and menu are available free until June 1, 2007. Go to www.cooksillustrated.com and click on the Cook's Extra button.

COOK'S extra

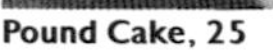
Pound Cake, 25

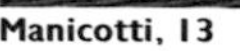
Manicotti, 13

Steak Frites, 9

Thai-Style Chicken Soup, 15

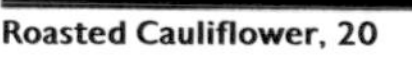
Roasted Cauliflower, 20

Rocky Road Fudge, 23

Herb-Crusted Pork Roast, 11

Sichuan Green Beans, 21

White Chicken Chili, 7

French Onion and Bacon Tart, 19

PHOTOGRAPHY: CARL TREMBLAY, STYLING: MARIE PIRAINO

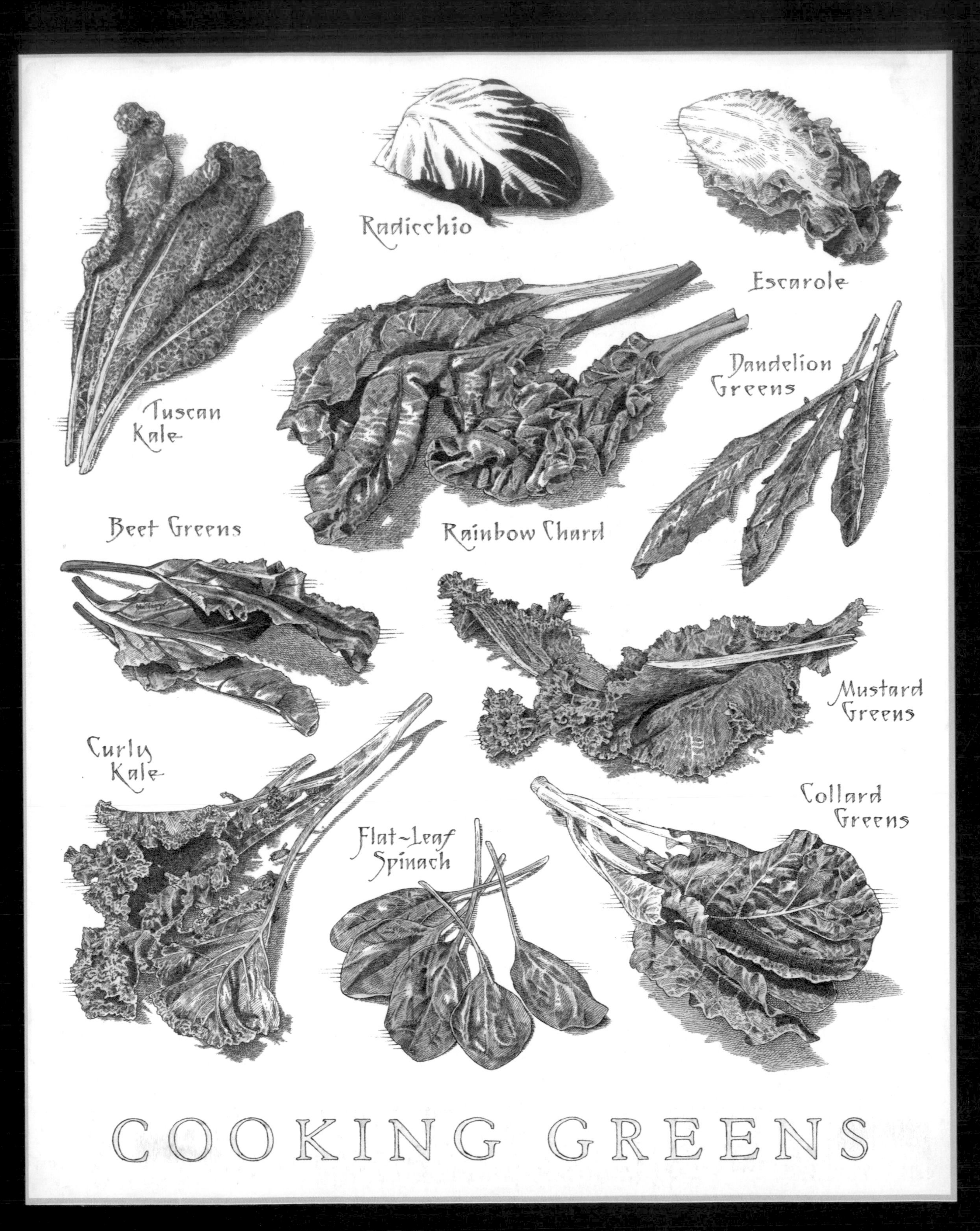
Radicchio
Escarole
Tuscan Kale
Dandelion Greens
Beet Greens
Rainbow Chard
Mustard Greens
Curly Kale
Collard Greens
Flat-Leaf Spinach
COOKING GREENS

NUMBER EIGHTY-FIVE

MARCH & APRIL 2007

Rating Chef's Knives
We Test Cutting-Edge Designs

Parmesan Chicken
Secrets to a Crispy, Cheesy Crust

Roasted Tomato Pasta Sauce
Big Flavor from Winter Tomatoes

Garlic-Butter Shrimp

Chinese BBQ Pork
Easy Oven Method

Lemon Layer Cake

Balsamic Vinegar Taste Test
Spend $2 or $200?

Bread Baking Demystified
Garlic-Potato Soup
Pan-Roasted Asparagus
Olive-Rosemary Bread
Brown Sugar Cookies

www.cooksillustrated.com
$5.95 U.S./$6.95 CANADA

CONTENTS

March & April 2007

FRENCH CHEESES Many French cheeses are subject to very strict production regulations, as governed by the Appellation d'Origine Contrôlée (AOC). Both Camembert and Brie de Meaux are made from cow's milk. Tangy and musky, Camembert should be very creamy when fully ripe; Brie de Meaux has a richer flavor and more compact texture. Epoisses is also made from cow's milk. Its odor can be quite pungent, but the flavor is smooth and nutty. Morbier, another cow's milk cheese, has a distinctive line of edible vegetable ash. Comté is a semifirm cow's milk cheese with a sweet, nutty flavor. Roquefort, a creamy blue cheese made from sheep's milk, is aged in caves. Valençay is a fresh goat cheese in a distinctive pyramid shape; it is tart and bright in flavor. Although not AOC labeled, many other French cheeses are of equal quality. The diminutive Crottin de Champcol is a goat cheese eaten fresh or aged. St. Agur, a cow's milk blue, is milder than Roquefort and very creamy. Tomme de Savoie is a cow's milk cheese with a thick rind and a semifirm, earthy interior. Brebis, a sheep's milk cheese, is firm and mildly nutty.

COVER (*Onions*): Elizabeth Brandon, BACK COVER (*French Cheeses*): John Burgoyne

For list rental information, contact: Specialists Marketing Services, Inc., 1200 Harbor Blvd., 9th Floor, Weehawken, NJ 07087; 201-865-5800.
Editorial Office: 17 Station St., Brookline, MA 02445; 617-232-1000; fax 617-232-1572. Subscription inquiries, call 800-526-8442.
Postmaster: Send all new orders, subscription inquiries, and change-of-address notices to Cook's Illustrated, P.O. Box 7446, Red Oak, IA 51591-0446.

COOK'S ILLUSTRATED
www.cooksillustrated.com
HOME OF AMERICA'S TEST KITCHEN

SEND IT DOWN, GABRIEL!

Harley Smith was a farmer who owned what is now the Haggerty place over on the west side of town. Our family now owns part of that property, the pastures across the road where his father's herd of Holsteins grazed during the summer. There is a good spring on the property, the water having been piped down the mountain and under the road to the milk house, where it cooled the large metal cans stored for pickup.

I have recounted in this column more than one story of Harley and his laconic wit, including the time he gave me a chain saw lesson without uttering a word (he just stood next to me and sawed through a log the right way) and his habit of showing up every Friday night at Tom and Nancy's farmhouse just in time for dessert. Harley and his wife, Dorothy, just sat against the wall, watching with anticipation as everyone finished supper.

Just after the first snow of the year, Tom and I were talking about snowplowing, and he told me about Harley's love of bad weather. As soon as a good size storm showed up, Tom's phone would ring and there would be Harley, shouting out with great enthusiasm, "Send it down, Gabriel!" Then he would go out, load up his spreader with sand and salt, and head out for the night. For some, the storm was a trial, but for Harley it was pure joy. His enthusiasm may have been fired by the notion of extra pocket money, but I doubt it. There was more to Harley Smith than that.

Last summer I stopped to talk with Gerald, a carpenter who used to work for Tom. He'd recently purchased a small red camp on the west side of town, and a few of the neighbors were complaining about the new piles of flotsam scattered about the yard. In response, and displaying a good helping of Vermont wit, he erected a fence to screen the yard—a bright red snow fence that, in places, was plastered with Tyvek (an industrial white paper-like material used to side houses). The fence was more of an eyesore than the junk.

Christopher Kimball

With our trucks parked nose to end, we chatted at the tail end of a tired August day. Gerald has not had an easy life. I remember in particular one hot summer when he impulsively abandoned his measuring tape and hammer to work as a barefoot flagman for the road crew standing on hot, soft macadam. Evenings, during the years when he was not living at home, there were reports of Gerald parked by the side of a dirt road in the woods, camping out in his junkyard pickup. Or I might drive by Gerald riding his electric golf cart around town, quite happily cruising at five miles an hour.

But that summer evening, he asked if I remembered the 10-point buck that we had seen in our lower field a half dozen years ago. I said I did. He had snapped a photo of it and said he was going to have it tattooed on his back just to keep the memory. He grinned big and rolled another cigarette, and when I left him, he was still sitting in his truck by the side of the road, enjoying a smoke and thinking of all 10 points.

For many years, Russell was the town metalworker. He would fix hay wagons, balers, plows—you name it. When he got older and his balance was shaky, he had to go live at the nursing home. On Sundays, Susy and Junior would pick him up and bring him back to their farm. They strapped him onto a Cub Cadet with extra seat belts, and then they would take a picture as he rode around, mowing the front yard. The photo was placed by his bedside table so that during the week he could smile and remember that he was still useful.

During summers, our kids do farm chores: graining the beefers; feeding the pigs corn mush; picking strawberries, blueberries, and raspberries; weeding the raised garden beds; taking out the compost; helping to groom the horses and clean the tack. Just at sunset, there is one last chore. The door to the henhouse has to be closed and locked to keep our small flock safe from raccoons and foxes.

The first few times our son, Charlie, was asked to step up and handle this slight task, there was a lot of complaining. "I set the table" or "I fed the pigs" was the typical response. And then, of course, he went AWOL every night just at sunset. But then, as with his two older sisters, Adrienne and I noticed the change. At first, he went down to the henhouse after just one or two reminders, and then, at last, he just got the job done on his own.

One night last summer, I was up by the sap house and happened to see Charlie heading down the driveway to close in the chickens. He was half-skipping down the road, talking to himself, the western sky pale with just a faint hint of baby blue and wisps of cirrus. I could hear the brook running—it had been a wet summer—and then I saw Charlie make his way back up to the house through the thickening green of the apple orchard. I could glimpse his face darkly as the sun set, and all I could think of was Harley Smith at the onset of a snowstorm. I whispered, "Send it down, Gabriel," and turned back to finish my chores.

FOR INQUIRIES, ORDERS, OR MORE INFORMATION:

www.cooksillustrated.com

At www.cooksillustrated.com, you can order books and subscriptions, sign up for our free e-newsletter, or renew your magazine subscription. Join the website and you'll have access to 14 years of *Cook's* recipes, cookware tests, ingredient tastings, and more.

COOKBOOKS

We sell more than 40 cookbooks by the editors of *Cook's Illustrated*. To order, visit our bookstore at www.cooksillustrated.com or call 800-611-0759 (or 515-246-6911 from outside the U.S.).

COOK'S ILLUSTRATED Magazine

Cook's Illustrated magazine (ISSN 1068-2821), number 84, is published bimonthly by Boston Common Press Limited Partnership, 17 Station St., Brookline, MA 02445. Copyright 2007 Boston Common Press Limited Partnership. Periodicals postage paid at Boston, Mass., and additional mailing offices USPS #012487. Publications Mail Agreement No. 40020778. Return undeliverable Canadian addresses to P.O. Box 875, Station A, Windsor, Ontario N9A 6P2. POSTMASTER: Send address changes to Cook's Illustrated, P.O. Box 7446, Red Oak, IA 51591-0446. For subscription and gift subscription orders, subscription inquiries, or change-of-address notices, call 800-526-8442 in the U.S. or 515-247-7571 from outside the U.S., or write us at Cook's Illustrated, P.O. Box 7446, Red Oak, IA 51591-0446.

ILLUSTRATION: RANDY GLASS

NOTES FROM READERS

COMPILED BY SANDRA WU

Storing Ginger

I don't use fresh ginger very often, so whenever I buy it, I end up having a lot left over. What's the best way to store it?

J.B. SIEGEL
SOMERVILLE, MASS.

➤We purchased several knobs of ginger, cut one end off of each to replicate the way they would normally be used in the kitchen, and stored them using several different methods: unwrapped in a cool, dark pantry; on the counter exposed to sunlight; in the refrigerator (unwrapped, wrapped in foil, wrapped in plastic wrap, and placed in a zipper lock bag); and in the freezer (wrapped in foil).

After two weeks, we examined the samples, all of which had dried out and sealed up where they had been cut. The frozen ginger fared the worst: Following a brief thaw, it was porous and mushy, rendering the process of grating or mincing nearly impossible. Both samples of room temperature–stored ginger were shriveled and had started to sprout. All of the wrapped, refrigerated ginger retained a smooth, taut exterior but exhibited spots of mold where condensation had gotten trapped in the wrapper. The unwrapped, refrigerated ginger, however, had a relatively fresh appearance, with no mold. So the next time you have a leftover knob of ginger, just toss it into the refrigerator unwrapped.

GINGER LIKES IT DRY
An unlikely method keeps ginger from becoming moldy.

Wax On, Wax Off

What's the best way to remove the wax from fruits and vegetables? I've seen vegetable wash at the supermarket, but it's rather expensive.

MARY MURPHY
MESA, ARIZ.

➤Our local supermarket carries a product called Veggie Wash, which purports to be significantly more effective at removing wax, soil, and chemicals from fruits and vegetables than rinsing with water alone. It contains water, corn and coconut derivatives, citrus oil, sodium citrate, glycerin, and grapefruit seed extract. Firm produce like cucumbers, apples, and oranges is to be sprayed with Veggie Wash, rubbed for 30 seconds, and then rinsed with water.

To find out just how effective this product is at removing surface residue, we peeled the waxiest cucumbers we could find. Then we weighed the strips of peel individually before cleaning them four different ways (repeated 10 times per method): under cold running water; hot running water; sprayed and rubbed with distilled white vinegar, followed by a cold-water rinse; and sprayed and rubbed with Veggie Wash, followed by a cold-water rinse. We also wiped down a set of cucumber peels with nail polish remover (a strong solvent) to use as a control by which to gauge the other methods.

THE PEEL TEST
We weighed cucumber peels before and after cleaning to measure four methods of removing wax from produce.

We weighed the cucumber peels again after washing and averaged the weight-loss results of the 10 tests. Of the food-safe methods, the Veggie Wash removed the most wax, with the peels averaging a weight loss of 7 percent post-washing. (The peels wiped with nail polish remover registered a 12.8 percent difference.) With a 6.3 percent difference, the vinegar-rubbed sample was a very close second, followed by the hot-water rinse (5.4 percent) and cold-water rinse (4.9 percent). While the 16-ounce bottle of Veggie Wash did produce a noticeably less-waxy surface, we don't think it's worth its $5.95 price tag. A spray bottle filled with vinegar works nearly as well at a fraction of the cost.

WAX BE GONE
Which product removes more wax from produce?

Odoriferous Oil

What causes oil to develop a fishy odor or taste when deep-frying?

DAVE NGUYEN
SAN MATEO, CALIF.

➤Oil is mainly composed of triglycerides, or fat molecules containing free fatty acids. When oil is heated, the fatty acids oxidize to form small volatile molecules (mostly peroxides and aldehydes) that produce a strong, rancid odor. The higher the heat and the longer the oil is used, the greater the likelihood that this effect will occur.

It's also worth noting that some oils are more susceptible to oxidation than others: Saturated fats are less likely to oxidize than unsaturated fats. Therefore, oils that are very low in saturated fat will deteriorate more quickly than oils with significant amounts of more stable saturated fats. Test kitchen taste tests of fried chicken proved that canola oil (6 percent saturated fat) and safflower oil (9 percent saturated fat) are more likely to lend a spoiled, "fishy" flavor to fried foods than refined peanut oil (17 percent saturated fat) or vegetable shortening (25 percent saturated fat), which generally produce clean-tasting fried foods.

Mollet Eggs

While flipping through French cookbooks, I came across references to mollet eggs. What are they, and what's the best way to prepare them?

MERLENE MOODY
WAUKESHA, WIS.

➤Mollet eggs are a category of cooked-in-shell eggs whose name is derived from the French word *molle*, meaning "soft." The texture of mollet eggs is somewhere between soft-boiled and hard-boiled. Mollet eggs have a dark yellow, semiliquid, gel-like yolk and a white that is firm enough for the egg to be peeled and served for breakfast or, more traditionally, as part of a composed salad.

We found the best way to produce this texture was to start with the test kitchen's standard procedure for boiling eggs. We placed 6 eggs in a medium saucepan, filled the pan with 2 quarts of cold water, brought the water to a boil, and shut off the heat. Hard-boiled eggs steep for 10 minutes before being transferred to a bowl of ice water, while soft-boiled eggs are removed right when the water comes to a boil. When we let these eggs steep in the hot water for 4 minutes, the yolks were still runny in the middle and the whites had barely set, making the eggs nearly impossible to peel. After 6 minutes, however, the yolks were just set and the whites had firmed up enough to make shelling easy. Voilà! Mollet eggs.

Avoiding the Daily Grind

I often buy a pound of coffee from my local coffee shop and have it ground for me so I don't have to deal with doing it myself. What's the best way to store it?

ROSECRANS BALDWIN
BROOKLYN, N.Y.

➤When it comes to coffee, we much prefer buying whole beans and grinding them ourselves in small batches, but we realize that most people don't want to bother with the mess (or noise) of grinding beans first thing every day. To determine the best storage method for ground coffee, we stored 1-pound batches using the best methods we have found for storing whole beans: on the counter, away from direct sunlight, in a zipper-lock bag with the air pressed out; and in the freezer (preferred over the counter or refrigerator for long-term storage), wrapped the same way.

After two weeks, we brewed both samples, as well as a third in which the frozen grounds were allowed to come to room temperature before brewing. Sipped black, the differences among the samples were fairly hard to detect, but tasters found the room temperature–stored coffee slightly harsher and more bitter than both freezer-stored samples. Additionally, letting the frozen grounds come to room temperature before brewing seemed to allow more of the essential oils to come out, resulting in an ever-so-slightly more flavorful cup.

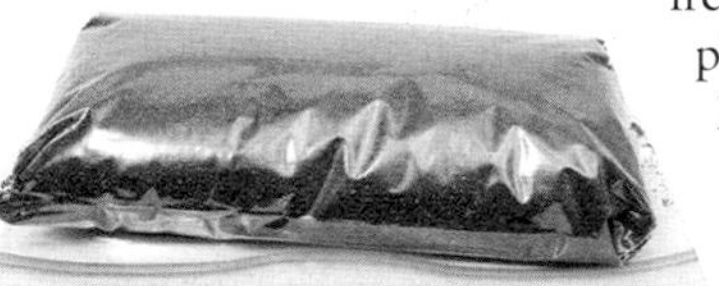

COFFEE STORAGE
Ground coffee fares best in the freezer.

After one month, the differences between the room temperature and frozen ground coffee were much more pronounced. The room temperature–stored coffee was undeniably harsher and more bitter than both freezer-stored samples, which had a smooth, well-rounded flavor. So if you buy ground beans, it makes sense to store them in the freezer, especially if you plan on having them around for a while. And if you have an extra 10 minutes, measure the frozen ground coffee into a filter and let it warm to room temperature before brewing.

Fat-Free Half-and-Half

I've heard that half-and-half is half milk and half cream. If this is true, then what is fat-free half-and-half, and how does it compare with regular half-and-half?

KRISTIN CLER
DALLAS, TEXAS

➢According to the U.S. Department of Agriculture, whole milk contains 3.5 percent fat and heavy cream contains 36 percent fat. Half-and-half falls somewhere in between, containing 10.5 percent to 18 percent fat. Fat-free half-and-half is made of skim milk, corn syrup, and a long list of natural and artificial additives that give it the color and consistency of the real deal. After an initial taste test pitting several national brands of nonfat half-and-half against bona fide half-and-half in cream of broccoli soup, tasters gave Land O'Lakes Fat Free Half-and-Half good marks. While not as rich or creamy as true half-and-half, it was at least edible, whereas other brands had a chemical aftertaste and curdled in the soup.

FAT-FREE HALF-AND-HALF
Can corn syrup and additives really take the place of fat?

Next, we compared Land O'Lakes Fat-Free Half-and-Half with real half-and-half in chocolate cream pie filling, mashed potatoes, light fettuccine Alfredo, and coffee. In the pie filling, the fat-free half-and-half offered smooth, creamy, pudding-like texture and decent—although slightly chalky—chocolate flavor. The problem? It wasn't firm enough to slice, making it unsuitable for pie but an acceptable choice for pudding. In the mashed potatoes, fat-free half-and-half provided a blander, leaner, watered-down version of the real thing, with a slightly sweet aftertaste. Tasters had a harder time distinguishing between the two samples of fettuccine Alfredo, which included a fair amount of Parmesan cheese. In the coffee, some tasters noticed a slight chemical aftertaste in the fat-free offering, while others couldn't tell the difference between the two.

In the end, we're not going to trade in proper half-and-half for the fat-free stuff. It just doesn't have the same body and flavor. But if you're going to replace half-and-half with a lower-fat dairy, Land O'Lakes Fat-Free Half-and-Half is a better choice than skim milk.

WHAT IS IT?

This shallow pan with 1-inch-deep cups is made of cast iron, just like my favorite skillet. What is it used for?

HELEN AVELIS
TERRE HAUTE, IND.

This item is a compartmentalized baking pan of the type manufactured from the mid-19th century through the 1920s. This heavy, cast-iron pan was known variously as a roll pan, muffin pan, or gem pan, depending on the shape of the baking cups and the cookbook recipes popular at the time. In researching this bakeware, we came across shapes ranging from simple—elliptical, round, square, rectangular, and diamond—to ornate designs reminiscent of miniature Bundt pans. The pans were used to bake quick bread batters, such as corn bread, biscuits, muffins, and gems (simple muffin-like breads).

The oval shape of your baking pan's cups and the gaps between them closely resemble a pan patented by Nathaniel Waterman and R&E Manufacturing Company in the late 1850s. According to David G. Smith, an avid collector of cast-iron cookware, Waterman patented the pan for "baking bread in small rolls." Unlike modern muffin tins, which are filled and baked right away, these pans were usually heated while empty in a very hot oven and then brushed with butter. This ensured that the baked goods would develop a handsome crust once the pans were filled with batter and returned to the oven.

This 19th-century cast-iron "roll pan" was used for baking corn bread, biscuits, muffins, and gems.

Carry-Over Cooking

Why does the phenomenon of carry-over cooking occur in large roasts but not in whole poultry or whole fish?

TONY POLOMBO
DELMONT, PA.

➢When it comes to red meat and pork, allowing a brief resting period after cooking enables the meat to continue to rise in temperature as the hotter exterior transfers heat to the cooler interior in the phenomenon known as carry-over cooking. The thicker the cut of meat and the higher the cooking temperature, the more the temperature of the meat will continue to rise. Thus, steaks and roasts should be taken off heat before they reach the desired temperature.

Both whole poultry and fish contain a hollow cavity, which provides a route for heat and steam to escape. Unlike a large beef roast, which can rise in temperature by 10 to 15 degrees over the course of 15 to 30 minutes, a whole chicken removed from the oven will not increase in temperature. To demonstrate this, we removed an undercooked chicken from the oven when the breast meat registered just 155 degrees, and, sure enough, carry-over heat didn't finish cooking the bird. In fact, the temperature immediately began to fall, hitting 140 degrees after 15 minutes. So always cook whole poultry and fish to the desired degree of doneness.

SEND US YOUR QUESTIONS We will provide a complimentary one-year subscription for each letter we print. Send your inquiry, name, address, and daytime telephone number to Notes from Readers, Cook's Illustrated, P.O. Box 470589, Brookline, MA 02447, or to notesfromreaders@americastestkitchen.com.

ILLUSTRATION: JOHN BURGOYNE

Quick Tips

⋟ COMPILED BY DAVID PAZMIÑO ⋞

Toast for a Crowd

Most electric toasters only accommodate 2 to 4 slices of bread—a problem if you're hosting a large group for breakfast or brunch. Mary Woosypiti of Cherokee, Okla., came up with an ingenious way to toast enough bread for a crowd.

Place an oven rack in the middle position; place a second rack in the lower-middle position; then place a baking sheet on the lower rack. Heat the oven to 450 degrees, then arrange bread slices between every other bar on the upper rack, resting on the baking sheet. Toast the bread until the top sides are lightly browned, about 6 minutes. Using tongs, flip the slices and continue toasting the second side, about 6 minutes longer.

Parchment Bags for Cooking

Cooking foods *en papillote,* or baked in a sealed parchment bag that traps steam, is a classic French technique, but the parchment bag can be difficult to fashion. Jana Volavka of Big Sky, Mont., devised this easy shortcut.

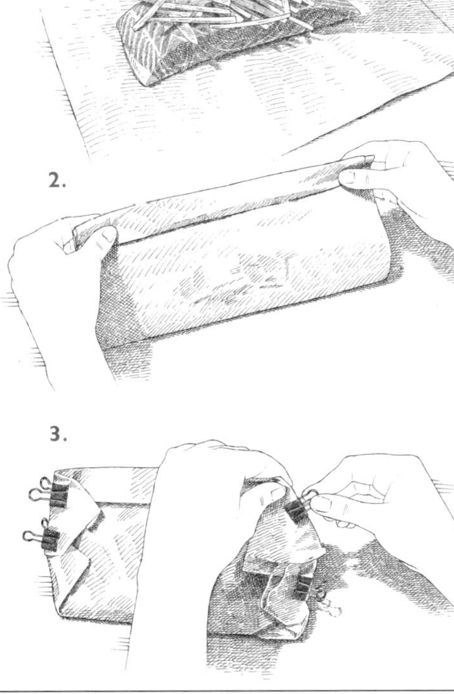

1. Place vegetables, fish, meat, or poultry and seasonings in the center of an oiled rectangle of parchment measuring 12 by 18 inches.
2. Lift the long edges of the parchment up toward the center and fold several times to create a closed package.
3. Secure folded edge with small metal binder-style clips.

Splash-Free Pouring

Tired of the splashes that occur when transferring tomato sauce, soup, or stew from a pot to a storage container, Adam Fontecchio of Exton, Pa., discovered that with the help of a spoon, the mess could be averted.

Place the backside of a large wooden or metal spoon under the pouring stream to deflect the liquid into the container.

Unwrapping Plastic Wrap

Dan Montgomery of Alexandria, Va., offers a clever way to find the beginning of a roll of plastic wrap that has torn and stuck to itself.

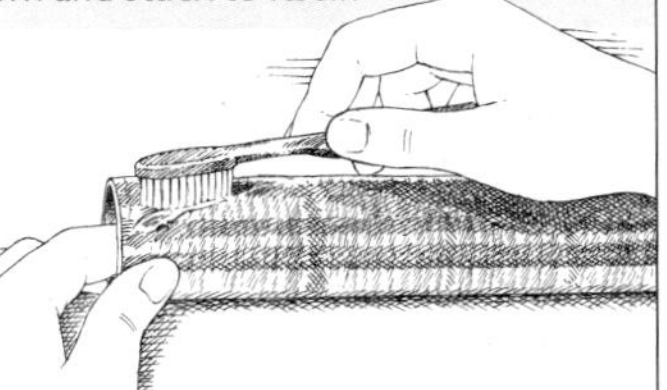

Hold a clean toothbrush or vegetable brush parallel to the roll of plastic wrap, rotating the roll and rubbing the bristles along the surface of the plastic until the hidden edge loosens and the plastic can be unwrapped.

Elevated Straining

When draining ingredients such as grated potatoes or yogurt in a mesh strainer set over a bowl, the strained liquid can sometimes rise back into the food, ruining the effort. Ashley Thibodaux-Jones of New Orleans, La., solves the problem this way.

1. Place an overturned ramekin or small bowl in a larger bowl that will catch the straining liquid.
2. Rest the strainer on the ramekin to elevate the food, preventing liquid from seeping back into it.

Snipping Green Beans

Bothered by the amount of time required to trim green beans, Lisa Green of New York, N.Y., came up with the following timesaving technique.

Gather 3 or 4 beans with the stem ends together in one hand. Use kitchen shears to trim the ends from the beans.

Seeding Cucumbers

Removing the seeds from cucumbers is a vital step toward avoiding soggy salads. Instead of dirtying a spoon, Dennis Walker of Menlo Park, Calif., uses the curved blade of the swivel-style peeler that he just used to peel the cucumber. After halving the cucumber lengthwise, use the tip of the blade to gently scrape out the seeds.

Send Us Your Tip We will provide a complimentary one-year subscription for each tip we print. Send your tip, name, and address to Quick Tips, Cook's Illustrated, P.O. Box 470589, Brookline, MA 02447, or to quicktips@americastestkitchen.com.

ILLUSTRATION: JOHN BURGOYNE

No More Beet Stains

Like many cooks, Adam Hulnick of New York, N.Y., always struggled to remove red stains from his hands after cutting fresh beets. He now wards off stains with vegetable oil.

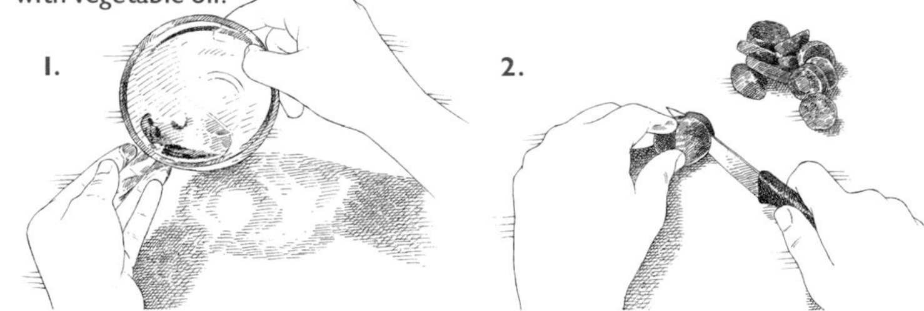

1. Rub the hand that will be holding the beets with about ½ teaspoon vegetable oil, taking care to keep the knife-holding hand dry.
2. Cut beets as desired, then wash hands with hot, soapy water.

Fresh Herbs, Fast

Fresh herbs are the finishing touch to countless recipes, but carefully plucking the leaves from a bunch of parsley or cilantro can be tedious. Vince Filippelli of Niagara Falls, N.Y., uses an everyday kitchen utensil to streamline the job.

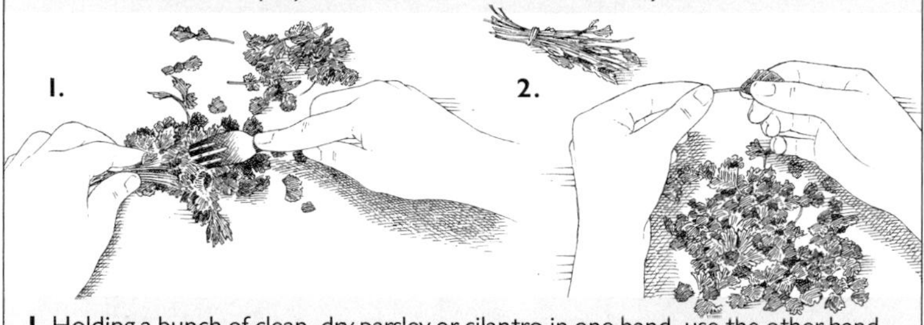

1. Holding a bunch of clean, dry parsley or cilantro in one hand, use the other hand to comb the tines of a dinner fork through the herbs to pull off the leaves.
2. Pick through the leaves to remove any remaining stems.

Spatula Holder

Instead of resting her rubber spatula on the counter after scraping down the sides of her food processor workbowl, Amanda Marion of Wyndmoor, Pa., keeps her counter clean with the following tip.

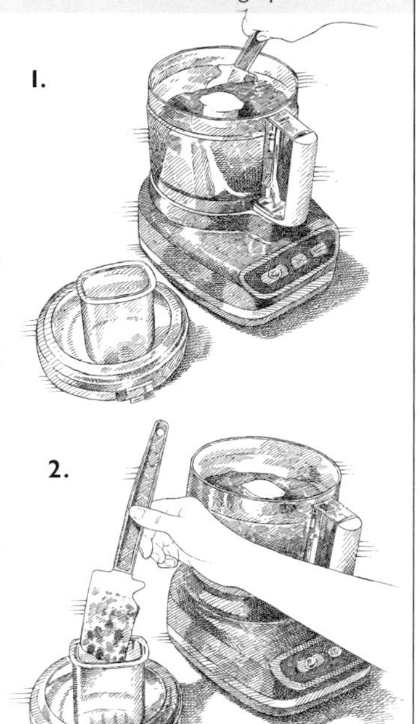

1. Scrape down the workbowl.
2. Rest the used spatula in the hollow feed tube of the food processor lid.

Handling Hot Pans

Pulling a hot baking sheet out of the oven while wearing oven mitts can be tricky, sometimes resulting in cookies with finger indents. Inspired by the cooks at his local pizzeria who use Channellock pliers to retrieve hot pizzas from the oven, John Watlington of Richmond, Va., put the tool to work in his own kitchen.

Use the pliers to latch onto metal baking sheets (or other bakeware without handles), then slide them out of the oven.

Separating Stuck Glass

Glass measuring cups and drinking glasses sometimes get locked together, with one cup stuck tightly inside the other. Rather than risk breaking the glass, John Colmers of Baltimore, Md., devised a novel way to release the seal.

1. Fill the top measuring cup or glass with ice cubes, then place the bottom cup in a bowl of warm tap water.
2. The contrast in temperatures between the cups will cause the seal to loosen, so the cups can be gently pulled apart.

Convenient Banana Slices

To avoid dirtying a cutting board when slicing bananas for his morning bowl of cereal, Michael Bibeault of Austin, Texas, came up with this trick.

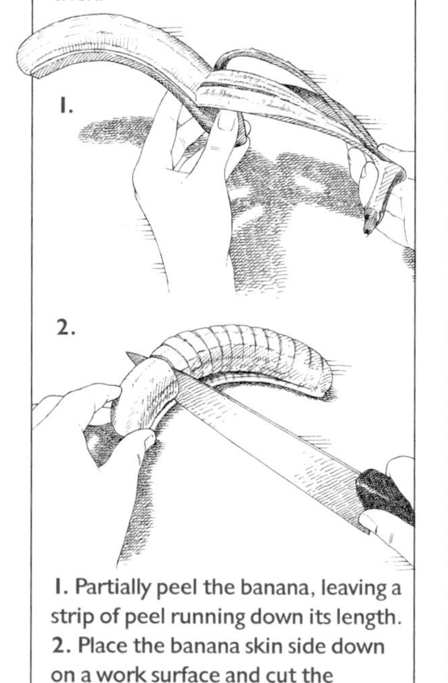

1. Partially peel the banana, leaving a strip of peel running down its length.
2. Place the banana skin side down on a work surface and cut the banana into slices.

Quicker Carrots Julienne

Cutting carrots into julienne—⅛-inch-thick by 2-inch-long strips—is painstaking work, even for cooks with advanced knife skills. Jolene Buccino of Ashland, Ore., saves time by starting with a bag of uniformly cut and peeled "snacking" carrots from the produce section of the supermarket.

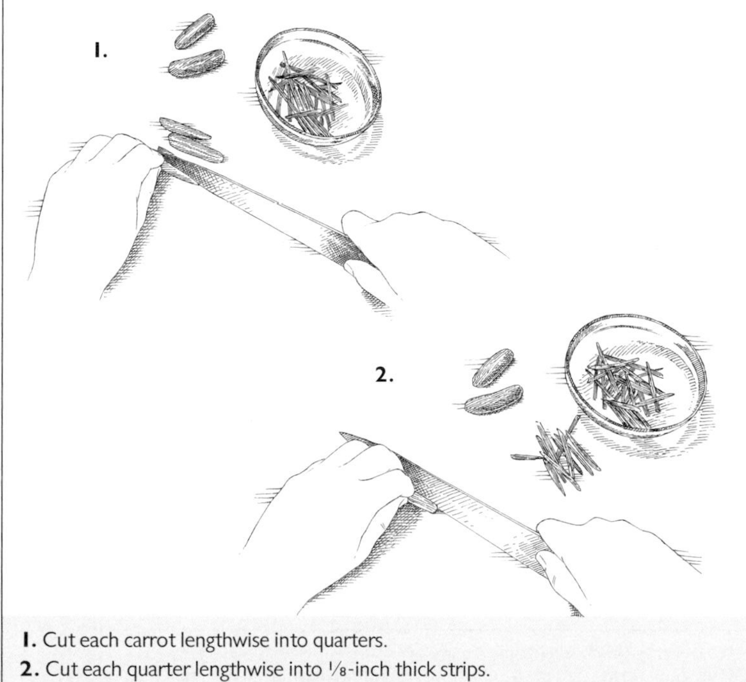

1. Cut each carrot lengthwise into quarters.
2. Cut each quarter lengthwise into ⅛-inch thick strips.

Parmesan-Crusted Chicken Cutlets

While chicken Milanese is defined by its thick, bready coating, this new classic skips the crumbs and puts cheese at the forefront. But the swap isn't as easy as it sounds.

BY SANDRA WU

When it comes to Italian-style chicken cutlets, most people are familiar with two classic recipes: chicken Parmesan (breaded chicken breasts topped with melted Parmesan and mozzarella cheeses and tomato sauce) and chicken Milanese (pan-fried cutlets with a Parmesan-accented breading). Although both offer some degree of Parmesan flavor, they're undeniably more focused on the bread crumbs. So it comes as no surprise that cookbook authors and food magazines have recently begun devising Italian-inspired chicken recipes that put the spotlight on the cheese. In place of the traditional thick layer of breading, Parmesan-crusted chicken offers a thinner, crispy-yet-chewy, wafer-like sheath of Parmesan cheese.

Lemon wedges provide a bright counterpoint to the rich cheese crust on these thin cutlets.

With short ingredient lists including only chicken breasts and Parmesan cheese plus one or two adherents such as eggs or flour, the recipes I found for this dish seemed straightforward and promising. But variations in cooking technique yielded samples that were far cries from their beautiful descriptions. A baked version was pale, wet, and gummy. And while several pan-fried recipes were nicely browned, their soft coatings were marred by bald spots and tasted surprisingly bitter and burnt. To come up with a superior dish, I'd have to conquer the problems of weak Parmesan flavor and mushy, patchy crusts. I also had to figure out what was causing the acrid flavor in so many recipes. After all, what good is a picture-perfect cutlet if it tastes like a charcoal briquette?

After some initial tests, I knew a few things for sure. First, the chicken would have to be pan-fried, not baked. While baking simply melted the cheese, pan-frying showed potential to deliver the crisp crust I was after. Second, the chicken would have to be cooked in a nonstick skillet to keep the crust from fusing to the bottom of the pan, and it would have to be cooked quickly to prevent the cheese from burning. Boneless, skinless chicken breasts, therefore, were a given, and they had to be fairly thin. For chicken that cooked through in just 3 minutes, I used ¼-inch-thick cutlets.

Modifying the Classics

For the coating, I began with the breading procedure for classic chicken Milanese (coating the cutlets in flour, followed by beaten egg, followed by bread crumbs), swapping grated Parmesan for both the flour and bread crumb layers. Unfortunately, the grated cheese didn't provide the smooth, dry base necessary for the beaten egg to cling to, producing an uneven crust with soft, eggy patches. After reintroducing flour as the base layer, the egg and cheese adhered more neatly to the cutlet. But the crust still had a slightly souffléed texture. Omitting the yolks greatly improved matters. The whites clung to the flour and acted like flavorless glue that helped the cheese stick to the chicken.

Now coated with flour, egg whites, and a thin layer of Parmesan, the chicken tasted only faintly of cheese. Looking for big cheese flavor, I tried adding a handful of grated Parmesan to the egg whites. Although cheesier, the mixture was thick, sludgy, and difficult to handle. Adding cheese to the dry base layer of flour was much more successful. Ultimately, I found that equal parts flour and grated cheese kept the binding qualities of the flour intact while contributing a powerful Parmesan boost. Now the coating had two distinct layers of cheese: a fresh, tangy base and a toastier exterior. But the crust was still a little thin and spotty for my liking.

To this point, I'd been using the smallest holes on the box grater to transform the Parmesan into a fine, powdery consistency, which was perfect for whisking into the flour but less impressive when it came to providing a significant outer crust—it was too delicate and lacy. It struck me that the thicker, coarser texture of shredded—rather than finely grated—cheese would provide the bulkier layer I was looking for. With ½ cup of shredded cheese per cutlet, the chicken finally had a substantial crust.

The key to crispness was revealed during a side tasting of preshredded supermarket Parmesan cheese. I noticed that while the flavor of the preshredded cheese was inferior to authentic Parmigiano-Reggiano, it produced chicken that was much crispier and less chewy. Knowing that many of these packaged tub cheeses include

RECIPE TESTING: When Parmesan-Crusted Chicken Goes Bad

Many of the recipes we tried fell short in terms of flavor and texture. Here are three common problems:

GUMMY
Baked chicken has a pale, damp, and gummy cheese coating.

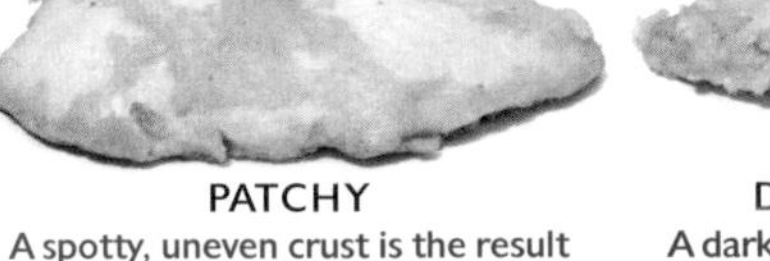

PATCHY
A spotty, uneven crust is the result of using the wrong "glue."

DARK AND BITTER
A dark brown crust looks appealing but tastes bitter and burnt.

Go to www.cooksillustrated.com
- Click on the **Cook's Extra** link for **Orange and Radish Salad with Arugula.**
- Recipe available until August 1, 2007.

PHOTOGRAPHY: CARL TREMBLAY

Two Ways to Cut the Parmesan

An ideal crust requires cheeses of two different textures. A base layer of finely grated Parmesan cut on the smallest holes of a box or Microplane grater (left) is paired with an exterior layer of coarsely shredded Parmesan cut on the largest holes of a box grater (right).

GRATED SHREDDED

starches to prevent caking, I wondered if adding flour to my Parmesan would do the same thing. The answer was yes: Tossing a mere tablespoon of flour with the outermost layer of shredded cheese filled in any gaps between the cheese and egg white layers, creating a crispier exterior.

Sour Notes

My recipe was coming along, but I still had a problem—a major problem. Whenever I cooked the chicken until it looked gorgeous—a deep, dark brown—it tasted burnt. When I under-browned the chicken (a counterintuitive move), it tasted fine. After some head scratching, I traced the problem back to the Maillard reaction. This chemical effect occurs when amino acids (building blocks for proteins) and sugars in foods are heated, causing them to combine and form new flavor compounds. Most cheeses undergo very little of this reaction when heated, because they don't contain much sugar. Parmesan cheese, however, contains fairly high levels of the sugar galactose, which undergoes the reaction quite readily. As the galactose reacts with sizable amounts of glutamic acid (an amino acid), the formation of bitter-tasting substances happens as soon as the cheese starts to brown. Turning the heat down to medium once the cutlets were in the pan—thus keeping browning at bay—allowed the chicken and cheese to cook through without tasting burnt.

I was confident that this Parmesan-crusted chicken, with a perfectly moist, tender interior and a crisp, flavorful cheese crust, could finally live up to its name. By emptying the serving platter in a flash, my tasters agreed without saying a word.

PARMESAN-CRUSTED CHICKEN CUTLETS

SERVES 4

The chicken breasts will be easier to slice into cutlets if you freeze them for 15 minutes until firm but not fully frozen. To slice in half, place one hand on top of the breast to secure it, hold a chef's knife parallel to the cutting board, and slice through the middle of the breast horizontally. Note that ½ ounce of Parmesan is grated on the smallest holes of a box grater (or Microplane rasp grater); the remaining 6 ounces are shredded on the largest holes of the box grater (see photos at left). We like the flavor that authentic Parmigiano-Reggiano lends to this recipe. Less-expensive DiGiorno Parmesan cheese can also be used, but the resulting cheese crust will be slightly saltier and chewier. Serve this chicken with a simple salad (see Cook's Extra, page 6). Although the portion size (1 cutlet per person) might seem small, these cutlets are rather rich due to the cheese content. To make 8 cutlets, double the ingredients and cook the chicken in 4 batches, transferring the cooked cutlets to a warm oven and wiping out the skillet after each batch.

- 2 boneless, skinless chicken breasts (8 ounces each), tenderloins removed, breasts trimmed of excess fat and halved horizontally (see note above)
- Table salt and ground black pepper
- ¼ cup plus 1 tablespoon all-purpose flour
- ½ ounce Parmesan cheese, grated (about ¼ cup) (see note above)
- 3 large egg whites
- 2 tablespoons minced fresh chives (optional)
- 6 ounces Parmesan cheese, shredded (about 2 cups) (see note above)
- 4 teaspoons olive oil
- 1 lemon, cut into wedges

1. Adjust oven rack to middle position and heat oven to 200 degrees. Place chicken between sheets of plastic wrap and pound to even ¼-inch thickness. Pat dry with paper towels and season both sides with salt and pepper.
2. Set wire rack on rimmed baking sheet. Whisk together ¼ cup flour and grated Parmesan cheese in pie plate. In medium bowl, whisk egg whites and chives (if using) together until slightly foamy. In second pie plate, combine 2 cups shredded Parmesan and remaining tablespoon flour.
3. Using tongs and working with 1 cutlet at a time, coat chicken in flour mixture, shaking off excess. Transfer chicken to egg-white mixture; coat evenly and let excess run off. Coat chicken with shredded Parmesan mixture, pressing gently so that cheese adheres. Place on wire rack.
4. Heat 2 teaspoons oil in 12-inch nonstick skillet over medium-high heat until shimmering. Place 2 cutlets in skillet and reduce heat to medium. Cook until cheese is pale golden brown, about 3 minutes. While chicken is cooking, use thin nonstick spatula to gently separate any cheesy edges that have melted together. Carefully flip cutlets and continue to cook until cheese is pale golden brown on second side and meat is no longer pink in center, about 3 minutes. Transfer chicken to wire rack set in rimmed baking sheet and keep warm in oven. Wipe out skillet with paper towel and return to medium heat. Add remaining 2 teaspoons oil and cook remaining 2 cutlets. Serve immediately with lemon wedges.

EQUIPMENT TESTING:

Box Graters

Food processors can swiftly shred pounds of cheese or vegetables, but lugging out the appliance for a chunk of Parmesan or a pair of russet potatoes is impractical. But do you need to risk slicing your knuckles in order to use a box grater? We tested eight models to find out.

Wobble Wobble After grating block mozzarella, Parmesan cheese, and raw potatoes on each of the graters in our lineup, we outlined the characteristics of a good box grater. The best models combine a stable base and comfortable handle with sharp blades set on a large shredding plane. Several models, including the wobbly Best Box Grater ($16.95) and the equally unsteady Progressive ProGrip Large Tower Grater ($12.99) quickly lost points for instability.

Shreds of Evidence As for grating ability, six of the eight graters featured classically deep punctures—fine for semisoft cheeses and softer vegetables, but no match to the shallower, razor-sharp edges on the Microplane 34005 Better Box Grater ($24.95) and the Cuisipro Accutec Box Grater ($35.99). Parmesan shreds, which occasionally chipped and flaked on the other models, fell lithely from these exceptionally sharp blades. However, the Microplane grater's unusually short (under five inches) shredding plane and poorly designed knuckle guard disqualified it from the top ranks. Meanwhile, the slender Accutec offered three shredding sizes—ultra-coarse, coarse, and fine—along with measurement-marked transparent walls, a snap-on base, and a comfortable, curved handle. Clearly, this was the sharpest tool in a box. –Elizabeth Bomze

BEST CHOICE

➢ **CUISIPRO Accutec Box Grater** ($35.99) Razor-sharp blades made short work of shredding potatoes and cheese.

TOO MANY SIDES

➢ **CUISIPRO 6-Sided Box Grater** ($25.89) Six blades seems excessive, but otherwise a solid choice.

COMES UP SHORT

➢ **MICROPLANE 34005 Better Box Grater** ($24.95) Though razor-sharp, an optional knuckle-saving door made shredding food difficult, as did the short shredding plane.

SLIPPERY SLOPE

➢ **PROGRESSIVE ProGrip Large Tower Grater** ($12.99) The nonskid rubber feet tore off with shredding pressure, making this tripod highly unsteady.

Chinese Barbecued Pork at Home

These lacquered strips of pork look exotic, but the meat is actually "barbecued" in the oven, making it an ideal candidate for home cooking—in theory, at least.

BY DAVID PAZMIÑO

With its ruby-red color, deeply browned and crusty edges, and sticky glazed exterior, Chinese barbecued pork (aka *char siu*) is eye candy for meat lovers. In Chinatown, these burnished strips of meat hang in storefront windows, enticing hungry passersby alongside Peking duck. This marketing ploy works. Whenever I'm in Boston's Chinatown, I buy barbecued pork and take it home to serve for dinner with steamed rice and greens. I make sure to buy enough to guarantee leftovers, which I recycle into wonton soup, fried rice, egg rolls, and more. But since I don't get to Chinatown all that often, I wondered if I could replicate this classic Chinese dish at home. After all, isn't it just barbecued meat?

Unlike American barbecue, where large cuts are cooked with smoke on outdoor cookers until they achieve a fall-apart tenderness, Chinese barbecued meats are usually cut into strips and cooked in an oven. Once the exterior is slightly charred, the meat is brushed with honey and cooked until a lacquered glaze forms. It's like having barbecue with almost all crust. Sounds simple enough.

There was just one hook—actually, more like eight hooks. Traditional recipes call for cutting the meat into thin strips and hanging the strips on metal rods that go inside refrigerator-sized ovens. The idea is that the heat can attack the meat from all sides and create a thick crust. I tried fabricating S-shaped hooks out of metal hangers and suspending the meat from the top rack of a test kitchen oven, but my forearms were soon covered with battle scars caused by my failed attempts to rescue dangling pieces of meat before they fell onto the floor of the oven. No meat—no matter how delicious—is worth second-degree burns. I needed to develop a cooking method suited to a home oven.

This oven-barbecue recipe relies on a sweet glaze to create a lacquered crust.

Thick and Thin

Traditional recipes cut pork butt into long strips. When I cut the meat into thicker steaks, it was much too fatty and tough. I concluded that cutting the meat into strips is a must, as it helps render fat during the relatively short cooking time. Working with a boneless pork butt (much easier than trying to remove the bone), I cut the pork in half lengthwise and then into eight long strips—removing some of the hard fat between the individual muscles. I marinated the meat in a classic mixture of light and dark soy sauces, Chinese rice wine, hoisin, spices, and either fermented red bean curd or red food coloring (red foods are seen as bringing good fortune in Chinese cuisine).

Suspending the meat from hooks was out, but what if I placed the strips of meat on a rack set over a baking sheet? Wouldn't an all-over crust form? I ran a series of tests with oven temperatures ranging from 350 to 500 degrees. The pork roasted in the cooler ovens remained moist and was less fatty, but it never achieved the characteristic browning and intense flavor; the meat cooked in the hotter ovens browned beautifully, but it was still too tough, with pockets of unrendered fat. Choosing the middle road (roasting at 425 degrees) didn't work, so I was left with one option—cooking the meat at a low temperature to render fat and then cranking up the heat to develop a burnished crust.

For my next tests, I lost the rack and placed the strips of meat on a big sheet of aluminum foil, poured the marinade over the top, and then tightly sealed the foil. After two hours, I opened the foil packet and browned the pork under the broiler. All the fat had been rendered, but the meat reminded my tasters of slightly charred pot roast—it simply fell apart at the approach of a fork. Like all good barbecue, char siu needs to have some chew to it.

I returned to cooking the meat on a rack set over a baking sheet, but this time I covered the pan with foil. After an hour at 300 degrees, I

Go to www.cooksillustrated.com
- Click on the **Cook's Extra** link for **Fried Rice with Shrimp, Pork, and Peas.**
- Recipe available until August 1, 2007.

AT A GLANCE | CHINESE BBQ

1. PRICK Using fork, prick pork 10 to 12 times on each side.

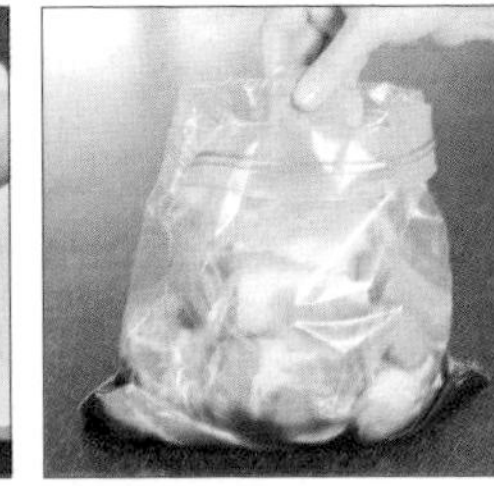

2. MARINATE Place pork and marinade in bag and refrigerate for 30 minutes.

3. ROAST Place pork on rack set in foil-covered baking sheet; add water.

4. GLAZE Turn oven to broil and brush pork with glaze.

PHOTOGRAPHY: CARL TREMBLAY

removed the foil and turned the oven to broil. The meat had a better crust, but it was still too tender. Eventually, I discovered that covering the meat for only 20 minutes during the initial hour of cooking was all that I needed to render excess fat and keep the meat tender. I then removed the foil and continued to cook the meat until a thick crust formed. A final blast of heat from the broiler produced a thick, slightly charred crust, and the meat was now tender but chewy.

A Flavorful Beginning and Glossy Finish

All the pork needed was a final adjustment of flavor in the marinade and glaze. First, I needed to tinker with the traditional marinade ingredients—light and dark soy sauces, rice wine, red fermented bean curd, hoisin sauce, and five-spice powder. In the end, my tasters were happy with just regular soy sauce and saw no harm in replacing the rice wine with dry sherry. The red bean curd was just too hard to find. Instead, I boosted the flavor of the marinade with ginger, garlic, toasted sesame oil, and white pepper.

Marinades are all about flavor penetration, but how long does that take? After four hours, the meat had soaked up the potent flavors of the marinade. Times in excess of four hours caused the meat to become too salty. But four hours was a long time to wait. Could I speed up this process? Pricking the meat with a fork before marinating enhanced the penetration of the marinade so much that just 30 minutes was sufficient.

To achieve a lacquered appearance, char siu requires the application of a honey glaze during the last few minutes of cooking. To mimic the traditional red color, I supplemented the honey with ketchup. I simmered honey and ketchup (along with some reserved marinade) to give it a syrupy consistency. I had finally replicated one of my favorite Chinese dishes at home. The solution wasn't obvious, but it was painless.

STEP-BY-STEP | BUTCHERING PORK BUTT

Pork butts are usually about 4 inches thick. If using a pork butt that is thinner than 4 inches, cut into six pieces instead of eight. For information on removing the bone from a bone-in pork butt, see page 31.

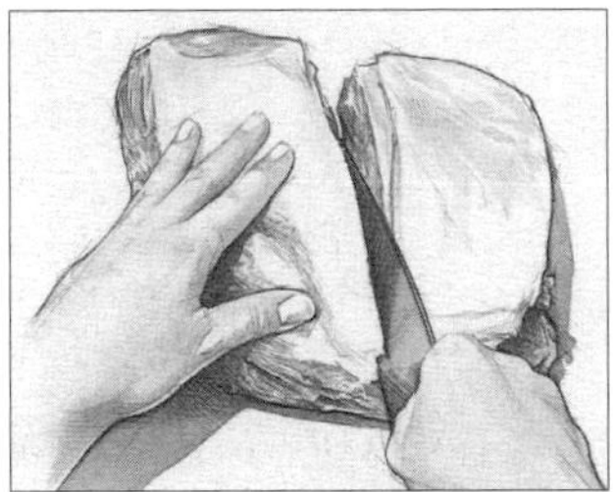

1. Cut roast in half lengthwise.

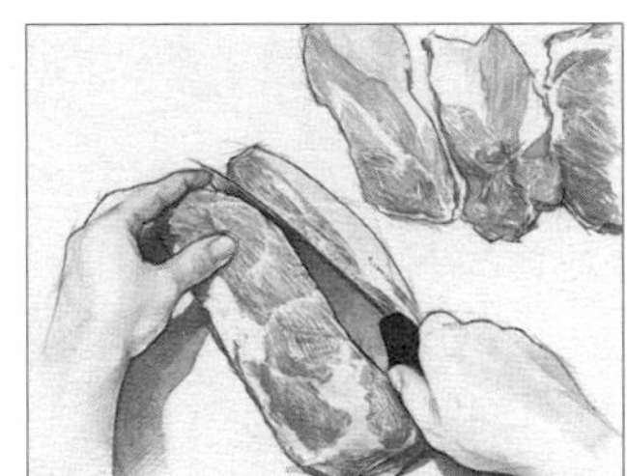

2. Turn each half on cut side and slice lengthwise into 4 equal pieces.

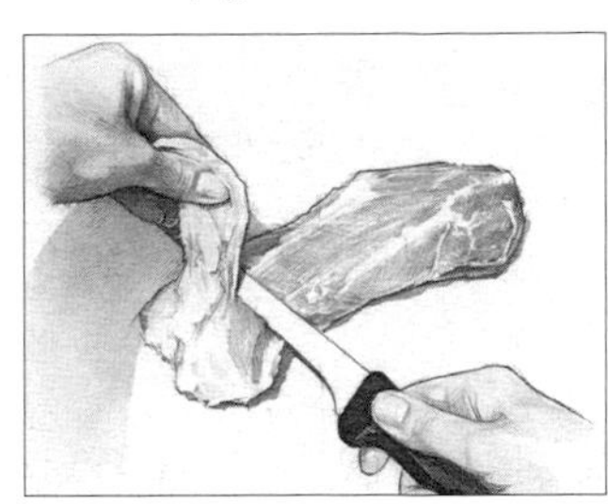

3. Trim excess hard, waxy fat, leaving some fat to render while cooking.

CHINESE BARBECUED PORK

SERVES 6

To facilitate cleanup, spray the rack and pan with vegetable oil spray. The pork will release liquid and fat during the cooking process, so be careful when removing the pan from the oven. If you don't have a wire rack that fits in a rimmed baking sheet, substitute a broiler pan, although the meat may not darken as much. Pay close attention to the meat when broiling—you are looking for it to darken and caramelize, not blacken. Do not use a drawer broiler—the heat source will be too close to the meat. Instead, increase the oven temperature in step 5 to 500 degrees and cook for 8 to 12 minutes before glazing and 6 to 8 minutes once the glaze has been applied; flip meat and repeat on second side. This recipe can be made with boneless country-style ribs, but the meat will be slightly drier and less flavorful. To use ribs, reduce the uncovered cooking time in step 4 to 20 minutes and increase the broiling and glazing times in step 5 by 2 to 3 minutes per side. This dish is best served with rice and a vegetable side dish. Leftover pork makes an excellent addition to fried rice (see Cook's Extra on page 8) or an Asian noodle soup.

- 1 (4-pound) boneless pork butt, cut into 8 strips and excess fat removed (see illustrations above)
- 1/2 cup sugar
- 1/2 cup soy sauce
- 6 tablespoons hoisin sauce
- 1/4 cup dry sherry
- 1/4 teaspoon ground white pepper
- 1 teaspoon five-spice powder
- 1 tablespoon toasted sesame oil
- 2 tablespoons grated fresh ginger (from 4- to 6-inch piece)
- 2 medium garlic cloves, minced or pressed through garlic press (about 2 teaspoons)
- 1/4 cup ketchup
- 1/3 cup honey

1. Using fork, prick pork 10 to 12 times on each side. Place pork in large plastic zipper-lock bag. Combine sugar, soy, hoisin, sherry, pepper, five-spice powder, sesame oil, ginger, and garlic in medium bowl. Measure out ½ cup marinade and set aside. Pour remaining marinade into bag with pork. Press out as much air as possible; seal bag. Refrigerate for at least 30 minutes or up to 4 hours.

2. While meat marinates, combine ketchup and honey with reserved marinade in small saucepan. Cook glaze over medium heat until syrupy and reduced to 1 cup, 4 to 6 minutes.

3. Adjust oven rack to middle position and heat oven to 300 degrees. Line rimmed baking sheet with aluminum foil and set wire rack on sheet.

4. Remove pork from marinade, letting any excess drip off, and place on wire rack. Pour 1/4 cup water into bottom of pan. Cover pan with heavy-duty aluminum foil, crimping edges tightly to seal. Cook pork for 20 minutes. Remove foil and continue to cook until edges of pork begin to brown, 40 to 45 minutes.

5. Turn on broiler. Broil pork until evenly caramelized, 7 to 9 minutes. Remove pan from oven and brush pork with half of glaze; broil until deep mahogany color, 3 to 5 minutes. Using tongs, flip meat and broil until other side caramelizes, 7 to 9 minutes. Brush meat with remaining glaze and continue to broil until second side is deep mahogany, 3 to 5 minutes. Cool for at least 10 minutes, then cut into thin strips and serve.

TASTING: Hoisin Sauce

Hoisin sauce is a thick, reddish brown mixture of soybeans, sugar, vinegar, garlic, and chiles used in many classic Chinese dishes, including barbecued pork, Peking duck, and moo shu pork. Spoonfuls of six hoisin sauces and forkfuls of our hoisin-basted barbecued pork indicated that no two brands of this staple condiment are identical; in fact, they vary dramatically in flavor, consistency, and even color—from gloppy and sweet, like plum sauce, to grainy and spicy, like Asian chili paste.

According to our tasters, the perfect hoisin sauce balances sweet, salty, pungent, and spicy elements so that no one flavor dominates. Kikkoman came closest to this ideal, with tasters praising its initial "burn," which mellowed into a harmonious blend of sweet and aromatic flavors. Two other brands also fared well in our tasting. Koon Chun was described as "fruity" (if a bit grainy), and Lee Kum Kee was deemed "plummy" but salty. Tasters were not impressed by the three remaining brands. Ka-Me was less interesting than our top choices, and no one liked House of Tsang's strange red color or Sun Luck's bitterness. —Elizabeth Bomze

BALANCING ACT Kikkoman's Hoisin Sauce won praise for its equilibrium of sweetness and salinity.

ILLUSTRATION: RANDY GLASS

Authentic Olive-Rosemary Bread

Really good olive bread can be made at home—but it requires a lot more than just adding a handful of olives to any bread recipe.

BY ERIKA BRUCE

My favorite rustic bread is flavored with olives and the subtle perfume of rosemary. This Italian-inspired bread has a coarse crumb, chewy interior, and thick, burnished crust.

But this hearty loaf is about as elusive as it is perfect, unless your neighborhood is blessed with a great bread bakery. And I've been hard-pressed to find a decent recipe to create this bread at home. My experience has been littered with homemade loaves that are more like sandwich bread than rustic bread, with a soft crumb and thin crust. And the olives are either forced into the dough early on and mixed to the point of disintegration or added at the very end as a sparse afterthought. To be able to enjoy this bread when and how I wanted, I first needed a recipe for really great homemade rustic bread, and then I needed to figure out a way to get good olive distribution without ruining the bread or the olives.

Crisp crust, chewy crumb, and big olive flavor equal one perfect loaf.

Dough Play

Rustic doughs are by nature lean, devoid of fat. But there are many other factors that come into play in the development of the characteristic holey crumb and chew; namely, the amount of water in the dough (the wetter the better), the type of flour, and the mixing, shaping, and baking techniques.

The test kitchen's Rustic Italian Bread (January/February 2003) calls for a lot of water: 68 percent hydration (measured by dividing the total weight of water by the total weight of flour), whereas most other breads have a hydration level of about 60 percent. But an initial test of adding moist olives to this recipe revealed a few problems. The first was an unmanageable, sticky mass of dough, which baked into a heavy, gummy bread. Second, the assertive flavor of the olives made the Rustic Italian Bread (with all bread flour) seem bland by comparison.

I reduced the hydration level to 64 percent (the olives would provide additional moisture) and replaced a portion of the bread flour with whole wheat flour. Honey added sweetness and helped bring out the savory flavor of the olives. Our Rustic Italian Bread requires an overnight sponge (a mixture of instant yeast, flour, and water allowed to rest overnight to build flavor in the dough). With whole wheat flour and honey in the dough, I hoped to save myself time by cutting this step. Indeed, once the olives were added to this same-day bread, the absent sponge was not noticeable.

The other production steps for making rustic breads were not as easily dismissed. Specifically, the *autolyse* (allowing the mixture of flours, water, and yeast to rest so that the flour has more time to absorb the water) was instrumental for more efficient kneading. But this was 20 minutes I could afford. Turning the dough during the first rise also drastically improved its elasticity and strength, which resulted in larger holes in the bread and a heartier chew (see "Turned, Not Punched," on page 11).

The Olive Branch

Now that I had the dough, I figured that gently working the olives into the risen dough by hand would keep them intact. I was wrong—the dough stubbornly spat out the olives at every turn. I began to understand why so many recipe writers add them earlier in the process.

But pitting the standing mixer against the olives was not a fair match. The olives and dough were like oil and water—resisting each other and leaving the olives to smear against the outside of the dough and the bottom of the bowl. I tried whole, halved, and diced olives; patting the olives dry; tossing them in flour; and even stuffing a pocket in the dough with olives. But every time, the olives were mashed and their briny liquid turned the loaf dense and gummy.

Adding the olives at the very end, during the shaping stage, started to look more attractive. I found a recipe that suggested folding the olives up into the shaped loaves, jellyroll-style. Unfortunately, this resulted in an insufficient distribution of olives—with large pockets in some places and none in others. But this technique gave me an idea: What if I rolled the olives up into the dough before the first and second rises? Success. I finally had a nicely textured loaf with evenly dispersed olives.

Turning next to the type of olives, I assumed I would be able to proclaim a test kitchen winner. But I discovered olive preference is highly subjective: After making bread with a dozen varieties, I realized that just about any brined or oil-cured olive good enough to eat out of hand will be fine in this bread. A preliminary quick rinse mediated excessive brine and controlled saltiness.

I've always perceived rosemary as being brutish; if used excessively, it can easily overpower a dish with its piney harshness. But I soon realized that this herb behaved differently when baked into bread—its flavor was as fleeting as the little specks were invisible. I needed a whopping 2 tablespoons to get a demure background flavor to complement the bright, fruity olives.

In the end, there were no mysteries to this recipe. Hearty, high-protein flours and the right techniques helped me create the characteristically chewy, rough-holed texture. Combined with a gentle yet thorough method for incorporating the olives, I was able to produce satisfying olive bread every time.

PHOTOGRAPHY: CARL TREMBLAY

OLIVE-ROSEMARY BREAD

MAKES TWO 12 BY 3-INCH LOAVES

Almost any variety of brined or oil-cured olive works in this recipe, although we preferred a mix of both green and black olives. Instant yeast is commonly labeled rapid-rise yeast. Use a spray bottle filled with water to mist the loaves. The bread will keep for up to 2 days, well wrapped and stored at room temperature. To recrisp the crust, place the bread in a 450-degree oven for 5 to 10 minutes. The bread will keep frozen for several months when wrapped in foil and placed in a large zipper-lock bag.

- 1¾ cups (14 ounces) water, room temperature
- 2 teaspoons instant yeast
- 2 tablespoons honey
- 3½ cups (19¼ ounces) bread flour, plus extra as needed for dough and counter
- ½ cup (2¾ ounces) whole wheat flour
- 2 teaspoons table salt
- 2 tablespoons chopped fresh rosemary
- 1½ cups (6 ounces) pitted olives, rinsed, chopped rough, and patted dry (see note above)

1. Whisk water, yeast, and honey in bowl of standing mixer. Add flours and mix on low speed with dough hook until cohesive dough is formed, about 3 minutes. Cover bowl with plastic wrap and let sit at room temperature for 20 minutes.

2. Remove plastic wrap; make well in center of dough and add salt and rosemary. Knead dough on low speed (speed 2 on KitchenAid) for 5 minutes (if dough creeps up attachment, stop mixer and scrape down). Increase speed to medium and continue to knead until dough is smooth and slightly tacky, about 1 minute. If dough is very sticky, add 1 to 2 tablespoons flour and continue mixing for 1 minute. Transfer dough to lightly floured counter and pat into 12 by 6-inch rectangle. Following illustration 1 below, press olives evenly into dough. Starting at long side, roll rectangle into tight log (illustration 2). With seam side facing up, roll log into coil (illustration 3). Transfer dough, spiral side up, to oiled container or bowl, at least 2 quarts in volume, and cover with plastic wrap. Let dough rise in warm, draft-free location until it increases in size by 50 percent, about 1 hour.

3. Fold partially risen dough over itself (illustration 4). Turn bowl 90 degrees; fold again. Turn bowl again; fold once more. Cover with plastic wrap (illustration 5) and let rise 30 minutes. Repeat folding, replace plastic wrap, and let rise until doubled in volume, about 30 minutes.

4. Transfer dough to lightly floured work surface, being careful not to deflate. Divide dough in half (illustration 6), loosely shape each piece into ball, and let rest 15 minutes. Flip each ball over and, starting from top, roll into tight oval shape (illustration 7). Using palms, roll each oval (seam side down) from center outward until 12-inch loaf is formed (illustration 8). Poke any olives that fall off into bottom seam, then pinch seam closed. Transfer each loaf, seam side down, to 12 by 6-inch piece of parchment and cover with plastic wrap. Let rise until doubled in size, 1 to 1½ hours (dough is ready when it springs back slowly when pressed lightly with finger). Meanwhile, adjust oven rack to lower-middle position, place baking stone on rack, and heat oven to 450 degrees at least 30 minutes before baking.

5. Slide parchment sheets with loaves onto peel or back of inverted baking sheet. Starting and stopping about 1 inch from each side, use razor blade or sharp knife to cut 3 ½-inch-deep slashes on diagonal along top of each fully risen loaf (illustration 9); spray loaves lightly with water. Carefully slide parchment with loaves into oven using jerking motion. Bake 15 minutes, spraying loaves with water twice more in first 5 minutes, and then reduce oven temperature to 375 degrees. Continue to bake until bread is deep golden brown and instant-read thermometer inserted into center of loaf registers 210 degrees, 25 to 30 minutes. Transfer to wire rack, discard parchment, and cool loaves to room temperature, about 2 hours.

SCIENCE: Turned, Not Punched

Most bread recipes call for punching down the dough between the first and second rises. Despite its name, punching down is best accomplished by pressing down gently on the dough. This process exposes the yeast to new food sources, which keeps it going strong longer. Punching also "degasses" the bread, resulting in a loaf with a fairly fine crumb—perfect for sandwich bread, but not a rustic loaf. To create a coarser crumb with better chew, we discovered that turning the dough (gently folding it over onto itself between the first and second rises) reactivates the yeast without pressing out as much air. –E.B.

PUNCHED Bread bakes up with a tight, more regular crumb better suited to sandwich bread.

TURNED Bread bakes up with a coarse, open crumb and chewy texture better suited to rustic bread.

EQUIPMENT TESTING: Bench Scrapers

Bread bakers rely on metal bench scrapers—broad, slightly blunt blades with handles that span the length of the metal—to cut through plump rounds of yeast bread or biscuit dough or to scrape sticky dough loose from the counter. We tested six models and quickly rejected three: the KitchenAid All-Purpose ($9.99) was too small, while the scrapers from Sur la Table ($6.95) and World Cuisine ($17.50) sported uncomfortable metal handles.

Testers preferred the flatter plastic, rubber, or nylon grips on the Dexter/Russell Dough Cutter/Scraper ($7.18), Forschner Dough Scraper ($6.95), and OXO Good Grips Stainless Steel Multi-Purpose Scraper & Chopper ($7.99). Though we had a slight preference for the slimmer handgrips on the Dexter/Russell and Forschner models, we sacrificed a bit of comfort for the added perks of OXO's ruler mark–engraved blade and its considerably thinner edge, which was perfectly suited to another common bench scraper task—scooping up chopped herbs and vegetables. –Elizabeth Bomze

BEST SCRAPER

The OXO Scraper ($7.99) combines the sharpest blade with ruler marks for easy measuring.

RECIPE SHORTHAND | SHAPING OLIVE-ROSEMARY BREAD

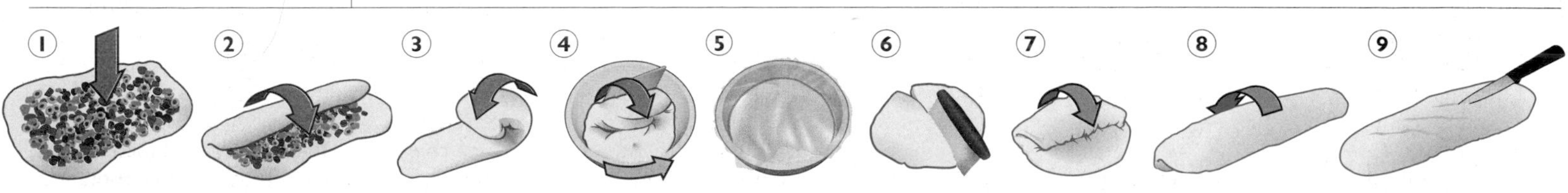

1. PRESS olives into dough. **2.** ROLL dough into tight log. **3.** COIL log into spiral and let RISE. **4.** FOLD partially risen dough. Turn bowl. Repeat twice. **5.** COVER with plastic wrap and let RISE. Repeat steps 4 and 5. **6.** DIVIDE dough and let REST. **7.** ROLL each ball into oval shape. **8.** ROLL each oval until loaf is formed; let RISE. **9.** SLASH each fully risen loaf.

ILLUSTRATION: JAY LAYMAN

Hearty Garlic-Potato Soup

A bowl of garlic-potato soup sounds appealing, but not if the assertive garlic overwhelms the mild-mannered potatoes. What are the secrets to this simple peasant dish?

⋟ BY REBECCA HAYS ⋞

In the middle of the 18th century, France's wheat crop failed and baguettes could no longer be found at the local boulangerie. On the verge of crisis, the Academy of Besançon held a competition to find a food "capable of reducing the calamities of famine." Enter Antoine-Augustin Parmentier, an entrepreneurial young soldier, who won the contest by championing the humble potato. He went on to open numerous potato soup kitchens in Paris, ladling out bowls of Potage Parmentier to hungry Frenchmen. The soup became a classic, and rustic potato soup is still the pinnacle of simple, economical fare. Pair the potatoes with heady garlic and what the duo lacks in glamour it makes up for with rich flavor and satisfying texture.

And yet an afternoon at the stove established that the stars of this soup can also ruin it. Take, for example, a recipe culled from the Internet calling for boiling 2 pounds of potatoes and a single clove of garlic in copious amounts of water. With zero flavor and a thin, gray broth, this potion was unfit for sampling. Then there was the concoction containing five whole heads of garlic, which obliterated any hint of potato. An idyllic garlic-potato soup recipe would have discernible garlic and potato flavors along with an agreeable (not-too-thick/not-too-thin) consistency.

A final garnish of toasted garlic chips finishes off this hearty soup.

One Potato, Two Potato

Working with a stripped-down recipe containing a spoonful of minced garlic, chicken broth, and a splash of cream (a common enrichment), I tested batches prepared with each of the three most common potato varieties, both peeled and unpeeled. From highest to lowest starch content, they are: russet, Yukon Gold, and Red Bliss. While the hearty flavor of unpeeled Red Bliss potatoes was appealing, tasters generally leaned toward soups made with peeled russets, praising the starchy spuds for the way they broke down and thickened the broth.

With my potato decision made, I moved on to the garlic. The few cloves of minced sautéed garlic in my working recipe added pleasant background notes, but I sought more complexity. It was not surprising that increasing the amount of garlic simply fortified the soup with overpowering flavor. Looking to temper the harshness, I turned to cooking techniques known for yielding milder, more approachable garlic flavor (see "Science: Three Ways to Great Garlic Flavor," page 13). A whole head or two of oven-roasted garlic added gentle sweetness to the soup, as did heads of garlic poached in water or milk. A more direct approach, poaching the garlic in the soup, worked just as well without requiring a second cooking vessel. The soup now tasted okay but wasn't really redolent of garlic. Maybe I'd dampened the flavor too much.

I was stuck. Sautéed garlic was too harsh, and poached was too mild. I regrouped and attempted a hybrid approach, finding that, for this recipe, two methods were better than one. Combining sautéed minced garlic with whole poached garlic heads lent the complexity I was after. However, now that I was satisfied with the layers of garlic flavor in the soup, I realized that I'd thrown off the overall balance, and the potato presence was meager.

As luck would have it, a colleague reminded me of the earlier test where we liked the earthy flavor of Red Bliss potatoes but rejected them in favor of starchier russets. After more tests, I found that keeping the russets but adding some Red Bliss ramped up the potato flavor nicely.

Souped-Up

In the lexicon of French cookery, there are three classifications for soup: *consommé* describes a clear, brothy soup; *soupe* refers to a thick, chunky, stew-like mixture; and *potage* is a hybrid of consommé and soupe, being at once partly chunky and partly smooth. For my country-style soup, I followed the lead of Parmentier, adopting the texture of a potage. I pureed a portion of the soup into a creamy, smooth consistency and left the remaining chunks untouched.

The framework of the soup was now complete, and it was time for refinements. Soup-making often starts with sautéed aromatics, so I added the classic trio of diced carrots, onion, and celery, or *mirepoix*, to my recipe. The mirepoix added flavor, but not the right kind: Tasters criticized the soup for being too vegetal. Leaving the carrots and celery

Two Spuds Are Better Than One

Our Garlic-Potato Soup uses both russet and Red Bliss potatoes for ultimate potato flavor and texture. Peeled starchy russet potatoes break down during cooking to thicken the soup, while unpeeled Red Bliss potatoes give the soup a rustic, chunky texture and rich potato flavor.

RED BLISS UNCOOKED

RED BLISS COOKED

RUSSET UNCOOKED

RUSSET COOKED

PHOTOGRAPHY: CARL TREMBLAY

SCIENCE: Three Ways to Great Garlic Flavor

Working my way through dozens of heads of garlic while developing this recipe, I clarified some of the mysteries surrounding the bulbous plant. First, the extent to which a garlic clove is cut determines the amount of flavor it will exude. When the cells of a garlic clove are ruptured, an odorless chemical called ***allyl sulfenic acid*** is released and comes into contact with an enzyme called ***alliinase***. The reaction of the two produces a new compound called ***allicin***, which is responsible for the characteristic fiery flavor and scent of garlic. The more a garlic clove is broken down, the more enzymes are released and the more allicin—and therefore flavor—is produced.

Second, cooking affects the flavor intensity of garlic. Garlic is at its sharpest when raw. When heated beyond 150 degrees, the enzymes in garlic are destroyed and no new flavor is produced; only flavor produced up to the inactivation temperature remains. One caveat: When garlic is browned at very high temperatures (300 to 350 degrees, as when making garlic chips), some of the flavor compounds are converted into slightly bitter molecules.

What does this mean for the garlic in our recipe? Whole heads of garlic yield mild, sweet flavor. Finely minced garlic produces pronounced flavor, and golden brown garlic chips deliver potent, pleasantly bitter notes. –R.H.

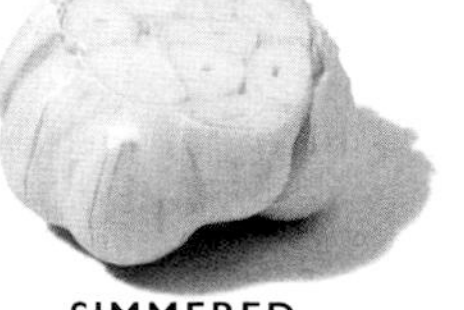

SIMMERED
Simmered in the soup, garlic heads add sweet, mild notes.

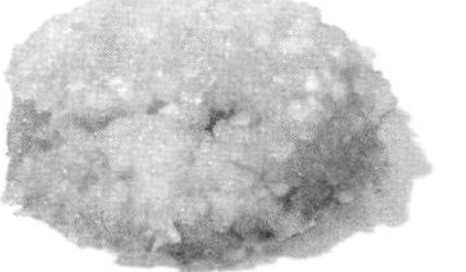

SAUTÉED
Three cloves of sautéed minced garlic contribute potent flavor.

TOASTED
A garnish of garlic chips adds bold, toasted flavor.

EQUIPMENT TESTING: Ladles

You might think one ladle is pretty much the same as the next. But after I had dunked eight stainless steel models (plastic stains and can melt on the stovetop) into pots of chicken noodle soup and hearty beef stew, scattered puddles on the test kitchen countertop made it clear that not all ladles are ergonomically equal.

Ladles with handles shorter than 9 inches, such as the KitchenAid Hollow Handle Serving Ladle ($14.99) and OXO Steel Serving Ladle ($7.95), simply sank in deeper pots; what's more, their small bowls were better suited to sauces than soups. However, more than 10 inches of grip on the Next Day Gourmet Stainless Steel Ladle ($17.70) and Fantes Stainless Steel Ladle ($4.49) proved cumbersome to maneuver, as did their lack of offset handles—a flaw shared by the Amco Stainless Steel Stand-Up Ladle ($12.99). Without some slight bend in the handle, cleanly transferring the ladle's contents into a bowl is nearly impossible.

A handle that bends too dramatically, however—the defect of the Cuisipro Tempo Serving Ladle ($14.95)—makes it difficult to dip the ladle into a tall, narrow stockpot. That left the Rösle Ladle with Pouring Rim & Hook Handle ($23.95), which worked very well. A hook handle and a drip-prevention pouring rim, which kept even wiggly noodles intact all the way to the bowl, earned the Rösle ladle our top rating.
–Elizabeth Bomze

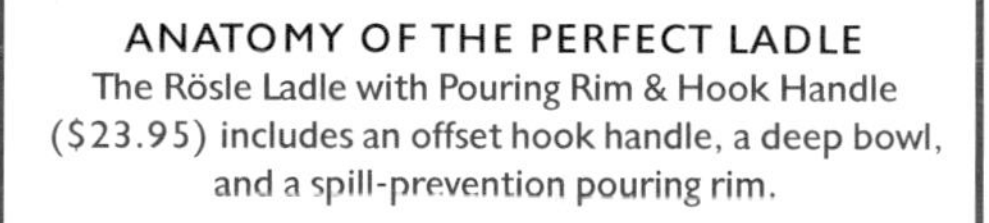

ANATOMY OF THE PERFECT LADLE
The Rösle Ladle with Pouring Rim & Hook Handle ($23.95) includes an offset hook handle, a deep bowl, and a spill-prevention pouring rim.

in the refrigerator, I prepared a batch of soup using onions alone. This was better, but not as good as the soup I prepared with leeks, a natural partner for potatoes. For the dairy component, cream was favored over milk and half-and-half for its richness. Finally, bay leaves and fresh thyme (the latter added at the end of cooking for maximum flavor) contributed a bright herbal dimension.

At this point, the soup tasted great but looked a bit drab and pale. My first instinct was to add a sprinkling of chives, and then the ideas kept rolling. Garlic chips, fried in olive oil, really hit the mark: Their toasty, pleasantly bitter flavor and crunchy texture pushed the soup over the top. I now had a peasant's soup fit for a king.

GARLIC-POTATO SOUP

SERVES 6 AS A MAIN COURSE

A garnish is essential to add crunch and flavor to this soup. We like garlic chips, but crisp bacon bits, fried leeks, or garlic croutons (see Cook's Extra at right for recipes) are good options, too. A potato masher can be used instead of an immersion blender to mash some of the potatoes right in the pot, though the consistency will not be as creamy. If leeks are not available, substitute an equal amount of yellow onion. The test kitchen prefers the soup made with chicken broth, but vegetable broth can be substituted.

- **3 tablespoons unsalted butter**
- **1 medium leek, white and light green parts halved lengthwise, washed, and chopped small (about 1 cup)**
- **3 medium garlic cloves, minced or pressed through garlic press (about 1 tablespoon), plus 2 whole heads garlic, rinsed, outer papery skins removed and top third of heads cut off and discarded**
- **6 cups low-sodium chicken broth, plus 1 cup to thin soup, if needed**
- **2 bay leaves**
- **Table salt**
- **1½ pounds russet potatoes, peeled and cut into ½-inch cubes (about 4½ cups)**
- **1 pound Red Bliss potatoes (unpeeled), cut into ½-inch cubes (about 3 cups)**
- **½ cup heavy cream**
- **1½ teaspoons minced fresh thyme leaves**
- **Ground black pepper**
- **¼ cup minced fresh chives**
- **Garlic Chips (recipe follows)**

1. Melt butter in Dutch oven over medium heat. When foaming subsides, add leeks and cook until soft (do not brown), 5 to 8 minutes. Stir in minced garlic and cook until fragrant, about 1 minute. Add garlic heads, broth, bay leaves, and ¾ teaspoon salt; partially cover pot and bring to simmer over medium-high heat. Reduce heat and simmer until garlic is very tender when pierced with tip of knife, 30 to 40 minutes. Add potatoes and continue to simmer, partially covered, until potatoes are tender, 15 to 20 minutes.

2. Discard bay leaves. Remove garlic heads; using tongs or paper towels, squeeze garlic heads at root end until cloves slip out of their skins. Using fork, mash garlic to smooth paste in bowl.

3. Stir cream, thyme, and half of mashed garlic into soup; heat soup until hot, about 2 minutes. Taste soup; add remaining garlic paste if desired. Using immersion blender, process soup until creamy, with some potato chunks remaining. Alternatively, transfer 1½ cups potatoes and 1 cup broth to blender or food processor and process until smooth. (Process more potatoes for thicker consistency.) Return puree to pot and stir to combine, adjusting consistency with more broth if necessary. Season with salt and pepper and serve, sprinkling each portion with chives and garlic chips.

GARLIC CHIPS

MAKES ABOUT ¼ CUP

- **3 tablespoons olive oil**
- **6 medium garlic cloves, sliced thin lengthwise**
- **Table salt**

Heat oil and garlic in 10-inch skillet over medium-high heat. Cook, turning frequently, until light golden brown, about 3 minutes. Using slotted spoon, transfer garlic to plate lined with paper towels; discard oil. Sprinkle lightly with salt.

COOK'S extra

Go to www.cooksillustrated.com
- Click on the **Cook's Extra** link for **Fried Leeks** or **Garlic Croutons** garnishes.
- Recipes available until August 1, 2007.

How to Make Potato Roesti

Achieving a crisp crust and creamy—not gummy—interior is easier said than done in this simple Swiss potato cake.

BY MATTHEW CARD

Sometimes simple really is best. Case in point: Switzerland's national dish, potato roesti (aka roschti or rosti). Grated potato—seasoned plainly with salt and pepper—is fried in loads of butter into a broad, golden-brown cake. The crunchy, crisp exterior encases a tender, creamy interior tasting of little but earthy potato and, of course, rich butter. It's sort of like a giant hash brown, just thicker and heartier—more dinner side dish than breakfast staple.

But as any cook knows, simple does not mean easy (think of a flaky pie crust or tender omelet). Few of the roesti I have tried measure up to their ideal; instead, most have suffered from a host of problems that make me wonder whether, perhaps, like crafting flawless watches or maintaining political neutrality in these trying times, preparing perfect roesti is a Swiss birthright. So, if you're not Swiss, how do you make roesti?

If at First You Don't Succeed . . .

Roesti can be prepared from either cooked or raw potatoes. Considering that cooked potatoes must be cooled overnight to be grated without crumbling, I favored raw potato versions. I found dozens of recipes that, despite differences, produced largely similar results: an attractive golden-brown crust concealing, to varying degrees, a gluey, gummy, half-cooked tangle of stringy potato. The big issue, then, wasn't browning the outside; it was cooking the inside.

The most successful recipes I tried—if you could call them that—followed a pretty basic protocol: Pat the grated potatoes dry with paper towels, season with salt and pepper, pack into a well-buttered nonstick skillet, fry over medium heat until browned, and flip to cook the second side. That being said, many of the recipes I collected had hooks, or tricks embedded in the basic technique that the authors promised were the secrets to success. These tips fell into two distinct categories: temperature and method.

This crisp potato cake is the perfect side dish for roasted meats.

Some of the recipes cranked the heat under the skillet to start the cake and dropped it to low to finish, or vice versa. Neither tactic really worked for me; medium heat proved best.

As for method-based tricks, a few recipes swore by covering the roesti as it cooked (in part or all the way through). I thought this would trap moisture and make the cake even denser and gummier than it already was, but just the opposite occurred. Roesti cooked covered for part of the time were surprisingly light, as if the moist heat cooked the potato through more fully than did dry heat alone. The gumminess was due in part to undercooked potatoes, and the cover addressed, but did not completely solve, that problem. After a few more batches, I found that cooking the cake for six minutes covered then another few minutes uncovered (until the bottom is a deep golden brown) before flipping yielded the best results yet.

Another recipe said the potato should be gently shaped into a cake, rather than packed tight into the pan. I used a rubber spatula and minimal force to persuade the potato into a round cake. As the cake cooked, you could see the steam escaping from the tangled potato and the resulting roesti was far lighter (and higher) and less gummy than a packed cake, though still not perfect.

Getting Closer

I wondered if the amount of butter—or the type of fat, for that matter—could have anything to do with success. Recipes almost universally favored butter, though a heretical few used oil, lard, or even goose fat. Outside of the goose fat—delicious but wholly impractical—nothing could touch the flavor or rich browning contributed by butter. For an exterior that was crisp but not greasy, I eventually settled on four tablespoons of butter—two for each side.

For the sake of testing, I had proceeded with the two potato varieties every recipe recommended: starchy russets and Yukon Golds. Could a different variety bring the recipe around? High-moisture Red Bliss potatoes made a roesti with a

RECIPE TESTING: 3 Swiss Misses

Here are three common problems we encountered when testing roesti recipes:

PROBLEM: BURNT
With too much butter in the pan or too much heat, the roesti burns in spots.

PROBLEM: GUMMY
Potatoes with excess moisture turn the roesti into a gray, sticky mess.

PROBLEM: CRUMBLY
Rinsing the potatoes washes away excess starch but can leave the roesti with no structure.

COOK'S extra

Go to www.cooksillustrated.com
- Click on the **Cook's Extra** link for **Roesti Serving Suggestions.**
- Information available until August 1, 2007.

PHOTOGRAPHY: CARL TREMBLAY

mushy, granular texture that fell apart in the pan. All-purpose potatoes were OK, but they couldn't compare with more flavorful russets and Yukons. Tasted head-to-head, Yukons won handily for their buttery flavor and sunny complexion, which emphasized the caramel-colored crust.

Watching me work one day, a colleague suggested I switch from paper towels to a dish towel and try wringing out the grated potatoes instead of simply patting them. With a bit of elbow grease, I was able to squeeze out a surprisingly large amount of moisture. Roesti cooked from these "dry" potatoes were better, but still not perfect.

A Quick Rinse

This being the modern age, I finally turned to Google for new ideas. After hours of surfing, I hit on the bulletin board of a professional chef's site. The responses to a query about roesti scrolled on for pages of tips that I had tried until the very last page, where one chef cited recipes from Madeleine Kamman and Craig Claiborne. The authors both rinsed the potatoes in cold water before squeezing them out and proceeding with the recipe.

I was skeptical about the rinsing. Wouldn't the potatoes absorb the water and become even wetter, effectively negating the squeezing? The proof, however, was in the roesti: rinsed, dried potatoes yielded the best cake yet: lighter, drier, and without a hint of gumminess. Rinsing, it seems, removed excess starch; squeezing removed the moisture. It was the combination of moisture and starch that was causing the gumminess, and I had now eliminated both.

But some of that starch was imperative for keeping the cake bound together. Kamman's roesti may have had the best interior, but it fell apart once sliced. Claiborne's recipe recommended collecting the potato starch that pooled at the bottom of the bowl after rinsing and tossing the potatoes with some of this starch before cooking. While the step seemed incredibly fussy, it made good sense. Looking to skip the tedious filtering of the potato starch from the rinsing water, I tossed the rinsed, squeezed-dry grated potato with a teaspoon of cornstarch.

The results were clear early on. Once I removed the lid and gave the skillet a shake, the strands of potato were stuck together in an airy nest—I hadn't even touched the potato with a spatula. I finished cooking the cake, and the results were near perfect: a caramel-gold crust, creamy, just-cooked-through interior, and airy, light texture that was perfectly sliceable.

STEP-BY-STEP | POTATO ROESTI

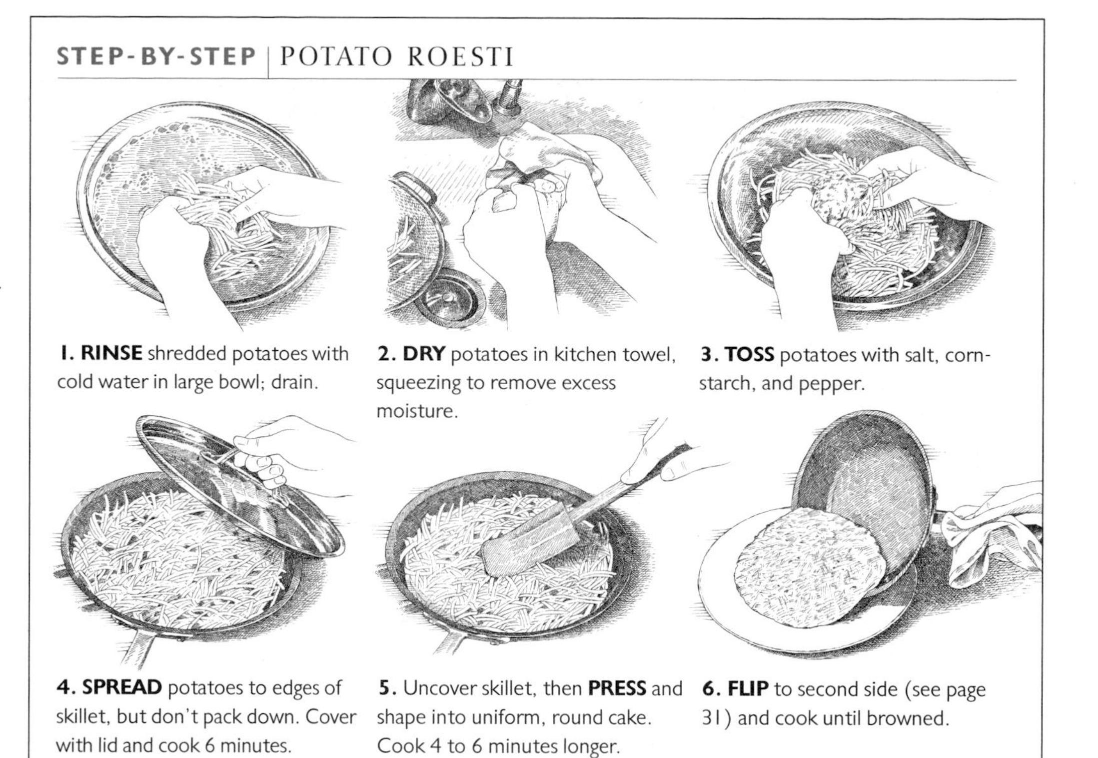

1. RINSE shredded potatoes with cold water in large bowl; drain.

2. DRY potatoes in kitchen towel, squeezing to remove excess moisture.

3. TOSS potatoes with salt, cornstarch, and pepper.

4. SPREAD potatoes to edges of skillet, but don't pack down. Cover with lid and cook 6 minutes.

5. Uncover skillet, then **PRESS** and shape into uniform, round cake. Cook 4 to 6 minutes longer.

6. FLIP to second side (see page 31) and cook until browned.

POTATO ROESTI

SERVES 4

The test kitchen prefers a roesti prepared with potatoes that have been cut through the large shredding disk of a food processor. It is possible to use a box grater to cut the potatoes, but they should be cut lengthwise, so you are left with long shreds. It is imperative to squeeze the potatoes as dry as possible. A well-seasoned cast-iron skillet can be used in place of the nonstick skillet. By adding fried eggs, ham, bacon, cheese, cooked onions, and/or tomatoes, roesti can be turned into a light meal (see Cook's Extra on page 14).

- 1½ pounds Yukon Gold potatoes (3 to 4 medium), peeled and shredded (see note above)
- ½ teaspoon table salt
- 1 teaspoon cornstarch
- Ground black pepper
- 4 tablespoons unsalted butter

1. Place potatoes in large bowl and fill with cold water. Using hands, swirl to remove excess starch, then drain in strainer.

2. Wipe bowl dry. Place half of potatoes in center of kitchen towel. Gather ends together and twist as tightly as possible to expel maximum moisture. Transfer potatoes to bowl and repeat process with remaining potatoes.

3. Sprinkle salt, cornstarch, and pepper to taste over potatoes. Using hands or fork, toss ingredients together until well blended.

4. Melt 2 tablespoons butter in 10-inch nonstick skillet over medium heat. When foaming subsides, add potato mixture and spread into even layer. Cover and cook 6 minutes. Remove cover and, using spatula, gently press potatoes down to form round cake. Cook, occasionally pressing on potatoes to shape into uniform round cake, until bottom is deep golden brown, 4 to 6 minutes longer.

5. Shake skillet to loosen roesti and slide onto large plate. Add remaining 2 tablespoons butter to skillet and swirl to coat pan. Invert roesti onto second plate and slide it, browned side up, back into skillet. Cook, occasionally pressing down on cake, until bottom is well browned, 7 to 9 minutes. Remove pan from heat and allow cake to cool in pan for 5 minutes. Transfer roesti to cutting board, cut into 4 pieces, and serve immediately.

FAMILY-SIZED POTATO ROESTI

SERVES 6

Follow recipe for Potato Roesti, increasing amount of potatoes to 2½ pounds. Squeeze potatoes in 3 batches (instead of 2) and increase salt to ¾ teaspoon and cornstarch to 1½ teaspoons. Cook roesti in 12-inch nonstick skillet, adding additional ½ tablespoon butter per side (5 tablespoons total). Increase uncovered cooking time in step 4 to 8 to 10 minutes and cooking time in step 5 to 8 to 10 minutes.

Yes, You Can "Juice" a Potato

Excess moisture in the potatoes will cause roesti to cook up gummy in the middle. To remove this moisture, squeeze the shredded potatoes in a kitchen towel. Expect to extract at least ¼ cup of liquid from 1½ pounds of potatoes.

ILLUSTRATION: JOHN BURGOYNE

Bread Baking Demystified

Bread baking is shrouded in mystery and plagued by misinformation and myths. After years of kitchen testing, we're ready to set the record straight. BY KEITH DRESSER

9 BREAD MYTHS YOU SHOULDN'T BELIEVE

MYTH #1: Bread Flour Is Best
FACT: All-Purpose Flour Is Fine We have found that unbleached all-purpose flour is the best choice in most bread recipes. Bread flour (which has more protein than all-purpose) is necessary only for rustic breads with a really sturdy crumb and thick crust.

MYTH #2: Tap Water Is Fine
FACT: Bottled Water Is Best
Water from the tap can contain many minerals and additives that adversely affect the flavor of bread. In our experience, bread made with bottled water has a sweeter, fuller flavor than bread made with tap water. If your tap water has an off taste or is particularly hard or soft, we recommend using bottled water.

MYTH #3: Salt Is Optional
FACT: Salt Is Essential If salt comes in direct contact with yeast, it will kill the yeast. Therefore, salt should be added to the dough after the yeast has been mixed with the flour. Because salt controls the activity of yeast, strengthens gluten, and accents the bread's flavor, it should never be omitted.

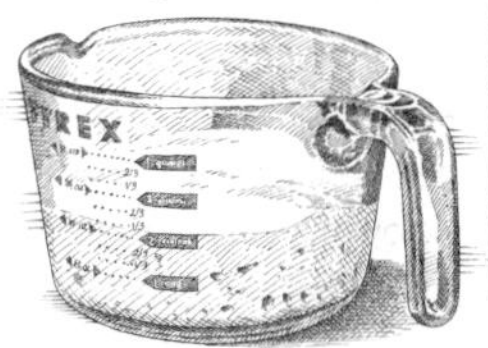

MYTH #4: Yeast Must Be Proofed
FACT: Proofing Is Unnecessary Older books tell you to sprinkle yeast over warm water and wait five minutes before proceeding. This process, called proofing the yeast, is no longer necessary. Our test kitchen relies on instant yeast (also labeled rapid-rise yeast) and adds the yeast directly to the dry ingredients.

MYTH #5: Always Start with a Sponge
FACT: Some Breads Don't Require a Sponge A sponge is made by mixing a portion of the flour, water, and yeast before the dough is made. This sponge (also called a biga or preferment) is then allowed to ferment for several hours or overnight before the dough is prepared. Although a sponge does impart a great deal of flavor to rustic breads, it isn't necessary with higher-fat loaf breads, for which all of the ingredients are usually just combined in a bowl.

MYTH #6: Hand-Kneading Is Better
FACT: You Should Use a Standing Mixer
In the test kitchen, kneading in a standing mixer is the technique of choice. (Use the paddle attachment to combine ingredients, then switch to the dough hook to knead.) This method ensures that we don't add too much flour to the dough (which can happen with hand-kneading and leads to dry, tough loaves). A standing mixer is especially suited for kneading wet or sticky dough. Once dough is kneaded, it may require a brief kneading by hand on the counter to form a cohesive ball.

MYTH #7: You Can't Overknead
FACT: Too Much Kneading Leads to Flavor Loss
Many bakers assume that the longer you knead bread, the better. However, prolonged kneading will overoxidize the dough, which leads to flavor loss. When properly kneaded, dough should have a smooth, almost shiny appearance. If you pull the dough, it should feel very stretchy and quickly spring back into place.

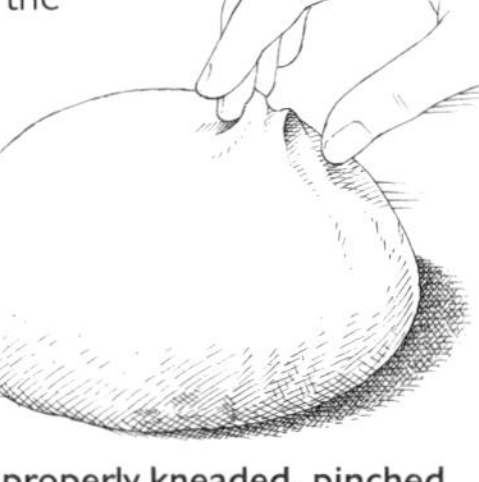
If properly kneaded, pinched portion of dough should spring back into shape quickly.

MYTH #8: Rising Times Are Flexible
FACT: Rising Times Should Be Followed
While there is some flexibility in the first rise (fermentation), we have found that it is important to pay close attention to the dough during the second rise (proofing). If underproofed, there is a chance that the dough will rise too much when baked, causing splitting and tearing. If overproofed, the dough may collapse when baked. A reliable way to test the dough's progress during proofing is to press it gently with a lightly moistened finger.

PROPERLY PROOFED
Dough will feel spongy rather than firm, and indentation will slowly fill in.

SCIENCE: AUTOLYSE
Autolyse (pronounced AUTO-lees) is a technique in which bread ingredients are briefly mixed and allowed to rest before kneading. This gives bread more flavor and better texture.

So how does autolyse work? When water and flour are combined, gluten forms in a random, disorganized matrix that is very weak. As the dough is kneaded, the disorganized bonds are pulled apart and reattached into straight, strong, orderly sheets. This must occur in order to give bread proper structure.

But excessive kneading can lead to flavor loss. The autolyse step reduces kneading time by allowing enzymes in the dough to break down disorganized bonds of gluten. Autolyse helps the gluten form a stronger, more organized network with less kneading.

MYTH #9: Baked Bread Will Sound Hollow
FACT: Thermometers Don't Lie Many recipes instruct the baker to tap the bottom of the loaf to check the bread's doneness—if it sounds hollow, then it's done. We have found this technique to be inexact. In our experience, it is much better to use an instant-read thermometer. Rustic breads should be baked to an internal temperature of 200 to 210 degrees, while richer breads are done at 190 to 195 degrees.

To test free-form loaf, turn bread over using oven mitt or potholder and insert thermometer through bottom crust into center of loaf.

To test bread baked in loaf pan, insert thermometer from side, just above edge of loaf pan, directing it at downward angle toward center of loaf.

Go to www.cooksillustrated.com
- Click on the **Cook's Extra** link for our list of **Gadgets and Gear for the Bread Baker.**
- Information available until August 1, 2007.

ILLUSTRATION: JOHN BURGOYNE

BREAD MAKING AT A GLANCE

Here's a brief overview of the steps you must follow to make most breads.

1. Measure

Carefully measuring ingredients is crucial to success. Because the ratio of flour to water greatly impacts the end result, we recommend weighing the ingredients before making bread.

2. Mix

Mixing distributes the ingredients, hydrates the flour, and starts the development of gluten.

3. Autolyse

Once the ingredients are fully combined, a 20-minute rest (called autolyse; see page 16) allows the flour to completely absorb the moisture and makes kneading quicker and easier.

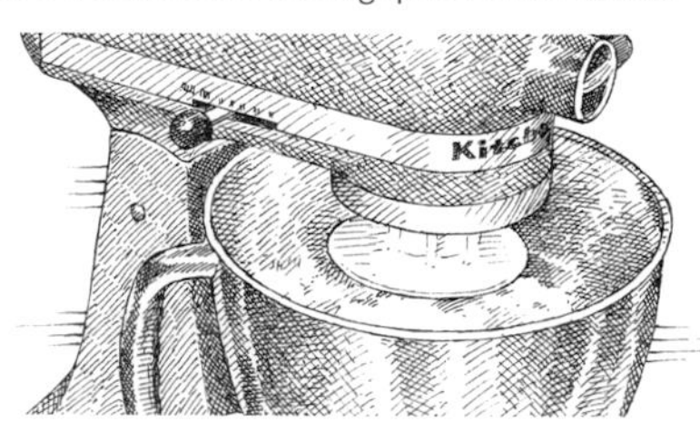

4. Knead

Kneading develops the gluten strands in the dough, which in turn provide the bread's structure. Resist the temptation to add excess flour, which will make the baked loaf dry.

5. Ferment

Fermentation is the process in which the starches in the flour break down to feed the yeast, which then releases carbon dioxide. This gas is trapped by the fibers of gluten, giving the bread lift. We like to ferment dough in a clear, straight-sided container, which allows us to easily judge when the dough has properly risen. It is also helpful to mark the height of the dough by placing a rubber band around the container.

6. Punch Down

Punching down helps to redistribute the yeast and allows it to find new food. This increases the yeast activity, ultimately leading to bread with a better texture. Punching down bread should not be violent. The simplest way is to pull the edges of the dough toward the center or push down gently on the dough.

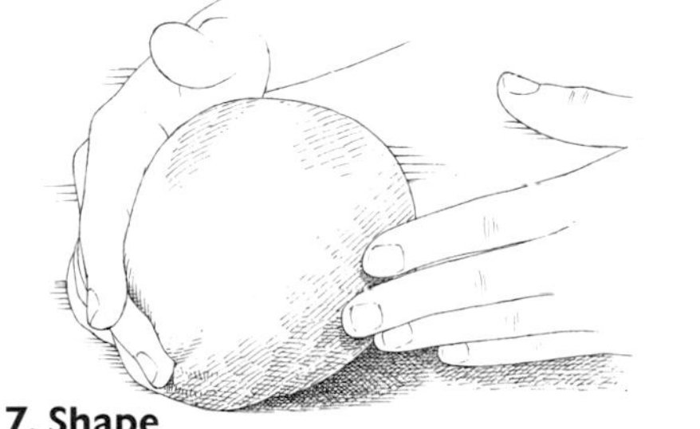

7. Shape

Form the dough into the desired shape on an unfloured work surface, which allows the dough to grip the counter, thus facilitating shaping.

8. Proof

Proofing is the dough's final rise before baking. When properly proofed, dough will have enough energy to provide the yeast with one last burst of activity (called oven spring) in the hot oven.

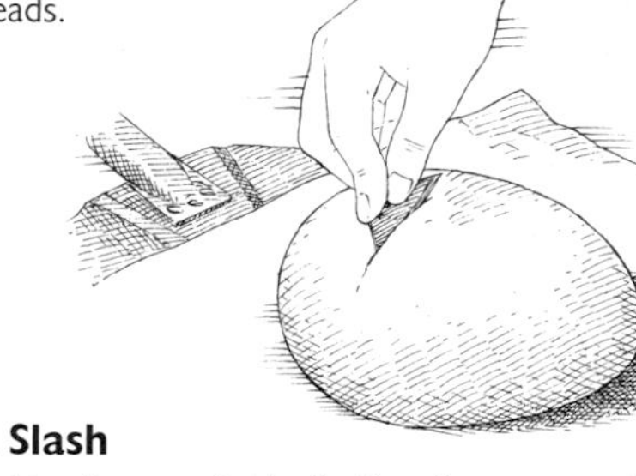

9. Slash

Slashing the proofed loaf with a sharp paring knife or razor allows the crust to expand and will prevent the bread from splitting in the oven.

10. Add Water

Misting the loaf right before it goes into the oven delays the formation of a crust, allowing the bread to fully expand without tearing or splitting. The steam also promotes the formation of a crispy, glossy crust.

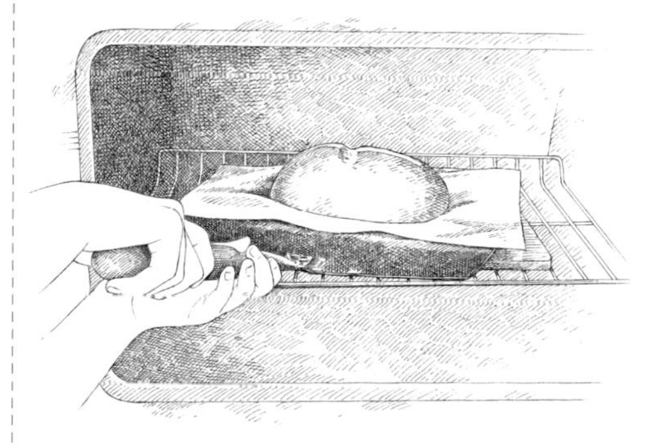

11. Bake

A baking stone will help keep the oven temperature steady and promote a thicker, crispier crust on free-form loaves.

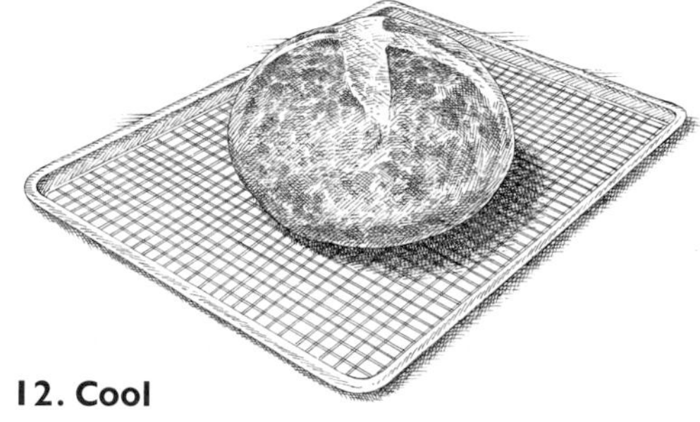

12. Cool

Cooling on a rack allows moisture to escape and keeps the bottom crust from becoming damp and soggy. Breads that are baked in a loaf pan should be removed from the pan as soon as they have cooled enough to be handled.

Roasted Tomato Sauce

Can a blast of heat transform unremarkable, out-of-season tomatoes into a vibrant sauce for pasta?

⋟ BY CHARLES KELSEY ⋞

I've become a bit of a tomato snob ever since getting into gardening. Tomatoes have to be deep red, ripe, and in-season to get my attention. And when it comes to tomato sauce, it had better be made with the plumpest garden-fresh fruit available. In my opinion, fresh tomato sauce has a hearty, almost meaty quality that can't be beat.

In the dead of winter, however, I rely on canned tomatoes—picked, cooked, and packed at peak ripeness—for sauce making. These convenient stand-ins make a good sauce, but I could do without their slightly tinny, stewed tomato flavor. A sauce made with canned tomatoes also lacks the meaty intensity of a sauce made with fresh tomatoes. Is there a way to make a great fresh tomato sauce when my garden is covered with snow?

Although my test kitchen colleagues expressed more than a little skepticism, I wondered if roasting could transform those characterless tomatoes that fill the supermarket produce section in the dead of winter. Roasting caramelizes natural sugars, intensifies flavors, and adds a light touch of smokiness. Just think what a hot oven does for plain-Jane potatoes and onions. Could roasting work its magic with crummy tomatoes?

Roasting the tomatoes until the skins char ensures a vibrant, smoky sauce with maximum flavor.

Some Like It Hot

Research turned up two basic approaches for making a roasted tomato sauce. The tomatoes could be roasted in a hot oven (about 450 degrees) for a short time (under an hour) or roasted "slow and low"—try eight hours in a 200-degree oven. Right off the bat, everyone in the test kitchen agreed that slow and low, albeit a great technique, took an unreasonable amount of time just to make a sauce.

The method in most of the quicker recipes was similar: Toss the tomatoes with oil, salt, and pepper, roast them on a rimmed baking sheet, and then transfer them to a food processor to finish the sauce. I prepared a dozen variations on this theme—almost all were bland and watery, but I learned a few things along the way.

I had expected to prefer plum tomatoes, but juicier vine-ripened tomatoes were actually the better choice. (For more information, see "The Right Tomato for the Job" on page 19.) Leaving the tomatoes whole prohibited the evaporation of moisture and thus stymied any flavor concentration. Recipes that called for peeled tomatoes had no roasted flavor at all. My conclusion: I would be cutting up vine-ripened tomatoes and leaving the skins in place so they could char and add smoky flavor to my sauce.

Seeding the tomatoes removed a lot of moisture from the outset, so the tomatoes got some good flavor concentration and a nice bit of caramelization. However, slicing and seeding 3 pounds of tomatoes (the amount needed to sauce a pound of pasta) was more prep work than I had in mind. But when I omitted the seeding step, the sauce had a stewed flavor that reminded me of canned tomatoes. Some oven-window observations revealed the culprit. The tomatoes were shedding their liquid early in the roasting process and stewing in that liquid for about 40 minutes, after which the liquid evaporated and the tomatoes started to dry out and char. I needed to find a way to minimize the time the tomatoes simmered in their liquid.

My gut response was to blast the oven temperature as high as it could go. My logic: Drive off the liquid as quickly as possible with intense heat. But the resulting sauce was watery and bitter from uneven cooking (and the same thing happened when I tried broiling the tomatoes). Next, I tried salting then pressing the moisture from the tomato slices before roasting. This technique required a colossal amount of prep work that wasn't worth the humdrum results.

I finally hit upon the solution when I added a wire rack to my baking sheet. Elevating the tomatoes on a rack set over the baking sheet eliminated the problem. The stewed tomato flavor was gone, because any tomato liquid simply fell through the rack and onto the tray. The rack also allowed for maximum air circulation and promoted better charring, which gave my sauce a more concentrated roasted tomato flavor.

The rack-roasting technique had earned a permanent spot in my recipe, but it was making the

RECIPE TESTING:

Digging Deeper for Tomato Flavor

We discovered that a couple tablespoons of tomato paste deepened the tomato flavor in our sauce and improved its color. We simply coated the fresh tomatoes, onion slices, and garlic cloves with tomato paste before they went into the oven. The paste darkened as it roasted, and its flavor became more intense. We've found that tomato paste performs a similar function in other recipes, adding depth to countless stews and sauces. We usually add the tomato paste once the aromatic vegetables have been cooked and before the liquid goes into the pan—exposing the tomato paste directly to dry heat intensifies its flavor and color. Sold in a no-fuss tube, Amore was the hands-down winner in a recent taste test.

BEST TOMATO PASTE

PHOTOGRAPHY: DANIEL J. VAN ACKERE

The Right Tomato for the Job

Most supermarkets offer three tomato choices. We roasted each variety and were surprised by the winner.

BEST BET
Vine-ripened tomatoes had the brightest flavor and best texture. These juicy tomatoes were absolutely consistent in our testing.

INCONSISTENT
Most plum tomatoes worked fine in our tests, but a few mealy samples created a sauce that was too dry.

NO THANKS
Large, out-of-season beefsteaks produced a watery, bland sauce.

finished sauce a bit dry and pulpy—too much moisture was being drained away during roasting. I started looking for a way to counterbalance the moisture loss, which led me to revisit the way I was cutting the tomatoes. I wondered if simply halving the tomatoes lengthwise then seeding them would work, the idea being that the less tomato flesh was exposed to the oven's dry heat, the more moisture the tomatoes would retain. I placed the tomato halves cut side down on the rack so that the tomato skins bore the brunt of the oven's heat and got an even better char.

I had some success with my first couple tries, but I found that I needed to ramp the oven temperature up to 475 degrees for well-charred skins. I thought I was done, until a fellow test cook questioned whether I really needed to seed the tomatoes now that I was using the rack. He reasoned that the extra moisture from the seeds might help my cause. I tried two sauces side by side, one with seeded tomatoes and one with seedless. Tasters preferred the sauce that contained tomato seeds, finding that it had the perfect balance of roasted and fresh flavor. Using the rack meant the only prep I had to do was slice the tomatoes in half.

Seeing Red

At this point my sauce had good tomato flavor but an unattractive, pale color. To improve the color and pump up the tomato flavor, I introduced tomato paste to my recipe. Tossing the halved tomatoes with tomato paste (as well as oil, salt, and pepper) was easy. As I had hoped, the tomato paste gave my sauce a deeper tomato flavor as well as a deeper red color. What I hadn't expected was more roasted flavor. The paste-coated tomatoes caramelized, and the skins blackened even more (a good thing) than tomatoes that were not coated. After some tinkering, I found that 2 tablespoons of paste was the perfect amount.

Garlic and onion seemed like a must, but the notion of sautéing them in a separate pan while the tomatoes roasted was unattractive. Could I add the garlic and onion to the rack with the tomatoes and roast them, too? To keep the garlic and onions from falling through the rack, I left the garlic cloves whole and sliced the onion thick. But pieces still fell down through the rack and failed to get much color or flavor development. I had better luck placing the garlic and onions on a sheet of foil set on the center of the rack, which kept them in place.

This method was simpler than sautéing the garlic and onion, but was it better? In a head-to-head test, tasters greatly favored the sauce with the roasted garlic and onion, praising its more complex, richer flavor. Tossing the garlic and onion with the tomato paste (as well as thyme and red pepper flakes) added another dimension to my sauce. To finish, tasters liked a drizzle of extra-virgin olive oil, a touch of sugar, and a splash of bright red wine vinegar. Fresh basil reinforced the garden-quality character of the sauce.

My recipe had good walk-away time and freed up burner space on the range. But most of all, it had a great technique for transforming dull, out-of-season tomatoes into a richly intense sauce that even a tomato snob couldn't resist.

ROASTED TOMATO SAUCE

MAKES 3 TO 3 1/2 CUPS, ENOUGH TO SAUCE 1 POUND OF PASTA

This sauce is best with short pasta shapes, such as ziti or penne. It can also be served over chicken Parmesan or grilled fish. If serving this sauce with pasta, save some of the pasta cooking water to adjust the sauce's consistency. Plum tomatoes can be used, but the sauce may require even more pasta cooking water. Because fresh tomatoes vary in sweetness, it's best to add sugar to taste before serving. The sauce can be refrigerated in an airtight container for up to 2 days; bring to a simmer before using.

- 2 tablespoons tomato paste
- 2 tablespoons extra-virgin olive oil
- 2 teaspoons minced fresh thyme leaves
- 1/8 teaspoon red pepper flakes
- Table salt and ground black pepper
- 3 pounds vine-ripened tomatoes (9 to 12 medium), cored and halved pole to pole
- 6 medium garlic cloves, peeled
- 1 small onion, peeled and cut into 1/2-inch rounds
- 1 teaspoon red wine vinegar
- Granulated sugar to taste (up to 2 teaspoons; see note above)
- 2 tablespoons chopped fresh basil leaves

1. Adjust oven rack to middle position and heat oven to 475 degrees. Combine tomato paste, 1 tablespoon oil, thyme, pepper flakes, 3/4 teaspoon salt, and 1/4 teaspoon pepper in large bowl. Toss tomatoes, garlic, and onion with tomato paste mixture until evenly coated. Place 4-inch square of foil in center of wire rack set in rimmed baking sheet lined with aluminum foil. Place garlic cloves and onion rounds on foil and arrange tomatoes, cut side down, around garlic and onion.

2. Roast until vegetables are soft and tomato skins are well charred, 45 to 55 minutes. Remove baking sheet from oven and let cool 5 minutes. Transfer garlic and onion to food processor; pulse until finely chopped, about five 1-second pulses. Add tomatoes, vinegar, and remaining tablespoon oil to food processor. Pulse until broken down but still chunky, about five 1-second pulses. Using rubber spatula, scrape down bowl; season with salt, pepper, and sugar to taste. Continue to process sauce until slightly chunky, about five 1-second pulses. Stir in basil.

ROASTED TOMATO SAUCE WITH ROSEMARY AND GOAT CHEESE

Follow recipe for Roasted Tomato Sauce, substituting 1 teaspoon minced fresh rosemary for thyme. Omit basil. After tossing sauce with pasta, sprinkle with 2 ounces crumbled fresh goat cheese.

ROASTED TOMATO SAUCE WITH FENNEL

Follow recipe for Roasted Tomato Sauce, adding 1/2 teaspoon fennel seed to tomato paste mixture in step 1. Replace onion with 1 small fennel bulb, trimmed, cored, and cut into 1/2-inch slices.

TECHNIQUE | SETTING UP THE TRAY

Elevating the vegetables on a rack set in a foil-lined rimmed baking sheet maximizes charring and flavor development. Position the garlic and onion on a small square of foil set in the center of the rack. Arrange the halved tomatoes, cut side down, around the edges of the rack.

Pan-Roasted Asparagus Side Dishes

A hot pan and complementary vegetables turn asparagus into a lively side dish.

BY DAVID PAZMIÑO

The test kitchen recently discovered a way to cook asparagus that adds roasted flavor without heating up either the grill or the oven (see "Pan-Roasted Asparagus", March/April 2005). This method uses the lid on a large skillet to trap steam, which cooks the asparagus through. When the lid is removed, the asparagus caramelizes. This cooking method concentrates the natural sweetness in this favorite spring vegetable while adding roasted flavor. Although the pan is quite crowded, I wondered if I could add other vegetables to make a more robust side dish.

I tried the easiest option first. In various tests, I added cherry tomatoes, onions, and bell peppers to the asparagus as it cooked. But I quickly discovered that excess moisture released from these vegetables (yes, even the onions) prevented the asparagus from browning and yielded a bland, soggy mess.

The best remedy for soggy vegetables was to divide and conquer: I cooked the accent vegetable first, removed it from the pan, and then wiped the pan clean. Then the asparagus could be cooked on its own in the now-empty pan, plated, and garnished with the second vegetable.

PAN-ROASTED ASPARAGUS

SERVES 4 TO 6

This recipe works best with asparagus that is at least ½ inch thick near the base. If using thinner spears, reduce the covered cooking time to 3 minutes and the uncovered cooking time to 5 minutes. Do not use pencil-thin asparagus; it cannot withstand the heat and overcooks too easily.

- 1 tablespoon olive oil
- 1 tablespoon unsalted butter
- 2 pounds thick asparagus spears (see note above), ends trimmed
- Kosher salt and ground black pepper
- 1 lemon, halved (optional)

1. Heat oil and butter in 12-inch skillet over medium-high heat. When butter has melted, add half of asparagus to skillet with tips pointed in one direction; add remaining spears with tips pointed in opposite direction. Using tongs, distribute spears evenly (spears will not quite fit into single layer); cover and cook until asparagus is bright green and still crisp, about 5 minutes.

2. Uncover and increase heat to high; season asparagus with salt and pepper. Cook until spears are tender and well browned along one side, using tongs to occasionally move spears from center of pan to edge of pan to ensure all are browned, 5 to 7 minutes. Transfer asparagus to serving dish, adjust seasonings with salt and pepper, and, if desired, squeeze lemon over spears. Serve immediately.

PAN-ROASTED ASPARAGUS WITH CHERRY TOMATOES AND BLACK OLIVES

SERVES 4 TO 6

- 1 tablespoon olive oil
- 2 medium garlic cloves, sliced thin
- 1 pint cherry tomatoes, halved
- ½ cup pitted black olives, such as kalamata or other brine-cured variety, chopped
- 1 recipe Pan-Roasted Asparagus
- 4 tablespoons chopped fresh basil leaves
- 1 ounce Parmesan cheese, grated (about ½ cup)

1. Heat oil and garlic in 12-inch skillet over medium heat. Cook, stirring occasionally, until garlic turns golden around edges but does not darken, 2 to 3 minutes. Add tomatoes and olives; cook until tomatoes begin to break down and release liquid, 1 to 2 minutes. Transfer mixture to bowl and cover with foil. Rinse skillet with water and dry well with paper towels.

2. Follow recipe for Pan-Roasted Asparagus.

3. After transferring asparagus to serving dish, top with tomato mixture. Adjust seasonings with salt and pepper; sprinkle with basil and Parmesan. Serve immediately.

PAN-ROASTED ASPARAGUS WITH RED ONION AND BACON

SERVES 4 TO 6

- 4 strips bacon, cut into ¼-inch-wide strips
- 1 large red onion, halved and sliced thin
- 2 tablespoons balsamic vinegar
- 1 tablespoon maple syrup
- 1 recipe Pan-Roasted Asparagus

1. Cook bacon in 12-inch skillet over medium heat until crisp, 8 to 10 minutes. Using slotted spoon, transfer bacon to paper towel–lined plate; set aside. Pour off and discard all but 1 tablespoon fat from pan.

2. Return skillet to medium-high heat and add onion. Cook, stirring occasionally, until edges darken and onions begin to soften, about 3 minutes. Add vinegar and maple syrup; cook until liquids reduce and cling to onions, about 2 minutes. Transfer onions to bowl and cover with foil. Rinse skillet with water and dry well with paper towels.

3. Follow recipe for Pan-Roasted Asparagus.

4. After transferring asparagus to serving dish, top with onion. Adjust seasonings with salt and pepper; sprinkle with bacon. Serve immediately.

PAN-ROASTED ASPARAGUS WITH RED PEPPERS AND GOAT CHEESE

SERVES 4 TO 6

- 1 tablespoon olive oil
- 2 medium red bell peppers, seeded and cut into ¼-inch-wide strips
- 1 recipe Pan-Roasted Asparagus
- 2 tablespoons chopped fresh mint leaves
- 4 ounces goat cheese, crumbled (about ½ cup)
- ¼ cup pine nuts, toasted

1. Heat oil in 12-inch skillet over medium-high heat until shimmering. Add peppers and cook, stirring occasionally, until skins begin to blister, 4 to 5 minutes. Transfer peppers to bowl and cover with foil. Rinse skillet with water and dry well with paper towels.

2. Follow recipe for Pan-Roasted Asparagus.

3. After transferring asparagus to serving dish, top with peppers. Adjust seasonings with salt and pepper; sprinkle with mint, goat cheese, and pine nuts. Serve immediately.

PAN-ROASTED ASPARAGUS (SMALL BATCH)

SERVES 2 TO 3

To make any of these recipes serve just 2 to 3 people, cut all ingredient amounts in half. Cook asparagus in 10-inch skillet over medium heat, covered, for 3 minutes. Remove cover and cook over medium-high heat until tender and browned, 3 to 4 minutes. Do not adjust heat when cooking garnishes; however, cooking times for garnishes should be reduced by 1 to 2 minutes.

Go to www.cooksillustrated.com

- Click on the **Cook's Extra** link for **Pan-Roasted Asparagus with Mushrooms and Tarragon** and **Pan-Roasted Asparagus with Red Onions, Hard-Boiled Eggs, Capers, and Tarragon.**
- Recipes available until August 1, 2007.

Garlicky Shrimp with Bread Crumbs

Saucy shrimp blanketed with toasted crumbs represents the best of old-fashioned American cooking, but not when the shrimp are waterlogged and tough.

BY SANDRA WU

Garlicky shrimp with buttery bread crumbs is classic American cooking. Look in any all-purpose cookbook and you'll find a recipe. I found dozens in our library, most of which followed the same basic formula: Poach the shrimp; place them in a baking dish; top with bread crumbs, sherry, melted butter, herbs, and garlic; and bake in a hot oven for 10 to 15 minutes. Unfortunately, the results did not make me nostalgic for the past.

The shrimp were often rubbery and bland (no surprise, since they were poached, then baked), while the topping—aside from its slightly crusty surface—was gluey and heavy on raw alcohol flavor. The combination of flavors and textures was appealing (in theory), but this dish needed some serious modernizing.

Extreme Makeover

To avoid poaching and then baking the shrimp, I tossed them with a mixture of melted butter, salt, pepper, garlic, shallots, sherry, and parsley; transferred everything to a baking dish; sprinkled buttered fresh bread crumbs on top; and popped the dish into the oven. After a dozen failures (the shrimp were always too bland and watery), I decided on a more radical solution: trading the baking dish in the oven for a skillet on the stovetop. This would allow me to sear the shrimp (and thus add a flavorful browned exterior) and concentrate the sauce by reducing liquids in the same pan. I planned to use the crumbs as a last-minute topping.

To start, I pan-seared the shrimp in two batches to promote browning rather than steaming. Cooking the shrimp completely through caused them to overcook when added to the sauce. Eventually, I hit upon the following strategy: Sear the shrimp on one side and remove them from the pan, build the sauce in the empty pan, and then return the shrimp to let them finish cooking in the sauce. Sprinkling the shrimp with a little sugar encouraged browning during their short stay in the skillet.

As for the sauce, I couldn't rely on sherry alone for my liquid component (it was too boozy). Cutting the sherry with bottled clam juice and letting the mixture simmer for several minutes concentrated the flavors and cooked off excess alcohol. To finish the sauce, I whisked in several tablespoons of cold butter, but the sauce was a bit thin. More butter just made the sauce greasy. I had better luck adding a pinch of flour.

Topping It Off

The crumb topping (toasted in the empty skillet before the shrimp were cooked) was easy. Japanese-style panko was too finely textured, while crumbs made from white sandwich bread became sandy on top and soggy underneath. Chewy supermarket baguette was sturdy enough to retain a crisp texture even after sitting on top of the saucy shrimp.

After sprinkling the flavorful topping onto the buttery, garlic-infused shrimp, I stepped back and offered up the results. My skillet "casserole" had all the potent flavors and contrasting textures my tasters wanted—but none of the usual problems.

GARLICKY SHRIMP WITH BUTTERED BREAD CRUMBS

SERVES 4

Vermouth can be substituted for the sherry. If using vermouth, increase the amount to ½ cup and reduce the amount of clam juice to ½ cup. To prepare this recipe in a 10-inch skillet, brown the shrimp in 3 batches for about 2 minutes each, using 2 teaspoons oil per batch. Serve the shrimp with rice and either broccoli or asparagus.

- 1 (3-inch) piece baguette, cut into small pieces
- 5 tablespoons unsalted butter, cut into 5 pieces
- 1 small shallot, minced (about 2 tablespoons)
- Table salt and ground black pepper
- 2 tablespoons minced fresh parsley leaves
- 2 pounds extra-large (21–25) shrimp, peeled and deveined
- ¼ teaspoon sugar
- 4 teaspoons vegetable oil
- 4 medium garlic cloves, minced or pressed through garlic press (about 4 teaspoons)
- ⅛ teaspoon red pepper flakes
- 2 teaspoons all-purpose flour
- ⅓ cup dry sherry
- ⅔ cup bottled clam juice
- 2 teaspoons juice from 1 lemon, plus 1 lemon, cut into wedges

1. Pulse bread in food processor until coarsely ground; you should have about 1 cup crumbs. Melt 1 tablespoon butter in 12-inch nonstick skillet over medium heat. When foaming subsides, add crumbs, shallot, ⅛ teaspoon salt, and ⅛ teaspoon pepper. Cook, stirring occasionally, until golden brown, 7 to 10 minutes. Stir in 1 tablespoon parsley and transfer to plate to cool. Wipe out skillet with paper towels.

2. Thoroughly dry shrimp with paper towels; toss with sugar, ¼ teaspoon salt, and ¼ teaspoon pepper in bowl. Return skillet to high heat, add 2 teaspoons oil, and heat until shimmering. Add half of shrimp in single layer and cook until spotty brown and edges turn pink, about 3 minutes (do not flip shrimp). Remove pan from heat and transfer shrimp to large plate. Wipe out skillet with paper towels. Repeat with remaining 2 teaspoons oil and shrimp; transfer shrimp to plate.

3. Return skillet to medium heat and add 1 tablespoon butter. When melted, add garlic and pepper flakes; cook, stirring frequently, until garlic just begins to color, about 1 minute. Add flour and cook, stirring frequently, for 1 minute. Increase heat to medium-high and slowly whisk in sherry and clam juice. Bring to simmer and cook until mixture reduces to ¾ cup, 3 to 4 minutes. Whisk in remaining 3 tablespoons butter, 1 tablespoon at a time. Stir in lemon juice and remaining tablespoon parsley.

4. Reduce heat to medium-low, return shrimp to pan, and toss to combine. Cook, covered, until shrimp are pink and cooked through, 2 to 3 minutes. Uncover and sprinkle with toasted bread crumbs. Serve with lemon wedges.

For best results, keep the toasted crumbs and buttery shrimp apart until the last possible moment.

PHOTOGRAPHY: CARL TREMBLAY

Ultimate Lemon Layer Cake

We carefully deconstructed this blue-ribbon recipe to create a light and lemony dessert.

BY ERIKA BRUCE

Special occasions deserve an exceptional dessert, and nothing fits the bill better than a sophisticated lemon layer cake. When made well, it is delicate and stylish, with an ideal contrast of sweet and tart. And yet this cake seems to have fallen out of favor, perhaps because most versions are poorly executed concoctions of heavy cake stacked with filling and frosting that taste more like butter than lemon. I wanted to produce a recipe for this old-fashioned cake in which tangy, creamy lemon filling divides layers of tender, delicate cake draped in sweet frosting.

Most layer cakes are made with substantial butter cakes, but I suspected that the light, fresh flavor of lemon would be better served by something more ethereal. I tried the test kitchen's recipes for all-purpose sponge cake, classic yellow cake, and white butter cake in a stripped-down lemon layer cake recipe. The yellow cake was somewhat dense and rich—great for a birthday cake, but not what I had in mind for a lighter lemon layer cake. And while the sponge cake was indeed light and fluffy, its crumb was coarse and not refined enough. The white butter cake, however, was the perfect compromise: nicely flavored by butter yet lighter than the yellow cake due to the use of egg whites only (no yolks), with a fine crumb and tender texture.

A fluffy, sweet frosting balances the tart lemon filling in this elegant cake.

Into the Thick

Lemon layer cake is often filled with lemon-scented buttercream, but this monotonic arrangement mutes the lemon flavor and makes the cake far too rich. I prefer the brightness of lemon curd, a combination of sugar, lemon juice, butter, and eggs cooked together until it reaches the consistency of custard. The mixture is simmered gently so as to not overcook the eggs, and the acidic lemon juice denatures the egg proteins, allowing them to form a fluid gel. The result is a creamy, smooth custard with lively lemon flavor.

Go to www.cooksillustrated.com

- Click on the **Cook's Extra** link for our **Fluffy Vanilla Icing, Tangy Orange Icing, Toasted Almond Icing,** and **Coconut Icing.**
- Click on the **Cook's Extra** link for **How to Make Lemon Curd** and **How to Frost a Layer Cake** illustrations.
- Information available until August 1, 2007.

Starting with 1 cup of lemon juice and 1½ cups of sugar for the right level of lemony tang, I tinkered with different amounts of eggs and butter, ultimately settling on a middle-of-the-road recipe containing 4 whole eggs plus 6 yolks and 8 tablespoons of butter. This curd was silky smooth and tasted great, but when I attempted to spread it over the cake, I realized it was too runny. I needed to create something sturdier. Adding more eggs thickened the curd so much that it became gluey. More butter thickened the curd but muted the lemon flavor. Cornstarch made the curd too pasty.

I was racking my brain for more ideas when a colleague suggested fruit pectin or gelatin. These ingredients can be a baker's secret weapons in helping to set finicky fillings. After a few tests, I found that both did a beautiful job of firming up the curd without marring its lush texture or changing its intense flavor. In the end, gelatin was easier to add, as it just needed to be hydrated in a little lemon juice, whereas pectin needed to be boiled with the sugar and lemon juice.

Icing on the Cake

Having successfully avoided rich buttercream for the filling, I was determined to find something lighter for the icing as well. I eventually landed on an old-fashioned classic: seven-minute icing. This pure white icing is exceptionally light and glossy, and tasters found it to be an ideal topping for my delicate cake. Prepared in the same manner as a Swiss meringue, it is made by whipping egg whites and sugar and a touch of water for precisely seven minutes over a pot of simmering water.

But this old model needed a new paint job. First, it was a little too sweet, almost candy-like. Second, it was slightly thick and chewy. Last, the cooking technique had me enduring the arm-numbing vibration of a hand-held mixer for longer than was comfortable.

Cutting back on the sugar (by a quarter) and adding a squeeze of lemon juice easily solved the first two problems, but the cooking technique took some finagling. I knew I needed to expose the egg mixture to a certain amount of heat (without it the mixture would not be stable; see "Seven-Minute Magic," page 23), but I wanted to rely on my standing mixer. After some trial and error, I learned that if I heated the mixture to at least 160 degrees and then transferred it to the standing mixer for whipping, the end result was just as billowy and shiny as the version whipped over constant heat.

With my adjustments to the recipe, it actually took 10 minutes, not seven, for the icing to form stiff peaks, but the mixer did the work—not me. (I also developed some flavor variations to use with other cakes; see Cook's Extra at left.) Finally, I added a spoonful of corn syrup to the icing, which lent an impressive luster. With swirling peaks of white icing, this light, lemony cake is fashionable enough for any special occasion.

LEMON LAYER CAKE

SERVES 10 TO 12

The filling can be made a day ahead and refrigerated, but it will become quite stiff; fold it with a rubber spatula to loosen it before spreading onto the cake. For neater slices, dip a knife into hot water before cutting the cake. Leftovers can be stored covered in the refrigerator, with the cut

PHOTOGRAPHY: CARL TREMBLAY

side of the cake covered tightly with plastic wrap, for up to 3 days.

Lemon Curd Filling

- 1 cup juice from about 6 lemons
- 1 teaspoon powdered gelatin
- 1 ½ cups (10 ½ ounces) granulated sugar
- ⅛ teaspoon table salt
- 4 large eggs
- 6 large egg yolks (reserve egg whites for cake)
- 8 tablespoons (1 stick) unsalted butter, cut into ½-inch cubes and frozen

Cake

- 2 ¼ cups (9 ounces) cake flour, plus extra for pans
- 1 cup whole milk, room temperature
- 6 large egg whites, room temperature
- 2 teaspoons vanilla extract
- 1 ¾ cups (12 ¼ ounces) granulated sugar
- 4 teaspoons baking powder
- 1 teaspoon table salt
- 12 tablespoons (1 ½ sticks) unsalted butter, cut into 12 pieces, softened but still cool

Fluffy White Icing

- 2 large egg whites
- 1 cup (7 ounces) granulated sugar
- ¼ cup water
- 1 tablespoon juice from 1 lemon
- 1 tablespoon corn syrup

1. **FOR THE FILLING:** Measure 1 tablespoon lemon juice into small bowl; sprinkle gelatin over top. Heat remaining lemon juice, sugar, and salt in medium nonreactive saucepan over medium-high heat, stirring occasionally, until sugar dissolves and mixture is hot but not boiling. Whisk eggs and yolks in large nonreactive bowl. Whisking constantly, slowly pour hot lemon-sugar mixture into eggs, then return mixture to saucepan. Cook over medium-low heat, stirring constantly with heatproof spatula, until mixture registers 170 degrees on instant-read thermometer and is thick enough to leave trail when spatula is scraped along pan bottom, 4 to 6 minutes. Immediately remove pan from heat and stir in gelatin mixture until dissolved. Stir in frozen butter until incorporated. Pour filling through fine-mesh strainer into nonreactive bowl (you should have 3 cups). Cover surface directly with plastic wrap; refrigerate until firm enough to spread, at least 4 hours.

2. **FOR THE CAKE:** Adjust oven rack to middle position and heat oven to 350 degrees. Grease and flour two 9-inch-wide by 2-inch-high round cake pans and line with parchment paper. In 2-cup liquid measure or medium bowl, whisk together milk, egg whites, and vanilla.

3. In bowl of standing mixer fitted with paddle attachment, mix flour, sugar, baking powder, and salt at low speed. With mixer running at low speed, add butter one piece at a time; continue beating until mixture resembles moist crumbs with no visible butter chunks. Add all but ½ cup milk mixture to crumbs and beat at medium speed until mixture is pale and fluffy, about 1½ minutes. With mixer running at low speed, add remaining ½ cup milk mixture; increase speed to medium and beat 30 seconds more. Stop mixer and scrape sides of bowl. Return mixer to medium speed and beat 20 seconds longer. Divide batter evenly between cake pans; using rubber spatula, spread batter to pan walls and smooth tops.

4. Bake until toothpick inserted in center of cakes comes out clean, 23 to 25 minutes. Loosen cakes from sides of pans with small knife, cool in pan 10 minutes, then invert onto greased wire rack; peel off parchment. Invert cakes again; cool completely on rack, about 1½ hours.

5. **TO ASSEMBLE:** Following illustrations above, use serrated knife to cut each cake into 2 even layers. Place bottom layer of 1 cake on cardboard round or cake plate. Using icing spatula, spread 1 cup lemon filling evenly on cake, leaving ½ inch border around edge; using cardboard round, gently replace top layer. Spread 1 cup filling on top. Using cardboard round, gently slide bottom half of second cake into place. Spread remaining cup filling on top. Using cardboard round, place top layer of second cake. Smooth out any filling that has leaked from sides of cake; cover with plastic wrap and refrigerate while making icing.

6. **FOR THE ICING:** Combine all ingredients in bowl of standing mixer or large heatproof bowl and set over medium saucepan filled with 1 inch of barely simmering water (do not let bowl touch water). Cook, stirring constantly, until mixture registers 160 degrees on instant-read thermometer, 5 to 10 minutes. Remove bowl from heat and transfer mixture to standing mixer fitted with whisk attachment. Beat on medium speed until soft peaks form, about 5 minutes. Increase speed to medium-high and continue to beat until mixture has cooled to room temperature and stiff peaks form, 5 minutes longer. Using icing spatula, spread frosting on cake. Serve. (Cake can be refrigerated for up to 1 day before serving.)

STEP-BY-STEP | ASSEMBLING A FOUR-LAYER CAKE

To create an elegant, four-tiered cake, you must split two cake layers in half horizontally. If you cut the layers a bit unevenly (which is bound to happen), the cake can lean to one side. Here's how to compensate for less-than-perfect cutting.

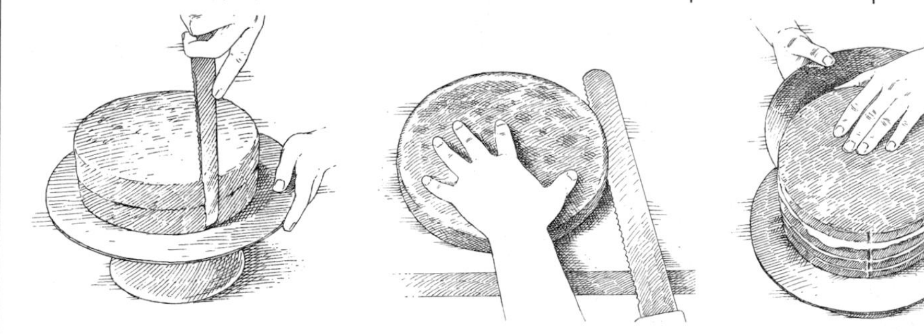
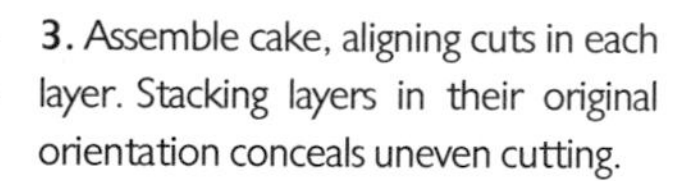

1. Place cooled cake layers on top of each other and make ⅛-inch-deep cut into side of each cake layer.

2. With long, serrated knife, use sawing motion to cut cakes in half horizontally so that each cake forms 2 layers.

3. Assemble cake, aligning cuts in each layer. Stacking layers in their original orientation conceals uneven cutting.

SCIENCE: Seven-Minute Magic

Along with its fluffy texture and glossy sheen, seven-minute icing offers the fringe benefit of retaining its volume for at least three days. What makes the egg whites in this old-fashioned recipe more stable than egg whites whipped for a mousse or a soufflé?

Beating raw egg whites and sugar temporarily relaxes the tightly wound egg proteins, allowing air to be trapped inside the resulting matrix. The foam this produces is impermanent, however, and will begin to deflate soon after being whipped.

Cooking the egg whites and sugar to 160 degrees causes the coiled egg proteins to permanently relax. When the warm mixture is then whipped, the egg proteins remain unraveled as they cool, forming a stable network that traps sugar and water. So the icing stays shiny, airy, and smooth long enough for you to enjoy the entire cake. –E.B.

NO HEAT = WEAK FOAM
After just 30 minutes, the foam made by whipping raw egg whites with sugar and other ingredients has lost most of its volume.

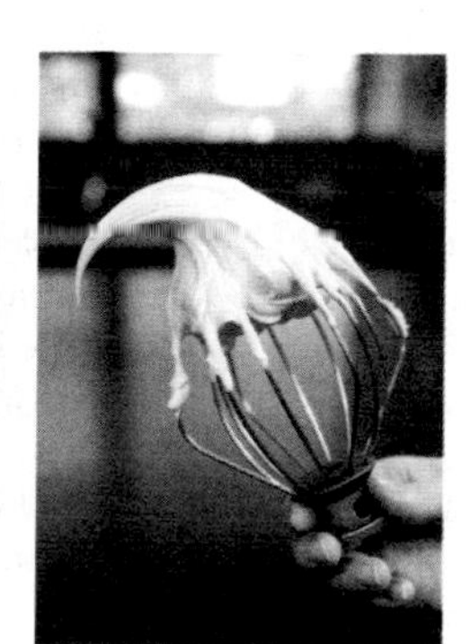

HEAT = STABLE FOAM
After 24 hours, the foam made by heating the egg whites with sugar and other ingredients and then whipping still holds its volume.

ILLUSTRATION: JOHN BURGOYNE

Brown Sugar Cookies

A chewy cookie with a crisp exterior and a big jolt of brown sugar flavor sounded easy to develop, but first we needed to understand the not-so-simple science of cookies.

⋟ BY CHARLES KELSEY ⋞

I'm not one for fancy cookies. No special nuts, exotic flavor extracts, or intricate decorating for me. I prefer simple cookies done well. Take sugar cookies, for example: Made of nothing more than butter, sugar, flour, eggs, and leavener, they're rich and buttery with a crisp sugary exterior. Big results from pantry ingredients . . . now that's what I like.

But a sugar cookie can seem too simple—even dull—at times. I love the butterscotch, vanilla, and caramel flavors that brown sugar gives coffeecakes and other baked goods. Could I replace the granulated sugar in a sugar cookie with brown sugar and create a simple cookie that was actually exciting? I had a clear vision of this cookie. It would be oversized, with a crackling crisp exterior and a chewy interior. And, like Mick Jagger, this cookie would scream "brown sugar."

I found a half-dozen recipes and got to work. Although they looked similar on paper, the baked cookies ranged in style from bite-sized puffs with a soft, cakey texture to thin disks with a short crumb. This first round of testing reminded me that cookies are deceptively difficult. Yes, most recipes can be executed by a young child, but even the tiniest alteration will make a significant difference in flavor and, especially, texture. To construct my ideal brown sugar cookie, I would need to brush up on the science of cookie making.

Let the cookies firm up on the hot baking sheet before transferring them to a cooling rack.

Basic Cookie Construction

Most sugar cookie recipes start by creaming softened butter with sugar until fluffy, beating in an egg or two, and then adding the dry ingredients (flour, baking powder, and salt). Vanilla is often incorporated along the way.

Butter was the obvious choice for optimal flavor, but creaming the fat and sugar beat tiny air bubbles into the dough and the resulting cookies were cakey and tender—not what I had in mind. I tried cutting the butter into the flour (like you do when making pie dough), but this method produced crumbly cookies with a texture akin to shortbread. When I melted the butter, the cookies finally had the chewy texture I wanted.

So why does melted butter make chewy cookies? Butter is actually 20 percent water and 80 percent fat. When melted, the water and fat separate and the proteins in the flour absorb some of the water and begin to form gluten, the protein that gives baked goods, including breads, their structure and chew.

Cookies made with melted butter and an entire 1-pound box of brown sugar had plenty of flavor, but these taffy-textured confections threatened to pull out my expensive dental work. Using dark brown sugar rather than light brown sugar allowed me to get more flavor from less sugar. Cookies made with 1¾ cups dark brown sugar had the best texture and decent flavor. I decided to nail down the rest of my recipe before circling back to flavor issues.

Eggs add richness and structure to cookies. A single egg didn't provide enough of the latter—the cookies were too candy-like. Thinking that two eggs would solve the problem, I was surprised when a test batch turned out dry and cakey. Splitting the difference, I added one whole egg plus a yolk and was pleased with the results.

Too much flour gave the cookies a homogenous texture; too little and that candy-like chew reemerged. Two cups flour, plus a couple extra tablespoons, was the perfect match for the amounts of butter, sugar, and egg I'd chosen.

The choice of leavener is probably the most confusing part of any cookie recipe. Sugar cookies typically contain baking powder—a mixture of baking soda and a weak acid (calcium acid phosphate) that is activated by moisture and heat. The soda and acid create gas bubbles, which expand cookies and other baked goods. However, many baked goods with brown sugar call for baking soda. While granulated sugar is neutral, dark brown sugar can be slightly acidic. When I used baking soda by itself, the cookies had an open, coarse crumb and craggy top. Tasters loved the craggy top but not the coarse crumb. When I used baking powder by itself, the cookies had a finer, tighter crumb but the craggy top disappeared. After a dozen rounds of testing, I found that ¼ teaspoon of baking powder mixed with ½ teaspoon of baking soda moderated the coarseness of the crumb without compromising the craggy tops.

Building Big Brown Sugar Flavor

Dark brown sugar was an obvious place to begin our efforts to create a cookie with a bold, nutty, butterscotch flavor. A whole tablespoon of vanilla helped, but everyone in the test kitchen was surprised how much impact browning the butter had on the flavor of these cookies.

DARK BROWN SUGAR — LOTS OF VANILLA — BROWNED BUTTER

PHOTOGRAPHY: CARL TREMBLAY

Browning Around

I had now developed a good cookie, but could I eke out even more brown sugar flavor? Riffing off a classic sugar cookie technique, I tried rolling the dough balls in brown sugar before baking them. The brown sugar clumped in some spots, but overall the crackling sugar exterior added good crunch and flavor. Cutting the brown sugar with granulated sugar solved the clumping problem.

To further ramp up the brown sugar flavor, I tested maple syrup, molasses, and vanilla extract. The maple and molasses were overpowering and masked the cookies' butterscotch flavor, but 1 tablespoon of vanilla extract properly reinforced the brown sugar flavor. A healthy dose of table salt (½ teaspoon) balanced the sweetness and helped accentuate the more interesting flavor components in brown sugar. But my biggest success came from an unlikely refinement.

Browned butter sauces add nutty flavor to delicate fish and pasta dishes. I wondered if browning the melted butter would add the same nutty flavor to my cookies. I was hoping for a modest improvement, but my tasters thought the complex nuttiness added by the browned butter made a substantial difference.

I noticed that cookies made with browned butter were slightly drier than cookies made with melted butter; some of the water in the butter was evaporating when I browned it. Adding an extra 2 tablespoons of butter and browning most (but not all) of the butter restored the chewy texture to my cookies.

TECHNIQUE | CHECKING DONENESS

Achieving the proper texture—crisp at the edges and chewy in the middle—is critical to this recipe. Because the cookies are so dark, it's hard to judge doneness by color. Instead, gently press halfway between the edge and center of the cookie. When it's done, it will form an indent with slight resistance. Check early and err on the side of underdone.

Final Baking Tests

I tried a range of baking temperatures between 300 and 400 degrees Fahrenheit and found that right down the middle (350 degrees) gave me the most consistent results. I had hoped to bake two sheets at the same time, but even with rotating and changing tray positions at different times during baking, I could not get two-tray baking to work. Some of the cookies had the right texture, but others were inexplicably dry. Baking one tray at a time allows for even heat distribution and ensures that every cookie has the same texture.

My final recipe relies on pantry staples and delivers big brown sugar flavor. And although my technique isn't difficult (the cookies can be in the oven after just 15 minutes of work), it did require me to learn some chemistry and physics. After baking 1,200 brown sugar cookies, I think I've earned advanced degrees in both subjects.

Getting the Cookies You Want

By adjusting key ingredients, you can change the texture of any cookie recipe.

IF YOU WANT . . .	ADD . . .	EXPLANATION
Chewy cookies	Melted butter	Butter is 20 percent water. Melting helps water in butter mix with flour to form gluten.
Thin, candy-like cookies	More sugar	Sugar becomes fluid in the oven and helps cookies spread.
Cakey cookies	More eggs	Yolks make cookies rich, and whites cause cookies to puff and dry out.
An open, coarse crumb and craggy top	Baking soda	Baking soda reacts quickly with acidic ingredients (such as brown sugar) to create lots of gas bubbles.
A fine, tight crumb and smooth top	Baking powder	Baking powder works slowly and allows for an even rise.

BROWN SUGAR COOKIES

MAKES 2 DOZEN COOKIES

The most efficient way to bake these cookies is to portion and bake half of the dough. While the first batch is in the oven, the remaining dough can be prepared for baking. Avoid using a nonstick skillet to brown the butter. The dark color of the nonstick coating makes it difficult to gauge when the butter is sufficiently browned. Use fresh brown sugar, as older (read: harder and drier) brown sugar will make the cookies too dry.

- 14 tablespoons (1 ¾ sticks) unsalted butter
- ¼ cup (about 1 ¾ ounces) granulated sugar
- 2 cups (14 ounces) packed dark brown sugar
- 2 cups plus 2 tablespoons (about 10 ½ ounces) unbleached all-purpose flour
- ½ teaspoon baking soda
- ¼ teaspoon baking powder
- ½ teaspoon table salt
- 1 large egg
- 1 large egg yolk
- 1 tablespoon vanilla extract

1. Heat 10 tablespoons butter in 10-inch skillet over medium-high heat until melted, about 2 minutes. Continue to cook, swirling pan constantly until butter is dark golden brown and has nutty aroma, 1 to 3 minutes. Remove skillet from heat and transfer browned butter to large heatproof bowl. Stir remaining 4 tablespoons butter into hot butter to melt; set aside for 15 minutes.

2. Meanwhile, adjust oven rack to middle position and heat oven to 350 degrees. Line 2 large (18 by 12-inch) baking sheets with parchment paper. In shallow baking dish or pie plate, mix granulated sugar and ¼ cup packed brown sugar, rubbing between fingers, until well combined; set aside. Whisk flour, baking soda, and baking powder together in medium bowl; set aside.

3. Add remaining 1¾ cups brown sugar and salt to bowl with cooled butter; mix until no sugar lumps remain, about 30 seconds. Scrape down sides of bowl with rubber spatula; add egg, yolk, and vanilla and mix until fully incorporated, about 30 seconds. Scrape down bowl. Add flour mixture and mix until just combined, about 1 minute. Give dough final stir with rubber spatula to ensure that no flour pockets remain and ingredients are evenly distributed.

4. Divide dough into 24 portions, each about 2 tablespoons, rolling between hands into balls about 1½ inches in diameter. Working in batches, toss balls in reserved sugar mixture to coat and set on prepared baking sheet, spacing them about 2 inches apart, 12 dough balls per sheet. (Smaller baking sheets can be used, but it will take 3 batches.)

5. Bake one sheet at a time until cookies are browned and still puffy and edges have begun to set but centers are still soft (cookies will look raw between cracks and seem underdone; see photo at left), 12 to 14 minutes, rotating baking sheet halfway through baking. Do not overbake.

6. Cool cookies on baking sheet 5 minutes; using wide metal spatula, transfer cookies to wire rack and cool to room temperature.

How to Buy a Good Balsamic Vinegar

Few foods demonstrate such a wide range in price—you can spend $2 or $200 for one bottle—or quality. Our tasters decode the mysteries of balsamico.

BY LISA McMANUS

Traditional aged balsamic vinegar, produced in the Emilia-Romagna region of Italy, can cost $200 per bottle, making even fine French perfume look like a bargain. You can also walk into any supermarket in America and fork over $2 or $3 for a big bottle of balsamic vinegar. What are you really buying in each case? And should you buy either product?

To find out, I purchased 13 balsamic vinegars ranging in price from $60 per ounce to just 18 cents per ounce. Before going into the tasting room, I wanted to figure out why the same product can cost so much and so little. A crash course in recent history helped.

Thirty years ago, almost no one in America had ever heard of (never mind tasted) balsamic vinegar. It was an obscure product made in northern Italy and so highly valued that many families passed along barrels of aged vinegar as part of a wedding dowry. Fast-forward a generation, and balsamic is now the best-selling vinegar in America, accounting for 45 percent of all supermarket vinegar sales. Intoxicated by its big, sweet, caramel flavor, Americans mix it in salad dressing; drizzle it on meat, fish, and vegetables; and add it to sauces, soups, and desserts. Of course, none of this popularity would have been possible if balsamic vinegar had remained a $100-an-ounce extravagance.

A Tale of Two Vinegars

It turns out there are two kinds of balsamic vinegar, and they're made by entirely different processes. The traditional technique takes a minimum of 12 years; the modern industrial method as little as a few hours. The centuries-old traditional way begins with late-harvest grapes (usually white Trebbiano) grown in Emilia-Romagna. The sweet, raisiny juice, skin, and seeds, called grape must, is boiled in open vats until reduced to about half its original volume. This concentrated must is added to the largest of a battery of wooden barrels, which are kept in uninsulated attics in this region where the summers are hot and the winters frosty. The battery comprises barrels of different woods—including oak, cherry, juniper, and mulberry—and sizes. The barrels aren't sealed; they have cloth-covered openings on top to allow evaporation. Each year, before the vinegar maker adds the new must to the largest barrel, he transfers some of its ever-more concentrated contents to the next largest, and so on down the line, before finally removing a liter or two of the oldest vinegar from the smallest barrel. This is traditional balsamic vinegar.

What's more, all this can only happen in two provinces of Emilia-Romagna: Modena and Reggio Emilia, an area designated as a government-protected denomination of origin, or DOP. Each province has its own consortium of experts who approve the balsamic before sealing it in its official 3-ounce bottle (an inverted tulip shape for Reggio Emilia; a ball with a neck for Modena). If you want a guarantee that you're getting true balsamic vinegar, look for the word *tradizionale* and these distinctive bottles—and be prepared to pay dearly.

All those rules are thrown out the window when it comes to commercial balsamic vinegar. With no law defining balsamic vinegar in the United States, manufacturers supply the huge demand any way they can, coloring and sweetening wine vinegar and calling it "balsamic vinegar of Modena." It may not be the real thing, but could I find one worth using until I hit the lottery?

I began by choosing 10 top-selling, nationally available supermarket balsamic vinegars. All were made in Italy, and their prices ranged from $2.39 to $14 a bottle. I tasted them plain, reduced to a glaze for roasted asparagus, and whipped into a vinaigrette. I also tasted a traditional balsamic vinegar for comparison (see "In Search of the Ultimate Drizzling Vinegar," below).

Now here's the bad news: Tasted straight from the bottle, there was no contest between supermarket and traditional balsamics. Even the best of the commercial bunch—while similarly sweet, brown, and viscous—couldn't compete with the complex, rich flavor of true balsamic vinegar. With notes of honey, fig, raisin, caramel, and wood; a smooth, lingering taste; and an aroma like fine port, traditional balsamic is good enough to sip like liqueur.

But the news is not all bad. You don't need to take out a loan to keep balsamic vinegar in your pantry. The test kitchen made vinaigrette with both a 25-year-old traditional balsamic from Reggio Emilia and the top supermarket brand from our taste tests—and frankly, in dressing, the traditional stuff did not justify its price tag. In a pan sauce, most of that fine aroma and depth of flavor was cooked away. The lesson was clear: Don't waste

In Search of the Ultimate Drizzling Vinegar

When it comes to drizzling vinegar over berries or a piece of grilled fish, do you have to shell out hundreds of dollars for a traditional vinegar aged for at least 12 years? To find out, we conducted another tasting that included a traditional balsamic approved and bottled by the Reggio Emilia vinegar consortium; Lucini Gran Riserva (winner of our supermarket tasting); and two high-priced commercial balsamics—the kind sold in gourmet stores.

The not-so-surprising news? The 25-year-old Cavalli Gold Seal Extra Vecchio Aceto Balsamico Tradizionale di Reggio Emilia, at $180 for 3 ounces, topped nearly everyone's list, with tasters waxing poetic about its "pomegranate," "caramel," "smoky" flavor that "coats the tongue" and tastes "amazing." In such rich company, our supermarket winner couldn't compete. Lucini finished last.

But the big surprise was the strong performance of the high-priced commercial vinegars I purchased at gourmet stores. They were nearly as good as the 25-year-old vinegar and cost just $3 to $4 per ounce. Tasters praised the Oliviers & Co. Premium Balsamic Vinegar of Modena ($27 for 8.5 ounces) as "fruity, raisiny, and complex," with notes of "wood, smoke, flowers," and described the Rubio Aceto Balsamico di Modena ($35 for 8.5 ounces) as "floral" and "aromatic." Made with aged grape must and, in the case of the Oliviers & Co., good wine vinegar, these gourmet commercial balsamics are reasonably priced options if you want to drizzle balsamic vinegar over food and don't want to pay a fortune. —L.M.

THE GOOD STUFF
The $60-per-ounce traditional balsamic vinegar (left) was tasters' favorite, but two reasonably priced gourmet brands (right) were nearly as good—and they cost just $3 to $4 per ounce.

your money on pricey traditional balsamic vinegar if you're going to toss it on salad or cook with it. The good stuff works best uncooked, as a drizzle to finish a dish. In vinaigrette or cooked sauce, the sharpness of a supermarket balsamic adds a pleasingly bright contrast to the vinegar's natural sweetness.

The Best Supermarket Option

Among the 10 supermarket vinegars we tasted, some were quite good, others quite awful. Why? An independent lab test supplied part of the answer. Our top choice contained the most sugar; vinegars with the lowest sugar content occupied four of the bottom five spots on the list. This makes sense—the sweeter supermarket vinegars tasted more like the traditional balsamic. It turns out that our tasters also wanted their supermarket balsamic vinegar to be viscous, like traditional balsamics. Lab tests confirmed that higher viscosity tracked with higher rankings.

But sweetness and thickness alone were not enough to guarantee a spot high on our list. The second-sweetest vinegar was also the second most viscous, and it broke the pattern by appearing near the bottom. We were puzzled, until we tested pH levels. This vinegar was the least acidic one tested, and tasters thought it was excessively sweet. So a good supermarket balsamic vinegar must be sweet and thick (like the real deal), but it should also offer a little jolt of acidity.

In the end, we found one supermarket vinegar—Lucini Gran Riserva—that appealed across the board, working well both plain and in the dishes we prepared. The manufacturer told us they use must that is aged in the artisanal way for 10 years, mixed with the company's own wine vinegar. It may have come across as "honey-sweet," but this vinegar offered "a nice compromise between sweet and tangy," with a "nuanced flavor" that came closest to traditional balsamic. I'll admit that it's no 25-year-old consortium-approved marvel. (That bottle is making its way home with me.) But Lucini Gran Riserva also didn't cost $60 per ounce. In fact, at about $2 per ounce, I'll use this supermarket vinegar at home—when my boss isn't paying the bill.

TASTING BALSAMIC VINEGARS

Twenty members of the *Cook's Illustrated* staff tasted 10 supermarket balsamic vinegars three ways: plain, in a vinaigrette with olive oil and mustard, and cooked into a glaze on asparagus topped with Parmesan cheese and olive oil. We measured pH in the test kitchen; higher numbers indicate lower acidity. An independent laboratory analyzed the vinegars' sugar content (in grams per 100 ml) and viscosity (in centipoise, or cP, a unit measure of viscosity in which water is 1 and olive oil 100). The balsamic vinegars are listed in order of preference based on their ranking across the three tastings.

RECOMMENDED

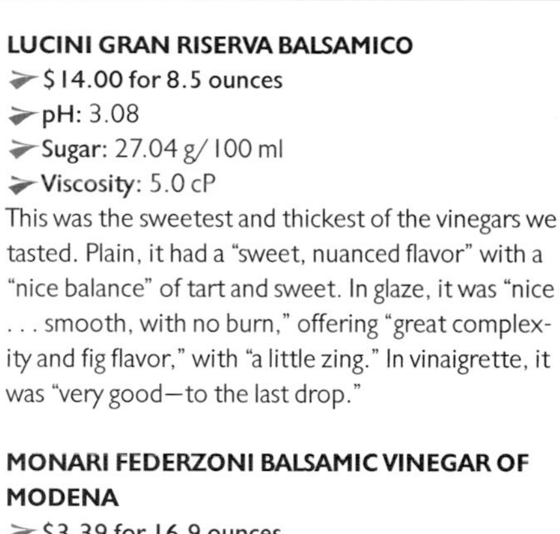

LUCINI GRAN RISERVA BALSAMICO
- **$14.00 for 8.5 ounces**
- **pH:** 3.08
- **Sugar:** 27.04 g/100 ml
- **Viscosity:** 5.0 cP

This was the sweetest and thickest of the vinegars we tasted. Plain, it had a "sweet, nuanced flavor" with a "nice balance" of tart and sweet. In glaze, it was "nice . . . smooth, with no burn," offering "great complexity and fig flavor," with "a little zing." In vinaigrette, it was "very good—to the last drop."

MONARI FEDERZONI BALSAMIC VINEGAR OF MODENA
- **$3.39 for 16.9 ounces**
- **pH:** 3.09
- **Sugar:** 19.71 g/100 ml
- **Viscosity:** 4.0 cP

A true standout in the vinaigrette, where its acidity lent brightness, winning raves as "extremely smooth and tangy." In glaze, it had "full-bodied" taste. Tasted plain, however, it lost points for harshness that "burns the back of your throat."

ORTALLI BALSAMIC VINEGAR OF MODENA
- **$4.69 for 16.9 ounces**
- **pH:** 3.17
- **Sugar:** 20.07 g/100 ml
- **Viscosity:** 4.0 cP

Tasters liked this vinegar's fruity flavor with "musky," "woody," "fermented" tones. In vinaigrette, it was a little too mellow, with tasters calling it "bland" and even a bit "boring." As a glaze, however, it was "very palatable," with "just the right amount of sweetness."

RECOMMENDED WITH RESERVATIONS

STAR BALSAMIC VINEGAR OF MODENA
- **$2.59 for 8.5 ounces**
- **pH:** 2.96
- **Sugar:** 22.36 g/100 ml
- **Viscosity:** 4.6 cP

Plain, it was "lightly fruity," but "too sharp," even "harsh." In glaze, it came across as "candy-like" and "one-dimensional." The tables were turned in the vinaigrette, where its sharpness and sweetness combined to make a "balanced" dressing that was "good, full, and complex."

COLAVITA BALSAMIC VINEGAR OF MODENA
- **$4.49 for 17 ounces**
- **pH:** 3.13
- **Sugar:** 20.71 g/100 ml
- **Viscosity:** 4.0 cP

"Floral and fruity," said a few tasters who favored this vinegar, though most found it humdrum. Plain, it was deemed "not impressive one way or another." In vinaigrette, again, it was "tasty enough, but bland"; in the glaze—you guessed it: "Nothing special."

RECOMMENDED WITH RESERVATIONS (cont.)

RIENZI BALSAMIC VINEGAR OF MODENA
- **$3.39 for 17 ounces**
- **pH:** 3.07
- **Sugar:** 15 g/100 ml
- **Viscosity:** 3.6 cP

Most tasters found this vinegar too tart, even "metallic." In vinaigrette, it was "crisp and light, but harsh." Cooked in glaze, it was more successful, with tasters calling it "complex and delicious, like a good red wine" and finding notes of "dried fruit" with "some heat."

PROGRESSO BALSAMIC VINEGAR
- **$2.39 for 12 ounces**
- **pH:** 3.06
- **Sugar:** 14.38 g/100 ml
- **Viscosity:** 3.6 cP

Tasters deemed this "more tangy than sweet," with a "rough finish." Several complained that it was "thin and astringent." Another wrote, "If it wasn't brown, I'm not sure I'd know it was balsamic." In glaze, it was praised for "oaky flavor."

ALESSI BALSAMIC VINEGAR
- **$3.85 for 8.5 ounces**
- **pH:** 3.20
- **Sugar:** 26.27 g/100 ml
- **Viscosity:** 4.6 cP

"Too sweet" was the consensus on this vinegar, described as "like vanilla on a bad day." In glaze, it was "like candy with red wine vinegar notes." Vinaigrette was "one-dimensional," with "very forward vinegar flavor and not much else."

MODENACETI BALSAMIC VINEGAR OF MODENA
- **$4.49 for 16.9 ounces**
- **pH:** 3.06
- **Sugar:** 14.33 g/100 ml
- **Viscosity:** 3.6 cP

Tasters noted "hints of richness with some nice fruit," but pointed out that it was "too harsh." "Tastes like wine vinegar with food coloring," noted one. Glaze was "too pungent," but vinaigrette was deemed "flavorful."

NOT RECOMMENDED

POMPEIAN BALSAMIC VINEGAR
- **$3.69 for 16 ounces**
- **pH:** 3.09
- **Sugar:** 15 g/100 ml
- **Viscosity:** 3.0 cP

"All harsh hit; no subtlety or character" was the majority opinion. "Bad flavor. I would only color Easter eggs with this," wrote one. "You know the drill: Sip, squint, wince, shudder."

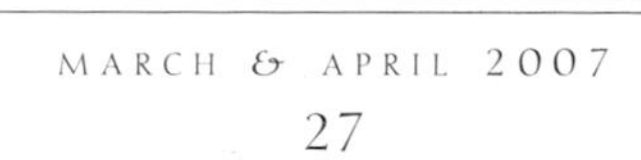

A Better Chef's Knife

In search of an improved mousetrap, we tested seven knives with innovative designs.

⋟ BY LISA McMANUS ⋞

We ask a lot of our chef's knives in the test kitchen. We want one that's versatile enough to handle almost any cutting task, whether it's mincing delicate herbs or cutting through meat and bones. We want a sharp blade that slices easily, without requiring a lot of force. We want a comfortable handle that doesn't hurt our hands or get slippery when wet or greasy.

We've tested 30 knives in recent years (see Cook's Extra, below), and we know what we like. But manufacturers have recently begun offering new designs that challenge many of our assumptions about the classic chef's knife. We've seen unusual handle angles and blades, ergonomic designs for reducing hand fatigue and improving grip, and a variety of other features that promise better handling and easier cutting. Would any of these prove to be a real improvement? We pitted seven innovative knives against the winners of our last comprehensive testing, the Victorinox Fibrox and the Wüsthof Grand Prix. (The Grand Prix has been replaced by the Grand Prix II; we used the new model for this test.)

Handle with Care

A good handle should virtually disappear in your grip, making the knife the oft-cited "extension of your hand." The knives in our lineup featured handles shaped like metal triangles or wedges, handles tilted upward, handles covered with spongy plastic or pebbled polypropylene, and handles with ergonomic bumps and bulges.

Metal handles on the Chroma Type 301 and Furi FX with Coppertail became slippery when wet or greasy. We continued slipping and sliding with the Wüsthof Grand Prix II's pebble-textured polypropylene handle. The slick plastic grip was heavy and uncomfortable, making the knife feel "angular and awkward."

Testers were more impressed by Alton's Angle, a striking knife designed by Food Network star Alton Brown. Instead of continuing straight from the blade, its handle rises in a 10-degree angle to keep knuckles clear of the cutting board. This provided leverage for hard cuts, but there were some complaints about the exaggerated rocking motion during mincing. The rounded, D-shaped grip was comfortable, but the handle's length made it bump above the wrists of some testers. Testers also had mixed feelings about the bright green ergonomic handle on the Sanelli Premana. Although they liked the "squishy" feel of the handle, chickeny hands had trouble gripping this knife.

The one innovative handle that really won testers over was on the Ken Onion knife by Kershaw Shun. (Ken Onion is a well-regarded knife-maker.) The short wooden handle arcs downward, with a pronounced bump on the belly. The metal bolster is cut away to help fingers grip the blade and mercifully extends over the sharp spine to protect the fingers. The wood did not become slippery, and testers reported that the knife felt natural and maneuverable as they worked. A nice touch: The bottom of the bolster stops ½ inch short of the knife's heel, allowing it to pass completely through a sharpening device.

Sticking Point

To keep food from sticking as you slice, designers cut dimples all over the blade surface on the Glestain Indented-Blade Gyutou; used rippled steel on the Ken Onion and Alton's Angle knives; and made the MAC Superior blade super-thin and light, with a roughened strip running just above the cutting edge. In contrast to most of the changes to traditional handle design, we found all of these blade innovations to be successful. These four knives received top scores, winning praise for their agility, ease of use, and precision cutting.

But what made them work, aside from the no-stick blades? One clue came when we realized they were all made by Japanese companies, which are known for their thin-profile knives. We measured the difference in width from spine to blade and found that, indeed, the Japanese knives started out thinner at the spine—as much as 40 percent thinner—than the losing knives and also narrowed less as they neared the cutting edge, with our top Japanese knife, the Glestain, varying by less than 1 millimeter from spine to edge. Why would this matter? As it enters food, your knife can either cut or act as a wedge that pushes the food apart. While a wedge-like blade can be useful for jobs like splitting open a heavy squash, it can rip food and make slicing slower and less precise.

Testers praised the Glestain for its "super-smooth" slicing. Mincing was so efficient it made "parsley almost like dust." It made quick work of raw chicken, onions, and squash, and it stayed sharp throughout testing. The MAC knife, lighter and more utilitarian than the Glestain, was equally sharp and efficient, and testers had high praise for the blades on both Kershaw knives.

So is there a new world order, with Japanese knives taking the lead from traditional Western styles? Not so fast. Our previous test kitchen winner, the very affordable Swiss-made Victorinox Fibrox ($22.95), defeated the best of the innovative newcomers, though just barely. A closer look revealed that, like the Japanese models, its spine starts out thinner and tapers less steeply than other Western knives. This lightweight knife is particularly agile, and the nonslip handle is very comfortable. We found plenty to admire among the top-rated Japanese knives in this test, but we are hard-pressed to pay a premium—sometimes as much as $175—for their innovations.

The $475 Chef's Knife

What do you get when you spend $475 on a chef's knife? You get handmade custom work by Master Bladesmith Bob Kramer of Olympia, Wash. Is this knife markedly better than the competition? Yes. The Kramer knife outperformed every knife we've ever rated. Testers found it exceptionally comfortable, sharp, and agile.

Kramer, a former professional chef, is one of only 100 Master Bladesmiths in America, having passed the American Bladesmith Society's rigorous series of tests. Unlike most bladesmiths, Kramer makes only kitchen cutlery. He uses carbon steel without chromium; this composition makes for a harder, thinner, and sharper blade than most kitchen knives. It will rust and discolor if you don't keep it clean and dry, but the blade is especially sharp and proved durable in our tests.

So why do his knives cost so much? Kramer heat-treats the blades, one at a time, in a seven-step process that takes six hours. He also makes the handles, polishing equatorial burl wood. As for the mass-produced knives made by the competition, Kramer says, "It's like comparing Twinkies to a Grand Marnier soufflé." We agree, but that's one expensive soufflé. –L.M.

HANDMADE PERFECTION
You get what you pay for.

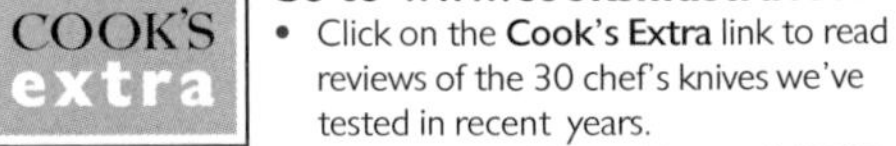

Go to www.cooksillustrated.com

- Click on the **Cook's Extra** link to read reviews of the 30 chef's knives we've tested in recent years.
- Reviews available until August 1, 2007.

RATING INNOVATIVE CHEF'S KNIVES

RATINGS
GOOD: ★★★
FAIR: ★★
POOR: ★

We tested nine chef's knives by butchering whole chickens, chopping butternut squash, mincing parsley, and dicing onions. We also evaluated their comfort and user-friendliness based on feedback from a variety of testers: right- and left-handed cooks; skilled professionals and untrained home cooks; cooks with small hands and cooks with large hands. We rated sharpness and edge retention by cutting ordinary sheets of 8½ by 11-inch paper before and after kitchen tests. Knives are listed in order of preference. See page 32 for sources.

HANDLE: Knives that were comfortable, fit securely, and resisted slipping in wet or greasy hands were preferred.

BLADE: Sharp, agile blades with sufficient curvature were preferred.

KITCHEN TESTS: We cut up whole chickens, chopped butternut squash, minced parsley, and diced onions. Knives were assigned a score for each task, which were averaged to get the overall rating.

EDGE RETENTION: Knives that maintained a sharp edge after testing was completed were preferred.

TESTERS' COMMENTS: General observations, including comfort, balance, perceived solidity and construction quality, and promotion of hand fatigue.

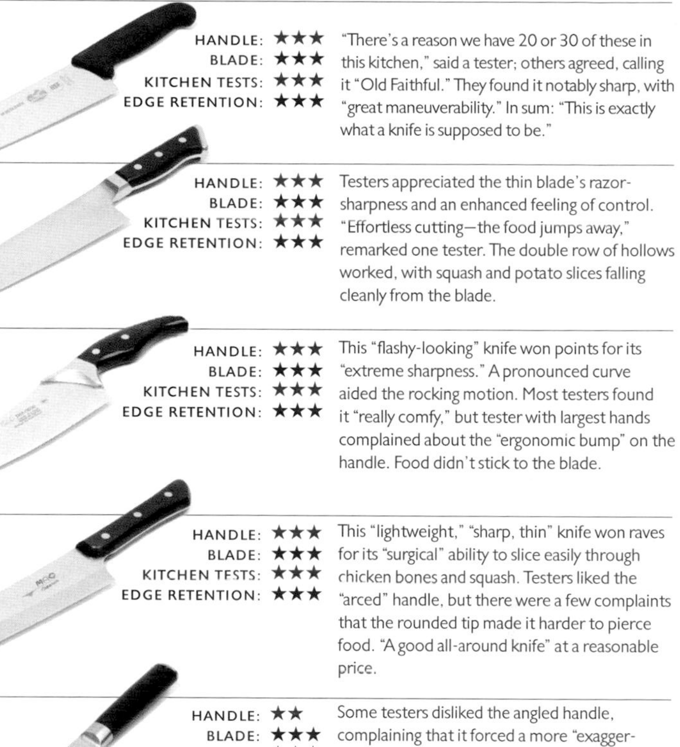

RECOMMENDED	PERFORMANCE	TESTERS' COMMENTS
BEST VALUE **Victorinox Fibrox 8-Inch Chef's Knife** PRICE: $22.95	HANDLE: ★★★ BLADE: ★★★ KITCHEN TESTS: ★★★ EDGE RETENTION: ★★★	"There's a reason we have 20 or 30 of these in this kitchen," said a tester; others agreed, calling it "Old Faithful." They found it notably sharp, with "great maneuverability." In sum: "This is exactly what a knife is supposed to be."
Glestain Indented-Blade 8.2-Inch Gyutou (Chef's Knife) PRICE: $210 INNOVATION: Double row of granton-style oval hollows on one side of blade to minimize resistance between blade and food.	HANDLE: ★★★ BLADE: ★★★ KITCHEN TESTS: ★★★ EDGE RETENTION: ★★★	Testers appreciated the thin blade's razor-sharpness and an enhanced feeling of control. "Effortless cutting—the food jumps away," remarked one tester. The double row of hollows worked, with squash and potato slices falling cleanly from the blade.
Kershaw Shun 8.25-Inch Ken Onion Chef's Knife PRICE: $193.95 INNOVATION: Damascus-look (wavy pattern on metal) blade designed to reduce sticking for faster prep time and less damage to food; curved bolster for comfortable grip.	HANDLE: ★★★ BLADE: ★★★ KITCHEN TESTS: ★★★ EDGE RETENTION: ★★★	This "flashy-looking" knife won points for its "extreme sharpness." A pronounced curve aided the rocking motion. Most testers found it "really comfy," but tester with largest hands complained about the "ergonomic bump" on the handle. Food didn't stick to the blade.
MAC Knives 8-Inch Chef's Knife, Superior PRICE: $54.95 INNOVATION: Ergonomic wooden handle; thin blade with rough strip along edge to release food; rounded tip, hole in blade for hanging.	HANDLE: ★★★ BLADE: ★★★ KITCHEN TESTS: ★★★ EDGE RETENTION: ★★★	This "lightweight," "sharp, thin" knife won raves for its "surgical" ability to slice easily through chicken bones and squash. Testers liked the "arced" handle, but there were a few complaints that the rounded tip made it harder to pierce food. "A good all-around knife" at a reasonable price.
Kershaw Shun 8-Inch Alton's Angle Chef's Knife PRICE: $130.95 INNOVATION: Blade set at 10-degree angle to reduce contact between knuckles and cutting surface; rippled metal blade to reduce sticking of food; D-shaped grip to prevent twisting in hand.	HANDLE: ★★ BLADE: ★★★ KITCHEN TESTS: ★★★ EDGE RETENTION: ★★★	Some testers disliked the angled handle, complaining that it forced a more "exaggerated rocking," while others liked the way it added leverage when cutting squash and bones. Everyone agreed that the blade "cuts beautifully" with "great control," splitting hard squash "like butter."

RECOMMENDED WITH RESERVATIONS	PERFORMANCE	TESTERS' COMMENTS
Sanelli 9.5-Inch Premana Professional Cook's Knife PRICE: $33.92 INNOVATION: Soft antislip ergonomic handle offers support when cook must use force; withstands sudden temperature change and is nonabsorbent and dishwasher-safe.	HANDLE: ★★★ BLADE: ★★★ KITCHEN TESTS: ★★ EDGE RETENTION: ★★	Testers liked the slightly squishy handle, saying "it would be great if it were attached to one of these fancy-pants blades." The lightweight blade did well with onions and parsley but on harder tasks felt "cheap" and "cumbersome" and "had trouble getting through bones."
Wüsthof Grand Prix II 8-Inch Cook's Knife PRICE: $94.95	HANDLE: ★★ BLADE: ★★★ KITCHEN TESTS: ★★ EDGE RETENTION: ★★★	This update performed worse than its well-regarded predecessor. The redesigned handle became very slippery when hands were wet. "Looks more comfortable than it actually is," said one tester. Testers complained that "knife is heavy" and "handle is too long."
Furi 8-Inch Cook's Knife with Coppertail, FX Forged PRICE: $94.95 INNOVATION: Blade, handle, and tang fused into one piece for added strength; wedge-shaped to keep hand from slipping forward; handle surface striated to prevent slippage; soft "coppertail" at end of handle can be filed down to rebalance knife after years of use.	HANDLE: ★★ BLADE: ★★★ KITCHEN TESTS: ★★ EDGE RETENTION: ★★★	According to one tester, this "heavier" knife "seems solid," but "I really had to push through the breast bone." It made "precision cuts" while dicing onion, but parsley seemed crushed. Testers with larger hands liked the handle more than did those with smaller hands, but all complained about slipperiness when hands were wet or greasy.
Chroma 8-Inch Chef's Knife, Type 301 PRICE: $81.95 INNOVATION: Ergonomic knife designed by Porsche (yes, the automaker); metal "pearl" at end of handle for control when cutting; seamless construction.	HANDLE: ★★ BLADE: ★★★ KITCHEN TESTS: ★★ EDGE RETENTION: ★★	Testers were surprised that the "weird-looking" triangular metal handle felt "bizarrely comfortable" in the palm, but all disliked the metal "nub," which "goes exactly where my thumb wants to go and puts pressure on it." One said simply, "It hurts." The knife was "very sharp."

KITCHEN NOTES

BY ERIKA BRUCE

As the Tomato Turns

For our Roasted Tomato Sauce (page 19), we discovered that vine-ripened tomatoes are the best choice at the supermarket. Their bright, uniformly red skin and juicy interior make them more attractive roasting candidates than pale, often mushy globe tomatoes. But despite their good looks, vine-ripened tomatoes taste only so-so and greatly benefit from roasting. Why do these tomatoes look so good but taste so mediocre?

It turns out that "vine-ripened" is a bit of a misnomer. These tomatoes are actually picked when their color starts to turn, a process known as "breaking." The tomatoes are picked when only 10 percent of the fruit has turned from green to red; this ensures that they can be transported without damage. In contrast, supermarket globe tomatoes are picked when still fully green. The longer time on the vine does improve the color and texture of "vine-ripened" tomatoes, but it is not so surprising that these ruby-red specimens don't really taste like in-season, truly vine-ripened tomatoes.

Storing Asparagus

In-season asparagus should be tender, sweet, and flavorful. But sometimes the supermarket pickings are less than stellar—usually because they've been stored too long. We wondered if there was a way to rescue those tired stalks.

We tried refrigerating bunches of asparagus three ways (always beginning by trimming an inch off the ends): wrapped in damp paper towels in an unsealed zipper-lock bag; cut side down in a cup of water with an unsealed bag over the top; and cut side down in a cup of sugar water with an unsealed bag over the top. The next day we steamed and tasted all three samples. Both water-soaked batches were sweeter and juicier than the towel-wrapped one, which had the toughest stalks and a slightly bitter flavor. We couldn't detect any significant difference between the asparagus soaked in sugar water and its plain-water counterpart.

So if you end up with asparagus that needs some sprucing up, trim the ends and store the stalks in cool water overnight—they will wake up the next day refreshed and ready to be eaten.

Picking Your Parmesan

We weren't surprised when tasters found that authentic Parmigiano-Reggiano really makes a difference in our Parmesan-Crusted Chicken Cutlets (page 7). But we noticed that some wedges of Parmesan seemed more flavorful than others, which left us wondering: How can you tell when you're buying good Parmigiano? Tasting the cheese isn't a realistic option at most markets.

Fortunately, when it comes to Parmesan, you can shop with your eyes. Look for pieces that have the rind still attached. To ensure that you're buying a properly aged (at least 18 months old) cheese, examine the condition of the rind. It should be a few shades darker than the straw-colored interior and penetrate about a half-inch deep (younger or improperly aged cheeses will have a paler, thinner rind). And closely scrutinize the center of the cheese. Those small white spots found on many samples are actually good things—they signify the presence of calcium phosphate crystals, which are formed only after the cheese has been aged for the proper amount of time. Also, check for the pin-dot writing—it should spell out some portion of the words Parmigiano-Reggiano.

SHOP WITH YOUR EYES
A thick, dark rind and the presence of white spots (in top sample) are signs of high-quality Parmigiano. A thin, pale rind and a smooth center (bottom sample) are signs of lower quality.

Sizing Up Onions

Many of our recipes call for a specific size of onion, and while we give cup measurements for the resulting chopped onion, that specification doesn't help much when you're shopping. So we grabbed a scale and a ruler and set out to find a shopper-friendly classification system.

Onions, Big and Small

	DIAMETER (Inches)	WEIGHT (Ounces)	VOLUME (Cups Chopped)
LARGE	4	16	2
MEDIUM	2 ½–3	8	1
SMALL	2	4	½

The Other White Vinegar

While shopping for supermarket balsamic vinegars (page 26), we came across a curious newcomer to the market, white balsamic vinegar. Ranging in color from clear to golden, white balsamic is actually a form of white wine vinegar to which grape must (freshly pressed juice, sometimes containing seeds, skin, or pulp) has been added. Although this grape must is sometimes made with the same Trebbiano grapes as real balsamic vinegar, it does not undergo any of the cooking down or caramelizing that is necessary to make authentic balsamic vinegar.

After sampling several brands of white balsamic vinegar, we weren't terribly impressed. Most of them came up short on flavor, having none of the tangy caramel notes characteristic of real balsamic. A few were mildly sweet and fruity, reminding us of white wine vinegar or cider vinegar, which you probably already have in your pantry.

Greater Ginger Grater

In many recipes, we prefer grated ginger to minced. Grated ginger is smooth, while minced is often fibrous. Grated ginger is also about twice as potent as minced. Although our first choice for grating ginger is a ceramic ginger grater (a shallow bowl with a raised center covered with small teeth), we realize that most kitchens do not stock such a tool. A Microplane rasp grater had been our second choice, but recent tests have revealed a better substitute: the small holes of a box grater. The box grater works more like the ceramic grater, leaving behind a smoother, more refined puree of ginger, whereas the Microplane produces a coarser mixture of both fibers and puree. Just be sure to work with a large nub of ginger—and watch your knuckles.

Why Refrigerated Baked Goods Go Stale

Our testing of Olive-Rosemary Bread (page 11) produced plenty of leftover loaves and reminded us once again that bread does not keep well in the refrigerator. In fact, past tests have shown that baked goods such as cookies, cakes, and muffins actually stale faster in the refrigerator than at room temperature. Yet these same items can be stored perfectly well in the freezer for long periods of time. Why doesn't the freezer have the same effect on breads and other baked goods as the refrigerator?

Staling is inevitable over time. In a process known as retrogradation, starch molecules reorganize to form

TECHNIQUE | REMOVING THE BONE

If you wind up purchasing a bone-in pork butt for Chinese Barbecued Pork (page 9), here's how to remove the bone before proceeding with the recipe.

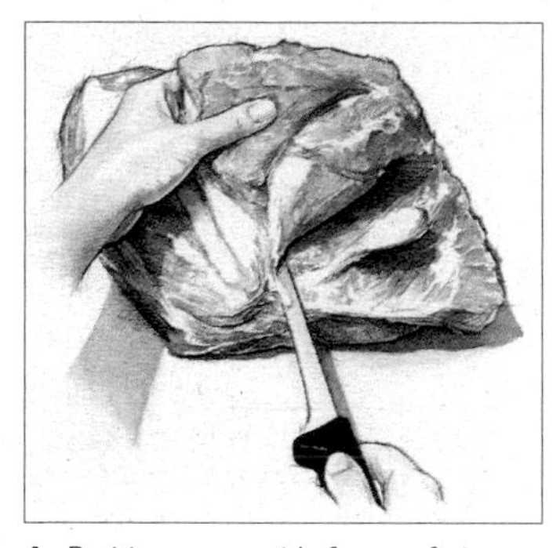

1. Position meat with fat cap facing up and visible part of bone facing you. Insert boning knife just above bone and, with short, sweeping strokes, follow the contour of the bone to separate the meat.

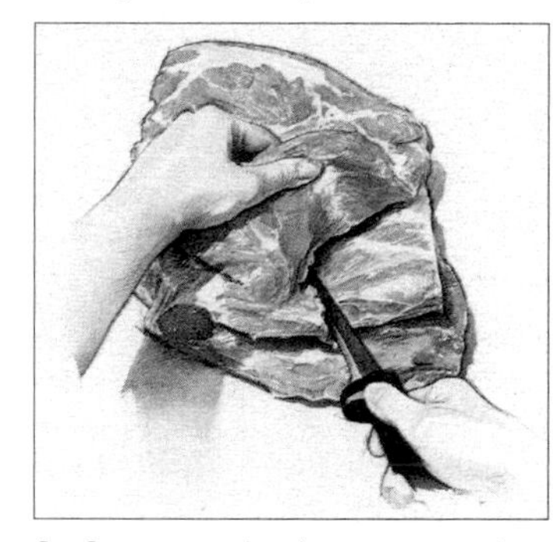

2. Once meat has been separated on top side, flip pork butt over and repeat on other side until bone is completely detached and can be easily removed with your hand.

crystalline structures in the presence of the moisture within the baked goods themselves. This eventually leads to a hard, dry texture at room temperature—no matter how well wrapped the item was during storage. The cooler temperature of the refrigerator speeds up this process, but the freezer actually halts it. The water molecules in the cake or bread freeze, which immobilizes the starch molecules and prevents them from forming the crystalline structures that translate to stale texture.

So if you aren't going to finish that loaf of Olive-Rosemary Bread right away, don't be tempted to pop it into the fridge. Instead, wrap it tightly, first in aluminum foil and then in a large zipper-lock bag, and store it in the freezer. Thaw the bread by taking it out of the plastic bag and placing it on the center rack of a 450-degree oven for 10 to 15 minutes. Then carefully remove the foil (watching for steam) and recrisp the crust in the oven for a few more minutes. Those leftovers will taste as good as fresh-baked bread.

Sugar Bear

We recently came across the terra-cotta Brown Sugar Bear ($3.25), a cuter and cuddlier alternative to our standby method of softening hardened brown sugar with a slice of fresh bread left in the bag of sugar overnight. But does cuter mean better? To find out, we left two bags of brown sugar open overnight to turn the sugar hard and lumpy. Then we put a bread slice into one and the Sugar Bear (which first gets a brief soak in water) into the other and sealed them up in zipper-lock bags. The next day, both bags of sugar were moist and pliable. But the Sugar Bear has one added bonus: Because it is nonperishable, it can be stored indefinitely in the sugar for ongoing insurance against drying.

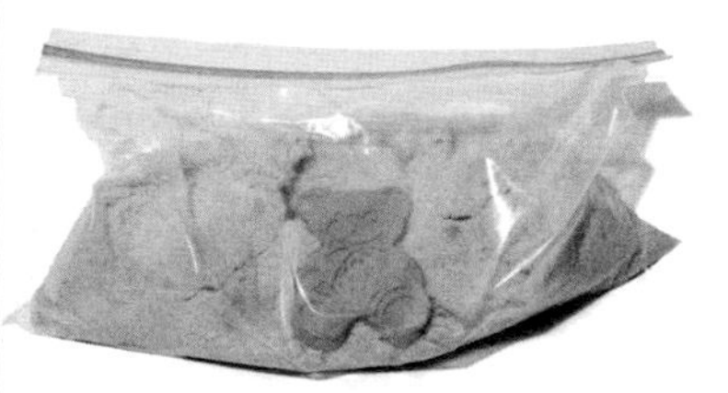

A BEAR IN THE KITCHEN
This clay bear keeps brown sugar soft.

Safer Flipping

While certain expert chefs (or particularly buff individuals) may think nothing of flipping over a piping hot skillet to turn a frittata or Potato Roesti (page 15) out onto a plate, it can be a scary endeavor for mere mortals. A slipped grip or faltering wrist can send dinner crashing to the floor. Fortunately, there is a safer and less intimidating way to turn something over in a large skillet. Working with two plates, slide whatever you wish to flip onto one plate and top it with the other. Then, holding the two plates together, flip them over and slide the inverted food back into the pan to finish cooking.

RECIPE UPDATE

A Wheaty

Several readers requested a whole wheat version of our **Pizza Margherita** (July/August 2006). We wanted to add enough whole wheat flour to impart a hearty wheat flavor but feared that too much would weigh down the distinctively light, thin Margherita crust created by a mix of 1 cup cake flour and 1 ¾ cups all-purpose flour. We started by swapping portions of the all-purpose/cake flour mix with small amounts of whole wheat flour and discovered that mixing in ¾ cup whole wheat flour gave our dough the best balance of nutty wheat flavor. Meanwhile, increasing the cake flour to 1 ½ cups and lowering the all-purpose to ½ cup kept our dough light. But the added heft of the whole wheat flour also caused our dough to rise more slowly. No worries, an extra half-hour of rising does the trick. See Cook's Extra, below, for the recipe.

Chicken ces

Fans of our **Chicken Chasseur** (November/December 2005)—which calls for bone-in, skin-on chicken breasts—wondered if this dish could be made with a combination of dark and white meat. In our original recipe, we brown the chicken pieces in a skillet on the stovetop and finish them on a baking sheet in the oven while we build the sauce in the skillet. We thought it might be as easy as trading in some of the breast meat for thighs, but we ran into a timing issue. White meat is done cooking when the internal temperature reaches 160 degrees, but dark meat needs to cook to 175 degrees. We found that the thighs need only 10 additional minutes. Simply remove the breasts from the oven and transfer them to a serving platter (tented loosely with foil), where they stay plenty warm while the thighs finish cooking. See Cook's Extra, below, for the recipe.

Milk Ch e

A number of chocolate lovers wrote us asking for the best way to make our **Pots de Crème** (November/December 2006) using milk chocolate. It sounded easy enough, but we found out otherwise when we tried simply replacing the bittersweet chocolate in our original recipe with milk chocolate. The resulting custards were cloying, with weak chocolate flavor and a runny texture. The solution turned out to be increasing the amount of chocolate, with 12 ounces of milk chocolate replacing the original 10 ounces of bittersweet. The extra milk chocolate gave the custards the proper stiffness and a more assertive flavor. Bumping the sugar in the custard down from 5 tablespoons to 2 guarded against excessive sweetness. See Cook's Extra, below, for the recipe. —Compiled by Charles Kelsey

Our original recipe made with mi chocolate instead of bittersweet ch late turned out runny (left). Incre the amount of milk chocolate help pots de crème to set properly (rig

IF YOU HAVE A QUESTION about a recipe, let us know. Send your inquiry, name, address, and daytime telephone number to Recipe Update, Cook's Illustrated, P.O. Box 470589, Brookline, MA 02447, or write to recipeupdate@americastestkitchen.com.

Go to www.cooksillustrated.com
Click on the **Cook's Extra** link for our recipes for **Whole Wheat Pizza Margherita, Chicken Chasseur with White and Dark Meat,** and **Milk Chocolate Pots de Crème.**
Recipes available until August 1, 2007.

ILLUSTRATION: RANDY GLASS

EQUIPMENT CORNER

BY ELIZABETH BOMZE

EQUIPMENT UPDATE: **Rasp Graters**

The Microplane has long been the test kitchen's first choice for grating Parmesan and zesting citrus fruit. Its rasp-like design was unique—until recently. We put three new rasp-style graters through their paces to see how they compare.

The results? The Kuhn Rikon required massive brute strength to produce even a few wisps of grated Parmesan. The Zyliss had the opposite problem—it gripped so well that it dug into the pith of the lemon. The Cuisipro felt flimsy and lacked a handle, which made it difficult to use. The Microplane 8.5-inch Grater/Zester ($12.95) breezed through all four tasks, producing piles of cheese, chocolate, zest, and ginger with minimal effort.

ANY WAY YOU GRATE IT
Microplane's razor sharp rasp grater still shreds the competition.

FOR MUSCLE-MEN ONLY
The Kuhn Rikon required massive brute force for paltry results.

EQUIPMENT UPDATE: **Potato Mashers**

After mashing thousands of pounds of potatoes over the years, we've concluded that disk-faced potato mashers work better than those with wavy wire loops. That's why we were intrigued when we ran across a new masher with two disks. Could two disks be better than one? Unfortunately, the double disks on the spring-loaded MIU France Double Disc Stainless Steel Potato Masher ($14.99) hurt rather than helped, producing potatoes that looked like they were pounded erratically with the palm of a hand. We'll stick with the single disk on our previous test kitchen winner, the WMF Profi Plus Stainless Steel Potato Masher ($17.99).

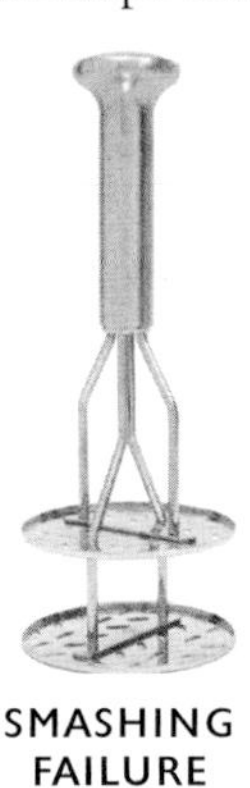

SMASHING FAILURE
This new potato masher was a dud.

DO YOU REALLY NEED THIS?
Microwave Popcorn Poppers

Bags of microwave popcorn are convenient, but the quality is mediocre. Here's how to spend fewer dollars and barely a minute longer to get a better-tasting result: Pour plain kernels into a microwave popcorn popper and press "start" on your microwave. We tested four all-plastic (glass can shatter and metal can spark) popcorn poppers.

After several batches, we realized the simplest popper style was best. Ashy fumes and grease spewed from the Miles Kimball ($7.99) "self-buttering" bowl, while the complicated Presto PowerPop ($18.10) demanded disposable (read: need-to-buy-more) cardboard disks. The Back to Basics and NordicWare poppers (both about $10) yielded fluffy popcorn, with few stragglers at the bottom, and were simple to clean.

EQUIPMENT UPDATE:
Goldtouch Cookie Sheet

In our testing of cookie sheets two years ago, we found that dark nonstick surfaces overbrowned cookies. We recommended a light-colored cookie sheet made by Vollrath ($24.95). For nonstick protection, we suggested lining this pan with parchment paper. But when we saw Williams-Sonoma's new light-colored nonstick Goldtouch pan ($26.95), we wondered if we could put our parchment away. To our surprise, batch after batch of lace cookies, butter cookies, and cream biscuits overbaked on the Goldtouch cookie sheet, even at the shortest recommended cooking time. And when we pulled the baked goods out early (before they looked too browned), they tasted dry. It turns out that a nonstick surface (whether light or dark) is highly water-repellent and speeds evaporation by driving moisture away, which can make cookies and biscuits too dry. We still recommend the light-colored Vollrath pan—and a roll of parchment paper.

NEW PRODUCT: **Nonskid Cutting Board**

We've used nonskid shelf liners to anchor our cutting boards for years in the test kitchen. The advent of the nonskid cutting board seemed long overdue. With dozens of counter-gripping rubber feet, the Architec Gripper Non-Slip Cutting Board ($14.95) combines the convenience of a skid-proof base with a knife blade–friendly polypropylene surface that readily cleans up in the dishwasher.

TOP

BOTTOM

GET A GRIP
The Architec Non-Slip Cutting Board ($14.95) stays anchored to the counter for every task.

Sources

The following are mail-order sources for items recommended in this issue. Prices were current at press time and do not include shipping. Contact companies to confirm information or visit www.cooksillustrated.com for updates.

Page 7: BOX GRATER
- Cuisipro Accutec Box Grater: $35.99, item #500170, Cooking.com (800-663-8810, www.cooking.com).

Page 11: BENCH SCRAPER
- OXO Good Grips Stainless Steel Multi-Purpose Scraper & Chopper: $7.99, item #73281, OXO (800-545-4411, www.oxo.com).

Page 13: LADLE
- Rösle Ladle: $23.95, item #10008, Chef's Resource (866-765-2433, www.chefsresource.com).

Page 26: PREMIUM BALSAMIC VINEGARS
- Cavalli Gold Seal Extra Vecchio Aceto Balsamico Tradizionale di Reggio Emilia: $180 for 3.3 fl. oz., Salumeria Italiana (800-400-5916, www.salumeriaitaliana.com).
- Rubio Aceto Balsamico di Modena: $35 for 8.5 fl. oz., Salumeria Italiana.
- Oliviers & Co. Premium Balsamic Vinegar of Modena: $27 for 8.5 fl. oz., item #7426, Oliviers & Co. (877-828-6620, www.oliviersandco.com).

Page 27: BALSAMIC VINEGAR
- Lucini Gran Riserva Balsamic Vinegar: $14 for 8.5 fl. oz., Specialty Food America! Inc. (888-881-1633, www.specialtyfoodamerica.com).

Page 29: CHEF'S KNIVES
- Victorinox Fibrox Chef's Knife: 8 inches: $22.95, item #40520, Cutlery and More (800-650-9866, www.cutleryandmore.com).
- Chef's Knife, European Line, 8 inches: $475, Kramer Knives (360-455-4357, www.kramerknives.com).

Page 31: BROWN SUGAR BEAR
- Brown Sugar Bear: $3.25, item #BSB, Sugar Bears Inc. (403-278-9947, www.sugarbearsinc.com).

Page 32: RASP GRATER
- Microplane 8.5-Inch Grater/Zester: $12.95, item #148189, Cooking.com.

Page 32: POTATO MASHER
- WMF Profi Plus 11 1/4-Inch Stainless Steel Potato Masher: $17.99, item #1871386030, Amazon.com.

Page 32: POPCORN POPPERS
- Back to Basics Microwave Popcorn Popper: $9.99, item #PCMP, The Mending Shed (800-339-9297, www.mendingshed.com).
- NordicWare Corn Popper: $10.50, item #60120, NordicWare (877-466-7342, www.nordicware.com).

Page 32: COOKIE SHEET
- Vollrath Cookie Sheet: $24.95, item #68085, Chef's Resource.

Page 32: NONSKID CUTTING BOARD
- Architec Gripper Non-Slip Cutting Board: $14.95, item #392076, Cooking.com.

RECIPES

March & April 2007

New Recipes Available on the Web

Go to www.cooksillustrated.com and click on the **Cook's Extra** link for the following recipes, available free until August 1, 2007.

Roasted Tomato Sauce, 19

Pan-Roasted Asparagus, 20

Lemon Layer Cake, 23

Garlicky Shrimp with Bread Crumbs, 21

Parmesan-Crusted Chicken Cutlets, 7

Olive-Rosemary Bread, 11

Garlic-Potato Soup, 13

Brown Sugar Cookies, 25

Potato Roesti, 15

Chinese Barbecued Pork, 9

PHOTOGRAPHY: CARL TREMBLAY, STYLING: MARIE PIRAINO

Crottin
de Champcol
Tomme
de Savoie
Brebis
Camembert
Valençay
Roquefort
Comté
Morbier
Brie
de Meaux
Epoisses
St. Agur
FRENCH CHEESES

NUMBER EIGHTY-SIX

MAY & JUNE 2007

How to Cook Steaks
New Oven-to-Skillet Method

Italian Skillet Chicken

Four-Cheese Lasagna
Smooth & Creamy, Not Greasy

Essential Gadgets
18 Tools You Should Own

Vegetable Curry
Secrets to Big Flavor Fast

Perfecting Crumb Cake

Tasting Crushed Tomatoes

Steak Marinades That Work
Rating $200 Toaster Ovens
Better Bran Muffins
Quick BBQ Ribs
Blackened Grilled Fish
Asparagus-Stuffed Omelets

www.cooksillustrated.com
$5.95 U.S./$6.95 CANADA

CONTENTS

May & June 2007

COOK'S ONLINE

Go to **www.cooksillustrated.com** to access all recipes from *Cook's Illustrated* since 1993 as well as updated tastings and testings. Watch videos of all the recipes in this issue and special reports on the crushed tomato taste test and toaster oven testing.

LATIN AMERICAN VEGETABLES Technically bananas, savory plantains can be prepared like potatoes. Chayote (or vegetable pear) has firm flesh and can be eaten raw in salads or cooked like squash. Even when cooked, jicama retains its crisp texture. Under their papery husks, tomatillos have firm, tart flesh that's used in sauces or soups. Nopales are the leaves or paddles of the prickly pear cactus. When boiled, their texture becomes similar to okra. Yuca (or cassava) is a root with a dark covering and a crisp, white interior. When cooked, its glutinous flesh turns almost translucent. The mild-tasting batata is a member of the sweet potato family and can be used in similar ways. Yams are tubers that resemble a waxy potato when cooked. Taro root has a dense, white flesh that tastes of coconut, chestnut, and potato. Calabaza is a pumpkin that's best used in soups, stews, or purees.

BACK COVER: *(Latin American Vegetables)*: John Burgoyne

FRONT COVER PAINTING: *Cucumbers* by Elizabeth Brandon. For more information, go to www.ElizabethBrandon.com.

For list rental information, contact: Specialists Marketing Services, Inc., 1200 Harbor Blvd., 9th Floor, Weehawken, NJ 07087; 201-865-5800.
Editorial Office: 17 Station St., Brookline, MA 02445; 617-232-1000; fax 617-232-1572. Subscription inquiries, call 800-526-8442.
Postmaster: Send all new orders, subscription inquiries, and change-of-address notices to Cook's Illustrated, P.O. Box 7446, Red Oak, IA 51591-0446.

COOK'S ILLUSTRATED
www.cooksillustrated.com
HOME OF AMERICA'S TEST KITCHEN

PRINTED IN THE USA

CHARLES BENTLEY, JR.

The road that travels by the Bentley farmhouse turns slightly to the left and then goes straight past the hayfields, down and over Tidd Brook, through the woods spotted with sunken hunting camps, and then up Red Mountain, where, on a fall day, the sun tries to force its way down through a stand of pine, spilling over the dead lower branches on its way to the forest floor. As a kid, Charlie started his walk to school on that road, going across the Green River and then up the valley past Hurd's General Store, whereas the Woodcocks—young Fred, Norman, Mary, and Charlotte—used to take the upper road that came out by Willie Lomberg's. When he was a young man, Charlie's father once stood by that road for a photograph, formally erect behind his parents, both dressed for church and sitting in ladder-back chairs, the farmhouse occupying the background much as it does today—not dressed up for visitors but comfortable in its purpose.

A visitor to town might remark on the old Methodist church, the renovated schoolhouse, or even the two-holer out back. And some of us remember the days when Charlie was still milking in the large red barn down on Route 313 where he kept his herd; we recall him harvesting corn with a knife and hooking teams up to a stone boat to practice for a horse draw; we envision Floyd Bentley cutting hay with a team, the clicking of the gears and the smell of cut timothy a balm of sorts even 40 years later. Of course, Charlie remembers the day in 1952 (the same year the schoolhouse was closed for lack of indoor plumbing) when the first baler showed up in Sandgate, how to use a side-hill plough, the day Uncle Fred mowed hay when you could spot icicles along the brook, the benefits of a hay loader, and the dance hall on Saturday nights, when Henry Squires had to keep order.

A curious fact about Charlie, however, is that he recalls the teams most. The old pair of sorrels, Jack and Jen, Pete and Dan, a roan and a gray, and Betsy and Debbie—Betsy was an inexperienced two-year-old, so he hitched her up with Debbie to show her the ropes. Charlie once told me why he preferred horses to tractors: "You always know that a horse is going to start on a cold morning." But, as Charlie puts it, "If they get loose once, they get a little foolish." One team took off in the field by Sam Pike's because the whippletree broke, and another time, the pull snapped as Charlie was using a dump rake on the bank by the church. He went over, holding desperately to the reins, but the horses stood fast until someone got hold of their heads. But his fondness for horses remains. If you are sharp-eyed during a visit to the Bentley homestead, you might notice a second-prize ribbon from the 1961 Bondville Fair in the 2800 Class or a faded envelope with a bit of Dan's hair. When Floyd died, Duke and Dan were never worked as a team again.

Christopher Kimball

The world is still filled with old farmers, old farmhouses, and old stories. But anyone expecting a trip down memory lane during a visit with Charlie might well be disappointed. It isn't about yesterday or tomorrow, but about the chance of rain this afternoon, or whether the corn shucker is working, or whether one should start up the arch in the saphouse. A lifetime of being useful changes a person. You stop talking about things that don't matter.

I am often asked what I have learned from Charlie Bentley. I've learned to not change gears when running a tractor downhill, to not use a milker on a cow with a sore teat, and how to throw a bale of hay to the top of a high load. I've learned how to move a horse around (push him in the direction opposite from where you want him to go), that knowing a place is better than always going somewhere new, and that when you shake hands with someone you don't know, make sure that they aren't holding on to an electric fence with the other hand. I've learned to appreciate the ground beneath my feet more than the view, the potatoes in the root cellar rather than the promise of next year's crop, and why you should never get into a fight that you aren't prepared to win. I've also learned at least a dozen things to do with a short stretch of baling twine, how to outrun a mad cow, and why a good dog is often worth two men.

I've also had the privilege of learning by watching. I've seen Charlie fix tractors with no more than a hammer and pliers. I have seen hayfields that seemed to stretch to the horizon but that got baled and picked before sunset. I have been in the woods, hopelessly searching in the dark, seeking wayward cows that, to my surprise, were quickly found by his more experienced eyes and ears.

I have also been taught the virtues of being common. Charlie doesn't drive a new pickup, tell others what to do with their property (although he did wonder why I didn't design my barn with a gambrel roof), complain about neighbors, or comment on the selection of hymns at the Methodist church. Not having to worry about self-expression leaves one with time for walking down River Road to take a drink at the spring that trickles down the embankment or to listen to the thumping mating call of partridges in the spring. Being common leaves time to appreciate the uncommon.

If someone really persisted, I would add that the biggest lesson learned was one of heart, not history. Of soldiering on and not yielding. Of getting up after being knocked down and doing it all over again. It is not a lesson of age or of youth. It is simply the lesson of Charlie Bentley.

We are not now that strength which in old days
Moved earth and heaven; that which we are,
we are; One equal temper of heroic hearts,
Made weak by time and fate, but strong in will
To strive, to seek, to find, and not to yield.

—*Alfred Lord Tennyson,* "Ulysses"

COOK'S ILLUSTRATED Magazine
Cook's Illustrated magazine (ISSN 1068-2821), number 86, is published bimonthly by Boston Common Press Limited Partnership, 17 Station St., Brookline, MA 02445. Copyright 2007 Boston Common Press Limited Partnership. Periodicals postage paid at Boston, Mass., and additional mailing offices USPS #012487. Publications Mail Agreement No. 40020778. Return undeliverable Canadian addresses to P.O. Box 875, Station A, Windsor, Ontario N9A 6P2. POSTMASTER: Send address changes to Cook's Illustrated, P.O. Box 7446, Red Oak, IA 51591-0446. For subscription and gift subscription orders, subscription inquiries, or change-of-address notices, call 800-526-8442 in the U.S. or 515-247-7571 from outside the U.S., or write us at Cook's Illustrated, P.O. Box 7446, Red Oak, IA 51591-0446.

ILLUSTRATION: RANDY GLASS

NOTES FROM READERS

COMPILED BY SANDRA WU

Turning Bread into Muffins

Is there a rule of thumb to follow for converting quick breads into muffins? For instance, can I convert a banana bread recipe into banana muffins?

DARLENE CHRISTOPHER
ALEXANDRIA, VA.

➢To answer your question, we chose four quick bread recipes with different ratios of liquid to dry ingredients and baked them as muffins: corn bread, banana bread, cranberry-nut bread, and date-nut bread. We didn't alter the batters and used them to fill standard 12-cup muffin tins (sprayed with nonstick cooking spray) three-quarters full.

We baked each batch on the middle rack of an oven heated to the temperature specified in the original bread recipe until a skewer inserted into the middle of a muffin came out with a few crumbs attached. With each recipe, the muffins required a little less than half the baking time of the original loaf version, and we had pretty good results across the board.

So the next time you want to transform your favorite quick bread into a batch of muffins, go ahead. Simply fill your muffin cups three-quarters full, bake the muffins for a few minutes less than half the time of the original recipe (checking several minutes early to prevent over-baking), and let them cool 5 to 10 minutes in the pan before turning them out onto a wire rack to cool completely.

MUFFIN METAMORPHOSIS
Quick breads make even quicker muffins.

Low-Sodium Salt

What do you think about Morton Lite Salt Mixture, which has half the sodium of table salt?

DAMIAN HANIEWICZ
DENVER, COLO.

➢Morton Lite Salt Mixture, introduced in 1973, is a combination of salt (sodium chloride), potassium chloride, potassium iodide, and several additional compounds (calcium silicate, magnesium carbonate, and dextrose) that make it free-flowing. According to the product's label, this "lite" salt can be used measure for measure in place of regular salt to cook, bake, or season at the table. Compared with regular salt, which has 590 mg of sodium per ¼ teaspoon, Morton Lite Salt contains only 290 mg sodium, or about half as much.

MORTON LITE SALT MIXTURE
Is this "lite" product worth its salt?

The key ingredient in Morton Lite Salt—potassium chloride—is closely related to sodium chloride. Both cause the production of saliva and enhance flavor. Sodium chloride is considered to have a pure salty taste, while potassium chloride is said to have a slightly bitter edge. Potassium chloride is not sold for commercial use in its pure form.

We compared Morton Lite Salt Mixture with table salt in several applications: roast chicken (brined), yellow cake, zucchini (salted, drained, rinsed, and sautéed), and scrambled eggs. When it came to the cake, zucchini, and scrambled eggs, tasters found it difficult to distinguish between the two salts and didn't notice any bitterness. In the brined roast chicken, however, tasters preferred the saltier, fuller flavor lent by table salt.

So if you're watching your sodium intake, give "lite" salt a try. Otherwise, stick to regular table salt, which costs only $0.59 for a 26-ounce canister, compared with $1.50 for an 11-ounce shaker jar of Morton Lite Salt Mixture.

Storing Leftover Pie

What's the best way to store leftover cream or fruit pie: on the counter or in the refrigerator?

NANCY PETERSON
LINCOLN, CALIF.

➢Because of their high dairy content, leftover custard- and cream-filled pies must be wrapped tightly in plastic wrap and stored in the refrigerator. They will generally last for a day or two stored this way. Whipped cream–topped pies do not store well, because the whipped cream breaks down and begins to weep within hours. If you're planning on serving only a few slices from a whipped cream–topped pie, top each slice individually with whipped cream and save the rest of the pie for later.

Double-crust and lattice-topped fruit pies such as apple, peach, blueberry, or cherry can be safely stored at room temperature because of their high sugar content and acidity, which retard the growth of bacteria. To find out if fruit pies fare better when refrigerated or stored at room temperature, we held a baking marathon, then stored pies both ways. In all cases, refrigeration turned the crisp crusts of the fruit pies gummy. This is a result of retrogradation, or the process by which the structure of the starch changes and becomes stale. So when it comes to fruit pies, storing at room temperature is the way to go. Wrapped well in foil, pies made with cooked fruit will last up to two days.

Note that pies made with fresh, uncooked fruit, such as strawberry pies, are a different story. These delicate pies often contain gelatin and should be stored in the refrigerator for no more than one day.

Turning Down the Heat

I have seen numerous references to adding raw potato to dishes that are too salty, but I have never seen anything written about how to reduce the heat of dishes that are too spicy. Any suggestions?

G.W. DECKER
SANTA BARBARA, CALIF.

➢First off, adding potatoes to oversalted foods simply doesn't work. But there is a way to tame the heat in foods that are too spicy: adding an ingredient that is on the opposite end of the flavor spectrum. Depending on the recipe, you can add a fat (such as butter, cream, sour cream, cheese, or oil) or a sweetener (such as sugar, honey, or maple syrup) to counteract the offending ingredient. Obviously, it wouldn't make sense to add cheese to a too-spicy Thai beef stir-fry, so use your best judgment.

We made five-alarm chili and salsa and attempted to remedy the situation. To bring down the heat of the chili, we added a small amount of sugar to one batch and served another with sour cream. Both worked, but the sour cream had a slightly more pronounced cooling effect. For the salsa, we added a small amount of sugar to one batch and olive oil to another. Both ingredients took the heat level down a notch, with neither being noticeably more successful.

While fat and sugar can balance out flavors, keep in mind that prevention is the best medicine: Whenever possible, begin with just a portion of the spice or chiles called for in a recipe and add more to taste later on.

WHAT IS IT?

I recently came across this tool while cleaning out my kitchen cabinets. It has no markings or brand labels, and no one seems to know what it is. I'm really stumped and would love your input.

MARY SCHEU, ST. PAUL, MINN.

This 5-inch-tall, stainless-steel contraption with a round, 4-inch-diameter rubber base resembles an improperly assembled hand-held mixer. But rather than mixing, whipping, or beating, it has an entirely different purpose: grating coconut. This device comes from India and is used to remove the firm, white flesh from fresh coconuts.

This nifty gadget is used to grate fresh coconut.

To use the grater, hold it with one hand to make sure the suction-cup base sits flush against the work surface. Next, turn the small metal foot toward you to fix the grater in place while you work. Place a shallow bowl or plate beneath the serrated blade, hold the cut side of a split coconut against the blade, and crank the handle, slowly turning the coconut as the flesh is removed. When you're finished, you'll be left with a pile of small, fluffy flakes of coconut.

Double-Strength Vanilla

I have seen double-strength vanilla for sale at specialty stores. Is it better than regular single-strength vanilla extract?

MICHAEL JURLANDO
PROSPECT, KY.

➢Most supermarket vanilla extracts are single-strength (a term used to describe the concentration of vanilla flavor) and must be made from 13.35 ounces of vanilla beans per gallon of liquid solvent, according to U.S. Food and Drug Administration standards. Double-strength, or two-fold, vanilla extract, which can be purchased from specialty stores and mail-order spice houses, is adjusted in the final stages of the manufacturing process to increase the "extractive matter" to 26.70 ounces (13.35 ounces doubled).

We purchased a bottle of double-strength vanilla extract from Penzeys Spices and tried it two ways—using half the amount of vanilla the recipe called for in one batch and using the full amount in another—in the following recipes: yellow cupcakes, vanilla frosting, pastry cream, and chocolate chip cookies. As a control, we also made the recipes using single-strength vanilla extract.

PENZEYS DOUBLE-STRENGTH VANILLA
Double the strength, double the flavor?

The differences in the uncooked applications—the frosting and pastry cream—were noticeable. While the samples that used the full amount of double-strength vanilla definitely had a more pronounced vanilla flavor, they didn't necessarily have a better flavor. In fact, several tasters found them too strong, citing "medicinal" or "alcohol" notes. When we compared single-strength versus halved double-strength vanilla, most tasters preferred the single-strength versions. In the baked goods, the differences were more difficult to detect. Some tasters appreciated the stronger vanilla flavor of the cupcakes that contained the full amount of double-strength vanilla. In contrast, several tasters complained that the double-strength vanilla was "overkill" in the cookies. In general, the single-strength vanilla was again preferred over the halved double-strength vanilla.

So if you have a bottle of double-strength vanilla on hand, use half the amount called for in most recipes, especially those in which the vanilla is stirred in raw. But don't run out and buy a bottle: Even though you only use half as much, a typical 4-ounce bottle costs about three times as much as single-strength supermarket vanilla.

"When Butter Stops Foaming"

Many of your recipes call for adding the ingredients to the skillet after the butter stops foaming. Why do you have to wait?

SUSAN WONG
HONOLULU, HAWAII

➢The simple answer is that it's an easy visual cue as to when the melted butter is ready for cooking. To be more specific, when the foaming stops, it's an indication that all the water in the butter (which is about 80 percent fat and 20 percent water) has evaporated. Melted butter starts out near 212 degrees, but as the water cooks off and the foaming subsides, the fat in the pan will continue to get hotter, starting to smoke when it reaches 250 degrees. Sautéing food in butter is most successful when the fat is at a higher temperature, which can only be reached when most of the water has been removed. Additionally, cooking food in the presence of water could produce unwanted steamed or boiled flavors rather than the dry-heat flavors and browning produced by straight-up fat.

Blending Soup Safely

I enjoy pureed soups but am wary of making them because the hot liquid occasionally explodes from the blender jar. Why does this happen?

SUE DENNEN
MANSFIELD, MASS.

➢Using a blender to make pureed vegetable soup makes perfect sense if you don't have an immersion blender. But blending hot soup can be dangerous if the blender jar is too full. As the blades rotate, the liquid in the jar forms a vortex, moving higher and higher up the sides of the jar. Hot liquids are generally thinner and less viscous than cold liquids, therefore forming a deeper vortex. If the jar is overfilled, the soup can move all the way to the top of the blender, forcing the top to pop off and causing the soup to fly everywhere. In addition, as hot liquids are blended, the steam trapped inside the liquid expands, making an explosion more likely. To make sure you don't get burned, let the soup cool down for 5 minutes or so before blending so it emits less steam, don't fill the blender jar past the halfway point, and hold the lid in place with a folded kitchen towel.

Frozen versus Fresh Herbs

While in my local grocery store I saw frozen basil, parsley, cilantro, and dill wrapped in small blister packs. How do they stand up to fresh herbs?

LIZ WOLLMAN
BROOKLYN, N.Y.

➢We found Dorot frozen herbs—stabilized with water, soybean oil, starch, dextrose, and salt—at the supermarket, packaged in small ice cube tray–like containers. According to the label, one cube is equivalent to 1 teaspoon of fresh chopped herbs. We tried them in six applications. Other than marinara sauce, tasters overwhelmingly preferred fresh herbs to their frozen counterparts. It is possible, however, to make decent homemade frozen herb cubes from parsley, sage, rosemary, or thyme. Place the chopped herbs in an ice cube tray, cover them with water, and freeze.

SEND US YOUR QUESTIONS We will provide a complimentary one-year subscription for each letter we print. Send your inquiry, name, address, and daytime telephone number to Notes from Readers, Cook's Illustrated, P.O. Box 470589, Brookline, MA 02447, or to notesfromreaders@americastestkitchen.com.

Quick Tips

COMPILED BY DAVID PAZMIÑO

Degreasing Stock

Spooning fat off of cooled stocks or broths can be tricky if the fat layer is thin and breaks into tiny pieces. Rosalie Blaze of San Francisco, Calif., uses cheesecloth to solve the problem.

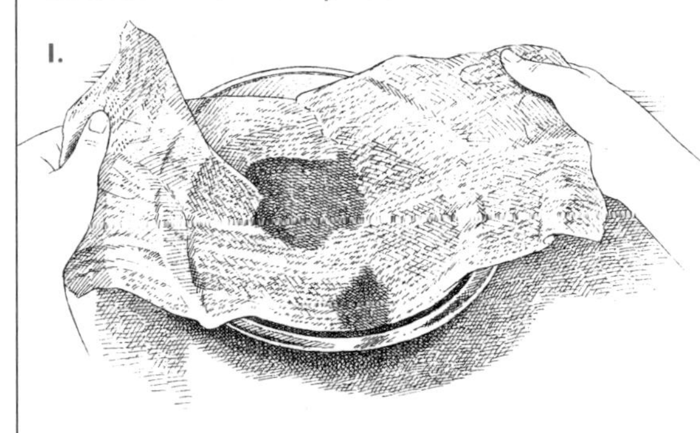

1.

2.

1. Cut a single layer of cheesecloth (or paper towel) to fit over the container of cooling stock or broth, with enough excess to drape over the sides. Place the cheesecloth so that it lies directly on top of the liquid and doesn't sink more than 1/4 inch below the surface.
2. Refrigerate. Gather the edges of the cheesecloth and carefully lift to remove the hardened fat.

Easy Garlic Prep

Smashing a garlic clove with the flat side of a knife is a great way to remove the peel if you intend to mince the clove but not if you intend to slice it. John Turati of Deerfield, Mass., has come up with a method that allows for slicing.

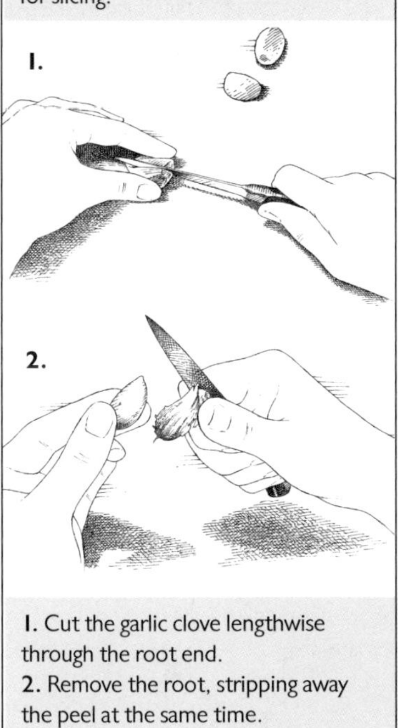

1.

2.

1. Cut the garlic clove lengthwise through the root end.
2. Remove the root, stripping away the peel at the same time.

Frying Oil Disposal

Instead of pouring a small amount of used frying oil into an empty bottle or can, Eda Burne of Hartsdale, N.Y., sops up the mess with the leftover flour, egg, and bread crumbs that were used to coat pan-fried foods.

1.

2.

1. Off heat, add leftover flour, egg, and bread crumbs to the hot oil; stir.
2. Once the oil has been absorbed by the flour mixture, cool and discard.

Dealing with Broken Corks

When you break a cork while opening a bottle of wine, little chunks tend to end up in each serving. Instead of fishing cork bits out of each glass with a spoon, Sorcha Byrne of San Francisco, Calif., reaches for a piece of cheesecloth and a rubber band.

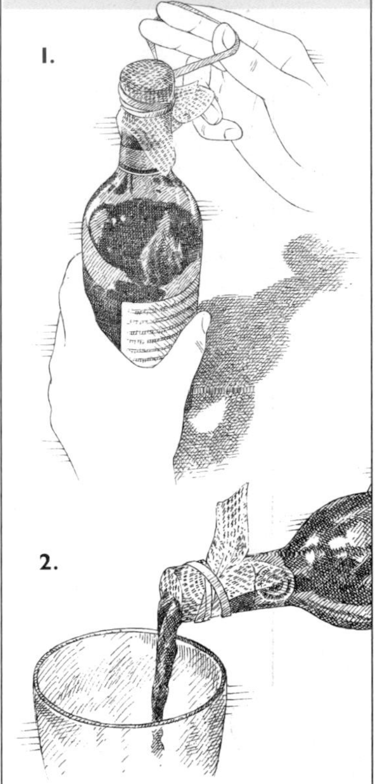

1.

2.

1. Cut cheesecloth into a 2-inch square, fit it over the wine bottle, and secure it with a rubber band.
2. Pour the wine through the cheesecloth, leaving any bits of cork behind.

Steady Stuffed Tomatoes

Baking stuffed tomatoes is a challenge when the fruit topples over and refuses to stay upright. Pat Wiemeler of Melbourne, Fla., uses a muffin tin to prevent wobbling.

Place tomato halves in the cups of a muffin tin sprayed with nonstick cooking spray. Top tomatoes with stuffing, then bake.

Send Us Your Tip We will provide a complimentary one-year subscription for each tip we print. Send your tip, name, and address to Quick Tips, Cook's Illustrated, P.O. Box 470589, Brookline, MA 02447, or to quicktips@americastestkitchen.com.

ILLUSTRATION: JOHN BURGOYNE

Using Up Leftover Brownies

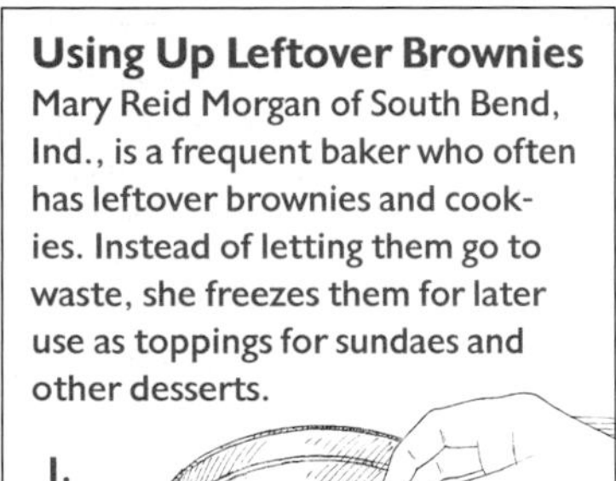

Mary Reid Morgan of South Bend, Ind., is a frequent baker who often has leftover brownies and cookies. Instead of letting them go to waste, she freezes them for later use as toppings for sundaes and other desserts.

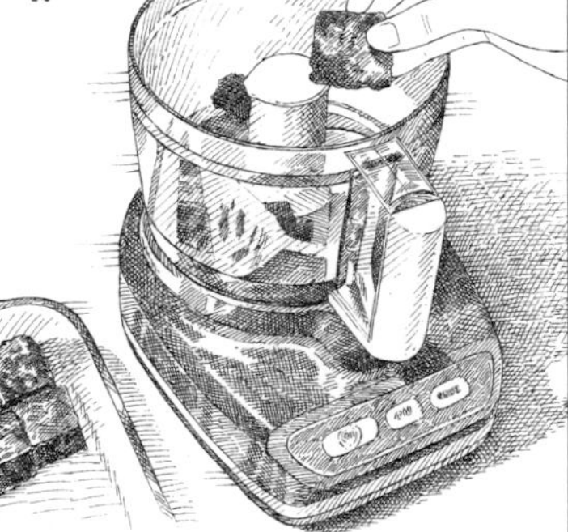

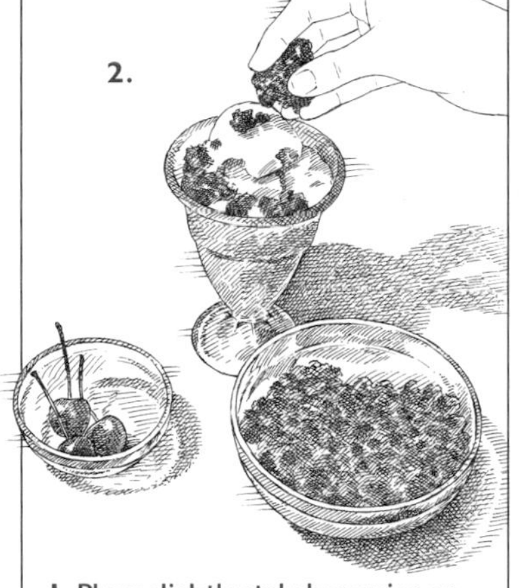

1. Place slightly stale brownies or cookies in the workbowl of a food processor and pulse until they form coarse crumbs. Store in a zipper-lock bag in the freezer.
2. Sprinkle frozen crumbs onto ice cream or other desserts.

No Match for Spaghetti

Flambéing alcohol in a skillet can be dangerous if you don't have a long, chimney-style match. Wary of singeing her fingers, Liz Babiak of Columbus, Ga., reaches for a single strand of dry spaghetti.

1. Light the spaghetti on the flame of a gas burner.
2. Use the spaghetti to safely ignite the alcohol.

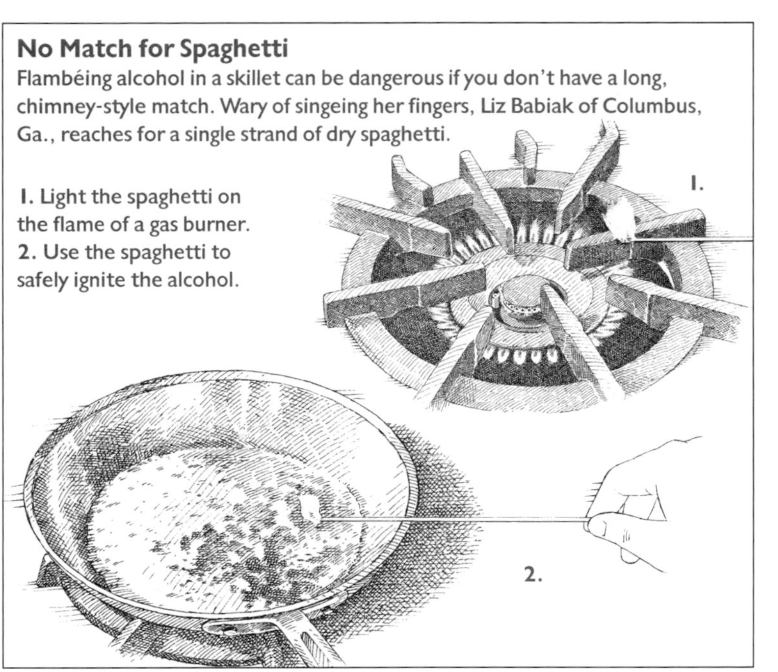

Removing Coffee Stains

Unable to adequately scrub the inside of her thermal coffee carafe, Lisa McDade of Alpine, Calif., devised this clever trick.

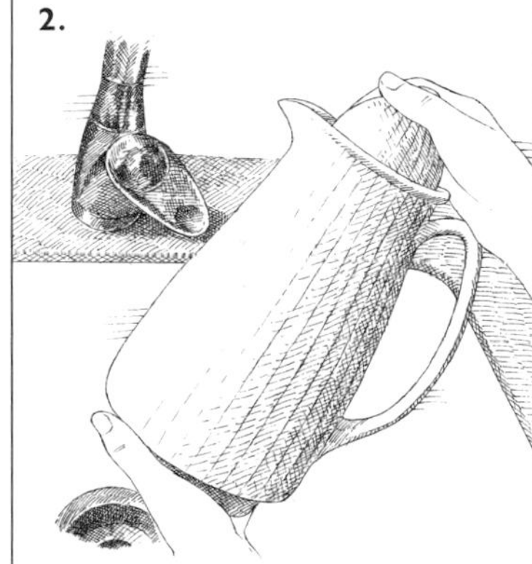

1. Fill a carafe with a handful of rice and a cup of hot water.
2. Cover, then swirl and shake the carafe vigorously. Once the inside is clean, discard the rice and water. Rinse several times with hot water to remove any remaining residue.

Maximizing Cabinet Space

Kitchen equipment that is stored in the back of deep cabinets can be difficult to reach. Rather than emptying out the front of the cabinet to reach items in the back, Patrice Alman of West Bloomfield, Mich., places cookware on a rimmed baking sheet on the bottom of the cabinet, then pulls the sheet out to access hard-to-reach items.

Straightening Out Parchment Paper

Parchment paper that has been cut from a roll almost always curls up when placed onto a baking sheet. To avoid this problem, Diane Schleppi of Dayton, Ohio, precuts sheets of parchment.

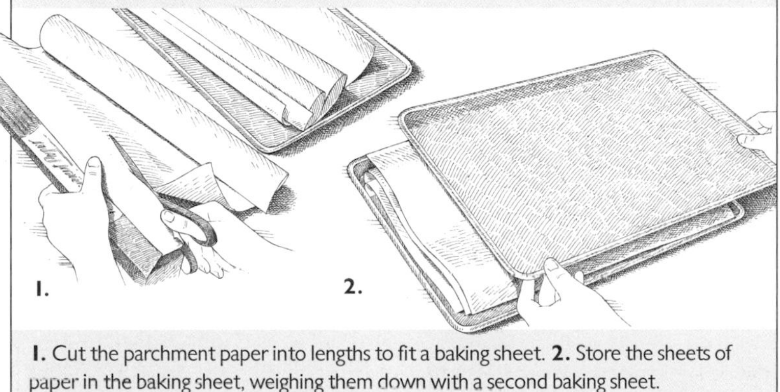

1. Cut the parchment paper into lengths to fit a baking sheet. **2.** Store the sheets of paper in the baking sheet, weighing them down with a second baking sheet.

Halve or Halve Not

Andrew Pimlott of Seaside, Calif., discovered an ingenious way to accurately measure 1/2 cup of liquid with a 1-cup dry measuring cup.

1. Fill a straight-sided, 1-cup measuring cup with liquid approximately halfway.
2. Tilt the cup diagonally. When the liquid touches the brim on one side of the cup and the edge of the flat bottom on the opposite side of the cup, you have measured exactly 1/2 cup. Use the same method to measure 1/4 cup from a 1/2-cup measure, 1/8 cup from a 1/4-cup measure, and so on.

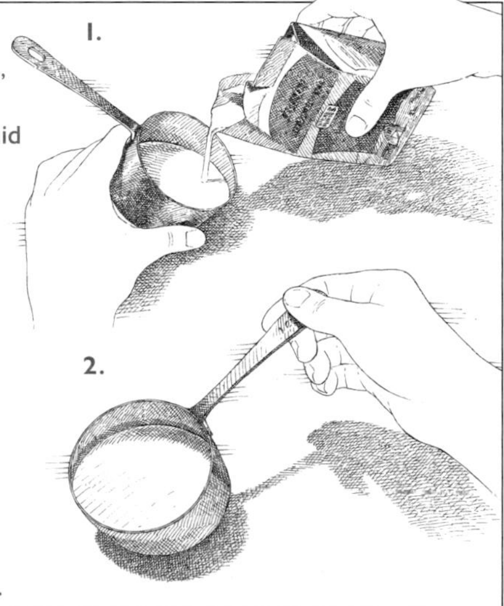

The Problem with Thick-Cut Steaks

The traditional pan-searing technique produces a brown crust, a pink center, and a gray band of overcooked meat in between. Could we eliminate the gray zone?

⋟ BY J. KENJI ALT ⋞

Cooking a standard supermarket steak is easy—we've been doing it for years; just get an oiled pan smoking hot and slap in your steak. A flip and a quick rest before serving, and you have dinner. But try this method with a thick cut strip steak (I'm talking almost as thick as it is wide) and you run into some problems. By the time a good crust has developed and the very center of the steak has reached medium-rare (130 degrees), the bulk of the meat is dry and gray. I was convinced that there was a better way to cook thick steaks, a new method that would give them the tender treatment they deserve.

A novel cooking method guarantees perfectly cooked, tender meat.

To begin, I had to figure out what was causing my meat to turn gray. When beef reaches temperatures above 140 degrees, it undergoes structural and chemical changes that cause it to dry out and toughen, as well as lose its red color. I wanted to keep as much of the meat under this critical temperature as possible. However, the Maillard reaction (which is responsible for the deep color and rich meaty flavor of a well-browned crust) occurs at temperatures closer to 300 degrees. The ideal technique would have to entail quickly searing the exterior to develop a crust while slowly cooking the interior to allow for more even heat distribution. My job was to reconcile these two conflicting goals.

My first attempt was using a technique proposed by food scientist and writer Harold McGee: By flipping the meat as often as once every 15 seconds, the heat will diffuse gradually through it, resulting in a steak that's cooked more evenly. This method did provide a uniform crust and a fairly evenly cooked interior, but to cook four steaks at a time, I had to flip one about every four seconds. With the 176 flips required over the course of the 11-minute cooking time, I'd flipped the equivalent of 88 pounds of meat—maybe doable for a short-order cook on steroids, but not for your average home cook.

Next I tried pan-roasting, which involves searing the steaks in a hot pan, then transferring them—pan and all—to a blazing 450-degree oven to quickly finish cooking. This resulted in the familiar gray band and chewy meat. I wanted my steaks to finish cooking more gently, so the next time around I transferred them out of the hot pan and onto a rack and lowered the oven temperature to a mild 275 degrees. Thirty-two minutes later, the steaks were noticeably more tender in the center—due to increased enzymatic action (see "Tender Steaks," page 7)—but still had ¼-inch-thick gray zones around their perimeters.

Comparing cross-sections of a steak at different cooking stages revealed that this gray band was created during the initial browning. It seemed that a low oven was the path to tender meat, but I needed to speed up the searing process so that the meat just underneath the surface would not have time to overcook.

The Crust of the Matter

Basic thermodynamics: When a 40-degree steak is placed in a 400-degree pan, the temperature of the pan drops significantly. Until it reheats to 300 degrees, no browning can take place. A cold, thick steak added to a hot pan can take upward of 4 minutes per side to form a good crust—during which time the meat beneath the surface is overcooking. Preheating the pan longer and with more oil only sent my hopes up in flames. But what if I upped the starting temperature of the meat? I put the steaks in a zipper-lock bag and submerged them in 120-degree tap water; 30 minutes later, they had reached 100 degrees. Convinced that this was the solution, I transferred the warmed steaks to a preheated pan—where, alas, it still took more than 6 minutes to brown both sides properly.

While racking my gray matter, I recalled a grade school science experiment. A paper cup full of water was placed directly over the flame of a candle, yet the paper did not burn. The cup was left over the flame until all the water had boiled away, at which point the cup finally ignited. Turned out that as long as there was still water in the cup, all the heat from the candle was being used to boil and vaporize the water,

Gray Matter

TRADITIONAL WAY
By the time thick steaks come up to temperature in the middle, a wide band of dry, gray meat has developed below the crust.

OUR METHOD
Our method starts the steaks in a low oven to gently raise their temperature. The rosy interior extends nearly to the crust.

PHOTOGRAPHY: CARL TREMBLAY

TECHNIQUE | TAKING SIDES

Use tongs to sear the sides of two steaks at a time.

preventing the cup from ever going above 212 degrees (the boiling point of water). My point? Just as a paper cup can't burn if there is any water in it, a steak can't brown until all of its surface moisture has evaporated.

That explained my failed zipper-lock bag test. The moisture that was sweating out of the warming steaks was coming into direct contact with the pan, thereby reducing the rate at which it could heat up. It struck me: To get well-browned, juicy steaks, start with dry meat. I seasoned some steaks as usual, this time moving them straight from the fridge into a 275-degree oven. After 25 minutes, they had warmed to 95 degrees and the surfaces looked like desiccated lunar landscapes. I began to doubt my theory, but then I seared them; they developed beautiful brown crusts in less than 4 minutes. I held my breath while they rested. As the knife cut through the crispy crust, it revealed pink, juicy, tender meat—the gray zone was all but gone.

PAN-SEARED THICK-CUT STRIP STEAKS

SERVES 4

Rib-eye or filet mignon of similar thickness can be substituted for strip steaks. If using filet mignon, buying a 2-pound center-cut tenderloin roast and portioning it into four 8-ounce steaks yourself will produce more consistent results. If using filet mignon, increase the oven time by about 5 minutes. When cooking lean strip steaks (without an external fat cap) or filet mignon, add an extra tablespoon of oil to the pan. If desired, serve with Red Wine–Mushroom Pan Sauce (recipe follows), Sun-Dried Tomato Relish, Tequila-Poblano Sauce, or Thai Chile Butter (recipes available free at www.cooksillustrated.com/june).

- 2 boneless strip steaks, 1 1/2 to 1 3/4 inches thick (about 1 pound each) (see note above)
- Kosher salt and ground black pepper
- 1 tablespoon vegetable oil

1. Adjust oven rack to middle position and heat oven to 275 degrees. Pat steaks dry with paper towels. Cut each steak in half vertically to create four 8-ounce steaks. Season steaks liberally with salt and pepper; using hands, gently shape into uniform thickness. Place steaks on wire rack set in rimmed baking sheet; transfer baking sheet to oven. Cook until instant-read thermometer inserted horizontally into center of steaks registers 90 to 95 degrees for rare to medium-rare, 20 to 25 minutes, or 100 to 105 degrees for medium, 25 to 30 minutes.

2. Heat oil in 12-inch heavy-bottomed skillet over high heat until smoking. Place steaks in skillet and sear until well browned and crusty, 1½ to 2 minutes, lifting once halfway through to redistribute fat underneath each steak. (Reduce heat if fond begins to burn.) Using tongs, turn steaks and cook until well browned on second side, 2 to 2½ minutes. Transfer steaks to clean rack and reduce heat under pan to medium. Use tongs to stand 2 steaks on their sides. Holding steaks together, return to skillet and sear on all edges until browned, about 1½ minutes (see photo above). Repeat with remaining 2 steaks.

3. Return steaks to wire rack and let rest, loosely tented with foil, for about 10 minutes. If desired, cook sauce in now-empty skillet. Serve immediately.

RED WINE–MUSHROOM PAN SAUCE

MAKES ABOUT 1 CUP

Prepare all the ingredients for the pan sauce while the steaks are in the oven.

- 1 tablespoon vegetable oil
- 8 ounces button mushrooms, trimmed and sliced thin (about 3 cups)
- 1 small shallot, minced (about 1 1/2 tablespoons)
- 1 cup dry red wine
- 1/2 cup low-sodium chicken broth
- 1 tablespoon balsamic vinegar
- 1 teaspoon Dijon mustard
- 2 tablespoons cold unsalted butter, cut into 4 pieces
- 1 teaspoon minced fresh thyme leaves
- Table salt and ground black pepper

Pour off fat from skillet in which steaks were cooked. Heat oil over medium-high heat until just smoking. Add mushrooms and cook, stirring occasionally, until beginning to brown and liquid has evaporated, about 5 minutes. Add shallot and cook, stirring frequently, until beginning to soften, about 1 minute. Increase heat to high; add red wine and broth, scraping bottom of skillet with wooden spoon to loosen any browned bits. Simmer rapidly until liquid and mushrooms are reduced to 1 cup, about 6 minutes. Add vinegar, mustard, and any juices from resting steaks; cook until thickened, about 1 minute. Off heat, whisk in butter and thyme; season with salt and pepper to taste. Spoon sauce over steaks and serve immediately.

SCIENCE: Tender Steaks

Our steaks spend a long time in a warm oven, yet taste more tender than traditionally prepared steaks, which can be tough and chewy. The explanation? Meat contains active enzymes called cathepsins, which break down connective tissues over time, increasing tenderness (a fact that is demonstrated to great effect in dry-aged meat). As the temperature of the meat rises, these enzymes work faster and faster until they reach 122 degrees, where all action stops. While our steaks are slowly heating up, the cathepsins are working overtime, in effect "aging" and tenderizing our steaks within half an hour. When steaks are cooked by conventional methods, their final temperature is reached much more rapidly, denying the cathepsins the time they need to properly do their job.—J.K.A.

COOK'S LIVE Original Test Kitchen Videos

www.cooksillustrated.com

RECIPE IN 60 SECONDS
- Pan-Seared Thick-Cut Strip Steaks

VIDEO TIPS
- What type of steak should I buy?
- Why do I need to let the steaks rest?
- Why does it matter when I salt the steaks?
- How should I prep my steaks for cooking?
- What's the difference between grades of beef?

TECHNIQUE | PREPARING 3 CUTS OF STEAK FOR PAN-SEARING

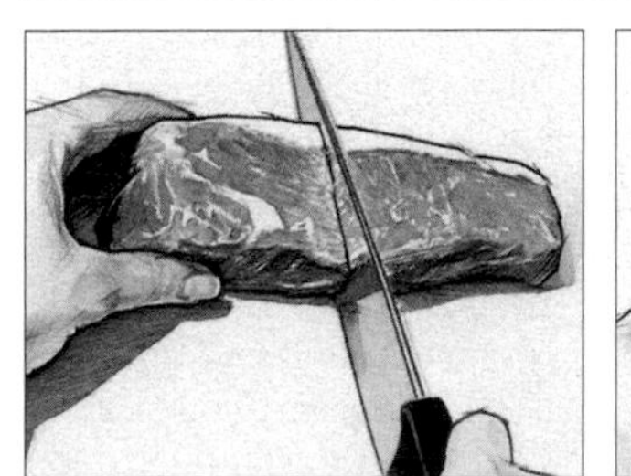

STRIP STEAKS
Buy two thick steaks and cut each in half.

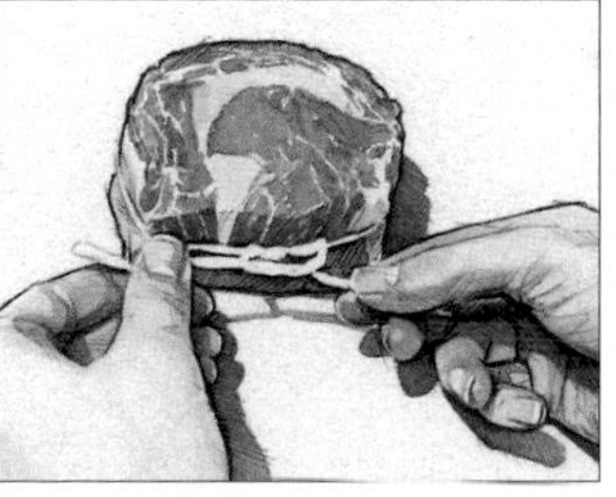

RIB-EYE STEAKS
Buy two thick steaks, cut each in half, and tie each piece with twine.

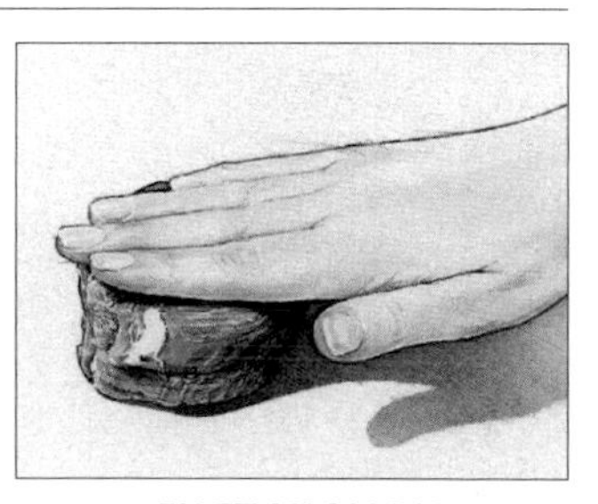

FILET MIGNON
Cut 2-pound roast into four steaks and press each piece to flatten.

ILLUSTRATION: RANDY GLASS

Rethinking Blackened Red Snapper

Transferring blackened fish from a cast-iron skillet to a grill may keep your kitchen from filling with smoke, but it creates a host of other problems, including sticking.

⪢ BY SANDRA WU ⪡

Ever since Paul Prudhomme popularized his signature dish of blackened redfish in the 1980s, blackened anything has become synonymous with nouvelle Cajun cookery. Creating the recipe's namesake crust required 3/4 pound of melted butter in two applications: First to coat the fish before it was dredged in a mixture of spices and again to drizzle over both sides of the fish as it seared in a white-hot cast-iron skillet. The result was a dark brown, crusty, sweet-smoky, toasted spice exterior that provided a rich contrast to the moist, mild-flavored fish inside. But achieving this meant cooking in a well-ventilated kitchen. In *The Prudhomme Family Cookbook*, the author recommends the recipe be made either outdoors or in a commercial kitchen, since the process creates "an incredible amount of smoke that will set off your own and your neighbors' smoke alarms."

Rub the toasted spice mixture into both sides of the fish.

I wanted to make this dish at home, but not if it necessitated a visit from the fire department. That left me with no choice but to take the entire project outdoors onto the grill. My first attempts revealed several challenges. The fish almost always stuck to the grates, leaving me with a pile of shredded fillets. They either burned on the outside by the time the flesh cooked through or failed to get dark and crusty enough. Complicating matters, the fillets often curled midway through cooking, resulting in burned edges and an arched, barely blackened center. Because redfish is found primarily near the Gulf Coast, I used nationally available red snapper—another mild fish with firm, white flesh. Red snapper's pinkish-red skin is delicious when cooked to a thin, crisp state. But like the redfish, whenever the snapper was placed skin side down over the high heat of the grates, it would buckle. By simply scoring the skin, the fillets stayed flat—an easy fix.

A cast-iron pan is another of the recipe's defining traits. I quickly cast it aside, however, as it couldn't comfortably hold two fillets and failed to deliver a full grilled flavor. Cooking directly on the grates eliminated the need to cook in batches. After some experimentation, I decided to use a modified two-level fire (see "The Right Fire," page 9). But even once I had my grilling technique down, the fillets had an annoying habit of sticking to the grates, and efforts to dislodge them resulted in the type of shredded fillets only a feline could love (see "Don't Get Stuck," page 9). The solution was right before my eyes: the aluminum pan that was serving as a holding tray for my grilling utensils. By inverting the pan over the grate while it preheated, I was able to get the grill super-hot—almost 200 degrees hotter than normal—and incinerate any nasty gunk. I now had a really clean surface on which to cook the fish.

The basic dry rub I'd been experimenting with remained unexciting, since so many spices burned on the grill. My blackened spirits were lifted when I added coriander, which could take the heat and gave the spice rub a bright floral note. Prudhomme's recipe calls for garlic powder and onion powder (fresh equivalents would burn), items not always stocked in our test kitchen. I found the powders gave the rub a robust flavor boost that tasters enjoyed.

Although my rub was improving, I wanted still more flavor, so I tried blooming the spices—that is, releasing their trapped flavors—by sautéing them in melted butter until they turned several shades darker (from bright red to dark, rusty brown) and emitted a deep, fragrant aroma. Once the spice mixture cooled to room temperature, I broke up any large clumps with a fork and applied it to the fish in a thin layer: no extra melted butter necessary. By the time the fillets were fully cooked, they were also well blackened on all sides, and—most important—the spice crust had finally acquired the proper depth and richness. At last, I had blackened fish that looked and tasted like it had come out of a bona fide New Orleans establishment, with no

Unbuckling

Skin-on fillets will buckle when grilled because the skin will shrink back, pulling the flesh along with it (left). They remain flat if the skin is scored first (right), which prevents it from contracting more quickly than the flesh.

A FISHY MESS
Cooked fillet with unscored skin, buckled

A FLAT FILLET
Cooked fillet with scored skin, perfectly flat

TASTING:
Blackening Spice Rubs

After sampling six store-bought Cajun spice rubs, we found that mixing your own delivers superior results. But if you really want to buy a rub, Paul Prudhomme's Blackened Redfish Magic has the best blend of flavors.

PHOTOGRAPHY: CARL TREMBLAY

TECHNIQUE | DON'T GET STUCK

I knew from past grilling stories that preheating the grate before scraping it with a grill brush was the most effective way to keep food from sticking. When it came to delicate fish, the grates had to be spotless. Thinking how the self-cleaning cycle in an oven transforms caked-on gunk into fine gray ash by superheating the interior, I decided to replicate the process with an inverted aluminum pan. This boosted the grill temperature to 818 degrees: Residue and stuck-on bits didn't stand a chance. This trick, along with a few others, will allow you to grill any fish without it sticking. –S.W.

1. CHILLING
Keep fish refrigerated until ready to grill. At room temperature, fillets become floppy.

2. SUPERHEATING
Place disposable aluminum pan upside down over hot side of grill. Cover and heat for 5 minutes.

3. SCRAPING/OILING
Scrape grate clean with grill brush. Then wipe grate with oil-dipped paper towels.

4. POSITIONING
Place fish perpendicular to grill grate with skin side facing down.

5. FLIPPING
Slide one spatula underneath fillet to lift; use another to support fish while it is being flipped.

indoor smell to mask, mess to clean up, or walls to repaint.

CHARCOAL-GRILLED BLACKENED RED SNAPPER

SERVES 4

If using fillets that are ½ inch or thinner, reduce cooking time to 3 minutes per side. If using fillets that are 1 inch or thicker, increase cooking time on second side by 2 minutes, moving the fish to the cooler side of the grill after the second side has browned. If you cannot find red snapper, substitute striped bass, halibut, or catfish. Making the slashes in the skin requires a sharp knife. If your knife isn't sharp enough, try cutting through the skin with a serrated knife. However, cut in one direction (don't saw) and be careful to not cut into the flesh. If you choose not to eat the skin, be sure to remove it after cooking rather than beforehand. Serve fish with lemon wedges and Rémoulade or Pineapple and Cucumber Salsa with Mint (recipes available free at www.cooksillustrated.com/june).

- 2 tablespoons sweet paprika
- 2 teaspoons onion powder
- 2 teaspoons garlic powder
- ¾ teaspoon ground coriander
- ¾ teaspoon table salt
- ¼ teaspoon cayenne pepper
- ¼ teaspoon ground black pepper
- ¼ teaspoon ground white pepper
- 3 tablespoons unsalted butter
- 13 by 9-inch disposable aluminum roasting pan
- 4 red snapper fillets, 6 to 8 ounces each, ¾ inch thick
- Vegetable oil for cooking grate

1. Combine paprika, onion powder, garlic powder, coriander, salt, and peppers in small bowl. Melt butter in 10-inch skillet over medium heat. When foaming subsides, stir in spice mixture. Cook, stirring frequently, until fragrant and spices turn dark rust color, 2 to 3 minutes. Transfer mixture to pie plate and cool, stirring occasionally, to room temperature, about 10 minutes. Once cooled, use fork to break up any large clumps.

2. Light large chimney starter filled two-thirds with charcoal (4 quarts, or about 65 briquettes) and allow to burn until coals are fully ignited and partially covered with thin layer of ash, 15 to 20 minutes. Build modified two-level fire by arranging coals to cover one half of grill. Position cooking grate over coals, place disposable roasting pan upside down on grate directly over coals, cover grill, and heat grate until hot, about 5 minutes. Remove roasting pan and scrape grate clean with grill brush. Grill is ready when coals are hot (you can hold your hand 5 inches above grate for 2 to 3 seconds).

3. Meanwhile, pat fillets dry on both sides with paper towels. Using sharp knife, make shallow diagonal slashes every inch along skin side of fish, being careful to not cut into flesh. Place fillets skin side up on rimmed baking sheet or large plate. Using fingers, rub spice mixture in thin, even layer on top and sides of fish. Flip fillets over and repeat on other side (you should use all of spice mixture). Refrigerate until needed.

4. Lightly dip wad of paper towels in oil; holding wad with tongs, wipe grill grate. Place fish perpendicular to grill grate, skin side down, on hot side of grill. Grill, uncovered, until skin is very dark brown and crisp, 3 to 4 minutes. Using thin metal spatula, carefully flip fish and continue to grill until dark brown and beginning to flake and center is opaque but still moist, about 5 minutes longer. Serve immediately.

TECHNIQUE | THE RIGHT FIRE

To concentrate heat and promote better blackening, we piled all the lit coals onto one side of the grill. The cooler side can be used to finish cooking fillets that are slightly thicker.

GAS-GRILLED BLACKENED RED SNAPPER

Follow recipe for Charcoal-Grilled Blackened Red Snapper, skipping step 2. Turn on all burners to high, cover, and heat grill until very hot, about 15 minutes. Use grill brush to scrape grill clean. Proceed with recipe from step 3, leaving burners on high and cooking with lid up.

COOK'S LIVE Original Test Kitchen Videos
www.cooksillustrated.com

RECIPE IN 60 SECONDS
- Grilled Blackened Red Snapper

VIDEO TIPS
- What's the best way to flip fish on the grill?
- Why do I need to score the fish?

Italian-Style Chicken with Sausage, Peppers, and Onions

This Italian American skillet dish makes a great weeknight meal—once you solve the problems of greasy sauce and flabby skin.

BY SANDRA WU

Just how chicken scarpariello came about is debatable, but its use of bright, flavorful ingredients is indisputable. Popularized in New York City restaurants opened by southern Italian immigrants, this dish was likely based on family recipes rather than a restaurant classic from the old country. In the Neapolitan dialect, scarpariello means "shoemaker-style." Most sources say this name refers to a meal that a poor cobbler could prepare with easy-to-find ingredients; others note the way the chicken bones stick out of your mouth as the dish is eaten, reminiscent of a shoemaker holding nails between his lips as he works.

This Little Italy specialty combines crisp, browned chicken pieces with sweet onions, hot Italian sausage, red bell peppers, and spicy pickled cherry peppers in a tart, vinegary sauce. Even though I'd never heard of chicken scarpariello, I couldn't resist the notion of an easy, home-style Italian dish that could be made in a skillet and on a weeknight.

Little Italy's "shoemaker" chicken is traditionally prepared entirely on the stovetop. To ensure crisp skin, we put the skillet in the oven to finish cooking.

Most recipes start by browning the sausage and then the chicken in a large skillet before sautéing the onions, bell peppers, jarred cherry peppers, and garlic. Once the vegetables have softened, the cooking liquid (typically the brine from the jar of cherry peppers supplemented by white wine vinegar) is added, followed by the browned chicken and sausage. By the time the chicken finishes cooking, the liquid has reduced into a sauce.

A day of experimentation left everyone in the test kitchen with a bad case of heartburn. The recipes I tried were all too greasy, too spicy, and too tart. Cobbling together a good recipe was going to take some work.

First I needed to get the meats squared away. Because the overall dish is so spicy, I immediately swapped hot Italian sausage for sweet. As for the chicken, most recipes call for hacking a whole bird into 18 to 22 pieces, a trying task for anyone who doesn't own a cleaver. Besides, dark and white meats cook at different rates. To streamline the process, I decided to use a single cut of chicken. Because the sausage already added plenty of richness to the dish, I opted for white meat. Split bone-in, skin-on chicken breasts cooked more quickly than thighs, and cutting each split breast into halves or thirds sped up the cooking process even further.

Reducing the fat in the sauce was easy—just wiping the skillet clean after sautéing the sausage and chicken did the trick. I cooked the vegetables in a little olive oil, and the finished sauce was no longer greasy. But tasters complained that my "low-fat" recipe wasn't very flavorful. Rather than sautéing the vegetables in oil, I cooked them in a light film of flavorful fat reserved from the sausage and chicken. Much better.

To keep the browned chicken from becoming soggy in the sauce, I nestled the pieces into the vegetables in the skillet, making sure to keep them skin side up. But this method caused the sauce to evaporate before the overprotected chicken could cook through. I tried speeding up the process with a lid, but the steam completely undid any crispness the skin had acquired from browning. Might some oven time be the answer? To find out, I put the uncovered skillet, with the assembled ingredients, into the oven and waited for the chicken to finish cooking. Once an instant-read thermometer inserted into the thickest piece of chicken registered 160 degrees, I put on oven mitts and removed the skillet from the oven. The chicken was perfectly done: Crisp on the outside, tender and moist on the inside. I set the chicken aside and went to work on the sauce.

Cry and Pucker

On the Scoville scale, which registers the level of capsaicin (the heat-providing component in chile peppers), cherry peppers can range from a warm 100 units to a mouth-scorching 5,000 units, the same as a jalapeño. But I didn't need a scientific scale to tell me what my mouth and tear ducts already knew. Cutting back on the number of cherry peppers was an essential step. But it was removing their seeds—which is where 80 percent of a chile's heat resides—that really tempered their fire.

With the heat adjusted, I needed to focus on the mouth-puckering elements in the sauce. Eliminating the cherry pepper brine and cutting the vinegar with chicken broth made the sauce richer and fuller. A couple of teaspoons of sugar successfully rounded it out. To prevent the crisp

SHOPPING: Cherry Picking

Cherry peppers are often found in the international section of the supermarket rather than the pickle aisle. Most jars feature a combination of the red and green peppers, which are equally hot. Don't confuse cherry peppers with roasted red peppers.

PHOTOGRAPHY: CARL TREMBLAY

chicken skin from soaking up the sauce and becoming soggy, I spooned the sauce, vegetables, and sausage around the platter of chicken.

I served this last batch of chicken scarpariello to tasters and waited for their verdict. Heartburn and heartache from previous recipes now a distant memory, they proclaimed that I had successfully tamed the big flavors in this rustic recipe.

SPICY ITALIAN-STYLE CHICKEN WITH SAUSAGE, PEPPERS, AND ONIONS

SERVES 4 TO 6

This dish is fairly spicy. To manage the heat, adjust the amount of cherry peppers as desired. If you cannot find hot cherry peppers, pickled banana pepper rings can be substituted. If your skillet is not ovensafe, add the cornstarch mixture to the skillet in step 3 (instead of step 5) along with the vinegar and simmer until slightly thickened, 3 to 4 minutes. Stir in the sausage and transfer mixture to 13 by 9-inch baking dish. Arrange the chicken over the mixture and bake as directed. To make this dish with chicken thighs, increase the cooking time in the oven to about 25 minutes, or until an instant-read thermometer inserted into the thickest part of chicken registers 175 degrees. Serve with a green salad and mashed potatoes, orzo, or soft polenta. (Polenta recipe available free at www.cooksillustrated.com/june.)

- 1 tablespoon vegetable oil
- 8 ounces sweet Italian sausage, casings removed
- 2 pounds bone-in, skin-on chicken breast halves, trimmed of excess fat and skin and cut crosswise into 2 or 3 pieces (see illustrations above)
- Table salt and ground black pepper
- 1 medium onion, halved and sliced ¼ inch thick (about 1 ¼ cups)
- 1 large red bell pepper, stemmed, seeded, and cut into ¼-inch strips (about 1 ½ cups)
- 3–5 pickled hot cherry peppers, stemmed, seeded, and cut into ¼-inch strips (about ¼ cup)
- 3 medium garlic cloves, minced or pressed through garlic press (about 1 tablespoon)
- 2 teaspoons granulated sugar
- ⅓ cup plus 2 tablespoons white wine vinegar
- ¾ cup plus 1 tablespoon low-sodium chicken broth
- 1 teaspoon cornstarch
- 1 teaspoon minced fresh thyme leaves
- 1 tablespoon minced fresh parsley leaves

1. Adjust oven rack to middle position and heat oven to 350 degrees. Heat 1 teaspoon oil in 12-inch skillet over medium-high heat until shimmering. Add sausage and cook, stirring to break sausage into ½-inch pieces, until browned, about 3 minutes. Transfer sausage to plate lined with paper towels. Remove skillet from heat; pour off fat into small bowl and reserve; wipe out skillet with paper towels.

2. Return skillet to medium-high heat and heat remaining 2 teaspoons oil until smoking. Pat chicken dry and liberally season with salt and pepper. Add chicken, skin side down, and cook without moving until well browned, 3 to 5 minutes. Using tongs, turn chicken and brown on other side, about 3 minutes. Transfer chicken to large plate. Remove skillet from heat and pour off fat into bowl with sausage fat; wipe out skillet with paper towels.

3. Return skillet to medium-high heat and heat 1 tablespoon reserved fat until shimmering. Add onion and cook until beginning to soften, about 2 minutes. Add bell pepper and cherry peppers and cook, stirring occasionally, until bell pepper begins to soften, about 4 minutes. Add garlic and cook, stirring frequently, until fragrant, about 30 seconds. Add sugar, ⅓ cup vinegar, and ¾ cup broth; bring mixture to boil, scraping up browned bits from pan bottom.

4. Add sausage and chicken (with any accumulated juices) to skillet, arranging chicken pieces in single layer, skin side up, on top of peppers and onion. Transfer skillet to oven and cook until instant-read thermometer inserted into thickest part of chicken registers 160 degrees, 18 to 22 minutes, removing smaller pieces sooner if necessary. Meanwhile, combine cornstarch, thyme, and remaining tablespoon broth in small bowl.

5. Carefully remove skillet from oven (handle will be very hot) and transfer chicken, skin side up, to platter or individual serving plates. Place skillet over medium-high heat and stir in cornstarch mixture. Simmer sauce mixture until slightly thickened, 2 to 3 minutes. Off heat, taste sauce and add up to 2 tablespoons vinegar. Adjust seasonings with salt and pepper. Spoon sauce around chicken, being careful not to pour it directly over chicken. Sprinkle with parsley and serve immediately.

TECHNIQUE

SPLITTING A BONE-IN CHICKEN BREAST

To make bone-in chicken breasts faster-cooking and more manageable to eat, we cut them into smaller pieces. If using large chicken breasts (about 1 pound each), cut each breast into three pieces. If using smaller breasts (10 to 12 ounces each), cut each breast into two pieces.

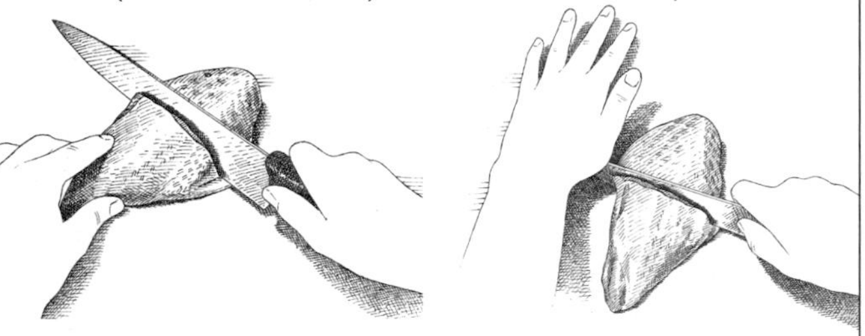

1. TO THE BONE: Using sharp chef's knife, cut into breast until knife hits bone.

2. ROCK ON: Rock knife back and forth through bone.

COOK'S LIVE Original Test Kitchen Videos

www.cooksillustrated.com

RECIPE IN 60 SECONDS

- Spicy Italian-Style Chicken with Sausage, Peppers, and Onions

VIDEO TIPS

- What's the best way to brown chicken?
- How do I cut bone-in chicken breasts?
- What size chef's knife should I use?

RECIPE SHORTHAND | CHICKEN WITH SAUSAGE, PEPPERS, AND ONIONS

To ensure properly cooked chicken pieces with crisp skin, our recipe requires transferring the skillet from the stovetop to the oven. This recipe takes about an hour to prepare and cook.

1. Brown sausage and set aside. **2.** Brown chicken and set aside. **3.** Sauté onion and peppers; add garlic. **4.** Add sugar, vinegar, and broth. **5.** Return sausage and chicken to skillet and place skillet in oven. **6.** Once chicken has cooked through, remove chicken to platter, thicken sauce, then spoon sauce around chicken.

ILLUSTRATION: JOHN BURGOYNE (ABOVE), JAY LAYMAN

10-Minute Barbecued Ribs

Koreans know how to take tough short ribs and transform them into tender barbecued beef in just minutes. Could we learn from their example?

BY DAVID PAZMIÑO

Koreans take their grilled beef as seriously as Americans do their grilled hamburgers and hot dogs. Although the preparations are worlds apart, both are highly seasoned with the barbecued flavor of the grill. While Americans might argue about the best fat percentage for hamburgers or if hot dogs should be all-beef or pork, Koreans debate the merits of various cuts of beef—the most prized being *kalbi*, or beef short ribs.

My first experience with kalbi came at a Korean restaurant, where each diner took his own slices of beef marinated in a sweet soy mixture with garlic and scallions and laid them across a hot grill in the center of the table. The result: crusty, browned meat that had a barbecued char but was nonetheless tender. Knowing that short ribs take hours of braising to become tender, I wondered how the Koreans accomplished this in only minutes.

When I grilled big short ribs from my supermarket, they were barely chewable and overly fatty, despite the "Great for Grilling" sticker. I quickly realized that how the ribs are butchered is essential to the success of this dish. Most short ribs sold in supermarkets are cut English-style—a single rib bone with a thick piece of meat attached to it. Korean short ribs are cut the opposite direction, across the bones, or flanken-style. Naturally, my first thought was to try flanken-style ribs. However, the markets that do sell them cut the ribs ½ to 1 inch thick—much too big to work in a quick Korean barbecue recipe. I eventually got the butcher to use a band saw to slice flanken-style ribs ¼ inch thick, like in Korean restaurants, but it was clear that my recipe would have to start with widely available English-style ribs.

A pear marinade flavors and tenderizes these barbecued short ribs.

I first tried removing the meat from the bone and butterflying it—cutting it nearly in half widthwise and opening it like a book. While better than the whole grilled rib, it was still tough. I suspected that slicing the meat into more uniform pieces might be the answer. I angled my knife against the meat and fabricated four slices from each rib. These pieces were large and chunky, but a quick pounding evened them out. On the grill, they looked much like a thinner, boneless version of the Asian cut. What's more, I didn't have to worry about removing bones before wrapping them up in lettuce like a Korean taco.

Tender Woes

Although the beef looked the part, it was still tough and chewy. Clearly, the secret to authentic Korean barbecued ribs was more than just proper butchering. The right marinade was critical, too. I lined up my ingredients for inspection: soy sauce, sugar, rice vinegar, garlic, and scallions. In previous test kitchen work, we have discovered that soy acts as a brine and helps tenderize meat, so I figured I was on the right track. For more flavor I added sesame oil and ginger. But surprisingly, the texture didn't change. Surely, upping the amount of vinegar would do the trick. No; more vinegar made the meat even tougher and imparted an unpleasant sour flavor.

I had one more series of tests to run. Many kalbi recipes add pureed pear to the marinade, claiming it acts as a tenderizer. Pineapple and papaya are well known for their tenderizing properties, but I had never heard of using pear. When I added pureed pear to my marinade, tasters unanimously thought the ribs were more tender. So maybe pear *is* a secret tenderizer? To test this hypothesis, I tried marinating the ribs

SHOPPING: Short Ribs

Depending on butchering technique, short ribs can vary markedly in appearance. Our recipe uses widely available English-style ribs; Korean-style and boneless ribs can also be used.

ENGLISH-STYLE
This common choice contains a single bone, about 4 to 5 inches long. Look for ribs that have at least 1 inch of meat above the bone.

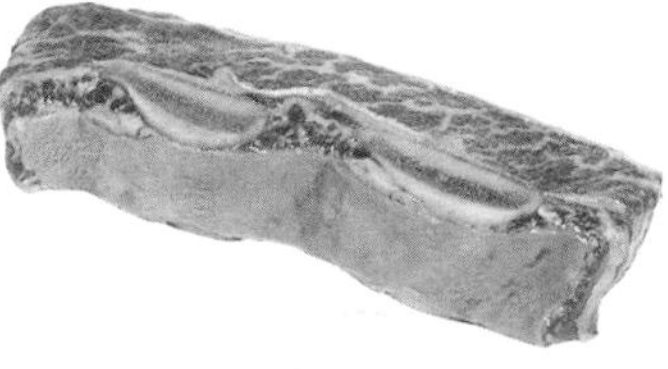

FLANKEN-STYLE
The meat has been cut across the ribs and contains 2 to 3 oval-shaped cross-sections of bone. These ribs can be difficult to find in the supermarket.

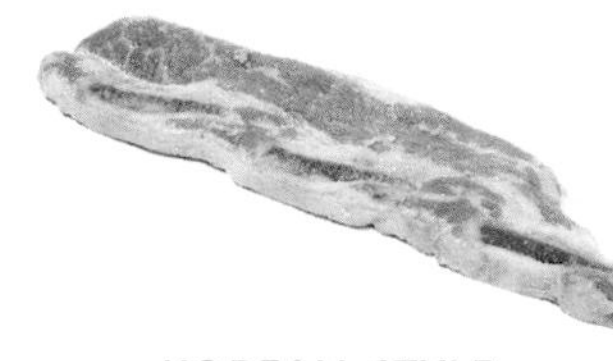

KOREAN-STYLE
The authentic choice (sold only in Asian markets) requires no butchering. The same as flanken-style ribs but cut much thinner, usually about ¼ inch thick.

BONELESS
A good option that is available at some markets. Make sure they are at least 4 inches long and 1 inch thick.

PHOTOGRAPHY: CARL TREMBLAY

STEP-BY-STEP | GETTING ENGLISH-STYLE RIBS READY TO GRILL

If using boneless ribs, skip to step 2.

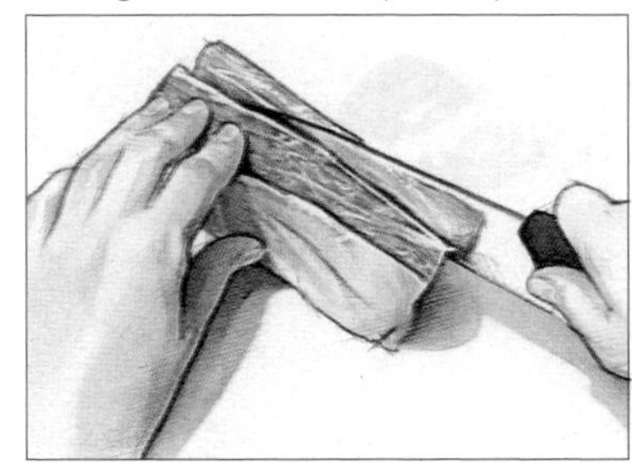

1. Remove meat from bone, positioning chef's knife as close as possible to bone.

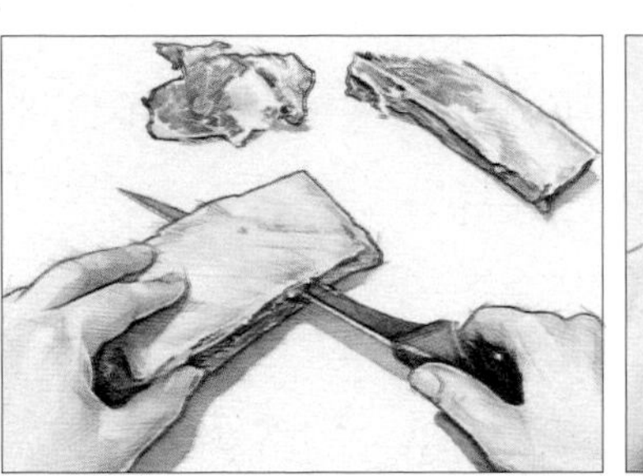

2. Trim excess hard fat and silver skin from both sides of meat.

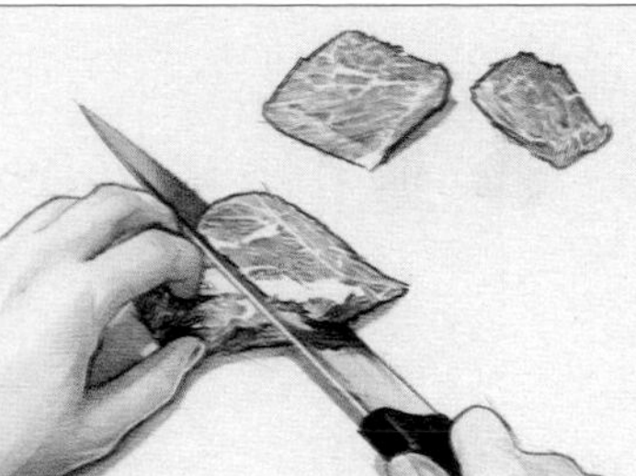

3. Slice meat at angle into 4 to 5 pieces ranging from ½ to ¾ inch thick.

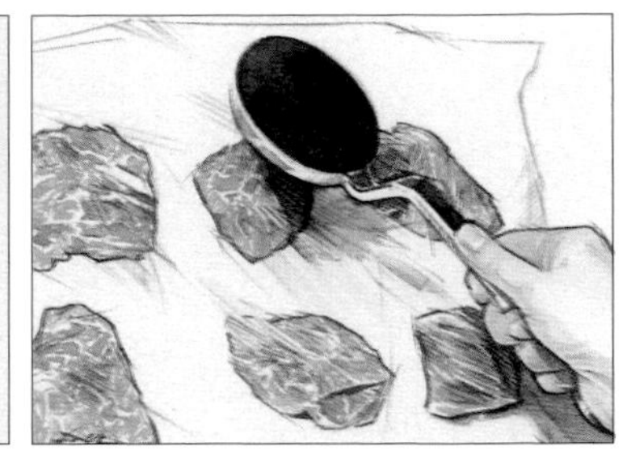

4. Place plastic wrap over meat and pound into even ¼-inch-thick pieces.

with pear alone, but the result, once again, was tough meat. Simple deduction told me that one of the ingredients in the marinade was working with the pear.

Conversations with food scientists taught me that the acidity in pears helps speed up the work of proteases, tenderizing compounds found in soy sauce. The rice vinegar does the same thing, only more so, which is why the pear-only marinade didn't have much effect on the meat. But rice vinegar can't do it alone. Remember, increasing the vinegar in the marinade made the meat taste sour. Besides acidity, pears add sweetness and a fruity flavor that complements the beefy char. The pear might have a modest role as a tenderizer, but it plays an important part in flavor development.

Now to the grill. To replicate the hot indoor restaurant grills that char the meat without making shoe leather, I tried banking the hot coals to one side of a kettle-style grill, creating what the test kitchen refers to as a modified two-level fire. This created the more intense heat that I needed to get a quick char without making the meat tough. Keeping the hot coals on one side also allowed me to move the meat to the cooler side when flare-ups occurred. With the marinade flavor and grilling technique perfected, I could now add short ribs to my shopping list, alongside the hot dogs and beef patties. And pears, too.

KOREAN GRILLED SHORT RIBS (KALBI)

SERVES 4 TO 6

If pressed for time, a 1-hour marinade will provide sufficient flavor, but it will not tenderize the meat as well as a longer marinade. Make sure to buy English-style ribs that have at least 1 inch of meat on top of the bone, avoiding ones that have little meat and large bones. Two pounds of boneless short ribs at least 4 inches long and 1 inch thick can be used instead of bone-in ribs. Alternatively, 2½ pounds of thinly sliced Korean-style ribs can be used (no butchering is required; recipe follows). For a spicier marinade, add ½ teaspoon or more hot red pepper flakes. Serve with steamed rice, kimchi (spicy pickled vegetables), and, if available, a spicy bean paste called *gochujang*. Traditionally, all these ingredients are wrapped in a lettuce leaf and eaten like a taco.

- 1 medium ripe pear, peeled, halved, cored, and roughly chopped
- 6 medium garlic cloves, peeled
- 4 teaspoons chopped fresh ginger
- ½ cup soy sauce
- 2 tablespoons toasted sesame oil
- 6 tablespoons sugar
- 1 tablespoon rice vinegar
- 3 scallions, green and white parts sliced thin
- 5 pounds English-style beef short ribs, meat removed from bone, trimmed of excess fat, sliced widthwise at angle into ½- to ¾-inch-thick pieces, and pounded ¼ inch thick (see illustrations above)
- Vegetable oil for grill grate

1. Process pear, garlic, ginger, soy sauce, oil, sugar, and vinegar in food processor until smooth, 20 to 30 seconds, scraping down sides of bowl as needed. Transfer to medium bowl and stir in scallions.

2. Spread one-third of marinade in 13 by 9-inch pan or other suitable container that will hold ribs in 2 layers. Place half of meat in single layer over marinade. Pour half of remaining marinade over meat, followed by remaining meat and marinade. Cover tightly with plastic wrap and place in refrigerator. Marinate ribs for at least 4 hours and up to 12 hours, turning meat once or twice to ensure that it marinates evenly.

3. Light large chimney starter filled two-thirds with charcoal (4 quarts, or about 65 briquettes) and allow to burn until coals are fully ignited and partially covered with thin layer of ash, 15 to 20 minutes. Build modified two-level fire by arranging coals to cover half of grill. Position grill grate over coals, cover grill, and heat grate until hot, about 5 minutes; scrape grate clean with grill brush. Lightly dip wad of paper towels in oil; holding wad with tongs, wipe grill grate.

4. Grill half of meat directly over coals, turning 3 or 4 times, until well browned on both sides, 7 to 12 minutes. If flare-ups occur, move meat to cooler side of grill until flames die down. Move first batch of meat to cooler side of grill and repeat browning with second batch. Transfer second batch of meat to platter. Return first batch of meat to hot side of grill and warm for 30 seconds; transfer to platter and serve immediately.

KOREAN GRILLED SHORT RIBS FOR GAS GRILL

In order to maximize heat on a gas grill, keep all burners on high and remain vigilant about flare-ups, spraying flames with water from squirt bottle if necessary. Note that cooking time on gas will be slightly longer than times on a charcoal grill.

Follow recipe for Korean Grilled Short Ribs through step 2. Turn all burners to high, close lid, and heat grill until very hot, about 15 minutes. Scrape cooking grate clean with grill brush and wipe with wad of oil-soaked paper towels, holding towels with tongs. Continue with recipe from step 4, cooking meat in 2 batches with lid down for 10 to 14 minutes per batch.

KOREAN GRILLED SHORT RIBS (KOREAN-STYLE RIB VARIATION)

Korean-style ribs are fattier than English style ribs, so watch for flare-ups at the grill.

Follow recipe for Korean Grilled Short Ribs, substituting 2½ pounds Korean-style beef short ribs that are trimmed of excess fat and cut no more than ¼ inch thick. Reduce amount of charcoal to 3 quarts.

COOK'S LIVE Original Test Kitchen Videos
www.cooksillustrated.com

RECIPE IN 60 SECONDS
- Korean Grilled Short Ribs

VIDEO TIPS
- How do I prevent flare-ups on the grill (and stop them when they happen)?
- What kind of ribs should I buy?

ILLUSTRATION: RANDY GLASS

Best Vegetable Curry

We wanted a quick meatless curry in which the vegetables stood up to the sauce. We took this dish from bland to bold.

BY REBECCA HAYS

The term "curry" is derived from the Tamil word *kari*, which simply means "sauce" or "gravy." There are thousands of ways to make curry. When flavorful beef or lamb is the main ingredient, even a mediocre recipe usually yields a decent outcome. But vegetable curry is a different story: It's all too easy to turn out a second-rate, if not awful, dish. Delicate vegetables are often watery carriers for the sauce, offering little personality of their own.

Vegetable curries can be complicated affairs, with lengthy ingredient lists and fussy techniques meant to compensate for the lack of meat. But I wanted something simpler—a curry I could make on a weeknight in less than an hour. Most streamlined recipes I tried, however, were uninspired. A few attempted to make up for the flavor deficit by overloading the dish with spices, and the results were harsh and overpowering. I had my work cut out for me.

To quickly build flavor, we toasted curry powder and garam masala in a skillet, then added an unexpected spoonful of tomato paste.

While some curries are made with exotic whole and ground spices (fenugreek, asafetida, dried rose petals, and so on), I decided to limit myself to everyday ground spices such as cumin, cloves, cardamom, cinnamon, and coriander. My testing dragged on for days, and it was hard to reach consensus in the test kitchen. Frankly, most of the homemade spice mixtures I tried were fine.

I had been reluctant to use store-bought curry powder, assuming its flavor would be inferior to a homemade blend, but it seemed worth a try. I was surprised when tasters liked the curry powder nearly as well as a homemade mixture made with seven spices. It turns out that store-bought curry powder contains some of the exotic spices I had dismissed at the outset. As long as I used enough, my recipe had decent flavor.

Looking for ways to improve the flavor of the curry powder, I tried toasting the spices in a skillet until their seductive aroma emerged. This simple step took just one minute and turned commercial curry powder into a flavor powerhouse. Why was toasting so beneficial? When added to a simmering sauce, spices can be heated to only 212 degrees. In a dry skillet, temperatures can exceed 500 degrees, causing flavors to explode.

With the spices settled, I turned to building the rest of my flavor base. Many classic recipes begin with a generous amount of sautéed onion, which adds depth and body to the sauce, and I followed suit. Ghee (clarified butter) is traditionally used to sauté the onions. It adds terrific richness, though I found that vegetable oil was a fine substitute. Almost all curry recipes—meat and vegetable alike—add equal amounts of garlic and ginger to the onions, and I found no reason to stray from this well-balanced tradition. Wanting to take my meatless sauce to the next level, I stirred in a minced fresh chile for heat and a spoonful of tomato paste for sweetness. The latter ingredient was decidedly inauthentic, but I found it really helped. As the onions caramelized with the other ingredients, fond (flavorful dark bits) developed in the bottom of the pan, mimicking the phenomenon that occurs when browning meat. I then added the toasted curry powder to the pan and let it dissolve. Creating a supercharged base for my curry took just 15 minutes.

Vegetable Picking

I decided to include chickpeas and potatoes for heartiness, along with one firm and one soft vegetable. Eventually, I settled on a classic pairing of cauliflower and peas. Although the combination of textures and colors was good, the vegetables were a bit bland. For meat curries, the beef or lamb is often added to the sauce without any prior flavor development, but I figured my vegetables should bring something to the dish. Oven roasting them definitely helped but took too much time. Instead, I tried browning the potatoes along with the onions. This unconventional move was an unqualified success, substantially boosting the flavor of the potatoes.

Could other vegetables come up in flavor, too? An Indian cooking method called *bhuna* involves sautéing the spices and main ingredients together to enhance and meld flavors. I tried this technique with cauliflower, as well as eggplant and green beans (used in a recipe variation), and they all developed a richer, more complex flavor. Next, I determined that a combination of water and pureed canned tomatoes, along with a splash of cream or coconut milk, allowed the delicate vegetables and fragrant spices to shine.

Lastly, I experimented with garam masala, a spice blend often sprinkled onto Indian dishes before serving. Like curry powder, garam masala varies among cooks but usually

Curry in a Hurry

Hoping we could skip the step of grinding our own spices for curry, we substituted store-bought curry powder and garam masala. Tasters found this shortcut to be long on flavor, provided we chose the right brands and toasted the spice blends in a dry skillet. For complete tasting results, go to www.cooksillustrated.com/june.

TEST KITCHEN WINNERS
Penzeys Curry Powder (left) and McCormick Garam Masala (right)

PHOTOGRAPHY: CARL TREMBLAY

STEP-BY-STEP | KEY STEPS FOR BUILDING FLAVOR

Indian curries are defined by lengthy ingredient lists that result in complex layers of flavor. Here are the key steps we took to create big flavors using supermarket staples.

1. Toast the curry powder and garam masala in a dry skillet.

2. Rather than simmering potatoes in the curry, brown them with the onions.

3. Add tomato paste to the traditional garlic, ginger, and chiles for sweetness and depth.

4. Add the toasted spices to the pot to infuse the dish with flavor.

5. Sauté vegetables in spices following a simple Indian technique called *bhuna*.

includes warm spices such as black pepper, cinnamon, coriander, and cardamom (its name means "hot spice" in Hindi). Following my success with the curry powder, I decided to buy a jar of commercial garam masala. But when I added a few pinches to the curry postcooking, the result was raw and harsh-tasting. What if I toasted the garam masala in a skillet along with the curry powder? Lightning did strike twice, as the garam masala mellowed into a second wave of flavor that helped the curry reach an even more layered complexity. Here was a robust, satisfying vegetable curry that relied on supermarket staples.

INDIAN-STYLE CURRY WITH POTATOES, CAULIFLOWER, PEAS, AND CHICKPEAS

SERVES 4 TO 6 AS A MAIN COURSE

This curry is moderately spicy when made with one chile. For more heat, use an additional half chile. For a mild curry, remove the chile's ribs and seeds before mincing. Onions can be pulsed in a food processor. You can substitute 2 teaspoons ground coriander, ½ teaspoon ground black pepper, ¼ teaspoon ground cardamom, and ¼ teaspoon ground cinnamon for the garam masala. Serve with Basmati Rice Pilaf (recipe available free at www.cooksillustrated.com/june), passing yogurt and at least one type of chutney or relish at the table. For our Cilantro-Mint Chutney recipe and mango chutney taste test results, go to www.cooksillustrated.com/june.

- 2 tablespoons sweet or mild curry powder (see photo on page 14)
- 1½ teaspoons garam masala (see note above and photo on page 14)
- ¼ cup vegetable oil
- 2 medium onions, chopped fine (about 2 cups)
- 12 ounces Red Bliss potatoes, scrubbed and cut into ½-inch pieces (about 2 cups)
- 3 medium garlic cloves, minced or pressed through garlic press (about 1 tablespoon)
- 1 tablespoon finely grated fresh ginger
- 1–1½ serrano chiles, ribs, seeds, and flesh minced (see note above)
- 1 tablespoon tomato paste
- ½ medium head cauliflower, trimmed, cored, and cut into 1-inch florets (about 4 cups)
- 1 (14.5-ounce) can diced tomatoes, pulsed in food processor until nearly smooth with ¼-inch pieces visible
- 1¼ cups water
- 1 (15-ounce) can chickpeas, drained and rinsed
- Table salt
- 8 ounces frozen peas (about 1½ cups)
- ¼ cup heavy cream or coconut milk

Condiments

- Plain whole-milk yogurt
- Onion Relish (recipe follows)
- Cilantro-Mint Chutney (see note above)
- Mango chutney (see note above)

1. Toast curry powder and garam masala in small skillet over medium-high heat, stirring constantly, until spices darken slightly and become fragrant, about 1 minute. Remove spices from skillet and set aside.

2. Heat 3 tablespoons oil in large Dutch oven over medium-high heat until shimmering. Add onions and potatoes and cook, stirring occasionally, until onions are caramelized and potatoes are golden brown on edges, about 10 minutes. (Reduce heat to medium if onions darken too quickly.)

3. Reduce heat to medium. Clear center of pan and add remaining tablespoon oil, garlic, ginger, chile, and tomato paste; cook, stirring constantly, until fragrant, about 30 seconds. Add toasted spices and cook, stirring constantly, about 1 minute longer. Add cauliflower and cook, stirring constantly, until spices coat florets, about 2 minutes longer.

4. Add tomatoes, water, chickpeas, and 1 teaspoon salt; increase heat to medium-high and bring mixture to boil, scraping bottom of pan with wooden spoon to loosen browned bits. Cover and reduce heat to medium. Simmer briskly, stirring occasionally, until vegetables are tender, 10 to 15 minutes. Stir in peas and cream or coconut milk; continue to cook until heated through, about 2 minutes longer. Adjust seasoning with salt and serve immediately, passing condiments separately.

INDIAN-STYLE CURRY WITH SWEET POTATOES, EGGPLANT, GREEN BEANS, AND CHICKPEAS

Follow recipe for Indian-Style Curry with Potatoes, Cauliflower, Peas, and Chickpeas, substituting peeled sweet potatoes, cut into ½-inch dice, for Red Bliss potatoes. Substitute 1½ cups green beans, trimmed and cut into 1-inch pieces, and 1 medium eggplant, cut into ½-inch pieces (about 3 cups), for cauliflower. Omit peas.

ONION RELISH

MAKES ABOUT 1 CUP

If using a regular yellow onion, increase the sugar to 1 teaspoon. The relish can be refrigerated in an airtight container for 1 day.

- 1 medium Vidalia onion, finely diced (about 1 cup) (see note above)
- ½ teaspoon sweet paprika
- 1 tablespoon juice from 1 lime
- ½ teaspoon sugar
- Pinch cayenne
- ⅛ teaspoon table salt

Mix all ingredients in medium bowl.

COOK'S LIVE Original Test Kitchen Videos

www.cooksillustrated.com

RECIPE IN 60 SECONDS

- Indian-Style Curry with Potatoes, Cauliflower, Peas, and Chickpeas

VIDEO TIPS

- What's the best way to chop cauliflower?
- What should I do if the curry is too spicy?

The Best Kitchen Tools

Countless gadgets promise convenience but deliver disappointment and lost drawer space. Here are 18 tools that really work. BY KEITH DRESSER

SALAD SPINNER

Why You Need It: Wet greens can't be dressed properly and result in a soggy salad. We also use a salad spinner to wash and dry herbs.

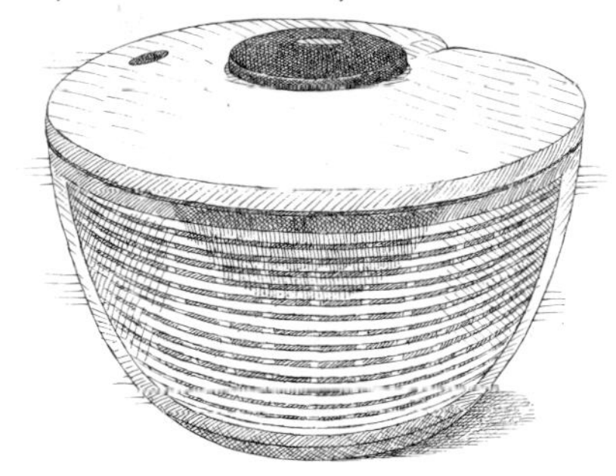

TEST KITCHEN FAVORITE:
➢OXO Good Grips Salad Spinner ($24.95)

Why We Like It: Its sturdy, leakproof bowl allows us to wash greens right in the bowl rather than in the sink. Its top-mounted pump knob requires little effort to use. We like that the top locks into place for storage, and a nonskid bottom holds the spinner in place.

VEGETABLE PEELERS

Why You Need Them: Most people have some kind of peeler that does an OK job on carrots and potatoes. But for other peeling jobs—say, the thick peel of a winter squash or the delicate skin of a pear—we rely on vegetable peelers that have maneuverable blades.

TEST KITCHEN FAVORITE:
➢OXO I-Series Swivel Peeler ($9.95)

Why We Like It: Given that our hands are constantly wet in the kitchen, we like that its rubberized handle is easy to grip. We find its hefty weight adds force to the sharpness of the blade, which can easily follow rounded contours. The blade is replaceable, but our OXO peelers have remained durable and sharp for years.

SERRATED PEELER

While not an everyday tool, this peeler's sharp serrated blade cleanly pulls the skin off difficult-to-peel produce such as tomatoes and easy-to-bruise peaches.

TEST KITCHEN FAVORITE:
➢MESSERMEISTER Peeler ($4.95)

COLANDER

Why You Need It: How else are you going to drain pasta and vegetables?

TEST KITCHEN FAVORITE:
➢ENDURANCE Pierced Colander/Strainer, 3-quart ($20.95) and 5-quart ($27.95)

Why We Like It: This large capacity colander contains minute, mesh-like perforations that drain in seconds, even when we have it overloaded with 2 pounds of cooked pasta. A wide base means it can sit in the sink without tipping or spilling.

HEATPROOF RUBBER SPATULA

Why You Need It: Nothing is better suited to a multitude of tasks, be it cleaning out the corners of bowls and pots, stirring batters, icing cakes, or folding egg whites. With the introduction of heat-resistant models, the tool is even more indispensable.

TEST KITCHEN FAVORITE:
➢RUBBERMAID 13.5-inch High Heat Scraper ($10.48)

Why We Like It: The wide, firm blade is rigid enough to mix the stiffest batter yet flexible enough to reach into the tightest of spaces. Unlike some rubber spatulas, the Rubbermaid doesn't stain or carry odors—even when used to stir chili. Rubbermaid's high-heat material is truly heatproof, something we've proved time and time again by leaving them in hot skillets and soup pots.

TONGS

Why You Need Them: Acting like an extension of the hand, tongs can lift, flip, turn, and rotate most any type of food, from small shrimp to a 5-pound rib roast. And unlike a hand, no burned fingers.

TEST KITCHEN FAVORITES:
➢OXO Good Grips 12-inch Locking Tongs ($9.95) and OXO Good Grips Tongs with Nylon Heads ($9.95)

Why We Like Them: These stainless steel tongs have rubber grips that help secure them in your hand. While they can open wide enough to pick up large items, they have springs that enable them to pick up the smallest of vegetables. Available with nonstick, nylon heads. Buy one of each.

GARLIC PRESS

Why You Need It: In our test kitchen, we press hundreds of garlic cloves each month. In numerous tests, we've found that a garlic press does a better job of mincing than one can do by hand—producing a fuller, less acrid flavor that is more evenly distributed throughout a dish. Keeps the garlic off your fingers, too.

TEST KITCHEN FAVORITE:
➢ZYLISS Jumbo Aluminum Garlic Press ($16.95)

Why We Like It: The Zyliss's sturdy construction has consistently delivered, making quick work of two garlic cloves at once. We like how the cleaner attachment stores cleverly in the handle.

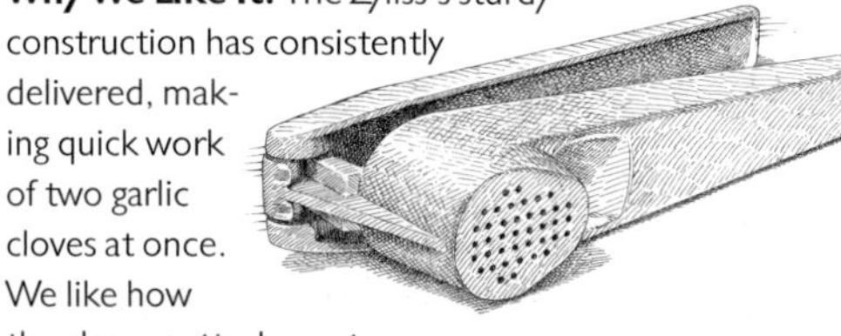

WHISK

Why You Need It: Useful for not only whipping cream and egg whites, a whisk can also mix batters and make pan sauces and gravies. Judging from all the shapes and sizes that whisks come in, you might think you need a different one for every task. Not so.

TEST KITCHEN FAVORITE:
➢BEST MANUFACTURERS 12-inch Standard French Whip ($9.95)

Why We Like It: This long whisk boasts a tight radius that can easily reach into all areas of a saucepan or bowl. Though agile, we've found its tines do not bend and twist with prolonged use.

MEASURING CUPS AND SPOONS

Why You Need Them: Inaccurate measuring of ingredients is one of the most common reasons recipes fail. Just ask any of us in the test kitchen: The need for a collection of measuring cups and spoons that efficiently and accurately measure ingredients is not debatable.

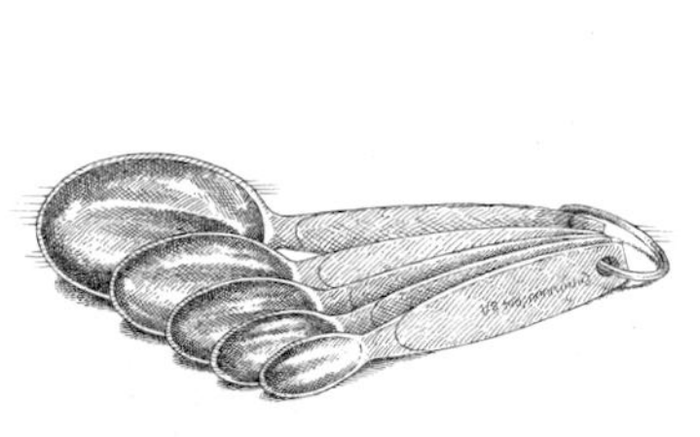

TEST KITCHEN FAVORITE:
➛AMCO Stainless Steel Dry Measuring Cups ($14.95)
Why We Like Them: These straight-sided cups have tops that are level with their handles, which makes for accurate measurement of dry ingredients. Set comes in fractional measurements such as ¾ and ⅔ cups, too.

TEST KITCHEN FAVORITE:
➛RUBBERMAID Liquid Measuring Cups ($4.49 for 2-cup; $5.99 for 4-cup)
Why We Like Them: These roomy cups are lightweight, able to pour without spilling a drop, and made of unbreakable plastic. Buy both the 2-cup and 4-cup sizes.

TEST KITCHEN FAVORITE:
➛CUISIPRO Stainless Steel Oval Measuring Spoons ($11.95)
Why We Like Them: The handles and bowl are flush, which facilitates the leveling of dry ingredients. Deep bowls make measuring liquids easier. And they're slim enough to be scooped into narrow spice jars.

GRATERS

Why You Need Them: A sharp box grater is indispensable for many tasks, from uniformly grating blocks of cheddar cheese to shredding potatoes. A finely textured rasp grater—so called because it's modeled after the woodworker's file-like tool—is portable, allowing you to grate or zest at the stove or table.

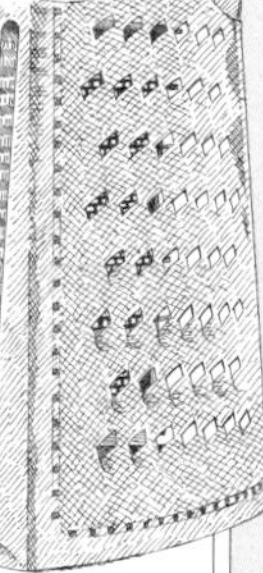

TEST KITCHEN FAVORITES:
➛CUISIPRO ACCUTEC Box Grater ($35.99)

Why We Like It: This razor-sharp box grater requires little effort or pressure to get results. We like its measurement-marked transparent walls, snap-on base, and comfortable, curved handle.

➛MICROPLANE Grater/Zester ($12.95)
Why We Like It: This handheld grater has razor-sharp teeth that can finely grate Parmesan in a flash. In addition to cheese, it can handle shallots, garlic, ginger, nutmeg, chocolate, and citrus zest.

INSTANT-READ THERMOMETER

Why You Need It: With an instant-read thermometer, you'll never again overcook a steak or undercook a chicken. We use them for everything from sauces and breads to cheesecakes.

TEST KITCHEN FAVORITE:
➛THERMOWORKS Super-Fast Thermapen ($85)

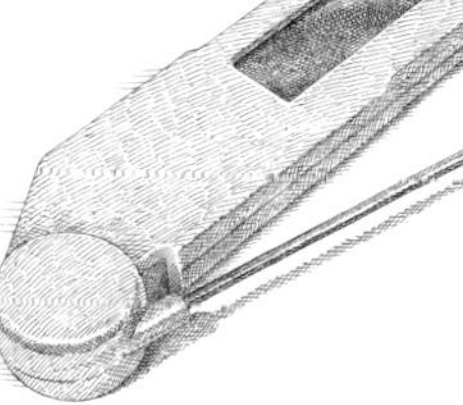

Why We Like It: In the test kitchen, we call it the Ferrari of thermometers. Besides providing an accurate read each time, its qualities include a quick response, thin probe, and large display. It can register temperatures from −58 to 572 degrees.

OVEN THERMOMETER

Why You Need It: While we calibrate the test kitchen ovens every two months, a survey of our ovens at home found that temperatures varied as much as 90 degrees from oven to oven. Knowing that, we always recommend checking an oven's temperature with a reliable thermometer.

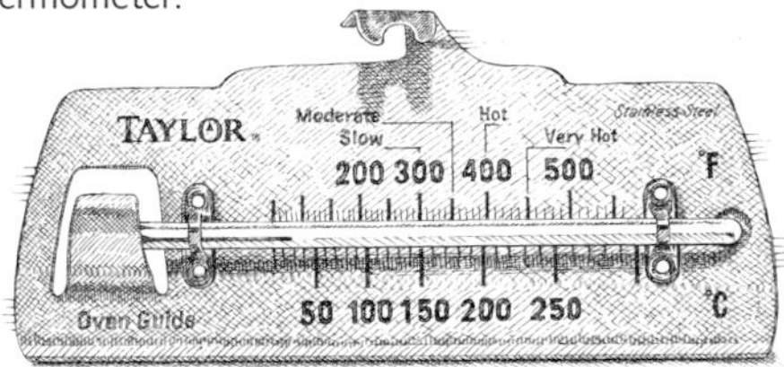

TEST KITCHEN FAVORITE:
➛TAYLOR Classic Oven Guide Thermometer ($14.99)

Why We Like It: We've found this oven thermometer to be the most accurate. It's also easy to read and hard to knock loose from an oven rack.

KITCHEN SHEARS

Why You Need Them: Our favorite tool for cutting up and trimming chickens, versatile kitchen shears are ideal for trimming pie dough, snipping herbs, and cutting parchment paper rounds. Try severing twine without them.

TEST KITCHEN FAVORITE:
➛MESSERMEISTER Take-Apart Shears ($23.99)

Why We Like Them: Precise, super-sharp, and agile. We like their slip-resistant handles and—especially when butchering chicken—the fact that they can be taken apart and cleaned thoroughly.

PEPPER MILL

Why You Need It: Because the preground stuff sold in bottles is insipid when compared with freshly ground. But grinding pepper shouldn't be a wrist-wrenching chore.

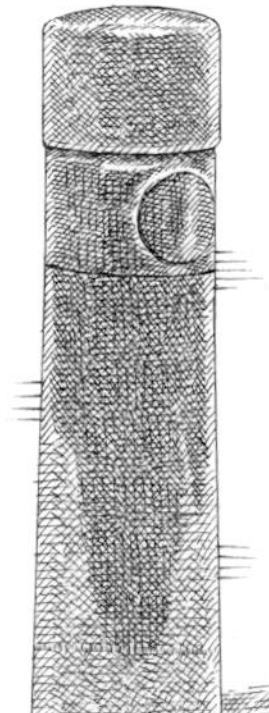

TEST KITCHEN FAVORITE:
➛UNICORN Magnum Plus Peppermill ($44.95)

Why We Like It: Whether coarse or fine, it quickly yields a consistent grind and requires little wrist action to operate. Its large capacity hopper requires infrequent filling. Best of all, it's easy to fill—no taking apart.

FINE-MESH STRAINER

Why You Need It: Essential for such tasks as dusting a tart with powdered sugar, removing bits of curdled egg from a pudding, or turning cooked raspberries into a seedless sauce. It also makes an excellent stand-in for a sifter.

TEST KITCHEN FAVORITE:
➛OXO Steel Strainer ($24.95)

Why We Like It: While other strainers in the test kitchen have bent or twisted over the years, the OXO has kept its shape. The ergonomic handle and deep bowl are nice, too.

SOURCES

www.cooksillustrated.com

Sources and ratings for recommended products are available at www.cooksillustrated.com/june.

ILLUSTRATION: JOHN BURGOYNE

Introducing Four-Cheese Lasagna

Choosing the right cheeses for this elegant lasagna is a good first step. Knowing how they melt results in a perfectly smooth and creamy sauce.

⋟ BY KEITH DRESSER ⋞

For most people, lasagna brings to mind a thick square with alternating layers of pasta, tomato sauce, gooey cheese, and chunks of ground meat—an unquestionably tasty combination. Four-cheese lasagna offers layers of pasta and cheese bound together with a creamy béchamel sauce. Discerning the uniqueness of each cheese flavor is part of the eating experience. Undeniably rich, but not prohibitively so, this lasagna is not meant to be eaten on its own. It is best served with a green salad, which both complements its richness and frames the dish as an elegant meal.

Many of the recipes I tried were heavy and bland, due in large part to the use of plain-tasting cheeses like mozzarella and ricotta. Though some recipes achieved good cheese flavor, they were either soupy, dry, or greasy. Because this lasagna lacked a meat sauce, the filling was thin and the finished product looked flat and insubstantial. I was determined to create a robust cheese lasagna with great structure, creamy texture, and great flavor.

Although ricotta isn't a big-flavor cheese, it adds structure to our lasagna.

Cheesy Come, Cheesy Go

Several quattro formaggi recipes from northern Italy used a combination of local cheeses, namely fontina, Parmesan, Gorgonzola, and Gruyère. When I tested a lasagna with a mixture of reasonably priced supermarket versions of these varieties, I was greeted by happy tasters. I saw no reason to vary.

The glue that holds the dish together is the béchamel sauce, which is made by thickening milk with a small amount of cooked butter and flour (called a roux). Though this classic white sauce is easy to prepare, finding the right amount and proper texture was a challenge. I made many loose, slippery pans of lasagna, and a number of bone-dry ones, before settling on a sauce made with 3 tablespoons of butter, 1/3 cup of flour, and 4 cups of milk. Making the sauce with a high ratio of flour to butter (traditional béchamel uses equal amounts) created a thick binder that provided enough heft to keep the layers together. The one remaining problem was the bland, milky flavor, which dulled the overall cheesiness of the dish. The solution lay in a classic French sauce called velouté, basically roux-thickened broth. Replacing 1½ cups of the milk with chicken broth was the key to balancing the richness of the sauce and bringing forward the cheese flavor. To give the sauce more complexity, I added a shallot and a garlic clove. A bay leaf and a pinch of cayenne stirred into the sauce as it simmered added backbone without overshadowing the other components.

To counter the recurring problem of all that cheese causing the lasagna to bake up with pools of unseemly grease on the surface and a slightly curdled texture, I took a cue from the Swiss. Classic fondue recipes include a starch when melting the cheese in order to keep it from becoming oily and gritty. In my next test, I incorporated the cheeses into the béchamel sauce, which contained a significant amount of flour, and hoped the starch would trap the oil and keep it from pooling on top of the lasagna. As I pulled the lasagna from the oven, I was thrilled to see no more puddles. After consulting with our science editor about the chemical structure of various cheeses (see "How Cheese Melts," page 19), I decided that the Gruyère was best mixed into the sauce, as it produced the most oil when cooked, while the fontina belonged between the pasta layers, where it helped maintain the dish's creamy texture.

RECIPE DIAGNOSIS: **Four Common Problems with Four-Cheese Lasagna**

PROBLEM: TOO RUNNY
SOLUTION: Make the béchamel sauce thicker by adding more flour than usual.

PROBLEM: TOO DRY
SOLUTION: Soak the no-boil noodles in hot water and don't skimp on the béchamel sauce.

PROBLEM: TOO GRAINY
SOLUTION: Bake the lasagna as gently as possible to keep the sauce from curdling.

PROBLEM: TOO GREASY
SOLUTION: Stabilize the Gruyère with some flour to keep it from leaving behind pools of grease.

PHOTOGRAPHY: CARL TREMBLAY

But even after I'd addressed the flavor and texture problems, my assembled lasagna was still squat and dense. Adding more noodles and cheese only made the entire dish heavier and starchier. The value of an open mind was demonstrated when I returned to an ingredient I had rejected early on, ricotta. It had the characteristics I was looking for: a flavor that didn't stand in the way of the others and a texture that gave the lasagna body without compromising the creamy nature of the sauce. Who knew? The secret to great four-cheese lasagna was a fifth cheese.

Baking the lasagna was my last hurdle, as it was quite delicate and would need only limited time in the oven. Using a technique that has served the test kitchen well, I presoaked the no-boil noodles for 10 minutes before layering them with the other ingredients, which shortened the lasagna's baking time. But the real key was to employ a low-heat/high-heat method. I baked the lasagna, covered, at 350 degrees until it just started to bubble around the edges. I then removed the cover and quickly broiled the lasagna to brown the top. Tasters agreed that this combination cooking method was the final touch that allowed me to deliver on my initial promise to create a sophisticated lasagna.

FOUR-CHEESE LASAGNA

SERVES 8 TO 10

It's important to not overbake the lasagna. Once the sauce starts bubbling around the edges, uncover the lasagna and turn the oven to broil. If your lasagna pan is not broiler-safe, brown the lasagna at 500 degrees for about 10 minutes. Whole milk is best in the sauce, but skim and low-fat milk also work. Supermarket-brand cheeses work fine in this recipe. The Gorgonzola may be omitted, but the flavor of the lasagna won't be as complex. The test kitchen prefers the flavor and texture of Barilla no-boil noodles, but this recipe will work with most brands. One box of Barilla will yield enough noodles for this recipe; you may need 2 boxes of other brands. The lasagna is rich; serve small portions with a green salad. Our recipe for Four-Cheese Lasagna with Artichokes and Prosciutto is available free at www.cooksillustrated.com/june.

- 6 ounces Gruyère cheese, shredded (about 1½ cups)
- 2 ounces finely grated Parmesan (about 1 cup)
- 1½ cups part-skim ricotta cheese
- 1 large egg, lightly beaten
- ¼ teaspoon ground black pepper
- 2 tablespoons plus 2 teaspoons minced fresh parsley leaves
- 3 tablespoons unsalted butter
- 1 medium shallot, minced (about 3 tablespoons)
- 1 medium garlic clove, minced or pressed through garlic press (about 1 teaspoon)
- ⅓ cup all-purpose flour
- 2½ cups whole milk
- 1½ cups low-sodium chicken broth
- ½ teaspoon table salt
- 1 bay leaf
- Pinch cayenne pepper
- 15 no-boil lasagna noodles
- 8 ounces fontina cheese, rind removed, shredded (about 2 cups)
- 3 ounces Gorgonzola cheese, finely crumbled (about ¾ cup)

1. Place Gruyère and ½ cup Parmesan in large heatproof bowl. Combine ricotta, egg, black pepper, and 2 tablespoons parsley in medium bowl. Set both bowls aside.

2. Melt butter in medium saucepan over medium heat until foaming; add shallot and garlic and cook, stirring frequently, until beginning to soften, about 2 minutes. Add flour and cook, stirring constantly, until thoroughly combined, about 1½ minutes; mixture should not brown. Gradually whisk in milk and broth; increase heat to medium-high and bring to full boil, whisking frequently. Add salt, bay leaf, and cayenne; reduce heat to medium-low and simmer until sauce thickens and coats the back of a spoon, about 10 minutes, stirring occasionally with heatproof rubber spatula or wooden spoon and making sure to scrape bottom and corners of saucepan (you should have about 4 cups sauce).

3. Remove saucepan from heat and discard bay leaf. Gradually whisk ¼ cup sauce into ricotta mixture. Pour remaining sauce over Gruyère mixture and stir until smooth; set aside.

4. Adjust oven rack to upper-middle position and heat oven to 350 degrees. Place noodles in 13 by 9-inch baking dish and cover with very hot tap water; soak 10 minutes, agitating noodles occasionally to prevent sticking. Remove noodles from water, place in single layer on kitchen towel, and pat dry. Wipe out baking dish and spray lightly with nonstick cooking spray.

5. Distribute ½ cup sauce in bottom of baking dish. Place 3 noodles in single layer on top of sauce. Spread ½ cup ricotta mixture evenly over noodles and sprinkle evenly with ½ cup fontina and 3 tablespoons Gorgonzola. Drizzle ½ cup sauce evenly over cheese. Repeat layering of noodles, ricotta, fontina, Gorgonzola, and sauce 3 more times. Place final 3 noodles on top and cover completely with remaining sauce, spreading with rubber spatula and allowing to spill over noodles. Sprinkle evenly with remaining ½ cup Parmesan.

6. Spray large sheet foil with nonstick cooking spray and cover lasagna; bake until edges are just bubbling, 25 to 30 minutes, rotating pan halfway through baking time. Remove foil and turn oven to broil. Broil until surface is spotty brown, 3 to 5 minutes. Cool 15 minutes. Sprinkle with remaining 2 teaspoons parsley; cut into pieces and serve.

SCIENCE: How Cheese Melts

While developing this recipe, I was surprised by how the cheeses reacted in very different ways when melted. The fontina melted into a creamy, cohesive mass, whereas the Gruyère became greasy and slightly grainy when heated. Why the difference?

It helps to understand that cheese doesn't melt in the true sense, like an ice cube. The protein casein, the solid component that gives cheese its structure, breaks down in the presence of heat. The protein molecules then separate and flow, which gives the appearance of melting.

Relatively young cheeses, such as fontina and mozzarella, have a high moisture content and a weaker protein structure, allowing for the protein to flow at lower temperatures. This higher moisture content means these cheeses have less of a tendency to "break" and become greasy when they melt. On the other hand, aged cheeses, such as Gruyère and cheddar, have less moisture and a stronger protein network, which means they melt at higher temperatures. Once melted, the more-developed protein structures in these cheeses break down, leaving behind a gritty texture. Because there is less moisture in these aged cheeses, they can become unstable and break when melted, releasing the fat and creating the greasiness I had noted in so many of my tests. –K.D.

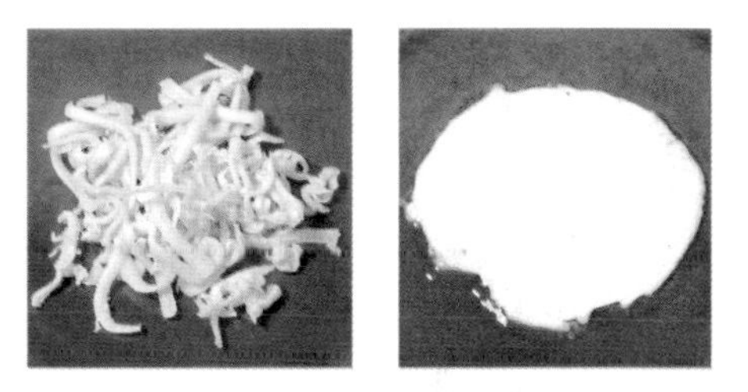

SHREDDED FONTINA MELTED FONTINA
Young, high-moisture fontina cheese melts smoothly.

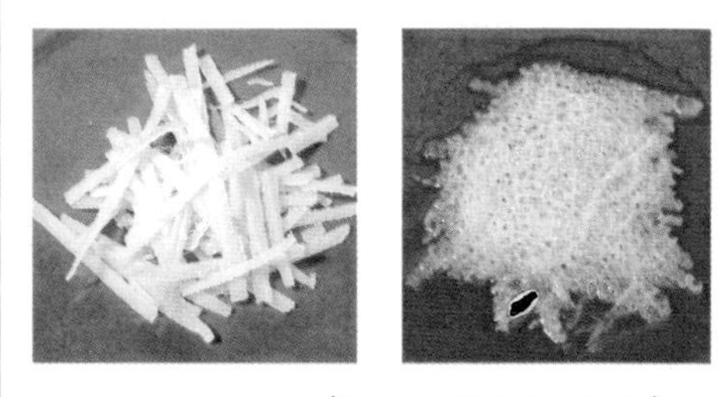

SHREDDED GRUYÈRE MELTED GRUYÈRE
Aged, low-moisture Gruyère separates when melted.

COOK'S LIVE Original Test Kitchen Videos
www.cooksillustrated.com

RECIPE IN 60 SECONDS
- Four-Cheese Lasagna

VIDEO TIP
- Why do I need to soak no-boil lasagna noodles?

Steak Marinades That Work

Most marinades fail miserably, neither tenderizing meat nor adding much flavor. We found a way to quickly do both: double dipping.

BY DAVID PAZMIÑO

Marinades are supposed to make steaks more flavorful and tender, but most do neither. Past experiments in the test kitchen have shown us that soy sauce is a good starting point. The salt in the soy sauce acts much like a brine, helping the meat retain moisture during cooking and making it more tender. Omitting any citrus juice and vinegar until serving time also improves texture. In large amounts, these acidic ingredients can make meat tough.

But what about flavor? A one-note Kikkoman kick wasn't what I had in mind. I figured that I needed strong seasonings to stand up to the soy sauce, and I found them in the international section of my supermarket, with ingredients as diverse as red curry paste, Dijon mustard, and chipotle chiles. I now needed to find out how long it would take my seasoned marinades to penetrate the steak with the exciting flavor I wanted. After numerous tests, tasters agreed that the clear front-runner was the steak that had been marinated for 24 hours, which translated to: Marinate today, grill tomorrow. No way.

How could I quickly intensify the flavors? I remembered that one of our recent stories on grilled shrimp called for marinating the shrimp after it was cooked, rather than before. Could I use a quick premarinade to do the tenderizing work of a brine and then employ a postmarinade—done while the steaks are resting—to heighten the flavor?

Setting a one-hour time limit, I combined the meat and all but ¼ cup of the marinade. The reserved marinade was then combined with vinegar or citrus juice—I knew these ingredients harm texture if added before cooking, but I wanted their bright flavors. Once the beef was pulled off the grill, I sliced it and placed it into this mixture. The marinade flavors were now quite obvious; in fact, some tasters thought the marinades were too intense. So instead of slicing the beef, I simply dipped the whole steak into the marinade, flipping it once while it rested. Then I sliced the meat and served the postmarinade on the side.

I ran six more tests to make sure this technique worked with a variety of cuts. While the looser-textured skirt, flank, and sirloin tip steaks absorbed the marinade better than the thicker rib-eye, strip, and blade steaks, they all benefited from the one-hour precooking marinade and the 10-minute postcooking marinade. This is one case where double dipping is a good thing.

BETTER THAN A-1 MARINADE

MAKES ENOUGH TO MARINATE 4 TO 6 INDIVIDUAL STEAKS OR ONE 2 POUND STEAK

Go to www.cooksillustrated.com/june for free information on grilling steak. You'll also find an additional recipe for Mojo Marinade.

- ½ cup soy sauce
- ⅓ cup vegetable oil
- 2 tablespoons dark brown sugar
- ¼ cup Worcestershire sauce
- 4 medium garlic cloves, minced or pressed through garlic press (about 4 teaspoons)
- 2 tablespoons minced chives
- 1½ teaspoons ground black pepper
- 2 teaspoons balsamic vinegar

1. Combine soy, oil, sugar, Worcestershire, garlic, chives, and pepper in medium bowl. Remove ¼ cup marinade and combine with vinegar in small bowl; set aside.
2. Place remaining marinade and steaks in gallon-size zipper-lock bag; press out as much air as possible and seal bag. Refrigerate 1 hour, flipping bag after 30 minutes to ensure that steaks marinate evenly.
3. Remove steaks from marinade, letting any excess marinade drip back into bag. Discard bag and marinade. Grill steaks as desired.
4. Transfer steaks to shallow pan and pour reserved marinade over top. Tent loosely with foil and let rest 10 minutes, turning meat halfway through. Slice steak or serve whole, passing reserved marinade if desired.

HONEY MUSTARD MARINADE

MAKES ENOUGH TO MARINATE 4 TO 6 INDIVIDUAL STEAKS OR ONE 2-POUND STEAK

- ½ cup soy sauce
- ⅓ cup vegetable oil
- 4 teaspoons honey
- 3 tablespoons Dijon mustard
- 2 tablespoons chopped fresh tarragon leaves
- 4 medium garlic cloves, minced or pressed through garlic press (about 4 teaspoons)
- 1½ teaspoons ground black pepper
- 1 teaspoon cider vinegar

Combine soy, oil, honey, mustard, tarragon, garlic, and pepper in medium bowl. Remove ¼ cup marinade and combine with vinegar in small bowl; set aside. Follow recipe for Better Than A-1 Marinade from step 2.

SOUTHEAST ASIAN MARINADE

MAKES ENOUGH TO MARINATE 4 TO 6 INDIVIDUAL STEAKS OR ONE 2-POUND STEAK

- ⅓ cup soy sauce
- ⅓ cup vegetable oil
- 2 tablespoons dark brown sugar
- 2 tablespoons fish sauce
- 2 tablespoons red curry paste
- 2 tablespoons grated fresh ginger
- 4 medium garlic cloves, minced or pressed through garlic press (about 4 teaspoons)
- 2 tablespoons juice from 1 lime

Combine soy, oil, sugar, fish sauce, curry paste, ginger, and garlic in medium bowl. Remove ¼ cup marinade and combine with lime juice in small bowl; set aside. Follow recipe for Better Than A-1 Marinade from step 2.

MOLE MARINADE

MAKES ENOUGH TO MARINATE 4 TO 6 INDIVIDUAL STEAKS OR ONE 2-POUND STEAK

- ½ cup soy sauce
- ⅓ cup vegetable oil
- 2 tablespoons dark brown sugar
- 4 chipotle chiles in adobo sauce, minced
- 4 teaspoons cocoa powder
- 1½ teaspoons dried oregano
- 4 medium garlic cloves, minced or pressed through garlic press (about 4 teaspoons)
- 1 teaspoon ground black pepper
- 2 tablespoons juice from 1 lime

Combine soy, oil, sugar, chiles, cocoa, oregano, garlic, and pepper in medium bowl. Remove ¼ cup marinade and combine with lime juice in small bowl; set aside. Follow recipe for Better Than A-1 Marinade from step 2.

COOK'S LIVE Original Test Kitchen Videos

www.cooksillustrated.com

VIDEO TIPS

- How do I prepare a charcoal grill for cooking steaks?
- How do I slice flank steak against the grain?
- What's the best way to slice sirloin tip or skirt steak?

Hearty Asparagus-Stuffed Omelets

How do you make a sturdy omelet that isn't tough?

BY MATTHEW CARD

There are two distinct styles of omelets: trifolded French omelets (also called rolled omelets) and bifolded diner omelets. The former is a delicate affair in which the tender texture and subtle flavor of the eggs, offset by a spoonful or two of filling, takes center stage; the latter is a far less refined dish in which a sturdy, lightly browned omelet shares equal billing with a substantial filling. I've got nothing against the French, but I'm a greater fan of the heartier brand of omelet, especially when packed with asparagus and cheese. It's a satisfying one-pan meal that can be readied in minutes.

That said, I have a few issues with diner-style omelets, the biggest being that the eggs are usually overcooked to lend the omelet enough structure to contain the filling without ripping or breaking. A rich filling can compensate for some of an omelet's dryness, but is it possible to synthesize the best of French- and diner-style omelets to make one that is moist, tender, and sturdy?

After making a few dozen omelets, it became clear that there are two primary issues to consider: the method in which the eggs are manipulated in the pan and the temperature at which the omelet is cooked. Classic recipes shake and swirl the pan to facilitate even cooking, but I opted for the easier approach of lifting the setting omelet with a rubber spatula to allow the uncooked egg to pool underneath and cook. Lifting in a circular fashion around the circumference of the skillet set the omelet evenly—no peaks, valleys, or lumps.

Using medium-high heat, the omelet wasn't fully cooked by the time the bottom was done. Dialing down to medium-low allowed the eggs to set more slowly and thoroughly, but this didn't eliminate the wet egg on top. Some recipes allow the omelet to sit covered off heat to finish cooking. I slid the pan off its burner, covered it, and waited. Seconds blurred into minutes before the egg dried and the cheese melted. I assumed the omelet would be tough, but it was as tender as any French-style omelet. As the pan cooled, however, it allowed the omelet to gain traction. I refired the pan, and within seconds my meal slid free.

Five eggs were the most I could cook in a 10-inch skillet, which yielded an omelet large enough, once filled, to serve two. A little salt and pepper were the only worthwhile additions to the eggs; neither milk, cream, nor water, which are often added to omelets to lighten their texture, made a difference. As for the filling, it made sense to sauté the asparagus in the same skillet in which the omelet was to be prepared. Tasters liked the subtly nutty flavor and smooth texture of finely grated Gruyère, which melted easily to become one with the eggs.

ASPARAGUS OMELET

SERVES 2

When cooking the eggs, it is important to lift the edges of the omelet rather than push them toward the center. Our recipe for Asparagus Omelet with Roasted Red Peppers and Garlic is available free at www.cooksillustrated.com/june.

- 2 tablespoons unsalted butter
- ½ pound asparagus, trimmed of tough ends and cut on bias into ¼-inch pieces (about 1 ¼ cups)
- Table salt and ground black pepper
- 1 medium shallot, halved and sliced thin
- 1 teaspoon juice from 1 lemon
- 5 large eggs
- 1 ½ ounces finely grated Gruyère cheese (about ½ cup)

1. Heat 1 tablespoon butter in 10-inch nonstick skillet over medium-high heat; when foaming subsides, add asparagus, pinch salt, and pepper to taste. Cook, stirring occasionally, for 2 minutes. Add shallot and continue cooking, stirring occasionally, until asparagus is lightly browned and tender, 2 to 4 minutes longer. Add lemon juice and toss to coat; transfer to bowl. While asparagus cooks, beat eggs and salt and pepper to taste with fork in small bowl until combined.

2. Wipe skillet clean with paper towel. Heat remaining 1 tablespoon butter in skillet over medium-low heat; when foaming subsides, pour in eggs. Cook, without stirring, until eggs begin to set, 45 seconds to 1 minute. Using rubber spatula, lift edge of cooked egg, then tilt pan to one side so that uncooked egg runs underneath. Repeat process, working around pan edge. Using spatula, gently scrape uncooked egg toward rim of skillet, until top is just slightly wet. Entire process should take 1½ to 2 minutes. Let pan sit on heat without moving for 30 seconds. Remove pan from heat, sprinkle asparagus mixture in even layer over omelet, then sprinkle cheese evenly over asparagus. Cover and let stand until eggs no longer appear wet, 4 to 5 minutes.

3. Return skillet to medium heat for 30 seconds. Using rubber spatula, loosen edges of omelet from skillet. Slide omelet halfway out of pan onto serving plate. Tilt pan so top of omelet folds over itself. Cut omelet in half; using large, thin spatula, transfer to individual plates and serve immediately.

ASPARAGUS OMELET WITH BLACK FOREST HAM AND MUSTARD

Follow recipe for Asparagus Omelet, adding 2 teaspoons whole-grain mustard to asparagus along with lemon juice in step 1. Add 3 ounces Black Forest ham, cut into ¼-inch dice, along with asparagus mixture in step 2.

COOK'S LIVE Original Test Kitchen Videos
www.cooksillustrated.com
RECIPE IN 60 SECONDS
- Asparagus Omelet

STEP-BY-STEP | MAKING AN OMELET

1. Once omelet begins to set, use spatula to lift edges, tilting pan so raw egg runs underneath.

2. When all but top of omelet has set, gently pull remaining uncooked egg to pan edges.

3. Remove filled omelet from heat, cover, and let stand until eggs are no longer wet.

4. Slide omelet halfway out of pan onto serving plate, tilting pan so omelet folds over itself.

Ultimate Crumb Cake

We wanted to bring this New York classic home—but not from the supermarket.

BY ERIKA BRUCE

Crumb cake has been around for a long time, but surprisingly few people can distinguish it from a regular streusel-topped coffeecake. This is because this quirky yet elegant cake has its origins deeply rooted in just one part of the United States, New York, where it arrived with the influx of German immigrants who came to the area in the late 1800s, their recipes for *krummelkuchen* in hand. The New York bakeries that originally made this especially rich yeasted Danish dough topped with thick chunks of lightly spiced crumb topping are all but extinct. My research uncovered only one still operating, the family-run Holtermann's Bakery on Staten Island.

Many people associate crumb cake with Entenmann's, a Brooklyn bakery that has expanded into a national supermarket brand. Laden with shelf-stabilizing preservatives, this popular version of crumb cake doesn't do justice to the bakery-fresh original. Because I think everyone deserves a proper taste of this classic confection, my goal was to come up with a recipe to make at home—one that would stand up to the legacy of authentic crumb cake.

Golden-edged crumbs are the mark of a great crumb cake.

A sampling of recipes showed that many modern versions are made with butter cake (even Entenmann's now offers this style). Though committed to making the best possible crumb cake, this was good news for me, as I didn't want to spend all day watching dough rise in order to do it. These recipes served as a primer on the potential problems with crumb cake. If the cake was too tender and delicate, the crumbs had a tendency to sink in the center. Drier, sturdier cakes provided little contrast between cake and crumb. Skimping on crumb topping—which is how some recipe writers avoid sinking crumbs—was not an option.

I decided to try one promising approach. Some recipes call for combining all of the flour, sugar, and butter and then reserving a portion for the topping and adding the remaining ingredients—such as eggs, milk, and baking powder—to the rest to make the cake batter. While this method was efficient, tasters found the results to be lackluster. The crumb needed more butter and sugar than flour, and the cake cried out for just the opposite. Clearly a wrong turn: For the ultimate crumb cake, each component would need its own recipe.

Starting with the test kitchen's favorite yellow cake recipe (March/April 1999), I divided it in half to make room for the crumb layer. Part of this cake's appeal is its rich butteriness; once topped with redundantly buttery crumbs, it crossed over the line to greasiness. Reducing the butter lightened the cake but also made it dry and lean. Increasing the milk moistened the cake but made it less sturdy; while in the oven, the crumbs promptly sank through the wet batter. I tried thicker dairy ingredients: buttermilk, sour cream, and yogurt. Buttermilk was the clear winner, although it required a switch from baking powder to baking soda to neutralize some of its acidity.

The cake was still a little too rubbery, which I suspected was due to its being egg-heavy. I tried removing an egg, but again the careful structure of the cake was compromised. I added back a yolk, and my cake problems were finally solved.

Don't Be Tempted

SUNKEN CAKE

If you use powdered buttermilk instead of the real thing, your crumb cake may sink as the batter will be thinner.

DRY CAKE

Using all-purpose flour in place of cake flour will make the crumb cake dry.

Surviving the Crunch

The pièce de résistance of all crumb cakes is, of course, the crumb topping. And this is where many recipes go wrong, veering more toward a streusel topping than a crumb topping. While these both begin with the same ingredients—flour, sugar, butter, and a pinch of salt—a subtle shift in the ratios gives very different results. Streusel is fine and crunchy and may include other textural additions such as nuts or oatmeal. It's more of a sugary topping, while a crumb topping is less sweet and more substantial, sharing equal billing with the cake. Streusel also has less butter, giving it a sandy quality. Crumb topping is softer, more cookie-like, and contains only cinnamon as a flavoring.

Once I had acknowledged these distinctions, I adjusted my recipe. Less sugar, however, gave my crumbs the texture of powdery snow. To make them more cohesive, I tried using brown sugar instead of granulated. These crumbs were too chewy but had a welcome butterscotch flavor; half of each sugar was the winning compromise. Getting the butter right proved to be even more challenging. Too much and the crumbs melted into a solid mass when baked; too little and they reverted back to streusel. Switching from softened butter to melted butter gave the raw topping a

PHOTOGRAPHY: CARL TREMBLAY

TECHNIQUE | SECRETS TO BIGGER CRUMBS

Using both hands, break apart the crumb dough, rolling the broken dough between your thumb and forefinger to form crumbs about the size of large peas. Continue until all the dough has been broken down into crumbs. Sprinkle crumbs evenly over the cake batter, breaking apart any larger chunks. Spread crumbs from the outside of the cake toward the center so as to not make the center too heavy.

BREAKING THE DOUGH

PERFECT-SIZED CRUMBS

unified, dough-like consistency—one I broke apart with my fingers before sprinkling over the cake batter. As I had hoped, these cohesive little nuggets held together when baked, giving me the quintessential crumb cake crumbs: sturdy on the outside, moist and tender on the inside.

Just the right amount of cinnamon (¾ teaspoon) finished the crumbs off with some warm spice. Reducing the oven temperature, lengthening the baking time, and raising the oven rack to the upper-middle position gave the crumbs their irresistible golden edges. I had finally captured the essence of what made this cake a classic. Plus I could enjoy it at home whenever I wanted, still warm from the oven—something you can't get out of any cake box.

NEW YORK-STYLE CRUMB CAKE

SERVES 8 TO 10

Don't be tempted to substitute all-purpose flour for the cake flour, as doing so will make a dry, tough cake. If you can't find buttermilk, you can substitute an equal amount of plain, low-fat yogurt. When topping the cake, take care to not push the crumbs into the batter. This recipe can be easily doubled and baked in a 13 by 9-inch baking dish. If doubling, increase the baking time to about 45 minutes. Cooled leftovers can be wrapped in plastic wrap and stored at room temperature for up to 2 days.

Crumb Topping

- ⅓ cup (2⅔ ounces) granulated sugar
- ⅓ cup (2⅔ ounces) dark brown sugar
- ¾ teaspoon ground cinnamon
- ⅛ teaspoon salt
- 8 tablespoons (1 stick) unsalted butter, melted and still warm
- 1¾ cups (7 ounces) cake flour

Cake

- 1¼ cups (5 ounces) cake flour
- ½ cup (3½ ounces) granulated sugar
- ¼ teaspoon baking soda
- ¼ teaspoon salt
- 6 tablespoons (¾ stick) unsalted butter, cut into 6 pieces, softened but still cool
- 1 large egg plus 1 large yolk
- 1 teaspoon vanilla extract
- ⅓ cup buttermilk
- Confectioners' sugar for dusting

1. **FOR THE TOPPING:** Whisk sugars, cinnamon, salt, and butter in medium bowl to combine. Add flour and stir with rubber spatula or wooden spoon until mixture resembles thick, cohesive dough; set aside to cool to room temperature, 10 to 15 minutes.

2. **FOR THE CAKE:** Adjust oven rack to upper-middle position and heat oven to 325 degrees. Cut 16-inch length parchment paper or aluminum foil and fold lengthwise to 7-inch width. Spray 8-inch square baking dish with nonstick cooking spray and fit parchment into dish, pushing it into corners and up sides; allow excess to overhang edges of dish.

3. In bowl of standing mixer fitted with paddle attachment, mix flour, sugar, baking soda, and salt on low speed to combine. With mixer running at low speed, add butter one piece at a time; continue beating until mixture resembles moist crumbs, with no visible butter chunks remaining, 1 to 2 minutes. Add egg, yolk, vanilla, and buttermilk; beat on medium-high speed until light and fluffy, about 1 minute, scraping once if necessary.

4. Transfer batter to baking pan; using rubber spatula, spread batter into even layer. Following photos at left, break apart crumb topping into large pea-sized pieces and spread in even layer over batter, beginning with edges and then working toward center. Bake until crumbs are golden and wooden skewer inserted into center of cake comes out clean, 35 to 40 minutes. Cool on wire rack at least 30 minutes. Remove cake from pan by lifting parchment overhang. Dust with confectioners' sugar just before serving.

EQUIPMENT TESTING:

Square Cake Pans

A square cake pan is a kitchen essential, but should you buy a glass, nonstick, or traditional metal model? We tested crumb cakes and corn bread in seven 8-inch pans to see how the various options performed. Pallid crusts plagued items baked in shiny metal pans made by Kaiser Tinplate ($6), Magic Line ($17.50), and Kitchen Supply ($14.98). The Pyrex Square Glass Pan ($9) turned out respectable color on our corn bread and crumb cake, though it was outshone by the deep, evenly golden sides and bottoms on baked goods prepared in the three nonstick options—Chicago Metallic Gourmetware ($5.50), Calphalon Classic Nonstick ($18.27), and Williams-Sonoma Goldtouch Nonstick Square Pan ($21). The Williams-Sonoma pan yielded baked goods that stood a full 2 inches tall and sported straight (rather than flared) sides, making it easier to cut symmetrical pieces and split cakes into two even layers. It is our top choice, although all three of the nonstick pans we tested are good options. For complete testing results, go to www.cooksillustrated.com/june. —Elizabeth Bomze

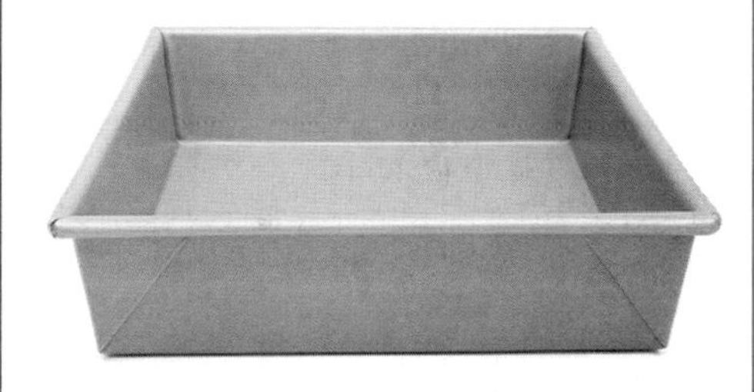

TOP PAN
WILLIAMS-SONOMA Goldtouch Nonstick ($21) is deeper than the competition and yields nicely browned cakes with perfectly straight edges.

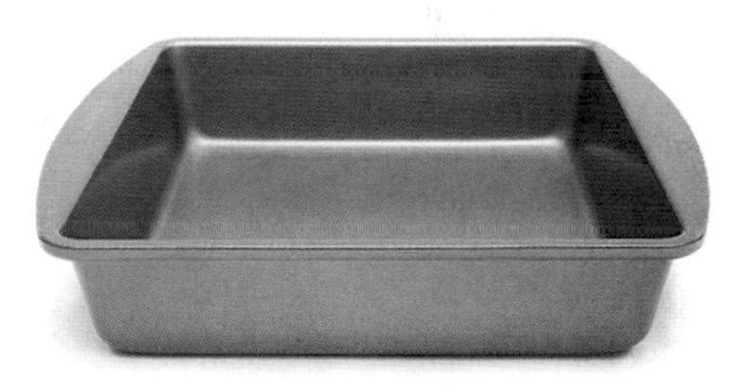

BEST BUY
CHICAGO METALLIC Gourmetware ($5.99) has sloped sides and is a bit shallow, but it delivers excellent browning and boasts convenient handles.

COOK'S LIVE Original Test Kitchen Videos
www.cooksillustrated.com

RECIPE IN 60 SECONDS
- New York-Style Crumb Cake

VIDEO TIPS
- What kind of cake pan should I use?
- How should I prepare my cake pan?
- Can I substitute all-purpose flour for the cake flour?

An Easier (and Better) Bran Muffin

We wanted a bran muffin that didn't require a trip to the health food store.

BY CHARLES KELSEY

The idea of using bran cereal to make muffins is nothing new. One of the first such recipes appeared on the package of Kellogg's Krumbled Bran in 1916, a time when mass-marketed bran cereals were a novel concept. Today, however, store shelves are chockablock with bran-based cereals that come in various shapes and sizes, fashioned as twigs, flakes, and granules. Many have other ingredients added, such as oats, corn, rice, barley, figs, raisins, and fruit juices. Most have accompanying bran muffin recipes.

In the past, I have made bran muffins with unprocessed wheat bran from the health food store. So I know what the real thing should be—a moist, hearty muffin redolent of bran's rich, earthy flavor. But these muffins require a special shopping trip. Could a commercial cereal sold at the supermarket deliver good results? If so, which one?

I wanted cereals in which wheat bran—the wheat kernel's papery, nutritious outer skin—was the major ingredient. That narrowed the field (goodbye to oat bran) and lightened my shopping cart, though not the "health nut" look from the checkout lady. After trying a number of back-of-the-box recipes, I'll admit I found a few muffins with decent bran flavor. But all of them came out squat and dry, desperate for moisture. Certainly none of them would inspire me to jump out of bed in the morning and get out the mixing bowl. I had my work cut out for me.

We made a great muffin using supermarket bran cereal. The tricks were to not presoak the cereal in milk and to choose the right brand.

Taking Control

My first goal was to clearly determine how each bran cereal functioned when baked into a muffin. I stitched together a recipe consisting of all-purpose flour, butter, sugar, molasses, milk, eggs, baking powder, and raisins and began testing cereals one at a time.

The recipes I tested with flakes came out flavorless and looked like springy cupcakes instead of the rustic muffins I had in mind. The muffins made with granules were also flavorless, and their texture was dense and pasty. The twigs provided a deep bran flavor, but getting them to bend to my will was another matter. They weren't fully dissolving into the batter and were even sticking out of the tops of the baked muffins.

Presoaking the twigs in the milk (as recommended in most recipes) didn't really work and made the muffins as dense as hockey pucks. The cereal was soaking up all the moisture, which dried out the batter. Heating the cereal in milk before adding it to the batter made it even worse, causing the muffins to bake up gummy. I decided to switch gears. Rather than soaking the cereal and then building the batter in the same bowl, I made the muffin batter first and tried adding the bran later. I hoped this would eliminate the guesswork regarding how much liquid the cereal was going to absorb.

Just adding the twigs to the batter didn't soften them enough. For my next test, I tried grinding the twigs to a powder in a food processor before adding them to the batter. Much better—the muffins had an even crumb, but they were a bit heavy. A compromise was in order. I pulverized half of the cereal and kept the other half whole. When I combined the pulverized and intact bran and added them to the batter, they softened perfectly in only five minutes. I finally had the chewy, rustic texture I wanted.

I had been using Kellogg's All-Bran Original for my testing, but I circled back to try other brands of twig-style bran cereal. General Mills Fiber One produced bland muffins—which made sense when I read the label more carefully and saw that wheat, not bran, was the primary ingredient. And tasters had a hard time getting past Post 100% Bran's malted, fruity flavor, which was explained by an ingredient list containing malted barley flour as well as fig and prune juice concentrates. In the end, tasters deemed Kellogg's All-Bran Original the winner for its deep, complex bran flavor.

SHOPPING: Bran Cereal

Bran is the outer layer of the wheat grain that is removed during milling. Bran cereal comes in various forms. Here's how they stack up in muffins.

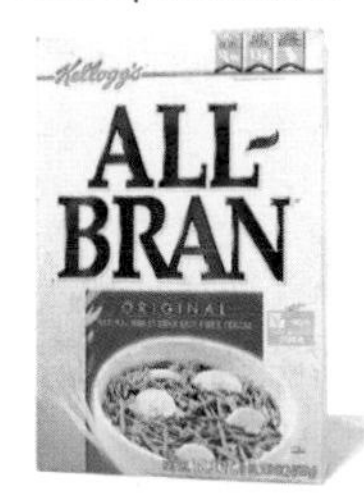

TWIGS
We found that All-Bran Original gave our muffins the most robust bran flavor.

FLAKES
Bran flakes use whole wheat and made muffins with very little bran flavor.

GRANULES
Small granules of bran buds made dense muffins with almost no bran flavor.

WITH RAISINS
This cereal seemed like a good idea, but the raisins cooked up dry and tough.

PHOTOGRAPHY: CARL TREMBLAY

TECHNIQUE | SOFTENING THE BRAN

When we added the cereal directly to the batter, the muffins were marred by crunchy bits and twigs sticking out of the top. When we processed all of the cereal into a fine powder, the muffins were too dense. By processing just half of the cereal and leaving the other half in twig form, we created muffins with an even, but not heavy, texture.

Measure for Measure

With the cereal mystery finally solved, I could fine-tune my recipe. I discovered that one egg didn't add enough structure, and two eggs made the muffins too springy. A whole egg plus a yolk worked best, giving the muffins a fluffy, but not bouncy, texture. But my muffins still seemed too lean and dry. More than 6 tablespoons of butter made the muffins greasy, so I turned to the dairy element. Swapping the milk for sour cream was overkill. Buttermilk was an improvement over plain milk, but whole milk yogurt was the tasters' first choice. And replacing the baking powder with baking soda gave me a coarser crumb that tasters liked.

Mixing some whole wheat flour with the all-purpose flour reinforced the flavor of the bran, as did replacing the granulated sugar with brown sugar and increasing the molasses. After complaints that the raisins didn't soften enough during baking, I plumped them in the microwave with a little water. I had finally used a supermarket cereal to create a moist, tender muffin with big bran flavor.

TECHNIQUE | FILL 'ER UP

For big, hearty muffins, fill the muffin cups to the rim. And for nicely domed muffins, mound the batter in the cups and don't level it off.

BETTER BRAN MUFFINS

MAKES 12 MUFFINS

The test kitchen prefers Kellogg's All-Bran Original cereal in this recipe. Dried cranberries or dried cherries may be substituted for raisins. Low-fat or nonfat yogurt can be substituted for whole milk yogurt, though the muffins will be slightly less flavorful.

- 1 cup raisins
- 1 teaspoon water
- 2¼ cups (5 ounces) All-Bran Original cereal
- 1¼ cups (6¼ ounces) unbleached all-purpose flour
- ½ cup (2½ ounces) whole wheat flour
- 2 teaspoons baking soda
- ½ teaspoon table salt
- 1 large egg plus 1 large yolk
- ⅔ cup (4⅔ ounces) packed light brown sugar
- 3 tablespoons mild or light molasses
- 1 teaspoon vanilla extract
- 6 tablespoons (¾ stick) unsalted butter, melted and cooled
- 1¾ cups plain whole milk yogurt

1. Adjust oven rack to middle position and heat oven to 400 degrees. Spray standard-sized muffin pan with nonstick cooking spray. Combine raisins and water in small microwave-safe bowl, cover with plastic wrap, cut several steam vents in plastic with paring knife, and microwave on high power for 30 seconds. Let stand, covered, until raisins are softened and plump, about 5 minutes. Transfer raisins to paper towel–lined plate to cool.

2. Process half of bran cereal in food processor until finely ground, about 1 minute. Whisk flours, baking soda, and salt in large bowl to combine; set aside. Whisk egg and yolk together in medium bowl until well-combined and light-colored, about 20 seconds. Add sugar, molasses, and vanilla; whisk until mixture is thick, about 30 seconds. Add melted butter and whisk to combine; add yogurt and whisk to combine. Stir in processed cereal and unprocessed cereal; let mixture sit until cereal is evenly moistened (there will still be some small lumps), about 5 minutes.

3. Add wet ingredients to dry ingredients and gently mix with rubber spatula until batter is combined and evenly moistened. Do not overmix. Gently fold raisins into batter. Using ⅓-cup measure or ice cream scoop, divide batter evenly among muffin cups, dropping batter to form mounds. Do not level or flatten surfaces of mounds.

4. Bake until muffins are dark golden and toothpick inserted into center of muffin comes out with a few crumbs attached, 16 to 20 minutes, rotating pan halfway through baking. Cool muffins in pan for 5 minutes, then transfer to wire rack and cool for 10 minutes before serving.

EQUIPMENT TESTING:

Kitchen Timers

In the test kitchen, timing is everything. To that end, we tested 10 new models designed to handle multitask timing. We were looking for timers with a range of at least 10 hours (for longer braises, brines, and barbecues) that could count up after the alarm and display two times simultaneously. The compact, easy-to-use Polder Dual Timer/Stopwatch ($19.99) impressed us the most (the previous test kitchen favorite was the Polder Electronic Clock, Timer and Stopwatch, at $5 less). The Taylor Two Event Big Digit Timer/Clock ($10.99) offers the same functions but isn't so easy to use. At half the price, it's our choice for best buy. For complete testing results, go to www.cooksillustrated.com/june.

—Meredith Smith

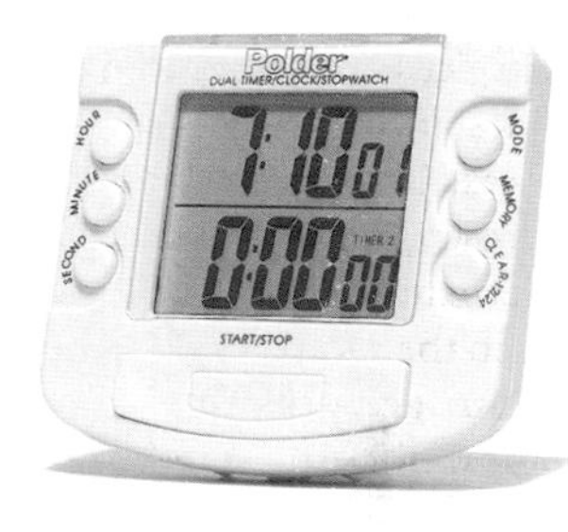

TOP TIMER

POLDER Dual Timer/Stopwatch #893 ($19.99) Our favorite does everything we want: Times up to 20 hours, has two easy-to-read countdown timers, and continues counting up after the alarm is silenced. Easiest to use, even if a bit wobbly sitting on the counter.

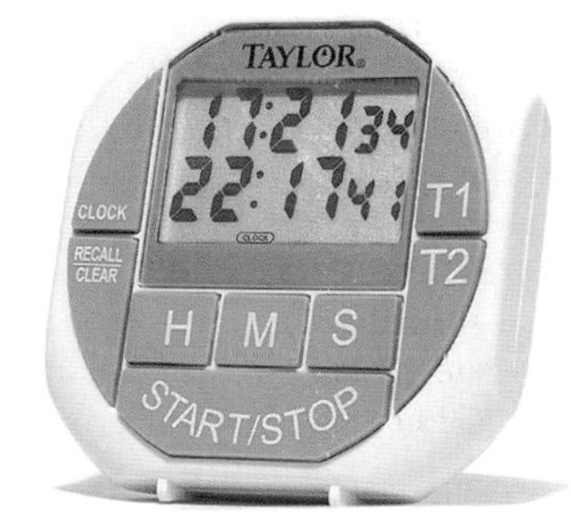

BEST BUY

TAYLOR Two Event Big Digit Timer/Clock Model #5809 ($10.99)
All the features at half the price. Trouble is, it's not intuitive to operate; you'll need to keep the instruction booklet close by.

COOK'S LIVE Original Test Kitchen Videos
www.cooksillustrated.com

RECIPE IN 60 SECONDS
- Better Bran Muffins

VIDEO TIP
- How can I make sure I don't overmix the batter? (And what will happen if I do?)

Crush Course

We knew that using the wrong kind of crushed tomatoes could ruin a dish. But learning just what's in those cans took some unusual testing.

BY LISA McMANUS

In the test kitchen, we've often avoided using crushed tomatoes because the differences among leading brands are so dramatic. The textures vary from watery and thin to so thick you could stand a spoon in it. You might get peels or no peels; plentiful seeds or none; big, rough-cut chunks of tomato or a smooth, sauce-like consistency with no chunks at all.

Why is it that manufacturers can't seem to agree on what crushed tomatoes are? Simple. The United States government regulates the appearance and consistency of other types of canned tomatoes, but not crushed tomatoes. As a result, each brand offers its own definition of "crushed."

Our solution to this problem has been to crush our own tomatoes by pulsing whole or diced canned tomatoes in the food processor. Given the extra work (and mess) this entails, it seemed time to tackle the issue head-on.

So Long, Food Processor

In our quest to find the perfect canned crushed tomatoes, we bought 10 varieties to test alongside our preferred brands of whole and diced tomatoes (which we pulsed in the food processor). We started by tasting them all uncooked. Then we reduced them on the stove to a thick, spoonable consistency, adding olive oil and garlic, per our recipe for Quick Tomato Sauce for Pizza (May/June 1995). A panel of 20 tasters rated the tomatoes, both cooked and raw, on their freshness of flavor, sweetness, acidity, and overall appeal.

Separating Liquids from Solids

To measure tomato solids, we poured each brand into a strainer lined with a coffee filter and covered the tomatoes with a bowl to prevent evaporation.

The good news is that we can put away the food processor. Our tasters liked some brands of crushed tomatoes more than the diced or whole tomatoes pulsed in the machine, which fell into the middle of the rankings.

So what makes a great can of crushed tomatoes? We knew texture would be very important. To get to the bottom of this, we investigated how much solid tomato—as opposed to liquid—you get in each can. We poured them into sieves suspended over glass measuring cups, wrapped them in plastic to prevent evaporation, and let the liquids drain for 24 hours. When we weighed the solids that remained, the results were dramatic: Tomato solids in the different brands ranged from a high of 71 percent to a low of 50 percent. But did more tomatoes equal better crushed tomatoes? Surprisingly, no. The thickest samples were criticized for having a "tomato paste" consistency, while the top two brands were 51 percent and 57 percent tomatoes, respectively. Looking over tasters' comments, it was clear that we preferred our crushed tomatoes chunky, not thick like tomato paste or smooth like tomato sauce. The ideal can of crushed tomatoes contains actual tomato pieces and a fair amount of liquid.

Hot and Cold

Fresh tomato taste is another essential. Canned tomatoes can actually have a fresher taste than supermarket tomatoes, as those tomatoes in the produce section are picked green and hard in order to survive shipping, then sprayed with ethylene gas—which, though it turns them red, can't do much about their undeveloped flavor. By contrast, tomatoes destined for the can are picked ripe and processed quickly. But which of these brands did the best job of preserving that vine-ripened flavor?

How they're processed makes a big difference, experts say. Generally, the fruit that will become canned crushed tomatoes is harvested by machine, explained Rich Rostomily, formerly of Morning Star Packing Company in Williams, Calif., one of the largest tomato-packing companies in the world. If they are to be peeled, this is done either by steam or with a lye bath. Next, he said, the tomatoes are sorted to remove those with "yellow shoulders" (parts that are not red), blemishes, and, if the product is to be peel-free, any peel still attached. The tomatoes are crushed by a machine called a disintegrator, described by Gerald Harter, who works in Morning Star's Santa Nella, Calif., canning facility, as "looking like a big cheese grater." Then they're heated to remove microorganisms, either at a lower temperature (between 160 and 185 degrees) for a longer time or a higher temperature (over 200 degrees) for a shorter time.

Here is where the flavor is most affected. "Typically, you'll have a better-tasting tomato if it's processed at a lower temperature," Rostomily said. Lower temperatures preserve an enzyme called lipoxygenase, which is vital to the formulation of the volatiles that contain tomato flavor. So why the high temperatures? For texture, he said. Heating tomatoes over 185 degrees, a process called "hot break," deactivates enzymes that would break down the pectin binding the cells together in the tomatoes. Though heat will give you a thicker product that won't separate, you'll lose tomato taste.

When we separated liquids from solids in the sieve, we were surprised to see that after 24 hours, our top-ranking tomatoes had exuded a golden-colored liquid, while the lower-ranked ones had produced bright red juice. Rostomily said the golden juice is a product of cooler-temperature processing, where the enzymes were left to break down the pectin, leading to what he called serum separation. Our tasters confirmed Rostomily's claim: Better-tasting crushed tomatoes are processed at a lower temperature.

In the next step of processing, the cans are topped with tomato puree or juice, according to

Going for Gold

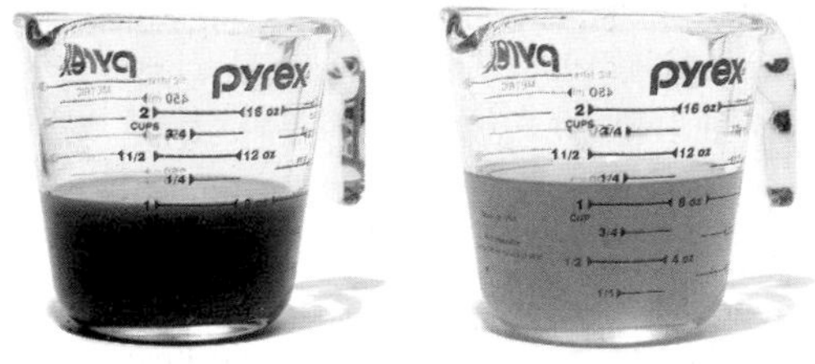

SEEING RED | GOLD STANDARD

At cooler processing temperatures, tomato liquids are gold instead of bright red. Our top tomatoes had golden juice.

COOK'S LIVE Original Test Kitchen Video
www.cooksillustrated.com
- Behind the Scenes: Crushed Tomato Tasting

manufacturer preference. Puree must be cooked for a long time to break down the tomatoes, and therefore imparts a more cooked—rather than fresh—taste to the final product, Rostomily said. Indeed, the lower-ranking crushed tomatoes in our lineup generally featured tomato puree as the first ingredient on the label, while the top four all started their ingredient lists with tomatoes. What's more, Rostomily noted, manufacturers often disguise less-than-perfect tomatoes with puree, which imparts a deeper red color to the contents of the can. The lesson? A fresh-tasting can of crushed tomatoes won't list puree first on the ingredient list.

Sweet and Sour

While sugar levels differ from brand to brand, no sugar is added. Manufacturers do add salt to boost the flavor and help preserve the contents. Some added salt is a good thing, Harter said, as it makes the tomatoes taste sweeter: "Too much and the tomatoes will taste salty; too little and they're bland." Indeed, our lowest-ranking tomato had no added salt.

Manufacturers may also add calcium chloride to maintain a firm texture. Amounts matter, says Harter: "If you get too high, you'll have a metallic taste." Rostomily added that too much can also give a "rubbery" texture to the tomato pieces. In our lineup, three of the four lowest-ranking tomatoes contained calcium chloride, while none of the top-ranked ones did.

Finally, citric acid appeared in every brand except our lowest-ranked. It's there to correct the acid level of the tomatoes, Harter said. "You want to balance the sugar-to-acid ratio," he explained. "An overripe tomato will have more sugar than acid, and you want a certain pH, usually 4.2 or lower, in a canned tomato." Our lowest-ranked brand came in at 4.3, meaning it was the least acidic of the bunch, leading to less-than-bright flavor. A lower pH also means more acid to preserve the tomatoes, so they will require less cooking, Harter said, and you'll get fresher taste.

Our two top-ranked crushed tomatoes, Tuttorosso and Muir Glen, brought all these desirable attributes together. Tuttorosso is only available in New York, New England, and Florida, but Muir Glen tomatoes are distributed nationally. Both are recommended. Tuttorosso crushed tomatoes also come in "New World Style," in a green can; this is not the same product and was disliked by many of our tasters.

TASTING CRUSHED TOMATOES

Twenty members of the *Cook's Illustrated* staff tasted 10 brands of crushed tomatoes. We tasted them poured from the can and reduced with olive oil and garlic to a spoonable consistency. We rated the crushed tomatoes on their freshness of flavor, sweetness, acidity, and overall appeal. Sugar and sodium amounts, found on the label, are shown per half-cup serving. Scores from the two tastings were averaged, and products appear in order of preference.

RECOMMENDED

TUTTOROSSO CRUSHED TOMATOES IN THICK PUREE WITH BASIL
- **pH:** 4.09
- **Tomato solids:** 51 percent
- **Sugar:** 4 g
- **Sodium:** 240 mg

Tasters declared Tuttorosso "chunky, with dimensional flavor and bright tomato taste"; "I'd use this." In the sauce, we liked its "deep roasted tomato flavor."

MUIR GLEN ORGANIC CRUSHED TOMATOES WITH BASIL
- **pH:** 4.09
- **Tomato solids:** 57 percent
- **Sugar:** 6 g
- **Sodium:** 380 mg

"Very fresh, spicy, like pizza topping," with "good-sized chunks of tomato." In sauce, tasters said it "tastes like a well-cooked marinara," with a "balanced," "bright tomato flavor."

HUNT'S ORGANIC CRUSHED TOMATOES

- **pH:** 4.11
- **Tomato solids:** 64 percent
- **Sugar:** 6 g
- **Sodium:** 220 mg

Right out of the can, this came across as "fresh and peppery" and "thick, rich, and tomatoey," with a "smooth, thick texture" and "bits of skin." In sauce, it was "ultrathick, with great flavor, not overly sweet or acidic."

REDPACK CRUSHED TOMATOES IN THICK PUREE

- **pH:** 4.11
- **Tomato solids:** 55 percent
- **Sugar:** 4 g
- **Sodium:** 240 mg

"Actually tastes like real tomatoes!" "Very fresh," with a "very tomato-forward flavor," "has body without being too chunky." In sauce, several complained that it was "bland."

PROGRESSO CRUSHED TOMATOES WITH ADDED PUREE

- **pH:** 4.13
- **Tomato solids:** 55 percent
- **Sugar:** 4 g
- **Sodium:** 190 mg

Tasters praised the "large, diced chunks," like "chopped tomato," and "nice, clear, clean flavor," though they disliked the "thin, watery" consistency. Well-liked "sweet, roasted tomato" taste in sauce.

RECOMMENDED WITH RESERVATIONS

PASTENE KITCHEN READY GROUND PEELED TOMATOES
- **pH:** 4.22
- **Tomato solids:** 71 percent
- **Sugar:** 8 g
- **Sodium:** 170 mg

"Too sweet" and "ketchupy" to many, with a "mushy" texture. In sauce, tasters found "good, meaty tomato flavor," with a texture "similar to a paste."

HUNT'S CRUSHED TOMATOES

- **pH:** 4.14
- **Tomato solids:** 59 percent
- **Sugar:** 5 g
- **Sodium:** 340 mg

"Candy-like but bold" in sauce, these tomatoes were drubbed for having a "pureed" texture and "lots of skins." One taster complained: "Tastes like someone used the best bits of the tomato and left me with the core and skin."

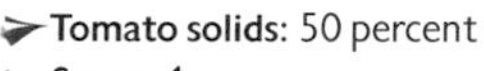

DEL MONTE ORGANIC CRUSHED TOMATOES

- **pH:** 4.01
- **Tomato solids:** 50 percent
- **Sugar:** 4 g
- **Sodium:** 300 mg

"Thin" and "watery" came up again and again. In sauce, some tasters found it gained a "good texture," with a "nice balance of sweet and acidic"; to others it was "uninspired."

CONTADINA CRUSHED ROMA STYLE TOMATOES
- **pH:** 4.03
- **Tomato solids:** 52 percent
- **Sugar:** 4 g
- **Sodium:** 300 mg

"Watery, awful texture," with "lots of skin and seeds," "rich tomato flavor, but not very fresh." Cooked, these tomatoes took on an "Olive Garden-esque" marinara flavor.

NOT RECOMMENDED

CENTO ALL-PURPOSE CRUSHED TOMATOES

- **pH:** 4.30
- **Tomato solids:** 68 percent
- **Sugar:** 8 g
- **Sodium:** 40 mg

"Flat," with a "canned puree flavor" that's "megathick" and "sweet." "This isn't crushed, it's puree." Cooked, it made a "vegetal," "pasty," "bland" sauce. "I feel like I'm eating tomato baby food."

Test Driving the $200 Toaster Oven

Can it roast chicken, cook pizza, and bake cookies? How about toast bread?

BY LISA McMANUS

If you're like a lot of people, you grew up using toaster ovens to make toast, melt cheese on sandwiches, or crisp up cold slices of pizza. But if you were to go shopping to replace that simple toaster oven, you'd be in for a surprise. Today, manufacturers are building toaster ovens bigger and fancier than they've ever been. Custom settings, convection capability, sleek design, digital displays, and their own cookware come along with higher prices—up to $200 for what used to be a pretty humble appliance in the $25 to $30 range.

Are these tricked-out toaster ovens really useful? Or have manufacturers gone too far and made something nobody needs? We bought eight models, all claiming to be big enough for six slices of toast or a 12-inch pizza and all with convection, the most widespread new feature. With their inflated size, they are sometimes called countertop ovens and are promoted as being able to do anything a full-size oven can do. We decided to find out if they really deliver.

This much was obvious: These bigger toaster ovens can't approach the capacity of a full-size oven. A standard 13 by 9-inch casserole dish could not fit inside any of the models in our lineup. If you want to bake cookies, you're restricted to the tiny baking sheet that comes with the appliance, which is capable of baking only six to eight cookies at a time. And only smaller whole chickens (less than 3½ pounds) fit without being too close to the heating elements.

Toaster ovens' smaller size means they preheat quickly, which is great if you're in a rush or don't want to heat up the kitchen. Even the slowest model in our lineup took half the time of a full-size oven, reaching 350 degrees in just over five minutes, compared with 11 to 12 minutes for a full-size oven. (The fastest took 1 minute, 47 seconds.) A toaster oven also uses roughly half the energy of a full-size oven. Still, if we are going to invest in a high-priced, souped-up toaster oven, we want oven-like consistency of cooking. We decided to test six foods that would each address a different aspect of the ovens' performance.

We were surprised to find that it is possible to roast a decent whole chicken in a toaster oven, though you get much better results using convection, in which a fan circulates the heat. If you don't use convection, the chicken browns only on top, where it faces the heating elements, leaving yellow skin on the sides and bottom. Without convection, we found that the side of the chicken near the back of the oven tended to cook faster, overcooking before the "door side" was done.

Getting Burned

Even in these new and improved models, toast still came out lousy. When we tried toasting six slices together, some burned and others were unevenly browned.

Broil Treatment

All the ovens claimed they could cook a frozen, 12-inch pizza, but not one model produced a great-looking pie. All were patchy; some areas were overbrowned, while in other spots the cheese barely melted. The instruction booklet for the Krups model suggested rotating the pizza halfway through cooking, which helped. With less surface area, tuna melts fared better.

Switching to delicate baked goods, we prepared our own slice-and-bake lemon cookies on both convection and regular settings. Though convection proved a little better, most ovens baked up cookies with varying degrees of doneness, from too brown to slightly underdone. Getting a baked potato cooked just right allowed all the ovens to shine.

Traditionally, toaster ovens have been known for making lousy toast, brown on top and white on the bottom. Since a recent appliance industry survey found that most people still buy toaster ovens primarily for making toast, we set toast as our gold standard. All of our models claimed they could fit six slices of bread, though several of them couldn't. On the medium setting, after nearly five minutes, two of the toaster ovens produced a barely crisped slice of white bread. With most of the others, the top of the toast browned but the bottom remained predominantly white. On the dark setting, half of the ovens produced charcoal. In this critical test, only two, by Black & Decker and Krups, made good-looking stacks of toast in short order.

So why did these toaster ovens perform so inconsistently? While manufacturers have given them a sleek new look, few have actually improved on the traditional problem of toaster oven cooking: The heating elements tend to be nothing more than pairs of narrow, exposed bars across the top and the bottom of the oven. You get intense heat in proximity to the bars, which cycle on and off to regulate overall temperature. (The bars contain a nickel-chromium wire coil—the same wire that heats up inside a regular toaster—covered in ceramic and metal.) Their position also explains why toasting is so inefficient in a toaster oven. Bread might be four or more inches from the elements. Ordinary toasters, however, have eight to 10 wires on each side of the toaster slot, less than an inch from the surface of the bread.

Manufacturers have made a few technical advances, most notably adding convection, which helps with heat distribution. Others simply cover the bars with pierced metal shields to help diffuse the heat or vary the number and placement of the bars. A few of the newest models sheath the bars with quartz instead of steel. "Quartz has less thermal mass [than metal], so the coil starts to radiate the heat out a lot quicker," said John Stein, president of Quartz Tubing Inc. of Bensalem, Pa. He explained that quartz also cools down more quickly, which makes the ovens less prone to overheating. With the most heating elements (six quartz bars), we found that the Krups cooked food more evenly than the other models.

Rapid Fire

With their fast cooking and tendency to scorch, you must be vigilant when cooking with toaster ovens. For multitasking cooks, toaster ovens with automatic shut-off and a digital countdown timer rather than a hard-to-interpret dial are valuable features. Krups was one of the few models we tested to offer these. After poring over instruction booklets with charts of rack positions and settings for every cooking task, we came to prefer toaster ovens in which the controls were self-evident. Again, the Krups oven stood out, with basic buttons that quickly became familiar.

Offering reliable cooking, user-friendly controls, solid construction, and even decent toast, the Krups emerged as the model that performed most like a full-size oven. If you want to invest in a higher-end toaster oven for small cooking projects, the $200 Krups might deserve a place in your kitchen. But you can do equally well (and save a lot of money) with an ordinary toaster and your full-size oven.

COOK'S LIVE Original Test Kitchen Video
www.cooksillustrated.com
- Behind the Scenes: Toaster Oven Testing

RATINGS
GOOD: ★★★
FAIR: ★★
POOR: ★

RATING TOASTER OVENS

We tested eight toaster ovens, all with convection capability and all claiming to hold a 12-inch pizza or six slices of toast. We made single slices of toast on medium and dark settings. To see if an oven could handle toast for a crowd, we made three batches of six slices in rapid succession. We also baked potatoes and lemon cookies; melted cheese on tuna sandwiches; heated frozen pizzas; and roasted whole chickens on regular and convection settings. We measured the accuracy of temperature controls and evaluated ease of operation and cleanup. Functionality of layout and user-friendliness received major emphasis. Ovens are listed in order of preference. See page 32 for sources.

PRICE: Prices were found online or at Boston-area retail outlets.

TOASTING: Toaster ovens were preferred if toast cooked on the medium setting was evenly golden brown, front and back, with a crisp exterior and moist interior; dark toast was deep brown, not burned; and batches of toast came out well and quickly. Scores on these tasks were averaged.

SPEED: Time to make one slice of toast on medium setting.

COOKING: Scores for baked potato, tuna melt, pizza, cookie, and roast chicken tests were averaged.

DESIGN: We looked for solid construction and straightforward controls that didn't constantly send us back to the manual.

ACCURACY: We tested how well the ovens held the temperature set by the user.

CLEANUP: We preferred ovens with accessible crumb trays and pans and interiors that easily released cooked-on food.

RECOMMENDED	PERFORMANCE	TESTERS' COMMENTS
Krups 6-Slice Digital Convection Toaster Oven FBC412 PRICE: $199.99	TOASTING: ★★★ TIME TO MAKE TOAST: 3 minutes, 8 seconds COOKING: ★★★ DESIGN: ★★★ ACCURACY: ★★★ CLEANUP: ★★	Easiest to use of all the ovens, with clear instructions and digital controls. Display counts down cook time. Dark toast was "beautiful deep brown, still moist inside." Cooked quickly, cleaned up easily. The baking pan's nonstick coating peeled in a few coin-sized spots, however.

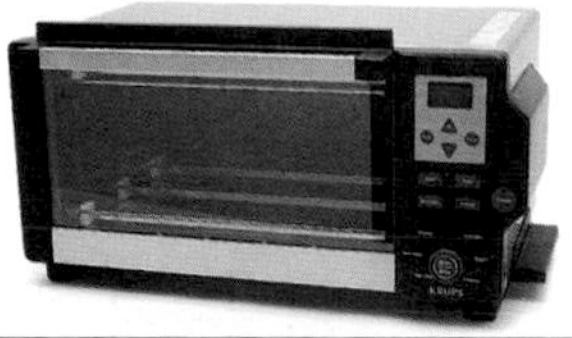

RECOMMENDED WITH RESERVATIONS	PERFORMANCE	TESTERS' COMMENTS
Oster Counterforms Digital Convection 6-Slice Toaster Oven 6292 PRICE: $98.95	TOASTING: ★ TIME TO MAKE TOAST: 5 minutes, 15 seconds COOKING: ★★ DESIGN: ★★★ ACCURACY: ★★★ CLEANUP: ★	Easy digital controls. Interior light a plus; lack of countdown timer a minus. Pans hard to clean; pieces of coating broke off. Toast incinerated on dark setting; burned underside of toast and cookies (on regular bake). Convection-baked cookies and pizza browned unevenly. Can't fit 6 slices of bread.
Cuisinart Toaster Oven Broiler TOB-175BC PRICE: $179	TOASTING: ★ TIME TO MAKE TOAST: 3 minutes, 34 seconds COOKING: ★★ DESIGN: ★★★ ACCURACY: ★★★ CLEANUP: ★	Easy-to-use touch-pad controls. Does not quite fit 12-inch pizza or 6 slices of toast. Toast browned on top, stayed white on bottom, on medium setting; burned on dark. Only oven in this lineup whose crumb tray must be emptied from back, requiring ample counter space; pans hard to clean.

NOT RECOMMENDED	PERFORMANCE	TESTERS' COMMENTS
Hamilton Beach Toaster Oven 31180 PRICE: $75.33	TOASTING: ★★ TIME TO MAKE TOAST: 5 minutes, 30 seconds COOKING: ★★ DESIGN: ★ ACCURACY: ★ CLEANUP: ★★★	Took "forever" to bake, broil, or roast; temperature controls were too low by 50 degrees. Timer/toast knob must be dialed past 10 minutes before setting, and must be set to "stay on" if cook time is to exceed 30 minutes. Confusing toast diagrams on timer to select toast shade.
De'Longhi Convection Oven EO1258 PRICE: $129.95	TOASTING: ★★ TIME TO MAKE TOAST: 4 minutes, 24 seconds COOKING: ★★★ DESIGN: no stars ACCURACY: ★ CLEANUP: ★★★	Cooks well, but the oven door snapped closed when inserting racks, resulting in burned forearms on 2 testers. Lacks timer or automatic shut-off (except for toasting). Small print on metal knobs hard to read. Runs more than 50 degrees hotter than setting.
Rival Counter Top Oven CO606 PRICE: $69.95	TOASTING: ★ TIME TO MAKE TOAST: 5 minutes, 9 seconds COOKING: ★★ DESIGN: ★★ ACCURACY: ★★★ CLEANUP: ★	Can't hold 6 slices of toast. Toast was blond underneath on medium setting, scorched on dark setting and in batches. Pizza overcooked along front and back, undercooked in center. Pans difficult to clean. Timer/toast knob hard to read; user must dial beyond 5 minutes before setting. Convection only.
Black & Decker Countertop Convection Oven CTO100 PRICE: $86	TOASTING: ★★ TIME TO MAKE TOAST: 5 minutes, 30 seconds COOKING: ★★ DESIGN: ★ ACCURACY: ★ CLEANUP: ★★	Timer knob imprecise and hard to read. Oven too tall to brown foods. Piece of toast still white after 5½ minutes. Cookies pale on top, overbrowned beneath. Helpful dial shows when oven is preheated. Easy to clean, but pan looked mottled after first use. Runs hot; averaged 400 degrees when set to 350.
Toastmaster Convection Toaster Oven Broiler COV760B PRICE: $49.99	TOASTING: ★ TIME TO MAKE TOAST: 7 minutes, 3 seconds COOKING: ★★ DESIGN: ★ ACCURACY: ★★★ CLEANUP: ★	Took almost twice as long as winning oven to make toast. Imprecise, illegible controls are metal-painted plastic knobs with raised arrows. Browning uneven; toast and cookies scorched. Had to place rack on bottom of oven to fit chicken. Pans required lots of scrubbing. Convection only.

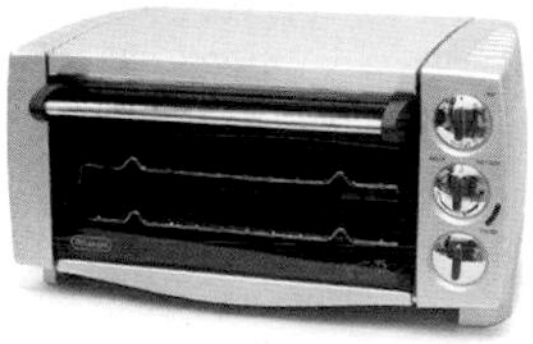

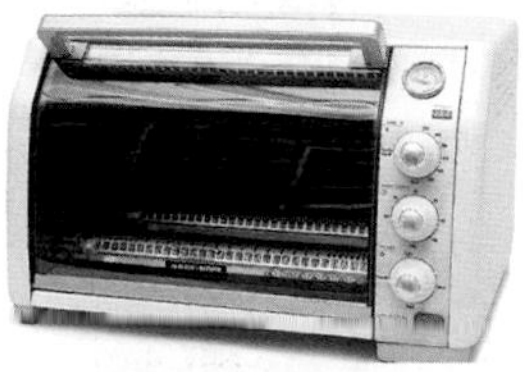

KITCHEN NOTES

BY ERIKA BRUCE AND J. KENJI ALT

The Best Pan for Pan-Searing

What's the best pan for searing meat and making a pan sauce? Some sources tout the benefits of cast iron, which browns food nicely, but others warn that acidic ingredients such as wine or lemon juice can introduce off-flavors and colors to your sauce. Nonstick pans are easy to clean but don't allow much fond to develop. (Fond is the bits of browned food that get stuck to the bottom of the pan and help flavor your sauce.) A conventional metal surface such as stainless steel or anodized aluminum sounded best.

To make sure, we seared chicken breasts in three different skillets: stainless steel, cast iron, and nonstick. We then deglazed the pans with 2 cups of water, which we reduced down to 1 cup before tasting all three samples. The results? The liquid from the nonstick pan was nearly flavorless, while the water from the cast-iron pan had metallic overtones and such faint chicken flavor that one taster likened it to "canned tap water." Only the liquid produced in the stainless-steel skillet developed a golden-brown hue and a distinct chicken flavor. So the lesson is clear: If you're making a pan sauce, choose a pan with a conventional metal surface.

NONSTICK PAN
This sauce was nearly indistinguishable from water.

CAST-IRON PAN
This sauce tasted faintly like chicken, with metallic off-flavors.

STAINLESS-STEEL PAN
This sauce acquired a golden-brown color and distinct chicken flavor.

Cake Pan Prep School

Correct preparation of cake pans is essential—there's not much you can do to save a cake that tears apart while being released from the pan. Different cooks in our test kitchen have championed various methods over the years. To find out which ones are best, we baked a few dozen butter cakes, pound cakes, sponge cakes, and Bundt cakes, using all manner of pan preparations.

With their bumps and ridges, Bundt cakes proved the trickiest. Greasing with softened butter and then dusting the pans with flour left us with a streaky, frosted look on our finished cakes (think bad dye job). A paste made of melted butter and flour (or cocoa for chocolate Bundt cakes), or just plain baking spray (which is cooking spray with flour added), produced clean, perfectly released cakes every time.

The best way to coat a loaf pan for a pound cake turned out to be applying a thick coating of softened butter followed by an even dusting of flour; the flour provided an added layer of protection against sticking and made for an easy and clean release.

As for regular nonstick cake pans, the traditional parchment-paper lining called for in most recipes wasn't necessary—even when making sponge cakes. The same buttered-and-floured pan method we used for the loaf pans produced the cleanest release.

How to Prepare a Cake Pan

PAN	METHOD
Bundt	Coat with baking spray or 1 tablespoon melted butter mixed with 1 tablespoon flour or cocoa powder (for chocolate cakes).
Loaf	Brush with softened butter, then dust with flour, tapping out excess.
Cake	Brush with softened butter, then dust with flour, tapping out excess.

Salting Meat

We have repeatedly warned against seasoning steaks until right before they're going to hit the pan. Past tests have proven that salt left sitting on the surface of meat will merely draw out moisture through a process known as osmosis. This is detrimental for developing any kind of brown, flavorful crust while searing the steak, no matter how hot the pan; the meat essentially steams in its own juice. But recent testing has caused us to reverse this opinion, at least partially: Salting meat for long periods of time improves flavor without adversely affecting crust formation, as the salt actually penetrates beyond the surface of the meat.

While we found the deepest flavor occurred after salting for about four hours, we wanted to see just how long it

TECHNIQUE | PORTIONING MEAT

While portioning tenderloin for our Pan-Seared Thick-Cut Strip Steaks (page 7), we found that to get a good sear it was important for the cut sides to be absolutely smooth and flat. We discovered the best way to achieve uniform cuts was to avoid any kind of sawing motion (which would cause jagged ridges to appear on the meat) and pull the blade in only one direction. Use either a very sharp chef's knife or a carving knife, preferably one at least 8 inches long. This same technique can be used when portioning any other type of boneless meat.

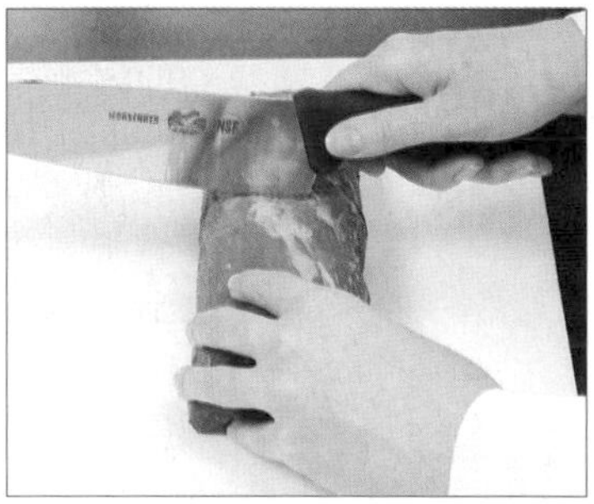

1. Hold knife parallel to work surface and start slicing with very heel of blade. Apply very gentle downward pressure as you pull knife toward your body, letting weight of knife do most of the work.

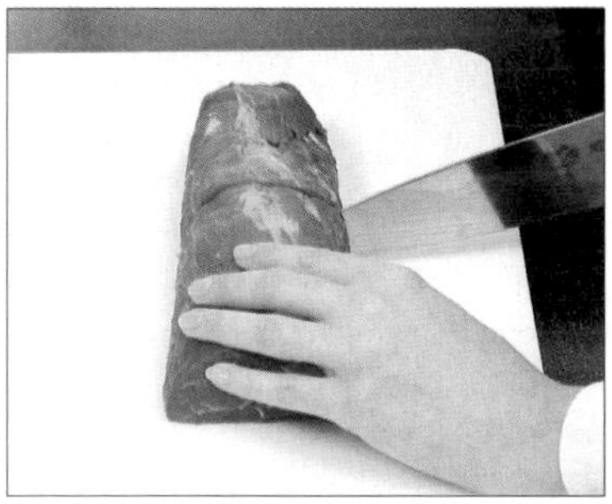

2. Use entire length of blade, from heel to tip, keeping pressure and motion both gentle and constant. If meat starts to stick, straddle blade with free hand and use thumb and forefinger to hold meat in place on either side of blade.

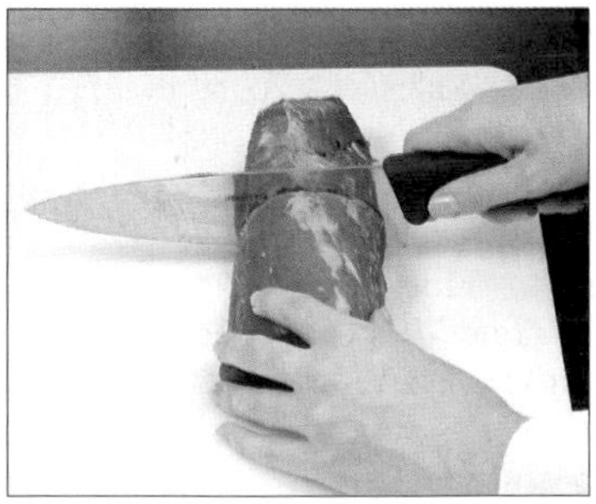

3. If you can't get through entire piece of meat in one stroke, don't saw back and forth. Instead, lift your knife, place heel back onto cut section, and continue slicing by pulling blade toward you.

SHOPPING: Asparagus

While shopping for asparagus to fill our Asparagus Omelet (page 21), we bought stalks as thin as pencils and others as fat as nickels. To find out how size affects flavor or texture, we steamed, broiled, and sautéed both thin and thick spears, adjusting the cooking times to make up for the difference in size.

While both groups were tender when steamed, the slender spears were less watery and had a more intense asparagus flavor than the fat ones. Inversely, broiling and sautéing both produced perfectly cooked thick asparagus—tender, moist interiors surrounded by crisp, browned skin—but left the delicate, thin asparagus emaciated inside of their shriveled, tough skins.

THICK SPEARS
Best for broiling or sautéing

THIN SPEARS
Best for steaming

took for the meat to start absorbing the salt. After 20 minutes, the salt had dissolved in the layer of liquid that it had drawn to the surface of the meat. This salty liquid then broke down and loosened some of the dense fibers in the meat, allowing the meat to reabsorb both its own liquid and the salt—a process that took another 20 minutes.

This same 40-minute time frame extended to different cuts of beef (from loose, fibrous cuts such as flank to the compact, lean tenderloin), as well as lamb chops and unbrined pork chops.

So when pan-searing, don't be afraid to season steaks and chops ahead of time—just be sure you have at least 40 minutes to wait for the moisture and salt to be absorbed back into the meat. To view a time-lapse video of salted meat, go to www.cooksillustrated.com/june.

Noodling Around

We have tried—and failed—in the past to substitute regular boiled lasagna noodles in recipes designed for no-boil noodles. Recipes using no-boil noodles need more liquid, and substituting regular boiled noodles leads to soupy lasagna. However, since the no-boil noodles for our Four-Cheese Lasagna (page 19) are first soaked in hot water and the sauce isn't so watery, we wondered if this finding would still hold true.

We used regular boiled noodles in this recipe, and the lasagna looked fine—no excessive soupiness. Unfortunately, the lasagna tasted too starchy and heavy. The regular lasagna noodles were so thick and bulky that they overpowered the delicate balance of pasta to sauce, adding excessive starchiness to the dish.

When we compared the actual weight of each type of pasta, we found that an uncooked regular lasagna noodle weighed almost twice as much as a no-boil noodle. So for creamy, delicate lasagnas (where fresh noodles are traditionally used), thinner, no-boil noodles are not only faster than regular dried lasagna noodles—they are also better.

Marinating Thin Cuts

Although we usually marinate meat in a zipper-lock bag to save refrigerator space and avoid dirtying dishes, during our development of Korean Grilled Short Ribs (page 13), we had some trouble with uneven marinating, because the long, thin slices of meat were sticking together. Layering the meat and marinade into a large baking dish before covering it with plastic wrap proved to be the better choice for this recipe. This method also works for other thin cuts of meat where sticking could be a problem, such as pounded chicken breasts or pork cutlets.

RECIPE UPDATE

Stir-Fried Sichuan Broccoli

Readers wanted to know if they could substitute broccoli for the green beans in our **Stir-Fried Sichuan Green Beans** (January/February 2007). To make this recipe, the beans are stir-fried until fully cooked, then removed from the skillet, in which the Sichuan sauce is promptly made. Having learned a thing or two about sautéing broccoli over the years, we knew it would be best to trim the florets into small pieces and slice the stalks into oblong coins before cooking. Because the stalks took longer to cook, they went into the pan first, followed by the florets. A little water helped to steam and evenly cook the broccoli. We found that the sauce needed a little extra sugar to balance the stronger broccoli flavor. Go to www.cooksillustrated.com/june for our free recipe for Stir-Fried Sichuan Broccoli.

Grill-Roasted Leg of Lamb

Grilling enthusiasts wrote in asking for a way to cook our **Garlic-Roasted Leg of Lamb** (March/April 2006) on their backyard grills. Our indoor recipe calls for portioning a boneless leg of lamb into three smaller roasts that are browned in a skillet and finished in the oven. We needed a grill setup with a hot side to sear the meat and a cool side where the roasts could finish gently cooking. A modified two-level fire—all the lit coals piled onto one side of the grill, leaving the other side empty—did the trick. Coating the meat with the amount of oil (3 tablespoons) in our original recipe created too many flare-ups. Rubbing the roasts with just 4 teaspoons of oil before grilling encouraged great browning without flare-ups. Go to www.cooksillustrated.com/june for our free recipe for Grill-Roasted Leg of Lamb.

Make-Ahead Sticky Buns

Fans of our **Sticky Buns with Pecans** (September/October 2004) wanted to know if they could do most of the work for this time-consuming recipe in advance. We had no trouble freezing the fully risen buns, but baking the pan of frozen buns per our original instructions—on a preheated baking stone on the lower rack for 25 to 30 minutes—proved disastrous. The caramel layer on the bottom of the pan burned before the frozen dough baked completely through. We needed to slow down the caramel cooking time. Adjusting the oven rack to the middle position and baking the buns on top of a baking sheet for 50 minutes helped the caramel to cook more gently. Keeping the pan of buns wrapped tightly with aluminum foil for the first stage of baking created an intense amount of heat in the pan, kick-starting the dough's thaw. After 20 to 25 minutes, we removed the foil to allow the buns to adequately brown. Go to www.cooksillustrated.com/june for our free recipe for Make-Ahead Sticky Buns.

—Compiled by Charles Kelsey

TOO HOT

JUST RIGHT

A pan of regular sticky buns must be baked on a pizza stone to cook the caramel properly. When we tried the same regimen with frozen buns, the caramel burned (left) by the time the buns were cooked through. Replacing the stone with a baking sheet yielded better results (right).

IF YOU HAVE A QUESTION about a recipe, let us know. Send your inquiry, name, address, and daytime telephone number to Recipe Update, Cook's Illustrated, P.O. Box 470589, Brookline, MA 02447, or write to recipeupdate@americastestkitchen.com.

EQUIPMENT CORNER

BY ELIZABETH BOMZE

EQUIPMENT UPDATE: Steak Knives

When we last tested steak knives (September/October 2001), we came to two conclusions: First, although top dollar may buy top quality, there are reasonably priced knives that perform quite well. Second, we found that serrated edges—designed to tackle tough meat—actually make jagged tears in the beef and are unnecessary if your straight-edged knife is sharp. With that in mind, we decided to test seven new sets of relatively inexpensive steak knives, all priced at $100 or less for a set of four or six. Could they cut it?

Despite our bias against serrated knives, we couldn't resist trying the Messermeister Four Seasons Steak Knife ($39.99 for a set of four) and the Sabatier Laguiole Steak Knife ($29.99 for a set of six), which both sported miniscule serrations. Size didn't matter here, because they still produced ragged slices of meat. As for straight-edged knives, the Wüsthof Gourmet Steak Knife ($49.95 for a set of four) wobbled, as did the skimpy, wavy-edged Henckels Gourmet Hollow Edge Steak Knife ($99.95 for a set of four). We found that our previous best buy, the Chicago Cutlery Walnut Tradition Steak Knife ($19.95 for a set of four), was no match for the sleek and sturdy Cuisinart CA4 Steak Knife ($29.95 for a set of four) or our new favorite, the exceptionally sharp and nimble Forschner Rosewood Straight Edge Steak Knife ($79.95 for a set of six).

A CUT ABOVE
This super-sharp Forschner steak knife makes quick work of even a tough steak.

NEW PRODUCT: Jumbo Fish Tongs

When cooking fish fillets, we use two thin-bladed metal spatulas to flip the flesh without breaking it. While one spatula lifts the fish, the other supports it from the top as we turn it over. Could one tool be better than two? We tried the new LamsonSharp Jumbo Turner Tongs ($21.95), which is essentially two large fish spatulas bonded together to mimic the grasping ability of tongs. Unlike a pair of tongs with a pointed axis that allows for exceptionally wide opening, the grip on this tool is curved, which makes opening it wider than the 3⅝-inch resting position difficult. As neither blade is offset from the handle, sliding one under a piece of fish is a dicey task. We'll stick with our dual-spatula method.

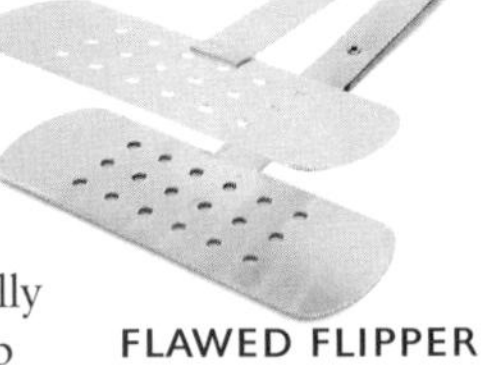

FLAWED FLIPPER
The LamsonSharp Jumbo Turner Tongs looks like an ingenious tool, but its flawed design makes it more cumbersome than cutting-edge.

NEW PRODUCT: Grill Wipes

Grate Chef Grill Wipes ($2.99 for a pack of six) are disposable, vegetable oil–soaked towelettes that promise to oil and clean your grates before you start cooking; using the bristles of your grill brush, you simply wipe the towelettes on the hot grill. Did they deliver? Yes. We got clean, slick grates and better grill marks on this issue's Grilled Blackened Red Snapper and Korean Grilled Short Ribs than those produced by oil-saturated paper towels. Be advised: These small wipes are flammable and can slip between the small rounded bars of a charcoal grill. Keep long-handled tongs on hand as a safety measure.

WON'T WIPE OUT
Grate Chef Grill Wipes clean and grease grills better than any homemade method.

EQUIPMENT UPDATE: Corkscrews

In the November/December 2006 issue, we recommended the Wine Enthusiast Zoom Corkscrew ($12.95) as a best-buy alternative to our top pick, the Screwpull Trigger ($99.95). Since then, this bargain item has been discontinued. In its place, we examined two other Wine Enthusiast models, the Lever Style Concorde Corkscrew Set ($19.95) and the ritzier QuickSilver Deluxe Corkscrew Set ($34.95), which comes with a display stand and bottle opener, foil cutter, and wax remover. Extras aside, its heavy chrome crank and handles and sleek lever helped the spiral screw twist through both plastic and cork. Though workable, the hard plastic mechanisms on the Concorde wobbled and shook in a rickety, stuttering motion during use. The QuickSilver is now our top-rated moderately priced corkscrew.

EQUIPMENT TESTING: Spice Toasters

Eastern cultures have long reaped more sensory benefits from spices by skillet-toasting them briefly before adding them to marinades, rubs, curries, and soups. Simple and quick as this technique is, some spices are prone to popping out of the open pan as they heat. A pair of mesh-lidded spice toasters that resemble tiny skillets, one from Williams-Sonoma ($14) and the other by Buck's Culinary Exotica ($12.95), claim to keep spices in the pan. Yes, they kept this promise. But compared with the generous 8 or 10 inches of cooking space in a skillet, the all-mesh Williams-Sonoma basket gave us fewer than 2½ inches, so some spices burned before others toasted. The 4½-inch diameter of the metal-bottomed Buck's model helped spices toast more evenly, but the lid latches on both sat so close to the hot toasting chamber that opening them scorched our fingers. We're going back to our skillet, confining jumpy spices with a splatter screen.

THEY'RE TOAST
These spice toasters are too small, and the lid latches scorched our fingers.

Sources

The following are sources for items recommended in this issue. Prices were current at press time and do not include shipping. Contact companies to confirm information or visit www.cooksillustrated.com for updates.

Page 3: COCONUT GRATER
- Coconut Grater: $24.50, Buck's Culinary Exotica (360-352-9301, www.culinaryexotica.com).

Page 23: SQUARE CAKE PANS
- Williams-Sonoma Goldtouch Nonstick 8" Square Cake Pan: $21, Williams-Sonoma (877-812-6235, www.williams-sonoma.com).
- Chicago Metallic Gourmetware Non-Stick 8" x 8" Square Cake Pan: $5.99, item #887, Kitchen Kapers (800-455-5567, www.kitchenkapers.com).

Page 25: TIMERS
- Polder Dual Timer/Stopwatch: $19.99, item #690738, Cooking.com (800-663-8810, www.cooking.com).
- Taylor Two Event Big Digit Timer/Clock: $10.99, item #B0007NIIPE, Amazon.com.

Page 29: TOASTER OVEN
- Krups FBC412 6-Slice Digital Convection Toaster Oven: $199.99, item #550157, Cooking.com.

Page 32: STEAK KNIVES
- Forschner Rosewood Straight Edge Steak Knife Set: $79.95 for 6, item #46059, Cutlery and More (800-650-9866, www.cutleryandmore.com).

Page 32: GRILL WIPES
- Grate Chef Grill Wipes: $2.99 for six, Gratechef.com (877-900-8415, www.gratechef.com).

Page 32: CORKSCREW
- Wine Enthusiast QuickSilver Deluxe Corkscrew Set: $34.95, item #4181945, Wine Enthusiast (800-356-8466, www.wineenthusiast.com).

INDEX

May & June 2007

RECIPES

Variations on these recipes and suggested side dishes are available free at www.cooksillustrated.com/june.

COOK'S LIVE Original Test Kitchen Videos www.cooksillustrated.com

MAIN DISHES
- **Asparagus Omelet in 60 Seconds**

- **Four-Cheese Lasagna in 60 Seconds**
- Why do I need to soak no-boil lasagna noodles?

- **Grilled Blackened Red Snapper in 60 Seconds**
- What's the best way to flip fish on the grill?
- Why do I need to score the fish?

- **Indian-Style Curry in 60 Seconds**
- What's the best way to chop cauliflower?
- What should I do if the curry is too spicy?

- **Korean Grilled Short Ribs in 60 Seconds**
- How do I prevent flare-ups on the grill?
- What kind of ribs should I buy?

- **Pan-Seared Thick-Cut Strip Steaks in 60 Seconds**
- What type of steak should I buy?
- Why do I need to let the steaks rest?
- Why does it matter when I salt the steaks?

- **Spicy Italian-Style Chicken in 60 Seconds**
- What's the best way to brown chicken?
- How do I cut bone-in chicken breasts?
- What size chef's knife should I use?

MARINADES
- How do you prepare a charcoal grill for cooking steaks?
- How do I slice flank steak against the grain?
- What's the best way to slice sirloin tip or skirt steak?

DESSERTS AND MUFFINS
- **Better Bran Muffins in 60 Seconds**
- How can I make sure I don't overmix the batter?

- **New York–Style Crumb Cake in 60 Seconds**
- What kind of cake pan should I use?
- How should I prepare my cake pan?
- Can I substitute all-purpose flour for the cake flour?

TASTINGS AND TESTINGS
- Behind the Scenes: Crushed Tomato Tasting
- Behind the Scenes: Toaster Oven Testing

AMERICA'S TEST KITCHEN
Public television's most popular cooking show

Join the millions of home cooks who watch our show, *America's Test Kitchen*, on public television every week. For more information, including recipes and program times, visit www.americastestkitchen.com.

Better Bran Muffins, 25

Pan-Seared Thick-Cut Strip Steaks, 7

Korean Grilled Short Ribs, 13

Spicy Italian-Style Chicken, 11

Asparagus Omelet, 21

New York–Style Crumb Cake, 23

Four-Cheese Lasagna, 19

Grilled Blackened Red Snapper, 9

Steak Marinades, 20

Vegetable Curry, 15

PHOTOGRAPHY: CARL TREMBLAY, STYLING: MARIE PIRAINO

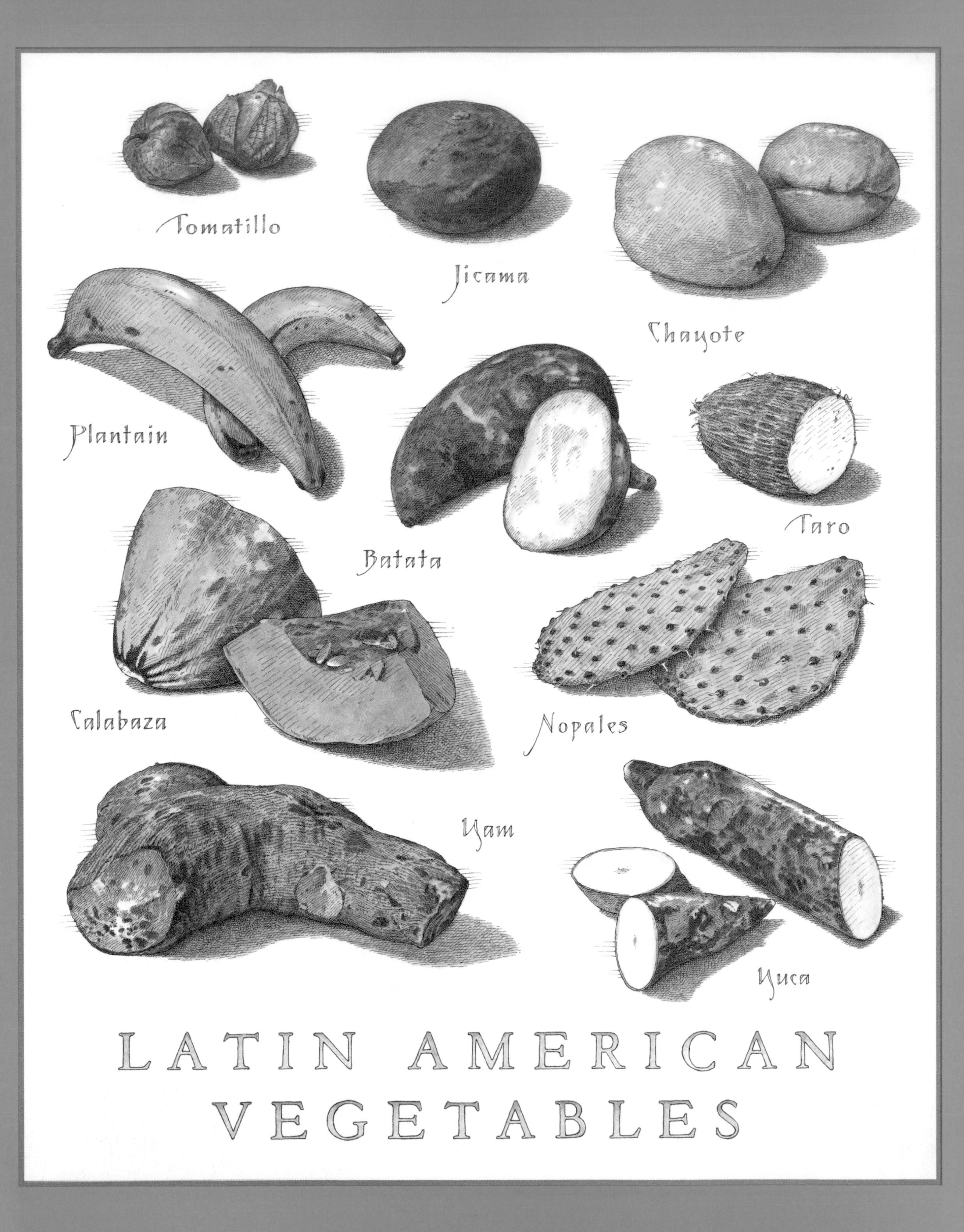
Tomatillo
Jicama
Chayote
Plantain
Batata
Taro
Calabaza
Nopales
Yam
Yuca
LATIN AMERICAN
VEGETABLES

NUMBER EIGHTY-SEVEN JULY & AUGUST 2007

Texas-Style Barbecue
Big Smoky Flavor, Rich Texas Crust

Best Grilled Chicken
A Marinade That Really Works!

Rating Garlic Presses
Big Winner Solves Garlic Problems

Perfecting Pasta Caprese
Tomatoes, Mozzarella, and Penne

Best Blueberry Scones
Rich, Light, and Flaky

Grilled Garlic Potatoes
New Method, Foolproof Grilling

Tasting Teas
Does Brand or Price Matter?

Perfect Plum Cake

Freezing Summer Produce 101

Summer Fruit Salads

How to Grill Game Hens

Improving Shrimp Salad

www.cooksillustrated.com

$5.95 U.S./$6.95 CANADA

CONTENTS

July & August 2007

COOK'S ONLINE

Go to **www.cooksillustrated.com** to access all recipes from *Cook's Illustrated* since 1993 as well as updated tastings and testings. Watch videos of all the recipes in this issue being prepared and special reports on the tea taste test and garlic press testing.

STONE FRUITS have a single large center pit, or stone. Peaches generally fall into two groups: clingstone, in which the flesh is firmly attached to the stone, and freestone, in which it is not. Yellow-fleshed peaches are the most widely available. White peaches are sweeter and less acidic. Donut peaches are named for their squat, rounded shape; they also have a sweet, white flesh. Nectarines are related to peaches but have thinner, smoother skin. The small honeydew nectarine is so named for its color rather than any relation to the melon. Plums range in size from the inch-long Damson plum (better for cooking) to the larger, ubiquitous black plum. In between are the medium yellow Shiro plum (a Japanese variety) and the oval-shaped Italian prune plum. Apricots have a pinkish-yellow color and very tender skins that do not require peeling. The pluot is a cross between a plum and an apricot. The best way to remove the pit from any stone fruit is to cut around the center of the fruit (along the stem crease), twist the two halves against each other, and then remove the stone.

BACK COVER: *Stone Fruit* by John Burgoyne

FRONT COVER PAINTING: *Peaches* by internationally renowned still-life artist Elizabeth Brandon, whose works are featured at www.elizabethbrandon.com

For list rental information, contact: Specialists Marketing Services, Inc., 1200 Harbor Blvd., 9th Floor, Weehawken, NJ 07087; 201-865-5800.
Editorial Office: 17 Station St., Brookline, MA 02445; 617-232-1000; fax 617-232-1572. Subscription inquiries, call 800-526-8442.
Postmaster: Send all new orders, subscription inquiries, and change-of-address notices to Cook's Illustrated, P.O. Box 7446, Red Oak, IA 51591-0446.

COOK'S ILLUSTRATED
www.cooksillustrated.com
HOME OF AMERICA'S TEST KITCHEN

ONE STEP AWAY

Trapping is a vocation that most folks don't want to hear much about. It seems as out-of-date as sap buckets, divining rods, and two-holers, yet it wasn't too long ago that many Vermonters made their living in the woods. O.M. Butcher had a trapping supply store just down the valley that attracted customers from all over (the sign just fell down last year). Stan Lincoln, who lived at the four corners, used to check his traps before and after school, making enough money during the Depression to help support his family. He'd get up early, hike up into the mountains to check the trap lines, and be back in time for school. Then he would do it all over again before dinner.

Some neighbors are still at it, so when our friend Tom purchased a piece of land two years back, I wasn't surprised that it came with a small shed that contained dozens of traps of all sizes plus bottles of scent and wicker baskets used to carry the tools of the trade up into the woods. I never had much stomach for trapping until last summer, when we thought a fox was eating our chickens. After a dozen or so went missing, our neighbor Jean called a trapper, but he came up empty. Turns out it was a red-tailed hawk; I caught him at it one morning as I walked outside with my first cup of coffee.

You can drive through Vermont and miss just about everything worth seeing. You wouldn't meet the Butler sisters, who have one pair of false teeth between them. (They switch off every Saturday night.) Or the farmer at the country store who, when he gets excited, flaps his large ears like an elephant. You wouldn't hear the story about the locals who got into a feud that saw the crazier of the two leave a dead cow on the other's front lawn. Or the bit about the carpenter who was working outside of a woman's house and happened to glance in the window. She was cleaning up in the kitchen. The next time he looked up, she was standing at the window topless, looking right at him. Or the woman who had her husband buried standing straight up. Or the local who weighed a good 300 pounds and was kindly referred to as "The Little Man." Or, my favorite, the woman who went to a Halloween party dressed as a front-loading washing machine complete with laundry, a box of detergent on top, and a cord with a plug sticking out the back.

Christopher Kimball

It is said that people in our town are just crazy. If you don't pay your snowplow bill on time, you'll get plowed in, not out, when the next storm hits. People build barns and paint the cupola before they close in the roof. When one man came home unexpectedly, he ended up chasing his near-naked wife and next-door neighbor through the woods at night until the state police showed up to restore the peace. Fights have been known to break out at the country store over a casual remark. And any piece of gossip worth its salt will make the rounds thanks to shopping at Wayside and Sherman's, breakfast at the State Line Diner, or the sometimes not-so-neighborly conversation at coffee hour after church.

The flatlander tourist will have no problem finding relics of the past—the old barns, the tedders and mowers rusting by the side of the road, the farmers who are still milking herds, the smell of liquid manure in April, and the cute country stores with signs that read, "If we don't have it, you don't need it." But they won't catch the essence of Vermonters, that we are barely a half-step away from who we have always been—a tough, self-reliant breed that Calvin Coolidge considered a reserve wellspring of liberty and independence in the event our national character ever required rebuilding.

Vermonters take pride in bad weather, look forward to a hard day's work, still think that one's reputation is worth defending, and cook their food at home—a place where, by the way, they were born and raised. For entertainment, they step outside to hunt, fish, barbecue, change the oil, watch the traffic from the front porch, or boil sap. They know how to tell a story and know that everyone has a story to tell. And if a neighbor needs help, well, you don't wait for them to ask for it. You just show up and stack the wood, jump-start the generator, fix the roof, cut down the tree, or drop off the casserole. And when someone dies, we don't talk about it much, because the race is over. There isn't time for regrets.

The world over, it would appear that life is lived countless miles from where we wish we still were. I know that to be true thanks to modern poets who, when they speak fondly of home, mean some other hallowed ground, either distant or in times past. Here in the mountains, life isn't always easy, but we are deeply rooted in the center of things, just a quick step away from where we have always wanted to be and the people that we had hoped to become.

FOR INQUIRIES, ORDERS, OR MORE INFORMATION:

www.cooksillustrated.com

At www.cooksillustrated.com, you can order books and subscriptions, sign up for our free e-newsletter, or renew your magazine subscription. Join the website and gain access to 15 years of *Cook's Illustrated* recipes, equipment tests, ingredient tastings, as well as *Cook's Live* companion videos for every recipe in this issue.

COOKBOOKS

We sell more than 50 cookbooks by the editors of *Cook's Illustrated*. To order, visit our bookstore at www.cooksillustrated.com or call 800-611-0759 (or 515-246-6911 from outside the U.S.).

COOK'S ILLUSTRATED Magazine

Cook's Illustrated magazine (ISSN 1068-2821), number 87, is published bimonthly by Boston Common Press Limited Partnership, 17 Station St., Brookline, MA 02445. Copyright 2007 Boston Common Press Limited Partnership. Periodicals postage paid at Boston, Mass., and additional mailing offices USPS #012487. Publications Mail Agreement No. 40020778. Return undeliverable Canadian addresses to P.O. Box 875, Station A, Windsor, Ontario N9A 6P2. POSTMASTER: Send address changes to Cook's Illustrated, P.O. Box 7446, Red Oak, IA 51591-0446. For subscription and gift subscription orders, subscription inquiries, or change-of-address notices, call 800-526-8442 in the U.S. or 515-247-7571 from outside the U.S., or write us at Cook's Illustrated, P.O. Box 7446, Red Oak, IA 51591-0446.

ILLUSTRATION: RANDY GLASS

NOTES FROM READERS

COMPILED BY SANDRA WU

Frothing Milk

When using my milk frother to make cappuccino, I've noticed that skim milk seems to foam up better than whole milk. Why is this?

SUSANNE NORWOOD
EAST BURKE, VT.

➢We poured 4-ounce samples of both nonfat and whole milk into oversized cups, whipped them up with a battery-operated milk frother, and compared the results. The skim milk indeed frothed better than the whole milk: The foam was thicker, more stable, and composed of finer bubbles; it rose up higher in the cup. The whole milk foam took longer to form and was made of larger bubbles that deflated in a matter of minutes.

As it turns out, milk fat contains monoglycerides and diglycerides, two substances that happen to be good emulsifiers but have a negative effect on the formation of foam. They destabilize the air bubbles introduced into milk when foam is made, thereby impeding the foam's formation. Skim milk contains a much smaller amount of these emulsifiers, thus making frothing easier.

Although most baristas wouldn't recommend using skim milk to make rich and creamy cappuccinos, if plenty of airy foam is your goal, the less fat in the milk, the better your results will be.

SKIM MILK FROTHED **WHOLE MILK FROTHED**

When frothing milk, less fat equals more foam.

Refreezing Thawed Meat

Sometimes when I thaw frozen meat, I can't use it all. Is it OK to refreeze meat for later use?

DONALD PACHOLSKI
WESTLAND, MICH.

➢According to the United States Department of Agriculture, food that is properly thawed in the refrigerator is safe to refreeze in its raw state. The only drawback is a reduction in quality due to moisture loss. The slow process of freezing that occurs in a home freezer (as compared with a commercial freezer) causes large ice crystals to form. The crystals rupture the cell walls of the meat, permitting the release of juices during cooking. A second freeze-thaw cycle aggravates the problem, as the meat's liquid-retaining capacity is further reduced, allowing even more moisture to escape from the meat as it cooks.

We wanted to see just how much moisture was lost from repeated freeze-thaw cycles. To find out, we cooked three 7-ounce samples of 85-percent lean ground beef—one straight from the store, one that we'd frozen and thawed once, and one that we'd frozen and thawed twice—over medium-high heat in a small skillet, drained them, and measured the amount of liquid released. We then repeated the test and averaged the results. The batches of ground beef that we hadn't frozen released ¾ teaspoon of liquid. The batches that had undergone a freeze-thaw cycle were dry-tasting, having released 2 teaspoons of liquid. The ground beef that had been frozen and thawed twice was even worse, releasing a full tablespoon of liquid. So while it's safe to refreeze defrosted meat, we don't recommend it.

Baking with Cold Eggs

I love to bake, and I was wondering why some recipes call for the eggs to be at room temperature. Does the temperature of the eggs really matter?

DANA ERIKSEN
JACKSON, N.J.

➢Cake recipes often call for room temperature eggs, which incorporate into the batter more readily than cold eggs.

We wondered, though, if the difference between room temperature and cold eggs was so great that it could actually ruin a basic cake recipe. To find out, we conducted a blind tasting of two yellow cakes: one made with room temperature eggs, the other with eggs pulled straight from the refrigerator. The cake prepared with cold eggs produced a slightly thicker batter and took five minutes longer to bake. The cake made with room temperature eggs had a slightly finer, more even crumb, but the cold-egg cake was entirely acceptable. Overall, tasters strained to detect differences between the two cakes, so it's fine to use cold eggs in most basic cake recipes.

However, cold eggs can cause problems in finicky cakes, such as pound, angel food, and chiffon, that rely on air incorporated into the beaten eggs as a primary means of leavening. In these cases, we found that cold eggs didn't whip nearly as well as room temperature eggs and the cakes didn't rise properly. As a result, these cakes were too dense when made with cold eggs.

To quickly warm whole eggs, place them in a bowl and cover them with hot—but not boiling—tap water for five minutes. Since it is easier to separate eggs when they are cold, eggs can be separated first and allowed to warm up while the remaining ingredients are assembled. If necessary, the whites or yolks can be placed in a bowl nestled within another bowl filled with warm water to speed up the process.

Odors Be Gone

What's the best way to remove strong odors, such as onion and garlic, from a cutting board?

MARY LOU ADAMS
HOUSTON, TEXAS

➢The dishwasher is the best way to clean plastic cutting boards, but often you can't wait two hours to reuse a malodorous board. To find the best way to remove odors without a dishwasher, we took four cutting boards and cut a large onion and made garlic paste out of raw minced garlic on each of them. Once they were nice and smelly, we used a different odor-removal method on each board before immediately washing it with hot, soapy water: spraying with a mixture of 1 tablespoon of bleach and 1 gallon of water; scrubbing with a paste of 1 tablespoon of baking soda and 1 teaspoon of water; spraying with distilled white vinegar; and doing nothing more than washing with hot, soapy water.

After the boards were wiped dry, we sliced apples on each one. Tasters were required not only to taste the apples for off-flavors but to sniff the boards as well. The results? Only the baking soda paste–treated board was odor-free; the other boards suffered from varying degrees of sulfurous odors and allium flavors. Tasters were nearly unanimous in finding the apples cut on the baking soda board "fine," with "no off-flavors." So the next time you stink up your cutting board, scrub it with a baking soda paste and follow up by washing it with hot, soapy water.

ODOR EATER

Baking soda removes odors from cutting boards.

Super-Soaked Beans

I often soak dried beans overnight with the intention of cooking them the next day, but sometimes I can't get to them until a couple of days later. Will there be any adverse effects if I still use them?

CHERYL VANNI
EUGENE, ORE.

➢Soaking dried beans helps them cook more quickly and evenly than beans that are used straight from the package, but is it possible to soak them for too long? We covered two batches of dried black beans with water and refrigerated them overnight. The next day, we drained the first batch and transferred the beans to a zipper-lock bag to be refrigerated for the next three days. We left the second batch in water in the refrigerator. On day four, we drained the beans held in water and prepared another batch using our quick-soak method (covering dried beans with boiling water and allowing them to sit, covered, for one hour).

We then prepared three separate batches of black bean soup and looked for differences in flavor and texture. Tasters liked the soups made with the quick-soaked beans and soaked, drained, and refrigerated beans: Both featured tender, moist, creamy beans accompanied by a rich, full-bodied broth. They did take issue, however, with the soup fashioned from beans that had been left soaking in water for four days. The beans lacked flavor, the skins were tough, and the interiors were mealy and a little too firm. In addition, the flavor of the soup was thin, watery, and bland, the beans having leached some of their sugars into the soaking water.

So if you soak beans overnight and can't use them right away, all is not lost. Simply drain the beans and refrigerate them in a zipper-lock bag or airtight container for up to four days before using them.

WHAT IS IT?

This tool has been in my family for over 50 years. I've kept it because I, like my grandmother, love to collect all kinds of kitchen gadgets. Can you tell me what it is?

GAYLE BAXLEY
DALTON GARDENS, IDAHO

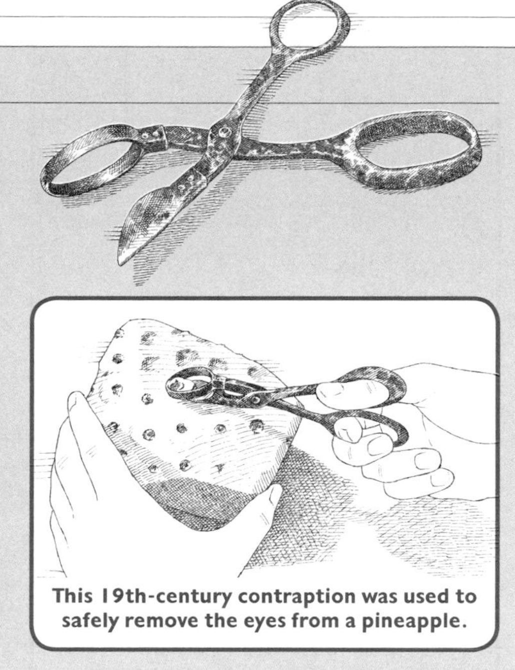

This 6-inch-long, scissor-like contraption is an iron pineapple-eye remover, or huller, from the 1880s. It was designed to remove the tough brown "eyes" embedded in a whole pineapple. After the crown and bottom are cut off of a pineapple and the skin is peeled off, the sharp spoon is used to dig underneath the eyes. Next, the handles are closed together, causing the open oval cutting edge to clamp down, extracting the eye. We found this tool quicker and safer than removing pineapple eyes with the tip of a paring knife. The downside? It took away a lot of the surrounding flesh in the process.

This 19th-century contraption was used to safely remove the eyes from a pineapple.

Keeping Cookies Soft

I've noticed that some of my favorite soft and chewy cookies taste fine the day I bake them but harden up after two or three days. What's the best way to store them so they stay soft?

VICTORIA O'NEILL
SAUNDERSTOWN, R.I.

➢When it comes to storing cookies (chewy or otherwise), too much air exposure dries them out and causes staling. To find the best method for storing chewy cookies, we baked three types—chocolate chip, molasses spice, and peanut butter—and stored them the following ways: in a zipper-lock bag with the air pressed out; in a zipper-lock bag with an apple slice; and in a zipper-lock bag with a slice of white sandwich bread thrown in. (The last two help keep brown sugar moist; we wondered if they would do the same for cookies.)

After five days, all three cookie samples exhibited negative traits. The ones simply placed in the bag had become dry on the edges but were still acceptable. Those stored with the apple slice were moist but had begun to pick up the odor and flavor of the apple. The cookies stored with a slice of bread became surprisingly damp in the areas where the bread touched the cookies. Nestled together in the same bag, the hygroscopic sugar in the cookies attracted some of the water from the bread. In fact, while the cookies became wetter, the bread dried out and became fairly brittle.

Because the bread was providing too much moisture, we wondered if using less bread would produce chewy, rather than soggy, cookies. No such luck. Half- and quarter-slices of bread produced similarly lackluster cookies. Though no longer wet, the cookies didn't seem any fresher than those stored by themselves. So the best way to store cookies is also the simplest: in a zipper-lock bag with the air pressed out. And, to return just-baked chewiness to cookies that have been stored for several days, place them on a microwave-safe plate and microwave at full power for 30 seconds.

Instant Espresso Substitute

Many chocolate desserts call for a small amount of instant espresso powder, which can be difficult to find. Is there a substitute?

ANGELA LOH
MENLO PARK, CALIF.

➢Instant espresso powder is often used to boost the intensity of chocolate flavor. Because instant espresso isn't always available, we often call for instant coffee as a substitute. To test just how much instant coffee should be used in place of instant espresso, we prepared three recipes—pots de crème, triple chocolate espresso brownies, and devil's food cake—each with the amount of instant espresso called for in the recipe, an equal amount of instant coffee, and twice the amount of instant coffee.

The pots de crème made with instant espresso had a rich, dark chocolate flavor. When the espresso was replaced with an equal amount of a popular brand of instant coffee, the chocolate flavor was weak and lacked depth. Doubling the amount of instant coffee, however, made the flavor comparable to the original recipe. The opposite was true with the espresso brownies, which exhibited a bitter, overwhelming coffee flavor when twice the amount of instant coffee was used. Tasters preferred the brownies made with a one-to-one conversion, which had a strong, but not undesirable, coffee flavor. As for the cake, tasters couldn't detect much of a difference among the three batches. In the end, if you can't find instant espresso powder, we recommend replacing it with the same amount of instant coffee in baked goods and with double the amount in creamy applications like puddings, frostings, and mousses, which contain proportionally more chocolate as a percentage of the total ingredients.

INSTANT FLAVOR
Instant espresso powder delivers the best flavor, but can instant coffee be used instead?

SEND US YOUR QUESTIONS We will provide a complimentary one-year subscription for each letter we print. Send your inquiry, name, address, and daytime telephone number to Notes from Readers, Cook's Illustrated, P.O. Box 470589, Brookline, MA 02447, or to notesfromreaders@americastestkitchen.com.

ILLUSTRATION: JOHN BURGOYNE

Quick Tips

COMPILED BY DAVID PAZMIÑO

Vegetable Timesaver

Instead of washing vegetables individually as she needs them, Millie Melendez of Airmont, N.Y., gets a head start by cleaning all of her vegetables as soon as she returns from her weekly trip to the supermarket.

1. Place the vegetables in a colander and wash with cool running water.
2. Dry the vegetables on a clean kitchen towel, then refrigerate in labeled zipper-lock bags.

Hot Coal Rake

Arranging lit coals in a grill with a pair of long-handled tongs requires patience: The tongs can only grasp one or two coals at a time. Stacy Olitsky of Philadelphia, Pa., uses a hand-held metal garden rake to arrange the coals as desired.

Wine Bottle Collar

To keep drips from staining her tablecloth, Su Chiang of Cambridge, Mass., ties a paper collar around wine bottles before pouring.

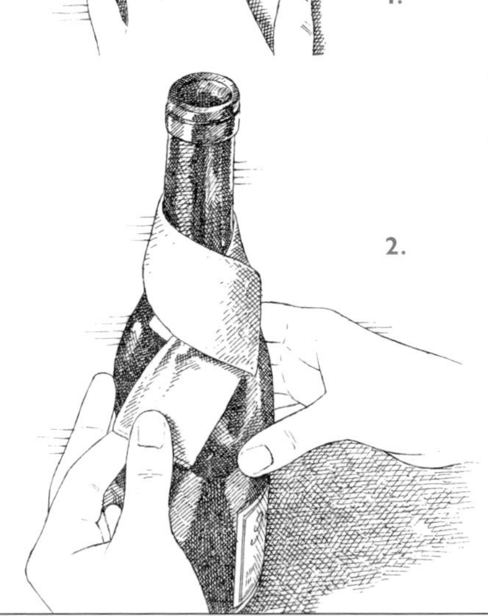

1. Fold a paper towel in half lengthwise, then fold it in thirds lengthwise (like a business letter). Wrap the strip around the neck of the wine bottle, overlapping the ends.
2. Tuck one end of the strip under the other and pull the free end to tighten the strip snugly around the neck of the bottle.

Oiled Grill Scraper

One of the test kitchen's favorite ways to clean a grill without a grill brush is to use balled-up aluminum foil. Dave Laatz of San Pedro, Calif., improved on the concept.

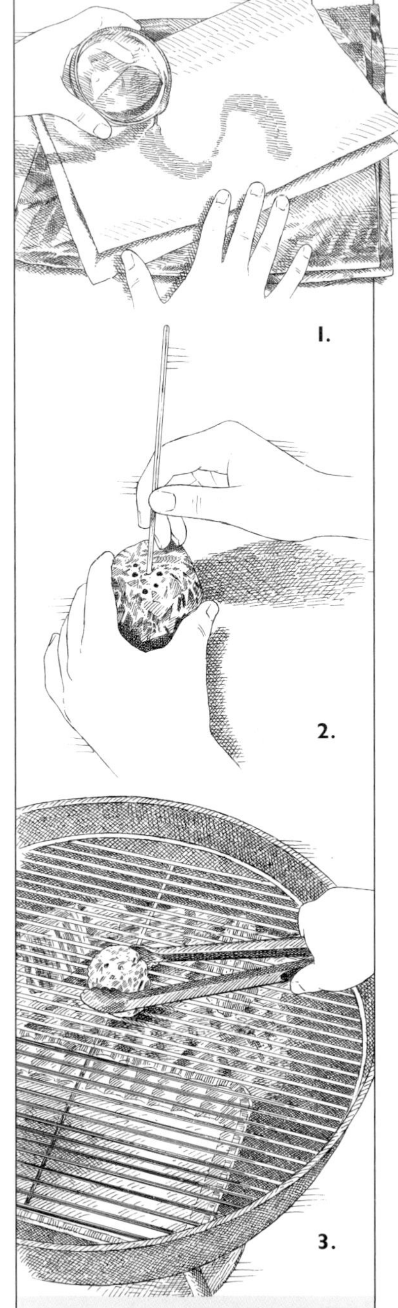

1. Lay a 12 by 18-inch piece of foil on the work surface, then center two paper towels on foil. Drizzle paper towels with 2 tablespoons vegetable oil.
2. Crumple the foil around the paper towels and poke several holes in it with a wooden skewer.
3. Using long-handled tongs, brush the hot grill surface with the aluminum foil, letting some of the oil leak out and season the grill.

Send Us Your Tip We will provide a complimentary one-year subscription for each tip we print. Send your tip, name, and address to Quick Tips, Cook's Illustrated, P.O. Box 470589, Brookline, MA 02447, or to quicktips@americastestkitchen.com.

ILLUSTRATION: JOHN BURGOYNE

Draining Wood Chips Outdoors

Soaking wood chips or chunks in water prevents them from burning too quickly on the hot coals. Rather than making a trip into the kitchen for a colander to drain soaked chips, Barbara Solbrig of Rochester, Minn., uses a clean, perforated flowerpot that she stores outside with her grilling tools. Dump the soaked chips into the flowerpot, allowing the water to drain out.

Grilling Small Items

There's nothing worse than watching perfectly grilled vegetables slip through the grill grates and scorch on the hot coals below. Kim Thom of Vancouver, B.C., uses a cooling rack to protect vegetables.

Place the wire cooling rack perpendicular to the grill grates. Heat for about five minutes, then rub the rack lightly with oil before grilling.

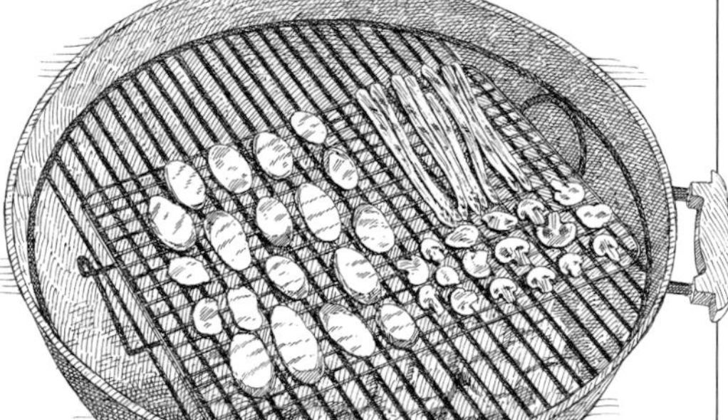

Last-Minute Smoke

Wood chips contribute smoky flavor to grill-roasted and barbecued meats. To prevent them from burning, they must be soaked in water for about an hour. Having forgotten to soak his wood chips ahead of time, Don Camp of Philadelphia, Pa., found that a 15-minute soak in boiling water adequately hydrated the chips and protected them from the heat of the grill.

Jiffy Tomato Seeding

Removing the seeds from one or two tomatoes is a snap, but the job becomes time-consuming when a recipe calls for several pounds of tomatoes. Justin Hutchinson of Flagstaff, Ariz., offers the following shortcut.

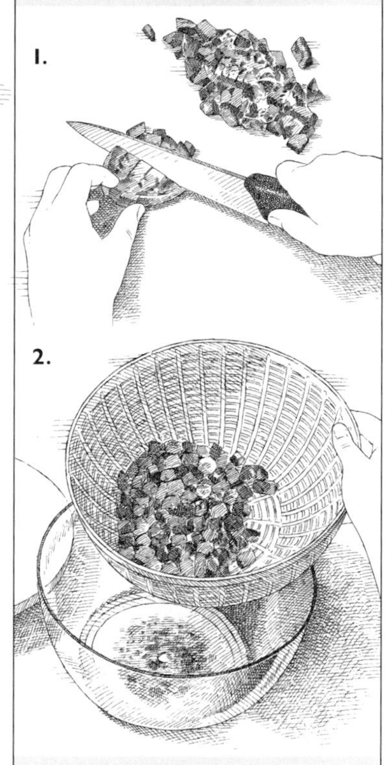

1. Core the tomatoes and cut them into pieces.
2. Spin the chopped tomatoes in the basket of a salad spinner until most of the seeds are released. Repeat the spinning process as necessary to remove excess seeds.

Foolproof Chimney Lighting

Attempting to light a chimney starter on a cold or blustery day can be frustrating. Adam Stoll of Wyoming, Mich., came up with a fail-safe way to accomplish the task while putting loose magazine insert cards to good use.

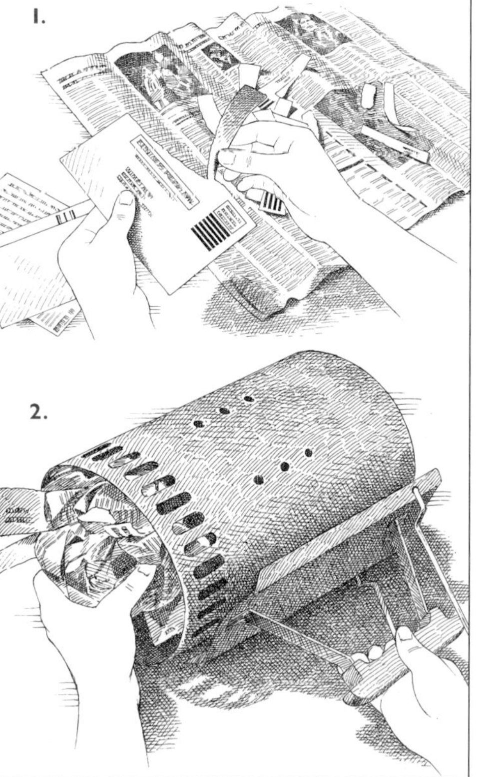

1. Place two or three magazine insert cards, torn into strips, on sheets of newspaper.
2. Crumple the newspaper and place in the bottom section of the chimney starter, taking care to not pack it too tightly; ignite. The thick paper will burn more slowly than the newspaper, providing longer-lasting flames to light the coals.

Removing Fruit Stickers

Fruit and vegetable stickers can be difficult to remove, especially from soft produce, such as plums and tomatoes. Misty Dawn Gaubatz of Missoula, Mont., came up with the following solution.

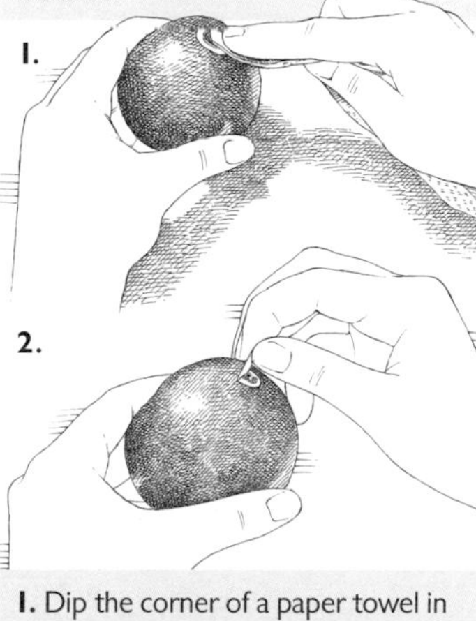

1. Dip the corner of a paper towel in vegetable oil. Rub the oiled towel over the sticker and let sit for about five minutes.
2. Peel off the offending sticker without damaging the fruit.

Impromptu Roasting Rack

Tim Grauzeau of Springfield, Ill., offers a novel way to cook a chicken or a roast without a roasting pan or V-rack. He places a round cake rack sprayed with nonstick cooking spray in a 12-inch skillet, then places a 3- to 4-pound chicken or roast on top of the rack. If the pan drippings start to burn during roasting, he adds a few ounces of water to the bottom of the pan.

Authentic Texas Brisket

Our mission was simple: We wanted a brisket with slow-cooked, pit barbecue flavor. Could we do it on a charcoal grill?

BY CHARLES KELSEY

It may or may not be true that everything is big in Texas, but one thing is for certain: Lone Star barbecue is big on flavor, especially barbecued beef brisket. I became addicted to this tender, deeply smoky beef years ago on a trip to the barbecue belt near Austin. This region is home to some of Texas's best barbecue joints, or "markets," butcher shops started by Czech and German immigrants in the mid-to-late 19th century who sold fresh as well as smoked meats. Today, the cold meat cases have been entirely replaced by massive smokers that cook meat slow and low. Although various kinds of pork barbecue and smoked sausage are available, brisket—sliced to order and served up on butcher paper—is the main attraction.

I will always remember the image of a sword-sized knife peeling off thin slices of juicy brisket outlined with its signature dark crust. More than anything, that crust—created by the low heat—is what sets Texas-style brisket apart from all others. Its intense, concentrated flavor is brought about by a melding of the meat's juices, smoke, and seasonings. And while other kinds of barbecue rely on fancy spice rubs or sticky sauces, in Texas the beef speaks for itself.

Slicing the meat against the grain ensures that our smoky barbecued brisket is tender.

Most barbecued brisket recipes designed for home cooks call for a backyard smoker—a smaller contraption functioning on the same indirect-heat cooking principles as large, commercial smokers. While a home smoker would be awfully convenient, in the test kitchen we try to avoid developing recipes based on specialized equipment. Besides, a basic kettle grill can do everything a smoker can.

Two Cuts of Brisket

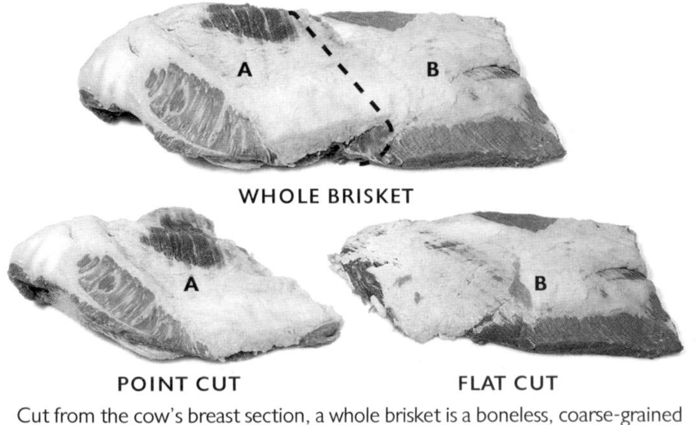

Cut from the cow's breast section, a whole brisket is a boneless, coarse-grained cut comprised of two smaller roasts: the flat (or first) cut and the point (or second) cut. The knobby point cut (A) overlaps the rectangular flat cut (B). The point cut has more marbling and fat, and the flat cut's meat is lean and topped with a thick fat cap. Our recipe calls for the widely available flat cut. Make sure that the fat cap isn't overtrimmed and is ⅓ to ½ inch thick.

To Build a Fire

Butchers usually divide the brisket into two cuts (see "Two Cuts of Brisket," left). The point cut has substantially more fat than the flat cut, so it was my first choice for barbecuing. Local butchers informed me, however, that they don't usually stock the point cut, as most customers prefer the leaner flat cut. I knew its lean meat was more prone to drying out, so down the line I'd have to find a way to keep it moist.

I came to work early on the first day of testing and set up my grill to emulate a barbecue pit. I built a medium-sized fire using 3 quarts of charcoal and rubbed a simple salt-and–black pepper mixture onto a 5-pound flat-cut brisket. I pushed all the coals to one side to create an indirect heat source and topped the coals with some water-soaked wood chunks (soaking causes them to smolder and slowly release smoke) to simulate a fire fueled by hardwood logs. I knew this method worked for barbecuing smaller pieces of meat, such as ribs and chicken, but I was concerned that my charcoal would burn out before the large brisket was cooked.

After placing the grill grate on, I put my brisket onto the cool side (as far from the fire as possible) and put the lid on. A thermometer tracked the grill's internal temperature, which I planned on maintaining at around 300 degrees by adding handfuls of unlit briquettes. Every hour or so, I removed the lid to refuel the fire, which caused the grill's internal temperature to plunge 100 degrees. Getting it back to 300 degrees took 45 minutes, and 15 minutes later the cycle began again. After six hours, the fire died. I headed into the test kitchen, where I transferred the underdone brisket to a low-temperature oven for an hour to finish cooking. While some of the meat was chewy and dry, tasters were nevertheless

PHOTOGRAPHY: CARL TREMBLAY

impressed with the brisket's intense beefiness and sweet smoky flavor. But the absence of a discernible crust was a big letdown.

What if I built a bigger, slightly hotter fire, one that wouldn't peter out? The next morning I lit a fire using 4 quarts of charcoal to see how long it would burn without interruption. This meant no refueling and no taking the lid off. According to my thermometer, the grill's internal temperature hovered around 300 degrees (just where I wanted it) until the fourth hour, when it dropped below 200 degrees. After a total of seven hours, the fire burned out and I removed the lid to retrieve the brisket. Though thoroughly cooked, the interior wasn't tender. But all wasn't lost: I learned that constant fueling wasn't necessary and, more important, keeping the lid on established a consistent temperature that created a darker crust.

During my next tests, I discovered that fires made with more than 4 quarts of charcoal caused the brisket to cook too quickly, making for extremely dry meat. About ready to pony up the plane fare to Austin, I had an epiphany of Texas proportions. The idea came to me while I watched candles on the table at a dinner party: Fire can burn down as well as up. So what if I laid down a bulk of unlit briquettes and then added 4 quarts of hot coals on top? I pictured the unlit briquettes slowly catching fire as the lit coals burned, creating a time-delayed fire of sorts—a changing of the guard.

To test my theory, I got up before dawn and banked unlit charcoal against one side of a grill, then lit a 4-quart fire in a chimney starter. When the hot coals were ready, I dumped them on the unlit briquettes. Then on went the grill grate, the brisket, and the lid. As I had hoped, the fire burned consistently in the 300-degree range for about six hours, before dropping too low. I later discovered that throwing 10 unlit briquettes onto the fire about halfway through cooking provided enough extra fuel to render the brisket perfectly tender.

A Crust as Big as Texas

To be up to Texas standards, my brisket needed an even thicker crust. In real Lone Star barbecue, the brisket turns crusty from slow, gentle browning of the meat, as well as from soot. All the salt-and-pepper formula needed was a little sugar; which turned the meat's exterior into a great dark-brown crust that tasters found addictive.

A few tricks—like leaving the fat cap intact and tenting the meat with aluminum foil for part of the cooking time—helped keep the lean flat-cut brisket moist but didn't offer a complete solution. Then I thought about how we usually treat lean proteins—chicken, turkey, and pork—in the test kitchen before grilling: We brine them. I didn't want to add any more time to my recipe, but I thought it would be worth it if it worked. Sure enough, brining the brisket for two hours ensured that each slice was juicy.

After barbecuing well over 100 pounds of beef, I had the real deal. I had cured my craving with a recipe for homemade barbecued brisket that no Texan could resist.

TECHNIQUE | TURNING YOUR GRILL INTO A SMOKER

The massive smokers used in Texas employ indirect-heat cooking to turn tough cuts like brisket tender. We did the same thing in a kettle grill by pushing the lit coals as far to one side as possible. Placing unlit coals beneath the lit coals keeps the fire going strong for hours. To ensure a slow release of smoke, we placed soaked wood chunks on the coals. We also put a disposable pan filled with water below the brisket to encourage the pink smoke ring under the crust.

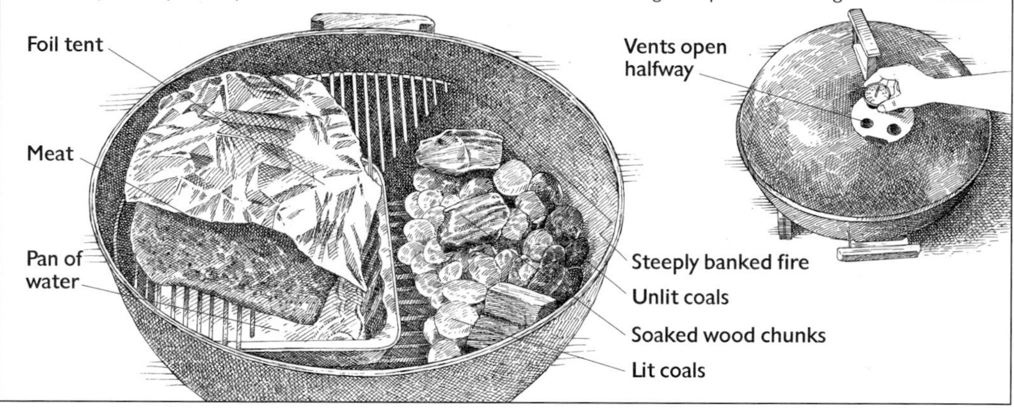

BARBECUED BEEF BRISKET

SERVES 8 TO 10

We prefer hickory wood chunks to smoke our brisket. Pecan, maple, oak, or fruitwoods such as apple, cherry, and peach also work well. It is best to avoid mesquite, which turns bitter during the long process of barbecuing. Use wood chunks that are about the size of a tennis ball. If your brisket is smaller than 5 pounds or the fat cap has been removed, or if you are using a small charcoal or 2-burner gas grill, it may be necessary to build a foil shield in order to keep the brisket from becoming too dark. (See illustration on page 8.) A 5- to 6-pound point-cut brisket can be used in the recipe, but because it is a thicker piece of meat it may need to be finished in the oven (see instructions in step 5 of recipe). If using the fattier point cut, omit the step of brining. Some of the traditional accompaniments to barbecued brisket include barbecue sauce (our recipe for Texas-Style Barbecue Sauce is available free at cooksillustrated.com/august), sliced white bread or saltine crackers, pickle chips (see the results of our bread-and-butter pickle tasting, on page 30), and thinly sliced onion.

- 1 flat-cut beef brisket, 5 to 6 pounds
- 2/3 cup table salt
- 1/2 cup plus 2 tablespoons sugar
- 3 (3-inch) wood chunks (see note above)
- 3 tablespoons kosher salt
- 2 tablespoons ground black pepper
- Disposable 13 by 9-inch aluminum roasting pan

1. Using sharp knife, cut slits in fat cap, spaced 1 inch apart, in crosshatch pattern, being careful to not cut into meat. Dissolve table salt and ½ cup sugar in 4 quarts cold water in stockpot or large bucket. Submerge brisket in brine and refrigerate for 2 hours.

RECIPE SHORTHAND | BARBECUED BRISKET

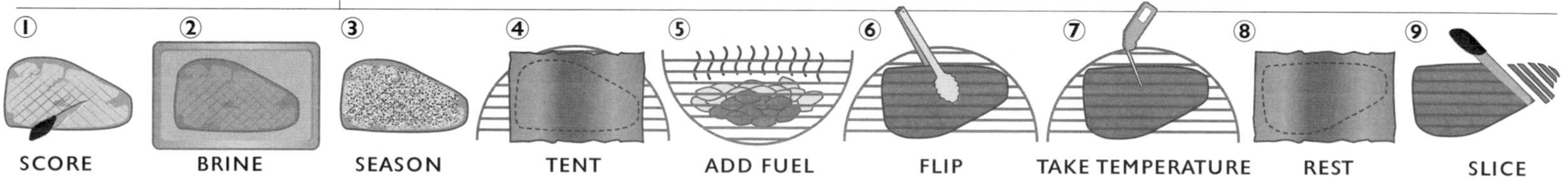

1. SCORE Use sharp knife to cut slits in fat cap 1 inch apart. **2. BRINE** Submerge brisket in brine and refrigerate for 2 hours. **3. SEASON** Rub salt-pepper-sugar mixture over entire brisket and into slits. **4. TENT** Place brisket on cooler side of grill and loosely cover with aluminum foil. **5. ADD FUEL** After 3 hours, quickly add 10 unlit briquettes to fire. **6. FLIP** Discard foil, flip meat, and rotate brisket so that side closest to fire is farthest away. **7. TAKE TEMPERATURE** Cook brisket for 2 to 4 more hours until thickest part of meat reaches 195 degrees. **8. REST** Transfer meat to cutting board, loosely tent with foil, and let rest for 30 minutes. **9. SLICE** Slice meat across grain into long, thin slices.

SCIENCE: Why Is Brisket Pink?

In the competitive barbecue world, championship brisket always contains a thick smoke ring—the ¼-inch pink layer just beneath the meat's surface. Often mistaken for underdone meat, smoke rings—which don't affect taste—occur in most barbecued meats. Despite the name, smoke doesn't play much of a role in creating a smoke ring. It's actually caused by reactions that occur when meat is cooked for a long time at a low temperature in a closed chamber (i.e., barbecued). The fire emits gasses that dissolve in the moisture on the surface of the meat to create new compounds similar to the nitrates that keep deli meats pink. I found that placing a pan of water in the grill added enough moisture to guarantee a proper smoke ring. —C.K.

2. While brisket brines, soak wood chunks in water for at least 1 hour; drain. Remove brisket from brine and pat dry with paper towels; transfer to rimmed baking sheet. Combine kosher salt, pepper, and remaining 2 tablespoons sugar in small bowl. Rub salt mixture over entire brisket and into slits.

3. About 20 minutes before grilling, open top and bottom grill vents halfway and arrange 3 quarts unlit charcoal (about 50 briquettes) banked against one side of grill. Place disposable pan filled with 2 cups of water on empty side of grill. Light large chimney starter filled two-thirds with charcoal (4 quarts, or about 65 briquettes) and allow to burn until coals are fully ignited and covered with thin layer of ash, 15 to 20 minutes. Empty coals into grill, on top of unlit briquettes, to cover one-third of grill with coals steeply banked against side of grill. Place soaked wood chunks on coals. Position cooking grate over coals, cover grill, and heat grate until hot, about 5 minutes; scrape grate clean with grill brush.

4. Place brisket fat-side down on grate over cooler side of grill, as far away from fire as possible without touching wall of grill. If brisket has pronounced thicker side, position it facing fire. Loosely tent meat with heavy-duty aluminum foil or build foil shield (see illustration at right). Cover grill, positioning top vent over brisket to draw smoke through grill. Cook brisket without removing lid for 3 hours. (Initial temperature of grill will be about 400 degrees and will drop to about 325 degrees after 3 hours.)

5. Working quickly, add 10 unlit briquettes to fire and open bottom vents all the way. Remove and discard foil from brisket; flip meat and rotate so side that was closest to fire is now farthest away. Cover grill with top vents over brisket and cook until tender and instant-read thermometer inserted into thickest part of meat registers 195 degrees, 2 to 4 more hours. (Final temperature of grill will be about 250 degrees.) If after 4 hours meat does not register 195 degrees, remove brisket from grill, transfer to wire rack set in rimmed baking sheet lined with aluminum foil, and place in 325-degree oven on middle rack until meat comes up to temperature.

6. Transfer brisket to cutting board and let rest 30 minutes, tented with foil. Cut meat across grain into long, thin slices; serve immediately.

BARBECUED BEEF BRISKET ON A GAS GRILL

It is necessary to divide the wood chips between two disposable aluminum pans, one with and one without water. The water in the one pan will delay the smoking of the chips, thus extending the time the brisket is exposed to smoke.

1. Follow recipe for Barbecued Beef Brisket through step 2, substituting 4 cups wood chips, soaked in water to cover for 30 minutes, for wood chunks. Drain chips and place 2 cups in small disposable aluminum pan. Place remaining 2 cups in another small disposable aluminum pan along with 1 cup water. Set pans on primary burner (burner that will remain on during barbecuing). Instead of large aluminum roasting pan, place 9-inch aluminum pie plate filled with 2 cups water on other burner(s). Position cooking grate over burners. Turn all burners to high and heat with lid down until very hot, about 15 minutes. Scrape grate clean with grill brush. Turn primary burner to medium-high and turn off other burner(s).

2. Place brisket fat-side down on grate over cooler side of grill, as far away from fire as possible without touching wall of grill. If brisket has pronounced thicker side, position it facing fire. Loosely tent meat with aluminum foil or build foil shield (see illustration above). Cook, without raising lid, for 3 hours. Transfer brisket to wire rack set in rimmed baking sheet lined with foil.

3. Meanwhile, adjust oven rack to middle position and heat oven to 325 degrees. Roast brisket until tender and instant-read thermometer inserted into thickest part of meat registers 195 degrees, 1½ to 2 hours. Transfer brisket to cutting board and let rest for 30 minutes, loosely tented with foil. Cut brisket across grain into long, thin slices and serve immediately.

TECHNIQUE | FOIL SHIELD FOR SMALLER GRILLS

When using a charcoal grill less than 22 inches in diameter or a gas grill with only two burners, or when barbecuing a small brisket without a fat cap, we found it necessary to make a foil shield to protect the brisket from getting too dark and leathery on the side closest to the heat. The shield is only needed for the first half of cooking.

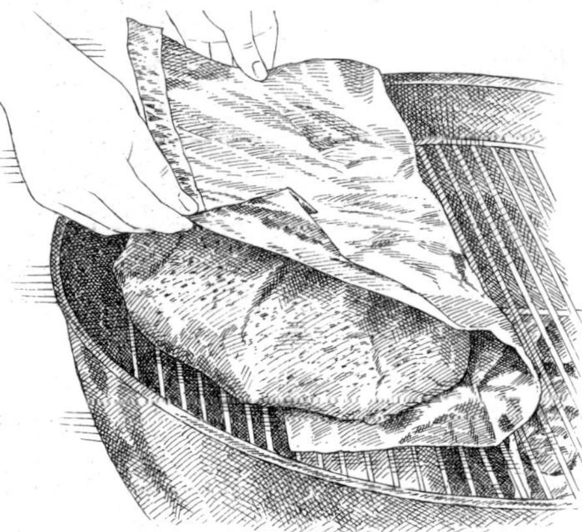

Make two ½-inch folds on long side of 18 by 20-inch piece of heavy-duty aluminum foil to form reinforced edge. Place foil on center of cooking grate, with reinforced edge over hot side of grill. Position brisket, fat-side down, over cool side of grill so that it covers about one-third of foil. Pull foil over brisket to loosely tent it; remove foil as directed in step 5.

EQUIPMENT TESTING: Barbecue Thermometers

With slow and low barbecuing, it's especially important to monitor the temperature of the fire without opening the grill lid. If your grill doesn't have a built-in thermometer, it's a good idea to buy one. We tested eight oven and barbecue thermometers, digital and dial-faced, all of which could slip through the grill lid's vent holes. We found a surprising range of features and prices—from $7.99 to $99. Our two favorites turned out to be the cheapest models tested: the Weber 9815 Replacement Food Thermometer ($7.99) and the Polder Stainless Steel Dual Oven/Meat Thermometer ($10). For a couple dollars more than the Weber, the Polder gives you simultaneous meat and oven temperature readings. On the grill, a heatproof silicone finger-grip under the dial allows you to take the thermometer out of the lid vents and check the temperature of the meat. For complete testing results, go to www.cooksillustrated.com/august. —Elizabeth Bomze

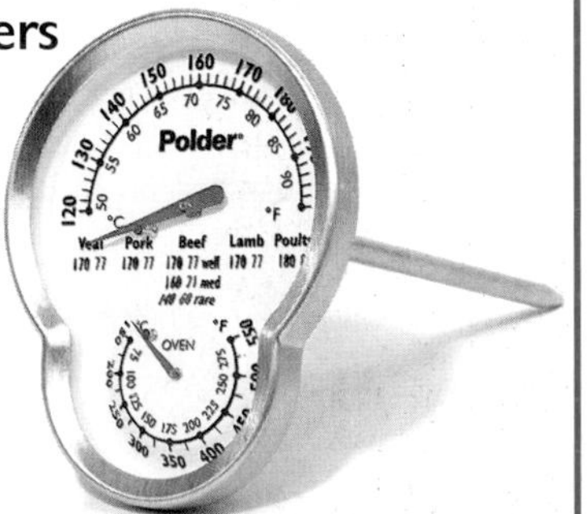

TOP THERMOMETER
The Polder Dual Oven/Meat Thermometer allows you to monitor the grill's internal temperature before checking the meat for doneness.

COOK'S LIVE Original Test Kitchen Videos
www.cooksillustrated.com

RECIPE IN 60 SECONDS
- Barbecued Beef Brisket

VIDEO TIPS
- Tips for better barbecuing
- How do I barbecue brisket on a gas grill?
- What is a smoke ring?

ILLUSTRATION: JOHN BURGOYNE

Grilled Garlic-Rosemary Potatoes

How could our recipe for plain grilled potatoes be improved? With rosemary, garlic, and a new technique.

BY KEITH DRESSER

The test kitchen's established technique for grilling potatoes needs no improvement: Halve and skewer small red potatoes, parboil them, brush them with olive oil, and then quickly place them on the hot grill. Besides yielding perfectly cooked potatoes—charred (not burnt) exteriors, smooth and creamy interiors, and plenty of smoky flavor—the skewers hold them together, allowing for hassle-free transfer from pot to grill to serving platter.

Seeing as there are no finer complements for potatoes than garlic and rosemary, I decided to see if I could incorporate this combination into our recipe. Coating the potatoes with oil, garlic, and rosemary prior to grilling seemed too easy, and it was: The garlic burned and became bitter, and the rosemary charred. I tried tossing the potatoes in the oil after they came off the grill, but the raw garlic was too harsh. Tasters winced.

Clearly, this was going to take some experimenting. One of my first ideas was to add crushed garlic cloves and rosemary sprigs to the water in which the potatoes were parboiled, hoping the potatoes would drink up their flavors. Hardly.

Switching gears, I decided to precook the skewered potatoes in the microwave. I brushed the potatoes with oil to prevent sticking, seasoned them with salt, microwaved them, and threw them on the grill. Although their texture was firmer and their skins saltier than when parboiled, the interiors remained unseasoned. Piercing each potato prior to microwaving encouraged the salt on the skin to migrate to the inside.

Now all I needed was to find a bold way to deliver the garlic and rosemary flavors. I slowly cooked nine cloves of garlic and 1 teaspoon of rosemary in ¼ cup of oil, then brushed the potatoes with this mixture prior to microwaving. But I didn't stop there. I brushed them with the infused oil again before grilling, and I tossed the potatoes with the garlic-and-rosemary oil yet again before serving. This repeated contact resulted in the potent flavor I was searching for.

TECHNIQUE | SKEWERING POTATOES FOR THE GRILL

Place potato half cut-side down on work surface and pierce through center with skewer. Repeat, holding already-skewered potatoes for better leverage.

ILLUSTRATION: RANDY GLASS

GRILLED POTATOES WITH GARLIC AND ROSEMARY

SERVES 4

This recipe allows you to grill an entree while the hot coals burn down in step 1. Once that item is done, start grilling the potatoes. This recipe works best with small potatoes that are about 1½ inches in diameter. If using medium potatoes, 2 to 3 inches in diameter, cut potatoes into quarters. If potatoes are larger than 3 inches in diameter, cut each potato into eighths. Since potatoes are cooked in microwave, use wooden skewers.

- Vegetable oil for cooking grate
- 4 tablespoons olive oil
- 9 medium garlic cloves, minced or pressed through garlic press (about 3 tablespoons)
- 1 teaspoon chopped fresh rosemary leaves
- Kosher salt
- 2 pounds small Red Bliss potatoes (about 18), scrubbed, halved, and skewered according to illustration at left (see note above)
- Ground black pepper
- Disposable 13 by 9-inch aluminum roasting pan
- 2 tablespoons chopped fresh chives

1. Light large chimney starter filled with charcoal (6 quarts, or about 100 briquettes) and allow to burn until coals are fully ignited and covered with thin layer of ash, about 20 minutes. Empty coals into grill; build two-level fire by arranging two-thirds of coals over half of grill and arranging remaining coals in single layer over other half. Position cooking grate over coals, cover grill, and heat grate until hot, about 5 minutes; scrape grate clean with grill brush. Remove lid and let coals burn until fire on hotter part of grill is medium (you can hold your hand 5 inches above grate for 5 to 6 seconds), about 10 minutes. Dip wad of paper towels in vegetable oil; holding wad with tongs, wipe cooking grate.

2. Meanwhile, heat olive oil, garlic, rosemary, and ½ teaspoon salt in small skillet over medium heat until sizzling, about 3 minutes. Reduce heat to medium-low and continue to cook until garlic is light blond, about 3 minutes. Pour mixture through fine-mesh strainer into small bowl; press on solids. Measure 1 tablespoon solids and 1 tablespoon oil into large bowl and set aside. Discard remaining solids but reserve remaining oil.

3. Place skewered potatoes in single layer on large microwave-safe plate and poke each potato several times with skewer. Brush with 1 tablespoon strained oil and season liberally with salt. Microwave on high power until potatoes offer slight resistance when pierced with tip of paring knife, about 8 minutes, turning them halfway through cooking time. Transfer potatoes to baking sheet coated with 1 tablespoon strained oil. Brush with remaining tablespoon strained oil; season with salt and pepper to taste.

4. Place potatoes on hotter side of grill. Cook, turning once, until grill marks appear, about 4 minutes. Move potatoes to cooler side of grill; cover with disposable pan and continue to cook until paring knife slips in and out of potatoes easily, 5 to 8 minutes longer. Remove potatoes from skewers and transfer to bowl with reserved garlic/oil mixture; add chives and toss until thoroughly coated. Serve immediately.

POTATOES WITH GARLIC AND ROSEMARY ON A GAS GRILL

Follow recipe for Grilled Potatoes with Garlic and Rosemary, skipping step 1. Turn all burners to high, cover, and heat grill until very hot, about 15 minutes. Use grill brush to scrape grill clean; oil cooking grate. Proceed with recipe from step 2, leaving primary burner on high and reducing other burner(s) to medium. Grill potatoes, omitting disposable pan, with lid down.

COOK'S LIVE Original Test Kitchen Video

www.cooksillustrated.com

RECIPE IN 60 SECONDS

- Grilled Potatoes with Garlic and Rosemary

Rethinking Grilled Chicken Breasts

We wanted boneless, skinless breasts that came off the grill juicy and flavorful. There had to be a solution better than bottled salad dressing.

⋟ BY SANDRA WU ⋞

Left to their own devices, boneless, skinless chicken breasts don't stand a chance on the backyard grill. Because they have no skin and little fat, untreated chicken breasts invariably turn out dry and leathery, with a mild—some might say bland—flavor. A quick and easy "solution" that millions of outdoor cooks commonly resort to is soaking the breasts in a store-bought marinade. Nice idea, but in a taste test we couldn't find one brand we could stomach, let alone recommend. Taking a few minutes to make my own marinade would yield better results.

I knew, though, that nothing else mattered if I couldn't produce perfectly grilled chicken breasts—moist, tender, and able to stand on their own flavor-wise. I didn't want to have to pound the chicken breasts or lose the tenderloin, which recipes usually recommend saving for "another use" (such as taking up permanent residence in the freezer). I wanted to keep things as simple as possible.

Cooked as most recipes suggest—that is, over a hot, single-level fire—the outsides of the breasts did what I expected: They turned into black shoe leather by the time the internal temperature reached 160 degrees. When cooked solely over indirect heat on the cooler side of a modified two-level fire (all the coals banked on one side of the grill), the interiors were noticeably moister, but the tough exteriors lacked color and true grilled flavor. Although searing the meat over the hotter side of the grill before moving it to the cool side to finish cooking offered a slight improvement, the chicken still wasn't where I wanted it to be.

Defying Convention

Were my conventional methods holding me back? Several test cooks suggested using a "hobo pack": wrapping the chicken up into a tight foil pouch to keep it moist while cooked over the grill. But without periodically opening the foil and risking a steam burn, I had no way of knowing when the chicken was ready. And when it was, it still lacked grilled texture and flavor. I needed a gentler cooking method. Since stovetop poaching does wonders for chicken, I wondered if I could make it work on the grill. I placed a disposable aluminum pan filled halfway with chicken broth over the grates, let it come up to a simmer, and added the chicken breasts. Once they reached 140 degrees, I finished them on the hot grates. Tasters complained that the texture was neither poached nor grilled but "weird."

The same ingredients used in the marinade see action again in a simple finishing sauce for our grilled chicken breasts.

Had I gone too far? Maybe not if I looked at things from a different perspective. Suppose I inverted the disposable pan over the chicken to trap the heat? Creating less temperature fluctuation would allow the breasts to cook more evenly. I started by searing the breasts on the hot side of the grill before moving them to the cooler side, where I covered them with the pan (I flipped them halfway through). Tasters noticed improved flavor and texture that were closer to what I wanted, but still no cigar. What if I tried reversing the cooking order, starting the covered breasts on the cooler side of the grill until they were nearly done (140 degrees), then giving them a quick sear afterward? The result was perfectly cooked boneless, skinless chicken breasts.

Proper Flow

I could now pursue my original goal of injecting some real flavor into the breasts by creating a marinade that could take the place of the test kitchen's standard practice of brining chicken. Lemon and garlic immediately came to mind, so I mixed together a combination of olive oil, lemon juice, garlic, salt, and pepper. I added some sugar to cut the acidity and help with browning. I quickly found that too much lemon juice caused the exterior of the chicken breasts to turn white. No good—I wasn't cooking seviche. But cutting the lemon juice down to 1 tablespoon made the interior bland and dry.

I knew from past brining experiences that without enough liquid, osmosis—the flow of water across a barrier from a place with a higher water concentration (the brine or marinade) to a place with a lower one (the chicken)—is inhibited. The liquid moving into the chicken should have carried with it some of the dissolved salt and flavor, but these molecules were too concentrated to penetrate the tissue. Adding 2 tablespoons of water diluted the concentration of salt and flavor molecules in the marinade enough for an exchange of dissolved molecules to flow in and out of the chicken. A 30-minute marinade did the trick.

RECIPE DIAGNOSIS: Avoiding Imperfect Chicken

PROBLEM: DRY, LEATHERY, AND UNEVENLY COOKED
SOLUTION: Trapping the heat under a disposable pan for most of the grilling time ensures even cooking and retains moisture.

PROBLEM: NO GRILL FLAVOR OR COLOR
SOLUTION: Cooking the chicken on the cool side of the grill imparts a smokier taste, and searing it afterward creates dark grill marks.

PHOTOGRAPHY: CARL TREMBLAY

RECIPE AT A GLANCE | GRILLING BONELESS, SKINLESS CHICKEN BREASTS

1. Place chicken on cool side of grill, with thicker ends facing coals.

2. Cover chicken with disposable aluminum roasting pan; cook 6 to 9 minutes.

3. Flip chicken so thinner ends face coals and continue grilling, covered, 6 to 9 minutes.

4. Finish chicken over coals until dark grill marks appear, 1 to 2 minutes on each side.

Fancy Finish

I thought I was finished, but tasters weren't ready to let me off the hook. I wanted to keep things simple, but they wanted a sauce. No problem: I could use the ingredients from the marinade—plus chopped parsley for color and Dijon mustard for extra flavor and emulsification—to spoon over the cooked chicken. This new complementary sauce added more moisture as well as another layer of flavor. These grilled chicken breasts were easy enough to make for myself on a weeknight (I could save the extras to top a salad the next day) and fancy enough to serve to guests at my next dinner party.

GRILLED LEMON-PARSLEY CHICKEN BREASTS

SERVES 4

This chicken can be served with a simply prepared vegetable for a light dinner. It can also be used in a sandwich or tossed with greens for a salad. The chicken should be marinated no less than 30 minutes and no more than 1 hour.

- 1 teaspoon Dijon mustard
- 2 tablespoons juice from 1 lemon
- 6 tablespoons olive oil
- 1 tablespoon minced fresh parsley leaves
- 1¼ teaspoons sugar
- Table salt and ground black pepper
- 3 medium garlic cloves, minced or pressed through garlic press (about 1 tablespoon)
- 2 tablespoons water
- 4 boneless, skinless chicken breasts (6 to 8 ounces each), trimmed of excess fat
- Vegetable oil for cooking grate
- Disposable 13 by 9-inch aluminum roasting pan

1. Whisk together mustard, 1 tablespoon lemon juice, 3 tablespoons olive oil, parsley, ¼ teaspoon sugar, ¼ teaspoon salt, and ¼ teaspoon pepper in small bowl; set aside.

2. Whisk together remaining tablespoon lemon juice, remaining 3 tablespoons olive oil, remaining teaspoon sugar, 1½ teaspoons salt, ½ teaspoon pepper, garlic, and water in medium bowl. Place marinade and chicken in gallon-size zipper-lock bag and toss to coat; press out as much air as possible and seal bag. Refrigerate 30 minutes, flipping bag after 15 minutes.

3. Meanwhile, light large chimney starter filled with charcoal (6 quarts, or about 100 briquettes) and allow to burn until coals are fully ignited and partially covered with thin layer of ash, about 20 minutes. Build modified two-level fire by arranging all coals over half of grill, leaving other half empty. Position cooking grate over coals, cover grill, and heat grate until hot, about 5 minutes; scrape grate clean with grill brush. Dip wad of paper towels in oil; holding wad with tongs, wipe cooking grate. Grill is ready when side with coals is medium-hot (you can hold your hand 5 inches above grate for 3 to 4 seconds).

4. Remove chicken from bag, allowing excess marinade to drip off. Place chicken on cooler side of grill, smooth-side down, with thicker side facing coals. Cover with disposable pan and cook until bottom of chicken just begins to develop light grill marks and is no longer translucent, 6 to 9 minutes. Using tongs, flip chicken and rotate so that thinner side faces coals. Cover with disposable pan and continue to cook until chicken is opaque and firm to touch and instant-read thermometer inserted into thickest part of chicken registers 140 degrees, 6 to 9 minutes longer.

5. Move chicken to hotter side of grill and cook, uncovered, until dark grill marks appear, 1 to 2 minutes. Using tongs, flip chicken and cook until dark grill marks appear and instant-read thermometer inserted into thickest part of chicken registers 160 degrees, 1 to 2 minutes longer. Transfer chicken to cutting board, let rest, tented with foil, 5 minutes. Slice each breast on bias into ¼-inch-thick slices and transfer to individual plates. Drizzle with reserved sauce and serve.

TASTING: Bottled Marinades

DON'T EVEN TRY THESE

We tried saving time by marinating our chicken breasts in four bottled lemon-and-herb marinades. Laden with sweeteners, stabilizers, and gums, their gelatinous consistencies and unnatural flavors were strongly disliked.

LEMON-PARSLEY CHICKEN BREASTS ON A GAS GRILL

Follow recipe for Grilled Lemon-Parsley Chicken Breasts through step 2. Turn all burners to high and heat with lid down until very hot, about 15 minutes. Scrape grate clean with grill brush. Dip wad of paper towels in oil; holding wad with tongs, wipe cooking grate. Leave primary burner on high and turn off other burner(s). Proceed with recipe from step 4, grilling with lid down and omitting disposable pan. Increase browning times in step 5 by 1 to 2 minutes.

GRILLED CHIPOTLE-LIME CHICKEN BREASTS

Follow recipe for Grilled Lemon-Parsley Chicken Breasts, substituting lime juice for lemon juice and using an extra teaspoon juice in reserved sauce in step 1. Substitute 1 teaspoon minced chipotle chile in adobo sauce for mustard and cilantro for parsley.

GRILLED ORANGE-TARRAGON CHICKEN BREASTS

Follow recipe for Grilled Lemon-Parsley Chicken Breasts, substituting orange juice for lemon juice and tarragon for parsley. Add ¼ teaspoon orange zest to reserved sauce in step 1.

COOK'S LIVE Original Test Kitchen Videos
www.cooksillustrated.com

RECIPE IN 60 SECONDS
- Grilled Lemon-Parsley Chicken Breasts

VIDEO TIP
- What does it mean to slice on the bias?

Bringing Gyros Home

We were craving restaurant-style Greek gyros that we could wrap our hands around. There was just one pressing problem: the meat.

⋡ BY SANDRA WU ⋠

I am hooked on gyros. What's not to love about these sandwiches of seasoned, marinated lamb, tomato, lettuce, and cucumber-yogurt tzatziki sauce stuffed inside a soft pita? During one of my latest cravings, I found myself at Farm Grill and Rotisserie, a Greek restaurant in Newton, Mass.

Hoping for some ideas on how to make them at home, I convinced chef Yousry Aly to take me into the kitchen and show me the traditional cooking method: Several pounds of marinated sliced leg of lamb are layered and stacked onto an electric vertical rotisserie to form a tightly packed cylinder of meat (gyro means "to turn" in Greek, hence "gyroscope"). After several hours of cooking, the meat is shaved with a long slicing knife. The pieces that fall off have crisp exteriors and moist interiors that are infused with garlic and oregano from the marinade. As appealing as it was, I knew this restaurant method wasn't going to translate to any home kitchen I knew of.

Flipping through cookbooks revealed that others had the same dilemma: how to cook the gyro's defining ingredient, the meat. One recipe called for quickly sautéing thin strips of marinated lamb. Trimming and slicing the fatty roast into thin strips required quite a bit of effort, and the end result resembled a bad stir-fry. A similar broiled version wasn't much better. Another recipe produced a lamb meatloaf sliced into thin strips: a novel approach, but one that took too long to prepare and yielded an odd, spongy texture.

I decided to try one last recipe: pan-fried ground lamb patties (reminiscent of Middle Eastern kefta) flavored with oregano and onion. While these patties sure didn't look like gyros, the texture was close, and they were really easy to make. I'd found my jumping-off point.

Our pita sandwich contains layers of lamb patties, tomato, lettuce, feta cheese, and a cooling yogurt-cucumber sauce.

Meaty Matters

To the ground lamb I added traditional Greek ingredients—oregano, finely chopped onion, and minced garlic—before rolling the mixture into balls and flattening them into small disks. But once the seasoned pan-fried patties were cooked through, tasters thought their texture was too dense and dry. Taking a cue from our recipe for Well-Done Hamburgers (July/August 2006), I incorporated a modified panade (a paste of fresh bread crumbs and milk) to make the meat juicier. But now tasters found the patties a little too mushy. At the supermarket, all I'd been able to find were pocketed pitas with tops that needed to be cut off before they could be filled. What if I replaced the white bread crumbs with crumbs from this drier bread? This gave the patties a sturdier structure along with fuller, more savory flavor. And no more waste.

In order to achieve the meat's traditional duality of texture—crisp outside, moist inside—I tried cooking the patties in a large oiled skillet over medium-high heat. Even though they didn't look like typical chipped gyro meat, they fooled my taste buds into believing what my eyes did not. With the lamb patties perfected, I decided to try my hand at making a just-as-good beef version. At 92-percent lean, ground sirloin was ruled out for being too dry and livery. Eighty-percent lean ground chuck won hands down.

Some Assembly Required

Just because I had nicely warmed pitas and well-seasoned meat didn't mean I was done. What's a gyro sandwich without the tzatziki sauce? The cooling combination of yogurt, garlic, cucumber, dill or mint, and lemon juice is more than just a condiment; it's a necessity. Since Greek yogurt can be difficult to find, I stuck to plain full-fat yogurt, which is better than low-fat at approximating the creamy texture of the real stuff. My first attempt at tzatziki was thin and watery; I'd have to remove some of the yogurt's excess whey.

RECIPE TESTING: Gyros Go Home

Here are three of the cooking methods we tried—and rejected—in our quest to make gyros at home.

TOO FUSSY
Sautéing strips of marinated lamb took effort, resulting in what looked like a bad stir-fry.

FLAWED TEXTURE
Packing the meat into a loaf shape yielded an odd, spongy texture with no crispy parts.

IMPRACTICAL
A vertical rotisserie produced flawless meat—crisp on the outside and moist inside—but isn't practical at home.

PHOTOGRAPHY: CARL TREMBLAY

RECIPE SHORTHAND | FOLDING A POCKETLESS PITA SANDWICH

Although pocketed pitas are easier to find, we prefer the pocketless versions for their thick, pillowy texture and deeper flavor. If you can't find them in your supermarket, look for them in Mediterranean grocery stores. They require a slightly different assembly technique, as shown here. When layering ingredients on the pita in step 1, leave a 1-inch border on all sides.

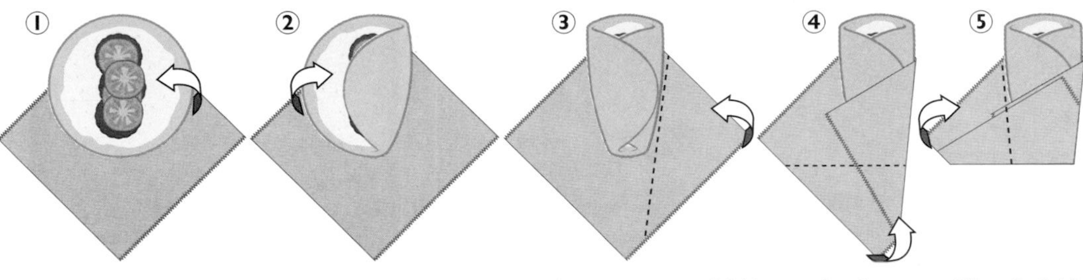

1. Place pita on top of aluminum foil, layer sandwich ingredients on pita, and fold one side of pita over filling. **2.** Fold opposite side of pita over filling so it overlaps first side. **3.** Fold one side of foil over sandwich. **4.** Fold up bottom of foil. **5.** Wrap other side of foil over sandwich to fully enclose it.

Drained for just 30 minutes over a paper towel– or coffee filter–lined strainer (a technique the test kitchen uses to make yogurt cheese), it attained a texture that was denser, richer, and much closer to the Greek variety. Salting the cucumber first also reduced excess moisture.

With my components ready, all I had to do now was put together the sandwich. Taking one warmed pita at a time, I spread a quarter of the sauce on one side before adding three lamb patties and filling the rest of the space with tomatoes, shredded lettuce, and an unconventional but welcome addition of feta cheese. A single bite confirmed that this was a great weeknight alternative to a cold cut sandwich or fast food burger.

GREEK-STYLE LAMB PITA SANDWICHES WITH TZATZIKI SAUCE

SERVES 4

Since the yogurt and cucumbers in the Tzatziki Sauce need to drain for 30 minutes, start making the sauce before the patties. To substitute beef for the lamb, use 80-percent lean ground chuck, decrease the amount of lemon juice to 1 tablespoon and increase the oregano to 2 tablespoons, garlic to 3 cloves, and oil to 1 tablespoon. The test kitchen prefers the flavor of fresh oregano, but 1 teaspoon of dried can be substituted. The skillet may appear crowded when you begin cooking the patties, but they will shrink slightly as they cook. If using pocketless pitas, heat them in a single layer on a baking sheet in a 350-degree oven for 5 minutes. Do not cut top quarters off pocketless pitas; instead, use a portion of a fifth pita to create crumbs in step 1. When cooking the patties, use a splatter screen to keep the mess to a minimum. The patties can be prepared through step 1 and refrigerated for up to a day or frozen before cooking as directed in step 2 (frozen patties should be thawed in refrigerator prior to cooking). This recipe can be doubled.

- 4 large (8-inch) pita breads (see note above)
- ½ medium onion, chopped coarse (about ¾ cup)
- 4 teaspoons juice from 1 lemon
- ½ teaspoon table salt
- ¼ teaspoon ground black pepper
- 1 tablespoon minced fresh oregano leaves
- 2 medium garlic cloves, minced or pressed through garlic press (about 2 teaspoons)
- 1 pound ground lamb (see note above for information on using beef)
- 2 teaspoons vegetable oil
- Tzatziki Sauce (recipe follows)
- 1 large tomato, sliced thin
- 2 cups shredded iceberg lettuce
- 2 ounces feta cheese, crumbled (about ½ cup)

1. Adjust oven rack to middle position and heat oven to 350 degrees. Cut top quarter off each pita bread. Tear quarters into 1-inch pieces. (You should have ¾ cup pita pieces.) Stack pitas and tightly wrap with aluminum foil. Process onion, lemon juice, salt, pepper, oregano, garlic, and pita bread pieces in food processor until smooth paste forms, about 30 seconds. Transfer onion mixture to large bowl; add lamb and gently mix with hands until thoroughly combined. Divide mixture into 12 equal pieces and roll into balls. Gently flatten balls into round disks, about ½ inch thick and 2½ inches in diameter.

2. Place foil-wrapped pitas directly on oven rack and heat for 10 minutes. Meanwhile, heat oil in 12-inch nonstick skillet over medium-high heat until just smoking. Add patties and cook until well browned and crust forms, 3 to 4 minutes. Flip patties, reduce heat to medium, and cook until well browned and crust forms on second side, about 5 minutes longer. (See page 31 for tips on flipping patties.) Transfer patties to paper towel–lined plate.

3. Using soupspoon, spread ¼ cup Tzatziki Sauce inside each pita. Divide patties evenly among pitas; top each sandwich with tomato slices, ½ cup shredded lettuce, and 2 tablespoons feta. Serve immediately.

TZATZIKI SAUCE

MAKES ABOUT 1 CUP

Although we prefer the richness of plain whole-milk yogurt, low-fat yogurt can be substituted. Greek yogurt can also be substituted, but use ½ cup and skip the step of draining. While we didn't like the flavor of dried mint, dried dill may be used in place of fresh, but reduce the amount to ½ teaspoon.

- 1 cup plain whole-milk yogurt
- ½ medium cucumber, peeled, seeded, and diced fine (about ½ cup)
- ⅜ teaspoon table salt
- 1 tablespoon juice from 1 lemon
- 1 small garlic clove, minced or pressed through garlic press (about ½ teaspoon)
- 1 tablespoon finely chopped fresh mint or dill

1. Line fine-mesh strainer set over deep container or bowl with 3 paper coffee filters or triple layer of paper towels. Spoon yogurt into lined strainer, cover, and refrigerate for 30 minutes.

2. Meanwhile, combine cucumber, ⅛ teaspoon salt, and lemon juice in colander set over bowl and let stand 30 minutes.

3. Discard drained liquid from yogurt. Combine thickened yogurt, drained cucumber, remaining ¼ teaspoon salt, garlic, and mint in clean bowl.

TASTING: Whole-Milk Yogurt

We call for plain whole-milk yogurt in our Tzatziki Sauce. It has three times as much fat as low-fat yogurt and far more flavor. Of the four national brands of whole-milk yogurt that we tasted, we found Horizon Organic Whole Milk Plain Yogurt and Dannon All Natural Plain Yogurt too sour. Tasters preferred the whole-milk yogurts with the most fat—Brown Cow Cream Top Plain Yogurt and Stonyfield Farm Organic Whole Milk Plain Yogurt. Brown Cow's slightly richer flavor profile made it the overall winner. For the complete results of this tasting, go to www.cooksillustrated.com/august. –Elizabeth Bomze

CREAM OF THE CROP
For smoothness and flavor, Brown Cow Cream Top Plain Yogurt trumped the leaner, more acidic competition.

ILLUSTRATION: JAY LAYMAN

Perfecting Pasta Caprese

This summer dish combines ripe tomatoes, fresh mozzarella, and fragrant basil with hot pasta. Preventing the cheese from turning into bubble gum presented a gooey problem.

BY REBECCA HAYS

Legend has it that the popular Caprese trio of garden tomatoes, fresh mozzarella, and basil leaves was introduced in the 1950s at Trattoria Da Vincenzo, a beachside restaurant on the Italian island of Capri. According to creator Margherita Cosentino, the red, white, and green salad of local produce and cheese allowed ladies to "have a nice lunch while still fitting into their bikinis." Swimsuit season or not, the combination became so popular that cooks everywhere took to mixing it with hot pasta, minced garlic, and extra-virgin olive oil for a 15-minute entrée that captures the flavors of summer.

We found that our Pasta Caprese required some help from the freezer.

Truth be told, I was skeptical that a recipe would really be required for such a clear-cut dish. Still, I gathered a representative sampling and went into the kitchen. The outcome? Instead of collecting the praise I had expected from my colleagues, I joined them for a few chuckles. The tomatoes, pasta, and basil weren't problems, but the cheese was. In each recipe, it had clumped into an intractable softball-sized wad in the bottom of the pasta bowl. After wrestling a serving out of the dish, things only got worse. The tangles of mozzarella bubble gum were difficult to chew, never mind swallow. The mozzarella was a classic case of Dr. Jekyll and Mr. Hyde: likable and tender at one moment, monstrously tough the next.

When the wisecracks and laughter subsided, several of my colleagues quietly confessed to having experienced the same problem at home.

Untangling the Cheese

For these first tests, I had purchased fresh mozzarella—the kind that comes immersed in plastic tubs of water and is shaped into irregular-sized balls—at the supermarket. What if I used regular block-style mozzarella (the low-moisture version often shredded for pizza) instead? It melted nicely and didn't turn chewy, but this inauthentic substitution cheated the dish of its star ingredient, and tasters complained about blandness.

For my next test, I took a big step in the opposite direction and tried water buffalo–milk mozzarella (***mozzarella di bufala***) from a specialty cheese shop. Much softer than the commercial fresh cheese, this handmade mozzarella melted into tender pillows when combined with the pasta—there were no rubbery bits to be found. In addition to the lovely consistency, tasters praised its flavor, which was dripping with milkiness and tang. The next day, I prepared pasta Caprese using handmade cow's-milk mozzarella and achieved the same impressive results. (Intrigued by the differences among the cheeses, I investigated the topic further; see "Shopping: Fresh Mozzarella," on page 15.)

Money Problem

So my problem was solved, as long as I had time to go to the cheese store and was willing to pay the big bucks for handmade cheese, which can easily top $9 per pound. Everyone in the test kitchen agreed this wasn't an acceptable solution. I needed to find a way to use fresh mozzarella from the supermarket.

My first thought was to thoroughly coat diced mozzarella cubes with olive oil before adding the steaming pasta. This was a step in the right direction, with the oil preventing sticking . . . initially. After a few minutes, however, the nasty clumping problem reemerged.

I wondered what would happen if I put the diced supermarket cheese in the freezer for a few minutes before combining it with the pasta. Could chilling the cheese keep it from melting fully and clumping into wads of bubble gum? I gave this approach a trial run, dicing the mozzarella and chilling it in the freezer for 10 minutes. I then proceeded as usual, combining the firmed-up cheese with the pasta and tomatoes. Success: When added to hot pasta, the cheese softened but did not fully melt, making the unattractive elastic ropes a thing of the past. It turns out that the proteins in fresh mozzarella begin to melt at about 130 degrees. As the temperature climbs past 130

RECIPE DIAGNOSIS: **Pasta Caprese**

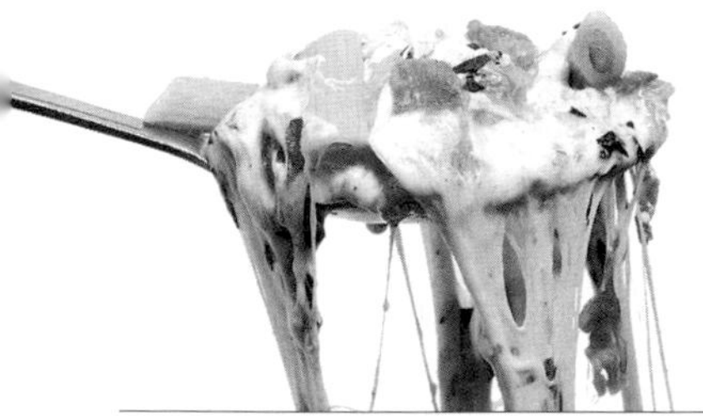

PROBLEM:
MOZZARELLA CHEWING GUM
Industrially produced mozzarella clumps into a rubbery, stringy mess when combined with hot pasta.

SOLUTION:
DICE, THEN FREEZE
Freezing the cheese for 10 minutes before combining it with the pasta prevents it from turning into taffy.

PHOTOGRAPHY: CARL TREMBLAY

degrees, the proteins clump together. Freezing the cheese kept it from overheating when tossed with the hot pasta.

Necessary Extras

With the cheese conundrum solved, I fine-tuned the rest of the recipe, starting with the tomatoes. Juicy, garden-ripe beauties need no adornment, but a sprinkle of sugar can replace the gentle sweetness that is often missing in less-than-perfect specimens. And while Italians would never add an acidic component to a true Caprese recipe, a squirt of fresh lemon juice (favored over all types of vinegar) did a great job of boosting the flavor of lackluster tomatoes. I also knew from experience that ridding the tomatoes of their seeds before dicing them would preclude a diluted, watery sauce.

In recipes that use raw olive oil, the fruity and spicy nuances of extra-virgin oil make a difference, and this dish is no exception. I added a healthy drizzle of the test kitchen's favorite extra-virgin olive oil, then stirred in a minced shallot, a sprinkle of salt, and a few twists of black pepper. Allowing the tomatoes and mozzarella to marinate while the pasta cooked infused them with fruity and subtle garlic flavors. Lengthy marinating times aren't recommended, however, as more than 45 minutes yielded mealy, broken-down tomatoes.

As for the pasta, tasters preferred penne, fusilli, and campanelle over spaghetti, which is commonly used. The short tubular or curly shapes trap the chunky sauce in their nooks and crannies. Freshly chopped basil was the finishing touch to pasta that tasted just like summer.

SHOPPING: Fresh Mozzarella

I found that artisanal-quality mozzarella melted beautifully in my recipe, but most of the fresh mozzarella I bought at supermarkets melted into bubble gum–like balls. Why the big difference?

To find out, I interviewed Al Scheps of Al Ducci's, a Vermont cheese maker with decades of experience. Scheps explained the art of making mozzarella: Blocks of curd (purchased wholesale or made from scratch) are cut into strips, then immersed in hot (roughly 180-degree) water, where they melt and amalgamate. The cheese maker then reaches into the hot water to gently knead and stretch the mozzarella like taffy, a process known as *pasta filata*. When the cheese is smooth and shiny, he cuts or tears the cheese into individual portions (the Italian verb *mozzare* means "to cut off"), carefully shapes them into balls, and places them in a salty brine. Freshly made mozzarella cheese, plump and bulging with whey, is extremely perishable and should be eaten within a few days.

WHAT'S IN THE TUB?
Just because it's packed in water doesn't mean this cheese is truly "fresh." Mass-produced brands with shelf lives measured in weeks (not days) will turn rubbery if they get too hot.

Commercial fresh mozzarella is manufactured in much the same way, with one important difference: To facilitate production, the cooking, stretching, kneading, and forming are done by machine, not by hand. Because of this rough handling, the cheese releases an abundance of butterfat and whey. With less fat and less moisture, the product is sturdier and has a shelf life of 90 to 120 days. But vigorous handling also strengthens the protein network in cheese, which causes it to turn tough and ropy when melted.

So what should you buy? In a taste test, the porcelain-white artisanal varieties were favored. Tasters praised their understated, milky flavor and soft texture. Fresh cheeses made by machine were tougher and not as flavorful, but still quite good. My advice: Buy a handmade cheese if you can. If you end up buying fresh mozzarella at the supermarket, my recipe will turn out great—as long as you remember to freeze the cheese. –R.H.

PASTA CAPRESE

SERVES 4 TO 6

This dish will be very warm, not hot. The success of this recipe depends on high-quality ingredients, including ripe, in-season tomatoes and a fruity olive oil (the test kitchen prefers Columela Extra-Virgin). Don't skip the step of freezing the mozzarella, as freezing prevents it from turning chewy when it comes in contact with the hot pasta. If handmade buffalo- or cow's-milk mozzarella is available (it's commonly found in gourmet and cheese shops packed in water), we highly recommend using it, but skip the step of freezing. Additional lemon juice or up to 1 teaspoon sugar can be added at the end to taste, depending on the ripeness of the tomatoes.

- **1/4 cup extra-virgin olive oil**
- **2–4 teaspoons juice from 1 lemon (see note above)**
- **1 small garlic clove, minced or pressed through garlic press (about 1/2 teaspoon)**
- **1 small shallot, minced fine (about 2 tablespoons) Table salt and ground black pepper**
- **1 1/2 pounds ripe tomatoes, cored, seeded, and cut into 1/2-inch dice**
- **12 ounces fresh mozzarella cheese, cut into 1/2-inch cubes (see note above)**
- **1 pound short tubular or curly pasta, such as penne, fusilli, or campanelle**
- **1/4 cup chopped fresh basil leaves**
- **1 teaspoon sugar (see note above)**

1. Whisk oil, 2 teaspoons lemon juice, garlic, shallot, 1/2 teaspoon salt, and 1/4 teaspoon pepper together in large bowl. Add tomatoes and gently toss to combine; set aside. Do not marinate tomatoes for longer than 45 minutes.

2. While tomatoes are marinating, place mozzarella on plate and freeze until slightly firm, about 10 minutes. Bring 4 quarts water to rolling boil in stockpot. Add 1 tablespoon salt and pasta, stir to separate, and cook until al dente. Drain well.

3. Add pasta and mozzarella to tomato mixture and gently toss to combine. Let stand 5 minutes. Stir in basil; adjust seasonings with salt, pepper, and additional lemon juice or sugar, if desired, and serve immediately.

COOK'S LIVE Original Test Kitchen Videos
www.cooksillustrated.com

RECIPE IN 60 SECONDS
- Pasta Caprese

VIDEO TIPS
- What happens if I don't freeze my mozzarella?
- What should I look for in a colander?

TASTING: High-End Pasta

Domestic brands of dried pasta, such as Ronzoni and Mueller's, have repeatedly won top honors with our testers, but now that more specialty brands and Italian imports have hit store shelves, we decided to give fancy pasta—this time in the form of penne—another taste. We tried eight brands, with some costing as much as $5 per pound. Though none were deemed unacceptable, there were significant differences among the brands we tasted.

PENNE WISE
Its box may be plain, but inexpensive Mueller's Penne Rigate rated tops with our tasters.

Many Italian brands claim to maintain traditional techniques and ingredients, such as slow kneading, mixing cold mountain spring water with hard durum semolina, extruding the dough through traditional bronze cast dies for a coarse texture, and prolonged air-drying. Supposedly, these practices make for stronger flavor and more rustic, sauce-gripping pasta. Yet three expensive imports (Bionaturae, Montebello, and Rustichella d'Abruzzo) landed at the bottom of our rankings. Ronzoni scored in the middle of the pack. Tasters liked three other Italian offerings (Benedetto Cavalieri, De Cecco, and Martelli), but top honors went to Mueller's. For complete tasting results, go to www.cooksillustrated.com/august. –Elizabeth Bomze

How to Freeze Summer Produce

We froze freshly picked summer fruits and vegetables last summer, then thawed them in the middle of winter to find out which methods of freezing work best. BY KEITH DRESSER

Our testing began last summer when we froze a variety of freshly picked fruits and vegetables to see which ones could be frozen and which method for preserving their freshness was the most effective. Follow our suggestions and you should be able to freeze produce for about six months—long enough to satisfy midwinter cravings for summer fruits and vegetables.

Science of Freezing

When fruits and vegetables freeze, the water that is contained in each cell turns into ice crystals. The size of these ice crystals depends on how rapidly the produce is frozen: Quick freezing yields smaller crystals; slow freezing creates larger crystals. As these ice crystals form, they rupture cell walls and internal cell organelles, which release enzymes from their locked compartments. When thawed, these enzymes cause produce to develop off-flavors and turn brown and soggy.

In vegetables, these enzymes can be deactivated by blanching. Because fruits are too delicate to blanch, sugar or sugar syrup is used to reduce the formation of ice crystals during freezing. In high concentrations, sugar acts as a barrier between fruit and oxygen. We also found it necessary to add ascorbic acid to peaches and nectarines when freezing, which deactivates the molecules that cause browning.

FREEZER BASICS

Some basic freezer knowledge will help you better preserve food.

AIRFLOW: To help cold air circulate, keep food away from freezer vents. For more efficiency and to maintain colder temps, vacuum filters and coils of your refrigerator/freezer periodically (unplug your fridge before doing so).

SHELF SPACE: The more quickly fruits and vegetables are frozen, the less they suffer when defrosted. Clearing shelf space will maximize airflow for a quicker freeze. Increase shelf space with portable wire cabinet shelving.

TEMPERATURE: A survey of test kitchen staff's home freezers showed temps ranged from 5 degrees to -10 degrees (0 degrees or below is optimal). Make sure your freezer is at the coldest possible setting (unlike your fridge, where the coldest setting is normally too cold).

THE COLDEST SPOT: The rear center is the coldest spot in most freezers, so place produce there.

HOW TO FREEZE FRUIT

We learned it's best to freeze fruit with sugar syrup or sugar to reduce the formation of damaging ice crystals (see "Science of Freezing," above). We found the bright color of strawberries and raspberries was best preserved in syrup. Sugar did a better job of protecting the flavor of blueberries and stone fruit. We found no good way of preserving fresh cherries.

FRUIT PREP

Fruits are best frozen in individual bags containing no more than 2 cups of fruit. The chart below gives the amount of syrup or sugar that should be added to every 2 cups of fruit. To avoid lowering freezer's temperature by overcrowding, freeze no more than 8 cups of fruit at a time. Wash and dry fruits before freezing.

SYRUP PACK: For every 2 cups of fruit, cover with the listed amount of syrup. To make 6 cups of syrup, heat 3 cups of sugar and 4 cups of water in a medium saucepan over medium-high heat, stirring occasionally, until sugar has dissolved, about 5 minutes. Cool to room temperature.

SUGAR PACK: Toss 2 cups of fruit with the listed amount of sugar before bagging and freezing. For peaches and nectarines, add 1 1/2 teaspoons of Fruit Fresh (or similar ascorbic acid–based product) to the sugar.

FRUIT	AMOUNT	PREPARATION	FREEZING METHOD	AMOUNT OF SUGAR OR SYRUP
Strawberries	2 cups	hulled and halved	Syrup	1 1/4 cups
Raspberries	2 cups	picked over	Syrup	1 1/4 cups
Blueberries	2 cups	picked over	Sugar	1/3 cup
Peaches or Nectarines	2 cups	pitted and cut into 1/2-inch-thick slices	Sugar	1/2 cup

Master Steps for Freezing Fruit

1. FILL BAG Fit labeled and dated quart-sized zipper-lock freezer bag into 2-cup liquid measuring cup. Spoon 2 cups prepared fruit into bag.

2. ADD SYRUP If using sugar syrup, pour syrup over fruit to cover.

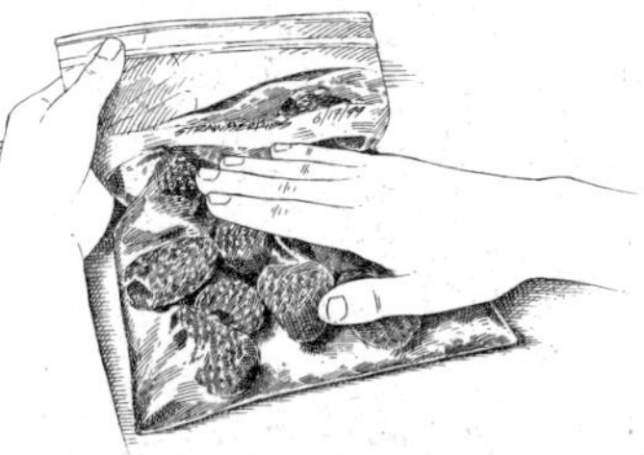

3. SEAL Remove as much air as possible from bag before sealing. Place bag into second zipper-lock bag.

4. FREEZE Lay bags flat in single layer on baking sheet. Freeze until solid, at least 24 hours, then store anywhere in freezer.

ILLUSTRATION: JOHN BURGOYNE

HOW TO FREEZE VEGETABLES

When freezing vegetables, blanching (briefly plunging the vegetables into boiling water) and shocking (moving them into cold water to stop the cooking process) is critical (see "Science of Freezing," on page 16). Work quickly and keep vegetables as cold as possible after they have been blanched and shocked. Freezing warm vegetables takes longer and creates large, damaging ice crystals.

VEGETABLE PREP

Blanch all vegetables in 6 quarts of water seasoned with 1 tablespoon of table salt. While we had success freezing corn, green beans, snow peas, snap peas, shell peas, and greens, we found tomatoes, cucumbers, zucchini, and eggplant didn't freeze well, due to their high water content and delicate cell structure. If you have an abundance of these vegetables, we suggest cooking them first, such as in a sauce, then freezing them. Go to www.cooksillustrated.com/august for the following free recipes: Quick Homemade Pickles, Quick Fresh Tomato Sauce, and Ratatouille.

VEGETABLE	AMOUNT	PREPARATION	BLANCHING TIME
Asparagus	1 pound	tough ends snapped off and discarded	2 minutes
Corn (Whole)	6 ears	husks and silks removed	3 ears at a time for 6 minutes
Corn (Kernels)	6 ears	kernels removed from cob	4 minutes
Green Beans	1 pound	ends trimmed and cut into 1½-inch pieces	2 minutes
Snow Peas	1 pound	strings removed	1 minute
Snap Peas	1 pound	strings removed	2 minutes
Shell Peas	2 pounds	shelled	2 minutes
Tender Greens (Spinach, Chard)	8 cups lightly packed (about 2 large bunches)	stemmed and washed	1 minute
Tough Greens (Kale)	8 cups lightly packed (about 2 large bunches)	stemmed and washed	2 minutes

Master Steps for Freezing Vegetables

1. BLANCH Cook prepared vegetables until color has brightened but vegetables are still very crisp (see times in chart at left).

2. SHOCK Transfer to bowl filled with ice water and cool for 1 minute. If needed, add more ice to water to keep cold.

3. DRY WELL Transfer to rimmed baking sheet covered with 3 layers of paper towels. Cover with another 2 layers and gently dry.

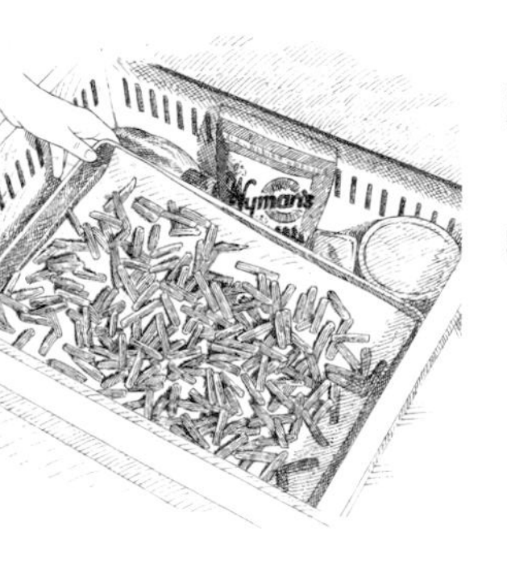

4. FREEZE Place in single layer on baking sheet lined with parchment paper and freeze until solid, 1 to 2 hours.

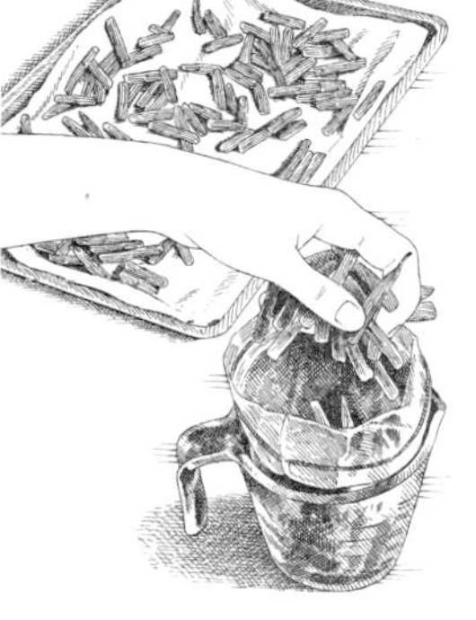

5. PACKAGE Once frozen, transfer 2 cups into labeled, dated zipper-lock freezer bag, squeezing out as much air as possible.

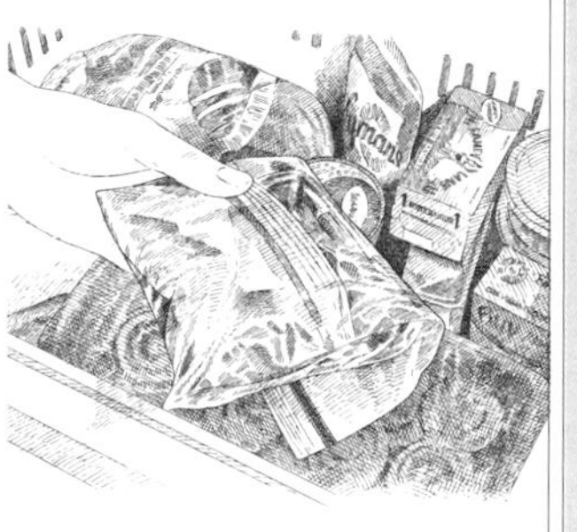

6. STORE Place bag into another zipper-lock freezer bag and store in coldest part of freezer.

TIPS FOR SUCCESS

1. Keep Air Out. When exposed to a freezer's arid environment, food becomes dry and discolored, a condition called freezer burn. We like to freeze in a double layer of zipper-lock freezer bags, finding this prevents freezer burn and keeps food from picking up odors and flavors.

2. Use Small Batches. Freezing a lot of fruits and vegetables at once will overload your freezer and cause its temperature to rise. Freezing no more than 2 pounds (8 cups) of produce at a time will keep the freezer as cold as possible and yield much better results over the long haul.

3. Freeze Quickly. See "Science of Freezing," on page 16.

4. Two Freezers Are Better Than One. We've found produce kept in a regularly used freezer has a shelf life two to three months shorter than produce stored in an infrequently used freezer. Normal, everyday use causes fluctuating temperatures. If you often freeze produce, we recommend a second freezer.

Thawing Vegetables and Fruit

VEGETABLES

When cooking with frozen vegetables, we mostly found it better to use the vegetables without thawing. This was the case with moist-heat cooking methods, such as steaming and boiling, or when the vegetables were added to soups, stews, and sauces. However, we did find cooking times for frozen vegetables were half as long as for their fresh counterparts. With dry-heat cooking methods such as sautéing, we found it best if the vegetables were partially thawed; again, they were done in about half the time. To partially thaw vegetables, allow them to slowly thaw in the refrigerator for about 4 hours. In a pinch, thaw the bag of frozen vegetables in cold water for 15 to 20 minutes.

FRUIT

After comparing quick thaws under cold water and slow thaws in the refrigerator overnight, we found slow thaws preserved more of the fruit's original flavor and texture. Once the fruit is thawed, transfer it to a colander and gently rinse it to remove excess syrup and sugar. Because the fruit's resiliency will have decreased, we prefer to use frozen fruit in applications where the fruit will be cooked.

How to Grill Cornish Game Hens

These birds provide crisp skin and delicate meat and are an elegant alternative to chicken.

⇛ BY DAVID PAZMIÑO ⇚

Cornish game hens look good on the plate, and since one hen makes a single serving, everyone gets tender portions of both white and dark meat. Most home cooks roast these elegant birds, but grilling has the potential to add smoky flavor and deliver really crisp skin. I started my testing by trying to adapt the test kitchen's method for grilling whole chickens (see "The Best Grill-Roasted Chicken," July/August 2000). After the chicken is treated to a short brine and spice rub, it's placed in the middle of a hot grill with coals and soaked wood chunks banked to either side. An hour later, the chicken emerges beautifully bronzed. I thought I could easily translate this method to game hens. Not quite.

My first modification was to put a drip pan under the hens to catch the rendered fat while also creating defined banks for the charcoal. Getting crisp skin without overcooking the delicate breast meat was trickier. The closest my initial testing came was spotty patches of browned and flabby skin. This was a hurdle I'd have to clear before I could begin worrying about a spice rub and finishing glaze.

A spice rub and glaze give these smoky birds their mahogany color.

Skewerin' Around

Whereas grill-roasting large birds for an hour produces mahogany skin and a juicy interior, keeping game hens on the grill for an hour made for bone-dry meat. Many recipes called for removing the backbone (a process called butterflying). This would put all of the skin on one side, which could face the coals and crisp more quickly. Butterflying also makes each bird a uniform thickness, which promotes even cooking. I used scissors to remove the delicate backbone and to cut the bone dividing the breast halves.

Although these splayed-open birds browned evenly and cooked uniformly, presentation was a whole other matter. Turning backboneless birds resulted in the legs flipping over the breast and the scant piece of skin holding the breast to the thighs tearing. Securing the legs to the body seemed like my best option. I used metal skewers to poke and stick a dozen hens into various contortionist positions before I landed on a method that worked (see "Butterflying and Skewering the Game Hens," on page 19). This kebab-like presentation also made it easier to fit the birds on the grill grates.

In flavor, texture, and appearance, tasters agreed these Cornish game hens were finally in a class by themselves. But I still thought they could benefit from a last blast of intense heat to make the skin crispier. To avoid charred birds, I found it best to sear them last, not first, as is traditionally the case with meats. Grill-roasting the birds with the lid down to an internal temperature of 160 to 165 degrees before finishing them over the now-cooler coals gave me just the right amount of browning and crispy skin. All I had left to do was build upon the grilled, smoky flavor via a rub and a glaze. After trying rubs with up to 20 ingredients, I settled on a seven-ingredient version that gave the hens a sweet and savory complexity. The rub helped crisp the skin even further, giving it a gorgeous mahogany hue. Finishing the birds with a quick glaze of ketchup, brown sugar, and soy sauce provided the crowning touch.

Game of Chance

Cooking whole game hens directly on the grill can produce skin that is burned in some parts and flabby in others. The interior fares no better, with unevenly cooked meat.

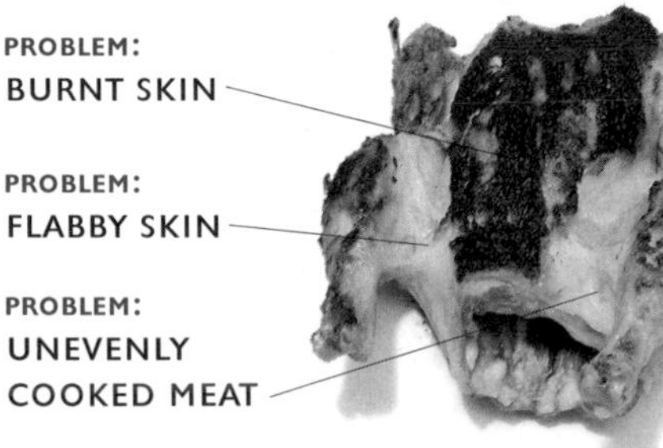

GRILL-ROASTED CORNISH GAME HENS

SERVES 4

If your hens weigh 1½ to 2 pounds, cook 3 instead of 4, brine them for an extra 15 minutes, and extend the cooking time in step 5 by 10 to 15 minutes. Thaw frozen game hens in the refrigerator for 24 to 36 hours before brining. To add smoke flavor to the hens, use the optional wood chunks. For the complete results from our tasting of Cornish game hens and our free recipe for Asian Barbecue Glaze, go to www.cooksillustrated.com/august.

Hens

- 1 cup table salt
- 4 Cornish game hens (1¼ to 1½ pounds each), butterflied according to illustrations 1 through 4 on page 19
- 2 tablespoons brown sugar
- 2 teaspoons garlic powder
- 1 tablespoon paprika
- 2 teaspoons chili powder
- 1 teaspoon ground black pepper
- 1 teaspoon ground coriander
- ⅛ teaspoon cayenne pepper
- 4 (3-inch) wood chunks (optional)
- Disposable 16 by 12-inch aluminum roasting pan
- Vegetable oil for cooking grate

Barbecue Glaze

- ½ cup ketchup
- 2 tablespoons brown sugar
- 1 tablespoon soy sauce
- 1 tablespoon distilled white vinegar
- 1 tablespoon prepared yellow mustard
- 1 medium garlic clove, minced or pressed through garlic press (about 1 teaspoon)

1. **FOR THE HENS:** Dissolve salt in 4 quarts cold water in large container. Submerge hens in brine, cover with plastic wrap, and refrigerate 1 hour.

PHOTOGRAPHY: CARL TREMBLAY

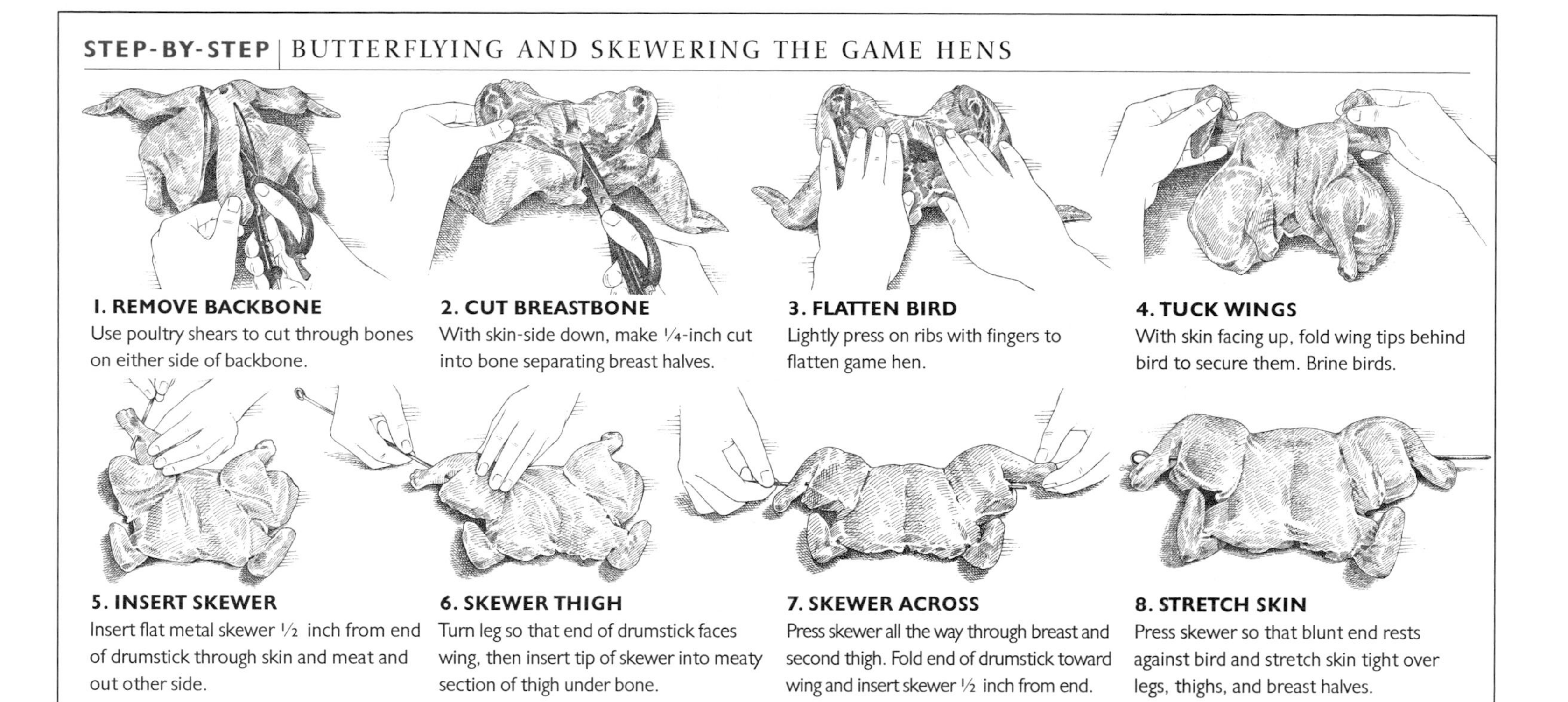

STEP-BY-STEP | BUTTERFLYING AND SKEWERING THE GAME HENS

1. REMOVE BACKBONE
Use poultry shears to cut through bones on either side of backbone.

2. CUT BREASTBONE
With skin-side down, make ¼-inch cut into bone separating breast halves.

3. FLATTEN BIRD
Lightly press on ribs with fingers to flatten game hen.

4. TUCK WINGS
With skin facing up, fold wing tips behind bird to secure them. Brine birds.

5. INSERT SKEWER
Insert flat metal skewer ½ inch from end of drumstick through skin and meat and out other side.

6. SKEWER THIGH
Turn leg so that end of drumstick faces wing, then insert tip of skewer into meaty section of thigh under bone.

7. SKEWER ACROSS
Press skewer all the way through breast and second thigh. Fold end of drumstick toward wing and insert skewer ½ inch from end.

8. STRETCH SKIN
Press skewer so that blunt end rests against bird and stretch skin tight over legs, thighs, and breast halves.

ILLUSTRATION: JOHN BURGOYNE

2. While hens brine, combine sugar and spices in small bowl. If using wood chunks, soak them in water for 1 hour; drain. Remove birds from brine and rinse inside and out with cold running water; pat dry with paper towels. Following illustrations 5 through 8, use 8- to 10-inch flat metal skewer to secure each hen. Rubs hens evenly with spice mixture and refrigerate while preparing grill.

3. TO MAKE GLAZE: Cook all ingredients in small saucepan over medium heat, stirring occasionally, until thick and slightly reduced, about 5 minutes.

4. TO GRILL HENS: Light large chimney starter filled with charcoal (6 quarts, or about 100 briquettes) and allow to burn until coals are fully ignited and partially covered with thin layer of ash, 20 to 25 minutes. Place disposable pan in center of grill. Empty coals into grill, creating equal-sized piles on each side of pan. Place 2 soaked wood chunks on each pile of coals, if using. Position cooking grate over coals, cover grill, and heat grate until hot, about 5 minutes; scrape grate clean with grill brush. Lightly dip wad of paper towels in oil; holding wad with tongs, wipe cooking grate.

5. Place hens, skin-side down, on center of grill over aluminum pan. Open grill lid vents completely and cover, positioning vents over hens. Grill-roast hens until instant-read thermometer inserted in thickest part of thigh registers 160 to 165 degrees and skin has started to turn golden brown, 20 to 30 minutes.

6. Using tongs, move birds to hot sides of grill (2 hens per side). Cover and continue to cook until browned, about 5 minutes. Brush birds with half of glaze; flip and cook for 2 minutes. Brush remaining glaze over hens; flip and continue to cook until instant-read thermometer inserted in thickest part of the thigh registers 170 to 175 degrees, 1 to 3 minutes longer.

7. Transfer hens to cutting board and let rest 10 minutes. Cut in half through breastbone and serve immediately.

GRILL-ROASTED CORNISH GAME HENS ON A GAS GRILL

1. Follow recipe for Grill-Roasted Cornish Game Hens through step 3, soaking 1 cup wood chips for 30 minutes if smoke flavor is desired. Drain chips and place in small disposable aluminum pan; set pan on one burner and replace cooking grate. Turn all burners to high, cover, and heat until very hot and chips are smoking, about 15 minutes (if chips ignite, use water-filled spray bottle to extinguish). Scrape grate clean with grill brush. Lightly dip wad of paper towels in oil; holding wad with tongs, wipe cooking grate. Turn all burners to medium.

2. Place hens, skin-side down, on grill grate. Cover and grill until skin is deeply browned and shows grill marks, 10 to 15 minutes. (If grill has hot spots, you might have to move hens on grill.) Using tongs, flip birds; cover and continue to grill until thickest part of thigh registers 160 to 165 degrees, 10 to 15 minutes more.

3. Brush birds with half of glaze. Using tongs, flip birds and cook until deeply browned, 2 to 3 minutes. Brush remaining glaze over hens; flip and continue to cook until deeply browned and thickest part of thigh registers 170 to 175 degrees, 2 to 3 minutes more.

4. Transfer hens to cutting board and let rest 10 minutes. Cut in half through breastbone and serve.

COOK'S LIVE Original Test Kitchen Videos
www.cooksillustrated.com

RECIPE IN 60 SECONDS
- Grill-Roasted Cornish Game Hens

VIDEO TIPS
- What's the easiest way to butterfly a game hen?
- How do I skewer a game hen?

EQUIPMENT TESTING:

Rotisserie Attachments

A rotisserie permits superior air circulation and natural self-basting, which makes poultry skin significantly crispier, with savory, juicy meat. However, so-called universal rotisseries designed to fit "most large grills" fit none of the three widely available grills that we use in our test kitchen. We fared much better when we paired rotisseries with grills from the same manufacturer. For complete results of our rotisserie attachment testing, go to www.cooksillustrated.com/august.—Elizabeth Bomze

FAVORITE ROTISSERIE
The BBQ Galore 31" Deluxe Stainless Steel Rotisserie ($149.99) is the perfect (albeit pricey) companion to our favorite charcoal grill.

Better Shrimp Salad

Deli-style shrimp salads are usually rubbery and bland. We fix the shrimp, then the dressing.

BY DAVID PAZMIÑO

Maybe it's a good thing that most shrimp salads are drowning in a sea of gloppy mayonnaise. The dressing might be bland, but at least it helps camouflage the sorry state of the rubbery, flavorless boiled shrimp. I wanted to find a cooking technique that would deliver perfectly cooked shrimp without the extra work of grilling, roasting, or sautéing. Was it too much to ask that the shrimp have some flavor of its own?

To begin, I rounded up some creamy-style shrimp salad recipes. Most call for boiling a flavorful liquid of white wine, lemon juice, herbs, spices, and water (called a court-bouillon by the French). After the shrimp are submerged into this hot liquid, the pot is removed from the heat and covered for about 10 minutes. Many of the recipes call for quickly shocking the shrimp in an ice bath to prevent overcooking. Although they looked perfect, shrimp prepared this way were in fact flavorless and tough. Reducing the time the shrimp spent in the liquid did make them more tender, but it did nothing to improve their flavor.

But I had a trick up my sleeve: a technique practiced in the 1970s by the French chef Michel Guérard. He poached proteins by starting them in cold liquid. The cold proteins and broth would heat simultaneously, unlike the traditional poaching technique in which the shrimp proteins immediately turn opaque (and rubbery) upon submersion in hot water. In this way the shrimp would better absorb flavors from the poaching liquid—a kind of turbocharged flavor injection.

In the test kitchen I took the court-bouillon ingredients—leaving out the white wine, which tasters found overwhelming—and added the shrimp. I then heated the liquid to various temperatures. Too low and the shrimp were mushy; too high and they turned tough. Eventually, I discovered that heating the liquid to a near simmer (165 degrees) was ideal. The shrimp were actually flavorful and their texture was so firm and crisp that several tasters compared them to lobster.

All I needed now was the perfect deli-style dressing. While mayonnaise provides creamy cohesiveness, I didn't want it to mask the shrimp's flavor or drown out the other ingredients. After testing several amounts, tasters felt a perfect coating was ¼ cup per 1 pound of shrimp. Diced celery, minced shallots, chopped herbs, and fresh lemon juice added unifying aromatic and herbal notes and a pleasant vegetal crunch and acidity. With less mayo, I found I could also add variety to the salads with bolder flavors like chipotle chile, orange, and roasted red pepper.

SHRIMP SALAD

SERVES 4

This recipe can also be prepared with large shrimp (26/30); the cooking time will be 1 to 2 minutes less. The shrimp can be cooked up to 24 hours in advance, but hold off on dressing the salad until ready to serve. The recipe can be easily doubled; cook the shrimp in a 7-quart Dutch oven and increase the cooking time to 12 to 14 minutes. Serve the salad on a bed of greens or on a buttered and grilled bun.

- 1 pound (21–25) extra-large shrimp, peeled, deveined, and tails removed
- ¼ cup plus 1 tablespoon juice from 2 to 3 lemons, spent halves reserved
- 5 sprigs plus 1 teaspoon minced fresh parsley leaves
- 3 sprigs plus 1 teaspoon minced fresh tarragon leaves
- 1 teaspoon whole black peppercorns plus ground black pepper
- 1 tablespoon sugar
- Table salt
- ¼ cup mayonnaise
- 1 small shallot, minced (about 2 tablespoons)
- 1 small celery stalk, minced (about ⅓ cup)

1. Combine shrimp, ¼ cup lemon juice, reserved lemon halves, parsley sprigs, tarragon sprigs, whole peppercorns, sugar, and 1 teaspoon salt with 2 cups cold water in medium saucepan. Place saucepan over medium heat and cook shrimp, stirring several times, until pink, firm to touch, and centers are no longer translucent, 8 to 10 minutes (water should be just bubbling around edge of pan and register 165 degrees on instant-read thermometer). Remove pan from heat, cover, and let shrimp sit in broth for 2 minutes.

2. Meanwhile, fill medium bowl with ice water. Drain shrimp into colander, discard lemon halves, herbs, and spices. Immediately transfer shrimp to ice water to stop cooking and chill thoroughly, about 3 minutes. Remove shrimp from ice water and pat dry with paper towels.

3. Whisk together mayonnaise, shallot, celery, remaining tablespoon lemon juice, minced parsley, and minced tarragon in medium bowl. Cut shrimp in half lengthwise and then each half into thirds; add shrimp to mayonnaise mixture and toss to combine. Adjust seasoning with salt and pepper and serve.

SHRIMP SALAD WITH ROASTED RED PEPPER AND BASIL

Follow recipe for Shrimp Salad, omitting tarragon sprigs from cooking liquid. Replace celery, minced parsley, and minced tarragon with ⅓ cup thinly sliced jarred roasted red peppers, 2 teaspoons rinsed capers, and 3 tablespoons chopped fresh basil leaves.

SHRIMP SALAD WITH AVOCADO AND ORANGE

Follow recipe for Shrimp Salad, omitting tarragon sprigs from cooking liquid. Replace celery, minced parsley, and minced tarragon with 4 halved and thinly sliced radishes; 1 large orange, peeled and cut into ½-inch pieces; ½ ripe avocado, cut into ½-inch pieces; and 2 teaspoons minced fresh mint leaves.

SPICY SHRIMP SALAD WITH CORN AND CHIPOTLE

Follow recipe for Shrimp Salad, substituting juice from 3 to 4 limes (save spent halves) for lemon juice and omitting tarragon sprigs from cooking liquid. Replace celery, minced parsley, and minced tarragon with ½ cup cooked corn kernels, 2 minced chipotle chiles in adobo sauce (about 2 tablespoons), and 1 tablespoon minced fresh cilantro leaves.

SHRIMP SALAD WITH WASABI AND PICKLED GINGER

Follow recipe for Shrimp Salad, omitting tarragon sprigs from cooking liquid. Replace shallot, minced parsley, and minced tarragon with 2 teaspoons wasabi powder; 2 scallions, white and green parts sliced thin; 2 tablespoons chopped pickled ginger; and 1 tablespoon toasted sesame seeds.

Summer Fruit Salads

Could an old bartending trick be the simple answer to a better fruit salad?

BY ERIN McMURRER

Most fruit salads betray neither rhyme nor reason regarding the fruit selection or assembly, and the customary heavy sprinkling of sugar seems designed to mask defects in the fruit. In cooking school, I learned to make simple syrup, which is nothing more than water and sugar boiled together. Unfortunately, most simple syrups are too sweet, and turning on the stove to make salad seems like a bother. With summer fruit at its peak, I marched into the test kitchen determined to redefine the rules.

Instead of the randomly hacked up chunks of fruit that one usually finds in salad, I cut the fruit into small, uniform pieces to allow the different flavors and textures to come through with each mouthful. So that each fruit could maintain its distinctiveness, I limited myself to three per salad. Although I wanted most of the sweetness to come from the fruit, I found it important to macerate it with a small amount of sugar to release the juice. To balance the sweetness, I added a squeeze of fresh lime juice.

Having created the proper foundation, I wanted to add more complexity of flavor and improve the texture. Though I got the flavors I wanted with fresh herbs (basil and mint) and citrus zest (lime and orange), texture was a problem. When I added small amounts of spices such as pepper, cardamom, and cayenne, it was difficult to guarantee even distribution. If not combined thoroughly, a pinch of cayenne could backfire.

I remembered the bartending technique of muddling, in which a small wooden dowel with a flattened end is used to mash sugar with herbs or citrus to extract bigger, fresher flavors in alcoholic drinks (think Mojito). Using a flexible rubber spatula, I applied this technique to my salads.

Mashing the sugar with the flavorings increased the intensity of the herbs and zest, meaning I could use less. And incorporating the spices with the sugar mixture allowed for even distribution. Once I tossed the sugar mixture with the fruit and allowed it to macerate for 30 minutes, a light, flavorful fruit syrup developed. I now had a fruit salad whose flavors and colors elegantly evoked summer.

Balancing Sweetness

Because riper fruits require more acid to balance their sweetness, the lime juice in our Summer Fruit Salads should be added to taste. Start with 1 tablespoon, then add 1 teaspoon at a time as necessary.

CANTALOUPE, PLUMS, AND CHERRIES WITH MINT AND VANILLA

SERVES 4 TO 6

Blueberries can be substituted for cherries.

- 4 teaspoons sugar
- 1–2 tablespoons minced fresh mint leaves
- 1/4 teaspoon vanilla extract
- 1/2 medium cantaloupe, rind and seeds removed, cut into 1/2-inch pieces (about 3 cups)
- 2 red or black plums (about 5 ounces each), pitted and cut into 1/2-inch pieces (about 2 cups)
- 8 ounces cherries, pitted and halved (about 2 cups)
- 1–2 tablespoons juice from 1 lime (see box)

Combine sugar and mint in large bowl. Using rubber spatula, press mixture into side of bowl until sugar becomes damp, about 30 seconds; add vanilla. Gently toss fruit with sugar mixture until combined. Let stand at room temperature, stirring occasionally, until fruit releases its juices, 15 to 30 minutes. Stir in lime juice to taste and serve.

HONEYDEW, MANGO, AND RASPBERRIES WITH LIME AND GINGER

SERVES 4

- 4 teaspoons sugar
- 2 teaspoons grated zest plus 1 to 2 tablespoons juice from 2 to 3 limes (see box)
- Pinch cayenne (optional)
- 1/2 medium honeydew, rind and seeds removed, cut into 1/2-inch pieces (about 3 cups)
- 1 mango (about 10 ounces), peeled, pitted, and cut into 1/2-inch pieces (about 1 1/2 cups)
- 1–2 teaspoons grated fresh ginger
- 1 half-pint container raspberries (about 1 cup), picked over

Combine sugar, zest, and cayenne (if using) in large bowl. Using rubber spatula, press mixture into side of bowl until sugar becomes damp, about 30 seconds. Gently toss melon, mango, and ginger with sugar mixture until combined. Let stand at room temperature, stirring occasionally, until fruit releases its juices, 15 to 30 minutes. Gently stir in raspberries. Stir in lime juice to taste and serve.

NECTARINES, GRAPES, AND BLUEBERRIES WITH ORANGE AND CARDAMOM

SERVES 4 TO 6

- 4 teaspoons sugar
- 1 teaspoon grated zest from 1 orange
- 1/8 teaspoon ground cardamom
- 3 medium nectarines (about 6 ounces each), pitted and cut into 1/2-inch pieces (about 3 cups)
- 9 ounces large green grapes, halved pole to pole (about 2 cups)
- 1 pint blueberries, picked over
- 1–2 tablespoons juice from 1 lime (see box)

Combine sugar, zest, and cardamom in large bowl. Using rubber spatula, press mixture into side of bowl until sugar becomes damp, about 30 seconds. Gently toss fruit with sugar mixture until combined. Let stand at room temperature, stirring occasionally, until fruit releases its juices, 15 to 30 minutes. Stir in lime juice to taste and serve.

PEACHES, BLACKBERRIES, AND STRAWBERRIES WITH BASIL AND PEPPER

SERVES 4 TO 6

- 4 teaspoons sugar
- 2 tablespoons minced fresh basil leaves
- 1/2 teaspoon ground black pepper
- 3 medium peaches (about 6 ounces each), pitted and cut into 1/2-inch pieces (about 3 cups)
- 2 half-pint containers blackberries (about 2 cups), picked over
- 1 pint strawberries, washed, hulled, and quartered lengthwise (about 2 cups)
- 1–2 tablespoons juice from 1 lime (see box)

Combine sugar, basil, and pepper in large bowl. Using rubber spatula, press mixture into side of bowl until sugar becomes damp, about 30 seconds. Gently toss fruit with sugar mixture until combined. Let stand at room temperature, stirring occasionally, until fruit releases its juices, 15 to 30 minutes. Stir in lime juice to taste and serve.

COOK'S LIVE Original Test Kitchen Videos
www.cooksillustrated.com

VIDEO TIPS
- Basic knife skills
- How should I take care of my knives?
- What's the best way to peel and chop a melon?
- What's the easiest way to cut a mango?
- What's the right way to zest citrus?

The Best Blueberry Scones

We already knew what a blueberry scone could be—dry, crumbly, or dense. We baked over 800 scones to achieve what we knew a blueberry scone should be—rich, light, and flaky.

BY J. KENJI ALT

Real British scones are like British humor—steeped in tradition, dry as a bone, and often tasteless. A distant relative of the crumpet and the English muffin, the first scones were cooked without the aid of an oven; they were prepared on a cast-iron griddle, like thick pancakes. With the addition of baking soda in Victorian times, scones in England took on the role of customizable teatime accompaniments. The dry, bland biscuits were rendered palatable by the addition of plenty of butter, clotted cream, or jam.

Americans, however, are used to having breakfast quickly and on the move. We like our pastries ready to go in single servings with the sweetness, richness, and fruit built in. We've been gradually remodeling scones to fit this image. These days, coffee shop samplings run the gamut from misshapen muffin-like objects to big-as-your-head cakes. It seemed like it was time to redefine the American scone.

Rather than reworking just one style, I decided to try to bring together the best qualities from the sweetness of a coffeehouse confection; the moist freshness of a muffin; the richness and fruit of clotted cream and jam; and the super-flaky crumb of a good biscuit. I wanted scones light enough to be eaten on the go, and, this being the season, with a healthy dose of fresh blueberries.

Our scones are rich enough to enjoy without accompaniments.

Scone Surgery

Traditional scone recipes call for a minimal amount of sugar and 2 to 3 tablespoons of butter per cup of flour. I found that a full 4 tablespoons of butter per cup of flour was ideal—any more and the dough became difficult to work with and baked up greasy. Adding ¼ cup sugar per cup of flour gave the scones subtle sweetness without being cloying, and a combination of sour cream and milk offered a contrasting tang.

Unfortunately, with all the added richness and sweetness, my scones were turning out heavy and under-risen. I was using the biscuit mixing method common to most scone recipes: cutting the cold butter into the dry ingredients with my fingertips and then quickly mixing in the wet ingredients. If I was going to capture the light flakiness I was after, my technique was going to need an overhaul.

I took a hint from puff pastry, where the power of steam is used to separate super-thin layers of dough into striated flakes. In a standard puff pastry recipe, a piece of dough will be turned, rolled, and folded about five times. With each fold, the number of layers of butter and dough increases exponentially. Upon baking, steam forces the layers apart and then escapes, causing the dough to puff up and crisp. I wasn't after the 768 layers produced by the standard five-turn puff pastry recipe, but adding a few quick folds to my recipe allowed the scones to gently rise and puff. Tasters appreciated that the scones were now much lighter, but I wondered if I could lighten them even more.

A good light pastry depends on distinct pieces of butter distributed throughout the dough that melt during baking and leave behind pockets of air. For this to happen, the butter needs to be as cold and solid as possible until baking. The problem with trying to cut butter into the flour with your fingers or a food processor is that the butter gets too warm during the distribution process. I tried every alternative form of butter incorporation I could think of before discovering that freezing a stick of butter and grating it on the large holes of a box grater works best. The butter could then be quickly and homogeneously cut into the flour while remaining cold. This new method of distributing the butter kept the interior of the scones tender and moist without being dense.

Blueberry Blues

Now that I'd made the ultimate plain scone, it was time to move on to adding the blueberries. Many recipes call for mixing blueberries in with the flour and butter and then adding the wet ingredients to form a dough. The results: scones that have been dyed blue by bludgeoned berries. What if I incorporated the berries into the already-mixed dough? No dice. I had to knead the dough an extra 10 to 12 times, which introduced friction and heat. The butter I'd taken such care to add in small flakes was melting into a homog-

RECIPE TESTING: Scone Confusion

Americans have embraced scones, but something has been lost in translation.

TRADITIONAL
The British original is lean, dry, and barely sweetened. Spoonfuls of jam and clotted cream are a must.

ARTIFICIALLY SWEET
This scone is shellacked with icing and has tiny flecks of artificial blueberries that add color but not flavor.

BIG BLOB
This scone is too large and amorphous to cook through, leaving the center doughy and unbaked.

PHOTOGRAPHY: CARL TREMBLAY

enous mass that wreaked havoc on the texture of the finished scones.

Low on ideas, I was running through a list of other foods that attempt a seamless marriage of distinct elements (sandwiches, napoleons, and sushi) when inspiration finally struck—cinnamon rolls. What if I were to distribute the berries evenly over a large, thin square of dough, roll the whole thing up like a cinnamon roll, and then flatten the log into a rectangle before cutting the scones out of it?

This worked even better than I had hoped. Rolling the blueberries and dough into a log not only distributed the berries much better but also created more flaky layers. My technique had captured the best elements from several styles of scone—sweet, moist, rich, flaky, tender, crisp, and full of fruit. Now I really might have a reason to take a break for tea every afternoon.

STEP-BY-STEP | FOLDING AND SHAPING THE SCONES

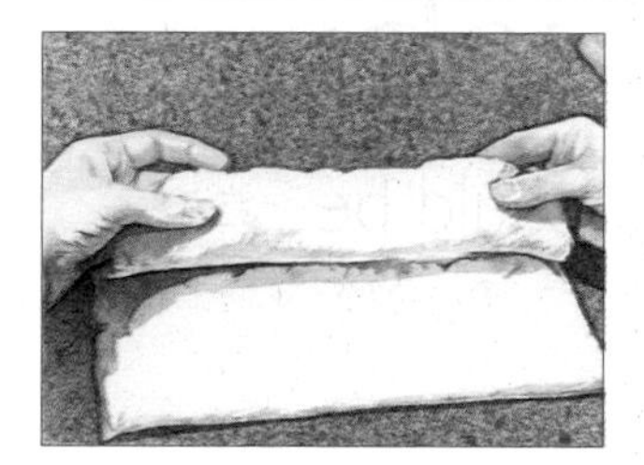

1. Fold dough into thirds (like a business letter).

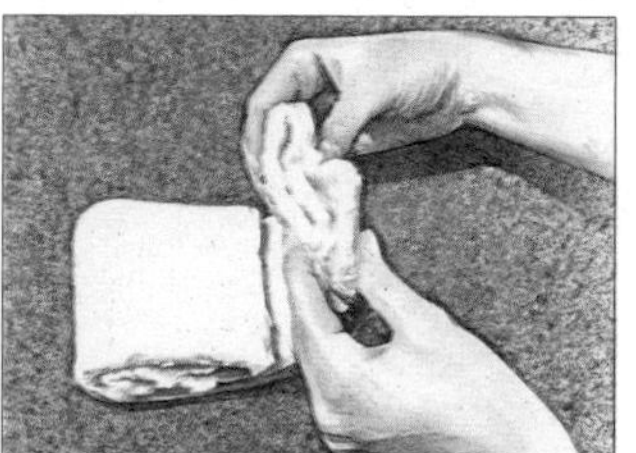

2. Fold in ends of dough to form 4-inch square. Chill dough.

3. Reroll dough into 12-inch square. Press berries into dough.

4. Roll dough into jellyroll-like log to incorporate blueberries.

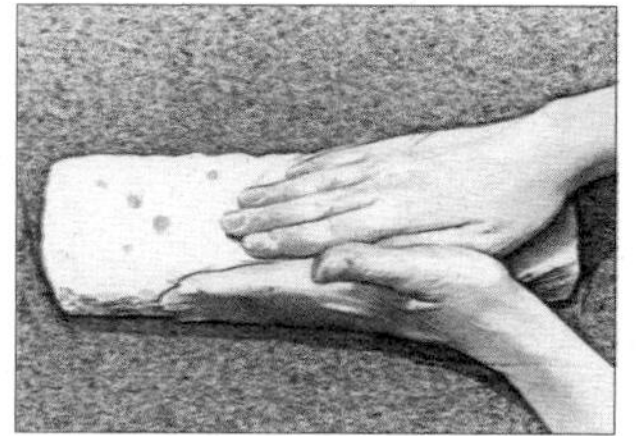

5. Lay log seam-side down and press into even 12 by 4-inch rectangle.

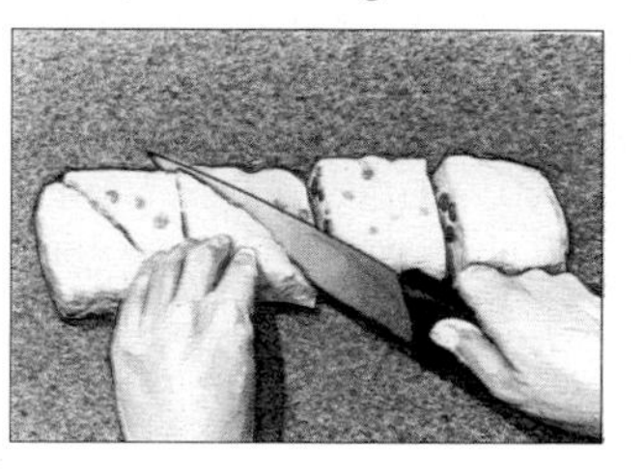

6. Cut dough into 8 triangular pieces.

BLUEBERRY SCONES

MAKES 8

It is important to work the dough as little as possible—work quickly and knead and fold the dough only the number of times called for. The butter should be frozen solid before grating. In hot or humid environments, chill the flour mixture and workbowls before use. While the recipe calls for 2 whole sticks of butter, only 10 tablespoons are actually used (see step 1). If fresh berries are unavailable, an equal amount of frozen berries (do not defrost) can be substituted. An equal amount of raspberries, blackberries, or strawberries can be used in place of the blueberries. Cut larger berries into ¼- to ½-inch pieces before incorporating. Refrigerate or freeze leftover scones, wrapped in foil, in an airtight container. To serve, remove foil and place scones on a baking sheet in a 375-degree oven. Heat until warmed through and recrisped, 8 to 10 minutes if refrigerated, 16 to 20 minutes if frozen. See page 30 for information on making the scone dough in advance.

- 16 tablespoons (2 sticks) butter, frozen whole (see note above)
- 1½ cups (about 7½ ounces) fresh blueberries, picked over (see note above)
- ½ cup whole milk
- ½ cup sour cream
- 2 cups (10 ounces) unbleached all-purpose flour, plus additional for work surface
- ½ cup (3½ ounces) sugar, plus 1 tablespoon for sprinkling
- 2 teaspoons baking powder
- ¼ teaspoon baking soda
- ½ teaspoon table salt
- 1 teaspoon finely grated zest from 1 lemon

1. Adjust oven rack to middle position and heat oven to 425 degrees. Score and remove half of wrapper from each stick of frozen butter. Following photo at left, grate unwrapped ends on large holes of box grater (you should grate total of 8 tablespoons). Place grated butter in freezer until needed. Melt 2 tablespoons of remaining ungrated butter and set aside. Save remaining 6 tablespoons butter for another use. Place blueberries in freezer until needed.

2. Whisk together milk and sour cream in medium bowl; refrigerate until needed. Whisk flour, ½ cup sugar, baking powder, baking soda, salt, and lemon zest in medium bowl. Add frozen butter to flour mixture and toss with fingers until thoroughly coated.

3. Add milk mixture to flour mixture; fold with spatula until just combined. With rubber spatula, transfer dough to liberally floured work surface. Dust surface of dough with flour; with floured hands, knead dough 6 to 8 times, until it just holds together in ragged ball, adding flour as needed to prevent sticking.

4. Roll dough into approximate 12-inch square. Following illustrations, fold dough into thirds like a business letter, using bench scraper or metal spatula to release dough if it sticks to countertop. Lift short ends of dough and fold into thirds again to form approximate 4-inch square. Transfer dough to plate lightly dusted with flour and chill in freezer 5 minutes.

5. Transfer dough to floured work surface and roll into approximate 12-inch square again. Sprinkle blueberries evenly over surface of dough, then press down so they are slightly embedded in dough. Using bench scraper or thin metal spatula, loosen dough from work surface. Roll dough, pressing to form tight log. Lay seam-side down and press log into 12 by 4-inch rectangle. Using sharp, floured knife, cut rectangle crosswise into 4 equal rectangles. Cut each rectangle diagonally to form 2 triangles and transfer to parchment-lined baking sheet.

6. Brush tops with melted butter and sprinkle with remaining tablespoon sugar. Bake until tops and bottoms are golden brown, 18 to 25 minutes. Transfer to wire rack and let cool 10 minutes before serving.

TECHNIQUE | GRATING BUTTER

Use the wrapper to hold the frozen butter while grating it on the large holes of a box grater. Grate 4 tablespoons from each stick of butter.

COOK'S LIVE Original Test Kitchen Videos

www.cooksillustrated.com

RECIPE IN 60 SECONDS

- Blueberry Scones

VIDEO TIPS

- Do I really need a bench scraper?
- When has my dough has been kneaded enough?
- What happens if I use butter that isn't cold?
- What's the best way to grate frozen butter?

ILLUSTRATION: RANDY GLASS

Rustic Plum Cake

Rustic plum cake should be an ideal showcase for summer-ripe plums, but it is often dry and short on fruit flavor.

BY ERIKA BRUCE

Zwetschgenkuchen is an Austrian specialty in which ripe, sweet plums (the regional variety *Zwetschgen*) are nestled into rich cake, or *Kuchen*. It is a simple way to enjoy a summertime fruit at its peak, but finding a promising recipe wasn't so easy. I consulted numerous cookbooks and even talked to Austrians who grew up on the dessert, and I learned that, depending on which country or region claimed credit, plum cake could be any thing from an Alsatian tart to a German yeasted bread. One friend recalled her grandmother shaking plums from a tree, then baking them into a cake, pits and all.

To get my bearings, I tried a variety of recipes. In most, the plums sank into the cake and created a sodden center. To get around this, some recipe writers placed a scant layer of thinly sliced plums on top, leaving behind mouthfuls of plain cake. Others mixed up a cake batter so dry and pancakey that the plums, having no choice but to be sponged up, did little to improve the cake's texture. What, I wondered, was the secret to this quintessential rustic treat?

It wasn't until a fellow test cook suggested I try a plum cake recipe that the *New York Times* ran every August from 1981 to 1996 that I found a style of cake I liked. This recipe was easy to make (a creamed cake batter spread into a springform pan, topped with plums, and baked), and it had a hefty plum presence. It called for Italian plums, which are well-suited to baking. Although this buttery yellow cake was sturdy enough to support all the fruit, tasters criticized it for being on the dry side. And the fruit was rather bland, needing embellishment beyond the uninspired sprinkling of cinnamon and sugar. I set out to add some finesse to this recipe.

Halved Italian prune plums work best in this Austrian-style cake.

Plum Options

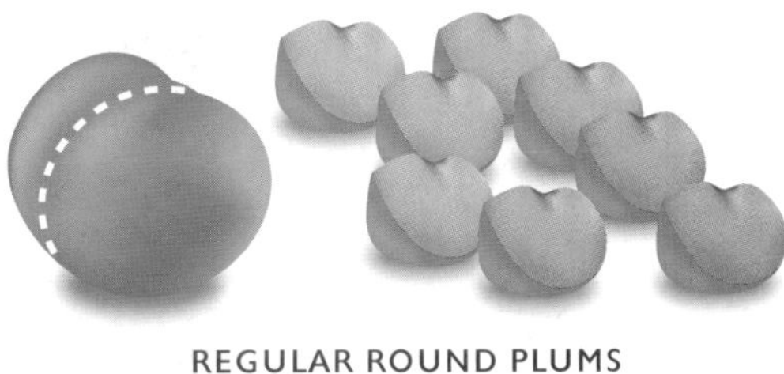

REGULAR ROUND PLUMS
Cut each plum in half, remove pit, and cut each half into 4 pieces.

ITALIAN PRUNE PLUMS
Cut each plum in half and remove pit.

Building a Better Cake

With its simple ingredient list of butter, sugar, flour, eggs, salt, and baking powder, my working recipe didn't contain any liquid dairy element, which explained why the batter was strong enough to support all those plums and also the dryness my tasters had complained about. I tried adding a little milk, but the cake turned light and fluffy, and the fruit plummeted to the bottom of the pan. This cake needs to be dense and sturdy.

Many rich European cakes replace some of the flour with ground nuts. I tried hazelnuts, walnuts, and almonds and found that in addition to a welcome flavor dimension (almonds were the preferred choice with plums), the nuts also added both bulk and richness. So rich was the cake, in fact, I had to cut back on the butter to avoid a greasy texture. The extra structure added by the nuts enabled me to both decrease the flour (making the cake even moister) and omit an egg white (making it more tender).

Adding nuts to the recipe also led me to reexamine the mixing method for this cake. I decided to try melting the butter and mixing everything in the food processor, which I was already using to grind the nuts, instead of the standard creaming method (whipping the sugar and butter together before adding the other ingredients). Not only was the food processor method more streamlined, but it also gave the cake a denser, chewier quality—a little too dense, even. A switch to softened butter, added to the dry ingredients before the eggs, made the cake lighter; this cake now offered the right textural contrast to the tender fruit.

Plum Assignment

The small Italian prune plums used in my working recipe are prized for baking due to their relatively dry, firm flesh and thin skin. But miss those few weeks when they're in season and you are plumb out of luck. I wanted a way to prepare this cake with any variety of fresh plum.

I found that even Italian prune plums needed some help to realize their full potential. I tried tossing the plum halves in sugar alone and then in melted butter and sugar, to little success. Realizing something more drastic was going to be necessary to get more than adequate plum flavor, I started with a battery of plum precooking methods. I tried roasting the plums (tossed in melted butter and sugar) and poaching them in

PHOTOGRAPHY: CARL TREMBLAY; ILLUSTRATION: JAY LAYMAN

AT A GLANCE | SECRETS TO A PERFECT PLUM CAKE

Cook the Plums: Gently heating plums in a few tablespoons of jam and brandy heightens their flavor without overcooking them.

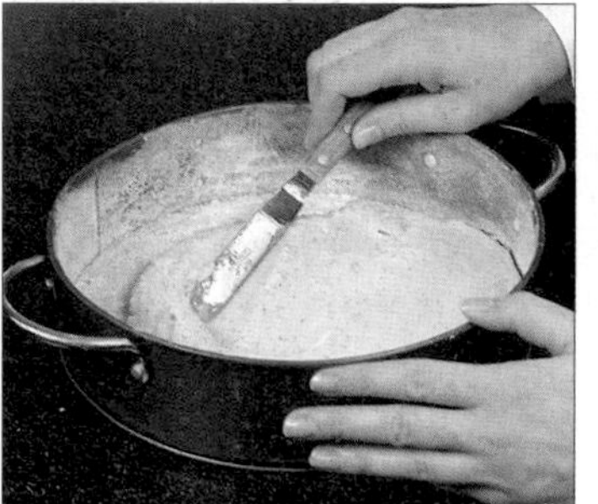

Use Thick, Rich Cake Batter: The batter must be thick enough to support the fruit, without being dry. The secret? Ground nuts.

Pack with Fruit: You want fruit in every bite, so place plums (skin-side down and not touching pan edges) over entire surface of batter.

sugar syrup. These methods intensified the flavor of the plums, but the fruit baked up overcooked and mushy.

Needing a quicker cooking method, I sautéed the plums, cut-side down, in butter and sugar in a skillet on the stovetop. Although the plums developed a nice golden color and caramelized flavor, the high heat caused the skins to peel back and the flesh to blow out—mushy fruit once again. I tried making caramel in the pan and then adding the fruit, but the caramel was still so hot that the fruit became overcooked. Cooling the caramel first caused it to harden, making it impossible to combine with the plums.

I was almost ready to give up on the skillet altogether when I decided to rethink how I was using it. What if I kept the plums in the skillet but cooked them over a gentler heat? True, I was forfeiting any chance of caramelizing the plums, but perhaps I could still coax more flavor without sacrificing texture. With just a sprinkling of sugar in the pan under the plums, I started them on medium heat. They slowly began to release their juices, which formed a syrup with the sugar. Effectively poached in their own juices, the plums were intensely flavored without being overcooked. And once in the cake, their syrupy surfaces stayed moist even after a spell in the oven. Best of all, this technique worked with every variety of plum I tested.

Excited about this solution, I explored other flavoring options, wondering if there was something more interesting to add than plain sugar. I tried brown sugar and cinnamon, but these both dumbed down the bright flavors of the fruit. Lemon juice gave a nice kick but was too assertive. I found red fruit jams enhanced the fruitiness of the plums better than plain sugar, and a shot of brandy added a nice tartness. Reducing the brandy with the jam first eliminated any harsh booziness. Finally, I had landed on a plum cake true to its name, and I knew eating it would be the highlight of my summer.

RUSTIC PLUM CAKE

SERVES 6 TO 8

This recipe works best with Italian plums, which are also called prune plums. If substituting regular red or black plums, use an equal weight of plums, cut them into eighths, and stir them a few times while cooking. Arrange slices, slightly overlapped, in two rings over surface of cake. Do not use canned Italian plums. Blanched whole almonds can be used but must be processed 30 seconds longer until finely ground. The brandy can be omitted, but then you will need to melt the jam with 1 tablespoon water before adding the plums. Don't add the leftover plum cooking liquid to the cake before baking; reserve it and serve with the finished cake or over ice cream. The cake can be served with lightly sweetened whipped cream.

- 2 tablespoons red currant or seedless raspberry jam
- 3 tablespoons brandy
- 1 pound (about 10 large or 14 small) Italian prune plums, halved and pitted (see note above)
- ¾ cup (3 ¾ ounces) unbleached all-purpose flour, plus extra for dusting pan
- ¾ cup (5¼ ounces) sugar
- ⅓ cup (1 ½ ounces) slivered almonds
- ½ teaspoon baking powder
- ¼ teaspoon table salt
- 6 tablespoons unsalted butter, cut into 6 pieces, softened but still cool
- 1 large egg plus 1 large yolk, room temperature
- 1 teaspoon vanilla extract
- ¼ teaspoon almond extract (optional)
- Confectioners' sugar for serving

1. Cook jam and brandy in 10-inch nonstick skillet over medium heat until reduced to thick syrup, 2 to 3 minutes. Remove skillet from heat and place plums cut-side down in syrup. Return skillet to medium heat and cook until plums shed their juices and thick syrup is again formed, about 5 minutes, shaking pan to prevent plums from sticking. Cool plums in pan, about 20 minutes.

2. Adjust oven rack to middle position and heat oven to 350 degrees. Grease and flour 9-inch springform pan. Process sugar and almonds in food processor until nuts are finely ground, about 1 minute. Add flour, baking powder, and salt; pulse to combine. Add butter and pulse until mixture resembles coarse sand, about ten 1-second pulses. Add eggs, vanilla, and almond extract (if using) and process until smooth, about 5 seconds, scraping bowl once if needed (batter will be very thick and heavy).

3. Transfer batter to prepared pan; using spatula, spread batter evenly to pan edges and smooth surface. Stir plums to coat with syrup. Arrange plum halves, skin-side down, evenly over surface of batter. Bake until cake is golden brown and wooden skewer inserted into center comes out with few crumbs attached, 40 to 50 minutes. Run paring knife around sides of cake to loosen. Cool in pan on wire rack until just warm or to room temperature, at least 30 minutes. Remove cake from pan and dust with confectioners' sugar. Cut into wedges and serve.

EQUIPMENT TESTING:

Mini Offset Spatulas

We've found that tasks like spreading batter in a cake pan or frosting cupcakes are a lot easier with a mini offset spatula. These moderately priced, blunt-edged metal pastry blades, which average about 4½ inches long, are especially helpful in spreading the sticky batter in our Rustic Plum Cake recipe. We tested five models and found significant differences. Thin blades wobbled and wooden handles absorbed odors. Our top choice, the Wilton Angled Comfort Grip 8-Inch Spatula ($4.49), has a sturdy, round-tipped blade and an easy-to-grip polypropylene handle. For complete testing results, go to www.cooksillustrated.com/august.

—Elizabeth Bomze

BEST OF THE MINIS
This Wilton mini spatula offers great control when spreading batter or icing.

COOK'S LIVE Original Test Kitchen Videos
www.cooksillustrated.com

RECIPE IN 60 SECONDS
- Rustic Plum Cake

VIDEO TIP
- What's the best way to measure flour?

Can You Buy Good Supermarket Tea?

Do upscale brands and higher price tags translate into a better cup of tea?

BY LISA MCMANUS

In our 2003 tasting of supermarket black teas, the test kitchen preferred Lipton, but we really weren't that impressed with any of them. Recently, tea companies have created many more options, including what they present as higher-quality offerings in the form of loose leaves, special blends, or new pyramid-shaped tea bags. We decided it's time to find out if the supermarket has the makings of a great cup of tea.

While you can find black, green, and even white tea on the shelves these days, it's all from the same plant, an evergreen called *Camellia sinensis*. The color and flavor differences come from the way the tea leaves are processed. Because 87 percent of all tea drunk in America is black, we decided to focus our tasting on black teas. We bought the more "upscale" offerings distributed by national brands, all labeled simply black tea or English breakfast–type blends, a popular mix of black teas designed to stand up to the milk and sugar popular among the Brits. We chose loose tea when it was available and tea bags when it was not, including three teas that came in the new pyramid-shaped bags, which are touted as having more room for the tea to expand for better flavor. A panel of 20 tasters from our staff sampled 10 teas, both plain and with milk.

My Cup of Tea

An ideal cup of black tea should taste fresh, with no stale overtones, and should not taste burnt, though a smoky or earthy flavor is acceptable. It should not be yeasty or sour. It should have a pleasing aroma, a bright color, and a crisp rather than heavy flavor, with some of the astringency tea professionals call "briskness." Black tea gets these characteristics from a number of factors, including where it is grown (cooler temperatures at higher elevations slow down the plant's growth and let it build more flavor), when it is picked (the often-prized "first flush" is the earliest), how it is picked (by hand is considered better; machines can be rough and tear up older, tougher leaves in addition to the desired top two leaves and bud), and how it is processed.

When making black tea, processors let the harvested leaves wither for up to 24 hours, then roll or cut them. This breaks the cell walls and releases enzymes that oxidize to develop the tea's flavor and color—in the case of black tea, turning the leaves black. Then they heat (or "fire") the leaves to stop oxidation before drying them until they look like familiar dry tea. The leaves are then sold to tea companies, which generally blend tea from several sources, although really fine-quality leaves are often kept unblended as single-estate teas.

Our tasters began by assessing the tea samples' aroma, followed by complexity of flavor, astringency, and overall appeal. Tasters' scores for aroma most closely tracked with their overall ranking of the teas. Whenever the tea failed to deliver on that aromatic promise, however, our tasters downgraded it. Our tasters also preferred teas with smoother, less astringent profiles.

Matters of Taste

For our next test, we examined the leaves, opening up the tea bags as needed. The leaves varied in size and texture from half-inch twiglike pieces of tightly rolled leaves to tiny flakes no bigger than coarse coffee grounds. While tea aficionados will tell you that bigger is better when it comes to leaf size, we disagree. Our top two teas had the seventh- and sixth-smallest leaves, respectively, out of the 10 teas we tasted. "While a larger leaf may give you more complexity of flavor, you always have to judge by what you taste in the cup," said Donna Fellman of the Specialty Tea Institute in New York.

In the plain tasting, our two highest-ranked teas were from British companies: Twinings English Breakfast (a loose tea) and PG Tips (in pyramid bags). These teas offered strong, bright flavor with just a little astringency—the balance that our tasters liked best without milk.

We had one more experiment. All three teas in pyramid-shaped bags had shown well, and the teas in traditional bags performed poorly. We decided to see if it was the bag or the tea by taking tea out of two traditional bags and brewing it instead in T-Sacs, fill-it-yourself paper bags with gusseted bottoms that give them a shape similar to the pyramid bag's. Regular Lipton tea still failed to impress tasters, but removed from its disk-shaped bag, Tetley performed much better. Evidently, the roomier pyramid bags (or T-Sacs) helped. Finally, better flavor didn't mean higher prices. While the teas in our lineup ranged from $.38 to $3.99 per ounce, our top two teas were $1.41 and $.47 per ounce.

Surprisingly, when we tried the teas again with milk, the results were nearly the opposite. Tea gets its astringency from tannic substances called catechins. Tasted plain, the teas that tasters rated lowest for astringency and highest for complexity of flavor rose in the rankings. When milk was added, teas deemed too harsh became quite palatable, and those that were smoother but less robustly flavored sank in our tasters' estimation.

There's a chemical explanation for this: Proteins in the milk called caseins bind with the tea's catechins, taking the edge off the astringent effect on your palate. A little astringency is considered a good characteristic in a black tea. But too much turned off tasters, unless it was masked by milk. Tea drinkers among us were firm about our preference for always drinking tea with—or without—milk. So we decided to present the top-ranked teas in each tasting and let you focus on the section that applies to the way you drink your tea.

Is Fancy Tea Any Better?

Premium teas are almost always picked by hand, sold loose, and mail-ordered. We chose English breakfast blends from five high-end tea companies—Harney & Sons, Upton Tea Imports, Mariage Frères, Mighty Leaf, and Adagio—and tasted them plain against our winning supermarket tea, Twinings English Breakfast, and again with milk against Tazo Awake, our favorite supermarket tea when milk is added. In the plain tasting, Mighty Leaf Organic English Breakfast Tea ($7.95 for 4 ounces, or $1.99 per ounce) won by a landslide. With milk, results changed dramatically. Harney & Sons English Breakfast Tea ($19 for 1 pound, or $1.19 per ounce) moved from fifth place in the plain tasting to the top. As for supermarket teas, Twinings and Tazo performed respectably in such rarified air, ranking in the middle of the pack in both the plain and with milk tastings. For complete tasting results, go to www.cooksillustrated.com/august. Sources for the winning teas are listed on page 32. –L.M.

MIGHTY LEAF
Our plain winner.

HARNEY & SONS
Shined with milk.

COOK'S LIVE Original Test Kitchen Video
www.cooksillustrated.com
- Behind the Scenes: Tea Tasting

TASTING SUPERMARKET TEA

Twenty *Cook's Illustrated* staff members tasted 10 teas, plain and with milk added. The top teas from each tasting are listed below in order of preference. Note that brands that showed well when tasted plain were generally quite dull when tasted with milk; likewise, brands that showed well when tasted with milk were generally too strong when tasted plain. Prices were paid at Boston-area supermarkets.

BEST TEAS PLAIN

TWININGS ENGLISH BREAKFAST TEA

➢ **Style:** Loose tea
➢ **Origin:** India, Kenya
➢ **Price:** $9.95 for 7.05-ounce tin ($1.41 per ounce)
➢ **Comments:** "Fruity and smooth," "floral, fragrant, nice and balanced," agreed tasters, who liked that this tea was "not too strong" but packed "a lot of flavor." "A good, bold cup of tea. Cheerio and all that."

PG TIPS

➢ **Style:** Pyramid paper tea bags
➢ **Origin:** India, Kenya, Sri Lanka
➢ **Price:** $12.50 for 240 bags ($.47 per ounce)
➢ **Comments:** "Not too astringent—clean-tasting and very nice," most tasters agreed, with a "lovely woodsy smell" and "a nice balance that matches the aroma," with hints of "citrus" and "tropical fruit."

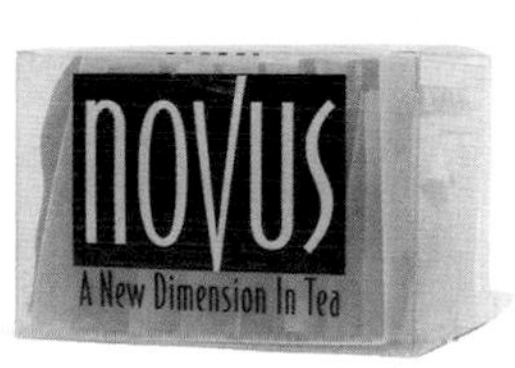

BIGELOW NOVUS KENILWORTH CEYLON

➢ **Style:** Pyramid nylon mesh tea bags
➢ **Origin:** Sri Lanka
➢ **Price:** $6.30 for 15 bags ($3.99 per ounce)
➢ **Comments:** Tasters appreciated an "earthy" quality in this tea, with a "lightly floral aroma and a super-smooth, almost honeyed flavor" and "moderate body."

LIPTON BLACK PEARL

➢ **Style:** Pyramid nylon mesh tea bags
➢ **Origin:** Sri Lanka
➢ **Price:** $3.39 for 20 bags ($2.42 per ounce)
➢ **Comments:** "Good and smooth," this tea was "fruity, pleasant, and mild," with a "clean taste" that "builds in the mouth," with a "surprisingly good aftertaste" and "slight astringency." Some, however, found it "nothing special."

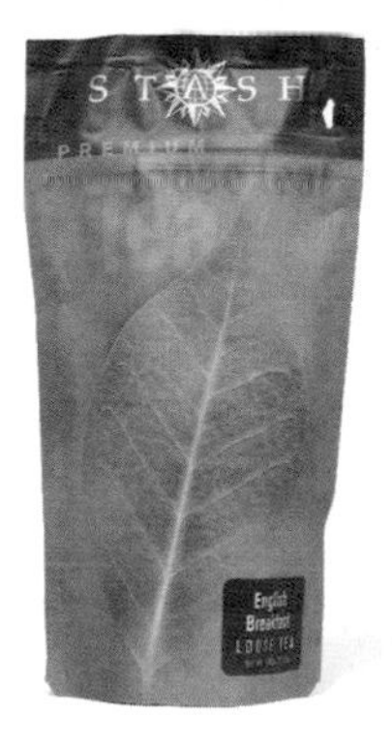

STASH ENGLISH BREAKFAST TEA

➢ **Style:** Loose tea
➢ **Origin:** Sri Lanka, India, and China
➢ **Price:** $5.95 for 3.5 ounces ($1.70 per ounce)
➢ **Comments:** "A strong smoky flavor and low astringency. I love it," said one taster, and others agreed—"quite smooth," "woodsy, floral, and sweet-smelling." However, a few found it "hoppy" and "musty like a barn."

BEST TEAS WITH MILK

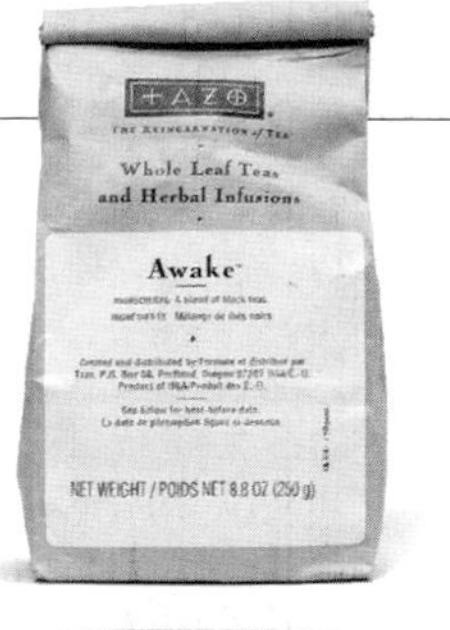

TAZO AWAKE

➢ **Style:** Loose tea
➢ **Origin:** Sri Lanka, India
➢ **Price:** $21.58 for 17.6 ounces ($1.23 per ounce)
➢ **Comments:** "Wow! Extremely smoky, with a strong, clean taste. Very good." "Fruity, delicious, and smooth, with a most pleasant aroma; perfumed but not overly precious." Tasters liked its spicy notes of clove, cinnamon, and vanilla. "Great balance of flavor and intensity."

TETLEY SPECIALTY TEA ENGLISH BREAKFAST

➢ **Style:** Disk-shaped paper tea bags
➢ **Origin:** India, Sri Lanka, Kenya
➢ **Price:** $3.19 for 20 bags ($2.28 per ounce)
➢ **Comments:** "Balanced; stands up to milk," with a "big flavor" that is "full-bodied" and "good and complex," with a "rich, steeped aroma."

RED ROSE

➢ **Style:** Loose tea
➢ **Origin:** Sri Lanka, India, Kenya, Indonesia
➢ **Price:** $3 for 8 ounces ($.38 per ounce)
➢ **Comments:** "Tea flavor comes through the milk," with an "almost savory," "strong," "complex and assertive" taste that has notes of "pumpkin" and "clove."

LIPTON TEA

➢ **Style:** Folded dual paper tea bags
➢ **Origin:** A changing blend from many countries around the world, such as Sri Lanka, India, Kenya, Indonesia, China, Brazil, Argentina, Ecuador, Malawi, Vietnam, and New Guinea
➢ **Price:** $4.99 for 100 bags ($.62 per ounce)
➢ **Comments:** Smelling "sweet," like "honey," and "yeasty, like dough," it came across as "plain-tasting," "not jarring," "strong but flavorful—very drinkable."

NOT RECOMMENDED

CELESTIAL SEASONINGS DEVONSHIRE ENGLISH BREAKFAST

➢ **Style:** Square paper tea bags
➢ **Origin:** India, Kenya
➢ **Price:** $2.99 for 20 bags ($2.14 per ounce)
➢ **Comments:** "Light aroma, light flavor, light everything" was the consensus here, with a few tasters liking its "roundness," but others calling it "one-note" or "dull and boring," adding that "nothing stands out." This tea ranked last in both tastings.

How We Brewed Our Tea

Tea experts recommend brewing black tea for three to five minutes, claiming that longer brewing brings out a harsh, bitter flavor. We put this to the test, tasting tea samples at three, four, and five minutes, and determined that four minutes was the best for full flavor without harshness. Clean-tasting water is the foundation of good tea, so we took fresh, cold spring water, brought it to a full boil, then immediately poured it over the tea bags in a prewarmed thermal carafe. (Boiling the water too long lets dissolved oxygen escape, leading to a flat-tasting cup of tea.) We used T-Sacs, fill-it-yourself paper tea bags sold in tea shops, to hold our loose tea and settled on 1/10 ounce (about 2 teaspoons, not packed down) of loose tea per T-Sac as an equivalent to one tea bag. We also used the tea industry standard of 6 ounces of water per teacup. For our second tasting, with milk, we tested proportions and decided to add 1 cup of milk to each half-gallon of tea before serving. –L.M.

In Search of the Perfect Garlic Press

Can your choice of garlic press affect the flavor of your dishes? You'd be surprised.

⋟ BY LISA McMANUS ⋞

We have a crush on garlic in the test kitchen. It appears in more than one-quarter of our recipes, and in most of those we suggest using a garlic press. This is heresy to some professional chefs. Why not just mince? Over the years, we've learned that for the average home cook, a garlic press is faster, easier, and more effective than trying to get a fine, even mince with a chef's knife. More important, garlic's flavor and aroma emerge only as its cell walls are ruptured and release an enzyme called alliinase, so a finely processed clove gives you a better distribution of garlic and fuller garlic flavor throughout the dish. Even our test cooks, trained to mince with a knife, generally grab a garlic press when cooking. And here's the best part: With a good garlic press, you don't even have to stop and peel the cloves.

Americans are using more garlic than ever, and it seems that every kitchen-tool manufacturer is trying to build a better garlic press. Many offer two or three models, traditional and innovative, hoping to catch the eye or the budget of every cook. Prices can range from less than $5 to more than $60. While you might imagine that the garlic press, which has been in America since the 1950s, has a pretty well-established design with all the kinks worked out, our tests quickly revealed that this is not the case. We rounded up nearly two dozen models and bushels of fresh garlic to find the best press for your kitchen.

The Case of the Peeling Press

When we first noticed that the coating had peeled off in patches on all of the Zyliss garlic presses in the test kitchen, we didn't worry. Recently, however, we noted that a tiny amount of black substance sometimes oozes onto our garlic as we press it. After some digging, we discovered that when the nonstick coating peels off, copper and iron in the aluminum base metal react with the air and sulfur compounds in the garlic to create oxides and sulfides, which we sometimes see as a black substance on our extruded garlic. It's similar to the discoloration from an old-fashioned carbon steel knife, and it's not toxic, according to science experts we spoke to. Patrice Gerber, director of product development international at Zyliss USA, concedes, "It doesn't look nice, for sure, but it's not dangerous." He said some peeling is normal inside the hopper, where the plunger "scratches against the basket." It might be normal, but it's not very appealing. –L.M.

COATS OFF
The nonstick coating peeled off our previously top-ranked presses, made by Zyliss, sending us back to the kitchen to test new models.

Flavor Find

But then it occurred to us: Beyond how easy it is to squeeze, does your garlic press really matter in your cooking? Will the right garlic press make your food taste better? We were skeptical, but a quick test revealed a surprising answer. We chose seven representative presses and used them to make seven batches of our Pasta with Garlic and Olive Oil (March/April 2001). It was remarkable to note the wide range of garlic flavor, from mild to robust, when the only difference was the press used to prepare the garlic. Larger chunks of garlic tended to drop to the bottom of the bowl, making most of the dish too bland. And when the pieces were uneven, tiny fragments overcooked to bitterness. Tasters overwhelmingly preferred the samples with the finest and most uniform garlic pieces, which produced a well-developed garlic flavor and consistent texture throughout the dish.

We decided that a garlic press's most important attribute was the ability to produce a fine and uniform garlic consistency. We also wanted a press that was simple and comfortable to operate and did not require the hand strength of Hercules. It should be solidly built, with no contest between the press and the garlic about which is going to break first. It should be able to hold more than one clove and should crush the garlic completely through the sieve, leaving little behind in the hopper. It should handle unpeeled cloves with ease. Finally, it should be simple to clean, by hand or dishwasher, and not require a toothpick to get the last pieces of garlic out.

A Pressing Problem

The more creative garlic gadgets were not successes. The Garlic Twist by NexTrend, a plastic pillbox-shaped device that you twist to chop the garlic inside, could only cut through a peeled, roughly chopped clove. The Genius Garlic Cutter (and a similar model by Moulinex) and the Chef'N Garlic Machine work like a peppermill. We found them slow to use and hard to clean. Such gimmicks sent us back to traditional lever-handled garlic presses. As we squeezed piles of pungent cloves, we began a process of elimination to decide on the 12 presses in our final lineup (see chart on page 29).

We had been satisfied with our previous favorite presses, the Zyliss Susi 2 and Zyliss Jumbo, until we noticed that the nonstick coating had peeled off each one in the test kitchen, particularly around the hopper; a tiny amount of black liquid was sometimes extruded along with the garlic. We sent a damaged press to an independent laboratory to determine what was happening and whether it could be unsafe (See "The Case of the Peeling Press," left). As we waited for the lab report, we tested the 12 finalists, including brand-new Zyliss presses. Since all were labeled dishwasher-safe, we ran them through a home dishwasher for 10 cycles. One model, by Amco, fell apart after just six cycles, leaving two halves and a missing hinge pin. And the nonstick coating on the brand-new Zyliss presses peeled—yet again.

We downgraded models with removable parts. The Cuisinart's hopper was too easy to put back in the wrong way or lose. We rejected designs such as the potato ricer–style Giant Garlic Press, which offered good leverage with its long handles but was cheaply executed, and the ridiculously expensive Eva Solo Garlic Press with Glass Container ($64.95), which was difficult to squeeze and quickly jammed up.

So which press is the best? Kuhn Rikon's Epicurean Garlic Press ($34.95) was the top performer, producing fine, uniform garlic with minimal effort. Made of solidly constructed stainless steel, it has a luxurious feel, with curved handles that are comfortable to squeeze and a hopper that smoothly and automatically lifts out for cleaning as you open the handles. However, at nearly $35, it's costly. At one-third the price, we found the chrome-plated Trudeau Garlic Press produced uniform pieces of garlic, had a generous hopper, and was easy to clean. It's our Best Buy.

COOK'S LIVE Original Test Kitchen Video
www.cooksillustrated.com
- Behind the Scenes: Garlic Press Testing

RATINGS
GOOD: ★★★
FAIR: ★★
POOR: ★

TESTING GARLIC PRESSES

We tested 12 garlic presses, pressing peeled and unpeeled cloves as well as multiple cloves. We ran the presses through a home dishwasher 10 times to evaluate durability. Presses are listed in order of preference. Sources for top model and Best Buy are listed on page 32.

PRICE: Retail price found online, in catalogs, or in Boston-area stores.

MATERIAL: Composition of press and handles.

CONSISTENCY OF GARLIC: We preferred presses that produced fine, uniform pieces of garlic.

PRESSING PERFORMANCE: We preferred models that were easy to press; handled peeled, unpeeled, and multiple garlic cloves; and left little waste.

DESIGN: We preferred devices that were comfortable, smooth, and intuitive to operate, with durable materials and construction.

CLEANUP: We wanted models that cleaned up easily by hand or dishwasher.

COMMENTS: Testers' observations.

RECOMMENDED	PERFORMANCE	TESTERS' COMMENTS
Kuhn Rikon 2315 Epicurean Garlic Press PRICE: $34.95 MATERIAL: Stainless steel 	CONSISTENCY OF GARLIC: ★★★ PRESSING PERFORMANCE: ★★★ DESIGN: ★★★ CLEANUP: ★★★	Heavy, solid gliding mechanism, with comfortably curved handles and hopper that lifts for easy cleaning. Mince is "very fine" and unpeeled garlic was "no problem." Overall, testers noted, "It pressed—and cleaned—like a dream."
RECOMMENDED WITH RESERVATIONS	**PERFORMANCE**	**TESTERS' COMMENTS**
Rösle Garlic Press PRICE: $34.95 MATERIAL: Stainless steel	CONSISTENCY OF GARLIC: ★★ PRESSING PERFORMANCE: ★★★ DESIGN: ★★ CLEANUP: ★★★	Solid, heavy press has pop-up hopper for cleaning. Straight, cylindrical, shiny handles "didn't feel perfectly ergonomic," but the press was "surprisingly easy to use and clean."
Trudeau Garlic Press **BEST BUY** PRICE: $11.99 MATERIAL: Chrome-plated metal with nonslip rubber handles	CONSISTENCY OF GARLIC: ★★ PRESSING PERFORMANCE: ★★ DESIGN: ★★★ CLEANUP: ★★★	"Good press" with a "solid" feel produced garlic pieces that were "uniform but a little chunky." Press was "very easy to clean," with flip handles and "generous" hopper.
Messermeister Pro-Touch Jumbo Garlic Press with Santoprene Handles PRICE: $9.95 MATERIAL: Zinc alloy, satin finished, with rubber handles	CONSISTENCY OF GARLIC: ★★ PRESSING PERFORMANCE: ★★ DESIGN: ★★★ CLEANUP: ★★★	"Sturdy and easy to squeeze," except for unpeeled cloves, which required more muscle. Garlic came out slightly "chunky" and "coarse." Construction is solid and heavy. "Jumbo" hopper no bigger than average.
Zyliss Susi 2 Garlic Press PRICE: $14.99 MATERIAL: Aluminum base with nonstick coating	CONSISTENCY OF GARLIC: ★★★ PRESSING PERFORMANCE: ★★★ DESIGN: ★ CLEANUP: ★★	Tapered holes shaped like tiny funnels gave "huge yield" of "fine-textured garlic" that was "super-easy" to press. "Effortless" with unpeeled cloves. Some testers preferred this lightweight model, but nonstick finish began to peel around the hopper.
Zyliss Jumbo Garlic Press PRICE: $16.99 MATERIAL: Aluminum base with nonstick coating	CONSISTENCY OF GARLIC: ★★★ PRESSING PERFORMANCE: ★★★ DESIGN: ★ CLEANUP: ★★	"Jumbo" press held four to five cloves; handled unpeeled cloves well, producing a "very good mince." Cleaning tool stores in the handle, but some found it "hard to figure out." Nonstick finish began to peel.
NOT RECOMMENDED	**PERFORMANCE**	**TESTERS' COMMENTS**
OXO Steel 58181 Garlic Press PRICE: $16.99 MATERIAL: Stainless steel with rubber handles, plastic cleaning spikes	CONSISTENCY OF GARLIC: ★ PRESSING PERFORMANCE: ★★ DESIGN: ★★ CLEANUP: ★★★	Plunger couldn't be fully depressed to bottom of hopper. "Inefficient," complained testers. Flip-handled model cleaned up easily. Testers deemed the sieve holes too large, producing "coarse," "chunky" pieces.
OXO Good Grips 28181 Garlic Press PRICE: $14.50 MATERIAL: Die-cast zinc, rubber handles, plastic cleaning spikes	CONSISTENCY OF GARLIC: ★★ PRESSING PERFORMANCE: ★ DESIGN: ★★ CLEANUP: ★★★	Plunger couldn't quite get to the bottom of the hopper, leaving some garlic unprocessed. Couldn't handle unpeeled cloves. Traditional flip-handled model rinsed out easily. Handles were comfortable and easy to press.
Giant Garlic Press PRICE: $14 MATERIAL: Stainless steel	CONSISTENCY OF GARLIC: ★★ PRESSING PERFORMANCE: ★★ DESIGN: ★★ CLEANUP: ★	Shaped like a potato ricer, this press struck testers as "flimsy." Hopper is "huge" but could press only three cloves, because plunger couldn't get into position with more. Press was "a pain to clean."
Cuisinart Red Garlic Press PRICE: $14.95 MATERIAL: Steel with plastic handles	CONSISTENCY OF GARLIC: ★★ PRESSING PERFORMANCE: ★ DESIGN: ★★ CLEANUP: ★★	Testers disliked "tiny hopper," which removes for cleaning. "I'd lose this in a second," complained one, "and it's too easy to put in backward." Unpeeled garlic "spattered and squished up the sides."
Amco Houseworks Garlic Press *Also sold as the Crate and Barrel Garlic Slicer and Press PRICE: $19.95 MATERIAL: Die-cast aluminum 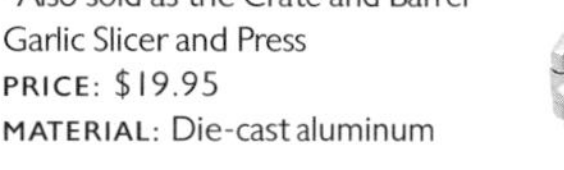	CONSISTENCY OF GARLIC: ★★ PRESSING PERFORMANCE: ★ DESIGN: ★ CLEANUP: ★	Fell completely apart in dishwasher after six washes. Press "left a lot behind," and pieces were somewhat uneven. Slices "too thick"; garlic looked "chewed-up" and stuck in the blades.
Eva Solo Stainless Steel Garlic Press with Glass Container PRICE: $64.95 MATERIAL: Stainless steel	CONSISTENCY OF GARLIC: ★★ PRESSING PERFORMANCE: ★ DESIGN: ★ CLEANUP: ★	"Too cool for its own good" and "very uncomfortable." "I used my whole body weight to press it," complained one tester. "Pathetic" output for peeled clove. Unpeeled cloves "almost impossible."

KITCHEN NOTES

⋟ BY J. KENJI ALT ⋞

Pickle Picks

Many barbecue aficionados are quick to point out that a plate of smoky brisket isn't complete without the sweet-and-sour tang and snappy crunch of bread-and-butter pickles. After topping our Barbecued Brisket (page 7) with seven brands, we learned that not just any crispy cuke will do. Though some form of sweetener is essential for preserving and flavoring a bread-and-butter chip, many brands have opted to replace real sugar with cheaper high-fructose corn syrup. Five of the seven pickle brands we sampled list this shelf-stable syrup as their second ingredient, which led to complaints about "artificial sweetness" and "syrupy" flavors. Our two favorites—Cascadian Farm and Bubbies—are made with real sugar, and our tasters could tell the difference. For the complete results of this tasting, go to www.cooksillustrated.com/august.

TOP PICKLE
We picked Cascadian Farm Bread & Butter Chips for their crunch and tang.

Make-Ahead Scones

Since not many people enjoy grating butter and rolling dough first thing in the morning, we decided to test whether our Blueberry Scones (page 23) could be made in advance. We mixed the dough, cut the scones, placed them on a parchment-lined baking sheet, and refrigerated them overnight before putting them straight into a preheated oven the next morning. The results were practically as good as a freshly mixed batch. We found that unbaked scones could actually be frozen and baked from the freezer without significant loss in quality. Why was this?

Today, most baking powder is "double-acting," meaning that in order to perform its leavening function, it must react in two stages. In the first stage, the baking powder dissolves in liquid and reacts to release carbon dioxide. In doughs with little liquid, such as our scone dough, the amount of leavening at this stage is minimal compared with that of thinner cake and pancake batters. The second stage of leavening requires heat. The thick dough in our scone recipe experiences most of its leavening during this second stage, in the oven.

To bake our Blueberry Scones from the refrigerator, heat oven to 425 degrees, then follow the directions on page 23 from step 6. For frozen scones, heat oven to 375 degrees, follow directions from step 6, and extend cooking time to 25 to 30 minutes. This same make-ahead method can be used for any baking powder–leavened dough recipe (such as cookie or biscuit dough).

As the Chimney Burns

For lighting coals on an outdoor grill, we like to use a chimney starter, but we've noticed that the time it takes to ignite the coals varies depending on weather conditions. We use our eyes to know when the coals are ready to spread over the grates. For a full (6 quarts, about 100 briquettes) or three-quarters-full chimney, the coals at the very top should be just starting to turn gray—large patches of black briquettes at this stage are OK, as lit coals at bottom of the chimney will get others going in no time, even after spreading. For a chimney that is less than three-quarters full (such as you might use for a smaller grill), make sure you wait until all the coals are entirely coated in a layer of gray ash before spreading them—once spread, the lower volume of briquettes will not get hot enough to ignite any unlit briquettes.

FULL CHIMNEY
A full chimney of charcoal should be unloaded when the top coals are just starting to become gray around the edges.

SMALL FIRE
For a chimney that is less than three-quarters full, wait until the top coals are fully covered in gray ash before dumping them.

Faster Defrosting

While testing our recipe for Grill-Roasted Cornish Game Hens (page 18), we occasionally hit a snag when the only ones available in the supermarket were frozen. We wanted a way to defrost our hens fast. Our recommended method, thawing them overnight in the refrigerator, can take 24 to 36 hours—not very convenient if you've got guests coming for dinner in a few hours (or if you have multiple rounds of recipe testing to conduct).

Our attempt to quickly defrost the Cornish hens in the microwave resulted in the protruding legs and wings being partially cooked. We found the quickest way to defrost Cornish hens without a significant loss in quality is to submerge them (unwrapped) in a bucket of cold tap water, changing the water every 15 minutes. After one hour, poke thickest part of the breast with a thin skewer to check if meat is fully thawed. If interior still feels frozen, change the water and check again at 10-minute intervals. Four giblet-free 1½-pound hens will take

TECHNIQUE | HOW TO PROLONG BERRY FRESHNESS

It's happened to all of us. Put a box of berries in the refrigerator, then throw them in the garbage a few days later, covered with mold. While we've advocated not washing berries until just before use (damp berries turn mushy faster than dry berries), we've discovered that cleaning with a mild vinegar solution and careful drying destroys bacteria and mold spores, extending the life of the berries. Here's how to do it:

1. Wash berries in bowl with 3 cups water mixed with 1 cup white vinegar. Drain in colander and rinse under running water.
2. Place berries in salad spinner lined with 3 layers of paper towels. Spin for 15 seconds or until berries are completely dry.
3. Store berries in paper towel–lined sealable container, keeping lid slightly open to allow excess moisture to escape.

ILLUSTRATION: JOHN BURGOYNE

Test Kitchen Tips: Better Barbecuing

Coaxing consistent results from a cooking method as inexact as barbecuing can be tricky, so we've put together some basic tips based on our years of experience.

MAKE SURE TO...	THIS ENSURES...
Shield grill from wind as much as possible.	Smoke stays in grill and fire burns at proper temperature.
Measure and/or count out briquettes.	Fire is consistently correct size and temperature.
Soak wood chunks or chips in water before cooking.	Smoke is slowly released over long period of time.
Bank coals as steeply as possible when barbecuing large cuts.	Proper indirect cooking by keeping meat as far as possible from fire.
Position lid vents directly above meat, not fire.	Smoke draws properly across meat.
Keep lid on as much as possible. (No peeking!)	Grill's internal temperature stays consistent.
Use a barbecue thermometer.	You know if your fire is too hot or dying out without lifting lid.

between one and 1½ hours to fully defrost. Extend the thawing time by half an hour if the hens come with giblets in the cavity.

Flip Tip

When cooking the patties for our Greek-Style Lamb Pita Sandwiches (page 13), we found that with 12 small patties all frying at once in a large pan, it was hard to keep track of when each patty needed to be flipped or removed. Laying the meat down in an organized spiral—working clockwise from the handle and toward the center of the pan—made it a simple matter of flipping the meat in the same order that it went into the pan.

This same technique can be applied any time you need to keep track of a large number of items in a pan, from searing scallops to frying meatballs. It's also helpful when managing a grill full of meat or vegetables (for rectangular grills, work in even rows, from left to right and back to front).

PAN MANAGEMENT
Arranging small items in a spiral pattern will help you keep track of when to flip and remove each piece.

Cleaner Cantaloupe

While researching various fresh fruits for our Summer Fruit Salads (page 21), we came across a surprising fact: Certain strains of salmonella can get into the nooks and crannies of cantaloupes' porous skin while they are growing in the field. Once there, they produce bacterial polymer biofilms—impermeable carbohydrate-based sheaths that protect the bacteria from even the most aggressive cleaning attempts. Our tests showed that even a scrub-down in antibacterial soap was completely ineffective in removing these dangerous bacteria, which reside only on the surface of the melons. To minimize the risk of salmonella infection, food safety experts suggest the following:

- **Choose clean, unbruised, unblemished melons and stay away from precut melons.**
- **Use a sharp knife to cut melons—a dull knife can push the rind into the flesh, causing contamination.**
- **Trim away the rind before eating or storing, and store any remaining flesh in the refrigerator within two hours of cutting.**
- **Wash your cutting board with hot, soapy water after cutting melons.**
- **Make sure you keep cut melon well refrigerated if you plan on bringing it on a picnic.**

RECIPE UPDATE

Thai-Style Soup with Pork or Shrimp

Readers wanted to know if they could substitute meat or shrimp for the chicken in our **Thai-Style Chicken Soup** (January/February 2007). To make this soup, we infuse a coconut milk/chicken broth base with intense Thai flavors: lemon grass, shallots, and fish sauce. Thin strips of chicken breast are simmered in the broth for a few minutes before serving. Thinly sliced pork and beef tenderloin, as well as peeled-and-deveined shrimp, cooked just as quickly as chicken breast in this soup. However, we don't recommend using beef, as it didn't pair well with the fish sauce. The sweet brininess of shrimp tasted great, and halving each one lengthwise ensured bite-sized pieces that cooked evenly. The supple texture and mild flavor of pork tenderloin make it a great substitute as well. For our free recipes for Thai-Style Soup with Shrimp and Thai-Style Soup with Pork, go to www.cooksillustrated.com/august.

Moroccan Chicken Breasts with Olives and Lemon

Fans of our **Moroccan Chicken with Olives and Lemon** recipe (May/June 2006)—which calls for a whole chicken cut up into pieces—wanted to know the best way to make it using boneless, skinless chicken breast. The original recipe was designed to cook white and dark meat—which cook at different rates—simultaneously. Using all white meat simplifies the original technique a bit, though the tender meat requires gentler treatment. First, to prevent the breasts from developing a tough exterior, we lightly brown them for a couple of minutes per side. Then, when it comes to finishing them in the sauce—chicken broth spiked with spices, lemon zest, onions, garlic, cilantro, carrots, and olives—it's best to prop up the chicken on the large carrot pieces and flip the breasts halfway through cooking. This technique promotes even cooking and prevents the meat from turning stringy. For our free recipe for Moroccan Chicken Breasts with Olives and Lemon, go to www.cooksillustrated.com/august.

Blueberry Yeasted Waffles

Our recipe for **Yeasted Waffles** (March/April 2004) seemed ideal for a blueberry variation. At first glance, it appeared as easy as folding a couple handfuls of fresh blueberries into the batter just before cooking. But the blueberries crushed inside the waffle iron, causing the juices to seep from the waffles and burn on the hot iron. Using frozen cultivated berries worked fairly well, as did using fresh wild blueberries, which are much smaller than cultivated berries. But we got the best results from frozen wild blueberries that we coated with flour before folding them into the batter. The frozen berries stay intact better after closing the lid, and the flour helps prevent the juices from bleeding. For our free recipe for Blueberry Yeasted Waffles, go to www.cooksillustrated.com/august.

—Compiled by Charles Kelsey

BIG BERRIES SMALL BERRIES

To avoid waffles with burnt blueberries (left), use frozen wild blueberries (right) and coat them with flour right before folding them into the batter.

IF YOU HAVE A QUESTION about a recipe, let us know. Send your inquiry, name, address, and daytime telephone number to Recipe Update, Cook's Illustrated, P.O. Box 470589, Brookline, MA 02447, or write to recipeupdate@americastestkitchen.com.

EQUIPMENT CORNER

BY ELIZABETH BOMZE

NEW PRODUCT: Grill Grate Lifter

Replenishing coals is a must for many slow-cooked barbecue recipes, but dealing with a blazing-hot grill can be a dicey task. As an alternative to grasping the grate with a mitt, the Barr Brothers Company offers its Grill Grabber Grate Lifter ($6.99). It looks like a skillet handle and measures just under 10 inches from polypropylene grip to stainless steel tip. Its curved, notched prongs securely hooked under the bars of the grate and steadily held its weight (it can support up to five pounds) as we poured more coals into the kettle. It also works indoors as an oven rack puller.

GRATE GRIP
Protect your hands (and your food) with the Grill Grabber Grate Lifter.

NEW PRODUCT: Onion Goggles

Chopping and dicing our way through 30 pounds of onions per week in the test kitchen, we're always interested in new methods of eye defense. And while they certainly look a bit goofy, the R.S.V.P. International Onion Goggles ($19.99) do help maintain focus on the onions—yellow, Vidalia, red, or otherwise—rather than the tissue box. We found that they block irritating fumes better than sunglasses, and the foam padding around the antifog lenses is a more comfortable alternative to swim goggles. Available in white or black with lime green trim.

NO MORE TEARS
R.S.V.P. International Onion Goggles protect your eyes when you're chopping onions.

EQUIPMENT UPDATE: Box Grater

Shortly after we proclaimed the Cuisipro Accutec Box Grater our favorite, several readers alerted us that the tool actually broke apart in their dishwashers. A call to Cuisipro revealed that they, too, have received a few complaints. The company will replace any box graters damaged by dishwashers. (Visit www.cuisipro.com for more information or call 302-326-4802.) If you own the Cuisipro grater, the company suggests washing it by hand. If you're in the market to buy a box grater, we now recommend the OXO Good Grips Box Grater ($14.99). This grater is sharp and slim and comes with a handy container marked with cup measurements that snaps onto the bottom.

NEW PRODUCT: Crumb Box

We love tearing into rustic boules and baguettes, but doing so leaves a crumby mess on the cutting board, countertop, or table. Tempted by the Bartelt Crumb Box ($27.95), a shoebox-sized hardwood box with a removable wooden grate on top, we placed a crusty loaf of Italian bread on the grate and began slicing. As promised, the crumbs fell through and collected in the bottom for easy disposal. What's more, the handsome grate serves as both a cooling surface for oven-fresh loaves and a serving platter for bread at the table.

EASY AS SLICED BREAD
The Bartelt Crumb Box functions as both a bread-slicing surface and a crumb-collection box.

EQUIPMENT TESTING: Tabletop Grills

We liked the idea of grilling shrimp or beef tableside, just like in restaurants, so we decided to test indoor grills. After dismissing models that required hard-to-find fondue fuel or denatured alcohol, we purchased six brands in two styles: electric and those designed to sit on a stovetop burner. The stovetop models didn't get hot enough and are not recommended. Among the electric versions, the Sanyo Smokeless Electric Indoor Grill ($39.95) was our favorite. It most closely mimicked the heat of an outdoor grill and produced the least smoke, due to a basin you must fill with water before cooking. For complete testing results, go to www.cooksillustrated.com/august.

BEST INDOOR GRILL
Of the six models tested, only the Sanyo Smokeless Electric Indoor Grill combined a large capacity with easy cleanup and minimal smoke.

EQUIPMENT UPDATE: Target Dutch Oven

In the January/February 2007 issue, we tested inexpensive Dutch ovens against our pricey favorites, the Le Creuset 7¼ Quart Round French Oven ($229.95) and the All-Clad Stainless 8-Quart Stockpot ($257.95). We were impressed by the significantly cheaper Round Enameled Cast Iron Casserole with Lid by Chefmate for Target ($39.99). Just as our article was published, however, Target's website sold out of this test kitchen Best Buy. Target assured us that the casserole will be available in stores through 2007. We suggest contacting Guest Services at a Target store and giving them the DPCI number (070/02/0962), so they can tell you if it's in stock.

Sources

The following are sources for items recommended in this issue. Prices were current at press time and do not include shipping. Contact companies to confirm information or visit www.cooksillustrated.com for updates.

Page 8: THERMOMETER
- Polder 12453 Dual Oven/Meat Thermometer: $10, item #B0002EXQHS, Amazon.com.

Page 19: GRILL ROTISSERIES
- BBQ Galore 31" Deluxe Stainless Steel Rotisserie: $149.99, item #287912, Barbeques Galore (800-752-3085, www.bbqgalore.com).
- Weber 9890 Gas Barbecue Rotisserie: $79.99, item #B00004RAMB, Amazon.com.
- Weber 2290 22½" Kettle Rotisserie: $119.99, item #B00004VWM1, Amazon.com.

Page 25: MINI OFFSET SPATULA
- Wilton Angled Comfort Grip 8" Spatula: $4.49, item# 409-6012, Wilton (800-794-5866, www.wilton.com).

Page 26: TEAS
- Mighty Leaf Organic English Breakfast Tea: $7.95 for 4 ounces, item #189349, Mighty Leaf Tea (877-698-5323, www.mightyleaf.com).
- Harney & Sons English Breakfast Tea: $19 per pound, Harney & Sons (888-427-6398, www.harney.com).

Page 29: GARLIC PRESSES
- Kuhn Rikon Epicurean Garlic Press: $34.95, item #189349, Cooking.com (800-663-8810, www.cooking.com).
- Trudeau Garlic Press: $11.99, item #B00062B0EM, Amazon.com.

Page 32: GRILL GRATE LIFTER
- Barr Brothers Company Grill Grabber Grate Lifter: $6.99, BBQ Tools (800-630-8665, www.bbq-tools.com).

Page 32: ONION GOGGLES
- R.S.V.P. International Onion Goggles: $19.99, item # B000H40QT4, Amazon.com.

Page 32: BOX GRATER
- OXO Good Grips Box Grater: $14.99, item #B0007VO0CQ, Amazon.com.

Page 32: CRUMB BOX
- Bartelt Crumb Box: $27.95, item #100442, Cooking.com.

Page 32: TABLETOP GRILL
- Sanyo Smokeless Electric Indoor Grill: $39.95, item #315062, Cooking.com.

Page 32: DUTCH OVEN
- Round Enameled Cast Iron Casserole with Lid by Chefmate for Target: $39.99, item #070/02/0962, in Target stores; see www.target.com for store locator.

INDEX

July & August 2007

RECIPES

COOK'S LIVE Original Test Kitchen Videos www.cooksillustrated.com

AMERICA'S TEST KITCHEN

Public television's most popular cooking show

Join the millions of home cooks who watch our show, *America's Test Kitchen*, on public television every week. For more information, including recipes and program times, visit www.americastestkitchen.com.

Barbecued Beef Brisket, 7

Summer Fruit Salads, 21

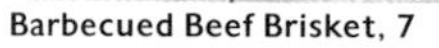

Shrimp Salads, 20

Grilled Potatoes, 9

Grilled Chicken Breasts, 11

Blueberry Scones, 23

Greek-Style Lamb Pita Sandwiches, 13

Grill-Roasted Cornish Game Hens, 18

Rustic Plum Cake, 25

Pasta Caprese, 15

PHOTOGRAPHY: CARL TREMBLAY, STYLING: MARIE PIRAINO

Damson Plum
Shiro Plum
Black Plum
Donut Peach
Yellow Peach
Pluot
Apricot
Honeydew Nectarine
Prune Plum
White Peach
Nectarine
STONE FRUIT

NUMBER EIGHTY-EIGHT SEPTEMBER & OCTOBER 2007

Perfecting Glazed Chicken

BBQ Pork Chops
New Indoor Skillet Recipe

Best Ways to Cook Common Vegetables

Cast Iron vs. Nonstick
Can Cast Iron Do It All?

Rating Parmesan
Are Italian Cheeses Really Best?

Ultimate Apple Tart
Flaky Crust, Caramelized Apples

Beef-Vegetable Soup
Big Flavor, Quick Cooking

Grilled Stuffed Pork Loin

Chicken Tikka Masala

Better Ricotta Gnocchi

Crispy Pear Crisp

www.cooksillustrated.com

$5.95 U.S./$6.95 CANADA

CONTENTS

September & October 2007

COOK'S ONLINE

Go to **www.cooksillustrated.com** to access all recipes from *Cook's Illustrated* since 1993 as well as updated tastings and testings. Watch videos of all the recipes in this issue being prepared and special reports on the Parmesan taste test and cast-iron skillet testing.

THAI HERBS & SPICES: A host of spicy, earthy, pungent, acidic, and sweet elements are essential to the dynamic flavors of Thai cooking. Where Western dishes would rely on lemons or limes to contribute acidity to a dish, Southeast Asian recipes draw from a more complex pool for the essence of citrus. Both the woody, bulbous base and lower portion of reed-like lemon grass stalks add peppery citrus notes to curries, stews, and stir-fries. The leaves and rind of tropical kaffir limes are used to impart an intense floral flavor to curry pastes. Galangal, a camphorous cousin of ginger, is also essential to curry pastes. These rhizomes are similar enough in flavor for Western interpretations of traditional Thai cuisine to use them interchangeably. A unique hint of anise distinguishes Thai basil from its Western counterparts. Culantro, used mostly in soups, stews, and noodle dishes, offers a more concentrated version of the soapy lemon flavor characteristic of cilantro. Tiny red Thai bird chiles impart a fierce heat to countless dishes. A garlicky nuance separates garlic chives from ordinary chives. The sweet and sour pulp of tamarind pods is used to lend tartness to soups and stews.

BACK COVER: *Thai Herbs & Spices* by John Burgoyne

FRONT COVER PAINTING: *Gourds*, by internationally renowned still-life artist Elizabeth Brandon, whose works are featured at www.elizabethbrandon.com.

For list rental information, contact: Specialists Marketing Services, Inc., 1200 Harbor Blvd., 9th Floor, Weehawken, NJ 07087; 201-865-5800.
Editorial Office: 17 Station St., Brookline, MA 02445; 617-232-1000; fax 617-232-1572. Subscription inquiries, call 800-526-8442.
Postmaster: Send all new orders, subscription inquiries, and change-of-address notices to Cook's Illustrated, P.O. Box 7446, Red Oak, IA 51591-0446.

THE ROAD TAKEN

The woods in our Vermont town are full of the unexpected. I've stumbled across black bears, coyotes, a rabid raccoon hiding in a hollow tree trunk, a young and gangly bull moose, a bobcat so large I thought it was a mountain lion, a glossy black porcupine with a face like a monkey, and once, during deer season, a fawn that walked right up, stared me down, and then slowly moved on after it had an eyeful. I've seen a large brown rabbit jump a 10-foot-wide stream without getting its feet wet, an eagle float over my head while I was standing on the top of Bear Mountain, and a red-tailed hawk launch itself out of a high perch and soar down to snatch one of our Rhode Island Reds.

Of course, there are the hunting stories. Nate tells about the time he shot two turkeys on the first day of the season with just one shot—a curious second turkey peeked around a tree at exactly the wrong moment. And the time he was sitting in a tree stand during deer season and watched a large coyote track his father, Tom, through the snow. And the time that Tom was rabbit hunting and watched his beagle run in circles following rabbit scent while, all the time, the rabbit was sitting plumb in the middle of the action on a tree stump, enjoying the show. Some people do some pretty stupid things in the woods, such as shooting a moose out of season while being shot themselves on videotape. (The judge had a good laugh.) And the half-wits who like to cruise back roads in the early morning or evening and shoot from their pickups. The game warden catches some of them by using his mechanical deer, Bambi, which he places strategically near the road. One out-of-towner, as he was being arrested, kept insisting that he had shot a real four-pointer and demanded the carcass.

On a few occasions, walks in the woods have led me to encounters with death—like the search for a neighbor who had a heart attack while looking for loose beefers—and then, while attending a three-day rock concert near Seattle in 1970, I saw a kid pulled stiff and bleached white out of a stream. And a few years back, the rescue squad was called in for a particularly bad turkey hunting accident—one hunter hid in the bushes and made turkey calls while his partner swung around and gave him both barrels.

Christopher Kimball

The longest walk I have ever taken was a recent hike through the Pyrenees with my wife, Adrienne. The hike was about eight miles, most of it spent on 4,000-foot ridgelines on the border between France and Spain. Around midday and after a series of wrong turns, we ended up at the end of the trail in a dark forest and with little idea where we were on the map. (The tour company had suggested bringing a flashlight, whistle, and compass; all three were left behind to make room for bread, charcuterie, and the local wine.) After climbing a boulder for a view, I discovered that we were at the head of a steep mountain ravine formed on two sides by high rocky ridgelines and filled in between with streams, gorges, and thick going. Miles in the distance, I could see a few houses. It was at least four hours of strenuous hiking back to our starting point, so we marched on. Then it darkened and started to rain.

After an hour of painful progress following what must have been a wild boar path, Adrienne finally said, "Let's follow the river back to civilization," a remark akin to "Use seat cushions for flotation." Without better options, we finally made it down to the river, found a trail, lost the trail, ended up at an impassable gorge, retraced our steps, found a parallel river, followed that, rejoined the original river, slogged through that for half a mile or so, and then picked up a trail that seemed promising. It was midafternoon but dark deep in the gorge, the forest more ragged and primeval than here in New England, as if its history were piled on top of itself, waiting patiently under our tired footsteps.

But, finally, we found the trailhead and a small settlement of houses, the roof tiles the color of pink peppercorns and the front yards sadly domesticated. Salvation had quickly turned to routine, and now it was just a question of reaching our final destination. We hitched a ride with a drunk school-bus driver and ended up in town, wearily ensconced in a small café. After two bracing, slightly bitter beers, I asked a local to point out where we were on the map. He looked perplexed for a few seconds and then, in a moment of enlightenment, turned it over and found the spot on the other side. We were a good 12 miles from our intended destination.

Robert Frost knew a lot about being lost and the deep longing to escape from earth for even just a moment. In his most famous poem, he chose, as Adrienne and I did by chance, the path with the ". . .better claim / Because it was grassy and wanted wear." Frost knew that life can be a ". . .pathless wood / Where your face burns and tickles with the cobwebs / Broken across it, and one eye is weeping / From a twig's having lashed across it open." He longed to get away from the mundane, to reach toward heaven for just a moment and then come back again, renewed. As the two of us emerged oddly exhilarated from the woods that day in the Pyrenees, I remembered the closing lines of Frost's "Birches."

Earth's the right place for love:
I don't know where it's likely to go better.
I'd like to go by climbing a birch tree,
And climb black branches up a snow-white trunk
Toward heaven, till the tree could bear no more,
But dipped its top and set me down again.
That would be good both going and coming back.
One could do worse than be a swinger of birches.

FOR INQUIRIES, ORDERS, OR MORE INFORMATION:

www.cooksillustrated.com

At www.cooksillustrated.com, you can order books and subscriptions, sign up for our free e-newsletter, or renew your magazine subscription. Join the website and gain access to 15 years of *Cook's Illustrated* recipes, equipment tests, ingredient tastings, as well as *Cook's Live* companion videos for every recipe in this issue.

COOKBOOKS

We sell more than 50 cookbooks by the editors of *Cook's Illustrated*. To order, visit our bookstore at www.cooksillustrated.com or call 800-611-0759 (or 515-246-6911 from outside the U.S.).

COOK'S ILLUSTRATED Magazine

Cook's Illustrated magazine (ISSN 1068-2821), number 88, is published bimonthly by Boston Common Press Limited Partnership, 17 Station St., Brookline, MA 02445. Copyright 2007 Boston Common Press Limited Partnership. Periodicals postage paid at Boston, Mass., and additional mailing offices USPS #012487. Publications Mail Agreement No. 40020778. Return undeliverable Canadian addresses to P.O. Box 875, Station A, Windsor, Ontario N9A 6P2. POSTMASTER: Send address changes to Cook's Illustrated, P.O. Box 7446, Red Oak, IA 51591-0446. For subscription and gift subscription orders, subscription inquiries, or change-of-address notices, call 800-526-8442 in the U.S. or 515-247-7571 from outside the U.S., or write us at Cook's Illustrated, P.O. Box 7446, Red Oak, IA 51591-0446.

ILLUSTRATION: RANDY GLASS

NOTES FROM READERS

COMPILED BY SANDRA WU

Getting Sprinkles to Stick

When I make butter cookies, I have the hardest time getting decorating sugar or sprinkles to stick to the tops. Can you offer some tips?

DEBBIE LA ROCCA
ALBANY, N.Y.

Simply dusting decorating sugar or sprinkles on top of cookies prior to baking will not work: Most of the granules will fall off by the time the cookies are removed from the baking sheet. A moist surface is necessary to help bind the sugar to the relatively dry dough.

We applied several different liquids—water, beaten egg, cooking spray, and corn syrup—to the tops of butter cookies before sprinkling them with an even layer of colored sugar to find out which was the best adhesive. After removing the cookies from the oven and allowing them to cool, we turned them upside down and shook them lightly to gauge how well the sugar stuck. The water, egg, and cooking spray all did an equally good job; a negligible amount of sugar fell from these cookies. The sugar also stuck to the cookies brushed with corn syrup, but the tops of these cookies became unacceptably darker, crunchier, and sweeter.

We recommend the easiest method of all: Lightly brush the tops of unbaked butter cookies with water before applying decorations.

STICKY SITUATION
To prevent sprinkles from falling off (left), brush cookies with water, then decorate and bake (right).

Soy Sauce Storage

Where should I store a bottle of soy sauce once it's open: in the pantry or in the refrigerator?

ESTHER KANG
CHICAGO, ILL.

Soy sauce is a fermented liquid made from soybeans and roasted wheat. The labels for some brands suggest refrigerating the bottle after opening, and others have no storage information at all. Although soy sauce will not actually spoil if left out at room temperature—it contains high levels of salt, sugar, and acid that provide protection against bacterial growth—we wondered if its flavor would deteriorate over time.

To find out, we stored our recommended brands of soy sauce, Lee Kum Kee Tabletop Soy Sauce and Ohsawa Nama Shoyu Organic Unpasteurized Soy Sauce, two ways: in a cool, dry cupboard and in the refrigerator. After a month had passed, we held a blind tasting of the soy sauces served with steamed white rice. The results? Tasters strained to detect differences, and all of the samples were deemed satisfactory. Wondering if additional storage time would prove detrimental, we sealed the bottles back up, waited four more months, then tasted the soy sauces again. Tasters found both samples of the pasteurized Lee Kum Kee soy sauce completely acceptable, but it was a different story for the unpasteurized Ohsawa soy sauce, which had taken on a fermented, somewhat fishy flavor after sitting in a cupboard for several months. The refrigerated sample had a sweeter, mellower profile.

Our conclusion? It doesn't hurt to refrigerate pasteurized soy sauce (and most brands are pasteurized), but it isn't necessary. Unpasteurized soy sauce, on the other hand, should be refrigerated.

Storing Anchovies

Whenever I open a tin of anchovies to use in a recipe, I end up with a lot of leftovers. What's the best way to store them?

A. DIMASSI
TORONTO, ONTARIO

Unless you plan on making Caesar salad, anchovy pizza, and spaghetti puttanesca all on the same day, you'd be hard-pressed to use up an entire tin of anchovies without having to store them. To find the best method for keeping anchovies, we stored leftovers three ways: covered with extra-virgin olive oil and refrigerated in an airtight container; covered with kosher salt and refrigerated in an airtight container; and coiled up individually, frozen on a plate, transferred to a zipper-lock bag, and returned to the freezer.

After two weeks, we removed the anchovies from the olive oil; brushed, rinsed, and patted dry the anchovies that were covered in salt; and defrosted the anchovies that had been frozen. Next, we tasted these samples plain and in Caesar salad dressing; we also included a freshly opened can of anchovies in the lineup. The only unacceptable fish were those that had been covered in kosher salt. Rinsing had mellowed their flavor, and those areas that hadn't been adequately rinsed were unacceptably salty.

The fish stored in olive oil had flavor that was nearly as good as the freshly opened can, but digging the fillets out of the partially congealed oil and blotting off the excess was a bit of a hassle. The frozen-and-thawed anchovies also tasted nearly as good as the fresh fillets and were much easier to handle. So the next time you have leftover anchovies, freezing is the way to go.

GOT ANCHOVIES?
Leftovers can be coiled up and frozen in a zipper-lock bag.

Freezing Pizza Dough

I've seen pizza dough for sale at the supermarket, but I prefer to make my own. Can homemade pizza dough be frozen?

DAN PICKARD
SEATTLE, WASH.

To answer your question, we made our basic pizza dough recipe (May/June 1995)—which makes enough for two pizza crusts—and froze it at two stages: immediately after mixing the dough and after allowing the dough to fully rise. After we shaped the dough into balls, we wrapped them in plastic wrap coated with nonstick cooking spray, placed them in zipper-lock bags, and froze them. A few days later, we thawed both doughs on the countertop, letting the unrisen dough rise for the two hours specified in the recipe. Next, we shaped both batches of dough—in addition to a freshly made batch and refrigerated dough from the supermarket—topped them with tomato sauce and mozzarella cheese, and baked them at 500 degrees for 10 minutes.

Tasted side by side, one of the frozen versions was nearly as good as the freshly made dough: The dough that had been frozen after rising was easy to shape (the gluten strands had had ample time to relax), crisp on the outside, chewy in the middle, and fresh-tasting. The dough that had been frozen before rising, on the other hand, was flatter and slightly tough. The freezing step had

WHAT IS IT?

I found this item at a garage sale and bought it without knowing what it's used for. Can you help me figure it out?

JANINE LEW
TEMPLE CITY, CALIF.

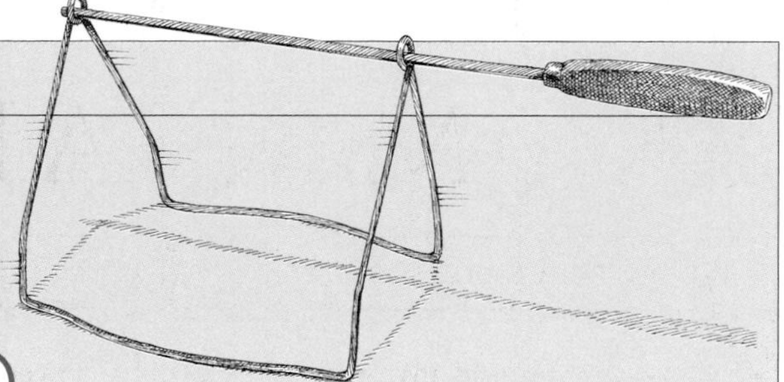

The vintage Pi-On Lifter is a cool tool for picking up hot pies and cakes.

The gadget you bought is a 1940s-era enameled wood and metal Pi-On Lifter from Wheeling, W.Va. This 13¼-inch device was used as an aid for picking up hot-from-the-oven pie plates and cake pans, providing a better grip than oven mitt–clad hands and reducing the risk of burns.

The instruction booklet touts the tool as being so simple that "a child can operate it," and it is indeed a cinch to use. To employ the Pi-On Lifter, hold the handle and twist it so that the free arm opens (one arm remains stationary). Hook the arms underneath the rim of the cake pan or pie plate and lift the pan up. The weight of the pie or cake will keep the Pi-On Lifter in place as dessert is transferred out of the oven and onto a cooling rack. To remove the lifter, simply twist the handle slightly to open the arms back up.

killed many of the yeast cells, resulting in a partially arrested rise and lackluster crust. Finally, the store-bought pizza dough received surprisingly good ratings from tasters.

If you have extra dough you'd like to keep around for later, be sure to let it rise fully before freezing. The best way to defrost dough is to let it sit on the countertop for a couple of hours or overnight in the refrigerator. (Thawing pizza dough in a microwave or low oven isn't recommended as it will dry the dough out.) And for last-minute pizza cravings, store-bought refrigerated dough is an entirely acceptable option.

Soaking Dried Mushrooms

Recipes that call for dried mushrooms often require soaking the mushrooms before use. For soups, isn't it fine to throw in the dried mushrooms as is, without the extra step of soaking?

SUSANNA LAAKSONEN
RICHMOND, CALIF.

➢Soaking dried mushrooms before cooking with them serves two purposes: First, it helps release dirt that can get stuck between the gills when the mushrooms are dried (rinsing them under cold running water doesn't always remove all of the dirt). Second, if you want to use dried mushrooms in minced form, they often require soaking before they can be properly chopped. This is especially true with potent dried porcini mushrooms, which are hardly ever used in the large slices in which they are sold. Therefore, we don't recommend adding dried, unsoaked mushrooms to any recipe, including soup. Be sure to save the flavorful soaking liquid; once filtered, it can be used to add mushroom essence to the recipe.

Best Way to Boil Potatoes

Is it important to start with cold water when boiling potatoes?

NANCY HANN
INDIANAPOLIS, IND.

➢Many cookbook authors suggest starting potatoes in cold, rather than boiling, water. The theory: Because potatoes take a while to cook, their exteriors tend to become mushy by the time their interiors cook through. Starting the potatoes in cold water allows their temperature to gradually increase, preventing excess softening of the exterior. We put the theory to the test by preparing plain whole unpeeled boiled potatoes, mashed potatoes (made with whole unpeeled potatoes that were boiled), and potato salad (made with potatoes that were peeled and cut into ¾-inch cubes before boiling) both ways—started in boiling water and kept at a simmer and started in cold water that was brought to a boil and lowered to a simmer—to see if one method was indeed better than the other.

Once the cubed potato pieces were cooled and tossed with mayonnaise and seasonings for the potato salad and the whole potatoes were peeled, pressed through a ricer, and combined with half-and-half and melted butter for the mashed potatoes, no differences between the two samples could be detected. In the case of the plain boiled whole potatoes, we did notice that the samples started in boiling water were softer on the exterior than on the interior. These boiled potatoes weren't terrible, but they weren't as good as the ones started in cold water.

In addition to slightly better texture in one test, the potatoes started in cold water were ready a few minutes earlier. Yes, the potatoes added to boiling water spent less time in the pot, but we had to wait for the water to boil before we could cook the potatoes. The bottom line is that starting the potatoes in cold water yields slightly better results in some applications and is always faster.

Refreshing Herbs

I've heard that it's better to refresh wilted herbs in tepid water rather than in cold water. Is this true?

TIM PIERSON
ABERDEEN, S.D.

➢After purposely letting several bunches of parsley, cilantro, and mint sit in the refrigerator until they became limp, sorry-looking versions of their former selves, we tried bringing the herbs back to life by soaking them in water. Soaking herbs in water restores the turgor pressure (the pressure of the cell contents against the cell wall), causing them to become firmer as the dehydrated cells plump up. This gives the herbs a fresher look and an improved texture, at least temporarily.

We divided each of the herbs into three smaller bunches, lopped off the stem ends, and soaked them in tepid and cold water. After 10 minutes, we removed the herbs from the water, spun them dry in a salad spinner, and compared them with the unsoaked samples.

All of the refreshed samples looked noticeably fresher than the originals, but some were clearly better than the others: The herbs soaked in standard cold tap water had perked up significantly and looked nearly as good as fresh. The herbs soaked in tepid water remained fairly droopy and resumed wilting a few minutes after being taken out of the water. The tepid water was less effective than the cold water because the enzymes that cause the breakdown of the cell walls become more active as the temperature rises.

We wondered if soaking the herbs in a solution of salt water or sugar water might yield an even better result. Neither worked any better than the plain cold-water soaking. In fact, they looked even more wilted. So to rejuvenate spent herbs, simply trim the stems and soak them for 10 minutes in cold water.

QUICK REJUVENATION
Old herbs (left) get a new life (right) after being refreshed in cold water for just 10 minutes.

SEND US YOUR QUESTIONS We will provide a complimentary one-year subscription for each letter we print. Send your inquiry, name, address, and daytime telephone number to Notes from Readers, Cook's Illustrated, P.O. Box 470589, Brookline, MA 02447, or to notesfromreaders@americastestkitchen.com.

ILLUSTRATION: JOHN BURGOYNE

Quick Tips

COMPILED BY DAVID PAZMIÑO

Proofing Bread Dough

Laura Liu of Brooklyn, N.Y., had trouble telling when her bread dough had properly risen inside a sloped bowl, so she came up with the following trick. Lightly spray a slow-cooker insert with nonstick cooking spray. Place the dough in the insert and cover until it has risen. The straight sides and glass lid of the insert allow the baker to easily gauge the dough's progress.

Securing Electric Cords

Marnie Drager of San Bernardino, Calif., found an inexpensive way to neatly contain appliance cords on her kitchen counter. Bundle the cord, then feed it into an empty cardboard toilet paper roll.

Rejuvenating Celery

Over time, even the crispest celery becomes limp. Mary Kariotis of Randallstown, Md., offers a simple technique for refreshing lifeless stalks.

1. Trim and discard the bottom end of each celery stalk.
2. Place the stalks cut-side down in a tall, narrow container with at least 2 inches of water. Refrigerate until the stalks are crisp and sprightly, six to 12 hours.

Saving Leftover Wine

Recorking a wine bottle to preserve leftovers can be a challenge if the cork no longer fits into the neck of the bottle. Dwight Collin of Pittsford, N.Y., uses his Microplane grater to shave off a portion of the cork so that it can be easily reinserted into the bottle.

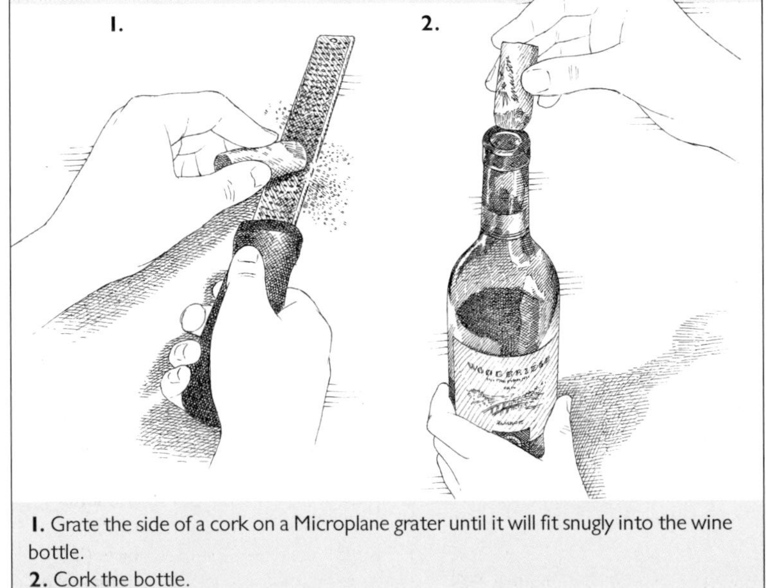

1. Grate the side of a cork on a Microplane grater until it will fit snugly into the wine bottle.
2. Cork the bottle.

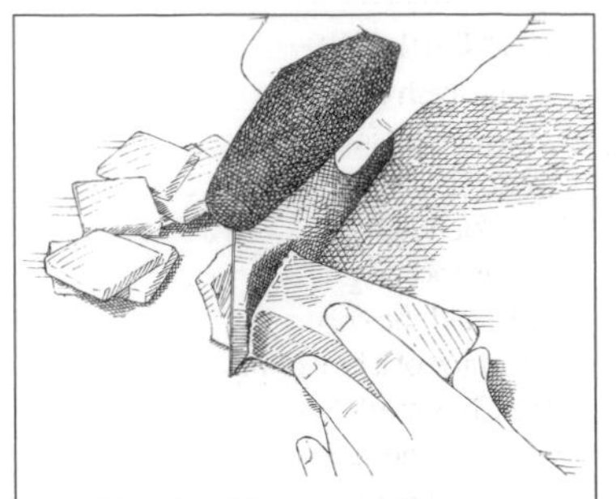

Better Butter Cutting

Cutting butter with a chef's knife can be a slippery proposition. Using butter straight from the refrigerator, Deborah Nelson of Lawrence, Kan., employs the sharp edge of a metal bench scraper to cut butter into uniform pieces.

No More Soggy Cheesecake

After refrigerating a baked and cooled cheesecake, Lori Johnson of Nordland, Wash., always found that unwanted moisture collected on the top of the cake, ruining her creation. Her solution is to arrange a layer of paper towels over the cheesecake before covering it with plastic wrap and refrigerating.

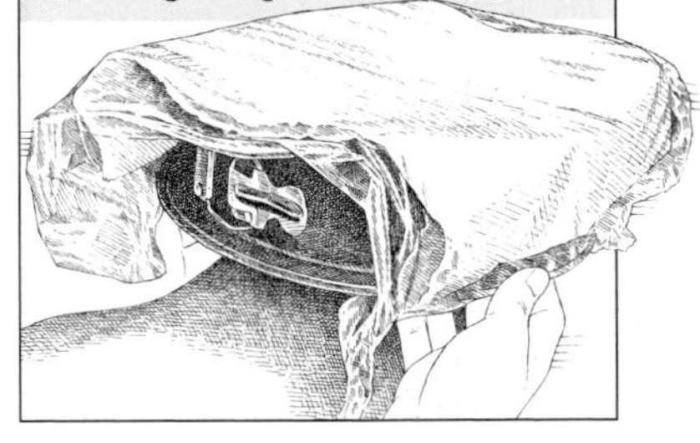

Cleaning Up Spills

Minor spills are a frequent occurrence in most kitchens. Roman Lasek of Berkeley, Calif., offers the following trick for keeping counters tidy. Use the small rimmed baking sheet from a toaster oven as a miniature dust pan, holding the pan under the edge of the counter and sweeping spilled food onto it for disposal.

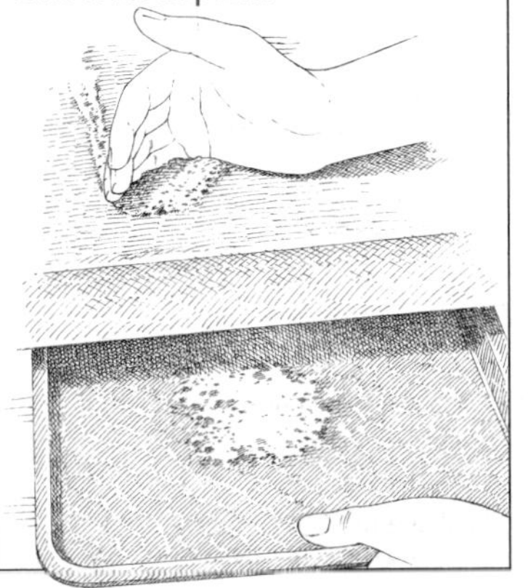

Send Us Your Tip We will provide a complimentary one-year subscription for each tip we print. Send your tip, name, and address to Quick Tips, Cook's Illustrated, P.O. Box 470589, Brookline, MA 02447, or to quicktips@americastestkitchen.com.

ILLUSTRATION: JOHN BURGOYNE

Safer Chile Handling

Mincing fresh chiles can lead to hand burns that last for hours. Tired of fiery fingers, Ellen Watson of Sacramento, Calif., found protection in a grater and a zipper-lock bag. Using the bag as a glove, hold the chile and grate it along the surface of a box or Microplane grater. This method doesn't allow you to remove the seeds, so you will get maximum heat from chiles prepared this way.

Cleaning and Drying Mushrooms

Some batches of mushrooms are so dirty that a cloth won't adequately clean them. Washing the mushrooms is a must, as is drying them. Riga Krienhoefer of Boise, Idaho, pulls out her salad spinner to perform both tasks.

1. Place the mushrooms in a salad spinner basket and spray with water until the dirt is removed.
2. Quickly place the basket into the salad spinner and spin the mushrooms dry.

Disposable Vegetable Scrubber

Finding herself in a kitchen without a vegetable scrubber, Carol Alexander of Charlottesville, Va., designed a homemade substitute.

1. Fold an empty perforated onion or citrus bag to form a compact shape, then secure it with a rubber band.
2. Use the scrubber to clean vegetables under cool running water, then discard the scrubber.

Impromptu Pan Lid

Finding himself short of lids to fit his skillets and sauté pans, Greg Evans of Jericho, N.Y., created a clever stand-in. Cover a splatter screen with two layers of aluminum foil, then place it on top of the skillet.

Powder-Free Chocolate

When chopped into chunks for cookies or bars, chocolate often shatters, leaving behind shavings and powder. Todd Nystul of Baltimore, Md., uses his microwave to solve the problem.

1. Place the chocolate bar on a microwave-safe plate and microwave on the lowest setting for about one minute, turning the chocolate halfway through. When the chocolate softens and begins to melt at the corners, remove it from the microwave. (If the chocolate bar is very thick, it may take longer to soften.)
2. Place the warm chocolate on a cutting board and chop it into chunks.

Makeshift Sifter

Using a small fine-mesh strainer to sift several cups of flour or confectioners' sugar often results in a powdery mess. Hanna Coleman of Potomac, Md., keeps her work space clean with the help of plastic wrap and a rubber band.

1. Place a small fine-mesh strainer over a small bowl to prevent it from tipping. Fill the strainer with flour or confectioners' sugar, cover with plastic wrap, and secure with a rubber band.
2. Shake the sifter over the bowl or dessert.

Pitting Olives

The most common way to remove pits from olives without an olive pitter is to smash them on a cutting board. Marci Abbrecht of Wellesley, Mass., came up with a more elegant—and equally effective—alternative. Place a funnel upside down on the work surface. Stand one end of the olive on the spout and press down, allowing the pit to fall through the funnel.

Skillet-Barbecued Pork Chops

The smoky, salty-sweet, charred flavor of grilled pork chops is easy to get on an outdoor grill. We wanted to bring that flavor indoors—keeping the smokiness but losing the smoke.

BY J. KENJI ALT

To enjoy the charred, salty-sweet flavor of grilled pork chops coated with spicy barbecue sauce in the off-season, I have two options: go to a restaurant with an indoor grill or attempt to make them in my own kitchen. Getting smoky flavor into the chops is almost assured when cooking over a live fire outdoors. Back inside, it can be more elusive.

Double-searing creates a charred, grill-like crust on pork chops.

Rubbing It In

The first order of business was to find a way of giving the pork a nice, evenly charred surface without overcooking the interior. I tried searing the chops in a blazing hot skillet and then turning the heat way down once they developed a good crust, a method I've used to good effect with steak and lamb chops. Aside from the fact that this technique filled the test kitchen with billowing smoke and splattered oil, the pork ended up stringy by the time a well-charred crust had developed. The problem? Pork chops are leaner than steaks and lamb chops and therefore more prone to drying out. Brining improved matters a bit, but it was clear that my technique was going to need an overhaul. Since I've successfully cooked charred, juicy pork chops on an outdoor grill, I wondered what was so different about cooking in a skillet.

For one thing, a piece of meat elevated above the heat source on a grill doesn't remain in contact with the juices released during cooking. In a pan, pork chops end up simmering in their own juices, which lowers the temperature of the cooking surface, leading to meat that overcooks before it can brown properly. If I couldn't get the pork itself to char, why not add another element that would char instead? I realized that there was already an outdoor technique that would accomplish this exact goal—the dry spice rub.

Though standard fare for a grill, a spice rub is rarely applied to meat cooked in a skillet—in a hot skillet, the rub (which darkens more readily than the pork proteins) doesn't just char, it blackens. But by starting with medium heat rather than high, I found I could let the spice rub char while the pork cooked at a gentler pace, which resulted in chops that were perfectly cooked both inside and out. Lowering the heat serendipitously solved my smoky kitchen problem, as well.

Smoking the Sauce

I turned my attention to the barbecue sauce. Starting with the requisite ketchup and molasses, I ran through a battery of taste tests. Hits of Worcestershire sauce and Dijon mustard gave the sauce complexity and heat, and onions and cider vinegar added a pungent kick. A spoonful of brown sugar helped mellow out and blend the sharper flavors. I figured a couple of teaspoons of my dry spice rub added to my sauce could only improve its flavor. Tasters confirmed my hunch.

Although my sauce was now balanced, I felt it needed more outdoor flavor. Without the benefit of a live fire with smoldering hickory chips, I had only one place to turn: liquid smoke. In the test kitchen, we generally shun artificial or synthetic ingredients, so I was pleased to learn that liquid smoke is a completely natural product (see "Smoke in the Water," page 30). All suspicions were laid to rest when a batch of sauce to which I had surreptitiously added a teaspoon of liquid smoke swept the next blind tasting. The key to keeping liquid smoke palatable is moderation.

Now I had my charred pork and my smoky sauce, but I also had a problem. I had been ignoring something every good outdoor cook knows: The sauce is not merely an accompaniment to the meat—it's an essential part of the cooking process. I had been treating the chops and the sauce as two discrete elements rather than parts of the same entity, applying the sauce only after the meat had been fully cooked. On an outdoor grill, the sauce caramelizes and intensifies, lacquering the chops in a sticky glaze. Could I re-create this process on my stovetop without ruining my pans and splattering hot barbecue sauce all over the kitchen?

Brushing the sauce directly onto the chops while they were still in the pan produced a sticky,

---

SHOPPING: **What's in the Package?**

Given the number of chops we went through to develop this recipe, we thought purchasing "family size" packs of pork chops would be the logical choice, but we ran into some unpleasant surprises at the bottom of the package.

LOOKS LIKE A GOOD VALUE
The chops on top look good, but beware of what lies beneath.

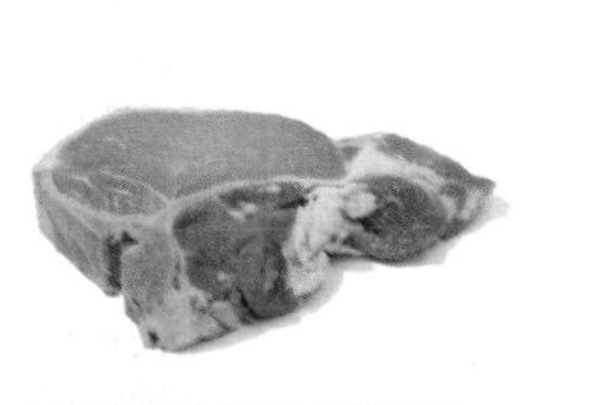

HIDDEN SURPRISES
The chops they don't want you to see are gristly and unevenly butchered.

BEST BET
Choose a smaller package in which the meat is laid in a single layer so you can see what you are paying for.

PHOTOGRAPHY: DANIEL J. VAN ACKERE

burnt mess and a stovetop splattered with sauce. What if instead of bringing the sauce to the pork, I brought the pork to the sauce? I cooked up a new batch of chops, this time removing them from the pan a few minutes early. After transferring the pork chops to a baking sheet, I brushed them with a thin coat of barbecue sauce and wiped out the skillet so I could finish cooking with a clean, hot surface. When the pork chops sizzled vigorously as they went back into the hot pan for their second sear, my hopes were high.

I flipped the chops and saw that the sauce had reduced to a sticky, smoky, caramelized glaze that firmly adhered to the meat. Served with the remaining reduced sauce, these skillet-barbecued pork chops with a rib-sticking sauce finally tasted like the real deal.

AT A GLANCE | BUILDING OUTDOOR FLAVOR ON THE STOVETOP

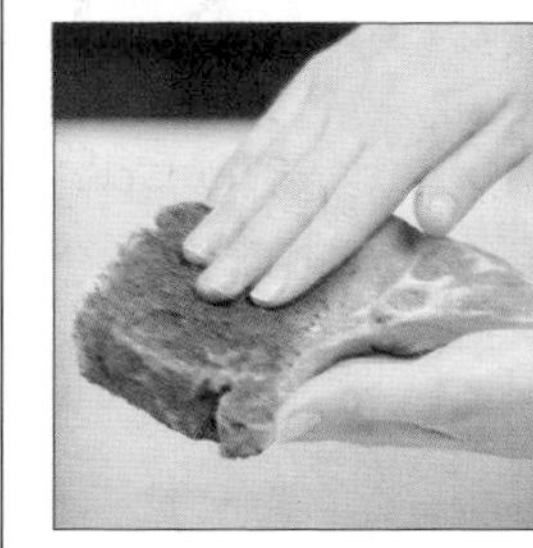

1. APPLY RUB
After brining chops, coat both sides with dry spice rub, pressing gently to adhere.

2. ADD SMOKE
Combine sauce ingredients, including 1 teaspoon of liquid smoke.

3. SEAR CHOPS
Place chops in skillet and don't move them until charred black spots develop.

4. BRUSH AND SEAR
Remove chops from pan, brush with sauce, and sear again to lacquer sauce onto the chops.

SKILLET-BARBECUED PORK CHOPS

SERVES 4

We prefer natural to enhanced pork (pork that has been injected with a salt solution to increase moistness and flavor) for this recipe, though enhanced pork can be used. If using enhanced pork, skip the brining in step 1 and add ½ teaspoon salt to the spice rub. Grate the onion on the large holes of a box grater. In step 5, check your chops after 3 minutes. If you don't hear a definite sizzle and the chops have not started to brown on the underside, increase the heat to medium-high and continue cooking as directed (follow indicated temperatures for remainder of recipe).

Pork Chops

- ½ cup table salt
- 4 bone-in pork rib chops, ¾ to 1 inch thick (8 to 10 ounces each), trimmed of excess fat, sides slit according to illustration at right (see note above)
- 4 teaspoons vegetable oil

Spice Rub

- 1 tablespoon paprika
- 1 tablespoon brown sugar
- 2 teaspoons ground coriander
- 1 teaspoon ground cumin
- 1 teaspoon ground black pepper

Sauce

- ½ cup ketchup
- 3 tablespoons light or mild molasses
- 2 tablespoons grated onion (see note above)
- 2 tablespoons Worcestershire sauce
- 2 tablespoons Dijon mustard
- 1 tablespoon cider vinegar
- 1 tablespoon brown sugar
- 1 teaspoon liquid smoke

1. **FOR THE PORK CHOPS:** Dissolve salt in 2 quarts water in large bowl or container. Submerge chops in brine, cover with plastic wrap, and refrigerate for 30 minutes.

2. **FOR THE SPICE RUB:** Combine ingredients in small bowl. Measure 2 teaspoons mixture into medium bowl and set aside for sauce. Transfer remaining spice rub to pie plate or large plate.

3. **FOR THE SAUCE:** Whisk ingredients in bowl with reserved spice mixture; set aside.

4. **TO COOK CHOPS:** Remove chops from brine and pat dry with paper towels. Coat both sides of chops with spice rub, pressing gently so rub adheres. Pat chops to remove excess rub; discard excess rub.

5. Heat 1 tablespoon oil in 12-inch heavy-bottomed nonstick skillet over medium heat until just smoking. Following illustration below, place chops in skillet in pinwheel formation; cook until charred in spots, 5 to 8 minutes. Flip chops and continue to cook until second side is browned and charred and center of chop registers 130 degrees on instant-read thermometer, 4 to 8 minutes. Remove skillet from heat and transfer chops to clean plate or baking sheet. Lightly brush top side of each chop with 2 teaspoons sauce.

6. Wipe out pan with paper towels and return to medium heat. Add remaining teaspoon oil and heat until just smoking. Add chops to pan, sauce-side down, and cook without moving until sauce has caramelized and charred in spots, about 1 minute. While cooking, lightly brush top side of each chop with 2 teaspoons sauce. Turn chops and cook until second side is charred and caramelized and center of chops registers 140 degrees on instant-read thermometer, 1 to 1½ minutes.

7. Transfer chops back to plate or baking sheet, tent with foil, and let rest 5 minutes. Internal temperature should rise to about 145 degrees. Meanwhile, add remaining sauce to pan and cook, scraping pan bottom, until thickened to ketchup-like consistency and reduced to ⅔ cup, about 3 minutes. Brush each chop with 1 tablespoon reduced sauce and serve immediately, passing remaining sauce at table.

TECHNIQUE | SEARING CHOPS

Getting pork chops to lie flat and cook evenly requires two simple techniques.

PROBLEM: Pork chops buckle during cooking.
SOLUTION: Cut two slits about 2 inches apart through fat and connective tissue.

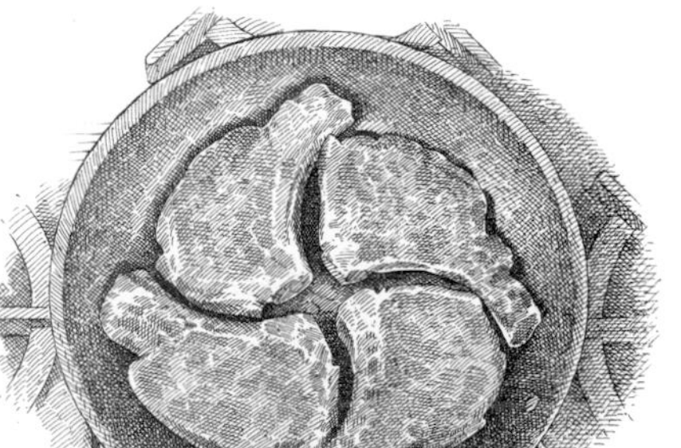

PROBLEM: Pork chops don't fit in pan.
SOLUTION: Arrange pork chops in pinwheel pattern with tips of ribs pointing toward edge of pan.

COOK'S LIVE Original Test Kitchen Videos
www.cooksillustrated.com

RECIPE IN 60 SECONDS
- Skillet-Barbecued Pork Chops

VIDEO TIPS
- What kind of pork chops should I buy?
- Should I buy enhanced pork?
- How can I protect my nonstick pans?

ILLUSTRATION: JOHN BURGOYNE

Quicker Beef Vegetable Soup

We found a faster path to a full-flavored soup.

BY DAVID PAZMIÑO

Given enough meat, bones, and time, a great beef soup isn't all that hard to make. Our Rich Beef Stock and Beef Noodle Soup (January/February 1998) are perfect examples. If you're willing to buy 6 pounds of beef shin meat and bones and invest 2½ hours, you can produce a fantastic stock (and a lot of leftover beef). Add another hour or so, and you have the ultimate beef soup. But I rarely have the time or energy to make this recipe.

When I want beef and vegetable soup in a hurry, I do what everyone else does—I open a can of soup and complain about its lackluster flavor. But is this all-or-nothing approach really necessary? Could I collapse the two separate steps of making stock and then soup into one and develop bold beef flavor in just 60 minutes?

To get my bearings, I prepared several traditional recipes (including ours) along with a handful of quick recipes. While every classic recipe yielded intense flavor, the quick soups were uniformly disappointing and lacked any real beef flavor. Most used either cubes of "stew meat"—a butcher's catchall for any relatively chunky scraps of beef—or more tender cuts like strip steak or rib eye. Although stew meat contributed a pleasant beefy flavor, it was barely chewable after simmering for half an hour. The strip and rib eye, though more tender, tasted livery and had a chalky, dry texture. My first and most important goal was to find a cut of meat that could give a quick beef and vegetable soup the same texture and flavor as one that cooked for hours.

A Tale of Two Meats

We tested nearly a dozen cuts of beef before settling on sirloin tip steaks as the best choice for our quick soup. Texture was a deciding factor.

TOO DENSE
Tender cuts such as strip steak and rib eye become tough, livery, and chalky when simmered in soup.

LOOSE AND TENDER
Cuts with a loose structure, such as sirloin tip steaks, give the impression that the meat has cooked for hours.

This hearty soup makes a meal and is ready in just 60 minutes.

What's the Beef?

Tasters praised the fall-apart tenderness of the shin meat in our original Beef Noodle Soup recipe, but it took hours to break down those tougher muscle fibers into anything remotely tender. After pulling out my diagrams for beef cuts, I tried to find a cut of meat that had the same textural characteristics of the shin meat but would cook in a quarter of the time. I cooked through various cuts, chasing them around the chart as if it was a carousel. I discovered that those with a loose, open grain—including hanger steak, flank steak, sirloin tip steak (or flap meat), and blade steak—had a shredded texture that fooled tasters into thinking I had cooked the meat for hours.

Of these four cuts, sirloin tip steaks offered the best balance of meaty flavor and tenderness. I just had to be careful how I cut the steaks. If the meat was cut too large, my soup seemed more like a stew. If I used too many small pieces, it resembled a watery chili. For six generous bowls of soup, I needed 1 pound of sirloin tip steaks cut into ½-inch pieces.

A Better Broth

I had found a cut of beef that cooked quickly and had the right texture, but it didn't do much for the rest of the soup. I would have to start with store-bought broth and engage in some serious flavor doctoring.

I tried reducing the broth to fortify its flavor, but when simmered by half, it turned ultra-salty and made the soup so harsh that many tasters mistook it for canned. I was getting nowhere fast.

Several of the quick soup recipes I uncovered took an "everything but the kitchen sink" approach to the vegetables. While these soups had flavor, it certainly wasn't beef flavor. I had better luck sticking to the basics: onions, carrots, and celery—safe, yes; exciting, not very. Then I remembered that many recipes for French onion soup rely on mountains of caramelized onions to up the meaty flavor of the broth. The liquid and sugars released by the onions leave a rich brown coating on the pan, contributing a depth of flavor that onions simply simmered in the broth can't attain. When I tested this idea, tasters praised the added complexity and sweetness, but I still had a long way to go.

It was time to do some research into what constitutes beefy flavor. I discovered that beef flavor is accentuated by naturally occurring compounds called glutamates, which are found in numerous foods (see "In Search of Glutamates," page 9). Like salt, glutamates stimulate receptors on the tongue, making food taste richer and meatier. Mushrooms, it turns out, are high in glutamates and for that reason are often paired with (or even substituted for) beef in many dishes. Thinking this might help, I prepared soups with white button, portobello, cremini, and porcini mushrooms. Portobellos imparted an overly murky flavor, and earthy porcinis overwhelmed any beef flavor I had already developed. Utilitarian white buttons were OK but a bit bland. Cremini mushrooms were perfect, providing mushroom intensity without being obtrusive.

I wondered what other ingredients high in glutamates could do. Worcestershire sauce, Parmesan cheese rinds, and miso paste competed with the beefiness of the dish. Less-intense tomato paste and red wine boosted the soup's meaty notes,

PHOTOGRAPHY: CARL TREMBLAY

TECHNIQUE |

THE FLAVOR BASE BEGINS

Before the beef is added to the pot, create a flavor base by browning chopped onions and cremini mushrooms. Stir frequently until the onions are really brown and dark bits form on the pan bottom. Don't shortcut this process or you will rob your soup of flavor.

especially when I browned the tomato paste with the meat and then deglazed the caramelized pan drippings with the red wine.

Though soy sauce is especially high in glutamates, I feared it might overpower the soup. But, to my surprise, it enhanced the beef flavor. I remembered, too, that soy sauce is a test kitchen favorite for quick marinades. Like a brine, the salt in soy sauce diffuses into the meat, allowing the individual muscle fibers to retain moisture while cooking. When I marinated the beef cubes with soy sauce for just 15 minutes, tasters commented on the improved flavor of the meat and also its softer texture.

My Soup Begins to Gel

I had now replicated the beef flavor of long-simmered soups but not the mouth-coating richness. This can only be created when collagen, the tough proteins in the meat and bones, breaks down into gelatin. Could I cheat and just add powdered gelatin instead? A tablespoon of gelatin softened in cold water and stirred into the finished soup provided the viscosity of traditional broths. This was an unlikely finish to a recipe that can stand up to soups that take hours to cook.

BEEF AND VEGETABLE SOUP

SERVES 6

Choose whole sirloin tip steaks over ones that have been cut into small pieces for stir-fries. If sirloin tip steaks are unavailable, substitute blade or flank steak, removing any hard gristle or excess fat. Button mushrooms can be used in place of the cremini mushrooms, with some trade-off in flavor. Our preferred brand of beef broth is Pacific. If you like, add 1 cup of frozen peas, frozen corn, or frozen cut green beans during the last 5 minutes of cooking. For a heartier soup, add 10 ounces of red-skinned potatoes, cut into ½-inch pieces (2 cups), during the last 15 minutes of cooking.

- 1 pound sirloin tip steaks, trimmed of excess fat and cut into ½-inch pieces (see note above)
- 2 tablespoons soy sauce
- 1 teaspoon vegetable oil
- 1 pound cremini mushrooms, stems trimmed, caps wiped clean and quartered
- 1 large onion, chopped medium (about 1½ cups)
- 2 tablespoons tomato paste
- 1 medium garlic clove, minced or pressed through garlic press (about 1 teaspoon)
- ½ cup red wine
- 4 cups beef broth (see note above)
- 1¾ cups low-sodium chicken broth
- 4 medium carrots, peeled and cut into ½-inch pieces (about 2 cups)
- 2 medium celery ribs, cut into ½-inch pieces (about ¾ cup)
- 1 bay leaf
- 1 tablespoon unflavored powdered gelatin
- ½ cup cold water
- 2 tablespoons minced fresh parsley leaves
- Table salt and ground black pepper

1. Combine beef and soy sauce in medium bowl; set aside for 15 minutes.

2. Heat oil in large Dutch oven over medium-high heat until just smoking. Add mushrooms and onion; cook, stirring frequently, until onion pieces are brown and dark bits form on pan bottom, 8 to 12 minutes. Transfer vegetables to bowl.

3. Add beef and cook, stirring occasionally, until liquid evaporates and meat starts to brown, 6 to 10 minutes. Add tomato paste and garlic; cook, stirring constantly, until aromatic, about 30 seconds. Add red wine, scraping bottom of pot with wooden spoon to loosen browned bits, and cook until syrupy, 1 to 2 minutes.

4. Add beef broth, chicken broth, carrots, celery, bay leaf, and browned mushrooms and onion; bring to boil. Reduce heat to low, cover, and simmer until vegetables and meat are tender, 25 to 30 minutes. While soup is simmering, sprinkle gelatin over cold water and let stand.

5. When soup is finished, turn off heat. Remove bay leaf. Add gelatin mixture and stir until completely dissolved. Stir in parsley; adjust seasonings with salt and pepper, and serve.

SCIENCE:

In Search of Glutamates

In grade school, we all learned that we experience four primary taste sensations: salty, sweet, bitter, and sour. But what makes savory foods taste meaty? Japanese physics professor Kidunae Ikeda answered this question in 1909 when he extracted a white compound from the giant sea kelp used to give Japanese broths a savory and meaty flavor, even when meat is absent. This substance, called glutamate, has been found to stimulate the tongue's taste receptors, just like salt and sugar. Ikeda named the resulting sensation *umami*, which translates as "deliciousness" and "savory." The American cook interprets this as "full," "meaty," and "robust." Naturally occurring glutamates are found in a wide variety of foods, some of which I used in my Beef and Vegetable Soup. –D.P.

GLUTAMATES IN COMMON FOODS

This scale shows the milligrams of glutamates per 100 grams (3½ ounces).

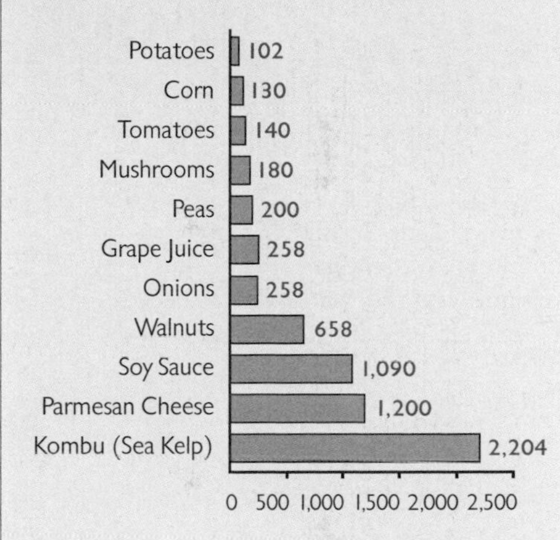

Building Meaty Flavor Quickly

These four glutamate-rich ingredients boosted meaty flavors in our quick soup.

MUSHROOMS
Sautéed cremini mushrooms begin to build flavor.

TOMATO PASTE
Thick tomato paste caramelizes in the pot to create more flavor.

SOY SAUCE
Strips of beef are marinated in soy sauce before being browned.

RED WINE
Red wine helps loosen flavorful browned bits from the pan bottom.

COOK'S LIVE Original Test Kitchen Videos

www.cooksillustrated.com

RECIPE IN 60 SECONDS
- Beef and Vegetable Soup

VIDEO TIP
- What's the right cut of beef for a quick soup?

Grilled Stuffed Pork Loin

Our moist stuffing works from the inside out to combat dryness in lean pork.

BY MATTHEW CARD

I'm fond of the meaty texture and moderate price of pork loin, but I'm annoyed by its tendency toward dryness. Most grilled pork loin recipes try to compensate with some combination of brining (soaking the meat in a salt-and-sugar solution prior to cooking), rubs, sauces, or condiments, but I was intrigued by something a little different: a stuffing. In theory, a rich filling could keep the loin moist and add aesthetic appeal to the otherwise plain-Jane cut of meat.

A spiced apple filling adds flavor and moisture to a lean pork loin.

Slice and Roll

In the test kitchen, we typically favor the blade-end pork roast for grilling because of its abundant fat. However, this asset became a liability when I tried to stuff a blade roast. As soon as I split it open, the meat fell apart into a lumpy mess of muscle, sinew, and fat. A center-cut loin roast proved the better choice because this solid muscle cut cleanly, but its leanness worried me.

I explored a variety of approaches to the stuffing, including recipes based on cheeses, cured meats, bread crumbs, and herbs. Most of the fillings oozed free of the roast, turned mushy, or were bland, but a chutney-like blend of dried fruits, spices, sugar, and vinegar caught my attention. Its flavor was unbalanced and its texture was dusty from dried spices, but the fruit's dense, chewy consistency and deep flavor were well suited to the pork, and the stuffing stayed put.

After testing various combinations of dried fruits, my tasters proclaimed apples and cranberries the perfect pairing. I poached the fruit in a blend of apple cider and apple cider vinegar until tender, then added cayenne, allspice, and grated fresh ginger. Brown sugar trumped white sugar and honey, and sliced shallot and mustard seeds added just the right zip to both the fruit and the pork. I strained off the excess poaching liquid to prevent the filling from being too wet, then ground the mixture to a coarse paste in the food processor.

Stuck in the Middle

How, exactly, do you stuff a pork loin? One popular method involves slicing the meat into a broad sheet onto which the filling is spread before the pork is rolled up tightly, like a jellyroll. Butchers call this a roll cut, and it sounds easy enough, but I found the knife work tricky. My early attempts looked amateurish, so I rethought the approach. I regarded the loin as more square than cylindrical and saw that just three or four straight, short cuts, like a triple butterfly (see illustrations on page 11), could produce the same results. Gentle persuasion with a meat pounder evened out any nicks and unevenness to give me a long, flat sheet that was easy to fill and roll up. Snugly tying up the rolled roast ensured a compact shape that cooked evenly and sliced easily.

To this point, I'd yet to try brining the roast. I hoped the filling would make brining redundant, and tests proved this to be the case. In fact, a stuffed and brined roast was, if possible, too moist. Turns out I'd made an unexpected scientific discovery, one our science editor confirmed. His analysis: Because the meat was sliced so thin (just ½ inch thick), the acids in the filling were denaturing the proteins in the meat and helping them hold onto moisture. The effects of acids on meat are limited to the area near the surface, so they don't usually do much for a thick pork loin. However, in this recipe, the entire roast was "surface," so I was essentially marinating the meat from the inside out.

Building a Burnished Exterior

To coax even more flavor out of the roast, most recipes sear the meat before or after cooking it, but my attempts to sear this leaner cut of pork left me with a tough exterior. I tried a variety of spice rubs but found them overpowering. A liberal coating of salt and pepper was more than sufficient.

Finally, I remembered our Maple-Glazed Pork Roast recipe (March/April 2003), in which the meat is rolled in the glaze after roasting. Didn't I have leftover liquid from preparing the filling? I reduced the sticky-sweet, spiced blend of sugar, cider, and vinegar down to a thick, spreadable consistency and lacquered the loin during its last few minutes on the grill. The mahogany glaze not only improved the look of the roast, it sharpened the flavor of the pork and filling alike.

SHOPPING: Not All Pork Loins Can Be Stuffed

Center-cut roasts come in various shapes, some of which are not suited to stuffing. Here's what to look for (and what to avoid).

LONG AND THIN
This roast is 12 inches long and just 3 inches wide . . .

TOO LITTLE ROOM
. . . so there's not much surface area for the stuffing.

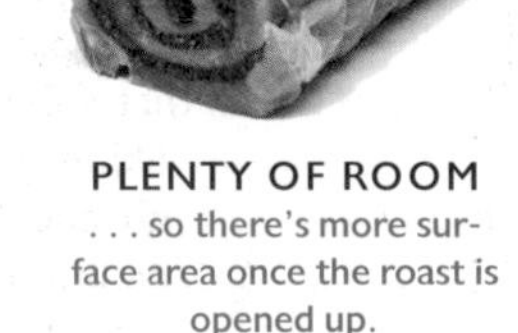

SHORT AND WIDE
This roast is just 8 inches long and nearly 5 inches wide . . .

PLENTY OF ROOM
. . . so there's more surface area once the roast is opened up.

PHOTOGRAPHY: CARL TREMBLAY

GRILLED PORK LOIN WITH APPLE-CRANBERRY FILLING

SERVES 6

This recipe is best prepared with a loin that is 7 to 8 inches long and 4 to 5 inches wide. To make cutting the pork easier, freeze it for 30 minutes. If mustard seeds are unavailable, stir an equal amount of whole-grain mustard into the filling after the apples have been processed. The pork loin can be stuffed and tied a day ahead of time, but don't season the exterior until you are ready to grill. Our recipe for Grilled Pork Loin with Apple-Cherry Filling with Caraway is available free at www.cooksillustrated.com/october.

Filling

- 1 cup apple cider
- ½ cup cider vinegar
- ¾ cup (5¼ ounces) packed light brown sugar
- 1 large shallot, halved lengthwise and sliced thin crosswise (about ¼ cup)
- 1½ cups (4 ounces) packed dried apples
- ½ cup (2½ ounces) packed dried cranberries
- 1 tablespoon grated fresh ginger
- 1 tablespoon yellow mustard seeds (see note above)
- ½ teaspoon ground allspice
- ⅛-¼ teaspoon cayenne

Pork

- 2 (3-inch) wood chunks
- 1 boneless center-cut pork loin roast, 2½ pounds (see note above)
- Kosher salt and ground black pepper
- Vegetable oil for cooking grate

1. **FOR THE FILLING:** Bring all ingredients to simmer in medium saucepan over medium-high heat. Cover, reduce heat to low, and cook until apples are very soft, about 20 minutes. Push mixture through fine-mesh strainer to extract as much liquid as possible. Return liquid to saucepan and simmer over medium-high heat until reduced to ⅓ cup, about 5 minutes; reserve glaze. Meanwhile, pulse apple mixture in food processor until uniformly coarsely chopped, about fifteen 1-second pulses. Transfer filling to bowl and refrigerate while preparing pork.

2. **FOR THE PORK:** Soak wood chunks in water for 1 hour. Meanwhile, following illustrations 1 through 3 above, cut meat to even ½-inch thickness. Season inside liberally with salt and spread apple filling in even layer, leaving ½-inch border (illustration 4). Roll tightly and tie with twine at 1-inch intervals (illustrations 5 and 6). Season exterior liberally with salt and pepper.

3. Light large chimney starter filled with 5 quarts of charcoal (about 85 briquettes) and allow to burn until coals are fully ignited and covered with thin layer of ash, about 20 minutes. Build modified two-level fire by arranging coals to cover one half of grill. Drain wood chunks and place on coals. Open bottom vent fully. Position cooking grate over coals, cover grill, and heat grate until hot, about 5 minutes; scrape grate clean with grill brush. Lightly dip wad of paper towels in oil; holding wad with tongs, wipe cooking grate.

4. Place roast, fat-side up, on grate over cool side of grill. Cover grill and position vent, halfway open, over roast to draw smoke through grill. Grill-roast until instant-read thermometer inserted into thickest part of roast registers 130 to 135 degrees, 55 to 70 minutes, flipping once halfway through cooking time. Brush roast with half of reserved glaze; flip and brush with remaining glaze. (You may need to reheat glaze briefly to make spreadable.) Continue to cook until glaze is glossy and sticky, about 5 minutes longer.

5. Transfer roast to cutting board, loosely tent with foil, and let rest for 15 minutes. (Internal temperature should rise to about 145 degrees.) Cut into ½-inch-thick slices, removing twine as you cut. Serve immediately.

STEP-BY-STEP | HOW TO STUFF A PORK LOIN

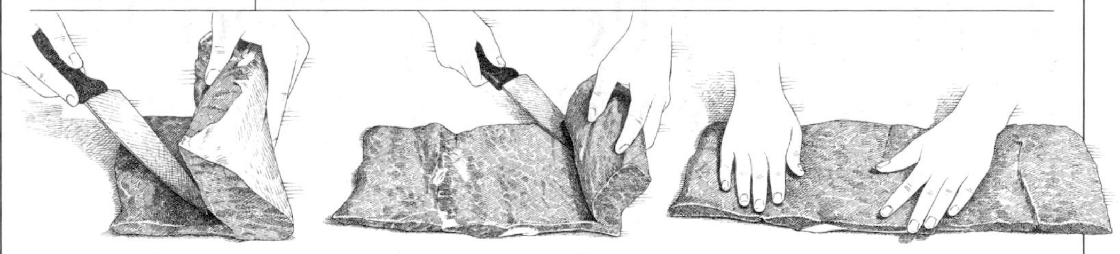

1. Position roast fat-side up. Insert knife ½ inch from bottom of roast and cut horizontally, stopping ½ inch before edge. Open this flap up.

2. Cut through thicker half of roast about ½ inch from bottom, stopping about ½ inch before edge. Open this flap up.

3. Repeat until pork loin is even ½ inch thickness throughout. If uneven, cover with plastic wrap and use meat pounder to even out.

4. With long side of meat facing you, season meat and spread filling, leaving ½-inch border on all sides.

5. Starting from short side, roll pork loin tightly.

6. Tie roast with twine at 1-inch intervals.

GRILLED PORK LOIN WITH APPLE-CRANBERRY FILLING ON A GAS GRILL

Follow recipe for Grilled Pork Loin with Apple-Cranberry Filling through step 2, substituting 2 cups wood chips for chunks and soaking them for 30 minutes. Drain chips and place in small disposable aluminum pan. About 20 minutes before grilling, place pan with chips on primary burner (burner that will remain on during cooking); position cooking grate over burners. Turn all burners to high and heat with lid down for 15 minutes. Scrape and oil grate. Leave primary burner on high and turn off other burner(s). Place roast, fat-side up, on side opposite primary burner and proceed with recipe from step 4.

COOK'S LIVE Original Test Kitchen Videos

www.cooksillustrated.com

RECIPE IN 60 SECONDS
- Grilled Pork Loin with Apple-Cranberry Filling

VIDEO TIPS
- What's the difference between pork loin cuts?
- What's the best way to stuff the pork loin?
- Is pink pork safe to eat?

EQUIPMENT TESTING:

Propane Level Indicators

You never want to run out of gas midway through grilling. To that end, we tested three propane level indicators, which are designed to show how much fuel you have in your tank. The Propane Genius ($14.99) sounds an alarm when you've got two hours of cooking time left. Unfortunately, it works only when the grill is ignited. The GrillPro EZ Check ($5.35) works like a mood ring, with sporadically illuminating color bars that we found nearly indecipherable. We much preferred the Original Grill Gauge ($13.99), which looks like a car gas gauge. You hook the indicator to the collar of the tank; when you lift the tank three inches off the ground, it registers the gas level by weight.

—Elizabeth Bomze

BEST GAS GAUGE
The Original Grill Gauge checks the gas level in a standard 20-gallon tank.

ILLUSTRATION: JOHN BURGOYNE

Introducing Ricotta Gnocchi

This elegant Florentine dish is the lighter cousin of potato gnocchi. But achieving the right texture requires more than a simple ricotta-for-potato swap.

⋡ BY SANDRA WU ⋠

As the petite divas of the pasta family, potato gnocchi (which, technically, aren't even pasta) have a reputation for being difficult to work with and not always worth the effort. The best ones start with baked potatoes and require at least 1½ hours just to make the dough, not to mention shape or cook them. And most of the flavor comes from the sauce rather than the gnocchi itself. It wasn't until a couple of years ago when I tried my first bite of tender, pillowy ricotta gnocchi that I realized gnocchi doesn't need to begin and end with spuds. A poll of the test kitchen revealed that many of my colleagues weren't too familiar with the ricotta version. This elegant, flavorful, and seemingly more straightforward dish was too good not to share with others, and I was determined to figure out how to make it at home.

Reviewing a wide swath of recipes revealed that, like many Italian dishes, this Florentine specialty doesn't require a long list of ingredients: just ricotta, eggs, flour, Parmesan cheese, salt, pepper, and sometimes herbs or spinach. The technique is quite simple, too. The dough is rolled out into ropes, cut into small pieces, and boiled. Even the two Italian names for ricotta gnocchi sound forgiving: *malfatti* ("badly made"), referring to their sometimes less-than-model-perfect appearance, and *gnudi* ("naked"), because they resemble ravioli without their pasta jackets.

Working the Cheese

I knew the success of this dish would hinge on its most prominent ingredient: ricotta cheese. Most recipes call for an entire pound. Tasters preferred whole-milk ricotta to the leaner, less flavorful part-skim variety. I began by forming a basic dough, combining a pound of ricotta with an egg, a cup of flour, ¼ cup of Parmesan cheese, and some salt and pepper. Instead of the pillowy bundles I'd been hoping for, I got dense, flour-laden blobs that lacked cheese flavor. More Parmesan helped ramp up the flavor, but I needed to use less flour. However, when I cut back on the flour, the dough was too sticky and unworkable.

When a fellow test cook commented on the wateriness of supermarket ricotta (in Italy, ricotta is creamy and dry, but American supermarket brands are curdy and wet), I saw an opportunity. In the test kitchen, we often thicken yogurt by draining it in the refrigerator. What if I drained the ricotta? Sure enough, the result was a slightly drier dough that had more structure. I felt I had made real progress. Now I could work on cutting back the flour.

Binding Techniques

Taking baby steps, I reduced the amount of flour to ¾ cup, which made the gnocchi slightly less gummy. At ½ cup, they were even better, but still not perfect. Any less flour and the dough became an overly sticky batter. I couldn't remove any more moisture from the ricotta, so I tried swapping potato starch and cornstarch for some of the flour. This just made the gnocchi gluey and slimy.

I thought back to one of the recipes I'd tried and dismissed for its use of an unexpected ingredient: fresh bread crumbs. Could this simple addition—one that's often coupled with milk or egg to add tenderness to meat loaf—absorb more of the moisture in the dough and allow me to add less flour? These gnocchi were a little better, but not enough to justify the extra effort. But I wasn't ready to give up. What if I toasted the crumbs? For my next test, I made a dough with just 6 tablespoons of flour and ½ cup of homemade dried bread crumbs. The resulting gnocchi held together and had the perfect combination of tenderness and structure. (Hoping to bow to convenience, I tried substituting store-bought bread crumbs, but they gave the gnocchi a stale taste.)

Handle Gently

There was one element still missing from this balancing act—proper technique. Before stepping out of the test kitchen one afternoon to run an errand, I put the gnocchi dough on hold in the refrigerator. When I returned 15 minutes later, I found that the refrigeration had helped the delicate dough stiffen and become more workable. Rolling it out afterward by hand wasn't difficult, provided I did it gently and worked with a little bit at a time.

The gnocchi were ready to be simmered. By the time they floated to the surface, they needed just two more minutes in the water before being scooped out with a slotted spoon. One last step

Gnocchi dough is rolled into thick ropes on a floured counter and then sliced into small, pillow-shaped pieces.

Two Kinds of Gnocchi

The more familiar potato gnocchi (left) has a texture that's between pasta and dumpling. The ricotta cheese version (right) is more delicate, with a texture like ravioli without the pasta jacket.

POTATO GNOCCHI RICOTTA GNOCCHI

PHOTOGRAPHY: CARL TREMBLAY

Proper Dough Consistency

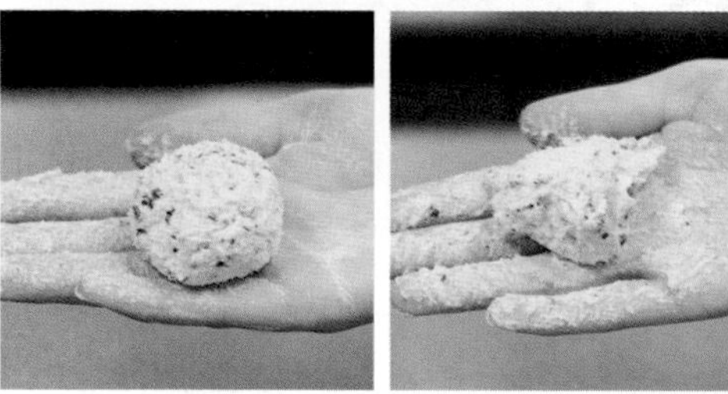

JUST RIGHT TOO SOFT

Gnocchi dough should be moist and slightly tacky to the touch. When the proper consistency is achieved, a few crumbs should stick to your finger (left). If the dough is too wet and a lot of crumbs stick to your finger (right), stir in additional flour, 1 tablespoon at a time.

remained: tossing the tender little dumplings in a simple sauce of browned butter, minced shallots, and sage. When I set the platter of gnocchi in front of my tasters, it took all of five minutes before the last piece disappeared. I guess they weren't so "badly made" after all.

RICOTTA GNOCCHI WITH BROWNED BUTTER AND SAGE SAUCE

SERVES 4 TO 6 AS FIRST COURSE OR 2 TO 3 AS MAIN DISH

We recommend using Calabro whole-milk ricotta, although other brands and part-skim cheese will work in this recipe. When rolling the gnocchi, use just enough flour to keep the dough from sticking to your hands and work surface; using too much flour will result in tough gnocchi. The gnocchi can be rolled, cut, and refrigerated for up to 24 hours. To freeze the uncooked gnocchi, place the baking sheet in the freezer until the gnocchi are firm (about 1 hour), then transfer them to a zipper-lock bag and store them for up to 1 month. Thaw frozen gnocchi overnight in the refrigerator or at room temperature for 1 hour before cooking as directed. To prevent the gnocchi from cooling too quickly, warm a serving platter or serving bowls in a 200-degree oven. If you prefer, replace the browned butter sauce with Tomato-Cream Sauce (recipe follows), Porcini Cream Sauce, or ½ cup Pesto (recipes available free at www.cooksillustrated.com/october).

Gnocchi

- 1 (15- or 16-ounce) container whole-milk ricotta cheese (see note above)
- 2 large slices white sandwich bread, crusts removed and bread torn into quarters
- 1 large egg
- 2 tablespoons minced fresh basil leaves
- 2 tablespoons minced fresh parsley leaves
- Table salt
- ¼ teaspoon ground black pepper
- 6 tablespoons all-purpose flour, plus additional for work surface
- 1 ounce Parmesan cheese, grated (about ½ cup)

Sauce

- 4 tablespoons unsalted butter, cut into 4 pieces
- 1 small shallot, minced (about 2 tablespoons)
- 2 teaspoons minced fresh sage leaves
- 1 teaspoon juice from 1 lemon
- ⅛ teaspoon table salt

1. **FOR THE GNOCCHI:** Line fine-mesh strainer set over deep container or bowl with 3 paper coffee filters or triple layer of paper towels. Place ricotta in lined strainer, cover, and refrigerate for 1 hour. Adjust oven rack to middle position and heat oven to 300 degrees.

2. Meanwhile, process bread in food processor until finely ground, about 10 seconds. Spread crumbs on rimmed baking sheet and bake until dry and just beginning to turn golden, about 10 minutes, stirring once during baking time. Let cool to room temperature. (You should have about ½ cup crumbs.)

3. Transfer drained ricotta to food processor and pulse until curds break down into fine, grainy consistency, about eight 1-second pulses. Using rubber spatula, combine ricotta, egg, basil, parsley, ½ teaspoon salt, and pepper in large bowl. Add flour, Parmesan, and bread crumbs; stir until well combined. Refrigerate dough for 15 minutes. Check texture of dough (see photos above) and add more flour if needed.

4. Lightly dust work surface with flour. With floured hands, roll lemon-sized piece of dough into ¾-inch-thick rope, rolling from center of dough outward. Cut rope into ¾-inch-long pieces and transfer to parchment paper–lined rimmed baking sheet. Repeat with remaining dough, dusting work surface with flour as needed.

5. **FOR THE SAUCE:** Melt butter in 12-inch skillet over medium-high heat, swirling occasionally, until butter is browned and releases nutty aroma, about 1½ minutes. Off heat, add shallot and sage, stirring until shallot is fragrant, about 1 minute. Stir in lemon juice and salt; cover to keep warm.

6. **TO COOK GNOCCHI:** Bring 4 quarts water to boil in large pot or Dutch oven over high heat. Add 1 tablespoon salt. Reduce heat so water is simmering, then gently drop half of gnocchi into water and cook until all pieces float to surface. Continue to simmer until gnocchi are cooked through, about 2 minutes longer, adjusting heat to maintain gentle simmer. Using slotted spoon, scoop gnocchi from water, allowing excess water to drain from spoon; transfer gnocchi to skillet with sauce and cover to keep warm. Repeat cooking process with remaining gnocchi. Using rubber spatula, gently toss gnocchi with sauce until uniformly coated. Divide among warmed bowls or serving platter and serve immediately.

Simmer, Don't Boil

Most pasta should be cooked at a full boil, but if gnocchi are cooked at a full boil they can fall apart from the vigorous churning. Once the water comes to a boil, reduce the heat, add the gnocchi, and make sure the water just simmers.

EQUIPMENT TESTING:

Slotted Spoons

A slotted spoon is indispensable for fishing food out of boiling water. But after damaging delicate gnocchi and dropping dozens of green peas as we tested nine models, we learned that not just any combination of handles and holes would do. Our testers preferred lengthy handles, deep bowls, and enough small slits or punctures to quickly drain water without losing as much as one petite pea. A stainless steel spoon from Calphalon ($9.95) and nonstick nylon models from Messermeister ($2.95) and OXO ($5.99) all met our demands, though the slightly flimsy Messermeister was downgraded for its smaller capacity. With its lighter weight and slimmer price tag, OXO just edged out Calphalon for top honors. For complete testing results, go to www.cooksillustrated.com/october.

—Elizabeth Bomze

TOP SLOT

The OXO Good Grips Nylon Slotted Spoon did the best job of retrieving gnocchi (and more) from a pot of boiling water.

TOMATO-CREAM SAUCE

MAKES ABOUT 1½ CUPS, ENOUGH FOR 1 RECIPE OF GNOCCHI

- 1 tablespoon extra-virgin olive oil
- 1 medium garlic clove, minced or pressed through garlic press (about 1 teaspoon)
- 1 (14½-ounce) can diced tomatoes, pureed in food processor until smooth
- ¼ teaspoon table salt
- ⅛ teaspoon sugar
- 2 tablespoons chopped fresh basil leaves
- 2 tablespoons heavy cream

Heat oil in 12-inch nonstick skillet over medium heat until shimmering. Add garlic and cook until fragrant but not brown, about 20 seconds. Stir in tomatoes, salt, and sugar; simmer until thickened slightly, 5 to 6 minutes. Remove pan from heat and stir in basil and cream. Cover to keep warm.

COOK'S LIVE Original Test Kitchen Videos

www.cooksillustrated.com

RECIPE IN 60 SECONDS
- Ricotta Gnocchi

VIDEO TIPS
- How can I prevent gnocchi from falling apart?
- Can I use store-bought bread crumbs in this recipe?

Chicken Tikka Masala at Home

Chicken tikka masala is the single most popular Indian restaurant dish in the world. Why is it so rarely made at home?

BY REBECCA HAYS

It is said that in the 1970s, a plateful of overcooked chicken tikka—boneless, skinless chicken chunks, skewered and cooked in a tandoor oven—was sent back to the kitchen of a London curry house by a disappointed patron. The Bangladeshi chef acted quickly, heating canned tomato soup with cream, sprinkling in Indian spices, and pouring it over the chicken before sending it back out to the dining room. His inventive creation of chicken tikka masala satisfied the demanding customer, and as the recipe was perfected, diners worldwide (including India) fell in love with the tender, moist pieces of chicken napped in a lightly spiced tomato cream sauce. In fact, chicken tikka masala is so adored that it went on to overtake the likes of Yorkshire pudding and fish and chips as the "true national dish" of Great Britain, according to former British Foreign Secretary Robin Cook.

A spiced tomato-cream sauce flavors broiled chunks of chicken.

Despite its popularity in restaurants, recipes for chicken tikka masala are absent from some of my favorite Indian cookbooks, a testament to its lack of authenticity in Indian cuisine. The recipes I did find had much in common. They all called for marinating chicken breast chunks in yogurt, often for 24 hours, then skewering them, kebab style, for cooking. The tandoor oven was replaced with a broiler or grill. The masala ingredients varied, but the sauces were all as easy to prepare as a quick Italian tomato sauce.

But the similarities didn't end there: In all of the recipes, the chicken was either mushy or dry and the sauces were unbearably rich and overspiced. The good news is that these problems did not seem impossible to overcome, and the promise of a new way to cook chicken with exotic flavors held plenty of appeal. I just needed a decent recipe.

SHOPPING: Key Ingredients

All of the ingredients for Chicken Tikka Masala are available at the supermarket. Here are notes on what to buy.

CHICKEN BREASTS
Lean white meat pairs well with the rich tomato-cream sauce. The test kitchen prefers Bell & Evans.

GARAM MASALA
This combination of warm spices seasons the masala sauce. McCormick won a recent test kitchen tasting.

PLAIN YOGURT
Whole-milk yogurt forms a protective barrier on the chicken. Brown Cow is our favorite brand.

CRUSHED TOMATOES
Crushed tomatoes form the base of the masala sauce. Muir Glen was highly rated in a recent tasting.

Tackling Tikka

I wanted a four-season dish, so I chose the broiler (not the grill). Cooking the boneless breasts whole and cutting them into pieces only after they were broiled was a step in the right direction. The larger pieces of chicken didn't dry out as quickly under the searing heat of the broiler. It also got rid of the fussy step of skewering raw, slippery chicken pieces. But the chicken still wasn't juicy enough.

The yogurt marinade is meant to tenderize the meat and infuse it with the essence of spices and aromatics. While overnight marinades did adequately flavor the chicken, they also made the texture too tender, bordering on mushy. Given enough time, the lactic acid in yogurt breaks down the protein strands in meat.

I was tempted to abandon the yogurt marinade altogether. But yogurt is so fundamental to this recipe that excluding it felt like a mistake. Could I find a different way to use it? I considered salting, a technique we have used for steaks, roasts, chicken parts, and whole turkeys. Salt initially draws moisture out of protein; then the reverse happens and the salt and moisture flow back in. What if I salted the chicken first, then dipped it in yogurt right before cooking?

I rubbed the chicken with a simple mixture of salt and everyday spices common in Indian cookery: coriander, cumin, and cayenne. I waited 30 minutes, which gave me time to prepare the masala sauce, then dunked the chicken in yogurt and broiled it. The result was the best tikka yet—nicely seasoned with spices and tender but not soft. In just half an hour's time, the salt rub had done its job of flavoring the chicken and keeping it moist, and the yogurt mixture acted as a protective barrier, shielding the lean meat from the powerful heat of the broiler.

To encourage gentle charring on the chicken, I fattened up the yogurt with two tablespoons of oil. I also took advantage of the yogurt's thick texture, mixing it with minced garlic and freshly grated ginger. The aromatics clung to the chicken as it cooked, producing tikka that was good enough to eat on its own.

Mastering Masala

Masala means "hot spice," and the ingredients in a masala sauce depend largely on the whims of the cook. When the masala is to be served as

PHOTOGRAPHY: CARL TREMBLAY

STEP-BY-STEP | CHICKEN TIKKA MASALA

1. RUB: Coat chicken in salt and spice mixture and refrigerate.

2. MAKE SAUCE: Prepare creamy tomato-masala sauce.

3. DIP: Dunk chicken in protective coating of yogurt and oil.

4. BROIL: Broil chicken, then allow to rest.

5. COMBINE: Cut chicken into chunks and add to sauce.

part of chicken tikka masala, however, tomatoes and cream always form the base. Working with a mixture of sautéed aromatics (onions, ginger, garlic, and chiles) simmered with tomatoes (crushed tomatoes were favored over diced canned or fresh because of their smoother consistency) and cream, I tested combination after combination of spices. With plenty of winners and no real losers, I eventually settled on the simplest choice of all: commercial garam masala. Garam masala blends warm spices such as cardamom, black pepper, cinnamon, and coriander in one jar. To bloom the flavor of the garam masala, I sautéed it in oil along with the aromatics instead of adding it to the simmering sauce, as some recipes suggest. There was just one problem: Many commercially prepared masala sauces contain tartrazine, an artificial coloring. Without it, the spices lent my sauce an ugly gray cast. A tablespoon of tomato paste easily restored a pleasant shade of red.

My recipe was getting rave reviews, but I had the nagging feeling that something was missing. I scanned through a flavor checklist in my mind: Salt? No. Acidity? No. Heat? No. Sweetness? That was it. I stirred a teaspoon of sugar into the pot, then another. My work was done, the sugar having successfully rounded out the flavors of the sauce. When I spooned the chicken over basmati rice and sprinkled it with cilantro, I knew I had a dish worth staying home for.

TASTING:

Basmati Rice

LONG ON FLAVOR

Prized for its nutty flavor and sweet aroma, basmati rice is eaten worldwide in pilafs and biryanis and as an accompaniment to curries. The best Indian-grown rice is said to come from the Himalaya foothills, where the snow-flooded soil and humid climate offer ideal growing conditions. Choosing among the multitude of boxes, bags, and burlap sacks available today on supermarket shelves can be confusing. To find a truly great grain, we steamed seven brands, five from India and two domestic options. Matched against Indian imports, domestic brands Lundberg and Della suffered. They were less aromatic, and the grains didn't elongate as much. Their overall texture was mushy, too. While all of the imported brands were acceptable, tasters overwhelmingly chose the longest sample—Tilda—as their favorite. For the complete results of this tasting, go to www.cooksillustrated.com/october.

—Elizabeth Bomze

CHICKEN TIKKA MASALA

SERVES 4 TO 6

This dish is best when prepared with whole-milk yogurt, but low-fat yogurt can be substituted. For a spicier dish, do not remove the ribs and seeds from the chile. If you prefer, substitute 2 teaspoons ground coriander, ¼ teaspoon ground cardamom, ¼ teaspoon ground cinnamon, and ½ teaspoon ground black pepper for the garam masala. The sauce can be made ahead, refrigerated for up to 4 days in an airtight container, and gently reheated before adding the hot chicken. Serve with basmati rice.

Chicken Tikka

- ½ teaspoon ground cumin
- ½ teaspoon ground coriander
- ¼ teaspoon cayenne
- 1 teaspoon table salt
- 2 pounds boneless, skinless chicken breasts, trimmed of fat
- 1 cup plain whole-milk yogurt (see note above)
- 2 tablespoons vegetable oil
- 2 medium garlic cloves, minced or pressed through garlic press (about 2 teaspoons)
- 1 tablespoon grated fresh ginger

Masala Sauce

- 3 tablespoons vegetable oil
- 1 medium onion, diced fine (about 1¼ cups)
- 2 medium garlic cloves, minced or pressed through garlic press (about 2 teaspoons)
- 2 teaspoons grated fresh ginger
- 1 serrano chile, ribs and seeds removed, flesh minced (see note above)
- 1 tablespoon tomato paste
- 1 tablespoon garam masala (see note above)
- 1 (28-ounce) can crushed tomatoes
- 2 teaspoons sugar
- ½ teaspoon table salt
- ⅔ cup heavy cream
- ¼ cup chopped fresh cilantro leaves

1. FOR THE CHICKEN: Combine cumin, coriander, cayenne, and salt in small bowl. Sprinkle both sides of chicken with spice mixture, pressing gently so mixture adheres. Place chicken on plate, cover with plastic wrap, and refrigerate for 30 to 60 minutes. In large bowl, whisk together yogurt, oil, garlic, and ginger; set aside.

2. FOR THE SAUCE: Heat oil in large Dutch oven over medium heat until shimmering. Add onion and cook, stirring frequently, until light golden, 8 to 10 minutes. Add garlic, ginger, chile, tomato paste, and garam masala; cook, stirring frequently, until fragrant, about 3 minutes. Add crushed tomatoes, sugar, and salt; bring to boil. Reduce heat to medium-low, cover, and simmer for 15 minutes, stirring occasionally. Stir in cream and return to simmer. Remove pan from heat and cover to keep warm.

3. While sauce simmers, adjust oven rack to upper-middle position (about 6 inches from heating element) and heat broiler. Using tongs, dip chicken into yogurt mixture (chicken should be coated with thick layer of yogurt) and arrange on wire rack set in foil-lined rimmed baking sheet or broiler pan. Discard excess yogurt mixture. Broil chicken until thickest parts register 160 degrees on instant-read thermometer and exterior is lightly charred in spots, 10 to 18 minutes, flipping chicken halfway through cooking.

4. Let chicken rest 5 minutes, then cut into 1-inch chunks and stir into warm sauce (do not simmer chicken in sauce). Stir in cilantro, adjust seasoning with salt, and serve.

COOK'S LIVE Original Test Kitchen Videos

www.cooksillustrated.com

RECIPE IN 60 SECONDS

- Chicken Tikka Masala

VIDEO TIP

- What's the best way to grate ginger?

ILLUSTRATION: JOHN BURGOYNE

The Best Way to Cook Vegetables

Vegetable side dishes often don't get much attention and taste rather dull. How do you build flavor with a minimum of work? BY KEITH DRESSER

One cookbook says to boil broccoli, another says to steam it. Neither method actually makes broccoli taste better. Over the years, the test kitchen has learned which methods work best with specific vegetables. Here's what you need to know about the most common techniques.

BOILING allows you to season vegetables as they cook (use 1 tablespoon table salt per 4 quarts water). However, it's easy to overcook vegetables when boiling, and this method washes away flavor. Boiled vegetables need further embellishment, such as a compound butter or vinaigrette. **Try with nonporous green vegetables, such as green beans and snap peas.**

STEAMING washes away less flavor than boiling and leaves vegetables crisper. Doesn't allow for seasoning vegetables and only works with small batches (1 pound or less). **Try with porous or delicate vegetables such as asparagus, broccoli, and cauliflower.**

SAUTÉING allows for the addition of everything from garlic to herbs but requires constant attention and a nonstick pan. **Try with peas and zucchini.**

PAN-ROASTING caramelizes natural sugars in vegetables and promotes browning. Doesn't work if the pan is overloaded, and most recipes rely on tight-fitting lid to capture steam and help cook vegetables through. **Try with asparagus and broccoli.**

ROASTING concentrates flavors by driving off excess moisture and makes vegetables crisp. Requires at least 30 minutes (including time to heat oven). **Try with asparagus, carrots, cauliflower, green beans, and zucchini.**

BROILING browns vegetables quickly and deeply. Broilers require constant attention; keep food at least 4 inches from the heating element to prevent flare-ups. **Try with asparagus and zucchini.**

So which techniques do we prefer? Our favorite indoor cooking methods, such as roasting, pan-roasting, and broiling, actually add flavor to vegetables. **Favorite recipes are available free at www.cooksillustrated.com/october, where you will also find our "Guide to Grilling Vegetables."**

BROCCOLI

Shopping Notes: The stalks are just as tasty as the florets, so make sure they aren't dry or cracked.

Preparation: Cut florets into 1 ½-inch pieces; peel stalks and cut on bias into ¼-inch-thick pieces.

Basic Cooking Method: Pan-roasting brings out broccoli's sweet rather than sulfurous flavors. Sauté peeled stalks from 1 ¾ pounds broccoli in 12-inch nonstick skillet filmed with 2 tablespoons oil for 2 minutes. To promote browning, cook over medium-high heat and do not stir. Add florets and cook until they start to brown (1 to 2 minutes), then add 3 tablespoons water, cover, and cook for 2 minutes. Remove lid and cook until water evaporates and broccoli is tender, another 2 minutes.

Favorite Recipe at CooksIllustrated.com

- Pan-Roasted Broccoli with Lemon Browned Butter

PREPARING BROCCOLI

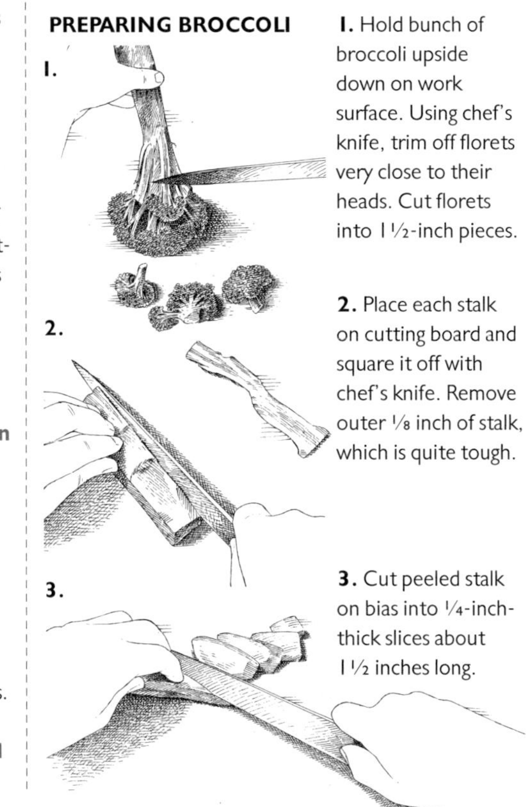

1. Hold bunch of broccoli upside down on work surface. Using chef's knife, trim off florets very close to their heads. Cut florets into 1 ½-inch pieces.

2. Place each stalk on cutting board and square it off with chef's knife. Remove outer ⅛ inch of stalk, which is quite tough.

3. Cut peeled stalk on bias into ¼-inch-thick slices about 1 ½ inches long.

ASPARAGUS

Shopping Notes: Pencil-thin asparagus are easily overcooked and thick spears are woody; choose asparagus ½ to ⅝ inch thick.

Preparation: Trim tough ends.

Basic Cooking Methods: Broiling and pan-roasting concentrate flavors in delicate asparagus. Toss 2 pounds trimmed asparagus with 1 tablespoon olive oil on baking sheet and broil, shaking pan once, for 8 to 10 minutes. Or heat 1 tablespoon each vegetable oil and butter in 12-inch nonstick skillet. Add 2 pounds trimmed asparagus, with half of tips pointing in one direction and other half pointing in opposite direction. Cover and cook over medium-high heat for 5 minutes. Uncover and cook over high heat until tender and browned, 5 to 7 minutes.

Favorite Recipes at CooksIllustrated.com

- Broiled Asparagus with Reduced Balsamic Vinaigrette and Parmesan
- Pan-Roasted Asparagus with Cherry Tomatoes and Black Olives

TRIMMING ASPARAGUS

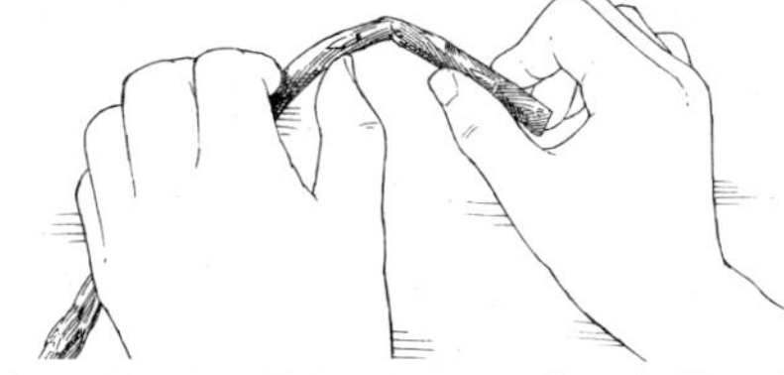

With one hand, hold the asparagus about halfway down stalk; with thumb and index finger of other hand, hold spear about an inch from bottom. Bend stalk until it snaps.

GREEN BEANS

Shopping Notes: Slender, crisp green beans are best boiled. Older, tougher green beans (the kind found in supermarkets at most times of the year) are best roasted.

Preparation: Trim ends.

Basic Cooking Method: Roasting promotes the conversion of starches to sugars, thus improving flavor. Toss 1 pound trimmed beans with 1 tablespoon olive oil and roast on foil-lined baking sheet in 450-degree oven for 20 minutes. Turn beans once for even browning.

Favorite Recipes at CooksIllustrated.com

- Roasted Green Beans with Red Onion and Walnuts
- Roasted Maple-Mustard Green Beans

TRIMMING ENDS FROM GREEN BEANS

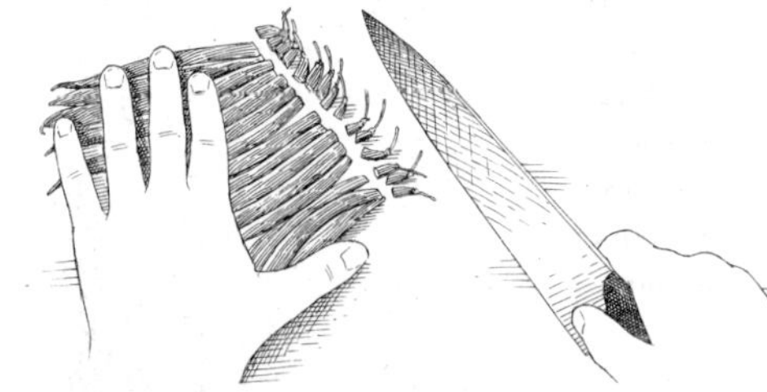

Line up beans on board and trim all ends with just one slice.

THREE COMMON COOKING MISTAKES (AND HOW TO AVOID THEM)

➢ **OVERCOOKING:** Vegetables will continue to soften as they make their way to the table. To keep vegetables crisp and tender, remove them from the heat when slightly underdone.

➢ **UNEVEN COOKING:** Make sure vegetables are cut uniformly. This is particularly important when steaming and sautéing.

➢ **SLOW COOKING:** Overloaded pans will cook very slowly. When roasting and sautéing, give vegetables room to brown. Piled on top of each other, they will steam and won't taste as good.

PEAS

Shopping Notes: Frozen peas are almost always better than fresh shell peas, which tend to be starchy.
Preparation: Frozen peas can be used without thawing.
Basic Cooking Method: Don't boil peas—they are much better sautéed. Add frozen peas directly to pan with sautéed aromatics (garlic and/or shallots cooked in a few tablespoons of butter until fragrant) and cover pan to trap steam and heat peas through (this will take about 4 minutes). Add 2 teaspoons sugar to 1 pound frozen peas to boost flavor.

Favorite Recipe at CooksIllustrated.com
- Sautéed Buttery Peas with Mint and Feta Cheese

ZUCCHINI

Shopping Notes: Zucchini weighing less than 8 ounces are more flavorful and less watery than larger ones.
Preparation: Shred, discarding seeds and core, then salt and squeeze dry.
Basic Cooking Method: Shredding, salting (use 1½ teaspoons salt with 2½ pounds zucchini), and squeezing removes moisture from this watery vegetable, as does a dry-heat cooking method, like sautéing. Toss dried zucchini with 2 teaspoons olive oil and then cook in 12-inch nonstick skillet filmed with 2 teaspoons additional oil over high heat for 4 minutes. Stir infrequently as zucchini cooks to promote browning.

Favorite Recipe at CooksIllustrated.com
- Zucchini with Tomatoes and Basil

SHREDDING AND SALTING ZUCCHINI

1. Cut zucchini into 3-inch pieces. Shred on large holes of box grater, rotating zucchini as needed to avoid shredding seeds and core.

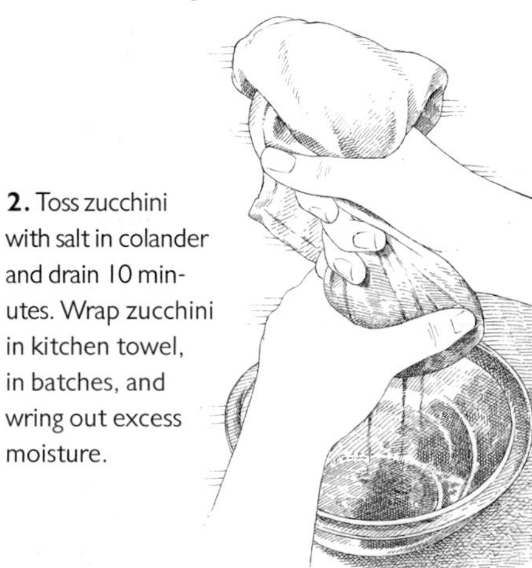

2. Toss zucchini with salt in colander and drain 10 minutes. Wrap zucchini in kitchen towel, in batches, and wring out excess moisture.

CAULIFLOWER

Shopping Notes: Buy heads of cauliflower with tight, firm florets without any discoloration.
Preparation: Trim leaves and stem, then cut into large wedges.
Basic Cooking Method: Roasting avoids the sulfurous smell that sometimes results when cauliflower is boiled or steamed. Toss wedges from 1 head cauliflower with 4 tablespoons olive oil and roast on foil-lined baking sheet in 475-degree oven for 25 to 35 minutes. Cover pan with foil for first 10 minutes of cooking time to ensure that cauliflower cooks through. Also, place baking sheet on bottom oven rack to maximize browning. Flip wedges once bottom has browned nicely (after about 20 minutes).

Favorite Recipe at CooksIllustrated.com
- Roasted Cauliflower with Soy-Ginger Sauce with Scallion

CUTTING UP CAULIFLOWER

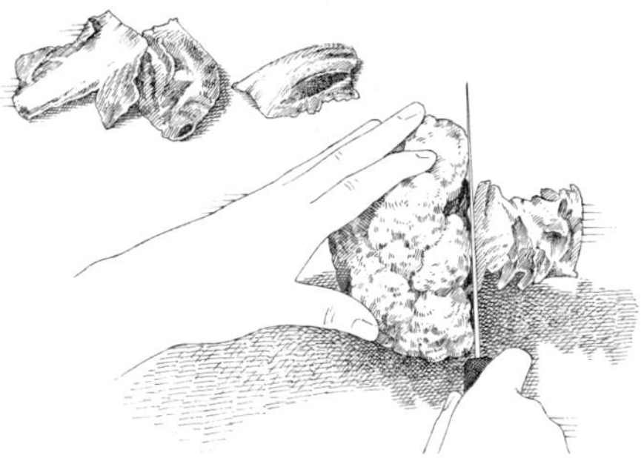

1. Pull off outer leaves and cut stem flush.

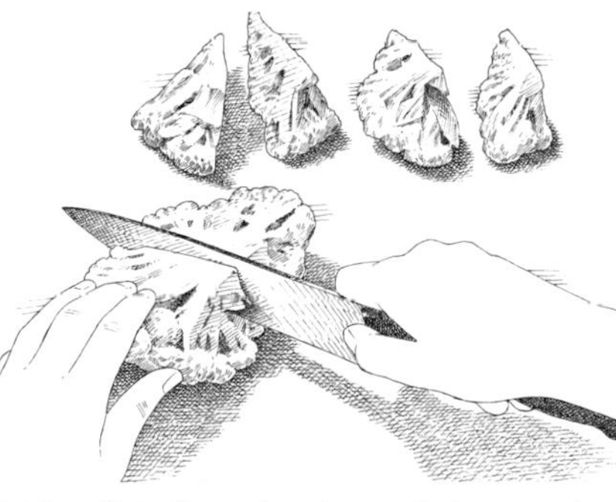

2. Cut head into 8 equal wedges so that core and florets remain intact.

ESSENTIAL EQUIPMENT

In addition to the usual suspects—knife and peeler—here are three items we use frequently when preparing vegetables.

TEST KITCHEN ESSENTIAL: COLANDER
The mega-perforated bowl of the **Precision Pierced Endurance Stainless Steel Colander ($29.99)** quickly and completely drains liquid from boiled vegetables. This 5-quart colander fits in a large Dutch oven, making it ideal for steaming.

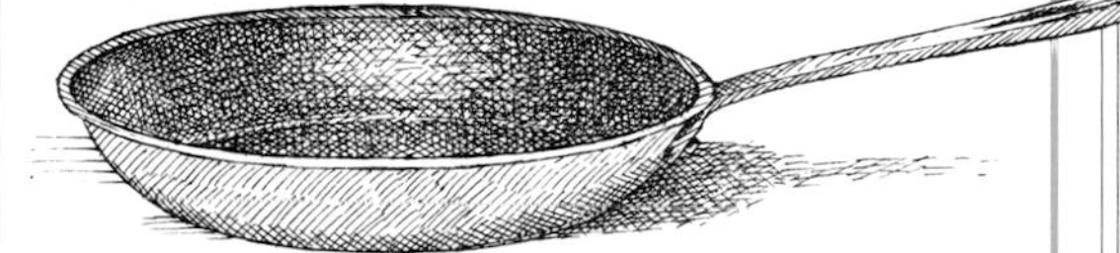

TEST KITCHEN ESSENTIAL: NONSTICK SKILLET
We use a large nonstick skillet to promote browning of sautéed or pan-roasted vegetables. The **All-Clad Stainless Nonstick 12-Inch Frypan ($160)** was the top performer in our kitchen tests.

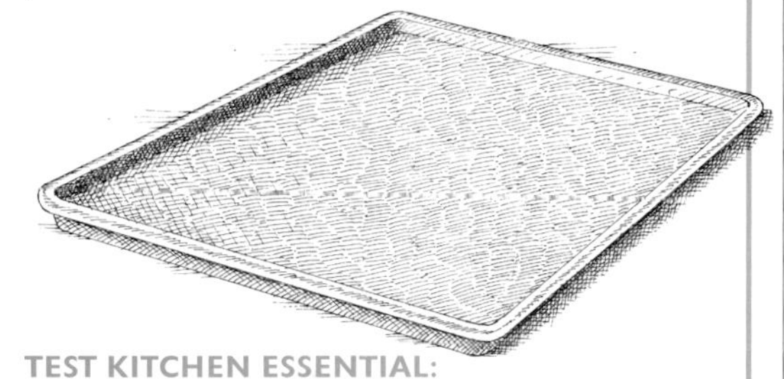

TEST KITCHEN ESSENTIAL: RIMMED BAKING SHEET
A sturdy baking sheet that won't buckle is a must when roasting at high temperatures. The **Lincoln Foodservice Half-Size Heavy-Duty Sheet Pan ($15.40)** is large enough to hold a big batch of vegetables and stays flat during roasting.

CARROTS

Shopping Notes: Avoid extra-large carrots, which are often woody and bitter. Baby carrots are fine for roasting but too thick for glazing.
Preparation: Peel regular carrots and slice on bias.
Basic Cooking Methods: Roasting intensifies sweetness without requiring other ingredients. Toss 1 pound baby carrots with 1 tablespoon olive oil in broiler-pan bottom and roast in 475-degree oven for 20 minutes, shaking pan several times to promote even browning. Glazing makes carrots even sweeter but requires more prep. Cook 1 pound sliced carrots with 1 tablespoon sugar and ½ cup chicken broth in covered 12-inch nonstick skillet for 5 minutes. Uncover and cook until liquid reduces to 2 tablespoons, 1 to 2 minutes. Add 1 tablespoon butter and additional 2 tablespoons sugar and cook, stirring frequently, until carrots are tender and evenly glazed, about 3 minutes.

Favorite Recipes at CooksIllustrated.com
- Roasted Baby Carrots with Ginger-Orange Glaze
- Glazed Carrots with Bacon and Pecans

SLICING CARROTS ON THE BIAS
Cut carrots on bias into pieces ¼ inch thick and 2 inches long.

ILLUSTRATION: JOHN BURGOYNE

Improving Glazed Chicken Breasts

We wanted to elevate this institutional standard to an elegant weeknight dinner. This required a glaze that would stick to the chicken and not taste like candy.

BY CHARLES KELSEY

On a recent flight to Paris, I chose the glazed chicken meal option. The flight attendant set down a plastic tray displaying a pale chicken breast with flabby skin smothered by a cloying glaze. I made it through two bites. That evening I found myself at an upscale restaurant ordering the house specialty: duck à l'orange. A silver platter arrived bearing carved duck pieces clad with deep-amber skin coated in a shiny, glazy sauce. The meat was perfectly moist, and each bite revealed the satisfying combination of roasted poultry and a citrus sauce balanced by sweet and sour flavors.

These contrasting experiences got me to thinking about glazed chicken's status in the American culinary repertoire. At best it's a humdrum weeknight dinner. Inspired by my French meal, I desired a glazed chicken breast with perfectly rendered skin and moist meat sufficiently coated with a complexly flavored glaze; one worthy of fine china but still something I could make after work on a Tuesday night.

Coming Home to Roast

When I got back home, I searched for glazed chicken recipes on the Internet, where I mostly found simple "dump-and-bake" versions. The instructions: Pour a jar of fruit preserves over raw chicken breasts and bake. I wasn't surprised when my attempt at one of these recipes emerged from the oven looking much like my airplane meal. Despite the dump-and-bake recipe's dismal results of flabby, pale skin and a candy-like glaze that pooled at the bottom of the pan, I did have to admire its simplicity. Browning the skin was an easy fix. I could brown the chicken in an ovenproof skillet on the stovetop before transferring the skillet to the oven to finish cooking (our standard test-kitchen method for cooking bone-in, skin-on breasts). I could add a glaze to the pan just after the chicken breasts were sufficiently browned.

But first I would have to fix the glaze. Every recipe I dug up in my research used a good deal of sticky, sweet ingredients for the base: fruit preserves, molasses, maple syrup, and brown sugar. How was it that my duck à l'orange sauce in Paris was glazy yet not cloying? My hunch was that it was some sort of reduction sauce. Flipping through French cookbooks, I found my answer: reduced orange juice. Orange juice is sticky, and its acidity helps balance the sugar—another key ingredient in the duck sauce. I wasn't interested in creating a recipe for chicken à l'orange, but using orange juice in my glaze seemed like a good place to start.

The chicken and glaze are conveniently cooked in the same pan.

If the Glaze Sticks

The recipes I found for classic orange sauce offered me enough guidance to piece together a working recipe. After browning some chicken breasts, I transferred the meat to a plate while I reduced orange juice and sugar in the empty skillet. I then returned the chicken breasts to the skillet, rolled them in the glaze, and finished them off in the oven. Tasters complained that the glaze was "too thin," "irresponsibly sweet," and "did not adhere to the chicken." More sugar would have been the ideal solution to the textural issue but was inappropriate for a glaze that was already too sweet.

Then I remembered a technique a test kitchen colleague used for her cake frosting recipe. She mixed in a small amount of light corn syrup to add luster and body—but, curiously, not sweetness. I'd always assumed corn syrup was supersweet, but when I tasted a lineup of sugar, brown sugar, maple syrup, and honey against corn syrup, I discovered otherwise. Nutrition labels on the sweeteners confirmed my palate's accuracy: Corn syrup contains half (and sometimes less than half) as much sugar as other sweeteners.

Excited by the prospect that corn syrup might help my cause, I immediately trimmed some chicken breasts, heated a skillet, and whipped up a new batch of glaze. Not only did this corn syrup–enhanced glaze cook up perfectly, the meat seemed juicier, almost as if I had brined the chicken. This warranted a quick call to our science editor, who told me that the concentrated glucose in corn syrup has a high affinity for water, which means it helps to hold moisture in the glaze, making the overall dish seem juicier. That same glucose also thickens and adds a gloss to the glaze.

However, as much as tasters liked the glaze's clean flavor, they now thought it wasn't sweet enough. A little honey instead of sugar gave the glaze just the right level of sweetness. And minced shallot, vinegar, Dijon mustard, and a pinch of pepper flakes created complexity.

Despite these improvements, there was one complaint—from me. I still felt the glaze should cling even more to the chicken. From past tests, I knew that adding cornstarch or flour to the glaze only made it gloppy. Maybe the problem

TECHNIQUE | MAKING TRAILS

To know when the sauce is ready after its second reduction in step 4, pull a heatproof rubber spatula through it. It should leave a wide trail.

PHOTOGRAPHY: CARL TREMBLAY

RECIPE SHORTHAND | GLAZED CHICKEN BREASTS

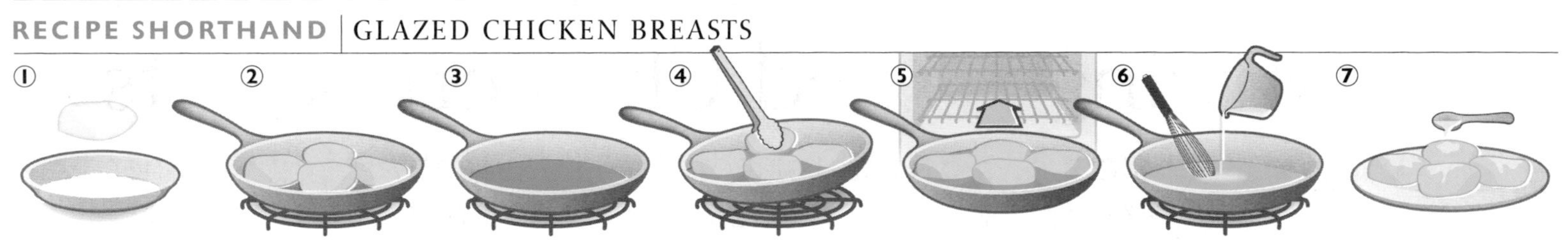

1. **COAT** chicken breasts with flour. 2. **BROWN** chicken in skillet. 3. **REDUCE** glaze in empty skillet. 4. **ROLL** each breast in glaze. 5. **TRANSFER** skillet to oven and finish cooking. 6. **WHISK** reserved orange juice into glaze. 7. **SPOON** glaze over chicken.

wasn't with the glaze but with the chicken. What if I added a thin layer of flour to the outside of the meat before browning it? In the test kitchen, we don't typically coat meat with flour before browning it, but it gave the chicken breasts a thin, crispy crust that served as a good grip for the glaze. (Cornstarch also held the glaze, but it turned the skin a bit slimy.)

I added a small amount of orange juice just before serving to brighten the glaze flavors even further. This finishing touch made all the difference. Now I had elevated glazed chicken to an elegant new height—far beyond 30,000 feet.

ORANGE-HONEY GLAZED CHICKEN BREASTS

SERVES 4

When reducing the glaze in step 4, remember that the skillet handle will be hot; use an oven mitt. To make sure the chicken cooks evenly, buy breasts that are similar in size—about 12 ounces apiece. If the glaze looks dry during baking, add up to 2 tablespoons of juice to the pan. If your skillet is not ovenproof, brown the chicken breasts and reduce the glaze as instructed, then transfer the chicken and glaze to a 13 by 9-inch baking dish and bake (don't wash the skillet). When the chicken is fully cooked, transfer it to a plate to rest and scrape the glaze back into the skillet to be reduced.

- 1½ cups plus 2 tablespoons orange juice
- ⅓ cup light corn syrup
- 3 tablespoons honey
- 1 tablespoon Dijon mustard
- 1 tablespoon distilled white vinegar
- ⅛ teaspoon red pepper flakes
- Table salt and ground black pepper
- ½ cup all-purpose flour
- 4 bone-in, skin-on chicken breast halves (about 12 ounces each), ribs removed, trimmed of excess fat and skin (see note above)
- 2 teaspoons vegetable oil
- 1 medium shallot, minced (about 3 tablespoons)

1. Adjust oven rack to middle position and heat oven to 375 degrees. Whisk 1½ cups orange juice, corn syrup, honey, mustard, vinegar, pepper flakes, ⅛ teaspoon salt, and ⅛ teaspoon pepper together in medium bowl. Place flour in pie plate, then season chicken on both sides with salt and pepper. Working with one chicken breast at a time, coat chicken with flour, patting off excess.

2. Heat oil in ovenproof 12-inch skillet over medium heat until shimmering. Add chicken breasts skin-side down; cook until well browned and most of fat has rendered from skin, 8 to 14 minutes. (If after 3 minutes you don't hear definite sizzling, increase heat to medium-high. If after 6 minutes chicken is darker than lightly browned, reduce heat slightly.) Turn chicken and lightly brown other side, about 5 minutes longer. Transfer chicken to plate.

3. Pour off all but 1 teaspoon fat from pan. Add shallot and cook until softened, 1 to 2 minutes. Increase heat to high and add orange juice mixture. Simmer, stirring occasionally, until syrupy and reduced to 1 cup (heatproof spatula should leave slight trail when dragged through glaze), 6 to 10 minutes. Remove skillet from heat and tilt to one side so glaze pools in corner of pan. Using tongs, roll each chicken breast in pooled glaze to coat evenly and place skin-side down in skillet.

4. Transfer skillet to oven and bake chicken until thickest part of breasts registers 160 degrees on instant-read thermometer, 25 to 30 minutes, turning chicken skin-side up halfway through cooking. Transfer chicken to platter and let rest 5 minutes. Return skillet to high heat (be careful—handle will be very hot) and cook glaze, stirring constantly, until thick and syrupy (heatproof spatula should leave wide trail when dragged through glaze), about 1 minute. Remove pan from heat and whisk in remaining 2 tablespoons orange juice. Spoon 1 teaspoon glaze over each breast and serve, passing remaining glaze at table.

APPLE-MAPLE GLAZED CHICKEN BREASTS

Follow recipe for Orange-Honey Glazed Chicken Breasts, substituting apple cider for orange juice and 2 tablespoons maple syrup for honey.

PINEAPPLE-BROWN SUGAR GLAZED CHICKEN BREASTS

Follow recipe for Orange-Honey Glazed Chicken Breasts, substituting pineapple juice for orange juice and 2 tablespoons brown sugar for honey.

EQUIPMENT TESTING:

Inexpensive Instant-Read Thermometers

An instant-read thermometer should have a broad range to cover high and low temperatures; a stem long enough to reach the interior of large cuts of meat; a way to recalibrate slips in accuracy; and, above all, speed, so you don't have to keep the oven door open too long. The most coveted instant-read thermometer in the test kitchen remains the ThermoWorks Super-Fast Thermapen, which meets all these criteria and produces readings in just four seconds. However, the $85 ticket begs for an affordable alternative.

We ran seven thermometers priced under $25 through a gauntlet of boiling water, ice water, hot oil, and thick-cut pork chops to compare accuracy, speed, and functionality. The Thermapen is outfitted with a thermocouple sensor, whereas the less expensive models register temperatures with a thermistor, which is a cheaper circuit that comes with a sacrifice in speed. However, our testing revealed a worthy stand-in that registered temperatures in only five additional seconds. The CDN ProAccurate Quick Tip Digital Cooking Thermometer DTQ450 ($17.95) further impressed us with a temperature range (–40 to 450 degrees) capable of handling every task we set before it. For the complete results of this testing, go to www.cooksillustrated.com/october.

–Meredith Smith

INSTANT WINNER
The CDN ProAccurate Quick Tip Digital Cooking Thermometer works quickly and is reasonably priced.

COOK'S LIVE Original Test Kitchen Videos
www.cooksillustrated.com

RECIPE IN 60 SECONDS
- Glazed Chicken Breasts

VIDEO TIPS
- How much fat and skin should I remove?
- Can I use a family pack of chicken for this recipe?

ILLUSTRATION: JAY LAYMAN

Secrets to Apple Galette

Getting a flaky crust and caramelized apples can make this simple French tart not so simple. We wanted both—every time.

⋟ BY DAVID PAZMIÑO ⋞

I was introduced to apple galette on my first visit to a French patisserie. One bite and I knew I had found a tart that I loved as much as apple pie. Galettes come in various shapes and sizes—from ones in which the dough is folded over a pile of apples to others that feature layers of sweet pastry, almond filling, and meticulously layered apples. I wanted to re-create the one I first fell in love with: This galette features a thin, crispy, flaky, sugary crust topped with a generous layer of apples sliced a mere ⅛ inch thick. There's not much to this galette besides flour, sugar, butter, and fruit, and you don't even need a fork to eat it. When baked properly, the pieces are sturdy enough to eat out of hand, just like a slice of pizza.

What I thought would be a simple task proved to be surprisingly tricky. Nearly all the recipes I tried were made from a simple dough (flour, sugar, salt, butter, and ice water) that claimed to produce the texture I was after. But in nearly every case, the dough was tough, cracker-like, and bland. I did learn a few things. Because of their size and thinness, round galettes were difficult to roll out and transfer to a baking sheet. I decided to stick with rectangular galettes. From the way even my mediocre attempts were being devoured by tasters, I knew that this dessert had to feed a crowd.

Picking Flours

For my early tests, I used a food processor to cut the butter completely into the dry ingredients. Although this is the test kitchen's preferred technique for classic American pie dough, I thought that a French dough might require a French technique. A few years ago, one of my colleagues experimented with fraisage (see "Freeform Fruit Tart," July/August 2004). This technique calls for partially cutting the butter into the dry ingredients, leaving large pea-sized pieces of fat

The ideal galette has the buttery flakiness of a croissant but is strong enough to support a generous layer of caramelized apples.

unmixed. But what makes fraisage truly unique is how the dough is combined. Small bits of the barely mixed dough are pressed firmly against the counter with the heel of the hand to create a uniform dough. As a result, the chunks of butter are pressed into long, thin sheets that create lots of flaky layers when the dough is baked.

Fraisage did indeed produce a flakier crust than had my initial tests, but tasters said it was tougher than they would have thought. Something wasn't making sense. Upon closer examination of the Freeform Fruit Tart recipe, it dawned on me. That recipe called for piling juicy summer fruit onto the dough and then folding the edges of the dough over the fruit. My recipe called for shingling a single layer of fairly dry apples on top. Without a mound of fruit to keep the dough moist, my crust was drying out before the apples could brown and caramelize. Adding a bit more butter to the dough increased tenderness slightly, but not enough.

I wondered if using a different flour could be the answer. Until now, I had been using all-purpose flour, even though many recipes for French pastry call for pastry flour. It was time to give this flour a try. Basically, the difference between these two flours is protein content. When mixed with water, the proteins (gliadin and glutenin) in flour create a stronger, more elastic protein called gluten. The higher the gluten content, the stronger and tougher the dough. Pastry flour has a protein content of 9 percent, and the protein content of all-purpose flour ranges from 10 percent to 12 percent. This difference might not seem like much, but when I made galettes from each type of flour the results were dramatic. The galette made with all-purpose flour was tough, and the one with pastry flour was flaky, tender, and sturdy. The only problem is that pastry flour is not widely available.

Looking for a more practical alternative, I tried cake flour, which is sold in supermarkets and has a protein content of just 8 percent. But when I substituted 1 cup, ½ cup, and even ¼ cup of cake flour for the equivalent amount of all-purpose flour, the dough—though tender—crumbled. It turns out that cake flour goes through a bleaching process (with chlorine gas) that affects how its proteins combine with water. As a result, weaker gluten is formed—perfect for a delicate cake but not for a pastry that must be tender *and* sturdy.

Casting a wider net, I looked through numerous French cookbooks. Although most recipes were nearly identical in ingredients, there were two that stood out. Tart doughs in Julia Child's *From Julia's Kitchen* and André Soltner's *Lutèce Cookbook* both touted instant flour (also called quick-mixing flour) as the essential ingredient for flaky yet tender tart crusts. I keep instant flour in the back of my cabinet to make lump-free gravies, but I had never thought of it for pastry-making. Instant flour is made by slightly moistening all-purpose flour with water. After being spray-dried, the tiny flour granules look like small clusters of grapes. Since these preclumped flour granules are larger than those of finer-ground all-purpose flour, they absorb less water, making it harder for the proteins to form gluten.

Instant Success

Mixing regular all-purpose flour with some instant flour creates a very flaky, tender crust. Both Wondra and Pillsbury Shake & Blend brands work well in our recipe and can be found near the cornstarch in the baking aisle of most supermarkets.

INSTANT FLOUR

PHOTOGRAPHY: CARL TREMBLAY

RECIPE AT A GLANCE | PREPARING APPLE GALETTE

1. **CUT** in butter. 2. **ADD** water to form dough. 3. **FORM** mound. 4. **FRAISAGE** and chill.

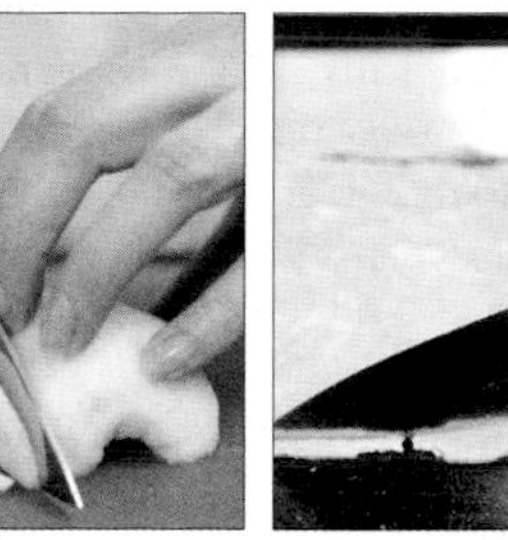
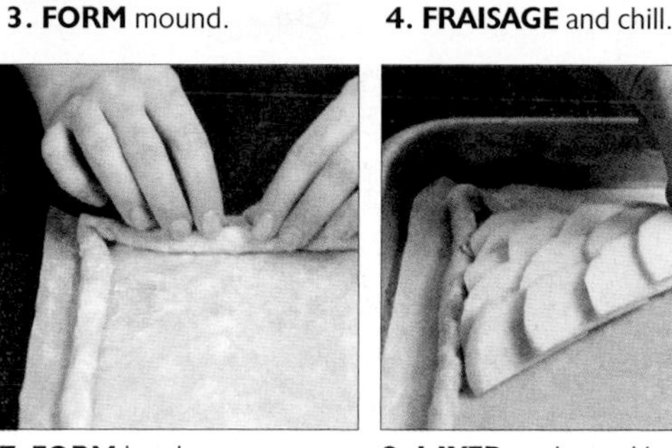

5. **CUT** apples. 6. **ROLL** and trim dough. 7. **FORM** border. 8. **LAYER** apples and bake.

I replaced some of the all-purpose flour with various amounts of instant flour. I found that ½ cup of instant flour kept the dough tender yet sturdy enough to cut neat slices of galette that could be eaten out of hand. An unlikely supermarket ingredient, along with a classic French mixing technique, had helped me create a remarkable crust.

Final Touches

The ideal galette should have both a crust and apples that are a deep golden-brown color. After several tests, most tasters felt that 400 degrees struck the right balance between intensely caramelized and simply burnt. Now the galette was perfect—almost. Although not all galette recipes called for it, many brush the hot-out-of-the-oven tart with apricot preserves. This glaze provided an attractive sheen and fruity tartness that tasters praised as they picked up another slice.

APPLE GALETTE

SERVES 8 TO 10

The galette can be made without instant flour, using 2 cups of all-purpose flour and 2 tablespoons of cornstarch. However, you might have to increase the amount of ice water. Although any apple will work in this recipe, we prefer Golden Delicious, Granny Smith, and Empire. If you don't have an apple corer, halve the peeled apples and then use a melon baller or paring knife to remove the core from each half. Make sure to cut the apples as thinly as possible. If they are cut thicker than ⅛ inch, they will be hard to shingle. If the dough has chilled longer than 1 hour, let it stand at room temperature for 15 to 20 minutes to soften. If the dough becomes soft and sticky while being rolled, transfer it to a baking sheet and refrigerate it for 10 to 15 minutes. Check the bottom of the galette halfway through baking—it should be a light golden brown. If it is darker, reduce the oven temperature to 375 degrees. Serve with vanilla ice cream, lightly sweetened whipped cream, or crème fraîche.

Dough

- 1½ cups (7½ ounces) unbleached all-purpose flour
- ½ cup (2½ ounces) instant flour (see page 20)
- ½ teaspoon table salt
- ½ teaspoon sugar
- 12 tablespoons (1½ sticks) cold unsalted butter, cut into ⅝-inch cubes
- 7–9 tablespoons ice water

Apple Filling

- 1½ pounds (3–4 medium or 4–5 small) apples (see note above)
- 2 tablespoons unsalted butter, cut into ¼-inch pieces
- ¼ cup sugar
- 2 tablespoons apricot preserves
- 1 tablespoon water

1. CUT IN BUTTER: Combine flours, salt, and sugar in food processor with three 1-second pulses. Scatter butter pieces over flour, pulse to cut butter into flour until butter pieces are size of large pebbles, about ½ inch, about six 1-second pulses.

2. ADD WATER: Sprinkle 1 tablespoon water over mixture and pulse once quickly to combine; repeat, adding water 1 tablespoon at a time and pulsing, until dough begins to form small curds that hold together when pinched with fingers (dough should look crumbly and should not form cohesive ball).

3. FORM MOUND: Empty dough onto work surface and gather into rough rectangular mound about 12 inches long and 5 inches wide.

4. FRAISAGE AND CHILL: Starting at farthest end, use heel of hand to smear small amount of dough against counter, pushing firmly down and away from you, to create separate pile of dough (flattened pieces of dough should look shaggy). Continue process until all dough has been worked. Gather dough into rough 12 by 5-inch mound and repeat smearing process. Dough will not have to be smeared as much as first time and should form cohesive ball once entire portion is worked. Form dough into 4-inch square, wrap in plastic, and refrigerate until cold and firm but still malleable, 30 minutes to 1 hour.

5. CUT APPLES: About 15 minutes before baking, adjust oven rack to middle position and heat oven to 400 degrees. Peel, core, and halve apples. Cut apple halves lengthwise into ⅛-inch-thick slices.

6. ROLL AND TRIM DOUGH: Place dough on floured 16 by 12-inch piece of parchment paper and dust with more flour. Roll dough until it just overhangs all four sides of parchment and is about ⅛ inch thick, dusting top and bottom of dough and rolling pin with flour as needed to keep dough from sticking. Trim dough so edges are even with parchment paper.

7. FORM BORDER: Roll up 1 inch of each edge and pinch firmly to create ½-inch-thick border. Transfer dough and parchment to rimmed baking sheet.

8. LAYER APPLES AND BAKE: Starting in one corner, shingle sliced apples to form even row across bottom of dough, overlapping each slice by about one-half. Continue to layer apples in rows, overlapping each row by half. Dot apples with butter and sprinkle evenly with sugar. Bake until bottom of tart is deep golden brown and apples have caramelized, 45 to 60 minutes.

9. GLAZE: While galette is cooking, combine apricot preserves and water in medium microwave-safe bowl. Microwave on medium power until mixture begins to bubble, about 1 minute. Pass through fine-mesh strainer to remove any large apricot pieces. Brush baked galette with glaze and cool on wire rack for 15 minutes. Transfer to cutting board. Cut in half lengthwise and then crosswise into individual portions; serve.

COOK'S LIVE Original Test Kitchen Videos

www.cooksillustrated.com

RECIPE IN 60 SECONDS

- Apple Galette

VIDEO TIPS

- When is the butter incorporated properly?
- How can I rescue problem pastry?
- What's the best way to peel and slice the apples?
- How can I tell if I've shingled the apples correctly?

Perfecting Pear Crisp

Simply substituting pears for apples in this classic American dessert is a recipe for disaster.

BY KEITH DRESSER

With its sweet filling and crunchy, buttery topping, a fruit crisp is a simple baked dessert, at least in theory. Apples are usually the fruit of choice for a crisp, but the delicate texture and subtle flavor of pears make this homey dessert a little more sophisticated. I was surprised to learn that the test kitchen had never developed a pear crisp recipe. But I wasn't worried. Believing that pears and apples are similar enough to substitute the former for the latter, I figured that with our recipe for Fruit Crisp (July/August 1998) in hand, things would work out fine.

No other way to say it: I paid for my culinary naiveté. Instead of a fruit crisp, my first attempt looked up at me with a face of watery pear sauce slathered with a gummy mixture of raw flour and soggy nuts. Other recipes I prepared didn't fare much better. Many consisted of hard, starchy chunks of pear with chewy granola bar–like toppings. It was obvious from my initial tests that pears react quite differently than apples when baked in a crisp. Further testing taught me that pear varieties, unlike many kinds of apples, are not always interchangeable. In the end, I found that Bartletts are best suited to a crisp (see "Three Kinds of Pears," page 23).

Pears might resemble apples, but they require different treatment in a crisp in order to ensure tender fruit and a crunchy topping.

Pear Warning

My first step toward perfecting a crisp recipe was to determine why pears react to baking so differently than do apples. Our science editor explained that pears and apples contain almost the same amount of moisture, but their cell walls are of very different strengths. During the ripening process, enzymes begin to break down the moisture-retaining cell walls in pears much faster than in apples. Cooking accelerates this process, which is why my impulse to use ripe pears for their more intense flavor resulted in mush. Unripe pears, on the other hand, retained their structure but cooked up starchy and dry. The solution was in the middle—using pears at the cusp of their ripeness. At this point, they have converted most of their starches into sugar but don't exude all of their juices when cooked.

Using ripe yet firm Bartlett pears reduced the wateriness, but my filling was still coming out too mushy, with a topping that tasted raw because it never completely cooked through. I thought about baking the filling and topping separately, but this seemed like too much trouble for such a simple dessert.

It occurred to me that maybe the pears weren't solely to blame. Was the sugar in the filling acting as an enabler, drawing out excess liquid? And wasn't the sugar turning to liquid itself when heated? When I tried omitting it, I was pleased to find that the amount of liquid in the bottom of the baking dish was significantly reduced and the topping was much drier. But now my crisp wasn't sweet enough. The apple crisp recipe I was using as a model called for 4 tablespoons of sugar. After some testing, I found the best balance between sweetness and moistness to be 2 tablespoons.

As a final refinement, I experimented with thickening the filling. This step isn't necessary in an apple crisp, because the apples don't give off much juice, but the pears needed help. I tested a handful of thickeners and settled on cornstarch. A teaspoon, mixed into a slurry with lemon juice, thickened the juices enough and unlike flour and tapioca, didn't leave a starchy taste or texture.

Top It Off

Every crisp needs a crunchy, sweet topping to provide textural contrast to the softer fruit. Our fruit crisp topping consists of cold butter cut into sugar, flour, and nuts, but this dry, powdery topping wasn't working for the pear crisp. Because pears release more juice than apples, the flour from the topping was being washed down into the filling. What I needed was a sturdier topping that would bake as a separate entity.

Borrowing from our Crumb Cake recipe (May/June 2007), I tried a streusel topping, in which melted butter is incorporated into flour (as opposed to cold butter being cut in), which helps to bind the flour to the other topping ingredients. Now when I took the dessert out of the oven, it had a crunchy topping that defined it as a true crisp.

RECIPE TESTING: **Getting the Topping Right**

Because pears exude so much juice when cooked, a traditional loose-and-sandy crisp topping will sink into the filling and won't get crunchy. We used a streusel technique that unified the ingredients to make a firmer topping that stays on top of the pears.

SOGGY CRISP
A sandy topping made with cold butter sinks into the filling.

CRISPY CRISP
A topping made with melted butter is more cohesive and stays in place.

COOK'S LIVE Original Test Kitchen Videos
www.cooksillustrated.com

RECIPE IN 60 SECONDS
- Pear Crisp

VIDEO TIPS
- How should I core the pears?
- What's the best way to ripen pears?

PHOTOGRAPHY: CARL TREMBLAY

STEP-BY-STEP | PREPARING PEARS

For this recipe, the pears are best peeled and halved, from stem to blossom end, and then cored and cut into pieces. We like to use a melon baller to core the fruit, but a paring knife also works.

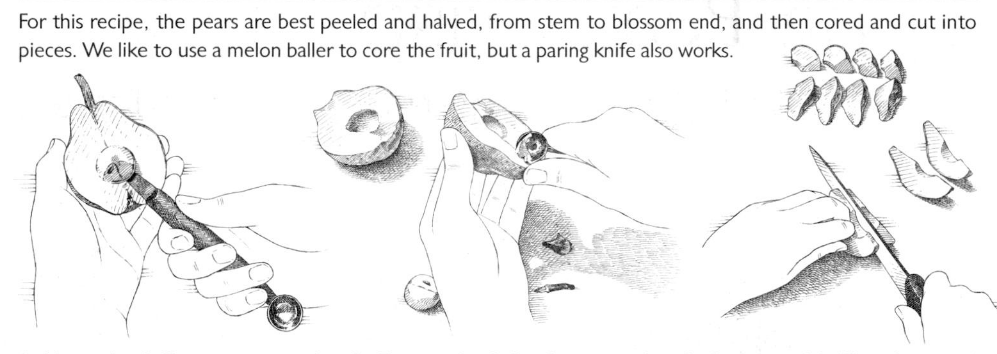

1. Use melon baller to cut around central core of halved, peeled pear with circular motion; remove core.

2. Draw melon baller from central core to top of pear, removing interior stem. Remove blossom end.

3. Quarter each half lengthwise and then cut each piece in half crosswise for eight pieces.

In my pear crisp adventure, I learned (as I should have known all along) that small details make all the difference. My final tweak to the recipe was to increase the oven temperature slightly from the 375 degrees we use to bake our apple crisp to 425 degrees, which made the topping even crunchier. Admittedly, this is a minor adjustment, but it is this kind of small detail that makes a great pear crisp.

PEAR CRISP

SERVES 6

The test kitchen prefers a crisp made with Bartlett pears, but Bosc pears can also be used. The pears should be ripe but firm, which means the flesh at the base of the stem should give slightly when gently pressed with a finger. Bartlett pears will turn from green to greenish-yellow when ripe. (See page 30 for information on ripening pears.) Although almost any unsalted nut may be used in the topping, we prefer almonds or pecans. Serve the crisp with lightly sweetened whipped cream or vanilla ice cream.

- ¾ cup (3 ounces) coarsely chopped nuts (see note above)
- ½ cup (2½ ounces) unbleached all-purpose flour
- ¼ cup (1¾ ounces) packed light brown sugar
- 4 tablespoons granulated sugar
- ¼ teaspoon ground cinnamon
- ⅛ teaspoon ground nutmeg
- Table salt
- 5 tablespoons unsalted butter, melted and cooled
- 1 teaspoon cornstarch
- 2 teaspoons juice from 1 lemon
- 3 pounds ripe but firm pears (6–7 medium) (see note above)

1. Adjust oven rack to lower-middle position and heat oven to 425 degrees. Process nuts, flour, brown sugar, 2 tablespoons granulated sugar, cinnamon, nutmeg, and ⅛ teaspoon salt in food processor until nuts are finely chopped, about nine 1-second pulses. Drizzle butter over flour mixture and pulse until mixture resembles crumbly wet sand, about five 1-second pulses, pausing halfway through to scrape down sides and bottom of workbowl. Set aside while preparing fruit.

2. Whisk remaining 2 tablespoons granulated sugar, cornstarch, lemon juice, and pinch of salt together in large bowl. Peel pears, then halve and core each (see illustrations above). Cut each half into 4 wedges and then cut in half crosswise (pieces should be about 1½ inches). Gently toss pears with sugar mixture and transfer to 8-inch-square baking dish.

3. Sprinkle topping evenly over fruit, breaking up any large chunks. Bake until fruit is bubbling around edges and topping is deep golden brown, 27 to 32 minutes. Cool on wire rack until warm, at least 15 minutes, and serve.

PEAR CRISP WITH OAT TOPPING

Follow recipe for Pear Crisp, reducing amount of nuts to ½ cup and increasing butter to 6 tablespoons. After incorporating butter into flour mixture in step 1, add ½ cup old-fashioned oats to food processor and process until evenly incorporated, about three 1-second pulses.

TRIPLE-GINGER PEAR CRISP

Follow recipe for Pear Crisp, using almonds and replacing cinnamon and nutmeg with ¾ teaspoon ground ginger. Process 2 tablespoons coarsely chopped crystallized ginger with nuts and flour in step 1. Reduce amount of lemon juice to 1 teaspoon and add 1 teaspoon grated fresh ginger to sugar-cornstarch mixture in step 2.

SHOPPING: **Three Kinds of Pears**

Although you may see as many as a half dozen pear varieties in some markets, these three are the most common. Our tasters found significant differences among them.

BARTLETT BOSC ANJOU

BARTLETT pears remained firm when baked, making them our top choice in a crisp. BOSC pears were a bit grainy when baked and are better poached. ANJOU pears are very juicy and were too soft in a crisp.

ILLUSTRATION: JOHN BURGOYNE

TASTING:

Light Vanilla Ice Cream

A new generation of light ice creams—appealingly described as "slow-churned," "double-churned," and the like—are filling supermarket freezer cases. How do they taste? To find out, we rounded up four samples.

Low-fat ice creams and ice milks used to be grainy and icy, because they didn't contain enough fat to counterbalance the ice crystals that inevitably form when ice cream is churned. For the last year or two, manufacturers have been using a process called low-temperature extrusion, which freezes light ice cream at an extremely low temperature. The idea is to freeze the ice cream so quickly that the air-fat-water emulsion does not break and grainy ice crystals never have a chance to form.

Overall, our tasters weren't terribly impressed. They gave low marks to Turkey Hill—the leanest sample in the group, with just 2.5 grams of fat per ½-cup serving. Breyers and Edy's (which is sold under the Dreyer's label on the West Coast) scored slightly higher but didn't elicit much enthusiasm. Tasters genuinely liked Häagen-Dazs, the only brand in the lineup made without stabilizers or emulsifiers. But with 7 grams per ½-cup serving, Häagen-Dazs Light has as much fat as many brands of regular ice cream.

How can something with so much fat be considered "light"? Federal labeling allows manufacturers to use the term "light" on ice cream with no more than half the fat and two-thirds the calories of the company's regular ice cream. Regular Häagen-Dazs has much more fat than the competition, so its light offering does, too.
—Elizabeth Bomze

TOP CHOICE, BUT NOT SO LIGHT
Tasters liked the "clean" vanilla flavor of Häagen-Dazs Light, which is made without stabilizers or emulsifiers.

A New Way with Sauces for Chicken

We rework classic French pan sauces to reduce the fat and punch up the flavor.

BY ERIN McMURRER

French pan sauces are made from the fond (intensely flavorful bits of browned protein) left in the skillet after you have cooked meat or poultry. These sauces are quick, reliable, and easy, but classic recipes require an awful lot of butter, usually about 1 tablespoon per serving. Newer sauces based on chutneys, relishes, and salsas have less fat, but they generally don't take advantage of the savory fond. I wanted to create lower-fat versions of classic French pan sauces for chicken.

First, a crash course in pan sauces. They must begin with an empty pan covered with fond. Aromatics, such as shallot or garlic, are quickly cooked in a thin film of oil on top of the fond. Next, a liquid (usually broth and/or wine) is added to loosen and dissolve the fond; scraping the pan bottom with a wooden spoon helps this process along. The sauce is then simmered rapidly to concentrate flavors and is finally enriched with a generous amount of cold butter.

Simply reducing the amount of butter left my sauces thin and brothy. But after some trial and error, I found that adding a teaspoon of flour with the aromatics helped to thicken the sauce, allowing me to reduce the butter to just 1 tablespoon. Using less butter had an unexpected benefit—the other flavors seemed amplified. Adding an acidic ingredient to the finished sauce (I had good luck with lemon juice, sherry, mustard, and brandy) provided a final blast of flavor.

SAUTÉED CHICKEN CUTLETS

SERVES 4

The chicken breasts will be easier to slice in half if you freeze them for 15 minutes. To slice in half, place one hand on top of the breast to secure it, hold a chef's knife parallel to the cutting board, and slice through the middle of the breast horizontally. Serve with any of the sauces that follow, or Brandy, Cream, and Chive Pan Sauce, available free at www.cooksillustrated.com/october.

- 4 boneless, skinless chicken breasts (6 to 8 ounces each), tenderloins removed, trimmed of excess fat, halved horizontally, and pounded ¼ inch thick (see note above)
- Table salt and ground black pepper
- 4 teaspoons vegetable oil

Adjust oven rack to middle position and heat oven to 200 degrees. Season both sides of each cutlet with salt and pepper. Heat 2 teaspoons oil in 12-inch skillet over medium-high heat until smoking. Place 4 cutlets in skillet and cook without moving them until browned, about 2 minutes. Flip cutlets and continue to cook until second sides are opaque, 15 to 20 seconds. Transfer to large ovensafe plate. Add remaining 2 teaspoons oil to now-empty skillet and repeat to cook remaining cutlets. Cover plate loosely with foil and transfer to oven to keep warm while making pan sauce.

VERMOUTH, LEEK, AND TARRAGON PAN SAUCE

MAKES ENOUGH FOR 8 CHICKEN CUTLETS (4 SERVINGS)

- 2 teaspoons vegetable oil
- 1 medium leek, white part only, halved lengthwise, sliced into ¼-inch-thick pieces, washed, and dried (about 1 cup)
- 1 teaspoon all-purpose flour
- ¾ cup low-sodium chicken broth
- ½ cup dry vermouth or white wine
- 1 teaspoon whole-grain mustard
- 2 teaspoons chopped fresh tarragon leaves
- 1 tablespoon cold unsalted butter
- Table salt and ground black pepper

Add oil to empty skillet used to cook chicken and return pan to medium heat. Add leek and cook, stirring often, until softened and browned around edges, 2 to 3 minutes. Add flour and cook, stirring constantly, 30 seconds. Add broth and vermouth, increase heat to medium-high, and bring to simmer, scraping pan bottom to loosen browned bits. Simmer rapidly until reduced to ¾ cup, 3 to 5 minutes. Stir in any accumulated chicken juices; return to simmer and cook 30 seconds. Off heat, whisk in mustard, tarragon, and butter; season with salt and pepper. Spoon over cutlets and serve immediately.

LEMON, CAPER, AND PARSLEY PAN SAUCE

MAKES ENOUGH FOR 8 CHICKEN CUTLETS (4 SERVINGS)

- 2 teaspoons vegetable oil
- 1 medium shallot, minced (about 3 tablespoons)
- 1 teaspoon all-purpose flour
- ¾ cup low-sodium chicken broth
- 2 teaspoons juice from 1 lemon
- 1 tablespoon capers, rinsed and chopped
- 1 tablespoon chopped fresh parsley leaves
- 1 tablespoon cold unsalted butter
- Table salt and ground black pepper

Add oil to empty skillet used to cook chicken and return pan to low heat. Add shallot and cook, stirring often, until softened, 1 to 1½ minutes. Add flour and cook, stirring constantly, 30 seconds. Add broth, increase heat to medium-high, and bring to simmer, scraping pan bottom to loosen browned bits. Simmer rapidly until reduced to ½ cup, 2 to 3 minutes. Stir in any accumulated chicken juices; return to simmer and cook 30 seconds. Off heat, whisk in lemon juice, capers, parsley, and butter; season with salt and pepper. Spoon over cutlets and serve immediately.

SHERRY, RED PEPPER, AND TOASTED GARLIC PAN SAUCE

MAKES ENOUGH FOR 8 CHICKEN CUTLETS (4 SERVINGS)

- 2 teaspoons vegetable oil
- 3 medium garlic cloves, minced or pressed through garlic press (about 1 tablespoon)
- 1 teaspoon all-purpose flour
- ¼ teaspoon paprika
- ¾ cup low-sodium chicken broth
- ½ cup plus 1 teaspoon dry sherry
- ¼ cup jarred roasted red peppers, patted dry and cut into ¼-inch dice
- ½ teaspoon chopped fresh thyme leaves
- 1 tablespoon cold unsalted butter
- Table salt and ground black pepper

Add oil to empty skillet used to cook chicken and return pan to low heat. Add garlic and cook, stirring constantly, until lightly browned, 30 to 60 seconds. Add flour and paprika; cook, stirring constantly, 30 seconds. Add broth and ½ cup sherry; increase heat to medium-high and bring to simmer, scraping pan bottom to loosen browned bits. Simmer rapidly until reduced to ¾ cup, 3 to 5 minutes. Stir in any accumulated chicken juices; return to simmer and cook 30 seconds. Off heat, whisk in peppers, thyme, butter, and remaining teaspoon sherry; season with salt and pepper. Spoon over cutlets and serve immediately.

COOK'S LIVE Original Test Kitchen Videos

www.cooksillustrated.com

RECIPE IN 60 SECONDS
- Pan Sauces

VIDEO TIPS
- How do I know when the sauce has reduced sufficiently?
- Why don't you make pan sauces in a nonstick pan?

Reconsidering Cast Iron

Is cast iron the original nonstick pan? Do recent innovations improve on this traditional kitchen workhorse?

BY LISA McMANUS

Centuries before DuPont invented Teflon in 1938, people were cooking with cast iron. Over the past 30 years, nonstick skillets have taken the place of cast iron in most homes. But with disturbing reports about the effects of nonstick coatings on the environment and our health, we decided to take another look at cast iron to see if it is worth bringing back into the kitchen.

Cast iron has always been known to have a few advantages over other types of cookware. Its material and weight give it excellent heat retention for high-heat cooking techniques such as frying and searing. You can use it on the stovetop or bake with it in the oven. Its durability is legendary—many people are still cooking with cast-iron pans handed down for generations. Unlike most consumer products, cast-iron pans actually improve with time and heavy use.

Cast iron also has disadvantages. It's heavy and needs special care. It must be seasoned to prevent it from rusting or reacting with the foods you cook. Until its seasoning is well established, food will stick to it. You shouldn't use soap or steel wool on it, lest you strip off the seasoning.

When we went shopping for cast-iron pans to test, we noticed that although you can still find traditional cast iron, manufacturers have been tweaking the design and materials to maintain its principal benefits while diminishing some of the downside. They have begun coating the surface with a variety of materials to either begin the seasoning process for you or render it unnecessary. In some cases, new coatings bonded onto the cast iron make soap and even the dishwasher no longer off-limits.

One thing that didn't always get better with innovation is price: Traditional unseasoned cast-iron skillets are a true bargain, costing between $11 and $20. Most preseasoned pans are also fairly cheap, at $15 to $30, but we found fancier pans that hovered around the $100 mark.

Seasoned Wisdom

"Seasoning" is a word you hear a lot around cast iron. It might sound mysterious, but it's just oil and carbon residue from cooking that polymerize when heated and bond to the cast iron, forming a smooth surface. You build up seasoning over time simply by cooking in the pan and doing routine maintenance (see "Taking Care of Cast Iron," page 26). Until recently, all cast-iron pans were purchased unseasoned. For our testing, we bought eight skillets, all about 12 inches in diameter: three factory-seasoned pans, three traditional unseasoned pans, and two with innovative finishes that required no seasoning. Le Creuset's skillet has a matte-textured black enamel interior, rather than the glossy cream-colored finish found inside the company's Dutch ovens. Newcomer Olvida offered the most unusual finish of all: nickel plating that made the pan shiny silver. The nickel finish is designed to be nonreactive and safe with metal utensils, soap, and the dishwasher. We followed manufacturer directions to prepare the unseasoned pans for cooking.

Our first goal was to see how the cast-iron pans stacked up against our favorite nonstick skillet, the All-Clad Nonstick 12-Inch Skillet ($159.95), and our favorite stainless-steel skillet, the All-Clad Stainless 12-Inch Skillet ($134.95), in a battery of cooking tasks.

One of the primary reasons to own a nonstick skillet is to cook eggs, so we started by rating each pan for sticking and ease of cleaning when cooking scrambled eggs. Next, we baked corn bread to test evenness of browning and oven performance. We pan seared steak to test

Cast-Iron History

Cast-iron cookware is formed by pouring molten iron into a mold made of sand, which is used only once, making each pan unique. The process originated in China in the 6th century B.C. and has been mostly unchanged for centuries, with the exception of machines that now pour the hot metal into the molds. Cast iron was the material of choice for cookware in America until the early 20th century, when aluminum became affordable. At one time, there were dozens of American companies making cast-iron cookware. Today, there are just two, Lodge and American Culinary (which sells pans under the Wagner label). Most of the pans we tested are made in China.—L.M.

OLDER, NOT BETTER
We purchased this 100-year-old Wagner pan from a collector for $110. This pan had a nice patina and aced the scrambled egg test, but it is lighter than the modern cast-iron pans in our lineup and didn't perform as well in the searing and frying tests.

AT A GLANCE: Nonstick vs. Cast Iron

Should you buy nonstick or cast-iron cookware? Here's how they stack up.

	NONSTICK	CAST IRON	NOTES
PRICE		√	The best nonstick pans cost at least $100. You can buy four good cast-iron pans for that money.
EASE OF USE	√		Cast-iron pans are heavy and hard to lift and maneuver.
CARE	√		Cast iron must be washed and dried carefully after each use and may require occasional reseasoning.
STICK-RESISTANCE	√		Preseasoned cast iron comes close to nonstick, especially with repeated use.
VERSATILITY		√	Cast iron is perfect for searing steaks and is ovensafe. Nonstick doesn't brown very well and can't go into a very hot oven.
DURABILITY		√	Cast iron will last a lifetime or longer. Nonstick might last a few years—at most.

Nonstick Surface Comes with Time

We found that all cast-iron pans will become more nonstick with time. While you might think this will take years, we found a significant difference after just a few weeks in the test kitchen.

STICKY MESS
Scrambled eggs stick to the surface of a new preseasoned cast-iron skillet just out of the box.

SEASONED PRO
After a few weeks, the same pan became more seasoned and released all but a few wisps of egg.

searing ability and made tomato-caper pan sauce with the resulting fond to see whether the cast iron would react with the acid in the sauce. We also shallow-fried breaded chicken cutlets while wiring the pans with a thermocouple to measure their responsiveness, conductivity, and heat retention—all reflecting their ability to evenly and crisply fry chicken.

In the egg test, the nonstick skillet was the runaway winner; the performance of the cast-iron pans ranged from mediocre to poor. The cast-iron pans were clearly superior in the corn bread tests, producing the brownest, crispest crust. They were on par with the stainless-steel pan in the steak and chicken tests. Though not unexpected, the results were somewhat disappointing.

However, we noticed that most of the cast-iron pans improved their ability to release food as our testing progressed. The seasoning (whether done by the manufacturer or us) was becoming thicker and more reliable. We decided to try the egg test again and were surprised by the dramatic improvement. Pans that had performed poorly in the first egg test did a decent job, and the preseasoned pans were now nearly as good as the nonstick pan in this test. Given such dramatic improvement over just a few weeks, we were not surprised when the cast-iron pans continued to become more "nonstick" with time.

At this point, we concluded that a cast-iron pan can combine the best traits of both nonstick and traditional cookware: You could make eggs and sear steak in the same pan. However, this endorsement comes with two important caveats—you must choose the right pan, and you must be willing to care for it.

Casting Call

So which of these eight cast-iron pans is our favorite? There were several factors that distinguished the high-ranked models. First, they were seasoned by the manufacturer. Seasoning new pans in the oven creates oily fumes and a mess as shortening drips off the pan. What's more, the unseasoned pans lagged behind the factory-seasoned pans in nonstick performance throughout our testing. Their lighter hue also produced lighter browning on the corn bread than the solidly black preseasoned pans. This year, Lodge discontinued selling unseasoned cast iron, stating that customers preferred the preseasoned pans by a wide margin. According to Lodge spokesperson Mark Kelly, the factory seasoning is "equivalent to seasoning it yourself 20 times." We think this leg up is well worth a few extra dollars.

Second, evenness of cooking without hot spots or heat surges was very important. We wanted a pan that wouldn't cool off too much when food was added and would quickly climb back to the desired temperature. The Bayou Classic skillet had trouble maintaining steady heat, a major flaw for this type of pan. When we weighed the pans and measured the thickness of their bottoms, we discovered that the Bayou was the thinnest. Our top-ranked pans were up to twice as thick and all demonstrated more even distribution and retention of heat.

A third key factor was the diameter of the interior cooking surface, which made a difference when trying to accommodate multiple chicken breasts or steaks without crowding or steaming. Despite averaging 12 inches from rim to rim, the interior cooking surfaces of the pans ranged from 9¼ inches to 10¾ inches. We have a strong preference for the larger pans.

Weight was a thorny issue. While we preferred the bigger pans, they tended to be heavy and difficult for a smaller cook to manipulate in tasks such as swirling melting butter, pouring off a pan sauce, and flipping to release corn bread. Good handle design can help offset the problem. Our top-ranked pans all featured helper handles opposite the main handle. Two pans (Le Creuset and Lodge Pro-Logic) also featured larger main handles, which made the pans easier for smaller cooks to use.

Durability is one of the biggest virtues of cast iron. And while the Le Creuset pan performed very well, the enameled bottom of the pan also became chipped and scratched with routine use during testing. (You also can't use metal utensils with this pan or stack other pans inside it.) If you want a kitchen workhorse, this isn't it. The nickel finish on the Olvida pan was durable and worked as described, but it didn't offer significant enough advantage over preseasoned cast iron to warrant spending nearly $100. While we often find that you get what you pay for, in the case of cast iron, you don't need to spend more to get more.

Taking Care of Cast Iron

Routine Maintenance

If you buy a preseasoned pan (and you should), you can use the pan with little fuss.

➢ Don't wash the pan with soap or leave it in the sink to soak. Rinse it out under hot running water, scrubbing with a brush to remove traces of food. (This is easiest if done while the pan is still warm.)

➢ Dry the pan thoroughly and put it back on the burner on low heat until all traces of moisture disappear (this keeps rusting at bay). Put a few drops of vegetable oil in the warm, dry pan and wipe the interior with a wad of paper towels until it is lightly covered with oil. Then, using fresh paper towels, rub more firmly to burnish the surface and remove all excess oil. The pan shouldn't look or feel oily to the touch. Turn off the heat and allow the pan to cool before putting it away.

Heavy-Duty Cleaning

If you have stuck-on food or you've inherited a pan that is rusty or gummy, scrub it with kosher salt.

➢ Pour in vegetable oil to a depth of ¼ inch, then place the pan on a stove set to medium-low for 5 minutes. Remove pan from heat and add ¼ cup kosher salt. Using potholder to grip hot handle, use thick cushion of paper towels to scrub pan. Warm oil will loosen food or rust, and kosher salt will have abrading effect. Rinse pan under hot running water, dry well, and repeat, if necessary.

Reseasoning

If cooking acidic foods or improper cleaning has removed the seasoning from your pan, it will look dull, patchy, and dry instead of a smooth, rich black. You need to restore the seasoning. We have found this stovetop method (rather than the usual oven method) to be the most effective way to season a cast-iron pan.

➢ Heat pan over medium-high heat until drop of water evaporates on contact. Wipe inside with wad of paper towels dipped in vegetable oil (hold towels with tongs to protect yourself). Wipe out excess oil and repeat as needed until pan is slick.

In the end, we preferred the classic design—with straight (rather than sloped) sides—and roomy interior of the preseasoned Lodge Logic Skillet ($26.95). It performed well in all our cooking tests, its surface gained seasoning in the course of testing, and it will last for generations. If you are strong and don't mind a truly heavy pan, the preseasoned Camp Chef skillet is a solid performer for only $17.99. It's our Best Buy.

COOK'S LIVE Original Test Kitchen Videos
www.cooksillustrated.com

BEHIND THE SCENES
- Cast-Iron Skillet Testing

VIDEO TIPS
- What's the right way to maintain a cast-iron skillet?

RATINGS
GOOD: ★★★
FAIR: ★★
POOR: ★

TESTING CAST-IRON SKILLETS

We tested eight cast-iron skillets, each approximately 12 inches in diameter, along with our top-rated nonstick and stainless-steel skillets. We compared the performance of these pans in a number of cooking tests. Mail-order sources for the top pans are on page 32.

MATERIAL: Metal and finish of pans.

PRICE: Retail price at Boston-area stores or online cookware sites.

COOKING SURFACE: Diameter of interior cooking surface measured (in inches) across the bottom of the skillet and thickness of pan bottom (in millimeters).

WEIGHT: Weight of skillet.

EGGS: We prepared scrambled eggs in each pan as the first test (after seasoning pans that required it), noting degree of sticking and ease of cleanup. We did it again after completing all other cooking tests, to observe whether pans became more seasoned during testing. Rating reflects performance in the second round.

STEAK: We pan-seared steaks and prepared a tomato-based pan sauce in each pan. We preferred pans that provided a well-browned crust and a good fond that led to a complex, flavorful pan sauce.

CORN BREAD: We put the pans in the oven; we preferred those that made corn bread that released easily from the pan and had a crisp, golden crust and moist interior.

CHICKEN: We looked for shallow-fried breaded chicken cutlets that were crisp and golden brown outside and moist inside, preferring pans that retained heat well, even when food was added, and did not get crowded.

DESIGN: We considered design features such as helper handles, weight, and shape, and performance features that helped make the pan easy to use and clean. Pans that required strong arms lost some points.

HIGHLY RECOMMENDED

	PERFORMANCE	TESTERS' COMMENTS
Lodge Logic 12-Inch Skillet MATERIAL: Cast iron, preseasoned PRICE: $26.95 COOKING SURFACE: diameter 10"; bottom thickness 5.66 mm. WEIGHT: 7.2 lb.	EGGS: ★★★ STEAK: ★★★ CORN BREAD: ★★★ CHICKEN: ★★★ DESIGN: ★★	Classic shape provided "plenty of room" in steak and chicken tests, but small handle made pan feel heavy when lifted. Eggs stuck "considerably" and took "tons of scrubbing" to clean the first time around but barely stuck and cleaned up easily the second time. Corn bread was crusty, with perfect release.
The Camp Chef SK-12 Cast Iron Skillet BEST BUY MATERIAL: Cast iron, preseasoned PRICE: $17.99 COOKING SURFACE: diameter 9 3/4"; bottom thickness 10.37 mm. WEIGHT: 9.2 lb.	EGGS: ★★★ STEAK: ★★★ CORN BREAD: ★★★ CHICKEN: ★★★ DESIGN: ★★	Heaviest and thickest pan in the lineup was "a beast" to handle, but its heft made it shine in our cooking tests, where a consistent heat and deep sear were desirable. Right out of the box, we made scrambled eggs that didn't stick and corn bread that browned well and released perfectly.

RECOMMENDED

	PERFORMANCE	TESTERS' COMMENTS
Lodge Pro-Logic 12-Inch Skillet MATERIAL: Cast iron, preseasoned PRICE: $29.95 COOKING SURFACE: diameter 9 1/4"; bottom thickness 5.44 mm. WEIGHT: 7.4 lb.	EGGS: ★★★ STEAK: ★★★ CORN BREAD: ★★★ CHICKEN: ★★★ DESIGN: ★★	"Gorgeous" browning on the fried chicken and steak. Eggs improved dramatically, from "horrible sticking" to "very easy to clean" by the end of testing. Handle is wide and well balanced, and loop-shaped helper handle is easy to grasp. Curved (rather than angled) sides make sauces easier to scrape up.
Le Creuset Round Skillet, 11-Inch MATERIAL: Enameled cast iron with matte-finish black enamel interior PRICE: $109.95 COOKING SURFACE: diameter 9 3/4"; bottom thickness 10.26 mm. WEIGHT: 6.5 lb.	EGGS: ★★★ STEAK: ★★★ CORN BREAD: ★★★ CHICKEN: ★★★ DESIGN: ★★	"Pretty" pan was well proportioned and easier to handle than others. Sloping sides made eggs and sauce easier to scrape up. Achieved "beautiful crust" on steak and corn bread. On first test, eggs stuck ferociously, but results improved dramatically in second round, with minimal sticking. Can't use metal utensils or stack anything inside without damaging enamel finish.
Olvida 13-Inch Skillet MATERIAL: Cast iron covered with nickel plate PRICE: $98.95 COOKING SURFACE: diameter 10 3/4"; bottom thickness 9.87 mm. WEIGHT: 8.65 lb.	EGGS: ★★ STEAK: ★★★ CORN BREAD: ★★★ CHICKEN: ★★★ DESIGN: ★★	Chicken and steak browned beautifully in this heavy, roomy, silver-colored pan with "steady heating." The fond for pan sauce was a little light on flavor, almost like the nonstick skillet. Eggs stuck a moderate amount, without much change as testing progressed; pan cleaned up easily. Dishwasher-safe.

RECOMMENDED WITH RESERVATIONS

	PERFORMANCE	TESTERS' COMMENTS
Wagner Collection Skillet, 11 3/4-Inch MATERIAL: Cast iron, unseasoned PRICE: $19 COOKING SURFACE: diameter 9 3/4" bottom thickness 5.82 mm. WEIGHT: 6.8 lb.	EGGS: ★★ STEAK: ★★★ CORN BREAD: ★★ CHICKEN: ★★★ DESIGN: ★★	Slightly less steady heating than higher-ranked pans, but good results shallow-frying chicken and searing steak. Eggs stuck moderately, even as testing progressed, and pan always required some scrubbing. Corn bread browned well but stuck to pan. Thumb-hold on handle is nice feature.
Cajun Classic 12-Inch Cast Iron Skillet MATERIAL: Cast iron, unseasoned PRICE: $16 COOKING SURFACE: diameter 9 1/2"; bottom thickness 8.15 mm. WEIGHT: 5.85 lb.	EGGS: ★★ STEAK: ★★ CORN BREAD: ★★★ CHICKEN: ★★★ DESIGN: ★★	Straight-sided pan was crowded while shallow-frying two chicken breasts and when searing a pair of steaks. Steak pan sauce had a slight metallic taste, indicating the acid had reacted with the pan. Eggs continued to stick in second round but cleaned up easily.
Bayou Classic Heavy Duty Cast Iron Skillet, 12 Inches MATERIAL: Cast iron, unseasoned PRICE: $11 COOKING SURFACE: diameter 9 1/2"; bottom thickness 4.06 mm. WEIGHT: 6.15 lb.	EGGS: ★ STEAK: ★★ CORN BREAD: ★★★ CHICKEN: ★★ DESIGN: ★★	Thin bottom caused steep temperature drop when chicken was added to hot oil. Steaks cooked unevenly and with unsteady temperatures (too hot, then too cool). Pan was crowded and began steaming steaks. Scrambled eggs stuck considerably throughout testing. Cooking surface was roughest of the lineup.

Is Wisconsin Parmesan a Player?

Do aging time, raw milk, and salt content really matter?

BY LISA McMANUS

The buttery, nutty, slightly fruity taste and crystalline crunch of genuine Parmigiano-Reggiano cheese is a one-of-a-kind experience. Produced using traditional methods for the past 800 years in one government-designated area of northern Italy, this hard cow's-milk cheese has a distinctive flavor that is touted as coming as much from the production process as from the region's geography. But is all of this regional emphasis for real, or can really good Parmesan be made anywhere?

Recently, many more brands of shrink-wrapped, wedge-style, American-made Parmesan have been appearing in supermarkets. They're sold at a fraction of the price of authentic stuff, which can cost up to $33 a pound.

To see how they stacked up, we bought eight nationally distributed brands at the supermarket: six domestic Parmesans and two imported Parmigiano-Reggianos. We also purchased Parmigiano-Reggiano from four gourmet mail-order companies. We paid from $13.99 to $33.60 per pound—plus shipping—for the high-end mail-order cheeses; the supermarket wedges ranged from $8.49 to $17.17 per pound.

The Making of Parmesan

In Italy, the making of Parmigiano-Reggiano is highly codified. Here's how the process works, in brief. Raw, partly skimmed milk from cows that graze in a small area of Emilia-Romagna in northern Italy is warmed and combined with a starter culture (think sourdough) to begin the curdling process. Rennet from calves' stomachs, which contains the coagulating enzyme rennin, is added to facilitate the formation of curds. The curds are stirred, which allows moisture and whey to escape. Eventually, the curds are formed into wheels that weigh about 80 pounds and have the words "Parmigiano-Reggiano" stenciled onto the exterior. The cheese is submerged in brine (salt water) for several days. This makes the rind a little salty, but most of the cheese is not exposed to the brine.

Finally, the cheese is aged. With aging, moisture levels decline and the cheese's characteristic crystals form. Aging also allows enzymes to break down the protein structure of the cheese, creating its signature crumbly, craggy texture. By law, Parmigiano-Reggiano must be aged for at least 12 months before it can be sold, and it is usually aged for 24 months.

The process is laborious and time-consuming, which explains the high price tag for this cheese. There are also plenty of places to cut corners, which is one reason domestic Parmesans are less expensive. But that's not the whole story.

An American Tale

What the cows eat will affect the flavor of their milk and the resulting cheese. In Italy, the cows designated for Parmigiano-Reggiano graze outdoors; in the United States, "most cows are not pastured," said Dean Sommer, cheese and food technologist at the Wisconsin Center for Dairy Research, at the University of Wisconsin-Madison. According to Sommer, American cows generally eat TMR, "total mixed ration," a concentrated feed.

In addition to the cows' diet, Sommer told us, "there are different and unique microflora and yeasts in the milk." The American practice of heating the milk for pasteurization kills these microorganisms. However, since Italians use raw milk to make Parmesan, these microorganisms add unique flavor components to the cheese. "With raw-milk cheeses, you get extreme highs and lows of flavor," Sommer said. "With pasteurized milk, you won't get those extreme highs, but you also won't get the lows. It's a more consistent product, and it saves money for the manufacturer."

It's not just the milk that's different in the United States. American cheese makers often use nonanimal rennet to curdle the milk. And the starter cultures differ, with Italians using the whey left from the cheese-making of the day before, while Americans generally purchase starters from enzyme manufacturers. Finally, each cheese-making company, and each plant of each company, will have slightly different microorganisms in its environment, which alters the flavor of the cheese being produced. "People will literally take bricks from the walls of the old plant with them to a new plant, in hopes of reestablishing the microflora," said Sommer.

Differences You Can Taste

Given all the differences in the manufacturing process on each side of the Atlantic, it shouldn't come as much of a surprise that our tasters easily picked out the imports in our lineup of eight supermarket cheeses (see chart on page 29). The two genuine Parmigiano-Reggianos, sold in supermarkets under brand names Boar's Head and Il Villaggio, were the panel's clear favorites. The domestic cheeses, all made in Wisconsin, presented a wide range of flavors and textures from quite good to rubbery, salty, and bland.

Tasting Mail-Order Parmigiano

We ordered Parmigiano-Reggiano from four gourmet websites: Zingermans.com ($22.50 per pound); Dean & Deluca, which imports a younger cheese to lower the cost ($21 per pound, 2-pound minimum, includes Parmigiano knife); Gustiamo.com, which boasts of a 36-month "extra-aged" cheese from a particular dairy ($42 for 1.25 pounds, $33.60 per pound); and iGourmet.com, where we chose both the regular Parmigiano-Reggiano ($13.99 per pound) and an intriguing Vacche Rosse ("Red Cow") Parmigiano-Reggiano ($12.99 for 8 ounces, $25.98 per pound).

We learned that this "Red Cow" Parmesan comes from the red-colored Reggiana cows that were the earliest breed native to northern Italy. Due to their lower milk yield, these cows were edged out by modern high-yield cows just after World War II. A few traditionalists are bringing them back to make cheese the old-fashioned way. Their milk has a naturally higher fat content, and the cheese is usually aged at least 30 months.

We preferred the iGourmet regular and Vacche Rosse Parmigiano-Reggiano by a landslide, ranking them significantly higher than the other cheeses for complexity of flavor and appealing texture. And when we tasted the regular Parmigiano from iGourmet against our supermarket cheeses, it was an easy winner. —L.M.

So what made the imported cheeses stand out? Though our test kitchen tasters usually like salty foods, the imports had the lowest salt content. Lab tests showed some cheeses to have nearly twice as much salt as others. That's because many American companies produce wheels of cheese that weigh just 20 to 24 pounds, not the 80-pound standard used in Italy. As a result, more of the cheese is exposed to salt during brining.

Texture was a big factor. The Italian imports had a drier, crumblier texture and a crystalline crunch. Nearly all of the American cheeses were noticeably moister, some even to the point of bounciness, with few or no crystals. The laboratory tests bore out our tasters' perceptions, with imported cheeses showing lower moisture levels in general.

TASTING SUPERMARKET PARMESAN CHEESE

Twenty *Cook's Illustrated* staff members tasted eight nationally available supermarket brands of Parmesan cheese three ways: broken into chunks, grated, and cooked in polenta. The results were averaged, and the cheeses are listed in order of preference. An independent laboratory measured the moisture level and salt content (both shown as grams per hundred). Information about aging was provided by manufacturers.

RECOMMENDED

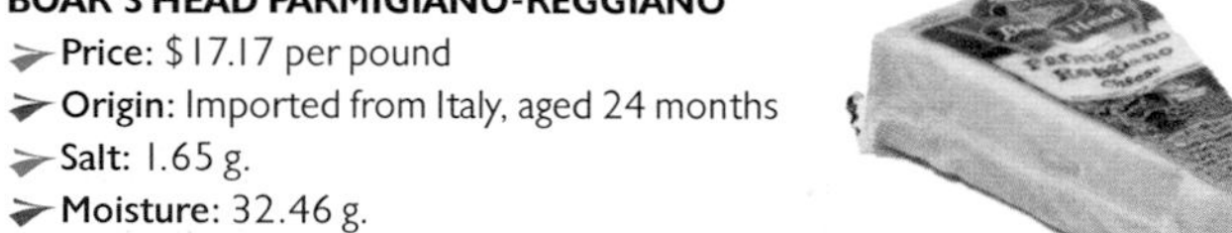

BOAR'S HEAD PARMIGIANO-REGGIANO
- **Price:** $17.17 per pound
- **Origin:** Imported from Italy, aged 24 months
- **Salt:** 1.65 g.
- **Moisture:** 32.46 g.
- **Comments:** Tasters deemed this sample "best in show" and "authentic," praising its "good crunch" and "nice tangy, nutty" flavor. "Rich" and "complex," this cheese had a "very good balance of acid/fruit/nutty/creamy."

IL VILLAGGIO PARMIGIANO-REGGIANO
- **Price:** $16.99 per pound
- **Origin:** Imported from Italy, aged 24 months
- **Salt:** 2.21 g.
- **Moisture:** 31.11 g.
- **Comments:** "Nutty, granular, tangy, and tasty" was the verdict, with tasters noting its "good, sharp flavor," "craggy" texture, "nice aroma," and "melt-on-your-tongue feel." In polenta, this cheese was "rich and bold."

BELGIOIOSO PARMESAN
BEST BUY
- **Price:** $8.99 per pound
- **Origin:** Domestic, aged at least 10 months
- **Salt:** 3.19 g.
- **Moisture:** 34.78 g.
- **Comments:** "Mild but complex," this cheese was a little "soft and creamy for a Parmesan," with a "too moist" texture. Grated, it had a "nice and tangy" aroma and "lovely, delicate flavor." In polenta, it was "nutty, well balanced, very good."

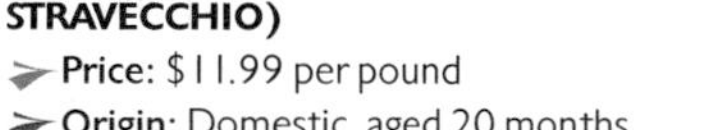

SARVECCHIO PARMESAN (FORMERLY STRAVECCHIO)
- **Price:** $11.99 per pound
- **Origin:** Domestic, aged 20 months
- **Salt:** 2.59 g.
- **Moisture:** 29.85 g.
- **Comments:** "Good, interesting flavor; almost has a sharp, lemony note," according to one taster. Another praised the "rich nuttiness" in this "crumbly" cheese "with a slight crunch." One taster summed up: "A Parm with guts!"

RECOMMENDED WITH RESERVATIONS

ROSALIA'S TRATTORIA PARMESAN
- **Price:** $8.49 per pound
- **Origin:** Domestic, aged at least 10 months
- **Salt:** 2.40 g.
- **Moisture:** 39.01 g.
- **Comments:** Tasters disliked its "plastic," "dense and rubbery," texture: "It's like I bit into food from a dollhouse." Grated, it had "nutty flavor and fresh aroma" but was "a bit one-dimensional." In polenta, it was "very cheesy," with "flavorful bite."

NOT RECOMMENDED

KRAFT GRATE-IT-FRESH PARMESAN
- **Price:** $11.40 per pound (sold in plastic grater, 7 ounces for $4.99)
- **Origin:** Domestic, aged 10 months
- **Salt:** 3.57 g.
- **Moisture:** 32.82 g.
- **Comments:** The high salt content showed: "I felt like a deer at a salt lick." Shredded with its own grater, the texture was "like dental floss," with flavor that was "artificial." One unhappy taster asked, "Was this grated from a Parm-scented candle?"

STELLA PARMESAN
- **Price:** $8.98 per pound
- **Origin:** Domestic, aged 10 months
- **Salt:** 2.90 g.
- **Moisture:** 33.48 g.
- **Comments:** In chunks, tasters were not impressed: "Soapy, fake, rubbery. Yuck." Grated, this sample fared better, with a "nutty, buttery aroma and flavor," though several deemed it "nothing special." In polenta, it was "very bland."

DIGIORNO PARMESAN
- **Price:** $8.49 per pound
- **Origin:** Domestic, aged at least 6 months
- **Salt:** 2.50 g.
- **Moisture:** 34.67 g.
- **Comments:** "Rubbery" came up over and over in tasters' comments. "Like eating candle wax, and the flavor's not much better." Grated, it was "blandsville." In polenta, it was "too mild." "Did you forget to put the cheese in here?"

Why is this so? First, even before the cheese is formed into wheels, the size of the curds influences its texture. In Italy, cheese makers use a giant whisk to break curds into pieces described as "the size of wheat grains," allowing moisture and whey to escape. American curds are broken up by machine and usually left larger, which causes them to retain more moisture, Sommer said.

Second, as Parmesan ages, it loses moisture and begins to form its characteristic crystals. At the same time, enzymes break down the protein structure, creating an increasingly crumbly, craggy texture, explained Pat Mugan, vice president of product innovation for Sartori Foods in Wisconsin, which produces SarVecchio Parmesan, the domestic cheese with the longest aging time (at least 20 months) and the lowest moisture level in our lineup. "At six months, the cheese would be able to bend; at twenty months, it crumbles," Mugan said. "You see a dramatic difference."

While Italian Parmigiano-Reggianos are all aged at least 12 and usually 24 months, for domestic Parmesan the federal standard is 10 months, though a few manufacturers petitioned (and got temporary permission) to shorten the aging standard to six months, claiming that it does not affect the quality of the cheese. Sommer disagrees: "For a Parmesan, especially, time is critical," he said. "For the first five months of aging, the cheese has hardly any flavor whatsoever. [Flavor development] gradually comes along, picking up speed from around eight months on, when you start getting some really nice flavors." Kraft now produces our previous favorite domestic Parmesan, DiGiorno, using this new shorter aging period, which helps explain why it rated so poorly with our tasters this time.

While our tasters clearly preferred Italian Parmigiano-Reggiano, they also praised the top two domestic cheeses for their pleasant nutty flavor. BelGioioso and SarVecchio were two of the longer-aged of the domestic cheeses, at 10 months and 20 months, respectively. While these cheeses can't really compete with our top-ranked imports, BelGioioso offered "lovely, delicate flavor" for just more than half the price.

KITCHEN NOTES

BY J. KENJI ALT

Smoke in the Water

We were among the many people who assume that there must be some kind of synthetic chemical chicanery going on in the making of "liquid smoke" flavoring. But according to the Colgin Company (which has been bottling liquid smoke since the 19th century), that's not the case. Liquid smoke is made by channeling smoke from smoldering wood chips through a condenser, which quickly cools the vapors, causing them to liquefy (just like the drops that form when you breathe on a piece of cold glass). The water-soluble flavor compounds in the smoke are trapped within this liquid, while the nonsoluble, carcinogenic tars and resins are removed by a series of filters, resulting in a clean, smoke-flavored liquid.

SMOKE SIGNALS
Test cook J. Kenji Alt turned a basic kettle grill into a homemade liquid smoke still. To view Kenji's slide show, go to www.cooksillustrated.com/october.

Curious about the manufacturing process for this product, we wondered if we could bottle up some smoke for ourselves. To do this, we created a small-scale mock-up of the commercial method, involving a kettle grill, a duct fan, a siphon, and an ice-chilled glass coil condenser.

In a comparison of homemade and store-bought liquid smoke, homemade was praised for its clean, intense, smoky flavor. But we spent an entire day and $50 on materials to produce 3 tablespoons of homemade liquid smoke. Commercial liquid smoke is just fine, especially if you avoid brands with additives such as salt, vinegar, and molasses. Wright's Liquid Smoke ($2.99 for 3.5 ounces) is our top-rated brand and contains nothing but smoke and water.

Cooling Soup

What's the best way to cool and store leftover soup? For safety reasons, the U.S. Food and Drug Administration (FDA) recommends cooling liquids to 70 degrees within the first two hours after cooking and 40 degrees within four hours after that.

The easiest method was to put the hot pot of soup in the refrigerator. The boiling soup cooled from 212 degrees to 40 degrees in a total time of four hours and 15 minutes. However, the fridge's temperature rose to nearly 50 degrees, which is unsafe for everything else being stored in there. We found that by letting the soup cool to 85 degrees on the countertop (which took only an hour) before transferring it to the fridge, we could bring it down to 40 degrees in a total time of four hours and 30 minutes (well within the FDA's recommended range), and the fridge never got above 40 degrees.

Ripening Pears

Most supermarket pears are rock-hard and must be ripened at home. What's the best way to accomplish this? Using Bartletts, we tested four methods: in a bowl on the counter; in a paper bag; in a paper bag with bananas (which give off ethylene gas, a ripening agent); and in the refrigerator. After two days, the pears in the bags were almost ripe and perfect for Pear Crisp (page 23) (the pears in the bag with bananas were slightly riper), but after just one more day they were too ripe. The pears in the bowl on the counter took four days to ripen, but they didn't exhibit the quick overripening that the pears in the bags did. Pears kept in the fridge were only slightly riper and softer after a week.

Our recommendation is to ripen pears in a bowl on the counter. If you need them sooner, ripen them in a bag with bananas. But check them frequently— they go from just right to mush in a matter of hours.

Cleaning Apples and Pears

In recent kitchen tests, we discovered that spraying produce with vinegar is the best way to remove surface wax and pesticides, but could this method destroy bacteria as well?

To find out, we cleaned apples and pears four different ways: rinsing under cold running tap water, scrubbing with a brush, washing with a vinegar solution, and scrubbing with antibacterial soap. (We also left one batch unwashed as a control.) We took surface samples from the produce and grew the bacteria in petri dishes. After four days, we compared the petri dishes and found that rinsing under cold water had removed only 25 percent of bacteria and scrubbing with a brush removed 85 percent. The vinegar removed 98 percent of surface bacteria, which made it nearly as effective as the antibacterial soap. The July 2002 issue of the journal *Microbiology* explains that the acetic acid in vinegar acts to lower the internal pH of bacterial cells, which in turn inhibits several key biochemical mechanisms, effectively destroying the bacteria.

UNWASHED
This petri dish shows the amount of bacteria present on the surface of an unwashed apple.

WASHED IN VINEGAR
This petri dish shows that washing apples in a mild vinegar solution cuts the bacteria level by 98 percent.

We recommend washing produce in a solution of 3 parts tap water to 1 part distilled vinegar applied with a spray bottle. This method should work for any firm, smooth-skinned produce. Just be sure to rinse them under cool running tap water afterward to remove any unwanted vinegary flavors.

SHOPPING: Wild Shrimp

Recently, we've been seeing producer-labeled "wild American shrimp" in our supermarkets. We held a blind tasting of frozen wild shrimp (caught in the Florida Keys); fresh (never-frozen) wild shrimp delivered overnight from Florida; and our favorite type of farm-raised shrimp (shell-on, individually quick-frozen). While both wild varieties had a sweeter, brinier flavor than the farm-raised shrimp, we found that the never-frozen wild shrimp had an off-putting mushy texture.

It turns out that fresh wild shrimp are minimally processed before delivery—they are almost always shipped head-on. The heads of shrimp contain digestive enzymes that can break down the muscle protein in the unfrozen shrimp's body rapidly after death, resulting in mushy meat. Frozen shrimp, on the other hand (both wild and farm-raised), have their heads removed and are frozen immediately after being caught, resulting in meat that stays plump and firm. If your supermarket carries frozen wild shrimp, we feel they are worth the extra money ($15.99 per pound versus $10.99 per pound for farm-raised at our local Whole Foods Market).

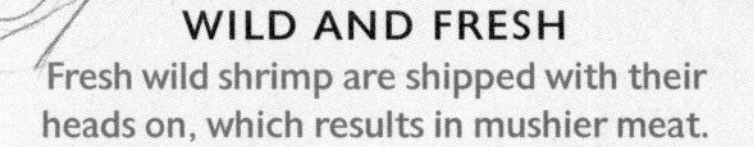

WILD AND FRESH
Fresh wild shrimp are shipped with their heads on, which results in mushier meat.

WILD BUT FROZEN
Frozen wild shrimp have their heads removed and a firmer, plumper texture.

SCIENCE: Brinerating

At one point during testing for our Skillet-Barbecued Pork Chops (page 6), the chops were flavored in a liquid-smoke marinade before being brined (the marinade was ultimately omitted; the powerful sauce provides enough flavor in this recipe). We tried to combine these steps by adding salt to the smoke-flavored marinade. Surprisingly, after cooking the chops, we found that compared with chops that were marinated then brined, the hybrid brine-marinated (or "brinerated") chops picked up very little smoke flavor.

The reason? The salt in brine binds to the muscle proteins in meat, increasing the electric charge on the proteins and making them less attractive to electrically neutral flavor molecules. It's as if the pork chop were a train with a line of salt and flavor molecules waiting to get on board. The stronger, electrically charged salt molecules barge their way onto the train and take all the seats, leaving most of the weaker, electrically neutral flavor molecules waiting at the station. If the meat is first placed in a salt-free marinade, however, the flavor molecules can get a seat and will stay on for the ride even after the meat is placed in a brine. Subsequent testing showed this to be true for a wide range of flavorings: fresh and dry herbs and spices, alliums, chiles, and citrus oils.

This explains why some of our brinerade recipes require super-saturating the brine with flavor. For example, our marinade for Cuban-Style Pork Roast (July/August, 2006) uses 2 full heads of garlic and 4 cups of orange juice. Adding a lot of flavor molecules to the brinerade gives a fighting chance for at least some of them to get on board.

FLAVOR FIRST
Marinating the meat first and then brining it produces flavorful and moist meat.

Marinade molecules
Salt molecules
Moist and flavorful meat

SALTY ATTRACTION
Salt has a stronger electrical charge than most flavor molecules and will bind easily with meat in a brinerade, making it less likely that other flavorings will penetrate.

Brinerade
Moist meat without much flavor

Brining Frozen Meat

Submerging small portions of frozen meat in a bucket of cold water on the counter speeds up the defrosting process. For recipes where the first step is a brine, we wondered if we could combine two steps into one by defrosting the meat directly in the brine. We partially thawed frozen chicken parts in fresh water, then completed the last half hour of thawing in the brine solution called for in the pan-roasted chicken recipe we were following. When cooked, the chicken was as well-seasoned and juicy as chicken that had been fully defrosted before brining.

Further testing showed that the same method can be used for any recipe that calls for brining small- to medium-sized pieces of meat. Simply cut the defrosting time by the amount of brining time the recipe calls for. For example, if your pork chops need to thaw for an hour and your recipe calls for a 45-minute brine, thaw the chops in fresh water for 15 minutes, then brine for 45 minutes. The chart below shows total thawing times for cuts that are frequently brined.

Thawing Times in Cold Water

FOOD	THAWING TIME
4 chicken parts (breasts or legs)	1 hour
4 Cornish hens (giblets removed)	1½ hours
1 whole chicken (3 to 4 pounds)	3 hours
4 pork chops (10 ounces each)	1 hour
1 pork loin (2 pounds)	2½ hours
2 pork tenderloins (1½ pounds each)	1½ hours

ILLUSTRATION: JAY LAYMAN

RECIPE UPDATE

Scalloped Potatoes with Root Vegetables

Fans of our **Scalloped Potatoes** (March/April 2003) asked for a version incorporating root vegetables. Our recipe starts on the stovetop, where the potatoes gently cook to partial doneness in chicken broth and cream. Then the mixture goes into a small casserole, gets topped with cheese, and finishes in the oven. Because root vegetables like celery root and parsnips (our favorite combo with these creamy potatoes) have such strong flavors, we found it best to use a little of each in place of the potatoes. Also, to avoid a casserole with perfectly tender potatoes and underdone root vegetables, we gave the celery root and parsnips a five-minute head start on the stovetop before adding the potatoes. Go to www.cooksillustrated.com/october for our free recipe for Scalloped Potatoes with Root Vegetables.

Cheese Muffins

We had a number of requests to transform our **Quick Cheese Bread** (May/June 2004) into muffins. It sounded as easy as plopping spoonfuls of the cheesy quick-bread batter into a prepared muffin tin, but the cheese chunks in the batter—designed to leave generous cheese pockets in the larger bread loaf—didn't distribute evenly in the muffins. Breaking the cheese into smaller pieces, however, solved the problem. Raising the oven temperature a bit to 375 degrees ensures moist muffins with the proper rise and browned exterior. Go to www.cooksillustrated.com/october for our free recipe for Quick Cheese Muffins.

BIG CHEESE — LITTLE CHEESE

While our Quick Cheese Bread benefits from large chunks of cheese, these oversized pieces caused problems in muffins (left). Smaller bits of cheese worked much better (right).

White Turkey Chili

Using turkey in place of chicken in our recipe for **White Chicken Chili** (January/February 2007) seemed worth a try. We discovered that the slightly gamey flavor of turkey works perfectly with the strong flavors of this brothy chili containing green chiles, lime, cilantro, and white beans. Turkey also takes well to the recipe technique: cooking the meat in the chili, cooling it, shredding it, and reintroducing it. However, simply replacing 3 pounds of bone-in, skin-on split chicken breasts with one 3-pound bone-in, skin-on split turkey breast did not work. The ratio of meat-to-bones wasn't the same, and we wound up with way too much turkey meat in the chili. A 2½-pound turkey breast yielded the right amount of meat for this recipe. Cooking the turkey breast takes about double the time; surprisingly, there's no need to increase the amount of liquid called for in the original recipe. Go to www.cooksillustrated.com/october for our free recipe for White Turkey Chili.

—Charles Kelsey

IF YOU HAVE A QUESTION about a recipe, let us know. Send your inquiry, name, address, and daytime telephone number to Recipe Update, Cook's Illustrated, P.O. Box 470589, Brookline, MA 02447, or write to recipeupdate@americastestkitchen.com.

EQUIPMENT CORNER

⋟ BY ELIZABETH BOMZE ⋞

EQUIPMENT TESTING Apple Corers

Rather than slicing an apple into quarters and then removing the core and seeds from each piece, we'd rather reach for an apple corer, which does the job in one fell swoop. We tested five models and found out the task wasn't always so cut and dried. Narrow blade diameters—less than ¾ inch—on the Henckels Twin Cuisine Apple Corer ($9.95) and Messermeister Serrated Apple Corer ($6.95) struggled to break through the firmer flesh on Granny Smith apples and forced us to poke and prod the core from the sharp metal teeth. The relatively stubby—3½ inches or less—metal tubes on the Henckels corer and the Leifheit Hinged Apple Corer ($11.99) came up short when asked to plow through large apples. We had much better results with the razor-sharp Rösle Fruit Corer ($21) and the OXO Good Grips Corer ($6.50). Testers preferred the more comfortable grip on the OXO model.

For the complete results of our Apple Corer testing, go to www.cooksillustrated.com/october.

CORE VALUE
We like the wide blade and long grip of the OXO Good Grips Corer.

COMES UP SHORT
The small blade on the Henckels Twin Cuisine Apple Corer couldn't cut it.

NEW PRODUCT
Cool Touch Oven Rack Guard

The JAZ Innovations Cool Touch Oven Rack Guard ($14.99) promises to protect hands and forearms from scorching oven racks. As we intentionally and unintentionally grazed our hands against the fabric while removing bubbling casserole dishes and baking sheets full of cookies, we noticed that the soft pad, though quite warm, was comfortably cooler than the exposed portion of the oven rack. Made from DuPont's flame-resistant Nomex fibers, the pad is not broiler-safe but does resist heat up to 500 degrees and can stay in your oven indefinitely. Just remember to take it out before turning the oven to broil or running the self-cleaning cycle.

PADDED PROTECTION
The JAZ Innovations Oven Rack Guard snaps around the front of a standard oven rack and protects against burns.

EQUIPMENT TESTING Knife Guards

If you store your knives loose in a drawer, you're putting the sharp edge of your blades—and your reaching hands—in danger. Blade sheaths are designed to protect against both risks, and we wondered if one style protected better and was easier to use than another. After some scary moments, we can safely say, yes. We rejected two models, the Messermeister 8-Inch Chef's Knife Edge-Guard ($2.50) and the Knife-Guard ($2.95), because they required "slicing" the knife into their slim, stiff polypropylene folds; what's more, the Knife-Guard's 1-inch depth barely covered our chef's knives. The magnetized Forschner 9-Inch Edge-Mag Knife Protector ($15.99 for three) was also disappointing. It opened easily, like a book, but its cheap, tape-like seam easily peeled or tore away from the cover and shut awkwardly over bulkier knife heels. We preferred Forschner's other model, the polypropylene BladeSafe case for 8- to 10-inch knives ($4.95). We liked its snap closure and its 2½-inch depth, which accommodated a variety of chef's, slicing, and paring knives. While it was a bit hard to open, it kept sharp blades safely covered.

For the complete results of our Knife Guard testing, go to www.cooksillustrated.com/october.

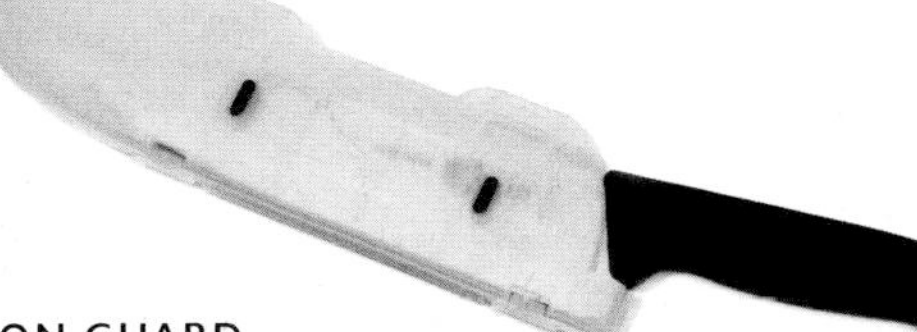

ON GUARD
The heavy-duty Forschner BladeSafe ($4.95) thoroughly shielded our hand from a wide array of knives.

NEW PRODUCT Utensil Pot Clips

Preparing soups, stews, and sautés with the kind of regular attention they need means keeping a stirring utensil on hand. A spoon rest can hold stirring utensils, but food can dribble off spoons and spatulas as you take them from the pot. The Trudeau Utensil Pot Clips ($13.50 for a set of two) keep drippy spoons and spatulas suspended over the food and actually do reduce mess at the stovetop. The silicone-covered stainless-steel pincher gripped the straight edge of a Dutch oven, saucepan, and sauté pan nicely, but it was a bit less sturdy on a slope-sided skillet.

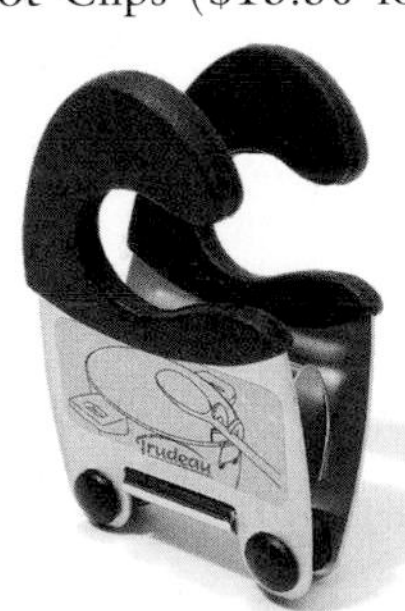

CLEVER CLIPS
Trudeau's Utensil Pot Clips keep drips in the pan.

DO YOU REALLY NEED THIS? Banana Hanger

Supermarkets suspend unripe bananas from tall poles covered with small hooks. The Nature's Way Banana Keeper ($3.99) miniaturizes this idea for the home kitchen. We hung underripe bananas from this plastic gadget and put others from the same bunch in a bowl. After monitoring the fruit for a week, we found that both bunches ripened and then turned spotty brown at the same rate. Our conclusion? Just stick with the bowl.

Sources

The following are mail-order sources for recommended items. Prices were current at press time and do not include shipping. Contact companies to confirm information or visit www.cooksillustrated.com for updates.

Page 11: GRILL GAUGE
- The Original Grill Gauge: $13.99, item GG1100, **Outdoor Cooking.com (866-674-0538, www.outdoorcooking.com).**

Page 13: SLOTTED SPOON
- OXO Good Grips Nylon Slotted Spoon: $5.99, item #77291, **OXO (800-545-4411, www.oxo.com).**

Page 15: BASMATI RICE
- Tilda Pure Basmati Rice: $7.99 for 4 lb. or 18.99 for 10 lb., **Kalustyan's (800-352-3451, www.kalustyans.com).**

Page 19: INSTANT-READ THERMOMETER
- CDN ProAccurate Quick Tip Digital Cooking Thermometer: $17.95, item#DTQ450, **Cutlery and More (800-650-9866, www.cutleryandmore.com).**

PAGE 27: CAST-IRON SKILLETS
- Lodge Logic 12-Inch Skillet: $26.95, item #L10SK3, **Lodge Manufacturing (423-837-7181, www.lodgemfg.com).**
- The Camp Chef SK-12 Cast Iron Skillet: $17.99, item #SK12, **Camp Chef (800-650-2433, www.campchef.com).**

Page 28: PARMESAN CHEESE
- iGourmet Parmigiano-Reggiano: $13.99/lb., item #208, **iGourmet (877-446-8763, www.igourmet.com).**

Page 32: APPLE CORER
- OXO Good Grips Corer: $6.50, item #112209, **Cooking.com (800-663-8810, www.cooking.com).**

Page 32: OVEN RACK GUARD
- JAZ Innovations Cool Touch Oven Rack Guard: $14.99, **Bed Bath and Beyond (800-462-3966, www.bedbathandbeyond.com).**

Page 32: KNIFE GUARD
- Forschner BladeSafe 8- to 10-Inch Blade Guard: $4.95, item #KS810, **The Knife Merchant (800-714-8226, www.knifemerchant.com).**

Page 32: POT CLIPS
- Trudeau Utensil Pot Clips: $13.50 for set of two, **Sur la Table (800-243-0852, www.surlatable.com).**

INDEX

September & October 2007

RECIPES

COOK'S LIVE Original Test Kitchen Videos www.cooksillustrated.com

MAIN DISHES
- **Beef and Vegetable Soup in 60 Seconds**
- What's the right cut of beef for a quick soup?

- **Chicken Tikka Masala in 60 Seconds**
- What's the best way to grate ginger?

- **Glazed Chicken Breasts in 60 Seconds**
- How much fat and skin should I remove?
- Can I use a family pack of chicken for this recipe?

- **Grilled Pork Loin with Apple-Cranberry Filling in 60 Seconds**
- What's the difference between pork loin cuts?
- What's the best way to stuff the pork loin?
- Is pink pork safe to eat?

- **Ricotta Gnocchi in 60 Seconds**
- How can I prevent gnocchi from falling apart?
- Can I use store-bought bread crumbs in this recipe?

- **Skillet-Barbecued Pork Chops in 60 Seconds**
- What kind of pork chops should I buy?
- Should I buy enhanced pork?
- How can I protect my nonstick pans?

SAUCES
- **Pan Sauces in 60 Seconds**
- How do I know when the sauce has reduced sufficiently?
- Why don't you make pan sauces in a non-stick pan?

DESSERTS
- **Apple Galette in 60 Seconds**
- When is the butter incorporated properly?
- How can I rescue problem pastry?
- What's the best way to peel and slice the apples?
- How can I tell if I've shingled the apples correctly?

- **Pear Crisp in 60 Seconds**
- How should I core the pears?
- What's the best way to ripen pears?

TASTING AND TESTING
- Behind the Scenes: Parmesan Tasting
- Behind the Scenes: Cast-Iron Skillet Testing
- What's the right way to maintain a cast-iron skillet?

AMERICA'S TEST KITCHEN
Public television's most popular cooking show
Join the millions of home cooks who watch our show, *America's Test Kitchen*, on public television every week. For more information, including recipes and program times, visit www.americastestkitchen.com.

Grilled Stuffed Pork Loin, 11

Beef and Vegetable Soup, 9

Skillet-Barbecued Pork Chops, 7

Chicken Tikka Masala, 15

Orange-Honey Glazed Chicken Breasts, 19

Ricotta Gnocchi, 13

Lemon, Caper, and Parsley Pan Sauce, 24

Apple Galette, 21

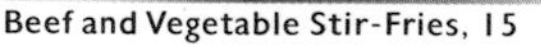
Beef and Vegetable Stir-Fries, 15

PHOTOGRAPHY: CARL TREMBLAY, STYLING: MARIE PIRAINO

Kaffir Lime Leaves
Culantro
Garlic Chives
Thai Basil
Tamarind
Galangal
Ginger
Thai Bird Chiles
Lemon Grass
THAI HERBS & SPICES

NUMBER EIGHTY-NINE

NOVEMBER & DECEMBER 2007

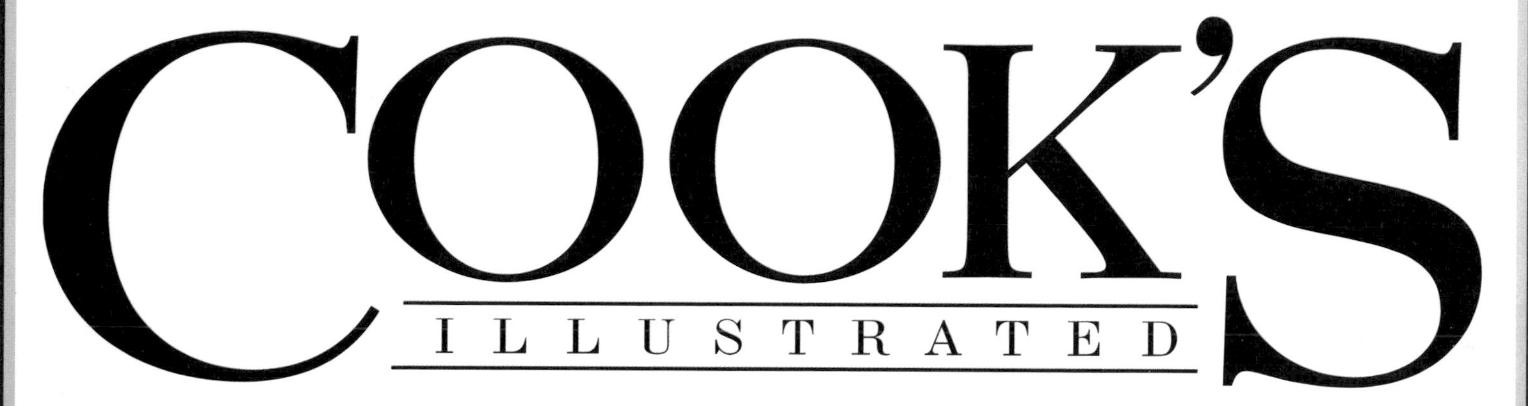

Foolproof & Flaky Pie Dough
Easy to Make, Easy to Roll

Holiday Ham 101
Test Kitchen Secrets

Turkey Taste-Test
Organic? Kosher? Butterball?

Mashed Potatoes and Root Vegetables

Best Drop Biscuits
No Roll, No Hassle

French Pot Roast

Rating Baking Sheets
Does Brand Matter? You Bet!

Perfect Apple-Cranberry Pie
Easy Roast Turkey Breast
Troubleshooting Tiramisù
Essential Ingredients for Baking
Beef and Vegetable Stir-Fries

www.cooksillustrated.com
$5.95 U.S./$6.95 CANADA

CONTENTS

November & December 2007

COOK'S ONLINE

Go to **www.cooksillustrated.com** to access all recipes from *Cook's Illustrated* since 1993 as well as updated tastings and testings. Watch videos of all the recipes in this issue being prepared and a special report on the baking sheet testing.

HOLIDAY BREADS *St. Lucia Buns*, or lussekatts, are sweet, raisin- or currant-studded saffron buns formed into "S" shapes for the Swedish festival of St. Lucia, which inaugurates the Christmas season. The Finnish spice their braided, briochelike *pulla* loaves with peppery cardamom. Golden-crusted *challah* is a rich Jewish egg bread served for everyday meals as well as on the Sabbath and other ceremonial occasions. Italians accent yeast bread with colorful candied or dried fruit to create the anise-enhanced *panettone* for Christmas celebrations. *Stollen*, Germany's oblong, sugar-dusted version of fruitcake, was originally intended to resemble baby Jesus in swaddling clothes. The Greeks make the cross-adorned *Christopsomo*, or Christ's bread—a rich, round loaf flavored with the licorice-like resin of the mastic tree. The Greek Easter bread *tsoureki* reflects the significance of the holiday through the red eggs, meant to represent new life, baked into the wreath-shaped loaf. Eastern European *potica* is essentially a strudel with a nut or poppy seed swirl. *Babka* is a traditional Polish Easter bread; the raisin-filled, rum-scented spongy yeast bread has become assimilated into Jewish holiday cooking, as well.

COVER: *Pears* by Robert Papp BACK COVER: *Holiday Breads* by John Burgoyne

For list rental information, contact: Specialists Marketing Services, Inc., 1200 Harbor Blvd., 9th Floor, Weehawken, NJ 07087; 201-865-5800.
Editorial Office: 17 Station St., Brookline, MA 02445; 617-232-1000; fax 617-232-1572. Subscription inquiries, call 800-526-8442.
Postmaster: Send all new orders, subscription inquiries, and change-of-address notices to Cook's Illustrated, P.O. Box 7446, Red Oak, IA 51591-0446

NOT ONE THING BUT THE OTHER

My mother was a doctor of sorts, a school psychologist who spent most of her career as a professor, both sober and respected. On a warm summer evening, however, she'd often enjoy a snort or two of Jack Daniel's, pack me and my younger sister into the back of an Army-surplus Jeep, and shoot up Southeast Corners Road like she was running moonshine, the bugs whipping into our faces like hail, the Jeep occasionally lifting up on two wheels like a catamaran sailing too close to the wind. Those days in Vermont were full of creosote, rough-sawn boards, homemade peach ice cream, mice nesting in waders, and swimming holes so cold they could shrink a full-grown sow down to the size of a woodchuck.

I know a successful New York book agent who traded in her flats for muck boots and now makes goat cheese. Lawyers have become pig farmers; a former librarian waits vigilantly, a .22 in hand, to shoot weasels that have acquired a taste for her turkeys; a backhoe operator and native Vermonter writes his invoices in a fine, feminine script; and a no-nonsense flatlander from Connecticut has become the local dowser. I wonder if the only things that are absolutely true to their nature are rabbit dogs and electric fences, since both are singular in purpose.

Many things in our bucolic small town in the Green Mountains of Vermont aren't what they appear to be. I hear rumors of girls flagging down truckers for a good time and the story of an otherwise-upstanding citizen who is a bit light-fingered when shopping in local stores. A hundred years ago, the local newspaper carried similar stories. In order to determine if a fence was of legal construction, our town had a unique approach. One police officer weighed 300 pounds, one was six feet eight, and the third was extremely small. "It was recently voted that all fences on which a fat man could sit, which the tall man couldn't step over, nor the little one crawl through should be deemed legal fences." And, in 1926, the paper printed the fish story of all time. "Clarence Holden who won a Mt. Anthony Club Tournament in 1910 has recovered the medal awarded him at that time...It was returned by Herbert Booth who said that he found the medal in the stomach of a big brown trout caught a short distance south of the point where the medal was lost ten years ago."

Christopher Kimball

Crime, especially violent crime, was common among our bustling community. Mrs. Philander Moffat was arrested on the charge of attempting to poison her husband. In 1894, a woman burned down the family barn with a cow in it. A kitchen dance in 1911 resulted in a fistfight over a young woman that ended in the death of a fiddler. In 1936, John Fox was found hanging from a large elm down on Lincoln Lane, and there are rumors to this day about foul play. A man who was alive when I first moved into town was said to have buried more than one body up in Beartown; a pair of entwined dead raccoons found on one's driveway was his special calling card—a warning to keep your distance.

Run-ins with wild animals were common if not exaggerated. A correspondent wrote to the local paper in the late 1800s that "two men, long since dead, rode a big bear down the side of the mountain. They got him pretty tired but...pretty soon, while they were having great sport, the bear got mad." The result was one badly injured Vermonter and a dead bear. Leroy Fitch was coming home down the western slope of Birch Hill when he heard, off to the left, "the quick tread of an animal," which he supposed to be a sheep. "Turning in that direction, he beheld, not over 7 rods distant, an animal that he declares to be a panther."

Over the years, a town is many things. It is an accumulation of histories, barns, kitchen dances, fish stories, practical jokes, fistfights, family grudges, teachers, ministers, loggers, hunters, and schoolhouses that have long sunk down into the weeds. Vermonters are not just New Englanders or Yankees. They come from Tidd or Kent Hollow, from the gentle lower slopes of Swearing or Minister Hill, from the old Ford farm up past the Bentley place. You live where you were born. The dirt under your boots tells a story. The saphouse may be where you had your first kiss. And you remember every hunting dog you've ever owned, every draft horse, and every deer that you have shot at and missed.

By the turn of the 20th century, our town had started to empty out, since better soil had been discovered by Vermonters called out of state by the Civil War. Yet our sense of place remained undiminished. A letter submitted to the newspaper in 1892 read, "We moved on to what is called the Bowen place and...from there you can...see the villages nestled among the hills and the long stretch of the Green Mountains losing itself away in the south beyond Bennington. The once comfortable farm buildings are a heap of ruins and where there were once splendid meadows and waving grain, now only sheep are pastured. Although the glory of the hill is...a thing of the past, it still holds loving places in the hearts of...its children."

That's the thing. We are in love with a place that has been many things. It may change again, it may have been something else, but the rocky ground beneath our feet, the first cold night in August, and the last run of sap tell us now and forever that we are home.

FOR INQUIRIES, ORDERS, OR MORE INFORMATION:

www.cooksillustrated.com

At www.cooksillustrated.com, you can order books and subscriptions, sign up for our free e-newsletter, or renew your magazine subscription. Join the website and gain access to 15 years of *Cook's Illustrated* recipes, equipment tests, ingredient tastings, as well as *Cook's Live* companion videos for every recipe in this issue.

COOKBOOKS

We sell more than 50 cookbooks by the editors of *Cook's Illustrated*. To order, visit our bookstore at www.cooksillustrated.com or call 800-611-0759 (or 515-246-6911 from outside the U.S.).

COOK'S ILLUSTRATED Magazine

Cook's Illustrated magazine (ISSN 1068-2821), number 89, is published bimonthly by Boston Common Press Limited Partnership, 17 Station St., Brookline, MA 02445. Copyright 2007 Boston Common Press Limited Partnership. Periodicals postage paid at Boston, Mass., and additional mailing offices USPS #012487. Publications Mail Agreement No. 40020778. Return undeliverable Canadian addresses to P.O. Box 875, Station A, Windsor, Ontario N9A 6P2. POSTMASTER: Send address changes to Cook's Illustrated, P.O. Box 7446, Red Oak, IA 51591-0446. For subscription and gift subscription orders, subscription inquiries, or change-of-address notices, call 800-526-8442 in the U.S. or 515-247-7571 from outside the U.S., or write us at Cook's Illustrated, P.O. Box 7446, Red Oak, IA 51591-0446.

ILLUSTRATION: RANDY GLASS

NOTES FROM READERS

⋙ COMPILED BY SANDRA WU ⋘

Good White Bread

Some of your recipes call for "high-quality white sandwich bread." What does that mean? Do you prefer a particular brand?

JUAN CARLOS RUAN
GAITHERSBURG, MD.

"High-quality white sandwich bread" does not refer to rustic artisanal loaves found in a bakery, but rather the classic white sandwich bread found sliced and packaged in the bread aisle of the supermarket. In the test kitchen, the refrigerator is always stocked with Pepperidge Farm Farmhouse Hearty White Bread and Arnold Country Classics White Bread. Both breads have a dense crumb and slightly sweet flavor that make them suitable for a variety of uses. Most traditional sandwich breads weigh between ½ ounce and 1 ounce per slice, but our two favorites weigh in at about 1¼ ounces per slice. This makes a difference in recipes that call for making the bread into crumbs. While 1 slice of this larger bread yields about a cup of finely processed bread crumbs, you may need 2 slices of smaller, thinner versions of classic white sandwich bread to yield the same amount.

Cheesy Cousins

I read your Parmesan cheese story (September/October 2007) with interest and I noticed you didn't include Grana Padano or Reggianito. How do these cheeses compare with Parmigiano-Reggiano in flavor and texture?

JOANN SHERMAN
EASTCHESTER, N.Y.

➤Parmigiano-Reggiano has two relatives that bear a family resemblance. Italy produces a cow's-milk cheese called Grana Padano. "Grana" describes its hard, granular texture and "Padano" refers to the Po River Valley where the cheese originated, which is outside the government-designated region for Parmigiano-Reggiano. Grana Padano is less expensive than Parmigiano-Reggiano—$11.99 per pound versus $16.99 per pound for the test kitchen's favorite grocery-store Parmigiano—and aged for at least 9 months and up to 24 months. (Parmigiano-Reggiano is usually aged for 24 months.) In Argentina, a cheese called Reggianito is made using methods brought in by northern Italian dairy farmers. Reggianito is aged no more than 12 months and, at $6.99 per pound, is significantly cheaper than the other options.

We compared small chunks of Parmigiano-Reggiano with samples of Grana Padano and Reggianito in a blind taste test. The Parmigiano-Reggiano was praised for its "sharp, complex, nutty" taste and slightly crunchy crystalline structure. It had the most "dimension and depth of flavor" of the three samples. Conversely, the Reggianito was given a firm thumbs-down for its moist, rubbery texture and bland flavor. The Grana Padano fell somewhere in between: a milder, less complex version of the Parmigiano-Reggiano, with fewer granular crystals.

Next, we tried the cheeses in a cooked application: polenta. Again, the Parmigiano-Reggiano came out on top, with the Grana Padano following in a close second. The Reggianito, which tasters described as being "super-bland," ranked at the bottom once again.

So the economical price of the Reggianito doesn't make up for its poor texture and lack of flavor. The Grana Padano, while acceptable, isn't that much cheaper than the real thing. We'll gladly pay a couple extra dollars for Parmigiano-Reggiano.

REGGIANITO **GRANA PADANO**
These two relatives don't measure up to Parmigiano-Reggiano.

Make-Ahead Holiday Pies

This holiday season, I plan on making a number of pies well in advance. Is it OK to freeze pies?

JAYA HARIHAR
BASKING RIDGE, N.J.

➤It depends on the pie. Apple pie (we tested our deep-dish version; September/October 2005) can be fully assembled and frozen before baking, though the crust will be slightly less crisp. To freeze, follow the recipe all the way through sealing the pie crust, but do not brush with egg wash. Freeze the pie for two to three hours, then wrap it tightly in a double layer of plastic wrap, followed by a layer of foil, and return it to the freezer for up to one month. On serving day, brush egg wash onto the frozen pie, sprinkle it with sugar, and bake it for 10 minutes longer than specified in the recipe.

Pecan pie (November/December 1995) can also be frozen for up to one month before baking. Fill the pie, then wrap it and freeze it using the same method as the apple pie and bake it straight from the freezer, adding 30 minutes to the baking time. (This pie is denser than apple pie and requires more time to cook through.)

Unfortunately, pumpkin pie cannot be successfully frozen. We tried baking and freezing our pumpkin pie (November/December 1993), but because it has a custard base, the texture was altered once the pie was frozen and defrosted. Rather than maintaining a smooth creaminess, it took on an unappealing grainy and separated consistency. Freezing places stress on the proteins in custards by concentrating the water into ice crystals, which pull away from the proteins and make them more susceptible to coagulation. Your best bet for making this pie ahead of time is baking it a day before it will be eaten, cooling it fully, wrapping it with plastic wrap, and storing it in the refrigerator.

How to Use Rose Water

I've seen rose water listed in recipes. What is it, and how is it used?

JACQUELINE RODMAN
SAN JOSE, CALIF.

➤Rose water is a floral, perfumelike flavoring made by boiling crushed rose petals and condensing the steam in a still. It is used in Middle Eastern and Indian desserts, sometimes in conjunction with orange blossom water. In Middle Eastern cooking, rose water is often used in cakes, puddings, fruit salads, confections, and baklava. It plays a similar role in sweets from northern India, such as *gulab jamun*, which are deep-fried milk powder balls soaked in a cardamom- and rose-flavored syrup. Rice pudding is another common application.

We purchased three brands of rose water—Maya, Alwadi Al Akhdar, and Cedar Phoenicia—and tasted them in a Middle Eastern rice pudding that calls for 2 tablespoons of the flavoring. Tasters found the Alwadi brand—the only one containing "natural flavors"—to have

FLOWER POWER
A little of this floral flavoring goes a long way.

the subtlest flavor, which they liked. The Maya rose water came in close behind, with a slightly stronger profile. On the opposite end of the spectrum, the Cedar rose water was described as being "fake-tasting" and "overwhelming." Rose water can be found in the international section of some supermarkets and at Middle Eastern and Indian grocers. If you're not used to its flavor, start out by using slightly less than the recipe calls for. A little goes a long way, and you can always add more.

WHAT IS IT?

I found this old tool in a box of household items. The wording on the handle reads Irvin Ware and Made in the U.S.A. I can't imagine what it was used for. Do you have any ideas?

STEPHANIE WOOD, PORTLAND, ORE.

For fresh lemon juice, just squeeze.

The gadget you found is a cast-aluminum citrus squeezer about 6 inches long and 3½ inches wide. To use it, place a quartered lemon or halved lime cut-side down in the perforated cup. Holding the device over a bowl, squeeze the handles together and allow the citrus juice to run through the holes.

While this antique contraption does what it is supposed to—the holes are just large enough to allow the juice to run through and just small enough to trap seeds—it still isn't as easy to use as our favorite modern reamers and juicers. The limited capacity of the holding cup makes it impossible to accommodate an entire lemon half. Additionally, if the fruit isn't properly positioned, with the peel touching both sides of the clamp, it runs the risk of slipping out or being juiced only halfway.

Sweetening Whipped Cream

I was intrigued when I saw that your basic recipe for whipped cream calls for adding the sugar at the beginning of whipping. I was always told the old wives' tale that you had to add it at the end, because otherwise the cream wouldn't whip properly. Can you clarify?

ROSA HAND
OXFORD, OHIO

➢First things first. The test kitchen has found granulated sugar to be the best sweetener for whipped cream. It takes twice as much confectioners' sugar to equal the sweetness of granulated sugar, and using so much inevitably lends a faint chalkiness to the end product. To answer your question, we made two batches of whipped cream with the sugar added at two different points: at the beginning of whipping and at the end. Although both batches whipped to the same volume, there was a difference in texture. When the sugar was added later in the process, the whipped cream had a slightly grainy texture. When added to the cream at the beginning of whipping, however, the granules had dissolved by the time the cream was fully whipped.

While sugar timing doesn't affect the cream's ability to whip up properly, the temperature of the cream does. Whipping the cream introduces air bubbles, whose walls are stabilized by tiny globules of fat. These fat globules hold the air bubbles in place as the whipping continues, forming what eventually becomes light, airy whipped cream. Because heat will soften the butterfat in the cream, the liquid fat globules will collapse completely rather than hold together the air bubbles, preventing the cream from whipping up properly. To keep this from happening, it is crucial to use cream straight from the refrigerator.

Microwavable Rice

I've noticed fully cooked microwavable rice at the supermarket. Would it work in recipes that call for cooked rice?

DAVE GODOWSKY
ARLINGTON, MASS.

➢Various types of instant white rice have been around for years to help time-crunched home cooks avoid the process of cooking rice. In addition to boil-in-bag rice and instant rice, there is another product that has cropped up more recently on supermarket shelves: fully cooked rice. This convenience product is coated with oil to keep the grains distinct and packaged in microwavable pouches.

We tried Uncle Ben's Ready Rice plain, in fried rice, and wrapped up in a burrito. Eaten on its own, the rice had an oddly waxy, super-smooth exterior and slightly artificial flavor, and the grains were too separate. While these same qualities were still present in the fried rice and burrito, the effects were less noticeable once the other recipe components were mixed in. Did we love it? No, but it can pass in a pinch if combined with other ingredients. If you plan on serving plain rice, however, we strongly recommend forgoing the bagged stuff and making it yourself.

READY RICE
Texture is a bit waxy, but acceptable in a pinch.

Cooling Cookie Sheets

When making multiple batches of cookies, can I scoop cookie dough onto the hot baking sheets, or do I need to let the baking sheets cool all the way down before using them again?

MAUREEN CONVERY
BROOKLINE, MASS.

➢While it's tempting to save time by portioning cookie dough onto a baking sheet that has just been removed from the oven, we don't recommend it. The dough begins to melt and spread before it even reaches the oven, which can adversely affect the texture of the cookies. We baked two batches each of our Thick and Chewy Chocolate Chip Cookies (January/February 1996) and Soft and Chewy Sugar Cookies (November/December 2002), the first using a cool baking sheet and the second using a hot baking sheet that had just been removed from the oven. Both baking sheets were lined with parchment paper. While differences between the two batches of chocolate chip cookies weren't too noticeable, the same couldn't be said of the thinner, more delicate sugar cookies. The sugar cookies baked on the hot cookie sheet spread more, had darker bottoms, and were noticeably thinner and crisper around the edges.

Here's our recommendation: After removing baked cookies from the oven and allowing the baking sheet to cool for a few minutes until warm but no longer hot, simply run the baking sheet under cold tap water to cool it down quickly, then wipe it dry. To make the operation even more efficient, line the cookie sheet with parchment paper. As the first batch bakes, load a second piece of parchment with dough. When the cookies come out of the oven, remove them, parchment and all, onto a cooling rack. Once the baking sheet is properly cooled, the next batch will be ready to go.

SEND US YOUR QUESTIONS We will provide a complimentary one-year subscription for each letter we print. Send your inquiry, name, address, and daytime telephone number to Notes from Readers, Cook's Illustrated, P.O. Box 470589, Brookline, MA 02447, or to notesfromreaders@americastestkitchen.com.

ILLUSTRATION: JOHN BURGOYNE

COMPILED BY DAVID PAZMIÑO

Cleaning Microplane Graters

A Microplane grater is invaluable, but food can get trapped in its holes, making it a challenge to clean. Ave Chuprevich of Monmouth, Maine, uses a clean toothbrush to scrub its hard-to-reach nooks and crannies.

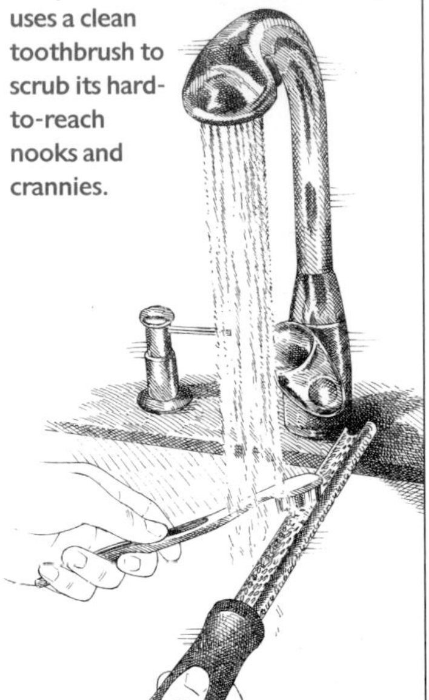

Rescuing Dry Vanilla Beans

Splitting dry, shriveled vanilla beans and removing their seeds is nearly impossible. Not wanting to waste this expensive ingredient, Carina Driscoll of Burlington, Vt., found a way to revive over-the-hill vanilla beans.

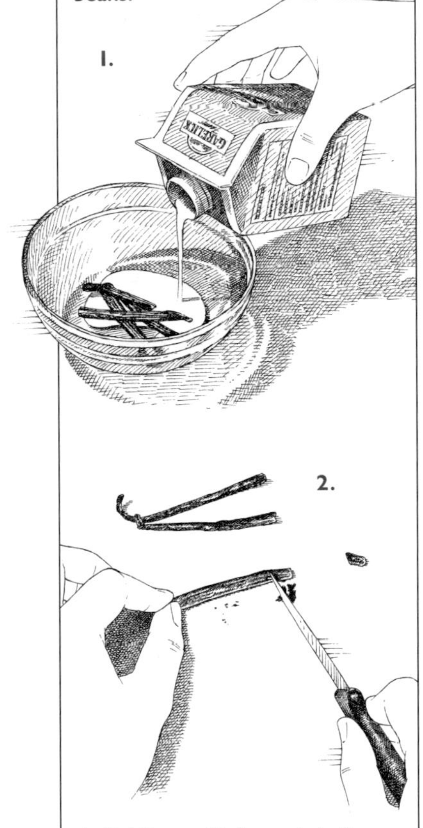

1. Cut the vanilla beans in half crosswise and place them in a microwave-safe bowl or measuring cup. Add enough cream or half-and-half to cover the beans.
2. Microwave the mixture on medium power for 1 to 2 minutes until the beans are soft and supple (cream should not boil). Remove the beans from the cream, split them lengthwise, and scrape out the seeds. Don't discard the vanilla-flavored cream: It can be cooled and used in coffee.

Smoothing Out Lumpy Gravy

Trying to thicken gravy by sprinkling in flour often results in unsightly lumps and a consistency that is still too thin because the starch is not dispersed. Dean Thomas of San Diego, Calif., solved the problem by coming up with the following plan. (This technique does not work with mushroom or giblet gravy.)

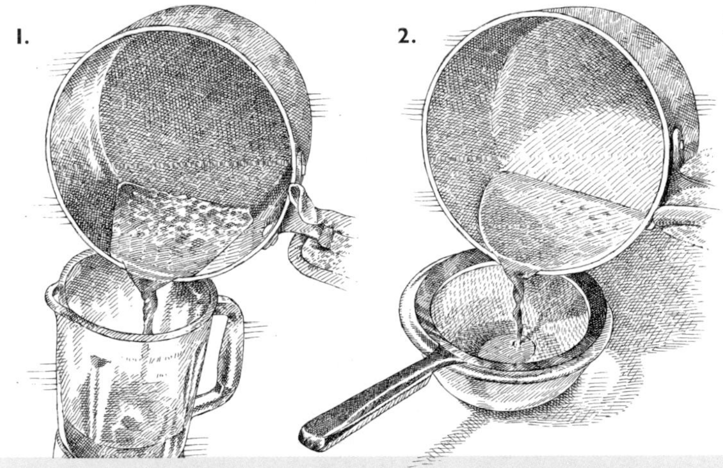

1. Fill a blender no more than half full with the lumpy gravy and process until the gravy is smooth, about 30 seconds.
2. To thicken the gravy, pour it back into a saucepan and bring it to a simmer. Any remaining small lumps can be strained out with a fine-mesh strainer.

No More Shrinking Pizza Dough

Even after allowing his pizza dough to rest, Robert Brandt of Tucson, Ariz., often had trouble rolling it out into a circle without it shrinking back. He came up with a clever remedy that uses gravity to help the process along.

1.

2.

1. Roll the dough into a 6-inch disk and place it on an overturned mixing bowl that has been lightly dusted with flour.
2. Gently pull the edges of the dough downward, stretching it over the bowl until it is the desired size.

Keeping Standing Mixers Clean

Batters and doughs can often find their way down to the spot where the bottom of the workbowl affixes to the base of a standing mixer, which is a difficult area to clean. To combat this problem, Erika Taylor of Pittsburgh, Pa., places a piece of plastic wrap between the base of the mixer and the bowl. This does not interfere with attaching the bowl to the base and provides a layer of protection so that food stays out of the cracks.

ILLUSTRATION: JOHN BURGOYNE

Send Us Your Tip We will provide a complimentary one-year subscription for each tip we print. Send your tip, name, and address to Quick Tips, Cook's Illustrated, P.O. Box 470589, Brookline, MA 02447, or to quicktips@americastestkitchen.com.

Homemade Knife Protector

Storing knives in a drawer not only is dangerous but can also damage the knives. Janet Van Liere of Boston, Mass., came up with a cheap way to protect her fingers and her knives.

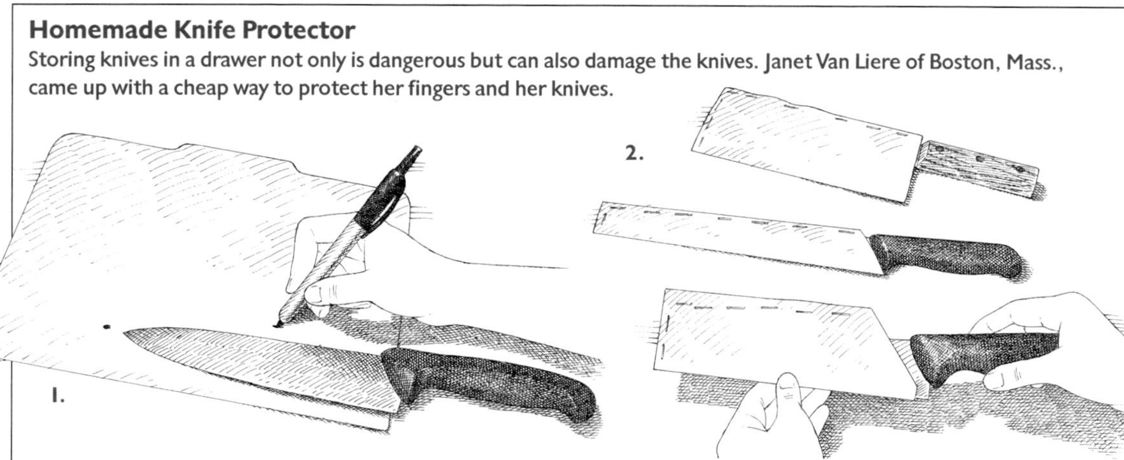

1. Set a knife on a manila folder, placing the blade of the knife parallel to the bottom edge of the folder. Use a pen to mark ½ inch beyond the tip and ½ inch above the spine.

2. Using these marks as guides, cut the folder into a rectangle. Staple the top edge and front of the rectangle at ½-inch intervals, leaving the back end open to slide in the knife.

Mess-Free Broiling

When broiling greasy meats such as ground beef, Tracey Frierson of Shaker Heights, Ohio, always found that the fat produced smoke and was hard to clean up. Lining the broiler pan with aluminum foil helps, and she takes this method one step further.

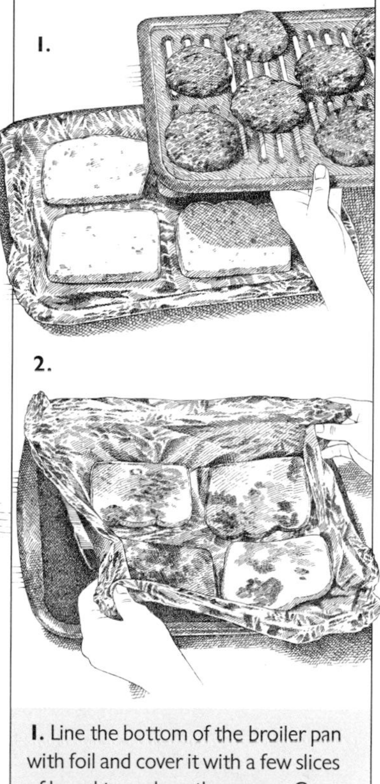

1. Line the bottom of the broiler pan with foil and cover it with a few slices of bread to soak up the grease. Cover with the perforated broiler pan top and proceed to broil the meat.

2. When it comes time to clean up, simply gather the foil and grease-soaked bread together and discard.

Easier Seed Removal

Splitting a pumpkin or winter squash is easy enough, but removing the tangled mess of seeds and pulp is another matter. Instead of using a spoon, Katie Graf of Lincoln, Neb., reaches for a round metal cookie cutter. The sharp edges conform to the curves of the squash, making it easy to remove the seeds and stringy pulp.

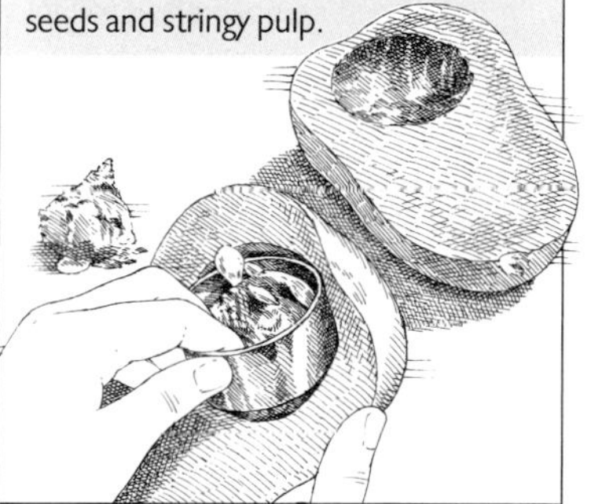

Fixing a Broken Cake

After removing a finicky cake from a pan, Lena Glaser of New York, N.Y., found herself with broken cake halves. She repaired the fracture by allowing the cakes to cool, then spreading a thin layer of soft buttercream frosting over the broken surfaces and reattaching the pieces. She then set the cake in the refrigerator for about an hour to allow the frosting to harden before continuing to assemble and frost it.

Blanched Almonds

When making a tart that called for blanched (skinned) almonds, Jeremy Turner of Brooklyn, N.Y., could find only whole, skin-on almonds at the supermarket. Here is the simple technique he used to remove the skins.

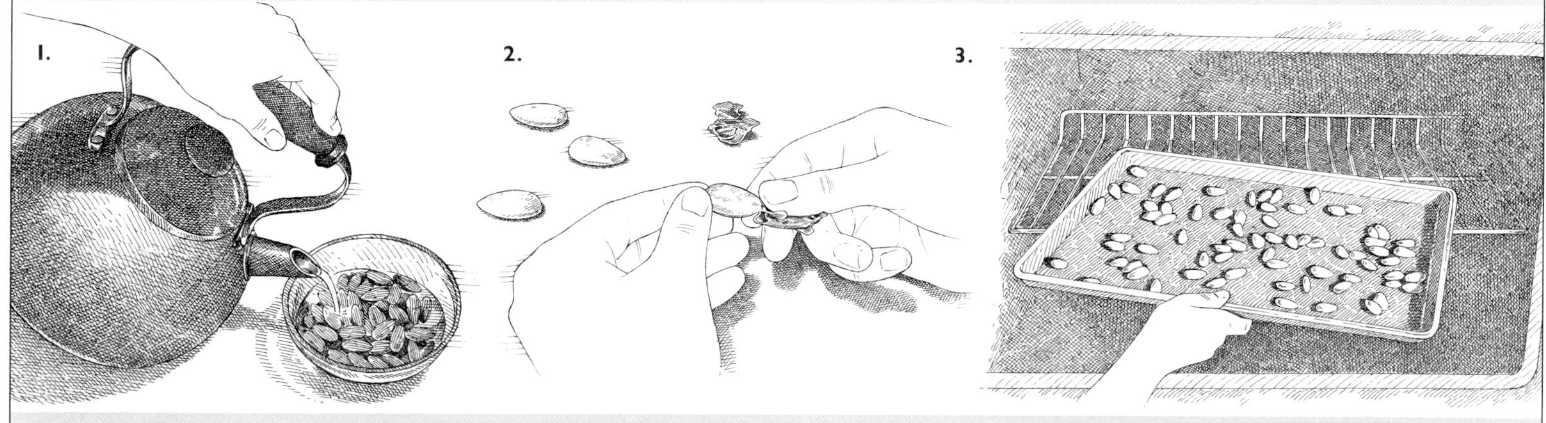

1. Place 1 cup almonds in a medium heatproof bowl and cover with 2 cups boiling water. Let the almonds stand for two minutes, then drain and rinse them under cold running water.

2. Press each almond between your thumb and index finger to slip off the skin.

3. To dry and lightly toast the skinned nuts, place them on a baking sheet in a 350-degree oven for seven to 10 minutes.

Modernizing French-Style Pot Roast

This 17th-century dish relies on lardons, pork trotters, and a 48-hour marinade to create the ultimate pot roast. It's time to bring this recipe into the 21st century.

BY SANDRA WU

Boeuf à la mode—"beef in the latest fashion"—is a classic French recipe that dates to a time when a multiday recipe was the rule rather than the exception. The earliest reference I found to this dish appeared in *Le Cuisinier François* (1651), an encyclopedic book that systematically catalogued French cuisine. Larding (inserting strips of marinated fat) and braising (searing the roast and simmering it partially submerged in liquid in a sealed pot) could transform an otherwise dry and chewy cut into a tender, moist, and flavorful roast. An added bonus of this cooking technique is that the braising liquid itself—red wine and beef stock—reduces into a thick, rich sauce to accompany the meat.

Although boeuf à la mode bears some similarity to American pot roast, this elegant French dish relies heavily on wine for flavor, adds collagen-rich veal and pork parts for body, and has a separately prepared mushroom-onion garnish. After spending days making five classic renditions of this old-fashioned recipe, I understood its allure—and its challenges. It is to pot roast what croissants are to refrigerated crescent rolls and, as such, required up to four days of preparation! To bring boeuf à la mode up to date for the modern home cook—the meats and times have changed, after all—some of the fussy techniques and hard-to-find ingredients would have to go. Still, I was willing to do just about anything to make this impressive dish, so long as it worked.

A concentrated red wine sauce is the hallmark of this elegant dish.

Bye, Bye Marinade

Traditionally, this recipe starts with threading strips of seasoned, brandy-soaked salt pork or fatback through the beef roast using a long needle, or *lardoir*. In addition to making up for the lack of marbling in the meat, larding adds flavor. I cut some fatback into thin strips, marinated them in brandy and seasonings, and struggled to pull them through the roast. For the amount of effort these steps took, I was disappointed when tasters felt the payoff wasn't that great. Today's grain-fed beef gets little exercise and has much more marbling than the leaner, grass-fed beef eaten in France when this recipe was created. As long as I chose the right cut (tasters liked a boneless chuck-eye roast best), there was plenty of fat in the meat and larding was just overkill. I was happy to ax this step from my recipe.

In all of the classic recipes I uncovered, the meat was marinated in a mixture of red wine and large-cut mirepoix (carrots, onions, and celery) for a significant period of time, up to three days in several cases. Testing various lengths of time, I found the effect superficial unless I was willing to invest at least two full days. Even then, the wine flavor penetrated only the outer part of the meat, and the vegetables didn't really add much. Frankly, the meat picked up so much wine flavor during the hours-long braising time that marinating didn't seem worth the effort.

In fact, some tasters actually complained that the meat was picking up too much wine flavor as it cooked; the beef tasted a bit sour and harsh. I reviewed a Julia Child recipe that called for marinating the roast in a mixture of wine and vegetables and then reducing that marinade by half before adding beef broth and beginning the braising process. I was intrigued. Would cooking the wine before braising the beef in it tame its unpleasant alcoholic punch? I put the wine in a saucepan and reduced it to 2 cups. When I combined the reduced wine with the beef broth and used this mixture as the braising liquid, tasters were much happier. The wine tasted complex and fruity, not sour and astringent.

Most of the vegetable flavor in this dish comes from the garnish of glazed pearl onions and button mushrooms, which is traditionally cooked separately and added just before serving. To speed up the process, I used frozen rather than fresh pearl onions. But the sauce needed some vegetables to balance the wine and meat flavors. Sautéed onion and garlic helped build depth in the early stages of cooking, and tasters liked the sweetness contributed by large chunks of carrots added to the braising liquid later in the cooking process.

The Sauce Matters

I had the wine and vegetables under control, but my recipe didn't seem as rich and meaty as some of the test recipes I had prepared. My first thought was to salt the meat, something we do in the test kitchen to improve the beefy flavor in thick-cut steaks. It works by drawing moisture out of the meat and forming a shallow brine. Over time, the salt migrates back into the meat, seasoning it throughout rather than just on the exterior. Tasters liked the effects of salting the roast overnight, but I was reluctant to make this a two-day recipe. Eventually, I discovered that salting the meat for just an hour was worth the minimal effort. The roast was nicely seasoned and tasted beefier.

Salt pork is traditionally added to the sauce for richness, but tasters preferred the smoky flavor of

One Roast Becomes Two

TOO FATTY — GOOD TO GO

The chuck-eye roast has great flavor, but we found that the interior fat is best trimmed before cooking. Simply pull the roast apart at the natural seam and trim away large knobs of fat from each half.

PHOTOGRAPHY: CARL TREMBLAY

TECHNIQUE | SECRETS TO MODERNIZING FRENCH POT ROAST

SALTING Instead of the usual two-day marinade, we improve the flavor of the beef by salting it for just one hour.

REDUCING For concentrated wine flavor without harshness or sour notes, we reduce an entire bottle of wine to just 2 cups.

GELATIN Soaked gelatin gives our sauce body and means that you don't need the traditional veal bones, calves' feet, and pork rind.

bacon. I decided to brown the meat in the bacon drippings and then add the bacon bits back to the braising liquid. My sauce was improving.

Compared with regular pot roast braising liquid, which is flavorful but relatively thin and brothy, the sauce that accompanies boeuf à la mode is richer and more akin to a sauce that might be found on a steak at a fine restaurant. Adding some flour to the sautéed onion and garlic helped with the overall consistency, but the sauce still lacked body. I tried adding pork rind, split calves' feet, and veal bones and liked the effect they had on the sauce—the collagen in these animal parts breaks down in the long cooking process and releases plenty of gelatin. But what if I went directly to the source instead?

I tried adding a tablespoon of powdered gelatin rehydrated in ¼ cup of cold water at the beginning of the recipe, but to no effect. The lengthy cooking time and high heat rendered the gelatin ineffective. I decided to try again, adding the gelatin during the sauce reduction stage. This helped, but not enough. It wasn't until I'd added the gelatin after the sauce had finished reducing that I got the results I had been looking for. Finally, it became rich and velvety, on par with the best classic recipe I'd tried at the beginning of my journey. Drizzled with this intense sauce and surrounded by the well-browned mushroom-onion garnish and tender carrots, this old-fashioned pot roast was the best I'd ever tasted.

FRENCH-STYLE POT ROAST

SERVES 6 TO 8

A medium-bodied, fruity red wine such as Côtes du Rhône or Pinot Noir is best for this recipe. If frozen pearl onions are unavailable, use fresh peeled pearl onions and follow the recipe as directed. The gelatin lends richness and body to the finished sauce; don't omit it. To prepare this dish in advance, follow the recipe through step 7, skipping the step of softening and adding the gelatin. Place the meat back into the reduced sauce, cool it to room temperature, cover it, and refrigerate it for up to 2 days. To serve, slice the beef and arrange it in a 13 by 9-inch baking dish. Bring the sauce to a simmer and stir in the gelatin until completely dissolved. Pour the warm sauce over the meat, cover it with aluminum foil, and bake it in a 350-degree oven until heated through, about 30 minutes. Serve this dish with boiled potatoes, buttered noodles, or steamed rice.

- 1 boneless chuck-eye roast (4 to 5 pounds), pulled apart into 2 pieces and fat trimmed (see page 6)
- 2 teaspoons kosher salt
- 1 bottle (750 ml) medium-bodied red wine (see note above)
- 10 sprigs fresh parsley, plus 2 tablespoons minced leaves
- 2 sprigs fresh thyme
- 2 bay leaves
- Ground black pepper
- 4 ounces bacon, preferably thick-cut, cut crosswise into ¼-inch pieces
- 1 medium onion, chopped fine (about 1 cup)
- 3 medium garlic cloves, minced or pressed through garlic press (about 1 tablespoon)
- 1 tablespoon unbleached all-purpose flour
- 2 cups beef broth
- 4 medium carrots, peeled and cut on bias into 1½-inch pieces
- 2 cups frozen pearl onions
- 3 tablespoons unsalted butter
- 2 teaspoons sugar
- ½ cup water, plus ¼ cup cold water to bloom gelatin
- 10 ounces white mushrooms, wiped clean, stems trimmed, halved if small and quartered if large
- Table salt
- 1 tablespoon powdered unflavored gelatin

1. Season meat with kosher salt, place on wire rack set in rimmed baking sheet, and let rest at room temperature for 1 hour.

2. Meanwhile, bring wine to simmer in large saucepan over medium-high heat. Cook until reduced to 2 cups, about 15 minutes. Using kitchen twine, tie parsley sprigs, thyme sprigs, and bay leaves into bundle.

3. Pat beef dry with paper towels and season generously with pepper. Tie three pieces of kitchen twine around each piece of meat to keep it from falling apart.

4. Adjust oven rack to lower-middle position and heat oven to 300 degrees. Cook bacon in large Dutch oven over medium-high heat, stirring occasionally, until crisp, 6 to 8 minutes. Using slotted spoon, transfer bacon to paper towel–lined plate and reserve. Pour off all but 2 tablespoons fat; return Dutch oven to medium-high heat and heat until fat begins to smoke. Add beef to pot and brown on all sides, 8 to 10 minutes total. Transfer beef to large plate and set aside.

5. Reduce heat to medium; add onion and cook, stirring occasionally, until beginning to soften, 2 to 4 minutes. Add garlic, flour, and reserved bacon; cook, stirring constantly, until fragrant, about 30 seconds. Add reduced wine, broth, and herb bundle, scraping bottom of pan with wooden spoon to loosen browned bits. Return roast and any accumulated juices to pot; increase heat to high and bring liquid to simmer, then place large sheet of foil over pot and cover tightly with lid. Set pot in oven and cook, using tongs to turn beef every hour, until dinner fork slips easily in and out of meat, 2½ to 3 hours, adding carrots to pot after 2 hours.

6. While meat cooks, bring pearl onions, butter, sugar, and ½ cup water to boil in large skillet over medium-high heat. Reduce heat to medium, cover, and cook until onions are tender, 5 to 8 minutes. Uncover, increase heat to medium-high, and cook until all liquid evaporates, 3 to 4 minutes. Add mushrooms and ¼ teaspoon table salt; cook, stirring occasionally, until vegetables are browned and glazed, 8 to 12 minutes. Remove from heat and set aside. Place remaining ¼ cup cold water in small bowl and sprinkle gelatin on top.

7. Transfer beef to cutting board; tent with foil to keep warm. Allow braising liquid to settle about 5 minutes; then, using wide, shallow spoon, skim fat off surface. Remove herb bundle and stir in onion-mushroom mixture. Bring liquid to simmer over medium-high heat and cook until mixture is slightly thickened and reduced to 3¼ cups, 20 to 30 minutes. Season sauce with salt and pepper. Add softened gelatin and stir until completely dissolved.

8. Remove kitchen twine from meat and discard. Using chef's or carving knife, cut meat against grain into ½-inch-thick slices. Divide meat among warmed bowls or transfer to platter; arrange vegetables around meat, pour sauce on top, and sprinkle with minced parsley. Serve immediately.

Improving Mashed Potatoes and Root Vegetables

Adding carrots, parsnips, turnips, or celery root to mashed potatoes sounds like a good idea—until the mash turns out too watery, too sweet, or too bitter.

BY REBECCA HAYS

Because mashed potatoes are relatively simple, many cookbook authors suggest that introducing root vegetables to the mash requires little forethought. In fact, most of the cookbooks I consulted didn't even devote a complete recipe to the topic; they merely tacked footnotes onto mashed potato recipes: "Try boiling parsnips along with the potatoes" or "Substitute celery root for half of the potatoes." The idea of adding the earthy, intriguing flavor of carrots, parsnips, turnips, or celery root to plain mashed potatoes is certainly appealing, but most of the recipes I tried failed miserably.

The trouble is that, despite being neighbors in the root cellar, root vegetables and potatoes (tubers) are quite different in three important ways. First, my preferred root vegetables contain more water (80 percent to 92 percent) than russet potatoes (about 79 percent), the test kitchen's first choice for mashing. Second, my root vegetables have less starch (between 0.2 percent and 6.2 percent) than potatoes (about 15 percent). Finally, many root vegetables are either noticeably sweet or slightly bitter—traits that can overwhelm mild potatoes. If you're not careful, these differences can add up to a watery, lean, or saccharine mash.

The Root of the Problem

In early rounds of recipe testing, I'd concluded that the 1–1 (or greater) ratio of root vegetables to potatoes that the majority of cookbooks advocate was much too heavy on the vegetable side. I experimented with a 1–2 ratio, boiling 12 ounces of root vegetables and 24 ounces of russet potatoes together in the same pot, draining them, mashing them with a potato masher, and stirring in cream and melted butter. This proportion didn't fare much better—the texture was still too thin. For optimal consistency, I had to go all the way down to a 1–3 ratio. But with only 8 ounces of root vegetables to 1½ pounds of potatoes, the distinctive flavor of the vegetables was barely recognizable.

COOK'S LIVE Original Test Kitchen Videos

www.cooksillustrated.com

HOW TO MAKE
- Mashed Potatoes and Root Vegetables

VIDEO TIPS
- How should I prepare parsnips?
- How should I prepare celery root?

A unique two-step cooking method is the key to a superior mash.

If I wanted to maintain an agreeable texture, I had to find a way to make the most of a small amount of vegetables. Could I enhance their character by cooking them separately and bolstering their flavor? Three possibilities sprang to mind: microwaving the root vegetables in chicken broth; sautéing them in butter; and roasting them in the oven with a coating of olive oil. I cooked one batch of vegetables using each technique, then mashed them with boiled potatoes. All of the samples were more appealing than the one made with potatoes and vegetables boiled in the same pot, but the mashes made with sautéed vegetables outshone the others because of their nutty, buttery qualities.

So cooking the vegetables separately amplified their flavor, and my problem was solved. Or was it? I envisioned the hectic predinner rush that is typical of holiday celebrations. Boiling potatoes in one pot and sautéing vegetables in another might be beyond the pale for a straightforward side dish. Could I come up with a more convenient one-burner, one-pot recipe? Paging through our archives, I came across the test kitchen's unusual recipe for Mashed Sweet Potatoes (November/December 2002), in which sweet potatoes are slowly cooked in a small amount of liquid in a tightly covered pot rather than boiled. What if I incorporated this technique into my recipe by sautéing the root vegetables first, then adding raw potatoes and braising them?

I returned to the kitchen and quickly sautéed some parsnips in a generous amount (4 tablespoons) of butter. Next, I added peeled and sliced potatoes to the pot, along with ⅓ cup of water and a dash of salt. After 30 minutes of gentle cooking, the potatoes and parsnips were completely tender and all of the water had been absorbed. I did some quick mashing, then folded in warm cream and black pepper. The flavor was good, but not remarkable. On my next try, I cooked the vegetables longer, allowing the butter to brown and the vegetables to caramelize, which accented their unique flavors. The flavor was now spot-on: rich, earthy, and well balanced. Swapping chicken broth (preferred to vegetable broth) for the water allowed the potatoes to soak up even more savory notes. As for dairy options, tasters didn't deviate from the test kitchen's usual choice

TECHNIQUE | RINSE CYCLE

Rinsing peeled, sliced potatoes in several changes of water removes excess starch and prevents gumminess once the potatoes are cooked and mashed.

PHOTOGRAPHY: CARL TREMBLAY

of half-and-half, preferring it to milk and cream. I let the potatoes drink up as much as they could, eventually settling on ¾ cup.

No Starch, Please

The flavor of my recipe was finally just right, but the texture had been thrown off in the meantime. When potatoes are boiled, some of their starch leaches out into the cooking water, never making it into the finished dish. With my unusual procedure, however, the starch could not escape and ended up being incorporated into the mash. The result was an overly starchy, almost gluey texture. Would switching to a lower-starch potato help? A batch made with Yukon Golds offered a modest improvement, but tasters still complained about excess starchiness. Thinking things over, I realized I needed to get rid of some starch before I cooked the potatoes. I rinsed some peeled, sliced potatoes in several changes of water (this took just a minute or two) and watched the cloudy, starch-filled rinsing liquid run down the drain. Once the potatoes were cooked and mashed, I knew that I'd found my solution—the starchiness was gone. Rinsing even made starchier russets an acceptable choice.

EQUIPMENT TESTING:

Vegetable Peelers

When we crowned the OXO I-Series Swivel Peeler ($9.99) our favorite a few years ago for its comfortably narrow grip and razor-sharp, replaceable stainless steel blade, we had one caveat: It weighed nearly four ounces. This isn't a problem when peeling a carrot or two, but when potatoes and apples are peeled in bulk, hand strain can become an issue. Hoping to find a lighter peeler that was just as sharp, we tested four new models.

The Zyliss Smoothglide Peeler ($6.99) simply wasn't sharp enough, and the stainless steel handle on the Giannini Swivel Peeler ($7.50) was slippery when wet. However, the Kyocera Ceramic Perfect Peeler ($17.95) and Messermeister Pro-Touch Swivel Peeler ($5.95) passed every peeling test with flying colors, including the toughest of all: tomatoes. Although we like the adjustable blade on the Kyocera (which weighs just 2.2 ounces), testers preferred the slightly smoother motion of the 1.5-ounce Messermeister peeler, which they found comfortable even after peeling piles of apples and potatoes. It's our new favorite. For the complete results of this testing, go to www.cooksillustrated.com/december. –Elizabeth Bomze

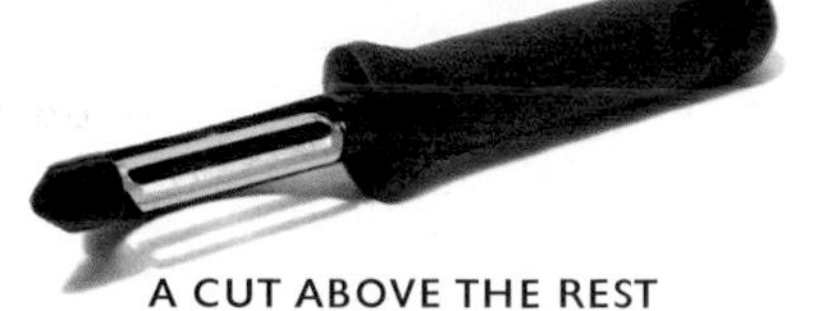

A CUT ABOVE THE REST
The Messermeister Pro-Touch Swivel Peeler is remarkably sharp and so light that hand strain is never a problem.

ILLUSTRATION: JOHN BURGOYNE

STEP-BY-STEP | MASHED POTATOES AND ROOT VEGETABLES

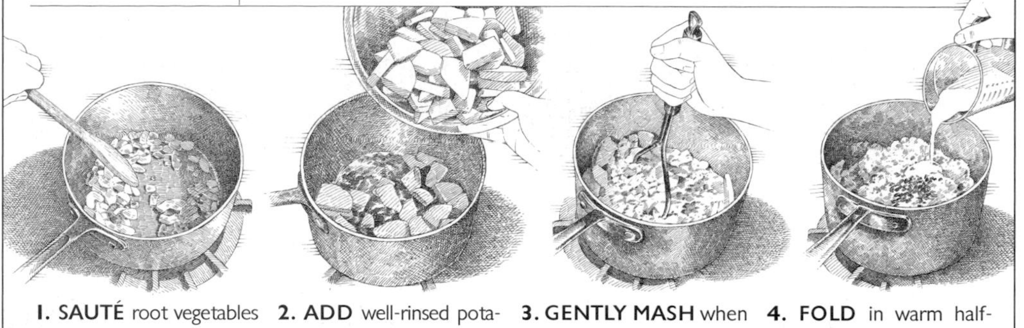

1. SAUTÉ root vegetables in butter until butter browns and vegetables caramelize.

2. ADD well-rinsed potatoes, chicken broth, and salt. Cover and simmer gently.

3. GENTLY MASH when liquid has been absorbed and vegetables are tender.

4. FOLD in warm half-and-half and chives.

To finish the potatoes off, a sprinkling of fresh herbs was in order. The delicate onion flavor of minced chives offered a nice counterpoint to the earthy vegetables. At last, I had a standout recipe for mashed potatoes and root vegetables that was more than just an afterthought.

MASHED POTATOES AND ROOT VEGETABLES

SERVES 4

Russet potatoes will yield a slightly fluffier, less creamy mash, but they can be used in place of the Yukon Gold potatoes if desired. Rinsing the potatoes in several changes of water reduces starch and prevents the mashed potatoes from becoming gluey. It is important to cut the potatoes and root vegetables into even-sized pieces so they cook at the same rate. This recipe can be doubled and cooked in a large Dutch oven. If doubling, increase the cooking time in step 2 to 40 minutes. See page 30 for information on preparing root vegetables. Recipes for Mashed Potatoes and Root Vegetables for Two are available free at www.cooksillustrated.com/december.

- 4 tablespoons unsalted butter
- 8 ounces either carrots, parsnips, turnips, or celery root, peeled; carrots or parsnips cut into ¼-inch-thick half-moons; turnips or celery root cut into ½-inch dice (about 1½ cups)
- 1½ pounds Yukon Gold potatoes, peeled, quartered lengthwise, and cut crosswise into ¼-inch-thick slices; rinsed well in 3 or 4 changes of cold water and drained well (see note above)
- ⅓ cup low-sodium chicken broth
- Table salt
- ¾ cup half-and-half, warmed
- 3 tablespoons minced fresh chives
- Ground black pepper

1. Melt butter in large saucepan over medium heat. When foaming subsides, add root vegetables and cook, stirring occasionally, until butter is browned and vegetables are dark brown and caramelized, 10 to 12 minutes. (If after 4 minutes vegetables have not started to brown, increase heat to medium-high.)

2. Add potatoes, broth, and ¾ teaspoon salt and stir to combine. Cook, covered, over low heat (broth should simmer gently; do not boil), stirring occasionally, until potatoes fall apart easily when poked with fork and all liquid has been absorbed, 25 to 30 minutes. (If liquid does not gently simmer after a few minutes, increase heat to medium-low.) Remove pan from heat; remove lid and allow steam to escape for 2 minutes.

3. Gently mash potatoes and root vegetables in saucepan with potato masher (do not mash vigorously). Gently fold in warm half-and-half and chives. Season with salt and pepper to taste; serve immediately.

MASHED POTATOES AND ROOT VEGETABLES WITH BACON AND THYME

This variation is particularly nice with turnips.

Cook 4 slices (about 4 ounces) bacon, cut into ½-inch pieces, in large saucepan over medium heat until browned and crisp, about 8 minutes. Using slotted spoon, transfer bacon to paper towel–lined plate; set aside. Remove all but 2 tablespoons bacon fat from pan. Add 2 tablespoons butter to pan and continue with recipe for Mashed Potatoes and Root Vegetables, cooking root vegetables in bacon fat–butter mixture instead of butter. Substitute 1 teaspoon minced fresh thyme leaves for chives and fold reserved bacon into potatoes along with thyme.

MASHED POTATOES AND ROOT VEGETABLES WITH PAPRIKA AND PARSLEY

This variation is particularly nice with carrots.

Toast 1½ teaspoons smoked or regular paprika in small skillet over medium heat until fragrant, about 30 seconds. Follow recipe for Mashed Potatoes and Root Vegetables, substituting parsley for chives and folding toasted paprika into potatoes along with parsley.

Holiday Ham 101

Ham is appealingly simple but often comes out dry and jerkylike. Here's what you need to know to produce a top-notch glazed ham that is always moist and tender.

BY DAVID PAZMIÑO

Isn't cooking a ham remarkably simple? You just throw it in the oven, slather on some glaze, and wait. But this approach can often yield inferior results—dried-out, leathery meat that tastes like salty jerky with a sticky, saccharine exterior. Ideally, ham is moist and tender and the glaze complements but doesn't overwhelm the meat. We've cooked hundreds of hams in the test kitchen over the years and have had our share of disasters. We decided to reexamine this topic to learn what really works—and what doesn't.

Which kind of ham—and how much—should I buy?

➢ In most supermarkets, cured hams come in five forms: boneless, semiboneless, bone-in, whole, and half. Each of these types is available unsliced or presliced (often labeled "spiral-sliced"). After cooking up each in the test kitchen, we clearly favored bone-in hams that had been spiral-sliced, since they offered the best flavor with the least amount of postcooking carving. As a rule of thumb, you should allow about ½ pound of ham per person. This takes into consideration any weight lost during cooking as well as the weight of the bone. Unless you are feeding a very large crowd, we recommend a half ham.

Are all spiral-sliced hams the same?

➢ With all hams, it is important to read the label. Typically, supermarket hams are wet-cured, a process that involves soaking the ham in brine. During this process, the ham will absorb water and gain weight. Not surprisingly, we found hams that gained the least water weight (labeled "ham with natural juices") taste the best. Avoid labels that read "ham with water added" or "ham and water products." See page 11 for the results of our tasting of specific brands.

SHOPPING: **Meaty or Easy to Carve?**

SIRLOIN END
Meatier option, but bones make it harder to carve.

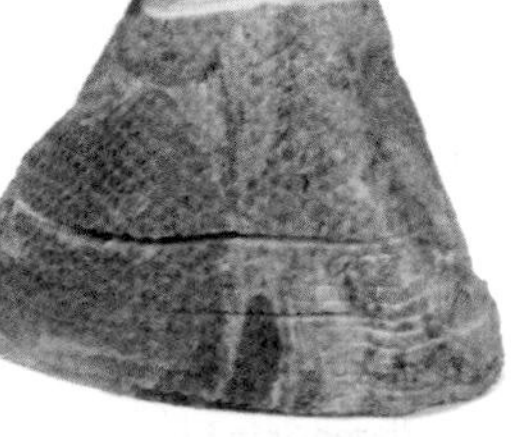

SHANK END
Easy-to-carve, but not quite as meaty.

A late blast of heat creates a glazed exterior without drying out the ham.

The hams in the market come in various shapes. What is the difference?

➢ Whole ham is the entire leg of the animal. Half hams are available in two distinct cuts: shank end (the bottom part of the leg) and sirloin end (the portion of the leg closer to the rump). If labeling is unclear, it's easy to identify half hams by their shape—shank hams have a pointed end much smaller than the larger end, whereas the sirloin (or butt) end is rounded. In the past, we have recommended the shank end for ease of carving, since the bone is relatively straight compared with the odder-shaped bones in the sirloin end. However, in our most recent round of tastings, we found the sirloin end to be meatier and less fatty. If you're up for a slightly more challenging carving job, the larger sirloin end will not disappoint.

If a spiral-sliced ham is already cooked, why do I have to cook it?

➢ There is nothing you have to do to serve a cured and cooked ham other than cut it off the bone. When ham is the centerpiece of a holiday dinner, however, most people prefer to have it served warm, and often with a glaze. After roasting many hams to temperatures ranging from 100 to 160 degrees, we found the ideal temperature to be between 110 and 120 degrees. This was enough to take the chill off the meat without drying it out. Cooking the ham to a higher internal temperature (as many sources suggest) guarantees dry meat.

My ham often dries out. What's the best way to keep ham moist?

➢ Most recipes cook the ham at 350 degrees, so by the time the center finally comes up to temperature, the exterior is parched. We roast ham in a 250-degree oven, which lessens the temperature differential between the exterior and the interior. Also, rather than starting with an ice-cold ham, we found that we could cut oven time (and thus drying) by leaving the ham at room temperature for 90 minutes prior to cooking. But could we do even better? Soaking the ham in warm water for 90 minutes raises the temperature considerably and cuts oven time by a full hour. Finally, we've discovered that roasting the ham in an oven bag reduces roasting time even further. (The bag speeds cooking by providing insulation.) Compared with a cold ham shoved into a 350-degree oven, our method reduces moisture loss in a 10-pound ham by 50 percent.

Do I really have to use an oven bag?

➢ We've found that oven bags produce the moistest ham in the least amount of time. If unavailable, aluminum foil will work, but you will have to add three to four minutes of cooking time per pound of meat (between 21 and 40 minutes for a 7- to 10-pound ham). Remember, less oven time means a moister ham.

PHOTOGRAPHY: CARL TREMBLAY

When should I apply a glaze?

➢Almost all spiral hams come with a packet of premixed glaze and instructions to brush it on the ham while cooking. Glaze is a good idea, but the stuff in the packets tastes awful. Take 10 minutes to make your own glaze. Since we cook ham inside an oven bag, we needed to figure out a new approach to glazing. Once the internal temperature of the ham reaches 100 degrees, cut open the bag and increase the oven temperature to 350 degrees. Apply the glaze and bake the ham for 10 minutes. Remove the ham from the oven, apply more glaze, and then make a quick sauce with the remaining glaze and the drippings in the oven bag.

Should I let ham rest before carving it?

➢We've found that a 15-minute rest allows the internal temperature to increase by 5 to 15 degrees, which allows us to bake the ham less in order to reach the ideal serving temperature of 110 to 120 degrees. (Cover the ham with foil as it rests.)

RECIPE DIAGNOSIS:

How to Keep a Ham Moist

A big ham can take hours to heat through in the oven, by which time the meat becomes very dry. We found two tricks for reducing oven time and increasing moisture retention.

SOAKING: Placing the wrapped ham in warm water for 90 minutes raises its internal temperature and decreases the cooking time by over an hour.

WRAPPING: Cooking the ham in an oven bag reduces the oven time by another half hour or so.

TASTING:

Spiral-Sliced Hams

At their best, spiral-sliced hams balance sweet, smoky, and salty flavors with a firm, moist texture. Assuming you buy the same cut, does brand matter? To find out, we prepared three nationally available brands of honey- or brown sugar–cured hams.

Tasters' preferences approached unanimity. Falling hard to the bottom, the Hillshire Farm Bone-In Brown Sugar Cured Ham ($2.99 per pound) lost points on two accounts: Tasters described the meat as "utterly devoid of smoke flavor" and "spongy and cottony," and no one liked the "sweet, gummy" glaze applied at the factory. The thickly sliced Carando Honey-Cured Spiral Sliced Ham ($2.99 per pound) earned high marks for its "deep, smoky flavor," but tasters criticized the meat as "too wet" and "too sweet." Nearly every taster praised the "nice balance of smoke and salt" and "genuine ham flavor" in the Cook's Spiral Sliced Hickory Smoked Bone-In Honey Ham ($3.29 per pound). (The Cook's brand is unrelated to *Cook's Illustrated.*) For complete tasting results, go to www.cooksillustrated.com/december. –Elizabeth Bomze

PREMIUM PIG

Praised for its balance of sweetness, salt, and smoke, the Cook's Spiral Sliced Hickory Smoked Bone-In Honey Ham is the test kitchen's clear favorite.

GLAZED SPIRAL-SLICED HAM

SERVES 12 TO 14, WITH LEFTOVERS

You can bypass the 90-minute soaking time, but the heating time will increase to 18 to 20 minutes per pound for a cold ham. If there is a tear or hole in the ham's inner covering, wrap it in several layers of plastic wrap before soaking it in hot water. Instead of using the plastic oven bag, the ham may be placed cut-side down in the roasting pan and covered tightly with foil, but you will need to add 3 to 4 minutes per pound to the heating time. If using an oven bag, be sure to cut slits in the bag so it does not burst. Our recipe for Apple-Ginger Glaze is available free at www.cooksillustrated.com/december.

- 1 spiral-sliced bone-in half ham (7 to 10 pounds)
- 1 large plastic oven bag
- 1 recipe glaze (recipes follow)

1. Leaving ham's inner plastic or foil covering intact, place ham in large container and cover with hot tap water; set aside for 45 minutes. Drain and cover again with hot tap water; set aside for another 45 minutes.

2. Adjust oven rack to lowest position and heat oven to 250 degrees. Unwrap ham; remove and discard plastic disk covering bone. Place ham in oven bag. Gather top of bag tightly so bag fits snugly around ham, tie bag, and trim excess plastic. Set ham cut-side down in large roasting pan and cut 4 slits in top of bag with paring knife.

3. Bake ham until center registers 100 degrees on instant-read thermometer, 1 to 1½ hours (about 10 minutes per pound).

4. Remove ham from oven and increase oven temperature to 350 degrees. Cut open oven bag and roll back sides to expose ham. Brush ham with one-third of glaze and return to oven until glaze becomes sticky, about 10 minutes (if glaze is too thick to brush, return to heat to loosen).

5. Remove ham from oven, transfer to cutting board, and brush entire ham with another third of glaze. Let ham rest, loosely tented with foil, for 15 minutes. While ham rests, heat remaining third of glaze with 4 to 6 tablespoons of ham juices until it forms thick but fluid sauce. Carve and serve ham, passing sauce at table.

MAPLE-ORANGE GLAZE

MAKES 1 CUP, ENOUGH TO GLAZE 1 HAM

- ¾ cup maple syrup
- ½ cup orange marmalade
- 2 tablespoons unsalted butter
- 1 tablespoon Dijon mustard
- 1 teaspoon ground black pepper
- ¼ teaspoon ground cinnamon

Combine all ingredients in small saucepan. Cook over medium heat, stirring occasionally, until mixture is thick, syrupy, and reduced to 1 cup, 5 to 10 minutes; set aside.

CHERRY-PORT GLAZE

MAKES 1 CUP, ENOUGH TO GLAZE 1 HAM

- ½ cup ruby port
- ½ cup cherry preserves
- 1 cup packed dark brown sugar
- 1 teaspoon ground black pepper

Simmer port in small saucepan over medium heat until reduced to 2 tablespoons, about 5 minutes. Add remaining ingredients and cook, stirring occasionally, until sugar dissolves and mixture is thick, syrupy, and reduced to 1 cup, 5 to 10 minutes; set aside.

COOK'S LIVE Original Test Kitchen Videos
www.cooksillustrated.com

HOW TO MAKE
- Glazed Spiral-Sliced Ham

VIDEO TIP
- What's the best way to carve a ham?

Beef and Vegetable Stir-Fries

Home stovetops often yield watery stir-fries with steamed meat and underdone vegetables. But with the proper technique, you can stir-fry like a pro.

BY DAVID PAZMIÑO

Stir-frying requires blazing heat to cook food quickly. In kitchen tests on several stoves, I found that the bottom of a traditional round wok reached an average of 564 degrees (a temperature sufficient to brown meat and vegetables), but when I moved the thermometer halfway up the side of the wok, I saw that the temperature dropped more than 100 degrees. At the top edge of the wok, the temperature averaged just 336 degrees—perfect for steaming beef but useless for searing it.

For years, the test kitchen has advocated using a large nonstick pan for stir-fries. Because the pan is basically flat, its usable cooking surface is much larger than a wok's. In my tests, I found that temperature was remarkably consistent—it averaged 560 degrees in the center of the pan, 555 degrees halfway between the center and the edge of the pan, and 554 degrees at the edge of the cooking surface. So a nonstick skillet is a must, but so is the right technique. To find out what you need to know when it comes to beef stir-fries, see the box at right.

Better than takeout and easy to execute, if you follow key steps.

Beef Stir-Fries 101

START WITH THE RIGHT CUT. Flank steak is the obvious choice, but we also like sirloin tip steaks and blade steaks. You will need to remove excess fat and gristle from blade steaks, so start with 1 pound to compensate for trimmings.

CHILL, THEN SLICE. To make slicing easier, freeze the meat for 20 to 30 minutes. Cut across the grain so meat won't be tough.

MARINATE FOR MOISTURE. A 10-minute soy marinade adds flavor and helps the meat retain moisture. (The soy acts like a brine.) Drain the meat before searing to remove excess liquid.

USE A BIG PAN. Pan sizes are measured across the top. Make sure your pan measures at least 12 inches.

COOK IN BATCHES. You want the meat to brown, so give it some space (see photos, page 13). Once the meat is browned, empty the pan and add the slow-cooking vegetables first so they get a head start on softer vegetables.

ADD GARLIC AND GINGER LAST. Add aromatics late in the game so they don't burn.

TERIYAKI STIR-FRIED BEEF WITH GREEN BEANS AND SHIITAKES

SERVES 4 AS MAIN DISH WITH RICE

You can substitute 1 tablespoon white wine or sake mixed with 1 teaspoon sugar for the mirin. Recipes for Stir-Fried Red Curry Beef with Eggplant, Korean Stir-Fried Beef with Kimchi, and Beef and Vegetable Stir-Fries for Two are available free at www.cooksillustrated.com/december.

- 4 tablespoons soy sauce
- 1 teaspoon plus 2 tablespoons sugar
- 12 ounces flank steak, cut into 2-inch-wide strips with grain, then sliced across grain into 1/8-inch-thick slices
- 1/2 cup low-sodium chicken broth
- 1 tablespoon mirin
- 1/4 teaspoon red pepper flakes
- 1 teaspoon cornstarch
- 3 medium garlic cloves, minced or pressed through garlic press (about 1 tablespoon)
- 1 tablespoon minced fresh ginger
- 2 tablespoons vegetable oil
- 8 ounces shiitake mushrooms, wiped clean, stemmed, and cut into 1-inch pieces
- 12 ounces green beans, ends trimmed and halved
- 1/4 cup water
- 3 scallions, cut into 1 1/2-inch pieces, white and light green pieces quartered lengthwise

1. Combine 2 tablespoons soy sauce and 1 teaspoon sugar in medium bowl. Add beef, toss well, and marinate for at least 10 minutes or up to 1 hour, stirring once. Meanwhile, whisk remaining 2 tablespoons soy sauce, remaining 2 tablespoons sugar, broth, mirin, pepper flakes, and cornstarch in medium bowl. Combine garlic, ginger, and 1 teaspoon oil in small bowl.

2. Drain beef and discard liquid. Heat 1 teaspoon oil in 12-inch nonstick skillet over high heat until just smoking. Add half of beef in single layer, breaking up clumps. Cook, without stirring, for 1 minute, then stir and cook until browned, 1 to 2 minutes. Transfer beef to clean bowl. Heat 1 teaspoon oil in skillet and repeat with remaining beef. Rinse skillet and dry with paper towels.

3. Add remaining tablespoon oil to now-empty skillet and heat until just smoking. Add mushrooms and cook until beginning to brown, about 2 minutes. Add green beans and cook, stirring frequently, until spotty brown, 3 to 4 minutes. Add water and cover pan; continue to cook until green beans are crisp-tender, 2 to 3 minutes longer. Uncover skillet and push vegetables to sides to clear center; add garlic-ginger mixture to clearing and cook, mashing with spatula, until fragrant, 15 to 20 seconds. Combine garlic-ginger mixture with vegetables. Return beef and any juices to skillet, add scallions, and stir to combine. Whisk sauce to recombine, then add to skillet; cook, stirring constantly, until thickened, about 30 seconds. Serve.

STIR-FRIED BEEF WITH SNAP PEAS AND RED PEPPERS

SERVES 4 AS MAIN DISH WITH RICE

- 2 tablespoons soy sauce
- 1 teaspoon plus 1 tablespoon sugar
- 12 ounces flank steak, cut into 2-inch-wide strips with grain, then sliced across grain into 1/8-inch-thick slices

PHOTOGRAPHY: CARL TREMBLAY

2 tablespoons dry sherry
½ cup low-sodium chicken broth
¼ cup oyster sauce
1 teaspoon cornstarch
3 medium garlic cloves, minced or pressed through garlic press (about 1 tablespoon)
1 tablespoon minced fresh ginger
2 tablespoons vegetable oil
12 ounces sugar snap peas, ends trimmed and strings removed (about 4 cups)
1 medium red bell pepper, seeded and cut into ¼-inch slices
2 tablespoons water

1. Combine soy sauce and 1 teaspoon sugar in medium bowl. Add beef, toss well, and marinate for at least 10 minutes or up to 1 hour, stirring once. Meanwhile, whisk remaining tablespoon sugar, sherry, broth, oyster sauce, and cornstarch in medium bowl. Combine garlic, ginger, and 1 teaspoon oil in small bowl.

2. Drain beef and discard liquid. Heat 1 teaspoon oil in 12-inch nonstick skillet over high heat until just smoking. Add half of beef in single layer, breaking up clumps. Cook, without stirring, for 1 minute, then stir and cook until browned, 1 to 2 minutes. Transfer beef to clean bowl. Heat 1 teaspoon oil in skillet and repeat with remaining beef. Rinse skillet and dry with paper towels.

3. Add remaining tablespoon oil to now-empty skillet and heat until just smoking. Add snap peas and bell pepper; cook, stirring frequently, until vegetables begin to brown, 3 to 5 minutes. Add water and continue to cook until vegetables are crisp-tender, 1 to 2 minutes longer. Push vegetables to sides of skillet; add garlic-ginger mixture to clearing and cook, mashing with spatula, until fragrant, 15 to 20 seconds. Combine garlic-ginger mixture with vegetables. Return beef and any juices to skillet and stir to combine. Whisk sauce to recombine, then add to skillet; cook, stirring constantly, until thickened, about 30 seconds. Serve.

TANGERINE STIR-FRIED BEEF WITH ONIONS AND SNOW PEAS

SERVES 4 AS MAIN DISH WITH RICE

Two to 3 oranges can be substituted for the tangerines. If available, substitute 1 teaspoon toasted and ground Sichuan peppercorns for the red pepper flakes.

4 tablespoons soy sauce
1 teaspoon plus 1 tablespoon light brown sugar
12 ounces flank steak, cut into 2-inch-wide strips with grain, then sliced across grain into ⅛-inch-thick slices
¾ cup juice plus 1 teaspoon grated zest from 3 to 4 tangerines
1 teaspoon sesame oil
1 teaspoon cornstarch
3 medium garlic cloves, minced or pressed through garlic press (about 1 tablespoon)
1 tablespoon minced fresh ginger
1 tablespoon Chinese black bean sauce
¼–½ teaspoon red pepper flakes (see note above)
2 tablespoons vegetable oil
1 large onion, halved and cut into ½-inch wedges
10 ounces snow peas, ends trimmed and strings removed (about 4 cups)
2 tablespoons water

1. Combine 2 tablespoons soy sauce and 1 teaspoon sugar in medium bowl. Add beef, toss well, and marinate for at least 10 minutes or up to 1 hour, stirring once. Meanwhile, whisk remaining 2 tablespoons soy sauce, remaining tablespoon sugar, tangerine juice, sesame oil, and cornstarch in medium bowl. Combine tangerine zest, garlic, ginger, black bean sauce, pepper flakes, and 1 teaspoon vegetable oil in small bowl.

2. Drain beef and discard liquid. Heat 1 teaspoon vegetable oil in 12-inch nonstick skillet over high heat until just smoking. Add half of beef in single layer, breaking up clumps. Cook, without stirring, for 1 minute, then stir and cook until browned, 1 to 2 minutes. Transfer beef to clean bowl. Heat 1 teaspoon vegetable oil in skillet and repeat with remaining beef. Rinse skillet and dry with paper towels.

3. Add remaining tablespoon vegetable oil to now-empty skillet and heat until just smoking. Add onion and cook, stirring frequently, until beginning to brown, 3 to 5 minutes. Add snow peas and continue to cook until spotty brown, about 2 minutes longer. Add water and cook until vegetables are crisp-tender, about 1 minute. Push vegetables to sides of skillet; add zest-garlic mixture to clearing and cook, mashing with spatula, until fragrant, 15 to 20 seconds. Combine zest-garlic mixture with vegetables. Return beef and any juices to skillet and stir to combine. Whisk sauce to recombine, then add to skillet; cook, stirring constantly, until thickened, about 30 seconds. Serve.

RECIPE DIAGNOSIS:
Browning Meat for Stir-Fries

PROBLEM: Cooking the meat in one large batch causes it to steam in its own liquid. The meat will be chewy, dry, and gray.

SOLUTION: Cooking the meat in two smaller batches allows it to brown quickly without drying out or becoming tough.

EQUIPMENT TESTING:
Are Wok-Style Pans Any Better?

Over the years, we have tested traditional woks several times and reached the same conclusion: Their rounded, wobbly design is not suited for conventional, flat-topped American stoves. You're better off using a large nonstick skillet. But recently we've noticed wok-style pans that split the design differences between a skillet and a wok and wondered how they compare. To find out, we stir-fried beef and vegetables in three different wok descendants and measured the results against stir-fries cooked in a 12-inch nonstick skillet.

Although all three of the wok-style pans we tested performed ably, we're not willing to invest in a new pan just for stir-frying. The actual cooking surface on these pans measured less than 7 inches across—a full 2 inches smaller than the cooking surface on a standard 12-inch skillet. While these wok-style pans are better suited to a flat burner than is a traditional round wok, they can't beat the skillet for stir-frying. For the complete results of this testing, go to www.cooksillustrated.com/december. —Elizabeth Bomze

FLAT-BOTTOMED WOK
➤This 14-inch pan from **JOYCE CHEN** ($54.95) actually offers less than 7 inches of cooking surface, but it heated quickly and seared meat respectably.

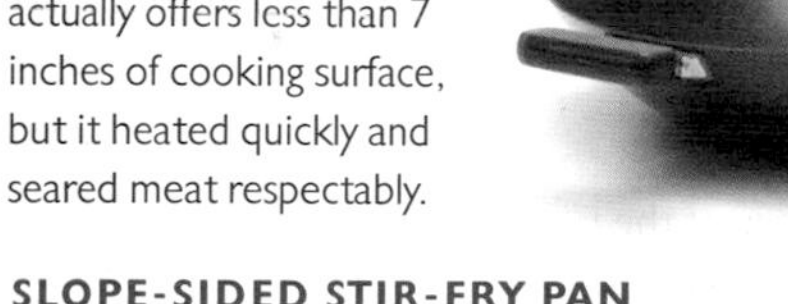

SLOPE-SIDED STIR-FRY PAN
➤Shallower than a flat-bottomed wok, this stir-fry pan from **ANOLON** ($39.99) has a nonstick coating (which we like) but not enough cooking space.

FLAT-BOTTOMED STIR-FRY PAN
➤This stainless steel beauty from **ALL-CLAD** ($159.95) performed well (although we used a bit more oil to prevent sticking), but its surface area can't match a skillet's.

COOK'S LIVE Original Test Kitchen Videos
www.cooksillustrated.com

HOW TO MAKE
- Beef and Vegetable Stir-Fries

VIDEO TIPS
- What's the best way to stir-fry meat?
- How do I know when my pan is hot enough?
- How do you make steamed rice?

Easy Roast Turkey Breast

Achieving crisp skin without drying out the delicate white meat is easier said than done when roasting a whole turkey breast.

BY CHARLES KELSEY

Roasting a whole turkey breast should be easy. The biggest challenge with the holiday bird is that the dark meat takes longer to cook than the white meat; this is neatly avoided by the all-white breast. And the stuffing, which slows down the whole process and makes it much more cumbersome, is a nonissue. You have no choice but to bake the holiday dressing separately. So why have I had such trouble with this seemingly easy recipe?

I like turkey and roast a whole breast several times a year. Sometimes the meat is moist and juicy, but more often than not the lean white meat comes out chalky and dry. The layers closest to the skin get especially parched as the meat near the bone takes its time coming up to temperature, and the skin is never as crisp as I'd like.

Back to Basics

Over the years, the test kitchen has discovered that brining (soaking in a saltwater solution for several hours) makes turkey moister. The salt changes the protein structure in the meat and helps it hold on to more moisture. Brining is especially helpful with delicate white meat, so it came as no surprise that brined turkey breasts were clearly juicier than unbrined turkey breasts. But brining is not enough. The right roasting technique is a must, too.

Thinking that a turkey breast is little more than a giant chicken breast, I looked to a method the test kitchen developed several years ago for roasting whole bone-in, skin-on chicken breasts. For this recipe, the skin on the whole chicken breasts is loosened and the meat is rubbed with softened butter. Loosening the skin helps it to lift and separate from the meat, which promotes even browning and creates crisper skin. The fat in the butter also keeps the breast meat moist and adds much-needed flavor. We found that roasting the chicken breasts skin-side up in a 450-degree oven delivered excellent results. Could I apply the same technique to a whole turkey breast that weighed four times as much?

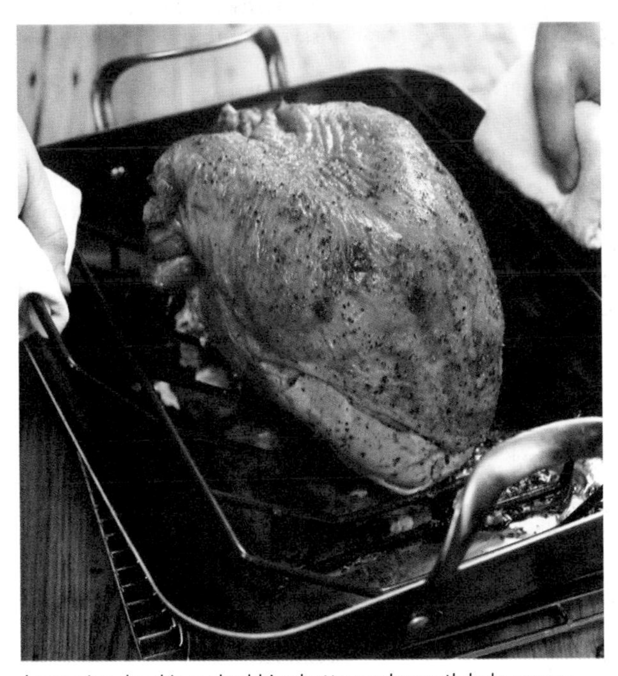

Loosening the skin and rubbing butter underneath help ensure flavorful, juicy results.

I brined a turkey breast, loosened the skin, rubbed the meat with butter, and set the breast skin-side up in a V-rack placed inside a roasting pan. (While chicken breasts can be roasted on a broiler-pan top, larger cuts like a bone-in turkey breast do better in a V-rack, which promotes better air circulation.) At 450 degrees, the skin scorched and the meat was much too dry. I tried the opposite approach and reduced the oven temperature to 325 degrees. After a couple of hours in the oven, my turkey breast emerged with flabby, straw-colored skin—certainly not the look I was going for. The meat, however, was a different story: It was tender and flavorful.

Desiring browner, crisper skin meant trying higher oven temperatures. I hoped that starting the turkey breast out at 325 degrees would conserve moisture in the meat and that a last-minute blast of heat would crisp the skin. But it was difficult to know when to crank up the heat. More worrisome, I found it hard to control the amount of browning, and the meat had a slightly leathery exterior. Not the best results, but I felt like I was getting somewhere using dual oven temperatures.

After testing several more oven temperature combinations, I finally found the best method: Starting the turkey breast in a 425-degree oven for the first half hour of cooking and then

How to Brine a Turkey Breast

A natural turkey breast works just fine for this recipe; however, to ensure that the meat turns out moist and well-seasoned, we suggest that you brine a natural turkey breast following the directions below. Do not brine a kosher or self-basting turkey breast.

Dissolve ½ cup of table salt (or ¾ cup of kosher salt) in 4 quarts of cold water in a large container; submerge the turkey breast in brine, cover it with plastic wrap, and refrigerate it for three to six hours. (Do not brine the turkey breast any longer, or it will be too salty.) Rinse the turkey breast under cold water and dry it thoroughly with paper towels.

STEP-BY-STEP | PREPARING A TURKEY BREAST FOR ROASTING

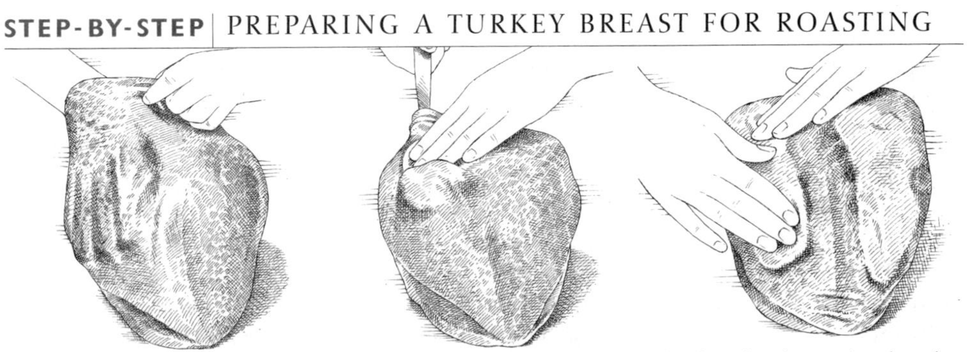

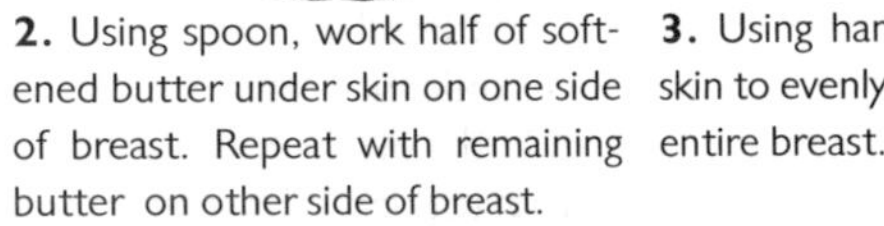

1. Using hands, separate skin from meat, taking care to not tear membrane around perimeter of breast; release skin on either side of breastbone.

2. Using spoon, work half of softened butter under skin on one side of breast. Repeat with remaining butter on other side of breast.

3. Using hands, gently rub turkey skin to evenly distribute butter over entire breast.

PHOTOGRAPHY: CARL TREMBLAY; ILLUSTRATION: JOHN BURGOYNE

TECHNIQUE | CARVING A TURKEY BREAST

To ensure that the juices in the meat have time to redistribute, let the roasted turkey breast rest for 20 minutes before attempting to carve it. Skipping this step will result in a flood of turkey juices on your carving board.

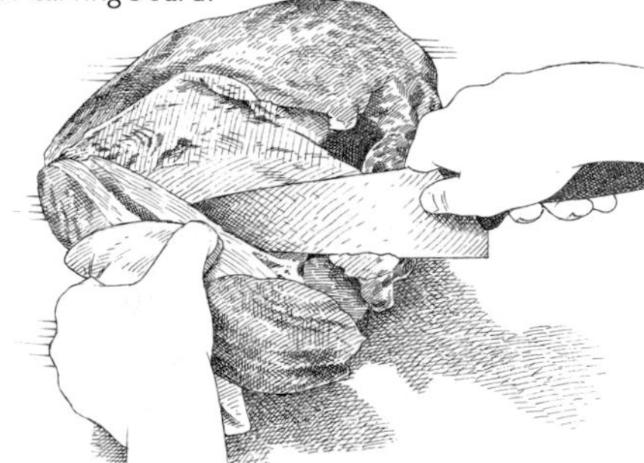

1. Run carving or chef's knife along one side of breastbone. Use other hand (with towel to protect it from heat) to pry entire breast half from bone while cutting, being mindful to keep skin intact.

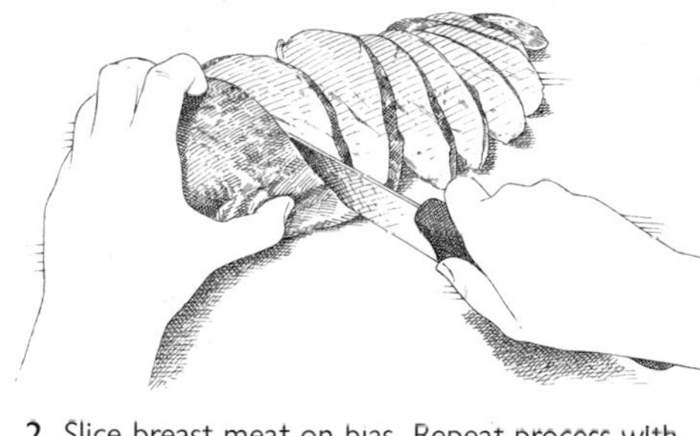

2. Slice breast meat on bias. Repeat process with meat on other side of breastbone.

reducing the heat to 325 degrees for the remaining hour. The initial blast of heat kick-starts the browning, ensuring the skin is beautifully golden by the end of the cooking time. And the low temperature gently finishes the turkey meat, helping it stay moist and tender.

One minor problem, though: During the high-heat roasting, the minimal drippings in the pan burned, smoking up the oven and, eventually, the test kitchen. A quick solution was to add water to the roasting pan before cooking. A cup was the perfect amount; any more and too much steam formed, prohibiting parts of the skin from browning properly.

Buttery Goodness

I had one last round of tests to conduct. I was adding salt and pepper to the 4 tablespoons of butter I was rubbing over the turkey meat, and I wondered what other flavors might work. Fresh herbs, citrus zest, garlic, and even ground spices were easy to incorporate into the softened butter mixture and gave the turkey a significant flavor boost. In order to make sure these flavors didn't overwhelm small patches of the turkey breast, I found it imperative to massage the butter evenly into the meat. Dividing the butter mixture in half and working each portion over one side of the breast guaranteed that the butter and seasonings were evenly applied.

My final recipe isn't any harder than the failed recipes I tried. But the butter and dual oven temperatures ensure that the skin is really crisp and the meat is flavorful and moist. I now have a recipe I look forward to making several times a year.

ILLUSTRATION: JOHN BURGOYNE

EASY ROAST TURKEY BREAST

SERVES 8 TO 10

This recipe works equally well with any type of turkey breast. We recommend brining (see page 14) if using a natural turkey breast (no salt added). Using a kosher turkey breast (soaked in salt water during processing) or self-basting turkey breast (injected with salt and water) eliminates the need for brining. The ingredient list on the turkey breast's package will say whether it's been treated with salt. If brining the turkey, omit the salt from the recipe. If the breast has a pop-up timer, do not remove it. Just ignore it (they pop too late) and follow the times and temperatures in the recipe. A turkey breast doesn't yield much in the way of drippings, so a classic pan gravy recipe is not an option. Instead, try our All-Purpose Gravy, available free at www.cooksillustrated.com/december, which doesn't require any drippings. Our Oven-Baked Holiday Stuffing recipes are also available free at www.cooksillustrated.com/december.

- 4 tablespoons (1/2 stick) unsalted butter, softened
- 3/4 teaspoon table salt
- 1/4 teaspoon ground black pepper
- 1 whole bone-in, skin-on turkey breast (6 to 7 pounds), trimmed of excess fat and patted dry with paper towels (see note above)
- 1 cup water

1. Adjust oven rack to middle position and heat oven to 425 degrees. Mix butter, salt, and pepper in medium bowl with rubber spatula until thoroughly combined. Following illustration 1 on page 14, carefully separate turkey skin from meat over breast; avoid breaking skin.

2. Following illustrations 2 and 3, work butter mixture under skin on both sides of breast and rub skin of turkey to evenly distribute butter over breast. Spray V-rack with nonstick cooking spray and set inside large roasting pan. Place turkey in rack with skin side facing up; pour water into roasting pan.

3. Roast turkey for 30 minutes. Reduce oven temperature to 325 degrees. Continue to roast turkey until thickest part of breast registers 160 degrees on instant-read thermometer, about 1 hour longer. Transfer turkey to carving board and let rest for 20 minutes. Carve (see illustrations above) and serve.

EQUIPMENT TESTING:

Refrigerator Thermometers

Holiday cooking means constantly opening your refrigerator and freezer, which can cause the temperatures to rise. To monitor the safety of our cold storage, we use refrigerator and freezer thermometers. We recently tested six models and ranked the Maverick Cold Check Digital Refrigerator/Freezer Thermometer ($34.95) first. Though relatively pricey, it is the only model that simultaneously monitors the temperature in both the freezer and refrigerator, thanks to a 75-inch wire probe that runs from the display (which you keep in the refrigerator) to the freezer. For complete results of this testing, go to www.cooksillustrated.com/december.
—Elizabeth Bomze

DOUBLE-DUTY THERMOMETER

EASY ROAST TURKEY BREAST WITH LEMON AND THYME

Follow recipe for Easy Roast Turkey Breast, adding 3 medium garlic cloves, minced or pressed through garlic press (about 1 tablespoon), 2 tablespoons minced fresh thyme leaves, and 1 teaspoon grated zest from 1 lemon to butter mixture in step 1.

EASY ROAST TURKEY BREAST WITH ORANGE AND ROSEMARY

Follow recipe for Easy Roast Turkey Breast, adding 3 medium garlic cloves, minced or pressed through garlic press (about 1 tablespoon), 1 tablespoon minced fresh rosemary, 1 teaspoon grated zest from 1 orange, and 1/4 teaspoon red pepper flakes to butter mixture in step 1.

EASY ROAST TURKEY BREAST WITH SOUTHWESTERN FLAVORS

Follow recipe for Easy Roast Turkey Breast, adding 3 medium garlic cloves, minced or pressed through garlic press (about 1 tablespoon), 1 tablespoon minced fresh oregano leaves, 2 teaspoons ground cumin, 2 teaspoons chili powder, 3/4 teaspoon cocoa powder, and 1/2 teaspoon cayenne pepper to butter mixture in step 1.

COOK'S LIVE Original Test Kitchen Videos
www.cooksillustrated.com

HOW TO MAKE
- Easy Roast Turkey Breast

VIDEO TIPS
- Which V-rack should I buy?
- How do you make All-Purpose Gravy?

Stocking a Baking Pantry

Here's what you need to have within reach. BY KEITH DRESSER

Baking demands attention to detail, which begins with the selection of the right ingredients. Here are the items we use most often in the test kitchen, along with common substitutes and tips for storing these staples.

SUGARS AND OTHER SWEETENERS

GRANULATED SUGAR: White, or granulated, sugar is commonly derived from either sugarcane or sugar beets, though flavor differences are imperceptible. We have not detected differences among brands of granulated sugar.

SUPERFINE SUGAR: This finely processed sugar has extra-small crystals that dissolve quickly. A must for drinks (such as iced tea), superfine sugar promotes a melt-in-the-mouth texture in delicate cookies such as shortbread and butter cookies.

TO REPLACE: 1 cup superfine sugar

- 1 cup granulated sugar pulverized in food processor for 30 seconds

CONFECTIONERS' SUGAR: To prevent clumping, this pulverized sugar contains a small amount of cornstarch, making it ideal for dusting over cakes or dissolving in a quick glaze.

TO REPLACE: 1 cup confectioners' sugar

- 1 cup granulated sugar + 1 teaspoon cornstarch ground in blender (not food processor)

MOLASSES: For most baking applications, we prefer to use light (or mild) molasses instead of dark (or robust). But if you want a fuller flavor, opt for the latter. Stay away from blackstrap, though; it can leave a bitter aftertaste.

HOW TO STORE: To keep the lids on molasses or honey jars from sticking, dip a small piece of paper towel into a bit of vegetable oil and wipe the threads of the jar. The bare film of oil prevents the lid from sticking.

BROWN SUGAR: When we want cookies with a serious chew, we get the best results from brown sugar, which is white sugar combined with molasses. Dark brown sugar contains 6.5 percent molasses as compared with light brown's 3.5 percent. Use light brown sugar unless a recipe specifically calls for dark brown.

HOW TO STORE: Airtight containers keep moisture at bay and make scooping and measuring easier, but brown sugar can still dry out, especially after several months. To revive hardened brown sugar, place it in a bowl with a slice of bread. Cover the bowl with plastic wrap and microwave it on high power for 10 to 20 seconds. This should soften the sugar enough so it can be measured (it will harden once cooled).

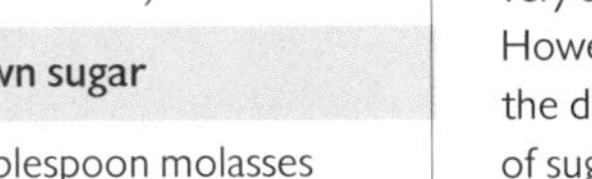

TO REPLACE: 1 cup light brown sugar

- 1 cup granulated sugar + 1 tablespoon molasses

TO REPLACE: 1 cup dark brown sugar

- 1 cup granulated sugar + 2 tablespoons molasses

MAPLE SYRUP: For most baking, the test kitchen prefers to use darker, grade B maple syrup because of its assertive flavor. Grade A dark amber is a close second.

HOW TO STORE: Because of its high moisture level and lack of preservatives, maple syrup is susceptible to the growth of yeasts, molds, and bacteria. Once opened, store it in the refrigerator, where it will keep for six months to a year.

HONEY: In baking, we prefer a mild-flavored honey, such as orange blossom or clover, which doesn't overpower other flavors.

HOW TO STORE: All honey will harden and crystallize over time, but that doesn't mean you have to throw it away. Place the open container of honey in a saucepan filled with 1 inch of water and stir over low heat until liquefied.

Why So Many Flours?

If you bake, you really should keep three flours (all-purpose, cake, and bread) on hand. Why? The protein content in flour varies significantly based on the type of wheat and the time of year the wheat was grown. Cake flour generally contains just 6 percent to 8 percent protein, whereas all-purpose flour has 10 percent to 12 percent protein and bread flour has 12 percent to 14 percent protein. Because of the variation in protein, these flours will absorb water differently—the same amount of water might make a soupy batter with a cup of cake flour but a nice, firm dough with bread flour. Protein content also affects gluten development. More protein leads to more gluten, which, in turn, can translate to coarseness, chewiness, toughness, or crispness. Depending on the recipe, these traits might be desirable or not.

FLOURS

ALL-PURPOSE FLOUR: We prefer unbleached to bleached flour, as we find bleaching imparts a slight chemical flavor that is detectable in very simple recipes such as biscuits. However, you'll never be able to tell the difference in recipes with a lot of sugar and/or fat, including cakes and cookies.

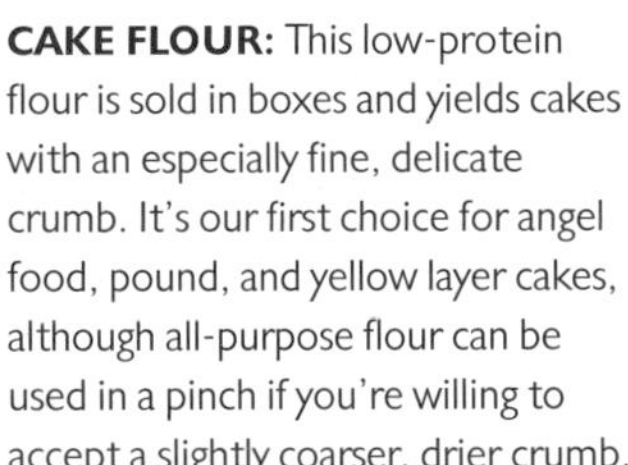

CAKE FLOUR: This low-protein flour is sold in boxes and yields cakes with an especially fine, delicate crumb. It's our first choice for angel food, pound, and yellow layer cakes, although all-purpose flour can be used in a pinch if you're willing to accept a slightly coarser, drier crumb.

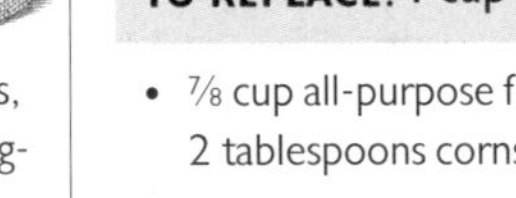

TO REPLACE: 1 cup cake flour

- ⅞ cup all-purpose flour + 2 tablespoons cornstarch

BREAD FLOUR: This high-protein flour (sometimes labeled "made for bread machines") is a must for rustic breads with a chewy crumb and crisp crust. However, we prefer all-purpose flour for American-style sandwich loaves, where a tender crumb is desirable.

HOW TO STORE: Don't keep flour in paper bags. It's messy, and the flour can pick up moisture, especially if your kitchen is humid. Flour belongs in an airtight container with an opening large enough to accommodate a 1-cup measure.

BAKING POWDER AND SODA

Although both are chemical leaveners, they react under different conditions and are not interchangeable. In our experience, there is no detectable difference among brands of baking soda or brands of baking powder.

HOW TO STORE: Moisture is the enemy of baking powder and baking soda, so keep them sealed in a cool, dry place. Baking powder will lose its effectiveness within a year, so it's wise to date the can when you open it.

TO REPLACE: 1 teaspoon baking powder

- ¼ teaspoon baking soda + ½ teaspoon cream of tartar

YEAST

We use instant yeast (also called rapid-rise yeast) exclusively in the test kitchen, as it is faster-acting and easier to use than active dry yeast. Instant yeast doesn't need to be proofed (mixed with warm water) and can be added directly to the dry ingredients. We've detected little difference among brands.

HOW TO STORE: Yeast should be stored in a cool environment, either in the refrigerator or the freezer. Because yeast is a living organism, the expiration date on the package should be observed.

TO REPLACE: 1 teaspoon instant yeast

- 1¼ teaspoons active dry yeast soaked in 105-degree liquid from recipe for 5 minutes

SALT

We use table salt in baking recipes. Its fine grains dissolve and distribute more readily than kosher or sea salt. There are no real flavor differences among brands of table or kosher salt.

TO REPLACE: 1 teaspoon table salt

- 1½ teaspoons Morton's kosher salt or 2 teaspoons Diamond Crystal kosher salt

CHOCOLATE

Unadulterated chocolate is sold as unsweetened or baking chocolate and packs the boldest chocolate punch. Most bittersweet and semisweet chocolates contain 50 percent to 70 percent chocolate; the rest is mostly sugar. We rely on both chocolates in many recipes. We generally use milk chocolate for snacking. For information on cocoa, chocolate chips, and everything else you need to know about chocolate, go to www.cooksillustrated.com/december to read our Chocolate 101 story.

HOW TO STORE: Never store chocolate in the refrigerator or freezer, as rapid changes in temperature or humidity can cause the exterior of the chocolate to bloom, a cosmetic defect that doesn't affect the flavor of the chocolate but is nonetheless undesirable. To extend the life of chocolate, wrap it tightly in plastic and store it in a cool, dry place. Milk and white chocolates will keep for at least six months; dark chocolates will be fine for a few years.

TO REPLACE: 1 ounce unsweetened chocolate

- 1½ ounces bittersweet or semisweet chocolate − 1 tablespoon sugar from recipe

TO REPLACE: 1 ounce bittersweet or semisweet chocolate

- 1⅔ ounces unsweetened chocolate + 2 teaspoons sugar

VANILLA

We have tasted both pure and imitation extracts side by side in numerous baked goods and have been shocked to find that we couldn't tell the difference between the two. (Custards are an exception; imitation extract will taste a bit off.) That said, imitation extract isn't all that cheap, and we prefer to buy the real thing; imitation vanilla is derived from wood pulp.

Thinking Outside the Pantry

While not necessarily pantry staples, there are a handful of ingredients in the test kitchen refrigerator that are crucial for baking.

BUTTER: When baking, we use unsalted butter exclusively. In our experience, we have found the amount of salt in salted butter to be inconsistent. Butter can pick up off-flavors and turn rancid if kept in the refrigerator for more than a month. If you don't use a lot of butter, freeze it and thaw it as needed.

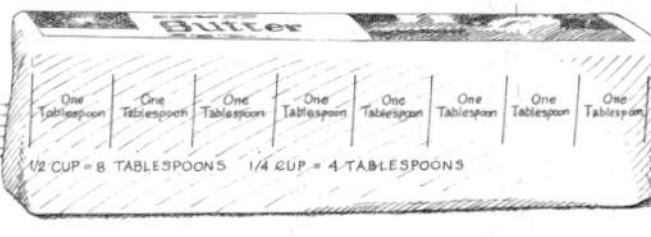

1 stick unsalted butter

- 1 stick salted butter − ½ teaspoon salt from recipe

EGGS: For consistency, we use large eggs in the test kitchen. To ensure freshness, store eggs in their original container in the coldest part of the fridge (not the egg tray in the door, where the eggs can easily pick up odors). Organic eggs performed slightly better than standard supermarket eggs in scrambled egg tests, but there is no detectable difference in baked goods.

BUTTERMILK: We find that buttermilk often gives a lighter, fluffier texture to cakes and biscuits. If you don't use a lot of buttermilk, there are some options: You can use powdered buttermilk (which can be stored in the pantry and reconstituted with water) or make clabbered or soured milk.

1 cup buttermilk

- 1 cup milk + 1 tablespoon lemon juice allowed to thicken for 10 minutes

MILK: Unless specified, we always bake with whole milk. Most recipes will turn out fine with low-fat milk, but skim milk will leave baked goods dry and tough.

1 cup whole milk

- ⅝ cup skim milk + ⅜ cup half-and-half

FATS AND OILS

OIL: We rarely use oil in baking (butter adds much more flavor), but when we do, we call for neutral-tasting canola or vegetable oil, which can be used interchangeably.

SHORTENING: We frequently use shortening in pie crust for extra flakiness. Because shortening doesn't contain water, it can add a desirable crispness to some cookies, such as snickerdoodles. Avoid butter-flavored shortening, which will give baked goods an unpleasant chemical flavor.

BAKING SPRAY: Baking spray—nonstick cooking spray with flour—creates an impenetrable nonstick surface without the mess of buttering and flouring pans. And baking sprays don't pool in pan corners like regular sprays.

ILLUSTRATION: JOHN BURGOYNE

The Best Drop Biscuits

Drop biscuits are the no-nonsense alternative to traditional rolled biscuits. Only one problem—they're often not very good.

BY SANDRA WU

Of the countless styles of biscuit out there, my favorite is the simple but often forgotten drop biscuit. This rustic biscuit offers a unique duality of textures: a crisp and craggy golden-brown exterior full of hills and valleys and a tender, fluffy interior. It's the savory, stand-alone cousin of shortcake or cobbler topping. Unlike fairly pale, flat-topped, uniformly tender baking-powder biscuits that are split in half and buttered, drop biscuits are meant to be broken apart and eaten as is, piece by buttery piece.

While both types of biscuit use the same handful of ingredients and are quick to prepare, drop biscuits don't rely on any of the finicky steps rolled biscuits require to get them just right. There's no need to cut super-cold butter into the dry ingredients. Kneading and rolling are not necessary, so you don't have to worry about overworking the dough. And there's no fussy biscuit cutter or rerolling of the scraps. Drop biscuits barely require a recipe. Flour, leavener, and salt are combined in a bowl; the wet ingredients (milk or buttermilk and either melted butter or vegetable oil) are stirred together in a measuring cup; the wet ingredients are stirred into the dry ingredients; and the resulting batter (which is wetter than traditional biscuit dough) is scooped up and dropped onto a baking sheet.

I headed into the kitchen to try a sampling of drop biscuit recipes. The techniques were as simple as I'd expected, but the texture of the biscuits often fell short, and the flavor was uninspiring. If they weren't dense, gummy, and doughy, my test biscuits were lean and dry. The generous amounts of leavener in most recipes gave the biscuits a bitter, metallic flavor. But the recipes that called for less than 1 tablespoon of baking powder were heavy and squat. Evidently, you need a lot of leavener to compensate for the lack of cold chunks of butter that produce steam and assist with the rise in classic rolled biscuits.

Back to Basics

Still, I had made some progress during this first round of testing. Oil-based biscuits were easy to work with but lacked the most important element: buttery flavor. So butter was a must. I'd also come to some conclusions about the flour.

While some rolled biscuits use softer, low-protein Southern brands of flour or a mixture of cake and all-purpose flours to achieve a light, cottony-soft texture, neither of these improved the texture of the drop biscuits. Instead, because the dough isn't kneaded—and therefore not much gluten development occurs—these softer flours made the biscuits too delicate and unable to form a substantial crust. I stuck with regular all-purpose flour, which provided the structure the drop biscuits needed.

A final brush with butter adds flavor to these craggy but tender biscuits.

My working recipe contained 2 cups of flour, 1 tablespoon of baking powder, ¾ teaspoon of salt, ¾ cup of milk, and 6 tablespoons of melted butter. Once the wet and dry ingredients were just combined, I used a ¼-cup dry measure to scoop the batter onto a parchment-lined baking sheet and baked the biscuits in a 475-degree oven. While this was definitely better than some of the recipes I'd tried early on, these biscuits were still far from perfect: They weren't quite buttery enough and still tasted of leavener.

Increasing the butter to 8 tablespoons answered my tasters' demand for deeper butter flavor, but something was still missing. Since milk didn't seem to be adding much flavor, I was tempted to try other dairy products in its place. Yogurt provided a tangy complexity, but at the price of unwanted gumminess. Sour cream made the biscuits way too rich. Buttermilk offered the best of both worlds: biscuits that had a rich, buttery tang and were also texturally appealing—crisper on the exterior and fluffier on the interior. Increasing the amount of buttermilk to a full cup amplified these effects.

Although one might think that more liquid would make the biscuits heavier and less crisp, just the opposite was happening. Discussions with several scientists cleared up the confusion. The more liquid I added to the dough, the more steam was created in the hot oven. This steam acts as a powerful leavener, which, in conjunction with the chemical leaveners, lightens the texture of the biscuits. And just as water sprayed on rustic bread dough helps crisp its crust, the additional steam was making the exterior of my biscuits seriously craggy, almost crunchy.

Switching to buttermilk meant that baking soda (not just baking powder) was now an option, as the soda would react with the acid in the buttermilk. After trying various combinations of baking soda and baking powder, I settled on what ended up being a fairly standard ratio for traditional rolled buttermilk biscuits: 2 teaspoons of baking powder to ½ teaspoon of baking soda. I knew I'd succeeded when the biscuits rose properly and I could no longer taste any metallic bitterness. As an added bonus, the baking soda aided browning, giving the biscuits a darker, more attractive crust. A mere teaspoon of sugar brought all the flavors into balance without making the biscuits sweet.

Keeping It Clumpy

There was just one aspect of my recipe that continued to bother me: the need to get the temperatures of the buttermilk and melted butter just right. For a quick and simple recipe, having to wait for two things to happen—for the buttermilk to come to room temperature and for the melted butter

PHOTOGRAPHY: CARL TREMBLAY

TECHNIQUE | CLUMPY BUTTER IS GOOD BUTTER

When you stir slightly cooled melted butter into cold buttermilk, the butter will clump. Although this might look like a mistake, it's one of the secrets to this recipe. The clumps of butter are similar to the small bits of cold butter in biscuits prepared according to the traditional method and help guarantee a light and fluffy interior.

to cool—in order for them to emulsify properly seemed like a hassle. But whenever I was impatient and tried to get away with combining the melted butter with straight-from-the-refrigerator buttermilk, the butter would start to form clumps. No matter how hard I whisked the mixture, the bits of butter would stubbornly remain.

In most cases, lumpy buttermilk is considered a mistake, but I wondered what would happen if I actually tried to use this mixture. Maybe the effects wouldn't be too noticeable. To find out, I made one batch of biscuits with a completely smooth buttermilk mixture and another with lumpy buttermilk. Compared side by side, the biscuits made with the lumpy buttermilk rose slightly higher and had a more distinct textural contrast between interior and exterior than did the batch made with the smooth buttermilk mixture.

A "mistake" turned out to be the final secret to my recipe. The lumps of butter turned to steam in the oven and helped create more rise. The clumpy buttermilk seemed to mimic the positive effects of making biscuits the old-fashioned way—with bits of cold butter left in the dough—but this method was better on two counts: It was more reliable and less messy. The only hard part was having the patience to wait for the biscuits to cool down before grabbing one to eat.

TECHNIQUE | SCOOP, DROP, AND BAKE

A greased ¼-cup measure is a great tool for scooping dough onto a parchment-lined baking sheet.

ILLUSTRATION: JOHN BURGOYNE

BEST DROP BISCUITS

MAKES 12 BISCUITS

If buttermilk isn't available, powdered buttermilk added according to package instructions or clabbered milk can be used instead. To make clabbered milk, mix 1 cup milk with 1 tablespoon lemon juice and let stand 10 minutes. A ¼-cup (#16) portion scoop (see page 31) can be used to portion the batter. To refresh day-old biscuits, heat them in a 300-degree oven for 10 minutes.

- 2 cups (10 ounces) unbleached all-purpose flour
- 2 teaspoons baking powder
- ½ teaspoon baking soda
- 1 teaspoon sugar
- ¾ teaspoon table salt
- 1 cup cold buttermilk
- 8 tablespoons unsalted butter, melted and cooled slightly (about 5 minutes), plus 2 tablespoons melted butter for brushing biscuits

1. Adjust oven rack to middle position and heat oven to 475 degrees. Whisk flour, baking powder, baking soda, sugar, and salt in large bowl. Combine buttermilk and 8 tablespoons melted butter in medium bowl, stirring until butter forms small clumps (see photo above).

2. Add buttermilk mixture to dry ingredients and stir with rubber spatula until just incorporated and batter pulls away from sides of bowl. Using greased ¼-cup dry measure, scoop level amount of batter and drop onto parchment-lined rimmed baking sheet (biscuits should measure about 2¼ inches in diameter and 1¼ inches high). Repeat with remaining batter, spacing biscuits about 1½ inches apart. Bake until tops are golden brown and crisp, 12 to 14 minutes.

3. Brush biscuit tops with remaining 2 tablespoons melted butter. Transfer to wire rack and let cool 5 minutes before serving.

BLACK PEPPER AND BACON DROP BISCUITS

Cut 6 strips bacon in half lengthwise and then crosswise into ¼-inch pieces; fry in 10-inch nonstick skillet over medium heat until crisp, 5 to 7 minutes. Using slotted spoon, transfer bacon to paper towel–lined plate and cool to room temperature. Follow recipe for Best Drop Biscuits, adding crisp bacon and 1 teaspoon coarsely ground black pepper to flour mixture in step 1.

EQUIPMENT TESTING: Reusable Pan Liners

Reusable nonstick baking-pan liners are relatively new and the choices are growing. We baked biscuits, ultrathin lace cookies, and berry-filled tarts on five nonstick liners made from various grades of silicone, silicone-reinforced woven fiberglass, and nonstick fiberglass to see if any could impress us more than a sheet of basic parchment paper.

The liners fell into two classes: lightweights and heavyweights. Baked goods made on lighter liners, like those produced by Wilton ($11) and Regency Wraps ($12), had bottoms with spotty browning. These liners can be cut to fit any pan, a definite plus, but the flimsy materials creased easily when washed by hand.

Mats made by SiliconeZone ($14.75) and KitchenAid ($14.99) were heavier but imparted plastic and chemical flavors to the cookies and biscuits. DeMarle's Silpat ($16.99) was clearly the best reusable liner we tested. However, these mats stain over time and can transfer flavors from previous uses. Also, unlike parchment, Silpat mats cannot be cut to fit specific pan sizes. Bottom line: We prefer parchment. For the complete results of this testing, go to www.cooksillustrated.com/december. –Meredith Smith

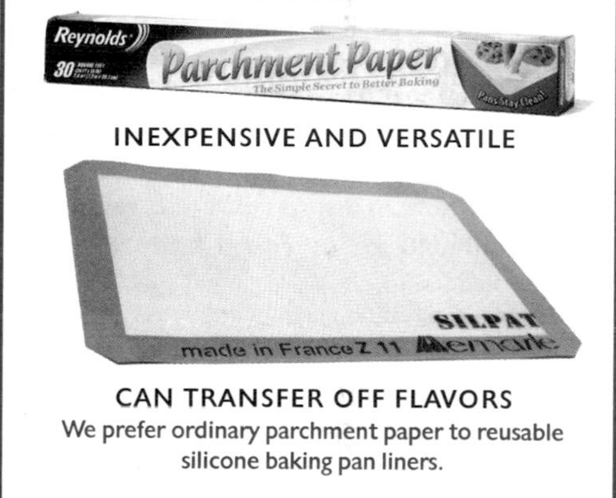

INEXPENSIVE AND VERSATILE

CAN TRANSFER OFF FLAVORS

We prefer ordinary parchment paper to reusable silicone baking pan liners.

CHEDDAR AND SCALLION DROP BISCUITS

Follow recipe for Best Drop Biscuits, adding ½ cup (2 ounces) shredded cheddar cheese and ¼ cup thinly sliced scallions to flour mixture in step 1.

ROSEMARY AND PARMESAN DROP BISCUITS

Follow recipe for Best Drop Biscuits, adding ¾ cup (1½ ounces) grated Parmesan cheese and ½ teaspoon finely minced fresh rosemary leaves to flour mixture in step 1.

COOK'S LIVE Original Test Kitchen Videos

www.cooksillustrated.com

HOW TO MAKE

- Best Drop Biscuits

VIDEO TIP

- How do I know if my baking powder is still good?

Perfecting Tiramisù

This new Italian classic has become a sad, soggy, tired excuse for a dessert. Could we inject new life into a dish whose name translates as "pick me up"?

BY DAWN YANAGIHARA

Like balsamic vinegar and polenta, tiramisù was virtually unheard of in the United States until about 20 years ago. Now it's everywhere from pizza parlors to chain restaurants. Unlike many Italian recipes, tiramisù hasn't been bastardized, but that's not to say it's generally well made. Despite tiramisù's simplicity (it requires just a handful of ingredients and no cooking), there is a lot that can go wrong. If it's soggy or parched, ponderously dense, sickly sweet, or fiery with alcohol, it's not worth the caloric cost.

The word tiramisù means "pick me up," a reference to the invigorating qualities of the dish's espresso, sugar, and alcohol. It's not an old-world dessert, but rather a 20th-century restaurant creation. Store-bought ladyfingers (spongecake-like cookies) are dipped into alcohol-spiked espresso and then layered into a dish along with buttery mascarpone (a thick cream) that has been enriched with sugar and eggs. The dish is dusted with cocoa or sprinkled with chocolate and served chilled.

A well-made, well-chilled tiramisù will cut into neat pieces for easy serving.

A good tiramisù is a seamless union of flavors and textures—it's difficult to tell where cookie ends and cream begins, where bitter espresso gives over to the bite of alcohol, and whether unctuous or uplifting is the better adjective to describe it. Rather than lament all the unworthy tiramisùs out there, I decided to make a batch…or two…or 40…to get to the bottom of a good one.

Filling First

I sorted through the dozens of recipes I had gathered. The most complicated ones involved making a *zabaglione*, a frothy custard, as the base of the mascarpone filling. This required a double boiler, vigilance, and a lot of whisking. I made six recipes and determined that a zabaglione base was not worth the trouble.

As such, the mechanics of making the mascarpone filling became quite simple: I combined raw egg yolks and sugar, mixed in the spirits, and finished with the mascarpone. My early tests taught me that a 13 by 9-inch dish was the right size and that the pound of mascarpone called for in most recipes was inadequate—the ladyfinger-to-cream ratio was off, and the tiramisù was slight in stature. Another ½ pound made the filling generous but not fulsome.

With too few yolks, the filling wasn't as rich as tasters liked, a problem that plagued several of the recipes I initially tested. Six yolks made the filling silky and suave, with a round, rich flavor. (For those wary of desserts made with raw eggs, I also created a slightly more involved variation that cooks the yolks.)

Next, I tested different amounts of sugar and decided that ⅔ cup provided the perfect amount of sweetness. I also added an ingredient—salt—that isn't found in most tiramisù recipes. (I saw only one that calls for salt, and it was just a pinch.) Salt greatly heightened all the flavors and made the most remarkable difference.

Tiramisù recipes fall into three camps: those that call for the addition of whipped egg whites to the filling; those that call for the addition of whipped cream; and those that call for neither. Without whipped whites or whipped cream, the filling was too heavy. Whipped egg whites watered down the flavor of the filling and made it too airy. Whipped cream lightened the texture without affecting the mascarpone's delicate flavor. I found that ¾ cup of cream (half the amount in many other recipes) was sufficient.

Stop, Drop, and Roll

To make tiramisù, ladyfingers are dipped into espresso spiked with alcohol so that the rather dry, bland cookies are moistened and flavored. Brewed espresso is not practical for many home cooks, so I tried three things in its stead: strong coffee made from espresso-roast beans; espresso made from instant espresso granules; and a rather wicked potion made by dissolving instant espresso in strong brewed coffee. Though it wasn't palatable straight from a cup, this last concoction tasted best in tiramisù.

Tiramisù recipes don't bother to give detailed instructions about how to dip the ladyfingers, but I found that the dipping or soaking technique greatly affects the outcome. A quick in-and-out dip wasn't adequate for moistening the cookies, and the result was a dry tiramisù. Fully submerging or otherwise saturating the ladyfingers yielded

TECHNIQUE | DIP, DON'T SUBMERGE

Both of the ladyfingers below were in the coffee mixture for the same amount of time, but different soaking techniques yielded very different results.

PERFECTLY SOAKED
This ladyfinger was dropped into the coffee mixture, rolled, and removed within 2 to 3 seconds. The coffee mixture has not completely saturated this cookie.

OVERSOAKED
This ladyfinger was fully submerged in the coffee mixture for 2 to 3 seconds. The coffee mixture has penetrated all the way to the center of the cookie.

PHOTOGRAPHY: CARL TREMBLAY

a wet, squishy tiramisù. Eventually, I found a method that worked reliably. One at a time, I dropped each ladyfinger into the liquid so that it floated on the surface, then without further ado I rolled it over to moisten the other side.

The only thing left to determine was the best spirit with which to spike the filling and the coffee-soaking mixture. Marsala gave the tiramisù a syrupy, citrusy overtone without appreciable alcohol character. Brandy gave it a lightly fruity flavor and good kick. Dark rum, with its caramel notes, complemented the rich, deep, toasty qualities of the coffee; it was the undisputed favorite. I started with a modest 4 tablespoons (divided between the filling and the coffee), but that was far too weak. I ratcheted up the rum several times before hitting the ideal amount—9 tablespoons.

My tiramisù was assembled like any other. I arranged half of the dipped ladyfingers in the dish and covered them with half of the mascarpone. I followed the lead of others and dusted the mascarpone with cocoa. The layering was repeated, and cocoa finished the tiramisù. (A sprinkling of grated chocolate was a nice addition.) The last detail: Tiramisù requires at least six hours in the fridge for the flavors and textures to meld.

Simple to prepare but grand enough to serve the most discerning *famiglia*, this tiramisù is an ideal holiday dessert. This pick-me-up is no longer a letdown—it's worth every creamy, coffee-flavored, rum-spiked calorie.

TIRAMISÙ

SERVES 10 TO 12

Brandy and even whiskey can stand in for the dark rum. The test kitchen prefers a tiramisù with a pronounced rum flavor; for a less potent rum flavor, halve the amount of rum added to the coffee mixture in step 1. Do not allow the mascarpone to warm to room temperature before using it; it has a tendency to break if allowed to do so. Recipes for Tiramisù with Sambuca and Lemon and Tiramisù with Frangelico and Orange are available free at www.cooksillustrated.com/december.

Is Mascarpone a Must?

Mascarpone, sometimes called mascarpone cheese because of its texture, is a rich cream thickened by acidification. In my tiramisù research, I came across suggestions for substitutes if mascarpone isn't available. Cream cheese was the base for all substitutions. To it, I added sour cream, heavy cream, pureed ricotta cheese, and softened butter in every combination and quantity. Though I came close to approximating the texture of mascarpone, the assertively tangy, salty flavor of the cream cheese (even when cut with other dairy products) made for a dastardly dessert. The lesson: There is no substitute for mascarpone. –D.Y.

ILLUSTRATION: JOHN BURGOYNE

STEP-BY-STEP | ASSEMBLING TIRAMISÙ

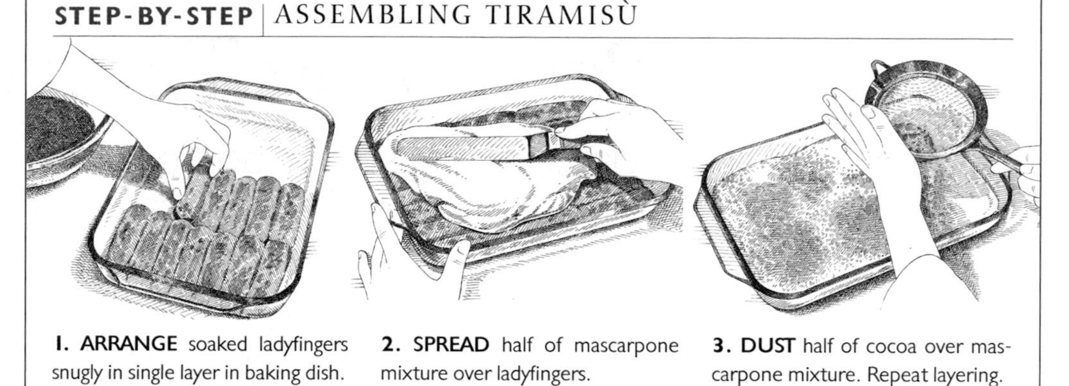

1. ARRANGE soaked ladyfingers snugly in single layer in baking dish.

2. SPREAD half of mascarpone mixture over ladyfingers.

3. DUST half of cocoa over mascarpone mixture. Repeat layering.

- 2½ cups strong brewed coffee, room temperature
- 1½ tablespoons instant espresso granules
- 9 tablespoons dark rum
- 6 large egg yolks
- ⅔ cup sugar
- ¼ teaspoon table salt
- 1½ pounds mascarpone
- ¾ cup cold heavy cream
- 14 ounces (42 to 60, depending on size) dried ladyfingers (savoiardi) (see page 30)
- 3½ tablespoons cocoa, preferably Dutch-processed
- ¼ cup grated semisweet or bittersweet chocolate (optional)

1. Stir coffee, espresso, and 5 tablespoons rum in wide bowl or baking dish until espresso dissolves; set aside.

2. In bowl of standing mixer fitted with whisk attachment, beat yolks at low speed until just combined. Add sugar and salt and beat at medium-high speed until pale yellow, 1½ to 2 minutes, scraping down bowl with rubber spatula once or twice. Add remaining 4 tablespoons rum and beat at medium speed until just combined, 20 to 30 seconds; scrape bowl. Add mascarpone and beat at medium speed until no lumps remain, 30 to 45 seconds, scraping down bowl once or twice. Transfer mixture to large bowl and set aside.

3. In now-empty mixer bowl (no need to clean bowl), beat cream at medium speed until frothy, 1 to 1½ minutes. Increase speed to high and continue to beat until cream holds stiff peaks, 1 to 1½ minutes longer. Using rubber spatula, fold one-third of whipped cream into mascarpone mixture to lighten, then gently fold in remaining whipped cream until no white streaks remain. Set mascarpone mixture aside.

4. Working one at a time, drop half of ladyfingers into coffee mixture, roll, remove, and transfer to 13 by 9-inch glass or ceramic baking dish. (Do not submerge ladyfingers in coffee mixture; entire process should take no longer than 2 to 3 seconds for each cookie.) Arrange soaked cookies in single layer in baking dish, breaking or trimming ladyfingers as needed to fit neatly into dish.

5. Spread half of mascarpone mixture over ladyfingers; use rubber spatula to spread mixture to sides and into corners of dish and smooth surface. Place 2 tablespoons cocoa in fine-mesh strainer and dust cocoa over mascarpone.

6. Repeat dipping and arrangement of ladyfingers; spread remaining mascarpone mixture over ladyfingers and dust with remaining 1½ tablespoons cocoa. Wipe edges of dish with dry paper towel. Cover with plastic wrap and refrigerate 6 to 24 hours. Sprinkle with grated chocolate, if using; cut into pieces and serve chilled.

TIRAMISÙ WITHOUT RAW EGGS

This recipe involves cooking the yolks in a double boiler, which requires a little more effort and makes for a slightly thicker mascarpone filling, but the results are just as good as with our traditional method. You will need an additional ⅓ cup of heavy cream.

Follow recipe for Tiramisù through step 1. In step 2, add ⅓ cup cream to yolks after sugar and salt; do not whisk in rum. Set bowl with yolks over medium saucepan containing 1 inch gently simmering water; cook, constantly scraping along bottom and sides of bowl with heatproof rubber spatula, until mixture coats back of spoon and registers 160 degrees on instant-read thermometer, 4 to 7 minutes. Remove from heat and stir vigorously to cool slightly, then set aside to cool to room temperature, about 15 minutes. Whisk in remaining 4 tablespoons rum until combined. Transfer bowl to standing mixer fitted with whisk attachment, add mascarpone, and beat at medium speed until no lumps remain, 30 to 45 seconds. Transfer mixture to large bowl and set aside. Continue with recipe from step 3, using the full amount of cream specified (¾ cup).

Foolproof Pie Dough

We wanted a recipe that is tender, flavorful, and—most important—consistent.

BY J. KENJI ALT

Pie crust in a nutshell: Mix flour, salt, and sugar together, cut in some fat, add water just until the dough sticks together, roll it out, and bake it. A study in simplicity. Yet it can all go wrong so easily. The dough is almost always too dry and crumbly to roll out successfully. The crust is either flaky but leathery or tender with no flakes. And the results are seemingly random: The recipe that gave you a perfect crust last month resulted in a tough-as-nails crust when you followed it this week.

I wanted to figure out exactly where a crust goes south, so I set out to sort through all the dubious science, purported secret ingredients, and perennial pie crust theories to separate fact from fiction and create a recipe that not only bakes up tender and flaky every single time, but also rolls out easily.

Our dough is well hydrated, so it rolls out easily.

The Theory of Pie

The first question was what type of fat to use. The test kitchen likes the rich flavor of an all-butter crust. Problem: Butter starts to soften at around 50 degrees and fully melts at around 100 degrees, which means the crust has to be worked very quickly. Also, butter's high water content (about 20 percent; the rest is fat) can lead to leathery crusts, as too much water will stimulate the formation of gluten, the protein matrix that provides structure in baked goods. Enter hydrogenated vegetable shortening, a soft fat that doesn't melt until a relatively high temperature and contains no water, just fat. But although crusts made with shortening are very tender, they have virtually no flavor. I ultimately found that a combination of butter and shortening provided the best balance of flavor and tenderness.

I moved on to the next step: cutting the fat into the flour. Of all the methods I tried (food processor, standing mixer, pastry blender, and by hand), the food processor was the fastest and most consistent. Even so, I ran into my first major hurdle—some recipes call for cutting the butter into walnut-sized pieces, and others say to incorporate the fat until it resembles wet sand. Which approach is better? And once you determine which method to use, is it possible to produce same-sized pieces of butter time after time?

What if I ran the food processor until the flour and fat were completely combined? This is simple to repeat every time, and there's no way to overprocess it. But dough is supposed to have pockets of fat in it, which melt upon baking to leave behind the gaps that create flaky layers. By fully incorporating the fat, I was left with no pockets, and sure enough, my dough baked up with no flakes. My next attempt was to process only a portion of the fat completely into the flour, freeze the rest of the fat, and grate it into the mixed dough to create those fat pockets. Consistent? Yes. But despite the fact that there were plenty of pockets of unmixed fat, my crust still came out flake-free.

While I was testing methods for incorporating the fat into the flour, I had been dealing with the frustrating issue of how much water to add to the dough. Some recipes call for a range of water that can vary by as much as 100 percent, claiming that a hot or humid day can throw measurements off. This excuse seemed a little suspicious, and I was eventually able to dismiss the theory by measuring the effects of humidity on flour (see page 31). It was time to step back and examine the structure of a pie crust.

Fat and Flour

When fat is being cut into flour, the flour is separated into two groups; some of the flour is coated with a layer of fat, which protects it from absorbing any water, while the uncoated flour will absorb water and form gluten. When the dough is rolled out, this gluten stretches into sheets separated by pockets of unmixed fat that melt upon baking, leaving behind crisp, separated sheets. The problem is that depending on who's making the crust, the exact temperature of the fat, and even the type of food processor being used, the ratio of fat-coated flour to uncoated flour can change drastically from batch to batch. This means a pie crust recipe that barely absorbed ¼ cup of water one time might readily absorb ½ cup the next. It also explains why the same recipe is flaky one day but not the next: For consistent flakiness, you need the same ratio of fat-coated flour to uncoated flour.

It's not just the chunks of fat that create flakiness. It's also the uncoated flour that mixes with water and forms gluten that guarantees a flaky crust. This explained the failure of the test in which I combined all the flour with some of the butter, then added grated butter to the dough. You need at least some flour that hasn't been

RECIPE DIAGNOSIS: **Why Traditional Pie Dough Fails**

Traditional pie dough is cold and dry, making it difficult to handle and leading to imperfect results.

PROBLEM: DOUGH CRACKS
Too much water makes crust tough, so most recipes call for the bare minimum. As a result, the dough cracks at the edges.

PROBLEM: DOUGH ROLLS OUT UNEVENLY
Dough must be chilled (so the butter won't melt), but cold dough is hard to roll out into an even circle.

PROBLEM: DOUGH STICKS AND TEARS
Most recipes call for using as little flour on the work surface as possible. As a result, butter sticks to the work surface and the dough sticks and tears.

PHOTOGRAPHY: CARL TREMBLAY

STEP-BY-STEP | KEY STEPS TO FOOLPROOF PIE DOUGH

1. MAKE A FAT AND FLOUR PASTE: Completely blending part of the flour with all of the butter ensures a consistent amount of fat-coated flour in the final dough.

2. ADD MORE FLOUR: Pulsing in the final cup of flour ensures a consistent amount of uncoated flour in the final dough.

3. ADD WATER AND VODKA: Sprinkling with water and vodka ensures even distribution. No need to skimp—unlike water, vodka won't make the dough tough.

coated with butter in the dough in order to create the gluten layers that form flakes. When processing the fat in a traditional crust, leaving some chunks of butter in the dough is a good sign that the dough hasn't been overprocessed (that is, chunks of butter in the dough are an indication that there is enough uncoated flour left to combine with water and create a flaky crust).

What if I measured out the two types of flour—the portion I wanted coated with fat and the portion I wanted to remain uncoated—separately? Rather than starting with all the flour in the processor, I put aside 1 cup of flour, then placed the remaining 1½ cups of flour in the food processor with all of the fat and processed it until it formed a unified paste. I then added the cup of reserved flour back to the bowl and pulsed it just until it was evenly distributed around the bowl. This would guarantee the dough had a constant amount of uncoated flour to mix with the water. After mixing in the water and rolling out the dough, I now theoretically had a dough with two distinct parts: long sheets of gluten separated by a flour-fat paste.

The dough baked up as flaky as could be. And since the stage in which the fat gets processed into the flour was no longer ambiguous, my new crusts came out identically, time and again.

SCIENCE: Vodka in Pie Dough?

Pie dough gets its structure from gluten, long chains of protein that form when flour mixes with water. But too much gluten will make pie dough tough. That's why traditional pie doughs are so stingy with the water. I discovered that vodka lets you add more liquid (so the dough is easy to roll out) without toughening the crust. Why?

Eighty-proof vodka consists of 60 percent water and 40 percent ethanol. While gluten forms readily in water, it does not form in ethanol. Thus, my recipe, which contains 4 tablespoons each of cold water and vodka, gets the benefits of 8 tablespoons of liquid (supple, easy-to-roll dough) but actually has the equivalent of about 6½ tablespoons of water—an amount that limits gluten formation and ensures tenderness. As for the alcohol? It vaporizes in the oven. –J.K.A.

DOUGH TENDERIZER

Hitting the Sauce

I had guaranteed flakiness, but tenderness was still a crapshoot. Most recipes with 2½ cups of flour call for 6 to 8 tablespoons of ice water. If I kept the water at the lower end of this range, the dough baked up very tender but was dry and hard to roll out. When I used the full 8 tablespoons, the dough was smooth and easy to roll out but baked up tough—too much gluten was forming. I had to figure out a way to tenderize the finished crust without reducing the amount of water I used.

Scanning through recipes turned up a common "miracle ingredient"—acid. Many recipes say that a teaspoon of vinegar or lemon juice can tenderize dough, claiming that gluten formation is inhibited at lower pH values. But after consulting our science editor, I learned that gluten formation is actually increased in slightly acidic environments (a pH of between 5 and 6) and doesn't begin to decrease until the pH drops below 5. This required replacing nearly half the water with lemon juice, by which point the crust was inedibly sour.

What about using lower-protein cake or pastry flour? No good. The crusts baked up sandy and too short. What about adding cream cheese or sour cream? Although this made the crust more tender, it had a strange, soft chewiness.

Let's review: In order to roll easily, dough needs more water, but more water makes crusts tough. Therefore, I needed something that's not water but is still wet. As the aromas from a nearby pan of reducing wine reached my nose, the answer hit me like a bottle to the head: alcohol.

Eighty-proof vodka is essentially 40 percent ethanol and 60 percent water. As it happens, gluten cannot form in alcohol, which means that for every tablespoon of vodka I added, only 60 percent of it contributed to gluten development.

I made a batch of pie dough with 4 tablespoons each of cold vodka and water. The resulting dough was as smooth as Play-Doh, and I couldn't have made it crack even if I'd wanted to. I was tempted to toss it, thinking it would bake up tough as leather, but giving good science the benefit of the doubt, I baked it anyway. It was an unparalleled success. The dough baked up every bit as tender and flaky as any crust I'd ever had, without a hint of booziness to give away its secret. One hundred forty-eight pie crusts later, I'd finally come up with a recipe that is 100 percent reliable.

FOOLPROOF PIE DOUGH

FOR ONE 9-INCH DOUBLE-CRUST PIE

Vodka is essential to the texture of the crust and imparts no flavor—do not substitute. This dough will be moister and more supple than most standard pie doughs and will require more flour to roll out (up to ¼ cup). Our recipe for Foolproof Pie Dough for a Single-Crust Pie is available free at www.cooksillustrated.com/december.

- 2½ cups (12½ ounces) unbleached all-purpose flour
- 1 teaspoon table salt
- 2 tablespoons sugar
- 12 tablespoons (1½ sticks) cold unsalted butter, cut into ¼-inch slices
- ½ cup cold vegetable shortening, cut into 4 pieces
- ¼ cup cold vodka
- ¼ cup cold water

1. Process 1½ cups flour, salt, and sugar in food processor until combined, about 2 one-second pulses. Add butter and shortening and process until homogenous dough just starts to collect in uneven clumps, about 15 seconds (dough will resemble cottage cheese curds and there should be no uncoated flour). Scrape bowl with rubber spatula and redistribute dough evenly around processor blade. Add remaining cup flour and pulse until mixture is evenly distributed around bowl and mass of dough has been broken up, 4 to 6 quick pulses. Empty mixture into medium bowl.

2. Sprinkle vodka and water over mixture. With rubber spatula, use folding motion to mix, pressing down on dough until dough is slightly tacky and sticks together. Divide dough into two even balls and flatten each into 4-inch disk. Wrap each in plastic wrap and refrigerate at least 45 minutes or up to 2 days.

COOK'S LIVE Original Test Kitchen Videos

www.cooksillustrated.com

HOW TO MAKE

- Foolproof Pie Dough

VIDEO TIPS

- How can I roll the dough into a perfect circle?
- Can I make this recipe without a food processor?

Apple-Cranberry Pie

Adding cranberries to an apple pie can result in out-of-balance flavors.

BY J. KENJI ALT

To prevent the tart cranberries from overpowering the subtle apples, we keep the fillings separate.

Apple pie is a balance between sweet and tart, tender and crisp. Adding cranberries upsets that delicate balance—the tart berries overwhelm the subtle perfume of the apples and shed a lot of liquid that makes the bottom crust soggy. My goal was to find a way to combine these two classic fall fruits in such a way that the full flavor of both came through and the crust remained crisp.

At first I thought it might be a simple matter of fine-tuning the proportion of cranberries to apples. I was wrong. No matter how few cranberries I used, adding them whole inevitably led to wincing when cranberries burst in tasters' mouths.

Thinking how cooking transforms whole cranberries into a stiff, sweet jelly, I assumed that precooking would at least solve the problem of excess juice from the cranberries. True, but it did little for their mouth-puckering flavor.

Most traditional apple pie recipes call for a balanced mix of sweet and tart apples. Instead, I tried using only sweet apples, figuring the cranberries would add plenty of tartness to this pie. Likewise, replacing the standard lemon juice with orange juice helped, but not enough. No matter what I tried, it seemed impossible to get the more subtle flavor of the apples to come through when combined with the cranberries. The solution? Don't combine them. I arranged the cooked cranberries and the apples in two distinct layers within the pie. This time, the flavor of both elements came through clearly.

I had one last test to run. The apple layer was mushier than I wanted, especially in comparison to the thick cranberry layer. When making Deep-Dish Apple Pie (September/October 2005), we discovered that precooking the apples actually made them firmer in the finished pie. It turns out that cooking apples over low heat converts the pectin within their cells to a more heat-stable form. As a result, the apples can tolerate nearly an hour in the oven without becoming excessively soft. Only one problem: Heating the apples on the stovetop released a lot of juice that made the crust soggy, and straining the apples and reducing their juice were extra steps I wanted to avoid.

I wondered if the microwave would be easier. Sure enough, 10 minutes in the microwave did the trick, making the apples firm but not soupy, with nicely thickened juices (thanks to a tablespoon of cornstarch). With distinct layers of pale yellow apples and deep-red cranberries, I had a pie that looked good and tasted even better.

APPLE-CRANBERRY PIE

MAKES ONE 9-INCH PIE

Use sweet, crisp apples, such as Golden Delicious, Jonagold, Fuji, or Braeburn. The two fillings can be made ahead, cooled, and stored separately in the refrigerator for up to 2 days.

- 2 cups frozen or fresh cranberries
- ¼ cup orange juice
- 1 cup (7 ounces) granulated sugar plus 1 tablespoon for top of pie
- ½ teaspoon ground cinnamon
- ½ teaspoon table salt
- ¼ cup water
- 1 tablespoon cornstarch
- 3½ pounds sweet apples (6 to 7 medium), peeled, cored, and cut into ¼-inch-thick slices (see note above)
- 1 recipe Foolproof Pie Dough (page 23)
- 1 egg white, beaten lightly

1. Bring cranberries, juice, ½ cup sugar, ¼ teaspoon cinnamon, and ¼ teaspoon salt to boil in medium saucepan over medium-high heat. Cook, stirring occasionally and pressing berries against side of pot, until berries have completely broken down and juices have thickened to jamlike consistency (wooden spoon scraped across bottom should leave clear trail that doesn't fill in), 10 to 12 minutes. Remove from heat, stir in water, and cool to room temperature, about 30 minutes.

2. Meanwhile, mix ½ cup sugar, remaining ¼ teaspoon cinnamon, remaining ¼ teaspoon salt, and cornstarch in large microwave-safe bowl; add apples and toss to combine. Microwave on high power, stirring with rubber spatula every 3 minutes, until apples are just starting to turn translucent around edges and liquid is thick and glossy, 10 to 14 minutes. Cool to room temperature, about 30 minutes.

3. While fillings cool, adjust oven rack to lowest position, place rimmed baking sheet on oven rack, and heat oven to 425 degrees. Remove 1 disk of dough from refrigerator and roll out on generously floured (up to ¼ cup) work surface to 12-inch circle about ⅛ inch thick. Roll dough loosely around rolling pin and unroll into pie plate, leaving at least 1 inch overhang. Ease dough into plate by gently lifting edge of dough with one hand while pressing into plate bottom with other hand. Leave dough that overhangs plate in place; refrigerate until dough is firm, about 30 minutes.

4. Transfer cooled cranberry mixture to dough-lined pie plate and spread into even layer. Place apple mixture on top of cranberries, mounding slightly in center; push down any sharp apple edges.

5. Roll second disk of dough on generously floured work surface (up to ¼ cup) to 12-inch circle about ⅛ inch thick. Roll dough loosely around rolling pin and unroll over pie, leaving at least 1-inch overhang on each side.

6. Using kitchen shears, cut evenly through both layers of overhanging dough, leaving ½-inch overhang. Fold dough under itself so that edge of fold is flush with outer rim of pie plate. Flute edges using thumb and forefinger or press with tines of fork to seal. Brush top and edges of pie with egg white and sprinkle with remaining tablespoon sugar. Using sharp paring knife, cut four 1½-inch slits in top of dough in cross pattern.

7. Place pie on preheated baking sheet and bake until top is light golden brown, 20 to 25 minutes. Reduce oven temperature to 375 degrees, rotate baking sheet, and continue to bake until crust is deep golden brown, 25 to 30 minutes longer. Transfer pie to wire rack to cool at least 2 hours. Cut into wedges and serve.

COOK'S LIVE Original Test Kitchen Videos

www.cooksillustrated.com

HOW TO MAKE
- Apple-Cranberry Pie

VIDEO TIP
- When should I take the apples out of the microwave?

PHOTOGRAPHY: CARL TREMBLAY

Seeking Pear Salad Perfection

Could we find a way to make lackluster pears shine in a holiday salad?

⋺ BY CHARLES KELSEY ⋲

Adding slices of perfectly ripe, juicy pear to a salad is a hit when using peak-season fruit. But what are you supposed to do the other 11 months of the year? Cooking mediocre supermarket pears until their exteriors caramelize is a great way to boost their flavor. Whether roasted in the oven or seared on the stovetop, heat heightens the pears' subtle complexity and intensifies their sweetness.

Most pear salad recipes offer complicated roasting instructions that yield overly soft pears better suited for a dessert. I wanted a simple technique for caramelizing pears that wouldn't overcook the fruit. Pan-roasting the pears on the stovetop, where I could easily control the heat and check the pears constantly, seemed like the way to go.

I heated a large skillet with oil over medium-high heat, added an even layer of ½-inch-thick pear slices, and cooked them on each side until brown. The cooked pears were OK when tossed with spicy greens, cheese, toasted nuts, and dressing. However, the slices continually turned out limp, no matter how I adjusted the heat.

The texture improved when I cut the pears bigger—into quarters. The exteriors still browned, but now the interiors weren't overcooked. Tossing the pears with sugar before cooking encouraged even better browning. After the pears cooled, I sliced each quarter crosswise to form bite-sized pieces.

As beautiful as the pears turned out, tasters complained that the fruit was still lacking presence in the salad. To this point, I had been using balsamic vinegar in my vinaigrette. Its mellow, fruity flavor worked perfectly to accentuate the perfumed essence of the pears. I wondered if the vinegar had a role outside the dressing. After caramelizing another batch of pears, I added a couple extra tablespoons of straight balsamic vinegar to the hot pan. Almost immediately, the vinegar reduced to form a glazy coating on the pears. When cooled, sliced, and tossed with the other salad ingredients, there was no doubt: These pears deserved top billing in the recipe title.

Watch Out for Too-Ripe Pears

MUSHY PERFECT

We found that completely ripe pears fell apart when pan-roasted (left). Instead, use ripe but firm pears, which will hold their shape when cooked (right). Even underripe pears will work—they'll just be firmer and less sweet.

PAN-ROASTED PEAR SALAD WITH WATERCRESS, PARMESAN, AND PECANS

SERVES 4 TO 6

The test kitchen prefers Bartlett pears for this recipe, but Bosc pears can also be used. With either variety, the pears should be ripe but firm; check the flesh at the neck of the pear—it should give slightly when pressed gently with a finger. If using Bartletts, look for pears that are starting to turn from green to yellow. Romaine lettuce may be substituted for green leaf. Recipes for Pan-Roasted Pear Salads for Two are available free at www.cooksillustrated.com/december.

- 3 ripe but firm pears (about 1½ pounds), quartered and cored (see note above)
- 2½ teaspoons sugar
- Table salt and ground black pepper
- 2 teaspoons plus 2 tablespoons olive oil
- 4 tablespoons balsamic vinegar
- 1 small shallot, minced (about 1 tablespoon)
- ½ medium head green leaf lettuce, washed, dried, and torn into 1-inch pieces (about 4 cups)
- 2 small bunches watercress, washed, dried, and stemmed (about 4 cups)
- 4 ounces Parmesan cheese, shaved into thin slices with vegetable peeler
- ¾ cup pecans, toasted and chopped

1. Toss pears, 2 teaspoons sugar, ¼ teaspoon salt, and ⅛ teaspoon pepper in medium bowl. Heat 2 teaspoons oil in large skillet over medium-high heat until just smoking. Add pears cut-side down in single layer and cook until golden brown, 2 to 4 minutes. Using small spatula or fork, tip each pear onto second cut side; continue to cook until second side is light brown, 2 to 4 minutes longer. Turn off heat, leave skillet on burner, and add 2 tablespoons vinegar; gently stir until vinegar becomes glazy and coats pears, about 30 seconds. Transfer pears to large plate and cool to room temperature, about 45 minutes. Cut each pear quarter crosswise into ½-inch pieces.

2. Whisk remaining 2 tablespoons oil, remaining 2 tablespoons vinegar, remaining ½ teaspoon sugar, and shallot together in large bowl; season to taste with salt and pepper. Add lettuce, watercress, and cooled pears to bowl; toss and adjust seasonings with salt and pepper. Divide salad among individual plates; top each with portions of cheese and nuts. Serve immediately.

PAN-ROASTED PEAR SALAD WITH RADICCHIO, BLUE CHEESE, AND WALNUTS

Follow recipe for Pan-Roasted Pear Salad with Watercress, Parmesan, and Pecans, substituting 1 large head radicchio, quartered, cored, and cut crosswise into ½-inch pieces (about 4 cups) for watercress, 4 ounces crumbled Gorgonzola or Stilton cheese (1 cup) for Parmesan, and ¾ cup toasted and chopped walnuts for pecans.

PAN-ROASTED PEAR SALAD WITH FRISÉE, GOAT CHEESE, AND ALMONDS

Follow recipe for Pan-Roasted Pear Salad with Watercress, Parmesan, and Pecans, substituting 1 head frisée, washed, dried, and torn into 1-inch pieces (about 4 cups) for watercress, 4 ounces crumbled goat cheese (1 cup) for Parmesan, and ¾ cup toasted sliced almonds for pecans.

COOK'S LIVE Original Test Kitchen Videos
www.cooksillustrated.com

HOW TO MAKE
- Pan-Roasted Pear Salads

VIDEO TIPS
- How do I cook pears for salad?
- What's the best way to wash and store salad greens?

TECHNIQUE

PAN-ROASTING PEARS

To maximize caramelization, arrange the pear quarters so that one of the cut sides is flush with the hot skillet. Once the first side is lightly browned, simply use a fork or small spatula to tip the pears over onto their uncooked cut side.

Should You Pay Top Dollar for Turkey?

Turkey is pretty bland, so why pay $100 for a mail-order bird when supermarket options cost less than $2 a pound?

BY LISA McMANUS

Over the years, we've offered a lot of advice about the best way to cook your holiday turkey. But does roasting a better bird start before you even get into the kitchen? Does it depend on which bird you buy? And is it ever worthwhile to mail-order a fancier turkey, which can run as much as $100 plus overnight shipping charges? To find out, we selected eight turkeys, including common supermarket brands as well as kosher, organic, pasture-raised, and heritage birds.

Talking Turkey

A great-tasting roast turkey is not just about turkey flavor; the texture and moisture of the meat are important, too, as anyone who has eaten a mouthful of dry, chewy turkey can attest. Wondering how big a role fat played, we sent the turkeys in our lineup to an independent laboratory to test samples from the skin, white meat, and dark meat; we also had the lab measure their salt content. As we awaited results, we talked with turkey experts about the factors that contribute to a turkey's quality, which include its breed, how it's raised and fed, and how it's processed for sale.

In a sense, modern commercial turkeys have been bred to have very little flavor, said Michael Lilburn, a professor of animal sciences at Ohio State University. "In the United States, we're a white-meat market. This created a heavy emphasis on genetic selection for breast-muscle growth."

The most common commercial turkey, the Broad-Breasted White, has been bred to grow bigger in less time and on less feed (to reduce costs) and to produce the maximum possible white meat, Lilburn said. Today's turkeys are up to 70 percent white meat, and they grow fast. Most Americans eat a hen (female) turkey on Thanksgiving. These birds are ready for market in just 14 weeks, when they weigh 16 to 22 pounds, which yields processed birds in the 12- to 18-pound range. (By contrast, older breeds of turkey, called heritage birds, need seven to eight months to grow to full size—roughly twice as long as modern turkeys.)

Rapid growth may be good for farmers, but it's not so great for cooks. Modern turkeys have less fat when fully grown, said Dong Ahn, a professor of animal science at Iowa State University, and fat is what provides meat with juiciness and flavor. "Fats contain more flavor compounds over time," Ahn said. "Commercial birds grow so fast, they don't have time to accumulate much flavor."

In Good Taste

Turkey growers have resorted to other means to return flavor—and fat—to the turkey, including injecting "basting" solutions during processing. These solutions can contain salt, turkey broth, oil, sugar, and sodium phosphate (which raises the meat's pH, binding water to the cells), all of which work to season the meat and keep it moist. Turkeys sold this way are often called "prebasted" and can be identified by the ingredient label. While our tasting panel generally liked Butterball and Jennie-O birds in this familiar style, some found them bland and "wet" rather than actually moist.

Another way turkey gains flavor is through koshering. Kosher birds start as the same breed of commercial large-breasted turkeys, but they are processed according to Jewish dietary law and under rabbinical supervision. The carcasses are covered in kosher salt and then rinsed multiple times in cold water, which works to season the meat, improve its texture, and help it retain moisture. Rubashkin's Aaron's Best and Empire Kosher were the two kosher birds in our lineup. While Aaron's Best ranked highly, tasters found the Empire to be decidedly bland. What made the difference? The lab tests were revealing. The Aaron's Best turkey had slightly more fat and nearly twice as much salt as the Empire turkey.

So what about the unconventional turkeys? The organic, pasture-raised bird from Good Earth Farms in Milladore, Wis. (purchased online through the independent farm cooperative Local Harvest) was the same breed as commercial turkeys, but it had been free to roam and eat foraged grass and insects. It also ate organic versions of the usual soy and cornmeal feed most turkeys consume, along with wheat. While all this sounds great, our tasters didn't notice a big improvement in flavor. Indeed, Ahn noted that unless the bird was eating 100 percent foraged food, most consumers could not taste a difference in the meat. The texture of this bird was slightly stringier and tougher than most tasters preferred, probably because it got more exercise. It finished second to last in our lineup.

Another unconventional turkey, from Diestel Family Turkey Ranch in Sonora, Calif., was raised on a vegetarian diet—meaning the bird ate none of the animal byproducts that can be part of commercial turkey diets—and was "range-grown," another term for pasture-raised. The company claims its birds are allowed to grow longer than average—in this case, about six months—for better flavor; however, tasters found that flavor "gamy" and "fishy," particularly in the dark meat. It finished last in the rankings.

Unlike the other two unconventional birds, the single heritage turkey in our lineup won favor, with tasters remarking on its "robust turkey flavor" that was "sweet" and "complex." Heritage turkeys are directly descended from wild turkeys and nearly disappeared in the mid-20th century as commercial Broad-Breasted Whites were created by the poultry industry. Heritage turkeys have colorful feathers, a more elongated frame, and a narrower breast.

The heritage turkey in our lineup, sold through Dean & Deluca for $100 plus shipping, had the most fat by far of the turkeys we tasted—lab results showed it had nearly three times the fat of the leanest bird. A call to its grower, Mike Walters of Walters Hatchery in Stilwell, Okla., revealed his secret for a sweeter bird. While most turkeys eat a ration of corn and soybean meal throughout their lives, Walters eliminates soy from his turkeys' diet in the final weeks, feeding them only sweet corn. "It gives the birds a layer of fat under

Fresh or Frozen?

When organizing our tasting, we decided to buy fresh turkeys wherever possible, assuming they would be better. But as we tallied the results of the tasting, we learned that most of our higher-ranked birds were, in fact, frozen. Our tasters consistently found the frozen birds to be moister than the fresh. This puzzled us until Professor Ahn explained that a "fresh" bird can actually be tougher and drier than a frozen one.

Turkeys may be labeled as "fresh" if they have been chilled to as low as 26 degrees. But at this temperature, tiny ice crystals can form in the meat. If the temperature fluctuates (during storage or transport, at the supermarket, or on the way to your home), these crystals can melt, combine with neighboring crystals, and then refreeze. According to Ahn, "Eventually, irregularly shaped ice crystals will start to poke the cell membranes in the meat. They make holes and the cell tissues in the muscles will start to lose their internal contents. Then when they are cooked, those birds will be dry." –L.M.

TASTING TURKEY

A panel of 24 tasters from the *Cook's Illustrated* staff sampled eight turkeys, each weighing 12 to 14 pounds. We prepared them all according to our recipe for Roasted Brined Turkey (November/December 2004). However, we did not brine the two kosher birds (which are salted as part of their koshering) or the two supermarket turkeys sold as "prebasted" with salt and other flavorings. Tasters rated the roasted birds on turkey flavor, texture, moistness, and overall appeal, taking into account both white and dark meat for each sample. They are listed below in order of preference. Prices were paid at Boston-area supermarkets or at online sources. Fat and salt content were determined by an independent laboratory. Rubashkin's Aaron's Best turkeys are distributed nationally in supermarkets. A source for the Walters Poultry turkey is on page 32.

HIGHLY RECOMMENDED

RUBASHKIN'S AARON'S BEST

- **Frozen kosher**
- **Price:** $1.99 per pound
- **Comments:** Lab tests revealed that this bird had the most salt and one of the highest levels of fat among the birds in our lineup; tasters noticed, finding this kosher turkey "very moist, with excellent texture" and boasting "both white and dark meat that are moist and flavorful."

WALTERS HATCHERY HERITAGE BREED

- **Frozen**
- **Price:** $7.14 per pound (plus shipping)
- **Comments:** Virtually tied for first place, this heritage bird had nearly three times as much fat as the leanest turkeys. It offered "robust turkey flavor" and was "very tender." "What I expect a turkey to be: mild, sweet, flavorful." Both the light and dark meat were juicy.

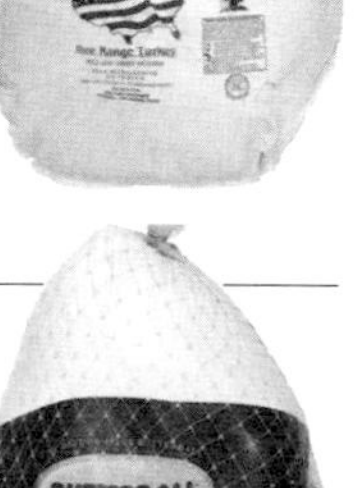

RECOMMENDED

BUTTERBALL

- **Frozen basted**
- **Price:** $1.49 per pound
- **Comments:** Tasters generally liked this self-basting turkey, calling it "nice and moist, with fairly good, unremarkable flavor," though some found it "too salty," "almost wet rather than moist," and "rather bland." Lab tests showed it had the second-highest salt level in the lineup.

JENNIE-O

- **Fresh basted**
- **Price:** $1.49 per pound
- **Comments:** Tasters dubbed this self-basting turkey "middle-of-the-road," with "mild flavor, but it's good." A few described it as tasting "more like chicken," calling the white meat "a bit dry and chewy." Its salt level was quite low, closer to the natural birds than to the self-basting Butterball.

RECOMMENDED WITH RESERVATIONS

EMPIRE KOSHER

- **Fresh kosher**
- **Price:** $2.69 per pound
- **Comments:** "A good consistency, with good moisture and texture, but lacking flavor" was the consensus on this kosher turkey. "White meat tastes like nothing: What am I eating?" A few noted a "metallic," "almost bitter" aftertaste. Lab tests revealed that this kosher bird had just over half the salt of the top-rated Aaron's bird.

SHADY BROOK FARMS

- **Fresh**
- **Price:** $1.29 per pound
- **Comments:** "Bland-o-rama" white meat, with a "chewy" texture that was "too dry." "Like my mother used to make, unfortunately." Tasters were divided on the dark meat, with some finding it good and others complaining of a "gamy" taste and "stringy" texture.

GOOD EARTH FARMS ORGANIC PASTURE-RAISED

- **Shipped frozen from Wisconsin farm**
- **Price:** $2.49 per pound (plus shipping)
- **Comments:** Tasters found this organic bird "tough," with a "dense, chewy quality." They noted its "clear turkey flavor," which was "very good," but felt it "needs gravy!" "Not a good stand-alone turkey." It had the lowest salt level in the lineup.

DIESTEL FAMILY TURKEY RANCH

- **Frozen**
- **Price:** $1.99 per pound
- **Comments:** "Even the dark meat is dry," tasters said of this California-raised bird, noting the dark meat was "rubbery, dark, and funky," with a "fishy flavor." The light meat fared better, with "great turkey flavor," but again, it was "too chewy."

the skin," Walters said. He also tastes the feed himself before he gives it to the turkeys. "I figure whatever residual flavor is in my mouth is the residual flavor that you will have after eating my turkey," he said. "If you ever ate a plain soybean, you know it's bitter. Why feed your birds a flavor that is bitter?" Walters said that he believes any breed of turkey would benefit from this feeding system, though he admits to having no science to back up this assertion, and the food scientists we spoke to were a bit skeptical.

Pecking Order

So what should you buy? It's hard to go wrong with the frozen kosher bird from Aaron's Best. It's moist, flavorful, and ready to cook, since no brining is needed. The prebasted birds from Butterball and Jennie-O finished a notch below our top choices, but they are consistent and also don't require brining. Although unremarkable, the frozen prebasted birds are certainly acceptable.

It's harder to give definitive advice about the less conventional choices. We didn't like the two pasture-raised birds we tasted, and heritage turkeys tend to be more variable in flavor than commercial options. Although the heritage bird from Walters Hatchery finished in the top tier, in a previous tasting of several heritage turkeys (November/December 2005), tasters complained that many of the birds were too gamy.

Finally, there's the cost issue. A 14-pound supermarket turkey sells for about $20. Order the same size bird by mail and the price tag could top $100 once you pay for overnight shipping. You might end up with a superior turkey, but it's a gamble. What's more, the smaller producers can undergo some upheaval, as we found with our favored heritage bird. After our tasting, we learned that the Walters family was moving their turkey business to Missouri and renaming it Walters Poultry, and while they plan to use the same breeder stock, growing conditions, and feed, there is no guarantee that this Thanksgiving's birds will be the same as the ones we tasted. We will be tasting this brand again just before the holidays; look for the results at www.cooksillustrated.com.

COOK'S LIVE Original Test Kitchen Videos
www.cooksillustrated.com

VIDEO TIPS

- What's the best way to carve a turkey?
- How do you make turkey gravy?

Why Don't You Own This Pan?

The flimsy jellyroll pans sold in most stores are useless. But a heavy-duty rimmed baking sheet is an unheralded workhorse every cook should own.

BY LISA McMANUS

Many times a day, our test cooks reach for a rimmed baking sheet. We use them for baking cookies, biscuits, scones, and jellyroll cakes, as well as for roasting oven fries and asparagus. With a wire cooling rack set inside, they're good for broiling or roasting meats and in prep work such as holding breaded cutlets before frying. Our baking sheets aren't just for baking—they are true kitchen workhorses.

But you'd be hard-pressed to find these essential pans in most cookware stores. Known as a half-sheet pan in restaurant supply stores, the real thing is made of heavy-gauge metal and measures 18 by 13 inches with a 1-inch rim all around. The closest thing you'll usually find in retail stores is a flimsy, too-small 15 by 10-inch "jellyroll pan."

If you happen to see a roomy rimmed baking sheet, stop and take a look. You want this pan. But are some models more useful and durable than others? After some digging, we found eight heavy-duty, full-sized rimmed baking sheets (traditional finish; nonstick can scratch or overbrown), priced from $9.95 to $59.95, and put them to the test.

Hidden Differences

If you glanced at the pans we gathered for this testing, you would be forgiven for wondering if it really matters which one you use. Our very first test convinced us that it does. We prepared a batch of our slice-and-bake Glazed Lemon Cookies (March/April 2003) in each of the eight baking sheets. Some pans gave us cookies that rose high and turned an evenly light golden brown across the baking sheet; others turned out burnt cookies—even when we repeated the test several times.

A closer look revealed that these pans are not identical. Rimmed baking sheets are formed by a machine that presses a flat metal sheet into a predetermined shape, maintaining consistent pressure so the metal will flow in without wrinkling or cracking, said Campbell Buchanan, technical manager for United Aluminum in North Haven, Conn. They can be made from different alloys and gauges of aluminum, aluminized steel (a thin coat of aluminum over steel), or a tri-ply sandwich of shiny stainless steel with an aluminum core.

We found that solid construction is more important than the choice of materials. A too-flimsy pan warps under high heat. We observed this when the oil pooled at one end of the warping Chicago Metallic baking sheet as we made fries in the 475-degree oven, resulting in uneven browning of the potatoes.

Aluminum sheet pans will soften slightly beginning at temperatures of 400 to 500 degrees, Buchanan said, and the metal will expand and contract. While steel won't soften significantly below 500 degrees, the combination of metals in aluminized steel can behave differently at high heat, leading to the warping we experienced. The thinner pans also seemed much more prone to warping. Buchanan echoed our findings. "The thicker the pan, the better," he told us.

A pan that is too lightweight also can transfer heat too intensely. We saw this with the lightest pan in our lineup (which was also one of the thinnest), by Wilton, which burned batch after batch of cookies. In this pan, oven fries also browned before they were cooked through, and the jellyroll cake finished before the recipe's recommended time. Other pans that overbrowned cookies, Anolon and NordicWare, were also among the thinnest in our testing.

RECIPE TESTING:

Burning Cookies and Pooling Oil

BURNT COOKIES

Pans with thin bottoms produced batches of burnt cookies.

POOLING OIL

Flimsy pans buckled during our oven-fry test.

Warped View

After all the cooking was done, we placed the pans on a countertop and pushed down on one corner of the rim. Some pans remained resolutely flat, others rocked—having been warped by our testing. We grasped the short sides of each pan and twisted. Again, some pans could be flexed easily, others could not. In general, the less flexible, flatter pans performed better in the kitchen.

So what should you buy? We loved almost everything about the Gourmet Standard pan. It was one of the thickest pans in the lineup and performed admirably in our kitchen tests. But one flaw kept this pan from claiming the top spot. The pan is 2 inches shorter than the competition, so parchment paper and standard cooling racks won't fit. And at $60, this flaw is hard to overlook.

The best rimmed baking sheet turned out to be a restaurant supply item available to retail consumers online. Lincoln Foodservice Products has been making cookware since 1903. Their Half-Size Heavy Duty Sheet Pan ($15.40), performed flawlessly, is one of the thickest pans we tested, sells at a reasonable price, and is our new favorite.

A Rack Above

A good rack should be sturdy, able to withstand a hot broiler, and clean up without warping or damage. It should also fit inside a standard 18 by 13-inch baking pan, which eliminated four of the six brands we purchased. Both the CIA Bakeware 12 x 17 Inch Cooling Rack ($14.95) and the Libertyware Cross Wire Cooling Rack Half Sheet Pan Size ($4.35) performed well. The CIA rack offered extra support, with a central brace and six feet, rather than four, and took top honors. But the inexpensive Libertyware rack is almost as good, and at one-third the price, it's our Best Buy. For complete results of the testing, go to www.cooksillustrated.com/december. –L.M.

ON THE GRID

A grid-style cooling rack turns a rimmed baking sheet into the perfect pan for broiling and roasting.

COOK'S LIVE Original Test Kitchen Videos

www.cooksillustrated.com

- Behind the Scenes: Baking Sheet Testing

VIDEO TIP

- Buying Guide to Baking Sheets

RATINGS
GOOD: ★★★
FAIR: ★★
POOR: ★

TESTING BAKING SHEETS

We tested eight brands of rimmed baking sheets according to the criteria listed below. The pans are listed in order of preference. The source for the winning pan is on page 32.

PRICE: Price paid in Boston-area retail stores or online cookware sites.

MATERIAL: Composition of pan.

SIZE: Outer dimensions of pan.

WEIGHT AND THICKNESS: Weight of pan, measured in the test kitchen; thickness of bottom, as reported by manufacturers.

COOKIES: We preferred pans that produced evenly golden brown cookies with a domed shape.

JELLYROLL: We preferred pans that made moist, evenly golden cake of a level thickness; released the cake easily; and produced a cake that rolled without cracking.

OVEN FRIES: Made with high heat in the oven, the fries were a good test of the pans' ability to cook without warping and evenly brown the potatoes.

PORK: Chinese Barbecued Pork was roasted on a wire rack set into the baking sheet. We preferred pans that held a standard wire rack; could be easily maneuvered into and out of the hot oven; and could be carried across the kitchen without bending and splashing or dumping hot drippings on the cook.

WIGGLE AND WARP: We attempted to twist the pans while grasping them along the short ends, preferring pans that could not be twisted or wiggled. After cooking tests were completed, we placed the pans on a level surface and tapped them hard on one corner to see if they rocked; if so, the pan had warped.

DESIGN: We preferred pans whose interior dimensions were a standard half-sheet size, so wire racks and parchment paper fit without gapping or adjustment; had a rolled edge that did not trap water; and had a durable finish.

COMMENTS: Testers' observations.

HIGHLY RECOMMENDED

	PERFORMANCE	TESTERS' COMMENTS
Lincoln Foodservice Half-Size Heavy Duty Sheet Pan PRICE: $15.40 MATERIAL: Aluminum alloy (13-gauge) SIZE: 18" x 13" x 1" WEIGHT AND THICKNESS: 1 lb., 14 oz.; 1.8 mm	COOKIES: ★★★ JELLYROLL: ★★★ OVEN FRIES: ★★★ PORK: ★★★ WIGGLE AND WARP: ★★★ DESIGN: ★★★	"Perfect" cookies, oven fries, and jellyroll in this "flawless" pan. Pork produced "lots of fat but no worries about spilling—pan is solid as a rock." Jellyroll browned and released perfectly. Pan can't be twisted, did not warp. "The search is over."

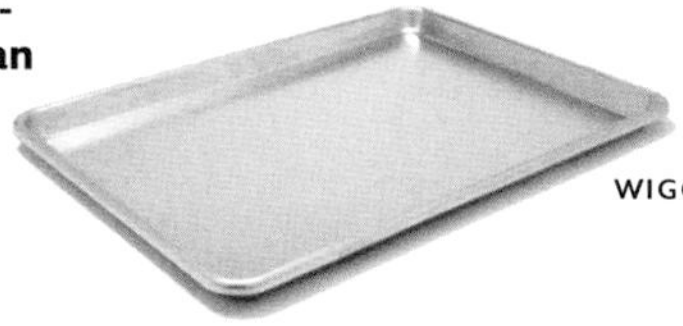

RECOMMENDED

	PERFORMANCE	TESTERS' COMMENTS
Norpro Heavy Gauge Aluminum Jelly Roll Pan PRICE: $17.99 MATERIAL: Aluminum SIZE: 18" x 12" x 1" WEIGHT AND THICKNESS: 1 lb., 15 oz.; 1.0 mm	COOKIES: ★★★ JELLYROLL: ★★★ OVEN FRIES: ★★★ PORK: ★★★ WIGGLE AND WARP: ★★ DESIGN: ★★★	Oven fries were evenly browned, as were cookies and jellyroll cake, and pan felt solid when we barbecued pork. However, while it felt sturdy, pan could be wiggled and had warped slightly by end of testing.
Gourmet Standard Tri-Ply Stainless Steel Jelly Roll Pan PRICE: $59.95 MATERIAL: Two layers of stainless steel sandwiching a layer of aluminum SIZE: 16" x 13" x 1" WEIGHT AND THICKNESS: 3 lb., 5 oz.; 1.8 mm	COOKIES: ★★★ JELLYROLL: ★★★ OVEN FRIES: ★★★ PORK: ★★★ WIGGLE AND WARP: ★★ DESIGN: ★★	Performed all cooking tests well, but this "pretty but pricey" pan's nonstandard size was a handicap: At just 16 inches long (15 inches once rims are discounted), it's too short for standard wire rack to fit inside, and parchment sheets must be trimmed.
Anolon Commercial Bakeware Jelly Roll Pan PRICE: $14.95 MATERIAL: Aluminized steel SIZE: 18" x 13" x 1" WEIGHT AND THICKNESS: 2 lb., 6 oz.; 0.5 mm	COOKIES: ★★ JELLYROLL: ★★★ OVEN FRIES: ★★★ PORK: ★★★ WIGGLE AND WARP: ★★★ DESIGN: ★★	"Sturdy" pan produced crisp, evenly cooked fries, released jellyroll easily, and was steady with hot pan full of barbecued pork and drippings. However, cookies baked up too dark, due to thinness of pan.
Vollrath Jelly Roll Pan PRICE: $9.95 MATERIAL: Aluminum alloy SIZE: 18" x 13" x 1" WEIGHT AND THICKNESS: 1 lb., 11 oz.; 1.02 mm	COOKIES: ★★★ JELLYROLL: ★★★ OVEN FRIES: ★★ PORK: ★★ WIGGLE AND WARP: ★★ DESIGN: ★★★	Cookies baked well, as did jellyroll, but fries were "a little uneven and not very crisp." Pan bent when full of hot barbecued pork, but did not spill. Was slightly warped after testing.
NordicWare Natural Commercial Bakeware Baker's Half Sheet PRICE: $14.99 MATERIAL: Aluminum SIZE: 18" x 13" x 1" WEIGHT AND THICKNESS: 1 lb., 10 oz.; 0.8 mm	COOKIES: ★★ JELLYROLL: ★★★ OVEN FRIES: ★★ PORK: ★★★ WIGGLE AND WARP: ★★★ DESIGN: ★★	While cookies baked evenly, they were too dark. Oven fries in middle of pan were "soggy, wimpy," and underdone, but those around edges of pan were too dark. Pan was stable with hot drippings. Soft surface scratched too easily: Butter knife used to loosen cake left deep hatches all around the pan.

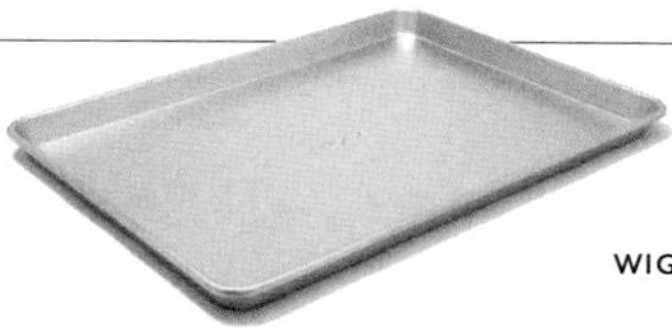

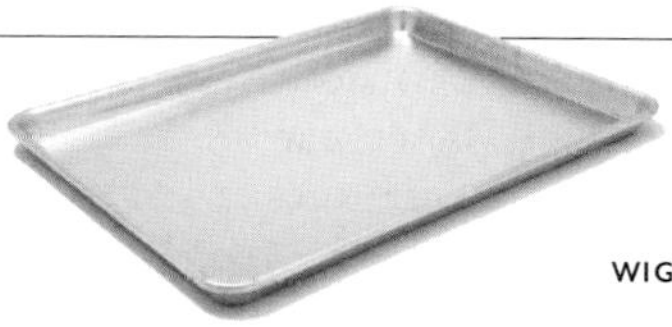

RECOMMENDED WITH RESERVATIONS

	PERFORMANCE	TESTERS' COMMENTS
Chicago Metallic Commercial Cookie/Jelly Roll Pan PRICE: $15.25 MATERIAL: Aluminized steel SIZE: 18" x 13" x 1" WEIGHT AND THICKNESS: 2 lb., 7 oz.; 0.5 mm	COOKIES: ★★ JELLYROLL: ★★★ OVEN FRIES: ★★ PORK: ★★ WIGGLE AND WARP: ★★ DESIGN: ★	Cookies and fries browned unevenly. Oil pooled at one end of pan after it warped under high heat while making fries; pan buckled a bit with pork, causing some hot fat to splash out as we moved pan. Rolled rim trapped dishwater.
Wilton Jelly Roll and Cookie Pan PRICE: $13.99 MATERIAL: Aluminum SIZE: 18" x 12" x 1" WEIGHT AND THICKNESS: 1 lb., 0.8 mm	COOKIES: ★ JELLYROLL: ★★ OVEN FRIES: ★ PORK: ★★ WIGGLE AND WARP: ★ DESIGN: ★	Light and "flimsy, bendy" ("It's flapping like a sail") pan transferred heat too rapidly: Cookies burned; jellyroll baked very quickly; oven fries were still uncooked inside when exteriors were deeply brown. Pan was "quite warped" by end of testing.

KITCHEN NOTES

BY J. KENJI ALT

Shopping for Ladyfingers

Ladyfingers, also called *savoiardi*, are spongecake-like cookies and an essential ingredient in tiramisù. The crisp, dry cookies can normally be found in the international or cookie aisle of the supermarket. Some supermarket bakeries also sell fresh ladyfingers with a soft, cakelike texture. Fresh ladyfingers will become mushy when soaked and aren't an option in our recipe for Tiramisù (page 21).

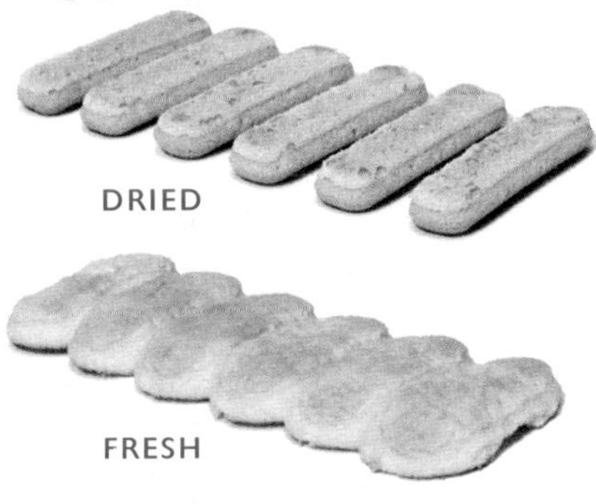

SCIENCE: What Happens to Alcohol in Stews?

Our recipe for French-Style Pot Roast (page 7) calls for both wine and beef broth. In an early version of the recipe, rather than reducing the wine on its own, we simply added all the liquid together at the beginning of the braise. We figured that 2½ hours in the oven would be plenty of time for the alcohol to cook off. We were surprised when the pot roast emerged from the oven with a strong booziness that didn't disappear even after the sauce was reduced on the stovetop.

When alcohol and water mix, they form a solution called an azeotrope—a mixture of two different liquids that behaves as if it were a single compound. Even though alcohol evaporates at a lower temperature than water, the vapors coming off of an alcohol-water azeotrope will contain both alcohol and water. While using a wider pan hastens the reduction process (simply switching from a 10-inch to a 12-inch pan can speed things up by 25 percent to 50 percent), as long as a liquid starts with an alcohol content higher than 5 percent, the final alcohol content will remain at about 5 percent. Theoretically, to lower the alcohol content we would need to first reduce the wine on its own before diluting it with broth.

To test this theory, we made two sauces. For the first, we reduced 2 cups of wine to ½ cup, added 2 cups of broth, and reduced everything to a final volume of 1 cup. For the second, we combined 2 cups of wine and 2 cups of broth and then reduced the mixture to 1 cup. Although they started with identical ingredients and ended up at the same final volume, our theory suggested that our second sauce would have about twice as much alcohol as our first. Our tasting confirmed this theory. The first had a smooth, clean flavor, and the second was overshadowed by booziness.

This fact is of particular importance in recipes with a lot of wine. If you want a strong wine flavor without the unpleasant hit of alcohol, don't be tempted to cheat by adding in your other liquids before the alcohol is fully reduced.

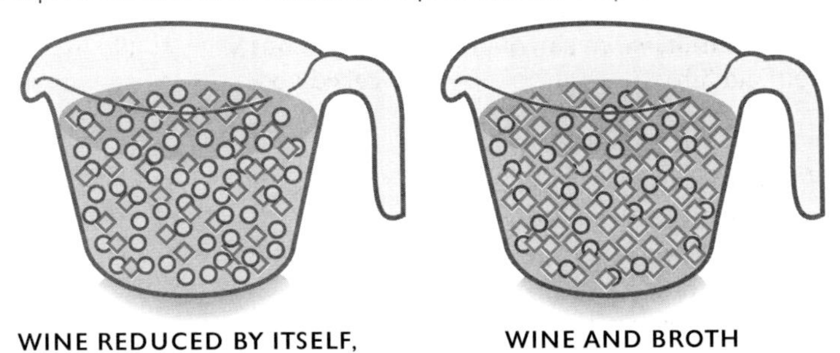

In the test kitchen, we reduced 2 cups of wine and 2 cups of broth to a final volume of 1 cup using two different methods. In the cup on the left, we reduced the wine first, then added broth, and reduced the mixture. In the cup on the right, we reduced the wine and broth together.

KEY: Water ○ Alcohol ◇

Humidity and Flour

Many baking experts claim that baking on very dry or very humid days can affect flour. We were a little skeptical but thought we'd run some tests while developing our recipe for Foolproof Pie Dough (page 23). We constructed a sealed humidity-controlled chamber in which we could simulate various types of weather. We made pie crusts at relative humidities of at least 85 percent (more humid than New Orleans in the wet season) and below 25 percent (drier than Phoenix in midsummer and the average air-conditioned office), leaving the lid to the flour container open for eight hours beforehand. We found that over the course of the test, the flour's weight varied by less than 0.5 percent between the two samples, and after being baked, the crusts were indistinguishable.

If an occasional humid day doesn't make a difference, what about long-term exposure to excess humidity? According to the King Arthur Flour Company, flour held in its paper packing bag (even unopened) can gain up to 5 percent of its weight in water after several months in a very humid environment. At this level, humidity might affect baked goods. But this problem is easily avoided by transferring flour to an airtight container (preferably one wide enough to accommodate a 1-cup measure) as soon as you get it home.

STEP-BY-STEP | PREPARING ROOT VEGETABLES

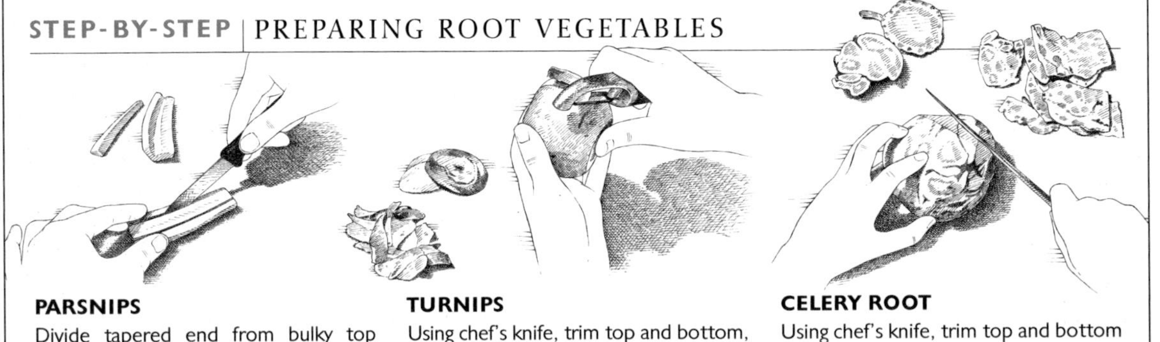

PARSNIPS
Divide tapered end from bulky top and halve top end lengthwise. Remove fibrous core by carefully cutting V-shaped channel down center of parsnip.

TURNIPS
Using chef's knife, trim top and bottom, then use vegetable peeler to remove thin skin.

CELERY ROOT
Using chef's knife, trim top and bottom so vegetable rests flat on work surface, then cut away thick, knobby skin in wide swaths.

Aged Balsamic for Less

Traditionally produced balsamic vinegar (labeled *tradizionale*) is used sparingly for drizzling or flavoring—never in salad dressings or vinaigrettes. It can also take over 25 years to produce and cost up to $60 per ounce. We wanted to find a way to reproduce some of the drizzle-worthy qualities of traditional balsamic without having to visit a specialty food store or a loan officer.

ILLUSTRATION: JAY LAYMAN (TOP), JOHN BURGOYNE (BOTTOM)

We started with a decent supermarket balsamic vinegar and tried reducing it with sugar and flavorings ranging from black currant juice to coffee. In the end, we found that a straight reduction of ⅓ cup of vinegar and 1 tablespoon of sugar worked well enough, but the addition of 1 tablespoon of port added the complexity we were after. Vigorous boiling destroyed nuances in the vinegar's flavor; the best results came from reducing this mixture for 30 to 40 minutes over extremely low heat (barely simmering) to about half of its original volume. While most tasters could distinguish this reduction from a traditional, 12-year-old balsamic, our homemade drizzling vinegar was surprisingly good. The flavor is very strong, so use sparingly over fresh fruit, ice cream, or grilled meats and fish.

Freezing Enhanced Meat

We know that freezing meat can reduce its moisture content, but sometimes those pork chops on sale are too cheap to pass up. Could we find an acceptable way to freeze our chops to minimize this moisture loss? We wrapped up a dozen chops using various combinations of plastic wrap, foil, and freezer bags, then froze them for six weeks. We found that only one method—multiple layers of plastic followed by a freezer bag with all the air squeezed out—kept moisture loss below 1 percent. After thawing, brining, and cooking the chops frozen this way, they were indistinguishable from fresh chops.

We then wondered if enhanced chops (injected with water, salt, and sodium phosphate) could be frozen with equal success. We found that with the exact same treatment, these chops lost nearly six times as much moisture as natural chops. Another reason why we'll stick to buying natural chops and brining them ourselves.

Measuring Matters

Variations in measurement can have a significant effect on baked goods. To prove this point, we asked 10 members of the kitchen staff to measure out 1 cup of flour and 3 tablespoons of water. The weights of the measured flour and water varied by as much as 20 percent.

From these findings, we recommend three things to guarantee more consistent results from your baked goods:

- **WEIGH FLOUR** Don't rely on cup measurements alone. (One cup all-purpose or bread flour weighs 5 ounces; 1 cup cake flour weighs 4 ounces.)
- **USE THE RIGHT MEASURING CUP** Liquid measurements ¼ cup or greater should be made in a liquid cup measure (not a dry cup measure). To measure accurately, place the cup on a level surface and bring your eyes down to the level of the measurement markings. Add liquid until the bottom of the curved top surface of the liquid (called the meniscus)—not the edges of the surface, which can cling and ride up the walls of the measuring cup—is level with the measurement marking.
- **BE PRECISE** When measuring tablespoon or teaspoon amounts of liquid, make sure that the teaspoon is completely filled and that there is no excess liquid clinging to the bottom of the spoon after pouring.

EQUIPMENT TESTING: What's the Scoop?

Portion scoops—essentially ice-cream dippers made in specific sizes—are popular in the hospitality industry for their ability to easily portion large quantities of foods such as cookie dough, tuna salad, or mashed potatoes. In the test kitchen, we find them very useful for neatly and evenly measuring batter-based baked goods like our Drop Biscuits (page 19). Scoop numbers stamped on the handle or spring-loaded trigger correspond to the number of level scoops it takes to equal 1 quart (32 fluid ounces; a fluid ounce is a unit of volume equal to 2 tablespoons). The #16 scoop we use for our Best Drop Biscuits, for example, equals 2 fluid ounces; the #8 scoop equals 4 fluid ounces. Handle colors often correspond to the numbers as well, but they vary from brand to brand. The test kitchen's preferred scoop is the Fantes #16 Stainless Steel Ice Cream Scoop ($11.99), an industrial-type model that's easy tosqueeze with either hand.

SURE SCOOP
Clear size marking and an easy-squeeze handle that's friendly to both left- and right-handers make the Fantes Stainless Steel Ice Cream Scoop our favorite.

RECIPE UPDATE

Make-Ahead Dinner Rolls

Readers requested a freezer make-ahead version of our **Rich and Tender American Dinner Rolls** (November/December 1999). The question was: At what point in the recipe's process do you freeze the rolls? Our recipe begins with mixing and kneading the dough, and then proofing it, after which the rolls are shaped, allowed to rise again, and then baked. Freezing the rolls after their second proofing worked best, but when we tried baking them right from the freezer, they turned out squatter and denser than usual. By the time the frozen center of the rolls started to bake, the exterior was already cooked and set, which prohibited the rolls from achieving their maximum oven rise. Thawing the rolls for 30 to 45 minutes allowed them to bake up light and fluffy. Go to www.cooksillustrated.com/december for our free recipe for Make-Ahead Rich and Tender American Dinner Rolls.

THAWED **NOT THAWED**

Allowing the dinner rolls to thaw and soften for half an hour or so ensures they rise properly (left) in the oven. Baking them straight from the freezer results in a dense, squat roll (right).

Broccoli Gratin

Using broccoli in place of cauliflower in our **Cauliflower Gratin** recipe (March/April 2002) seemed worth a try. Our recipe starts by blanching cauliflower and building a creamy sauce in a separate skillet. The two are combined in a casserole dish, topped with cheese and buttery bread crumbs, and finished in the oven. Simply substituting broccoli for cauliflower resulted in overcooked florets, and the rich sauce overwhelmed the flavor of the broccoli. Reducing the broccoli's blanching time by a minute or so guarded against overcooked florets, and using equal parts chicken broth and heavy cream (instead of all heavy cream) lightened the sauce just enough to allow the broccoli's flavor to shine through. Tasters strongly preferred sharp cheddar to Parmesan in this gratin. Go to www.cooksillustrated.com/december for our free recipe for Broccoli and Cheddar Gratin.

Grilled Shrimp Skewers Indoors

We wanted to find a way to make our **Charcoal-Grilled Shrimp Skewers** (July/August 2006) indoors under the broiler. The recipe's pregrilling preparation—skewers packed with peeled shrimp brushed with oil and seasoned with salt, pepper, and sugar (to promote better browning)—worked great for broiling as well. But cooking the skewers on a broiler pan or rimmed baking sheet produced pale, wet shrimp. Broiling the skewers on a wire rack set in a rimmed baking sheet solves the problem. The rack elevates the shrimp and allows for maximum air circulation, which means better browning and charring. Go to www.cooksillustrated.com/december for our free recipe for Broiled Shrimp Skewers.

—Charles Kelsey

IF YOU HAVE A QUESTION about a recipe, let us know. Send your inquiry, name, address, and daytime telephone number to Recipe Update, Cook's Illustrated, P.O. Box 470589, Brookline, MA 02447 or write to recipeupdate@americastestkitchen.com.

EQUIPMENT CORNER

BY ELIZABETH BOMZE WITH LOIS WEINBLATT

EQUIPMENT UPDATE: Mini Torches

Six years ago, we chose a mini kitchen torch by Bernzomatic as our favorite for preparing dishes like crème brûlée. The company recently replaced it with the new model ST2200T ($28.99). To see if it still passed muster, we sprinkled turbinado sugar on a baking dish of custard and torched half with the old model and half with the new. Both deeply caramelized the sugar, but the new model was even easier to use. The new model requires only one hand to operate and is triggered by the thumb rather than the forefinger, which we found far more comfortable. Also, the safety switch can be flicked off with the thumb, which is much easier than the two-handed pull-push trick required by the old torch. It's our new winner. (Butane is sold separately and is available at most hardware stores.)

FIRED UP
The remodeled Bernzomatic ST2200T improves on our former favorite with a more comfortable design, sturdier base, and simpler safety switch.

EQUIPMENT TESTING: Silicone Pot Handle Covers

When soup boils over, it's all too easy to grab a hot pan handle and burn yourself. Silicone handle sleeves promise a no-sear solution. We tested two models, from Le Creuset and HotSpot, and when they gripped a handle snugly, we liked their performance. The problem? Neither fits all pans. The hourglass-figured Le Creuset Cool Tool Silicone Handle Sleeve ($8.95) was designed for the brand's own cookware and was too slim and stumpy for longer, bulkier handles. Conversely, the HotSpot HotHandle Handle Holder ($7.95) fit nicely over only fatter handles. Our advice? Before you buy, try them in the store on your line of cookware. Note that neither model is designed to go into the oven.

NEW PRODUCT: Chestnutter

The Chestnutter ($24.95), a gadget shaped like an oversized garlic press, claims to streamline the chore of preparing chestnuts for roasting by cutting their tough shells to make a steam vent. We took 2 pounds of chestnuts into the test kitchen and pitted the device against the traditional method of scoring the nuts with a paring knife. Ten nuts in, one test cook cut herself with the knife, but even colleagues who emerged unscathed had to admit that driving a sharp knife into a round, slippery nut made them a little nervous. The Chestnutter worked as advertised, punching consistent X-shaped cuts regardless of a chestnut's shape or size. While the device does require a strong squeeze, it left our fingers unharmed and shaved three minutes off a seven-minute task.

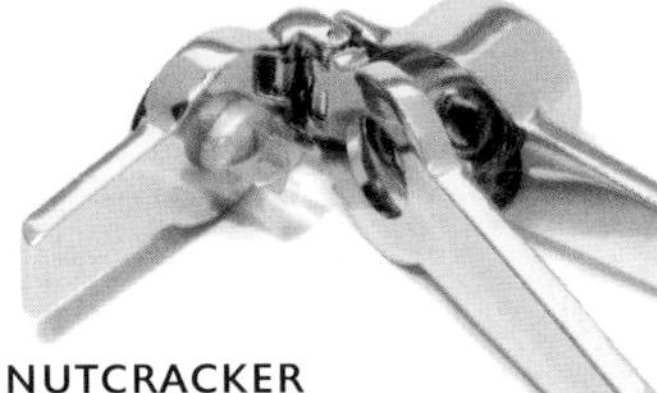

NUTCRACKER
Although a bit pricey for a single-use gadget, the Chestnutter does score nuts quickly and safely.

NEW PRODUCT: AeroGarden

Winter can be a gloomy time for cooking with fresh herbs. You can pay upward of $5 a bunch for herbs that don't last more than a week, which can be hard to justify when you need only a tablespoon or two. Enter the AeroGarden from AeroGrow. This produce-sprouting appliance claims to bring freshly grown herbs into your kitchen without bugs, dirt, or seasonal limitations. You drop in premade seed pods and add water and time-release nutrient tablets to the base. A grow lamp cycles on and off automatically, no sunlight (or even window) required.

We were pretty skeptical, especially of the $149.95 price, which also gets you a Gourmet Herb Kit of seven herbs. However, the AeroGarden performed as advertised. Setup and maintenance were easy, and within two weeks, six of the seven pods sprouted. (Cilantro remained dormant, but a call to AeroGrow customer service brought a free replacement, which grew as promised.) As we clipped and used sprigs from the plants, they continued to grow.

So is it worth it? It's pricey, and if you wanted to make a batch of pesto, you'd still have to go to the store for enough fresh basil. But for the cook who wants to keep a variety of fresh herbs (in small amounts only) on hand, the AeroGarden does deliver.

HIGH-TECH HERB GARDEN
This self-sufficient, hydroponic greenhouse is no bargain, but the AeroGarden offers fresh herbs without the hassle of dirt, bugs, or bad weather.

DO YOU REALLY NEED THIS? Stuffing Cage

The Stuffing Cage ($9.99) promises to eliminate the hassle of scooping stuffing out of a turkey. You pack stuffing into the hinged cage, latch it, and put it in the bird. But this gadget required some wrestling. The first unit we tried wouldn't latch closed. We were able to clamp a second cage shut, but not without a struggle. We recommend cooking stuffing separately (it's easier and safer). But if you insist on having the turkey juices baste the stuffing as it cooks, wrap the stuffing in a homemade cheesecloth sack cinched at one end with twine.

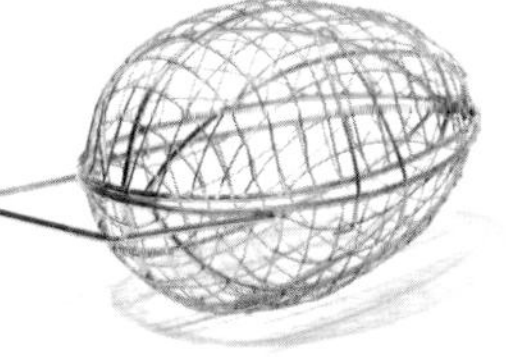

BIRD CAGE
The metal Stuffing Cage goes inside the bird to hold stuffing in place but offers no advantages over cheesecloth.

Sources

The following are sources for items recommended in this issue. Prices were current at press time and do not include shipping. Contact companies to confirm information or visit www.cooksillustrated.com for updates.

Page 9: VEGETABLE PEELER
- Messermeister Pro-Touch Swivel Peeler: $5.95, item #800-58, **CutleryAndMore.com (800-650-9866, www.cutleryandmore.com).**

Page 15: REFRIGERATOR/FREEZER THERMOMETER
- Maverick RF-02 Cold Check Digital Refrigerator/Freezer Thermometer: $34.95, item #B0000AQL26, **Amazon.com.**

Page 27: TURKEY
- Walters Poultry 14-lb. turkey: $100, **Dean & Deluca (800-221-7714, www.deandeluca.com).**

Page 28: COOLING RACKS
- CIA Bakeware 12 x 17 Inch Cooling Rack: $14.95, item #CIA-23304, **MetroKitchen (888-892-9911, www.metrokitchen.com).**
- Libertyware Cross Wire Cooling Rack Half Sheet Pan Size: $4.35, **Ram Kitchen Supplies (800-617-1187, www.ramkitchen.com).**

Page 29: BAKING SHEET
- Lincoln Foodservice Half-Size Heavy Duty Sheet Pan: $15.40, item #B0001MS3P6, **Amazon.com.**

Page 31: PORTION SCOOP
- Fantes Ice Cream Portioning Scoop #16: $11.99, item #1733, **Fantes (800-443-2683, www.fantes.com).**

Page 32: MINI TORCH
- Bernzomatic ST2200T: $28.99, item #20-376111, **USA Hardware (763-417-0094, www.usahardware.com).**

Page 32: CHESTNUTTER
- Chestnutter: $24.95, item #67-7314909, **Williams-Sonoma (877-812-6235, www.williams-sonoma.com).**

Page 32: AEROGARDEN
- AeroGarden: $149.95, item # 696835, **Cooking.com (800-663-8810, www.cooking.com).**

INDEX

November & December 2007

RECIPES

COOK'S LIVE Original Test Kitchen Videos www.cooksillustrated.com

Pan-Roasted Pear Salads, 25

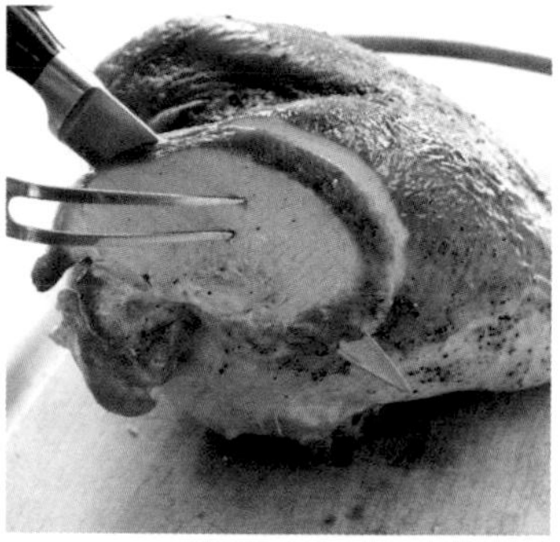

Easy Roast Turkey Breast, 15

Apple-Cranberry Pie, 24

Glazed Spiral-Sliced Ham, 11

Mashed Potatoes and Root Vegetables, 9

French-Style Pot Roast, 7

Tiramisù, 21

Best Drop Biscuits, 19

Beef and Vegetable Stir-Fries, 12

PHOTOGRAPHY: CARL TREMBLAY, KELLER + KELLER; STYLING: MARIE PIRAINO, MARY JANE SAWYER

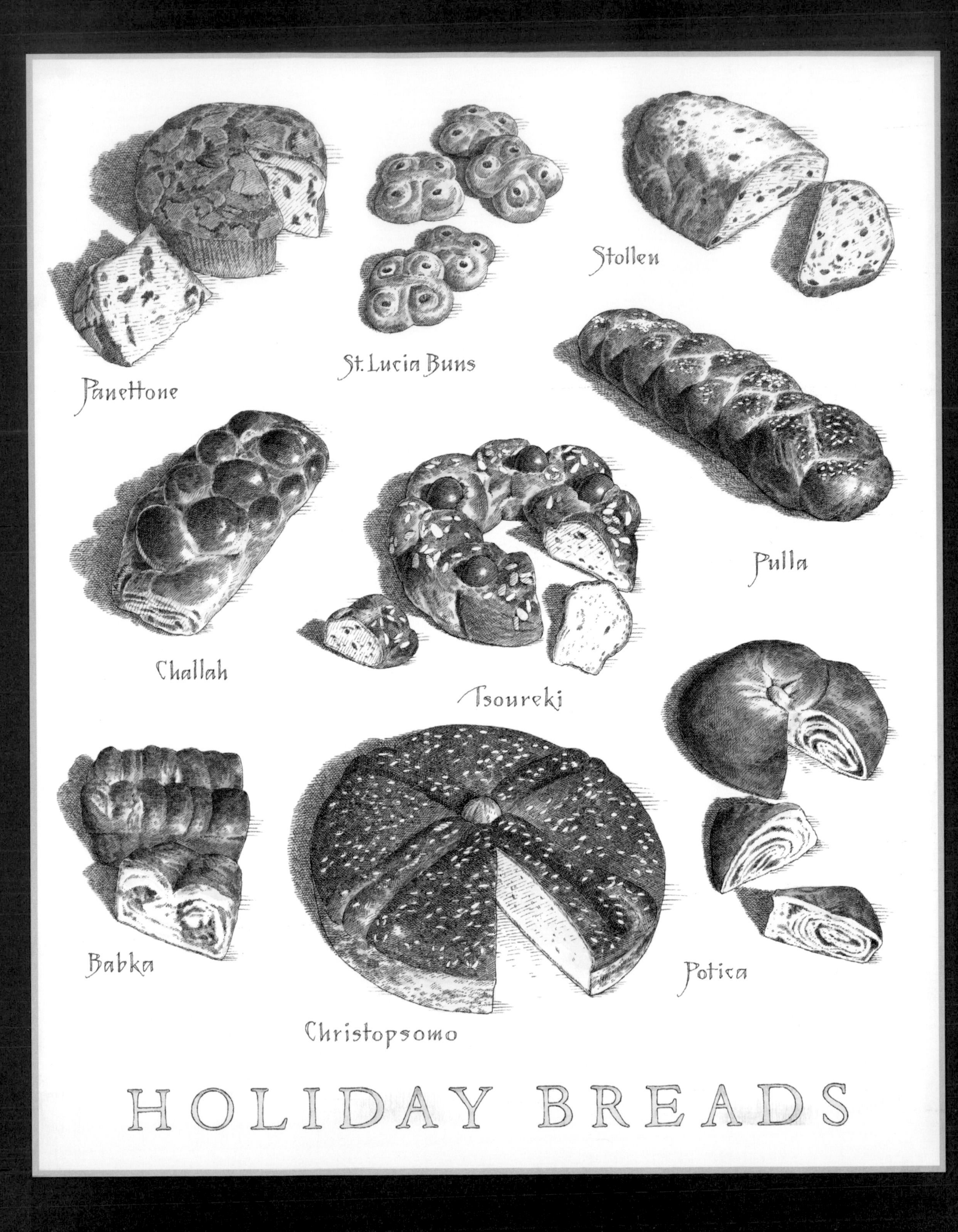
Panettone
St. Lucia Buns
Stollen
Pulla
Challah
Tsoureki
Babka
Christopsomo
Potica
HOLIDAY BREADS